CONSERVATION
Pride *and* Passion

The Alberta Fish and Game Association
1908-2008

DON MEREDITH • DUANE RADFORD

and the Alberta Fish and Game Association
Heritage 100 Committee

CONSERVATION
Pride *and* Passion

The Alberta Fish and Game Association
1908-2008

Written and edited by
Don Meredith and Duane Radford
and the
Alberta Fish and Game Association Heritage 100 Committee

Front cover photos (clockwise from upper left):
Children with rods: courtesy of Eva Tomaszewski,
Camrose and District Fish and Game Association
Hands holding yellow perch: courtesy of Duane Radford
Pheasant release: courtesy of Heinz Plontke,
Lethbridge Fish and Game Association
Mule deer buck and doe: stock photo
Background:
Southwest Alberta foothills/mountains scene with
Andy Russell's Hawk's Nest summer home: courtesy of Duane Radford
Back cover photos:
Myles Radford on a prairie deer hunt: courtesy of Duane Radford
Myles Radford (L) fly fishing on the Bow River,
and Don Pike, fishing guide in boat: courtesy of Duane Radford

Design and print production co-ordination by the

EDMONTON JOURNAL

a division of Canwest Publishing Inc.
10006-101 Street, Edmonton, Alberta, Canada T5J 0S1
Mailing Address:
P.O. Box 2421, Edmonton, Alberta, Canada T5J 2S6
Phone 780-429-5400
edmontonjournal.com

Production Manager - Louise L. Lozeau
Creative Director/Lead Designer - Annabelle Wright
Junior Designers - Amanda Dunlop and Lilla Pferschy
Copy Editors - Sandy Arndt and Sarah Pratt
Proofreaders - Connie Dennis, Yvonne Murphy
and Annabelle Wright
Image Production Co-ordinator - Shaun Cooney
Image Production Assistant - Terry Elniski
Technical Support - Donald Allen
Photo Support - Travel Alberta, Glenbow Museum
and Edmonton Archives

*The spellings of names, organizations and events are based on the AFGA records, and every attempt
was made to be accurate and consistent. The Heritage 100 Committee and the* Edmonton Journal
apologize if a name was misspelled or a person missed.
Published by the *Edmonton Journal*
Printed in Canada 2008
ISBN 978-0-9809772-0-2
Alberta Fish and Game Association
© 2008

CONSERVATION
Pride *and* Passion

The Alberta Fish and Game Association
1908-2008

TABLE OF CONTENTS

... continued

COURTESY OF TRAVEL ALBERTA
Bull moose in Rocky Mountains

Acknowledgements

The Heritage 100 Committee would like to acknowledge the following organizations and individuals for help in researching and writing sections of the book:

Organizations
Alberta Fish and Game Association: Wildlife Awards Competitions, Brad Fenson; Summary Report of Archival Information to the Heritage 100 Committee, Kandice Sharren; Alberta Professional Outfitters Society, Susan Feddema-Leonard and Bob Heyde; Ducks Unlimited Canada, Ron Montgomery; and Wildlife Habitat Canada, David Bracket.

Individuals
Bob Adams, Tom Bateman, Yvonne Baxter, Sylvia Birkholz, Frank Bishop, Dave Ealey, Lorne Fitch, Leo Gudmundson, Gordon Kerr, Brent Markham, Ray Makowecki, Paul Paetkau, Ernie Psikla, Lewis Ramstead, Blair Rippin and Gerry Thompson.

Clubs
All the members of the local fish and game clubs who were involved with the research and writing of their individual club history submissions, and the zone directors who encouraged each club to submit a history.

The AFGA would also like to acknowledge the financial contributions of the following Alberta Fish and Game Associations and zones, individuals and organizations in support of this publication:

Alberta Fish and Game Association Zones and Clubs
Athabasca, Beaver River, Brooks and District, Busby and District, Devon, Edmonton, Fort Saskatchewan, Fort Macleod, Hillcrest, Iron Creek, Lacombe, Lamont, Leduc, Lethbridge, Lloydminster, Morinville, Mundare, Onoway, Ponoka, Red Deer, Sherwood Park, Spedden, Spruce Grove, St. Albert and District, St. Paul, Sylvan Lake, Wheatland, Whitecourt, Willow Valley, zones 1, 2, 3, 4 and 5 who refer to themselves as North Eastern Alberta Fish and Game Association, zone 5.

Individuals
Randy Collins, Tony Ferguson, Jack Graham, Don Hayden, Ray Makowecki, Don Meredith, Gordon Poirier, Duane Radford, Carole Romaniuk, Carmen and Dan Roth and R.H. (Bob) Scammell.

Organizations
A.M. Consulting, Alberta Conservation Association, Alberta Environment, Alberta Historical Resources Foundation, Alberta Professional Outfitters Society, Atco Electric, Canadian Wildlife Federation, Ducks Unlimited Canada, Fishin' Hole Stores, Syncrude Canada, Wildlife Habitat Canada and The Association of Professional Engineers, Geologists and Geophysicists of Alberta.

Material in this book prior to 1945 was obtained primarily from a summary report of archival information from the Provincial Archives of Alberta on Roper Road in Edmonton and Glenbow Museum in Calgary, researched by Kandice Sharren in 2005.

In the interest of historical accuracy, "quotations" from the records (including the Resolutions) retain the original terminology.

If by chance we have missed anyone, it was certainly unintentional and everyone's help was truly appreciated.

The Authors

COURTESY OF DUANE RADFORD
Duane Radford with a mule deer buck shot on Alberta's prairies near Consort, 2006.

Duane Radford is a writer and photographer residing in Edmonton. He worked for the Fish and Wildlife Division for 34 years, retiring in 2002. In that time, he worked as a fisheries research biologist, regional fisheries biologist and regional director for the Southern Region, and assistant director-fisheries management and fisheries director. He is a member of the Outdoor Writers of Canada (currently the midwest director) and the Alberta Fish and Game Association. His home club is the Edmonton Trout Fishing Club. He has several award-winning articles and photographs for various publications. He writes two columns for *Alberta Outdoorsmen* magazine and is the Alberta North field editor for *The Canadian Fly Fisher Magazine*. Duane is also the author of the award-winning cookbook: *From the Field to the Table-Fish & Wild Game Recipes*.

COURTESY OF DON MEREDITH
Don Meredith with a white-tailed buck shot in Alberta's parkland near Keephills, 2000.

Don Meredith is a writer and biologist living west of Edmonton. He worked for the Alberta Fish and Wildlife Division in various capacities from 1978 to 2002, as both a contractor and full-time employee. He served as the co-ordinator of information and education for the division from 1996 to 2002. Don is a member of the Outdoor Writers of Canada (president, 2007-09) and the Stony Plain Fish and Game Association. He has written several award-winning articles for a variety of publications, and writes a monthly outdoor column for *Alberta Outdoorsmen* magazine. Don is also the author of two award-winning novels: *Dog Runner* and *The Search for Grizzly One*. Many of his articles can be read on his website: www.donmeredith.ca.

COURTESY OF ICON EXPERIENCE PHOTOGRAPHY
Kandice Sharren, AFGA researcher.

Kandice has had a passion for books ever since she was old enough to hold one. Born in Edmonton and raised in St. Albert, she spent many happy childhood days on the eastern slopes of the Rockies where she developed a deep understanding of nature. Enrolled in the full International Baccalaureate diploma program in high school, she received top marks for her research and writing of the program's final paper. At the time of this book's printing Kandice is in her last year of an honours degree in English at the University of Victoria.

CANADA

PRIME MINISTER · PREMIER MINISTRE

I am pleased to offer my sincere congratulations to the members of the Alberta Fish and Game Association on the occasion of its 100th anniversary.

The Alberta Fish and Game Association is Alberta's oldest and largest conservation organization with over 120 clubs. Through its involvement with programs like the Habitat Steward Program, the Heritage Farmstead Program and the AFGA Wildlife Trust Fund, the Association has set aside thousands of hectares for the preservation of wildlife habitat in Alberta.

As you celebrate this milestone, you have the opportunity to reflect upon all of your accomplishments. I commend everyone involved with this organization for your dedication to the maintenance, enhancement and retention of habitat, as well as your steadfast defence of the rights of hunters and anglers.

On behalf of the Government of Canada, please accept my best wishes for a memorable day, and for every future success.

OTTAWA
2008

Message from Honourable Ed Stelmach
Premier of Alberta

On behalf of the Government of Alberta, I would like to extend congratulations to the Alberta Fish and Game Association on 100 years of conservation work in Alberta.

From the onset, the Alberta Fish and Game Association has been a partner with Alberta government. The government worked with Alberta Fish and Game Association to educate hunters and anglers on fish and wildlife management and the necessity of legislation to ensure our resources would be enjoyed for many generations.

In the past 100 years, the Alberta Fish and Game Association has had many accomplishments. Recent accomplishments include the Wildlife Trust Fund, which has secured over 30,000 acres of critical habitat, and assistance in the Hunting, Fishing and Trapping Heritage Act, which the Alberta government passed this spring.

Today, Alberta is facing a new challenge with increased development in our province. The Alberta Fish and Game Association will be playing a vital role by ensuring all aspects are considered when decisions are made on the landscape, while ensuring the hunting and fishing tradition remains strong in Alberta.

I would like to thank all the volunteers that contributed to the success of your organization and helped in fish and wildlife management in Alberta. I look forward to continuing our strong partnership for years to come.

Ed Stelmach

Ed Stelmach

September 2008

Office of the Premier, Legislature Building, Edmonton, Alberta, Canada T5K 2B6
Telephone (780) 427-2251 Fax (780) 427-1349

Conservation

CONSERVE TODAY—FOR TOMORROW

"That the land

and all things there-on

belongs to a vast family,

of which

many are dead,

few still living, and

countless numbers are

still unborn."

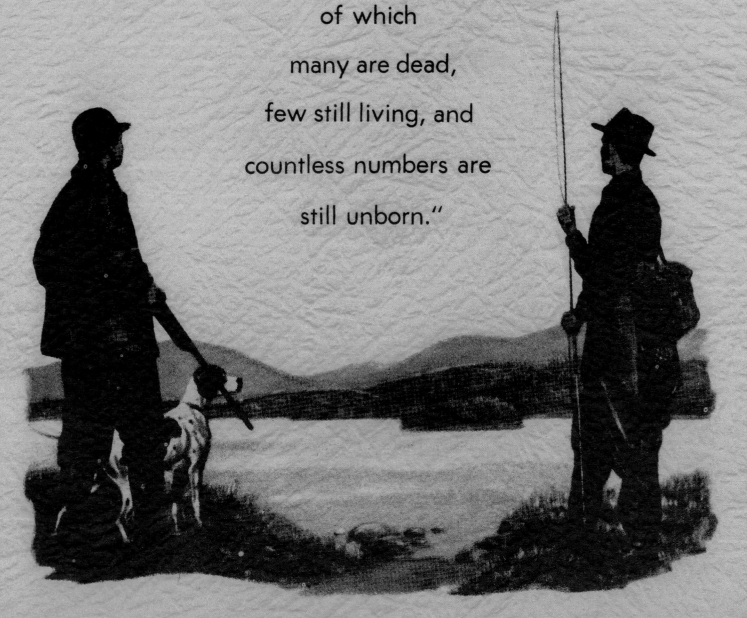

Introduction

The idea for a book commemorating the Alberta Fish and Game Association's (AFGA) first 100 years had its genesis in 2003 when then-president Ray Makowecki appointed past-president Don Hayden as chairman of the Heritage 100 Committee, which began to actively collect historical documents about the organization. Ray Makowecki deserves credit for coining the title of this book, *CONSERVATION Pride and Passion*, which was accepted as one of the favourites by delegates at the 2007 AFGA conference in Medicine Hat. The committee soon realized that current and future members of the AFGA, as well as Albertans in general, needed to know and understand the rich history of the organization to fully appreciate the long and ongoing heritage of conservation that has been passed down over the last century. Thus, the concept for a book about that history took form.

> **Y**ou hold in your hands a treasure of history and personal accounts of the AFGA. I hope that you enjoy it and learn from it; let the accomplishments as well as the failures of our past guide you into the future.
> — Maurice Nadeau, AFGA President 2007-09

The AFGA is a volunteer-based, not-for-profit, charitable organization that advocates the common interests of ethical hunters, anglers and outdoor enthusiasts dedicated to the responsible stewardship of Alberta's environment. Its mission is to promote, through education, lobbying and programs, the conservation and utilization of fish and wildlife and to protect and enhance the habitat they depend on. The AFGA is recognized by all levels of government as the official voice for organized hunters and anglers interested in the conservation of fish and wildlife. The motto of the organization is "The Alberta Fish and Game Association is Alberta's Voice for Conservation."

This book describes the history of the provincial organization as well as that of the individual clubs that make up the organization. The provincial history is broken into decades for clarity, starting with 1908-17 and concluding with 1998-2007. During the 1918-27 decade and until 1936, information contained in the annual chapters for each decade was obtained from notes from the minute books found in the Northern Alberta Game and Fish Protective League (NAGFPL) archival records. There are detailed, type-written records of notes from minute books of the NAGFPL from 1920-46. As such, the records in this history book until 1936 primarily represent this particular association and not the eventual AFGA parent body which was not organized until 1928. Notwithstanding this limitation, the issues and concerns of Alberta's pioneer sportsmen during this period of time are well documented in these particular records. Material in this book prior to 1945 was obtained primarily from a summary report of archival information researched by Kandice Sharren in 2005 under contract by the AFGA for use by the Heritage 100 Committee. The archival information is stored in the Alberta Provincial Archives building at 8555 Roper Road in Edmonton.

From 1945 onward, the bulk of material for the text in this book was obtained from the AFGA head office in Edmonton. There, the association maintains records of yearbooks, convention and conference minutes, resolutions, photographs as well as newspaper clippings, newsletters and magazines.

Information was also obtained from the AFGA and government correspondence in head office files, the AFGA executive meeting minutes and central office bulletins, government reports and brochures, hunting and fishing regulations, personal interviews with various officials in the AFGA and government, information supplied directly by (primarily former) employees of the Fish and Wildlife Division of the Alberta government, government news releases, magazines and newspaper clippings.

In the provincial history from 1945 onwards, the heading for each year represents the calendar year in which the annual reports were published in the conference yearbook as well as the conference minutes for that year. As such, much of the information presented for each year represents events and activities that occurred during the preceding year. For example, much of the information for 1993 is presented in the 1994 section because it was obtained from the 1994 conference yearbook where the reports of activities in 1993 were published. The information is presented in this way because it is difficult to chronologically separate events and activities from the policies and proposed activities reported in these documents.

The description of each decade includes information (when available) about membership, membership trends, the nature of the organization, the presidents and other key officials on the executive (particularly chairs of various standing committees), the major issues, trends in fish and game numbers (as reported primarily by members of the association), information on the numbers of hunters and anglers, accounts from key government officials and their staff, fish and game regulations, select AFGA resolutions submitted by the various clubs that were debated at the annual convention and conferences, and successes and failures over the years.

Information for the individual club histories was provided by the clubs (aptly named "locals" or "leagues" in the formative years of the organization), as well as the various zones. Clubs were provided guidelines for the club history reports and most of the clubs submitted a report; club histories were even provided for some clubs no longer in existence, such as Jasper Place in Edmonton.

Over the last century, the AFGA has been a major player in the conservation of Alberta's rich fish and wildlife legacy. The stories told in this book illustrate the perseverance and commitment of many individuals and organizations, and the struggles they waged to keep that legacy alive and well. There were arguments, protracted battles and ambitious projects that led to failures and triumphs. Through it all, individuals rose to the challenge and made the organization what it is today. The result has been an Alberta that continues to have one of the richest fish and wildlife resources in North America. These are stories that need to be told and retold to ensure future generations do not forget from where we have come.

Organizational Profile of the Alberta Fish and Game Association

In one form or another, the AFGA has been active since 1908; however, it wasn't until November of 1946 that it was registered under the Alberta Societies Act. As of 2008, the association has a total membership exceeding 17,000, representing 100 affiliated fish and game clubs in cities, towns and villages throughout the province. Members range in age from newborn to over 80 years and cover a broad cross-section of an urban/rural population. Policy and direction is established by a 15-member volunteer executive committee and governed by a five-member senior executive committee. The association is administered through a head office in Edmonton by a staff of approximately 10 full-time administrative and habitat staff. The AFGA is a founding member of the Canadian Wildlife Federation and maintains a fraternal relationship with all provincial affiliates.

COURTESY OF DUANE RADFORD

Cornwall Lake in northeast Alberta.

Prologue

The Good Old Daze *by Robert H. (Bob) Scammell*

Since the Alberta Fish and Game Association (AFGA) decided to celebrate its 100th anniversary with a book recounting its history, people have been interested and involved in the What, Where, When and How of the story. However, the most intriguing question for many of those people has been the Why. Why did sportsmen—hunters and anglers—organize in the first place so many years ago? What was the need? Weren't those the "good old days" hunters and anglers like to dream and drone on about, an earthly "happy hunting ground" in an Alberta of abundant fish and game? Anyone who delves even modestly into Alberta history, before and just after it became a province, is in a total daze if he still believes the myth that those were the good old days.

In the beginning on our frontier there was neither general rule of law nor any specific law protecting fish and game. But harvesting fish and game was serious, big business. Buffalo Lake, near Stettler, got its name because, when seen from above, it is buffalo-shaped. From where the tail would be on a buffalo, flows Tail Creek. In the 1870s, near where Tail Creek joins the Red Deer River, Alberta's largest community was located, a seasonal gathering of 4,000 whites and Indians, but mostly Métis, devoted exclusively to killing buffalo.

The great Métis buffalo hunters, like Gabriel Dumont, developed and enforced a few rules that governed the conduct of their hunts. Penalties for breaking the rules were ridicule, ostracism and beating. By 1875 those few rules had expanded to 25, including rules which, for the first time, showed concern for the future; for example, forbidding the wasting of buffalo carcasses and killing the great beasts solely for their hides or tongues.

Because buffalo herds continued their steep decline, in 1887 the Council of the Northwest Territories (N.W.T.) passed a tough law aimed at the preservation of the buffalo. It provided penalties for waste, prohibited the use of pounds or jumps (where buffalo were slaughtered in large numbers), actually attempted to put limits on how many buffalo any one hunter could kill, prohibited slaughter for amusement or "solely to secure their tongues, choice cuts or peltries," and for the first time prohibited killing of cow buffalo in certain seasons and the killing of calves under two years old.

The law caused such uproar that the very next year, 1888, it was repealed. The Indians objected because they believed the buffalo were the gift of their god, Manitou, and that the whites had no right to interfere. The Métis objected, despite their own rules governing their own hunts, because they felt the law discriminated against them in favour of the Indians. The white market hunters, of course, were not about to put up with any laws of any kind. To put it all into ironic perspective, most accounts indicate the last buffalo in Alberta was killed on the banks of the Red Deer River in 1886, one year before the first Territorial law protecting buffalo was passed, and two years before it was repealed—perhaps the classic legislative example of too little law, too late.

A land bereft of buffalo was an opportunity for the flood of settlers that began arriving in the province thanks to the Canadian Pacific Railroad, which reached Calgary in 1883. Generally speaking, the plague of exotic displaced humanity that descended on the North American west after 1885 was the hungriest horde of unrepentant poachers ever assembled in one place and time. The people who came first were not landed gentry and had no hunting rights in their homelands. We do owe a debt to those settlers for insisting on the unique North American principle that the game belongs to all the people, not just the privileged. But unfortunately they were also hungry, knew little of the principles of stewardship and husbandry that guided the hated gentry and gamekeepers in their homelands, and were completely ignorant of any concept of hunting ethics or sportsmanship. With regard to authority, all these people knew was that the gamekeeper kept them from the game. But on a frontier where there was no law and no gamekeepers, the prime poachers' rule prevailed: "the fish and gyme [sic] belongs to 'im as brings it to 'and," and was expanded in the new land to free game for all, to be taken freely by all.

With the buffalo about gone, the settlers had to resort, and apply their poachers' principles, to other species for sport and sustenance. Soon many game populations were in such peril that, in 1893, the legislative assembly of the Territories passed "The Game Ordinance." The radical new act closed the season between Feb. 1 and Oct. 1 on elk, moose, antelope, deer or their fawns, mountain sheep and goats, and imposed a limit of sorts on those species of "not more than six head per season, except for the purpose of food for a person, or his family."

The exception about hunting for food disappeared from the 1903 Territorial Ordinance, which also became much more sophisticated in the management sense of separate seasons for different species and was positively paranoid about penalties for anyone who would kill a buffalo. It was this 1903 NWT Ordinance, with a few amendments—the most important of which, strangely, was outlawing the use of dogs to hunt big game—that became Alberta's first *Game Act* in the first session of the first Alberta legislature after the province was carved out of the Territories and joined confederation on Sept. 1, 1905.

The first species prohibition was that "no person shall hunt, trap, take, shoot at, wound or kill any bison or buffalo at any time." An indication of just how bad things had become for other game is that the NWT Ordinance of 1903 permitted a season of only six weeks on any member of the deer family and that season continued intact into the first Alberta *Game Act*. Of course Alberta's first "Ordinance for the Protection of Game" stated that it did not apply in any part to Indians unless the Superintendent General of Indian Affairs of Canada said so, pursuant to section 133 of the federal *Indian Act*.

Other strange things appeared in the 1903 NWT Ordinance and the first Alberta *Game Act* regarding game birds. There was a two-month season on all manner of upland game birds, including partridge and pheasant, although there is no record that pheasants or Hungarian or European partridge, had been introduced anywhere in the Territories or Alberta at that time. The mystery and confusion is compounded by the following wording in the 1903 Territorial "Game Ordinance:" "Provided that no English pheasant shall be taken or killed at any time…" The "English" pheasant is really no different from the Chinese ring-neck that was not introduced in Alberta until 1908 at the earliest and not seriously until 1922. It is tempting to speculate that some of the British blimps in those old legislatures believed that "if we 'ad them at 'ome, we must bloody well 'ave them 'ere in the colonies."

By the turn of the century, Alberta was scorched earth like most of western North America, and there was little wildlife left to protect. Long grass, uneaten by buffalo, combined with rampant use of fire for preventing migration of what buffalo were left, had virtually wiped out most wildlife habitats. Wildlife populations, with the exception of migratory waterfowl, were near extinction from excessive, unregulated market and native hunting and some of what passed for sport hunting back then.

What modern biologists like to scorn as "anecdotal" evidence testifies that settlers at the turn of the century arrived in a blackened and burnt Alberta, like a theatre of war. In 1973 a gnarled, bent and retired old hunter sits near the pot-bellied stove in the kitchen beneath his two great trophy white-tail heads and reminisces about arriving from Sweden as a small boy with his parents at their homestead near Pine Lake. The wildlife consisted solely of waterfowl and muskrats. "We ate rats," he laughs, "because they was all I could catch." To the north were the breaks of the Red Deer River where he would see the odd mule deer. As the aspen parkland came back, so did the deer, even a new species. The old man's eyes take on a thousand-yard stare as he recalls the first time he ever saw a "floppy-tail" deer, a white tail. Farther south, a Hungarian settler tells a similar tale, only it was gophers he caught for the family to eat. His eyes twinkle. "Gopher goulash," he laughs, "not bad."

Five years after his arrival in Alberta, that Swedish immigrant kid, barely a teenager, might have seen, tacked to the wall in the Pine Lake Post Office, the one-page, legal-size *1908 GAME REGULATIONS, Province Of Alberta*. As we now annually expect the nearly 90-page modern *Alberta Guide to Hunting Regulations* we can also marvel at how they tried to deal with Alberta's greatest wildlife crisis with only one page containing all the hunting regulations that existed back in 1908. What a terrible tale those 1908 regulations tell, not the least of which is that the second largest print on the document, right near the top, is used to tell us only that "SUNDAY SHOOTING IS PROHIBITED." The priests and preachers had their say and way.

There was no season at all on buffalo, of course, but also no season on mountain sheep, goat and elk. But, by 1908, the deer family was so decimated in Alberta that the season was cut to the month of November. Things only got worse, so that by the 1922 version of Alberta's *Game Act*, there was no season at any time on "bison, buffalo, elk or wapiti," although there is no explanation of the difference between an elk and a wapiti. The season on deer, caribou and moose was the month of November, period, and the limit was one per year of one of these species. Exclude caribou, and we do much better than that today.

The unlicensed buying, selling, dealing and trafficking the flesh of big and bird game or unbranded heads was prohibited in 1908. Destroying game by "means of poison, narcotics, sunken punts, nightlights, traps, snares, swivel, spring, automatic or machine gun" was outlawed. The only bright spot in 1908 was migratory water fowl. There seems to have been no limit on ducks and swans and the season ran from the middle of August to the end of December.

What really shakes people up today is to see a yellowed, old copy of those 1908 game regulations and note there was no season at all on beaver. Curiously, wild geese head the list of "birds which may be killed at any time," along with most raptors, crows, English sparrows, loons, cormorants, pelicans and magpies. In most of North America today we still have too many geese, beavers have recovered and are out of control, and crows and magpies continue to flourish, as they always will.

Cynics will say that when the newspapers take notice, it is already too late. On Oct. 27, 1906 the *Calgary Herald* published an editorial titled "Alberta Losing a Valuable Asset."

"The necessity for stricter laws governing the protection of game is manifest," the first paragraph says, "from the reports of sportsmen all over the province, and their criticism of the lax way the present laws are carried out as regards ducks, chicken, fish, deer, sheep and goats."

The editorial goes on to decry a litany of abuses such as "pothunters" shooting waterfowl too young to fly and just leaving the birds, killing "chicken" out of season, and the running of lye from cattle-dipping vats into rivers and streams.

Surprising as it is to learn that the *Herald* thought there were any sportsmen at all in Alberta in those days, let alone "true sportsmen," it is absolutely astonishing that the editorial should exhort those sportsmen – rather than the government – to do something about the situation:

"Every true sportsman and property owner should take an interest in the preservation of the fish and game. It is one of our greatest assets. We should have strict laws passed and guardians appointed to see they are enforced…. Indians should not be allowed to kill in and out of season…."

Thus the stage is set, or unset—black and bare, empty. Whether in response to the cue of the *Calgary Herald*, or moved by the sad tale told by those 1908 regulations tacked to post office walls all over the province, sportsmen start to enter, stage right, left and centre. As usually happens on a frontier, the first flush of settlers was followed by some business and professional people, even many "remittance men"—the superfluous sons of landed gentry in the old countries. These people were of the class that could hunt and fish back home and wanted to do so in this new country and wanted to do so as sportsmen do, with concern for the quarry, the land and other sportsmen. They quickly saw that work had to be done and changes made if those goals were to be achieved.

Groups of sportsmen banded together to do their good works. It is generally conceded that what became the AFGA started in and around Calgary in 1908 with the efforts of a small group of sportsmen, led by lawyer Austin de B. Winter, Q.C., who released 15 pairs of Hungarian partridges near Midnapore on April 28, 1908. As introduced species sometimes do, the Huns multiplied like flies and there was an open season just six years later. From that success, through the 1920s, sportsmen were heavily involved in planting pheasants in many parts of Alberta, another successful introduction that culminated in the first open season in 1939.

Sportsmen's clubs also multiplied across the province. In March 1920 in downtown Edmonton, two organizational meetings took place of a sort of umbrella group for local clubs, the NAGFPL. The handwritten minutes of these two meetings reveal the major concerns of the day were understandably the stocking of fish and game birds, but also fish and game law enforcement, and the increase of league membership. More surprisingly, a group of Alberta sportsmen was even then trying to end the ban on Sunday hunting.

It quickly became obvious that a united voice of Alberta sportsmen was needed to deal with the two levels of government—Dominion and Provincial—that had jurisdiction over fish and game matters in the province. On July 11, 1928 the delegates of 22 local sportsmen's groups met in Calgary to form the AFGA. Exactly a year later, at the first annual convention of the AFGA, also in Calgary, C.A. Hayden, the first AFGA president, reported a good year of sound progress and that the association had nearly doubled from 22 to 38 "locals."

The organized sportsmen's movement had come to Alberta, uniting realistic, practical people who knew that the only good old days that really matter to avid hunters and anglers are here and now, and on into the future….

COURTESY OF DUANE RADFORD

Duane Radford in the Alberta Rockies.

Chapter One

The First One Hundred Years

As Bob Scammell outlined in his Prologue, when Alberta became a province in 1905, much of its fish and wildlife had been lost to poaching, market hunting and habitat change. Concerned citizens wanted better laws and programs to conserve and restore the resources. They began forming organizations to focus those concerns. As far as can be determined, these organizations began in 1908 and culminated in a province-wide organization in 1928. The following are descriptions of the history of the Alberta Fish and Game Association (AFGA) through the decades from 1908 to 2007.

- **1908-1917**
- **1918-1927**
- **1928-1937**
- **1938-1947**
- **1948-1957**
- **1958-1967**
- **1968-1977**
- **1978-1987**
- **1988-1997**
- **1998-2007**

John (L) and James Kerr with their horses Dan (L), Rags and Babe. Unknown location, probably heading to south country.

1908-1917
Summary

Major issues: Enforcement of closed seasons; bounty on crows and magpies; introduction of Chinese ring-necked pheasants and Hungarian partridge.

Highlights: *1908* - The Calgary Fish and Game Protective League is formed. The club apparently was inactive during World War I (1914-18).

Presidents: The first president of the Calgary club was Robert Alexander Darker (1908-09), followed by E.G. Mason (1910-11) and A.G. Wolley-Dod (1912-13).

The first decade of what eventually became the Alberta Fish and Game Association (AFGA) began during an economic boom for Canada, the world's fastest growing economy at the time. The industrial revolution, which began in the early 19th century, was providing new technologies, making labour-intensive tasks more efficient. Canada's agriculture-based economy benefited from these advancements and the fact that much farmland in the United States had been exhausted of nutrients. In 1911 Alberta had a human population of about 374,000 people (Statistics Canada), or roughly five percent of the Canadian population. One U.S. dollar in 1911 was worth $22.51 U.S. dollars (USD) in 2007 (based on Consumer Price Index; source: www.measuringworth.com). Note: over the following century, the Canadian dollar was either pegged or floated around the value of the U.S. dollar.

In 1908 Wilfrid Laurier of the federal Liberal Party was prime minister of Canada. He was replaced by Conservative Robert Borden in October of 1911. In Alberta, the infant province was led by its first premier, Alexander Rutherford of the Liberal Party. Arthur Sifton of the Liberals replaced Rutherford in 1910. Sifton was in turn replaced by Liberal Charles Stewart in 1917.

For its size, Canada made extraordinary contributions to the Allied effort in the First World War (1914-18). It sent hundreds of thousands of troops over to fight in Europe. As well, it was a chief supplier of grain and arms. Domestic labour was at a premium as industry and farms struggled to meet the war demand.

COURTESY OF THE GLENBOW MUSEUM NA-1993-8

Pioneers of Dorothy, Alberta.

Fish and wildlife conservation and management was in its infancy at this time. In the United States, Theodore Roosevelt founded the Boone and Crockett Club in 1887 "to establish a coalition of dedicated conservationists and sportsmen who would provide the leadership needed to address the issues that affect hunting, wildlife and wild habitat." That club spawned the creation of other like-minded groups across the continent.

In Alberta such clubs did not get started as early, but nonetheless there was concern over the plight of fish and wildlife in the province. Wainwright Buffalo National Park was established in 1909 to protect bison, and Nemiskam National Park was established to protect pronghorn antelope in 1914. The first federal trout hatchery was established in Banff in 1913.

Very few records related to the organizations that eventually formed the AFGA exist prior to 1920. Many subsequent records about the early years are notably brief (often not listing members of the executive) and contradictory. Much information presented here was gleaned primarily from reports from various sources, such as an article by George W. Colpitts in *Alberta History* (1994). According to Colpitts, the first conservation association began in 1907, when

COURTESY OF THE EDMONTON ARCHIVES EA-10-627

The Alberta Legislature building under construction, 1907.

COURTESY OF THE GLENBOW MUSEUM NA-3028-2

Settlers enroute to Irma from Edmonton in spring 1908.

the Alberta Fish and Game Protective Association was formed in Calgary under the leadership of Robert Alexander Darker. Colpitts reported that many such associations appeared in Alberta with urban settlement, gaining their greatest popularity after towns began growing in size along the foothills of the Rocky Mountains.

The Colpitts article contradicts the records filed in the Provincial Museum and Archives of Alberta. These files indicate that the AFGA was established on Feb. 20, 1908 as the Northern Alberta Game and Fish Protective League (NAGFPL) in Edmonton. The name was changed to the Alberta Fish and Game Association in 1909. However, it is the opinion of the AFGA Heritage 100 Committee that a mistake was made at the Provincial Archives when the AFGA records were deposited there in 1987. The committee believes it was the Calgary Fish and Game Protective League (CFGPL) which was formed in 1908, not the NAGFPL (which was formed in 1920). The first president of the CFGPL was Robert Alexander Darker, who served from 1908-09. He was followed by E.G. Mason from 1910-11 and A.G. Wolley-Dod, 1912-13. Apparently, this association was not active during World War I from 1914-18. The league's secretary, Austin de B. Winter, makes no reference to any activities during this time in his numerous letters to different parties in Canada and the U.S.

COURTESY OF THE GLENBOW MUSEUM NA-2084-22

G.E. Goddard after shooting expedition in the Cochrane area, circa 1900-03.

Mr. Benjamin Lawton of Lacombe was appointed Chief Game Guardian for the provincial government of Alberta in 1906. Records indicate he worked in close association with the early fish and game organizations.

The fish and game clubs in the province addressed many issues related to conservation, including enforcement of closed seasons, a desire to permit Sunday hunting, propagation and introduction of exotic game birds, protection of songbirds, concerns related to poor fishing in lakes and streams, use of distinct hunting garments for safety, and a bounty on crows and magpies because of their predation on game bird nests and nestlings.

COURTESY OF THE GLENBOW MUSEUM NA-297-4

Antelope hunt on prairie near Bassano, circa 1907-09.

COURTESY OF THE GLENBOW MUSEUM NA-2547-22

Fisherman in river, southern Alberta.

According to W. Ray Salt and A.L. Wilk (1966), whether the harm done by the crow outweighs the good is a controversial question whose answer probably varies throughout the province. They assert that various methods of crow control which have been tried indicate that the crow cannot be exterminated but that local populations can be kept within reasonable limits. The most expensive, and probably least effective, of these methods is apparently the bounty system. The most effective methods capitalize on their gregarious behaviour during the winter, using explosives to kill them at their roosts.

The first successful release of Hungarian partridge occurred in 1908 when 70 pairs were imported from Hungary and liberated at Midnapore (W. Ray Salt and A.L. Wilk, 1966) just south of Calgary. According to Lewis (1979), 15 pairs of Hungarian partridge were released on Dan Patton's farm, two miles south and two miles west of Midnapore on April 21, 1908. Another 95 pairs were introduced in 1909. These introduced 'huns' increased so rapidly that a hunting season was opened in 1913 and since that time they have spread throughout much of the settled area of southern and central Alberta.

As a result of the vastly diminished abundance of both fish and game in the province in 1905, many early settlers focused their attention on establishing familiar species of fish and game they knew from Europe and Eastern Canada. They worked to re-populate what they felt was suitable habitat with Chinese ring-necked pheasant, Hungarian (gray) partridge, eastern brook trout and bass, for example.

The introduction of Hungarian partridge was orchestrated by Austin de B. Winter, who served as secretary for the CFGPL during this period. Winter was born in England and studied law in London. He immigrated to Canada in 1903 and was the deputy clerk of the Supreme Court until 1910.

Austin de B. Winter was also credited with the introduction of Chinese ring-necked pheasants in 1928, according to some reports (Glenbow Museum and Archives). This record, however, is inconsistent with information provided by Lewis (1979), who noted that the first documented release of the Mongolian and

8th Avenue in Calgary in the early 1900s.

Chinese ring-necked pheasants was in 1908, although apparently some undocumented records indicate that Calgarians A.E. Cross and Pat Burns brought them into Alberta as early as 1905. *Fish, Fur & Feathers: Fish and Wildlife Conservation in Alberta 1905-2005 (2005)* indicated, "Several groups, including various Fish and Game and Rod and Gun Club members, started introducing the popular and remarkable ring-necked pheasant into Alberta in 1909."

According to the report of secretary treasurer George M. Spargo (1930-62) on the "History of Pheasants in Alberta," published in the AFGA agenda for the 18th annual convention (1947): "The first known planting [of pheasants] according to my records, advertises the fact that birds were planted in four locations around Calgary, namely Bragg Creek, Midnapore, Strathmore, and Rosebud Creek, in 1908, resulting in the aforementioned open season at Bragg Creek four years following. These were the result of the purchase of 50 hens and five cocks brought from Yardley, Pennsylvania, in 1908."

The early fish and game clubs jealously guarded British sporting values, and sought to incorporate them into law and the actions of members. As a result, the sporting nature of hunting and fishing became deeply rooted in the culture of the AFGA and is often referenced in various records, even when dealing with government and other organizations. For example, it would be considered unethical for members of the AFGA not to treat officials from government and other agencies in anything less than a "sporting manner" when dealing with various issues and concerns.

The first decade of what became the AFGA was largely formative, where citizens with concerns about fishing and hunting opportunities came together to form local organizations. In these early years, the groups focused their efforts on enforcement, propagation of game species and bounties on predators.

1908
GAME REGULATIONS
PROVINCE OF ALBERTA

SUNDAY SHOOTING IS PROHIBITED

OPEN AND CLOSE SEASONS. (WHITE, CLOSE SEASON; BLACK, OPEN SEASON)

Hunting over enclosed lands prohibited without having obtained the consent of the owner or occupant thereof.

	JANUARY	FEBRUARY	MARCH	APRIL	MAY	JUNE	JULY	AUGUST	SEPTEMBER	OCTOBER	NOVEMBER	DECEMBER
Buffalo, Mountain Sheep, Mountain Goat, Elk, Wapiti												
Antelope												
Deer, Caribou and Moose												
Ducks and Swans								AUG.23				
Cranes, Rails and Coots, Snipe, Plover, etc.									SEP15			
Prairie Chicken, Partridge, etc.												
Mink, Fisher or Marten												
Otter and Muskrats												
Beaver												

No person shall shoot or hunt between one hour after sunset and one hour before sunrise.

No person shall destroy game by means of poison, narcotics, sunken punts, nightlights, traps, snares, swivel, spring, automatic or machine shot gun.

No person shall export game without a permit from the Minister of Agriculture.

No person shall wilfully disturb, destroy or take the eggs of any game or other bird protected by the Game Act.

No dog shall be used by any one to hunt Big Game.

No person may shoot more than one deer, moose or caribou in any year.
No person shall hunt big game without a License.
No person shall buy or sell any game heads unless branded by the Department.
No person shall buy and sell, deal or traffic in the flesh of any big game or game bird without a License.
No person shall act as guide or camp helper without a License.

Birds which may be killed at any time are as follows: Wild geese, crows, eagles, goshawks, pigeon hawks, Cooper's hawks, hawk owls, blackbirds, grackles, English sparrows, loons, cormorants, pelicans and magpies. All other birds are protected.

PERMITS

Licenses entitling the holders thereof to shoot any kind of game (called General Game License) will be issued to nonresidents upon application to Game Guardians and payment of the fee of $25.00 for each license. The fee for a license to shoot game birds only (Bird Game License) is $15.00. The fee for a license to hunt and trap furbearing animals (nonresident Trapper's license) is $10.00. Resident's Big Game License $2.50. All game Licenses are good only if endorsed by the licensees and during calendar year in which they are issued.

FINES

Not exceeding $500.00 and costs may be imposed for infractions of the Game Act.

GEO. HARCOURT,
Deputy Minister.

Department of Agriculture,
Edmonton, Alta., March 1st, 1908.

PLEASE POST IN A CONSPICUOUS PLACE

of the Game Act may be had on application.

John Kerr (L) and his son James R. Kerr. John joined a rod and gun club in the Crowsnest in about 1908 and both he and his son were active members of the Alberta Fish and Game Association for many years. Picture taken circa 1925 on the Castle River. Grandson Gordon Kerr remembers his father telling how in those days it was a problem catching larger fish because they stayed at the bottom of the pools and it was hard getting a hook down to them before the smaller fish took it.

1918-1927
Summary

Major issues: Enforcement of closed seasons; bounty on crows and magpies; introduction of Chinese ring-necked pheasants and Hungarian partridge.

Highlights: *1908 - 1920* - Northern Alberta Game and Fish Protective League (NAGFPL) forms in Edmonton.
1922 - Second *Game Act* of Alberta passes.
1926 - Trout rearing ponds constructed on Raven River.

Presidents: (NAGFPL) Adam H. Esch (1920-21), A. Kinnaird (1922-23), Dr. R.A. Rooney (1924-26), E.P Hall (1927).

Immediately following World War I, the Canadian economy suffered a short but severe recession as it adjusted to the end of the war. However, by 1921 the economy was up and running, and rapidly expanding. The standard of living greatly increased as industry began mass producing what were formerly thought to be luxury items, such as flush toilets and automobiles. The boom lasted well into the late 1920s. In 1921 the population of Alberta numbered about 588,000, or roughly seven percent of the Canadian population. In 1921 the U.S. dollar was worth $11.58 in 2007 USD.

Borden led Canada through the war as prime minister. He was replaced by Arthur Meighen of the Conservative Party in 1920. Meighen led a minority government until it was defeated in an election by William Lyon Mackenzie King's Liberals in 1921. Meighen's Conservatives defeated Mackenzie King's government in June of 1926, again in a minority position, only to lose to King again in September of that year.

In Alberta, Charles Stewart of the Liberals served as premier until August 1921, when Herbert Greenfield of the new United Farmers of Alberta came to power. He resigned in 1925 in favour of John Brownlee of the United Farmers.

COURTESY OF THE GLENBOW MUSEUM NA-2635-86
Hunters with bear near Waterton Lakes, circa early 1920s.

The present-day Alberta Fish and Game Association arose from an alliance between the Calgary Fish and Game Protective League and the Northern Alberta Game and Fish Protective League (NAGFPL). The objective of NAGFPL, as stated in its constitution of 1920, was as follows: "Furthering the interest of sportsmen by planting game, birds and fish in the local fields and waters, giving all game protection during closed seasons, and to advance legislation that will be helpful toward the end of increasing game and fish." NAGFPL eventually became the Edmonton Fish and Game Association.

There is some confusion in the various records, some of which indicate that a Calgary branch of the AFGA was formed in 1920 and was known as the Southern Alberta Fish and Game Protective Association and carried on as such for the years 1921-25. This is contrary to information in George Colpitts' 1994 article in *Alberta History* on "The Fish and Game Associations in Southern Alberta, 1907-1928," wherein he noted, "In Alberta, the first conservation association began in 1907, when the Alberta Fish and Game Protective Association (AFGPS) was formed in Calgary under the leadership of Robert Alexander Darker, an Irish immigrant, who, after living in Quebec, had moved to Alberta in 1902." In 1926 and 1927 the Calgary association's letterhead read "Alberta Fish & Game Association Calgary Branch." In 1928 and 1929 the letterhead read "Calgary Fish and Game Association" with C.A. Hayden as president.

In reviewing these records, the editors of this book feel the two organizations (in Calgary and Edmonton) did not officially come together until 1928. Unfortunately, most of the records for the 1918 to 1927 decade concern only the NAGFPL, which was organized in 1920. Minutes from that organizational meeting on March 3, 1920 and a subsequent meeting on March 26, 1920 paint a disconcerting picture of issues on sportsmen's minds at that time. Because these are the first complete and official records of one of the fledgling organizations that eventually formed the AFGA, they are provided on page 28 in their entirety (unedited).

The NAGFPL minutes during the 1920s were spotted with references to requests for various exotic species of fish (bass, brown trout) and game birds (pheasants, Hungarian partridge and Bobwhite quail) to replenish diminished stocks of native fish and wildlife.

First Organizational Meeting

"A meeting was called to bring together sportsmen of Edmonton and district with the object of forming an association to look after Fish and Game interests in this district, and was called to order at the Hotel Macdonald at 8 p.m., March 3rd, 1920.

"On motion, a temporary chairman and secretary were nominated, A.H. Esch and C. Irgens respectively being named.

"The object of the meeting was put before those present and suggestions for a name were received. On motion, the name 'Northern Alberta Game and Fish Protection League' was adopted unanimously. It was moved, seconded, and passed that officers be elected to complete organization, draw up a constitution and submit same at the following meeting for approval. On nominations being call for, the following were chosen unanimously:

President:	A. H. Esch
Vice President:	P. E. Bowen
Secretary-Treasurer:	W. Holmes
Chairman Big Game Committee:	P. Anderson
Chairman Feathered Committee:	A. Hine
Chairman Fish Committee:	C. W. Boon

"Mr. B. J. Lawton, Provincial Game Guardian, addressed the meeting, speaking generally on the need of such an association, outlining the work before it, the advisability of having game sanctuaries, and other matters pertaining to game protection.

"Mr. E. S. Leonard of Minnesota, a visitor in the city, gave much valuable information regarding success that had been attained in Minnesota, particularly in introducing game fish into lakes in that state. The secretary was authorized to write the Minnesota State Game and Fish Association for information.

"Dr. Hope spoke of the advisability of farmers being secured who would interest themselves in protecting and feeding game birds throughout the closed seasons, especially during the winter, and the Executive was ordered to bring before the following meeting a scheme to secure the interest of farmers and get them to take such action.

"Several communications were read from parties in the United States who are dealers in game birds. These all explained the difficulty of securing Hungarian Partridges and Pheasants at this time.

"A communication from the Canadian Department of Fisheries regarding stocking Alberta waters was read. This was referred to the Executive.

"The meeting adjourned shortly before 10 o'clock, to meet again within two weeks.

"*Recorded by Walter Holmes, Secretary*"

Reproductions of the original minutes of the first organizational meeting of the AFGA held March 3, 1920.

"The second meeting

of the Northern Alberta Game and Fish Protection League was announced to be held Friday, March 26, 1920, at 8 p.m. at the Hotel Macdonald, but on account of the charge made for the use of the room, the meeting place was changed to the Board Room of the King Edward Hotel. The meeting was called to order at 8:20 p.m. President Esch explained to the meeting that whereas a charge of $20 was asked by the manager of the Macdonald Hotel, the King Edward management offered the use of the room without charge, which was greeted with applause.

"The minutes of the preceding meeting were read and adopted. The Constitution as drawn up by the Executive was submitted, clause by clause. It was adopted with one amendment. A later motion to add to the constitution was received and is dealt with in these minutes further on.

"Correspondence was read and ordered filed. This had to do with a letter from the Postmaster, C.E. Atter, Pine Lake, regarding bass in that lake; also a letter from Mr. M.M. Case in which the writer stated he had seen bass caught at Pine Lake during 1917; also a letter from the Fisheries Department stating that a report was being sought on Hastings and Ministik Lakes to ascertain their suitability to bass; and an acknowledgment by the Parks Branch of a letter asking for permission to place Hungarian Partridges in Dominion Parks.

"A note of thanks was passed to the management of the King Edward Hotel for the use of their Board Room.

"Under reports by committees, Chairman Boon named his appointees as Chris Irgens and J.C. McCaig to complete the Fish Committee.

"Chairman Hine named H. P. Warren and W. Wolfe to complete his Game Bird Committee. Mr. Hine also thought the ammunition makers should be asked for prizes to be offered in a crow-shooting contest. A crow shoot is to be organized throughout Northern Alberta, a given date to be set, and the co-operation of sportsmen in smaller centres to be enlisted.

"Chairman P. Anderson of the Big Game Committee made his first appearance before the members. He spoke very earnestly on the necessity of prosecuting violators of the closed season. Also, he spoke of the present law protecting cow moose and other big game, and expressed the opinion that each few years, the shooting of cows be allowed as otherwise the natural balance was upset: many dry cows resulted from lack of sufficient bulls and this could be avoided if each few years the shooting of cows was allowed.

"On motion, the reports of the committees were adopted.

"A recess was set by the President to allow those present to become affiliated as members of the League, E. Morris, J. Bowen and W. Mason be appointed to receive same.

"President Esch referred to the season suggested by the Provincial Game Guardian for Prairie Chicken for 1920; he stated that the Edmonton Gun Club had appointed a committee to interview the friends of the sportsmen in the Legislature and also to appear before the Committee on Agriculture to see if the season could be made the full month of October or the first two weeks. As President, he stated he had named a committee from the League to act in conjunction with the Gun Club Committee. Dr. Rooney speaking on this matter thought that the matter of having Sunday shooting allowed should also be brought up before the House. But as the Lord's Day Act, which prevents Sunday shooting is a Dominion Act, it was said the Dominion Government would have to be approached.

"A motion was proposed and seconded that a committee of this League be appointed to draw up a petition, secure signatures and submit it to the proper authorities asking that Sunday shooting be allowed. This was carried.

"Mr. J. D. Willson, Inspector of Fisheries, gave a comprehensive report of the game conditions as far as fish are concerned in this district. He spoke of difficulties, both arising from natural causes, and departmental regulations, that would have to be overcome if the League's proposal to introduce sporting fish in local waters was to be a success. The hearty co-operation of his department was assured to the League and much appreciated.

"Mr. E. S. Leonard told of the way Minnesota had overcome some of the difficulties mentioned by Mr. Wilson.

"Mr. H. Barry of Clover Bar suggested that the League should get in touch with the ABC Auto Club of Clover Bar District. Also he thought that the League would make friends with the farmers if the young boys were advised to leave their .22s at home, as the farmers were much more apprehensive of damage by careless handling of rifles than of shotguns.

"Mr. Hilton suggested that some action should be taken to teach the value of songbirds to the community and to do all possible to protect songbirds. He thought this work could be taken up in the schools by getting the school children interested in creating bird houses, feeding the birds, and such ways. He also suggested that a children's branch of the League should be formed with a low membership fee. Out of this suggestion, a motion was made and carried that the constitution be amended to allow for a Chairman of Songbirds Committee with two appointed members to complete the committee. Mr. Hilton was unanimously elected to this committee. The fee for the school children's branch, which will be under his direction, was set at 10 cents.

"The matter of a crow shoot was brought up and on motion; it was left for the Executive Committee to work out the details.

"In answer to a question, the President stated that meetings would be held from time to time as necessity arose, and whenever business of general interest could be put before the members.

"An active campaign for members is to be instituted several taking books of tickets for this purpose. The meeting adjourned at 10:45 p.m.

"Recorded by Walter Holmes, Secretary"

COURTESY OF JOHN KERR SR.

Kerr family fishing trip on the Crowsnest River, circa 1925. Mary Kerr (L), Mrs. John (Anne) Kerr (rear left), John Kerr Jr. (front left) James (Jim) R. Kerr (front right), and John Kerr Sr. (right). Kerr Sr. was an active photographer with good cameras, and did his own developing in the basement of his home as there were no commercial facilities at the time. Here, he used a timer and then got back into the photo himself, complete with teacup in hand!

1921 Adam Esch was the president of the NAGFPL. At a meeting in February 1921, Ben Lawton spoke in favour of "white coats" for hunters, presumably for their own safety; this was opposed by the members present. Minutes of this meeting also indicated that members were opposed to the protection of black bears.

At a March 10 supper meeting, however, the resolution regarding white coats for hunters was approved while it was resolved that market hunting be prohibited. During that meeting, a transfer of perch to Ministik and Hastings Lake was discussed—an example of some early fish propagation projects.

Also of note is a record at a meeting on May 2 of a protest sent to Ottawa regarding a drainage policy [for wetlands] in Alberta. There are also records in support of spring closures to protect spawning trout, because "...trout being caught early in [the] season were full of spawn."

1922 A. Kinnaird was the president of the NAGFPL. Records from a February 1922 meeting indicated the NAGFPL made requests of government for involvement in any amendments to the second *Game Act of Alberta*, indicative of early attempts by the organization to be part of the decision-making process that affected their interests.

1923 There is no record of the executive for this year. At a meeting on Feb. 26, there was a discussion regarding the advisability of changing the name of the NAGFPL, which had a connotation of being restrictive (i.e., the name could be interpreted as the league being opposed to hunting and fishing). Of interest at this meeting was a proposal to create a game commission. While details in support of this motion were not recorded, it is perhaps indicative of some early sportsmen's concerns that politics should be removed from fish and game management in Alberta, and a board of commissioners be held responsible for overall management, as is the case in most jurisdictions in the United States.

1924 Dr. Rooney was the president of the NAGFPL. Much of the business for this year dealt with propagation of fish and fowl, including requests for a permit to ship black bass from Ontario to Alberta to be stocked in Ministik Lake and the release of Hungarian partridge by the Whitecourt local. Ben Lawton reported that shooting crows on Sunday would not have official sanction. Professor Rowan (University of Alberta) suggested the formation of a scientific section of the AFGA, a first for the organization.

COURTESY OF GORDON KERR

Jim Kerr and his horse Rags near Castle River. In the 1920s there were a few old logging trails, but that was long before seismic lines and ATVs. Jim and Rags covered a lot of ground, but the rewards of the likes of this good mule deer from the Carbondale-Lynx Creek country was well worth the effort.

COURTESY OF GORDON KERR

Brother and sister Jim (L) and Mary Kerr fishing in the Crowsnest River, about 1924.
It was good fishing then too! Photographer John Kerr Sr. was active in rod and gun clubs as
early as 1909.

COURTESY OF GORDON KERR

During a visit to the Waterton Lakes Trout Rearing Station, are Jim Kerr (L), secretary
treasurer of the Coleman Fish and Game Association, and George E. Watt, president of the
AFGA, discussing trout stocking plans for the season ahead.

1925 Dr. Rooney remained president of the NAGFPL. Messrs. Rowan, Strickland, Fryer and R.T. Rodd were to act as the AFGA Scientific Committee.

There was a motion that the AFGA take steps to stop commercial fishing in Cold Lake and Trout Lake, and that the closing of trout streams tributary to the Elbow River be affected. During the first half of the century, commercial fishing was important to Alberta's economy and much of the attention of the fisheries branch was directed towards administration and management of various commercial fisheries.

There was a note in the Sept. 30 minutes that "…crows and magpies are a growing menace." Grouse were reported being scarce in 1925 while the population of Hungarian partridge appeared to be increasing.

1926 Dr. Rooney remained president of the NAGFPL. At the Feb. 25 meeting there was a motion that "That the government be asked to conduct a CROW CAMPAIGN," and that there be immediate protection for remnant elk in the Brazeau area. There was also discussion that permits should be granted for the serving of game at banquets, presumably to curtail consumption of illegally shot game animals in hotels. The hiring of salaried game guardians by government was discussed, along with diseased Hungarian partridge being reported from the Wainwright area.

At a meeting on Nov. 3 the association approved a motion that a fishing licence be required for children under 16.

1927 E.P Hall was elected president of the NAGFPL. Mr. Hall died while in office and was replaced by H.H. Cooper.

The AFGA has a long history in support of non-game programs and the executive appointed a songbird chairperson again in 1927. As well, there were committees responsible for big game, bird game, fish, membership and a scientific committee. In the educational area, Dr. Nicholls recommended the league should print a pamphlet about the objectives and accomplishments of the association to date. Once again, an independent commission was requested to administer the *Game Act*. Dr. Rooney and W. Mason were appointed to act as a committee to promote the establishment of a fish hatchery in Jasper National Park.

The association had long opposed the commercial harvest of game fish such as lake trout in Cold Lake. Records indicate that in 1927 it requested a limit of 30 tons of lake trout on Cold Lake as a conservation measure and wanted the season closed on this species.

COURTESY OF GORDON KERR

Morden, a real forester, later to be with forestry department. Date of photo unknown, probably in the 1920s.

There had been some discussion during the year to delete the word "northern" from the name of the local. However, it was decided not to make any changes until other leagues in the northern part of the province started functioning.

There was also discussion about requesting permits for the shooting of crows on Sunday. No shooting was permitted on the sabbath.

At the Dec. 6 meeting there was a discussion over a letter received from Mr. Hayden, Calgary, regarding the formation of a Provincial Game Protective Association. Dr. Wilson and Mr. Nicholls recommended that the league approve this plan.

On a more sinister note, Stan Clarke of Entrance recorded that he "...advocated further endeavour to have more protection for Big Game. Out of season killing by Half breeds was rampant."

COURTESY OF GORDON KERR

Family fishing trip on rocks near Waldon Bridge.

Farm near Consort.

SEASON 1934

GOVERNMENT OF THE PROVINCE OF ALBERTA
DEPARTMENT OF LANDS AND MINES
(FISHERIES SERVICE)

No. 6753

ANGLING PERMIT
(Issued under authority of The Fishery Act)

NAME OF PERMITTEE _James R. Kerr_

PLACE OF RESIDENCE _Maple Leaf, Alberta_

is hereby permitted to fish, by means of ANGLING, in all waters in the PROVINCE of ALBERTA, other than waters closed to fishing under The Fishery Act and Regulations thereunder, and in waters in the National Parks of Canada.

The fee for this permit is $2.25.

It is a condition of this permit that the person to whom it has been issued must comply fully with the provisions of The Fishery Act, and the Regulations made thereunder; also any instructions given verbally or in writing by Fishery Officers and Forestry Officers, and in default of compliance with any of these regulations or instructions this permit shall automatically become null and void and any privileges granted by the issue of this permit shall be forfeited forthwith, saving unto the Crown the right of any action that may be taken under The Fishery Act and Regulations.

The granting of this permit neither conveys nor implies any right or claim to its continuance beyond the period stated.

Permittees must carry their permits with them, and produce them when requested by any Fishery Officer, Fishery Guardian, Forestry Officer, or Police Officer.

R. T. RODD,
Director of Fisheries.

R. G. REID,
Minister of Lands and Mines.

This permit is valid from _16th June_ to _15th October_

Countersigned by _John Kerr_
Issuing Officer.

Dated at _Passburg_, Alberta, this _15th_ day of _June_ 1934.

THIS PERMIT IS NOT TRANSFERABLE.
"PREVENT FOREST FIRES"—(OBSERVE THE LAWS AND REGULATIONS)

General

"Minister" shall mean the Minister of Lands and Mines.
"Angling" shall include trolling and shall mean the taking of fish with hook and line held in the hand, or with hook and line and rod, the latter held in the hand, but shall not include set lines or lines tied to a boat.
"One day" shall mean during hours of daylight.
"Closed season" shall mean a specified time during which fish may not be taken.
A resident of the Province may angle in waters frequented by Trout, Grayling, or Rocky Mountain Whitefish, for a fee of two dollars and twenty-five cents.
Children under 16 years do not require an Angling permit providing their parents have obtained such permits.
Non-resident—A non-resident shall not engage in angling except under permit. The fee for such permit shall be two dollars and twenty-five cents.

Close Seasons
(Trout, Grayling, Rocky Mountain Whitefish)

Including Bow River and all streams south to International boundary, from October 16th to June 14th following, both days inclusive.
Red Deer River, North Saskatchewan River and tributaries, September 16th to May 15th following, both days inclusive.
Athabasca River and tributaries, October 16th to June 14th following, both days inclusive.
Lake Trout—from September 16th to May 15th following, both days inclusive.
Pike, Pickerel, Perch and Goldeyes—from April 1st to May 15th, both days inclusive.

Size Limits

Lake Trout under 15 inches in length, and all other Trout, Grayling, or Rocky Mountain Whitefish under 9 inches must be returned to the water alive and uninjured.

Per Diem Catch

Not more than 10 Lake Trout.
Not more than 20 of any other species of Trout, Grayling, or Rocky Mountain Whitefish, or of all combined amounting to not more than 20 fish.
Not more than 25 Perch or Goldeyes or both combined.
Not more than 15 Pike or Pickerel or both combined.
And not more of the four species combined that will in the aggregate exceed 20 fish.

Prohibitions

Gang hooks for Trout, Grayling and Rocky Mountain Whitefish fishing, explosives, firearms, spears, and snares prohibited.

Closed Waters (To All Fishing)

No fishing is permissible at any time in the following streams in Alberta, which streams are set apart for the purpose of natural propagation of fish.

Pine Creek and tributaries in Townships 2 and 3, Ranges 29 and 30, West of the 4th Meridian.
Camp and Coal Creeks tributary to Old Man River.
Cow or Camp Creek tributary to Tod Creek.
All tributaries to Crow's Nest River, west of and including Connelly Creek.
Burke or Brown Creek and tributaries and Quail Creek, tributary to Trout Creek.
All streams and their tributaries flowing into North and South branches of Willow Creek.
All tributaries of the Highwood River.
All tributaries of the Elbow River.
Spring Creek in Section 30, Township 20, Range 29, West of the 4th Meridian; and Section 25, Township 20, Range 1, West of the 5th Meridian.
Sand and Sullivan Creeks, in Townships 52 and 53, Range 23, West of the 5th Meridian.
Fish Creek, in Townships 51 and 52, Ranges 25 and 26, West of the 6th Meridian.
That part of Dog-pound Creek, West of the highway bridge at Bottrell, and in Townships 27 and 28, Ranges 4, 5 and 6, West of the 5th Meridian.

The Muskeg or Edson River and tributaries North and West of the forks in Section 26, Township 54, Range 18, West of the 5th Meridian.
That part of the Bow River and Canadian Pacific Irrigation Canal flowing through the Englewood Bird Sanctuary within the City of Calgary.
All waters within the Crow's Nest Forest Reserve except the main streams of the Old Man, Livingstone, Carbondale and Castle Rivers, West Branch of Castle River and Race Horse Creek from the mouth of Daisy Creek eastward and Yarrow and Drywood Creeks west to the falls.
All waters within the Bow River Forest Reserve except the main streams of the Red Deer, Bow, Elbow, and Highwood Rivers, Kananaskis Lakes and River and the Spray Lakes.
Shunda Creek and its tributaries within the Clearwater Forest Reserve.
All waters within the Brazeau Forest Reserve, except the main streams of the Brazeau, Cardinal, Pembina, Lovatt, Erith, Embarras and McLeod Rivers, and the following tributaries thereto:
McKenzie Creek, Mary Gregg Creek, Mary Gregg Lake, Drinnen Creek, Warden Creek, Berry's Creek, Gregg River, White Creek and the main stream of Beaver Dam Creek.

The above is not a complete transcript of the Regulations governing Angling. It is intended merely as a concise statement of the provisions most likely to be of general interest. For further information apply to the local Fishery Officer or Forestry Officer, or direct to the Department at Edmonton.

1934 angling permit.

1928-1937

Summary

Major issues: Bounty on crows and magpies; control of wolves, eagles, coyotes and pests; slaughter of moose, deer and caribou by Indians for their hides in northeastern Alberta; colour of hunting clothing.

Highlights: *1928* - First province-wide organizational meeting of the Alberta Fish and Game Association (AFGA) held in Calgary on July 11, 1928.
1929 - First annual convention held in Calgary.
1930 - Federal *Alberta Natural Resources Act* transferred jurisdiction for fish and wildlife management from the federal government to Alberta.
1937 - Chukar partridge first introduced.

Presidents: C.A. Hayden (1928-29), Dr. W.A. Wilson (1930), Frank Farley (1931), A.P. Burns (1932), Norman Frazer (1933-34), H.L. Wyman (1935), H.L. Wyman and L.E. Wise (each in part-1936), L.E. Wise (1937).

Canada's close economic links to the U.S. meant it quickly followed that country into the Great Depression that began in 1929. By 1933, 30 percent of the nation's labour force was out of work and 20 percent of the Canadian population was dependent on government assistance. However, on the Prairies, where the Depression coincided with a severe drought, conditions were much worse; close to two-thirds of the population was on government relief. Alberta's population in 1931 was about 732,000; and the U.S. dollar was worth $13.61 in 2007 USD.

The start of an economic recession/depression seldom benefits the party in power, and such was the case with Mackenzie King's federal Liberals. They lost to Richard Bennett's Conservatives in August 1930. That government held power until Mackenzie King once again won an election in 1935.

The United Farmer's John Brownlee held power in Alberta until 1934 when he resigned in favour of Richard Reid, also of the United Farmers. In 1935, Reid and the United Farmers were defeated by William Aberhart and the new Social Credit party, which promised a reorganization of the Alberta economy to bring it out of the Depression.

In 1933, American Aldo Leopold published *Game Management*, the founding text book of the new science of wildlife management.

1928 Fred Nicholls was the president of the Northern Alberta Game and Fish Protective League (NAGFPL). Records show there were discussions at the Feb. 24 meeting regarding the formation of a provincial association.

Records also show that the Alberta Fish and Game Association (AFGA) had asked the provincial government to set aside funds, in an amount at least equal to the total game licence fees, for game protection and propagation.

Concerns were being expressed about a proposal to drain Big Lake near St. Albert. The members went on record as being opposed.

The first record regarding fishing derbies is found during this year. It referenced a member-only "fishing contest" with $50 in prizes to be allotted. Surprisingly, it was a barbless-hooks-only contest.

Dr. Rooney advocated raising the membership fee to $2, but W. Mason "...objected strongly feeling that membership would thus be cut in half." This was the first of many references regarding membership fees in the history of the AFGA. After discussion, it was moved and carried that the annual fee remain at $1.

The provincial AFGA was organized in Calgary on July 11, 1928 with 22 local associations represented. C.A. (Charles) Hayden was elected president. The first annual meeting was held in Calgary in 1929.

> George M. Spargo, secretary treasurer of the AFGA from 1925-62, provided a report on the History of Pheasants in Alberta in the 18th annual convention yearbook in 1947, wherein he noted: "Since the organization of the parent body in 1928, the association was motivated from the start with a co-ordinating policy with which to assist locals in procuring birds by exchange, circulars indicating the care of pheasants, proper food and liberation, ratio of sex, supervision, laws and regulations, open and closed season, information as to hatch and finally, to the construction of the game bird farm at Brooks, now the sole agency through which pheasants are hatched and liberated."

The first two meetings of the AFGA in 1928-29 were provisional and organizational in nature.

1929 C.A. Hayden was president of the newly formed AFGA. Unfortunately, records of meetings and activities of the AFGA until about 1945 are missing and the authors have relied on the NAGFPL records to describe these early years.

Dr. W. A. Wilson was the president of NAGFPL. The question of hunting "costumes" was again a topic of discussion in 1929 and a committee of the NAGFPL was established to select a colour.

NAGFPL supported a motion that there be a bounty on coyotes. A novel idea to cull crows was put forward by Professor Rowan. He proposed releasing his captive crows bearing numbered tags on Nov. 9 and that five prizes of $5 be offered for shooting a tagged crow. Most crows would have been long departed by this late date in the season, as they are summer residents that do not winter in Alberta.

At the annual AFGA convention in Calgary on July 11, 1929, the following resolution was passed: "RESOLVED: That the Minister of Agriculture be further petitioned to still further extend his program for the extermination of crows, magpies, and other menaces to game birds and to this end to appoint an official, whose duty it will be to organize campaigns in various districts of the Province. And that the various branches of this association pledge practical support to such officials in said organization work."

At the first annual convention of the AFGA on July 11, 1929 (a year to the day since the provincial organization was formed), some 38 locals were represented. Hayden remarked, "I firmly believe that our association has justified its existence and that interest in it will grow and… be responsible for the creation of one of the finest fish and game countries in the world." According to the first bulletin issued by the association on Dec. 15, 1928, senior government officials responsible for fish and game management and protection in Alberta were of the unanimous opinion that a provincial association could bring about a definite improvement in regulations and conditions respecting wildlife (Lewis, 1979).

COURTESY OF GORDON KERR

Jim Kerr (L) and Andy Dow both of the Coleman Fish and Game Association on the Livingstone River, circa 1930s.

Alberta Natural Resources Act

Until 1930, matters concerning the management of fish, wildlife and other resources had been under the jurisdiction of the federal government. Thus, the early fish and game clubs had to petition the federal government to make changes to management policy and regulations, such as the earlier referenced water drainage projects. At the urging of the province, the federal government passed the *Alberta Natural Resources Act* in 1930. Key provisions include:

Alberta Natural Resources Act 1930, c. 3

FISHERIES

9. Except as herein otherwise provided, all rights of fishery shall, after the coming into force of this agreement, belong to and be administered by the Province, and the Province shall have the right to dispose of all such rights of fishery by sale, licence or otherwise, subject to the exercise by the Parliament of Canada of its legislative jurisdiction over sea-coast and inland fisheries.

INDIAN RESERVES

10. All lands included in Indian reserves within the Province, including those selected and surveyed but not yet confirmed, as well as those confirmed, shall continue to be vested in the Crown and administered by the Government of Canada for the purposes of Canada, and the Province will from time to time, upon the request of the Superintendent General of Indian Affairs, set aside, out of the unoccupied Crown lands hereby transferred to its administration, such further areas as the said Superintendent General may, in agreement with the appropriate Minister of the Province, select as necessary to enable Canada to fulfil its obligations under the treaties with the Indians of the Province, and such areas shall thereafter be administered by Canada in the same way in all respects as if they had never passed to the Province under the provisions hereof.

11. The provisions of paragraphs one to six inclusive and of paragraph eight of the agreement made between the Government of the Dominion of Canada and the Government of the Province of Ontario on the 24th day of March, 1924, which said agreement was confirmed by statute of Canada, fourteen and fifteen George the Fifth chapter forty-eight, shall (except so far as they relate to the *Bed of Navigable Waters Act*) apply to the lands included in such Indian reserves as may hereafter be set aside under the last preceding clause as if the said agreement had been made between the parties hereto, and the provisions of the said paragraphs shall likewise apply to the lands included in the reserves heretofore selected and surveyed, except that neither the said lands nor the proceeds of the disposition thereof shall in any circumstances become administrable by or be paid to the Province.

12. In order to secure to the Indians of the Province the continuance of the supply of game and fish for their support and subsistence, Canada agrees that the laws respecting game in force in the Province from time to time shall apply to the Indians within the boundaries thereof, provided however, that the said Indians shall have the right, which the Province hereby assures to them, of hunting, trapping and fishing game and fish for food at all seasons of the year on all unoccupied Crown lands and on any other lands to which the said Indians may have a right of access.

BIRD SANCTUARIES

19a. The Province may discontinue any bird sanctuary or public shooting ground which was transferred to the Province by virtue of this Agreement or which has since been established by the Province or which may hereafter be established by the Province pursuant to this Agreement in any case in which an agreement is entered into between the Minister of Mines and Resources of Canada and the Minister of Lands and Mines of Alberta approved by the Governor in Council and the Lieutenant Governor in Council respectively, providing for the discontinuance of any such bird sanctuary or public shooting ground.

Of interest was a motion that the AFGA go on record opposing the transfer of natural resources management to the provincial government, and that the federal government retain administration of the fisheries branch. The federal *Alberta Natural Resources Act* was passed in 1930 and gave authority to Alberta to manage its own fish and wildlife resources for the first time.

1930 Dr. W. A. Wilson was president of the AFGA and Frank Farley was vice president. The second annual convention was held at the Macdonald Hotel in Edmonton on Friday, July 18, 1930. It was hosted by NAGFPL. Cold Lake trout [lake trout], a gift of the federal Department of Marine and Fisheries, was served at the luncheon.

AFGA pressure to better enforce hunting seasons appeared to be paying off. The executive agreed to send a letter of appreciation to the minister responsible for the game ordinance, as well as Benjamin (Ben) Lawton, the provincial game guardian, for a "...noticeable improvement in enforcement of the *Game Act* during 1929." Ben Lawton had supplied the membership chairperson with a list of names of people who had purchased hunting and angling licences so the league could promote membership. Today, this would not be possible as such revealing of private information would be contrary to the *Freedom of Information and Protection of Privacy Act*.

Delegates were welcomed to the convention by H.A. Craig, deputy minister of the Department of Agriculture, who reminded them that they would have greater responsibilities as a result of the transfer of natural resources agreement coming into force.

The first resolution arising from business at the meeting stated, "That this Association is in favour of special licences being granted for moose, deer and caribou, north of the North Saskatchewan River, for the months of September and October." The resolution carried unanimously.

Distinguished patrons of the association were declared:
1. H.R.H. The Prince of Wales
2. Premier J.E. Brownlee
3. Senator Lessard, Edmonton
4. Senator W.A. Buchanan, Lethbridge
5. Senator Dan Riley, High River
6. Hon. R.B. Bennett, M.P., Calgary
7. K.A. Blatchford, M.P., Edmonton
8. J.W. Frame, M.L.A., Athabasca
9. Geo. McLachlan, M.L.A., Clyde
10. A.E. Cross, Calgary
11. P. Burns, Calgary

Lake sturgeon from North Saskatchewan River.

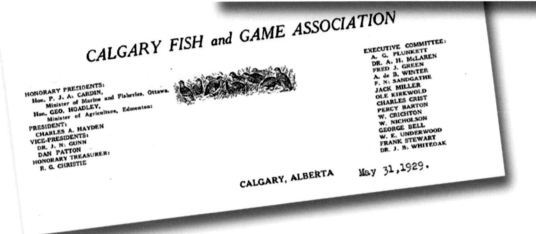

Early letterheads from the "Alberta Fish & Game Assn." and the "Calgary Fish and Game Association."

The following provincial committees were in force in 1930: angling committee, legislative committee, upland game birds committee, big game committee, constitutional and by-laws committee and a scientific committee.

The Hon. George Hoadley, Minister of Agriculture, addressed the delegates, reporting "…he was out to see that the Game and Fish of this Province should first of all be conserved for the people and sportsmen of this Province, primarily," adding "Secondly, to the sportsmen of Canada as a whole, and finally to the tourists and guests from other parts of the world."

Delegates must have been of a serious mind respecting Resolution No. 20, "That this Association write to the manufacturers of automobiles suggesting the placement of two ash trays in every car, thus assisting in the movement to 'Save the Forests.' It was further suggested that the association forward the above resolution to every Association, as well as the Dominion Fish and Game Association requesting co-operative assistance in the above regard."

Delegates carried a resolution calling for a halt to the slaughter of moose, primarily for their hides, in the area north of Cold Lake, Primrose Lake and surrounding districts. Apparently, hides of not only moose, but also deer and caribou, were being made into moccasins, mitts, gloves, coats, pants, robes and other apparel for sale. One dealer in Cold Lake was handling about 3,000 pairs of moccasins annually, another about the same amount, and other stores also in the thousands of pairs annually. According to the Cold Lake Big Game Guides Association

records published in the preliminary report of the AFGA second convention for 1930, "Roughly around eight thousand pairs of moccasins are handled annually by four merchants, representing the bounty on eight hundred head of moose, while Bonnyville and St. Paul handle considerable leather goods, most of which originally came from our district, that is east of the Sand River and north of the Beaver River."

The above report also noted, "The question of Indian privilege has been a sore spot. If Indians are subservient to our provincial game laws, then no attempt has been made to curb their depredations."

It wasn't just the Indians who raised cause for concern among members of the association. Resolution No. 26 moved, "That this association request that the Alberta Elk's Lodge consider the use of some emblem—other than elk teeth—to avoid the illegal killing of elk." This motion was carried. To carry on with this theme, Resolution No. 28 moved, "That this association request that the government place the following birds on the open vermin list: great horned owl, Snowy owl, goshawk." The motion carried.

Resolution No. 30 moved, "Whereas the provincial government of Alberta is to be commended for the splendid effort it has put forth to encourage the destruction of crows and magpies; and whereas the decrease in the number of these pests is quite noticeable in some districts; be it therefore resolved that the AFGA request the provincial government to continue in this good work and to also increase the competitions by creating one to be known as the 'Theatre Award'."

Group fishing expedition in the 1930s.

1931 Frank Farley was president of the AFGA.

Norman Frazer was president of the NAGFPL. George Spargo, secretary treasurer of the NAGFPL, had a salary of $120 as a paid employee in 1931. This position was [officially] filled by Spargo for the first time in 1930 although other records indicated he started work as secretary treasurer in 1925. Spargo replaced H.C. Tolchard who was secretary of the league during 1929.

Issues related to avian predators continued, and $150 was voted for the crow control program, with an alleged menace of eagles to the young of bighorn sheep being drawn to the attention of the big game committee.

W.J. Dick addressed the members with regard to fly casting and tying, the first time this subject appeared in the records.

The minutes also record a vote of condolences on the death of Ben Lawton, Alberta's chief game guardian, who passed away in 1931.

1932 A.P. Burns was president of the AFGA; and Norman Fraser remained as president of the NAGFPL. At the Feb. 9 executive meeting the minutes state the association should economize "...as a result of the DEPRESSION."

Records indicate that the executive recommended that the "President of the Alberta Association and the President of the Dominion [provincial] Association be approached regarding the formation of a Game Commission and that control of wolves, eagles, coyotes and pests be the primary objective of the appointed commissioner; a bounty on wolves was urged on the government."

Stan Clark became Alberta's new provincial government Chief Game Guardian in 1932, replacing Ben Lawton.

The annual conference was held in Lethbridge, Alberta.

1933 Norman Frazer became the president of the AFGA in 1933. The NAGFPL president was L.E. Wise. The minutes of the NAGFPL reflect that the fisheries branch had obtained a second consignment of Loch Leven fry [brown trout] for stocking in Lake Wabamun and Pigeon Lake; also rainbow trout fry for streams west of Edmonton.

A birdhouse contest with prizes was recorded for the first time. As well, the Royal Canadian Mounted Police offered its co-operation in enforcement for the first time. Also, a fly-and-bait cast contest at Elk Island National Park with prizes was recorded for the first time. R. T. Moore was the winner.

It wasn't just on matters of fish and game that AFGA lobbied the government. The association urged the government to gravel the road between Edmonton and Jasper. It also formed a committee to lobby the government to approach school boards advocating education in wildlife conservation policies.

The annual conference was scheduled for Edson.

A prize of $5 was approved for a bass (specimen) caught legitimately in Alberta waters.

COURTESY OF ANNE AND STEVE SAPETA

Walter (L), Bill and Steve Sapeta with their horse Phoenix on family farm north of Cowley, 1934.

1934 Norman Frazer continued as president of the AFGA. The NAGFPL president was Neville Lindsay. The convention was scheduled for High River. Some of the resolutions were earmarking licence fees for game protection and urging the Fish and Game Commission to implement bounties on predators.

A motion was made that the AFGA approach the premier recommending the commission be moved from the Department of Agriculture to the Department of Lands and Mines.

1935 H.L. Wyman was the AFGA president. The NAGFPL president was N. Lindsay. A controversial item was recorded in the minutes by H.A. Mason, who "...reported on Indian's disregard for Game life, describing conditions in the Brazeau area."

The *Edmonton Journal* was approached suggesting they follow the *Halifax Star* in reporting fish and game activities.

The 7th annual provincial convention was held in Edmonton at the Corona Hotel. There was a resolution banning duck shooting over water, but allowing stubble shooting, in the event of the U.S. declaring a closed season for migratory birds in 1935. This year marked the height of the depression which was characterized by a

pervasive drought that impacted waterfowl propagation throughout the Great Plains of North America.

Alberta Outdoors, a new magazine (publisher C. Groff) is mentioned with the promise of the AFGA endorsement.

The program for the annual convention highlights the name of the "Alberta Fish & Game Association" on the cover page, however, on the second page it features past presidents (C.A. Hayden, Dr. W.A. Wilson, A.P. Burns, F.L. Farley, and 1933-34: N. Fraser) along with the then present officers (president, 1935-36: H.L. Wyman, vice president: L.E. Wise, second vice president: L. Fairbairn and secretary treasurer: George M. Spargo) under the banner "Alberta Fish & Game Protective Association."

The Saturday evening game dinner was hosted by the NAGFPL with Neville R. Lindsay as toastmaster. Cold Lake trout were supplied courtesy of R.T. Rodd and the fisheries branch, and elk venison steak and moose steak courtesy of S.H. Clark and the game branch.

President Lindsay appealed to the executive for an extra effort toward increasing educational efforts as a primary AFGA objective. Essay contests were implemented in 1936 regarding fish and game conservation with $10 in awards as an incentive.

Another controversial report drew attention to the Minister of Lands and Mines about Indian depletion methods and their increasing sales of moose hides.

For the first time it is recorded that an AFGA member is honoured with a life membership: W.F.H. Mason, for "...his invaluable labours over the years."

1937 L.E. Wise remained as president of the AFGA. The NAGFPL president was S.A. Maddocks. The president's address called for the need for further education measures, following the lines of the AFGA essay contest. For example, in the Junior League, feeding of game birds in winter and construction of shelters; fish hatchery – restocking streams; restocking woodlands to support this league. C.I.L. [Canadian Industries Limited] was to be sent a thank you letter for their "SUPER Donation of 5,000 'MY PLEDGES' supplied towards the essay and drawing competitions." C.I.L. was the munitions giant of the day.

The Indian question [no elaboration given] was raised for discussion among the executive.

"Vermin control" was tabled as a serious issue, with a call for members "...truly interested to meet together at the close of the [March 8] meeting," at which time the Game Commissioner reported that "...his department was going all out to control predation and illegal hunting and fishing." As the year progressed, teams were formed and prize money set aside for an all-out vermin-control campaign. No actual details were provided on this campaign by Dr. Rooney, who was the secretary chairman of the crow and magpie [control] program.

A motion was made that it was time for the government to implement a game preserve in the Brazeau area. In addition, another motion was made that the government raise the hunting licence fee to $2.25 (a 25 cents increase) and also to raise big-game licences by 25 cents, the extra money obtained to be returned to the AFGA to be put towards game conservation projects.

The issue of hunting clothing remained, with a motion to require scarlet coats and caps, except above tree line.

At a meeting on Nov. 9, the crow campaign report indicated that 10,957 pairs of feet were turned in. The AFGA had been zealous in its crow-control program. By all reports, the AFGA had been zealous ever since its inception. Other predators were no exception and there is a report by Dr. Rooney that cougar killing by professional hunters was to be discontinued in parks. The organization urged a vigorous protest.

Of note was the retirement of George M. Spargo as secretary in 1937, presumably to take a job as fisheries director for the province. President Maddocks called on past president Lindsay to present Mr. Spargo with a distinguished service certificate, and expressions of sincere regret on the part of the executive and members at large.

As a result of a long lasting drought throughout the Great Plains of North America and its impact on waterfowl production, a group of far-sighted American sportsmen banded together to form Ducks Unlimited, incorporated on Jan. 29, 1937 in Washington, D.C. as a non-profit organization. The fledgling organization was "...dedicated to the wise management of waterfowl and the perpetuation of the noble heritage of water fowling." A sister organization, Ducks Unlimited (Canada), was created in 1938 to administer and construct waterfowl projects in Canada, where much of the waterfowl production occurred (Lewis, 1979).

COURTESY OF DUANE RADFORD

Flying R Ranch near the Cypress Hills.

COURTESY OF VERN MCINTOSH

Bill Kother, long-time member of Mayerthorpe Fish and Game, near Anselmo, 1946.

1938-1947

Summary

Major issues:	Predator control; re-stocking of lakes and streams; safe handling of firearms; sportsmen's stamp to raise money for conservation; financial constraints on the Alberta Fish and Game Association; Sunday hunting prohibition; lack of ammunition for firearms; killing of cow elk in the Castle-Carbondale area; lack of a fish management plan; closure of antelope season; stream improvement.
Highlights:	*1938* - Ducks Unlimited Canada established as a result of a pervasive drought during the 1930s.
	1940 - Calgary fish hatchery begins stocking fish.
	Terms of reference developed for local fish and game association clubs throughout the province.
	1942 - There is a record about the first white-tailed deer to be brought to Alberta.
	1943 - Fish and Game Advisory Council established.
	1945 - First AFGA wild game dinner for members of the Alberta government; the first year for which a president's report was available for the annual conference; Sportsman's Stamp petition originated; a seemingly bizarre motion was discussed by the executive to register rifles.
	1946 - The AFGA incorporated as a society.
Presidents:	L.E. Wise (1938-39), William Fisher (1940-41), Dr. R.A. Rooney (1942-43), J.A. McGhee (1944-46), G.E.Watt (1946-47)
Membership:	The first record of membership numbers (812) was in 1941, membership rose from 4,000 in 1943 to over 6,000 in 1944, 6,489 in 1945, 8,160 in 1945, 9,226 in 1947 (70 clubs).

Both Canada and the United States remained in economic depression until the outbreak of World War II in 1939. However, Canada had no national recovery program similar to that of President Franklin Roosevelt's New Deal in the United States. Also unlike the United States, Canada entered the war early alongside Great Britain in 1939. As factories turned to war production and soldiers were recruited to fight the war, unemployment virtually disappeared by 1940. In 1941, Alberta had a population of about 796,000; and the U.S. dollar was worth $14.08 in 2007 U.S. dollars.

Mackenzie King's Liberals held power federally for 13 years until 1948. In Alberta, William Aberhart's Social Credit government held power until Aberhart died in 1943. He was replaced by Ernest Manning, also of the Social Credit party. In 1947, the discovery of oil at Leduc transformed the economy of the province from mainly agricultural to industrial and agricultural.

1938 L.E. Wise continued as president of the AFGA. The Northern Alberta Game and Fish Protective League (NAGFPL) president was S.A. Maddocks.

As an example of just how high a priority predator control was with the AFGA executive, for the first time it struck a "vermin control" committee, chaired by Dr. Rooney. The executive decided that the Game Commissioner should be invited to a meeting and "...the question of needed CONTROL be put before him."

Of interest were all the deliberations that occurred at the executive meetings in 1938 to try to increase attendance at the AFGA meetings, from the need to show films to attract members, the timing of meetings so as not to conflict with "gardening" and the November hunting season, etc. Some things never seem to change.

Dr. Rooney advocated yet another crow and magpie campaign. Ducks Unlimited supported these campaigns and donated $1,300 towards crow and magpie control in 1938. The AFGA worked out a provincial strategy, complete with news coverage and prizes to encourage participation. A box of trap-load shotgun shells was awarded for each 15 pairs of crows' or magpies' feet turned in or five cents per pair of feet mailed in from rural areas. In September, the secretary reported that 4,600 pairs of crows' feet had been turned in for rewards. Today, these efforts appear almost comical, but early members of the AFGA were sincere in their belief that predators must be controlled to benefit game birds and big game.

In 1938, "Regulations Relating to Awarding of Prizes for the Destruction of the Following Agricultural Pests: Gophers, Crows, and Magpies" (Order in Council No. 319-32) were implemented. These regulations detailed cash prizes to be awarded for the destruction of these "pests" based on a point system and described rules of procedure for the awards. For example, "For each crow or magpie killed, four points shall be allowed (awards to be based on an allowance to two points for each foot produced). For each egg of a crow or magpie produced, four points should be allowed (unbroken eggs only to be counted). For each gopher killed, one point shall be allowed (tail only to be produced). Cash prizes will be awarded for eggs taken and birds or animals killed in 1938 on or before the 1st day of September." The awards were open to any gun club, game protective association, municipal district, or other organizations deemed acceptable by the local Justice of the peace; the awards were also open to schools and persons of school age. A first place prize of $200 was awarded for the top-seeded organization and $75 for the top individual resident of Alberta; a $70 prize was awarded for the top school competition.

During 1938 plans were made to raise and release additional chukar partridge following an initial introduction in 1937, even though the potential success of these introductions was questioned; preliminary reports indicated "chukar making good progress; test will be their SURVIVAL showing after the coming winter."

> *A*ccording to W. Ray Salt and A.L. Wilk (1966), the chukar partridge was first released in Alberta in the Calgary district in September 1937, but this implantation and others in immediately succeeding years were unsuccessful.
>
> In the 18th annual convention report for 1947, secretary manager George M. Spargo provided a report on the history of the introduction of Chukar Partridge. "The first shipment of 25 pairs of chukar was received and liberated at Dan Patton's farm at Midnapore. On Sept. 28, 1937 some 50 pair were imported and released in 1938, and over 500 birds were put down in April, 1939, in lots from 15 to 60 birds at selected posted places, with water and shelter, near the following: Calgary, Carseland, Champion, Stavely, Baintree, Kreoma, Didsbury, Vulcan, Midnapore, Castor, Indus, Lacombe, Drumheller, Innisfail, and Rockyford."
>
> Other releases were made by the NAGFPL in and around Edmonton.
>
> Spargo noted that two coveys were found in 1946 near Carseland and Innisfail and another covey was subsequently reported northwest of Cochrane, which was of interest because no chukar were ever planted in that district. He concluded: "It can be said on good ground that birds planted in our prairie region with the exception of the foregoing have simply vanished."

All attempts, by both the AFGA and officials in the Alberta government, to establish self-sustaining populations of chukar in Alberta failed.

In setting appropriations for the upcoming convention, the executive addressed various minutiae and details, with a note that "...member's ticket to the banquet [be] set at $1.00, with ladies admitted."

The first discussions took place in 1938 about the possibility of the government bringing in a biologist from Moose Jaw, Saskatchewan to survey Alberta waters, with Banff as a probable starting point. There was also a discussion about moving surplus deer in Elk Island National Park to the Cooking Lake Forest Reserve; that the reserve be fenced, with the idea of the area being made self-supporting through the sale of hunting licences. As time would tell, both Elk Island National Park and the Cooking Lake/Blackfoot Recreation Area (east of Edmonton) would be eventually fenced in. There were also discussions about urging the government to build a fish hatchery and rearing pond near Jasper.

1939 L.E. Wise continued as president of the AFGA and S.A. Maddocks continued as president of the NAGFPL. Maddocks retired during his term of office in 1939.

Dr. Rooney, vermin control chairman, kicked off the new year with a resolution at the Jan. 6 executive meeting urging that a $20 bounty on wolves be declared - a large sum of money in 1939. Later, reference was made by the president about making representation to the government about the "MAGPIE MENACE." Reports indicated that 2,107 pairs of crows' feet were sent in as a result of the crow campaign, with $100 being received from Ducks Unlimited to cover expenses. Controlled poisoning of magpies by paid officials was urged in the approved resolutions.

There was another resolution that the "...lending of hunting licences be punishable by a fine."

Despite unsuccessful attempts to rear and naturalize chukar, Dr. Rooney and other members pointed out the hardiness of the broods first hatched. They felt it was wise to continue the tests and make further purchases of eggs for propagation and release of birds to the wild.

"The Major," 1940s Ducks Unlimited Canada construction equipment fleet.

G.M. Spargo reported to the AFGA executive as director of fisheries in 1939, after having resigned from the AFGA as secretary treasurer in 1937.

> *A*t the December 21 general meeting, a report on angling stated, "Alberta fishing [was reported as] non-attractive to tourists," with a note that "Lakes and streams need re-stocking and hatcheries to replenish [fish]."

1940 The AFGA president for 1940 was William Fisher. G. Keltie became president of the NAGFPL. Just as certain as death and taxes, the AFGA executive advocated an early start of the crow and magpie campaign, and a bounty of five cents per pair of feet was approved; traps were advocated, with boys chosen to operate and move them. The president advised "…as to the increase of MAGPIES it being plain that winter control campaigns were necessary."

According to a guest speaker from Jasper, T. Young, "Control of cougar [is] now satisfactory. The $20.00 bounty being a very effective measure."

The AFGA was not solely focused on predator control, although it was certainly a high priority. They had songbird, publicity and education committees, for example, in addition to committees responsible for finance, membership, as well as big game and game birds.

There were ongoing resolutions in the late 1930s and again in 1940 to protect large pike in Jackfish Lake. Some fish were reported in the 20-pound range. The resolutions advocated special regulations to sustain the fishery, with a limit of one only 20-pound pike, for example, and a ban on use of live bait fish. G.M. Spargo, then provincial fisheries director, reported back to the AFGA that the department was unwilling to enforce the desired restrictions. The AFGA president G. Keltie made a motion, "We will try to prevail on Fishery Dept. to erect two SIGNS: CATCH LIMIT 20 lbs. and 1 fish; and Volunteer Wardens [be] appointed to give Service."

Hungarian partridge must have started to drop in abundance because Dr. Rooney made a motion that the "Bag limit on Huns (10 per day, 150/season) be changed." The season limit of 150 birds in 1940 is astounding by today's standards.

There was a report that the hatching success of chukar partridge was disappointing. The minutes recorded, "Assimilation and naturalization now deemed FAILURE as far as Alberta is concerned."

Reference is made that, "owing to unsettled conditions because of WAR and the satisfactory record of the present executive, especially that of the membership chairman Mr. Chadwick, who established a record for new members, THE PRESENT EXECUTIVE BE ELECTED TO REMAIN IN OFFICE FOR ANOTHER YEAR." The meeting was unanimous in favouring the election. No statistics are available regarding membership numbers, but it is rather striking that a record number of members joined the AFGA at the start of World War II.

> *C*orrespondence dated 1940 lays out the terms of reference for Fish and Game Protective Leagues affiliated with the AFGA. The "Organization: A league should have an enthusiastic group of Officers selected from among the ranks of Naturalists and Sportsmen because of their known interest in the Outdoors and League accredited objects. There should be a president, a vice president, a secretary, a treasurer (or secretary treasurer combined) with four other members, to wit:
> (a) Chairman of Game Animal Section.
> (b) Chairman of Game Bird Section.
> (c) Chairman of Songbird Section.
> (d) Chairman of Game-Fish Section.
> Each chairman should organize a sub-committee to secure interesting information regarding the Wild Life covered by his particular section. Aims and objects of the League should be generally:
> (a) Conservation of Alberta's Game Animals, Game Birds, Song Birds, and Game Fish.
> (b) Protection of Forests, Lakes and Streams.
> (c) Promotion of Protective Legislation for Wild-Life useful to man.
> (d) Dissemination of Knowledge to young and old in regard to Wild-Life.
> (e) Promotion of the true Spirit of Sportsmanship, with strict obedience to all law enactments. Members should never think of shooting or fishing without a license; should respect the Legal Limit; respect owner's rights, and see that others do likewise."

1941 William Fisher continued as president of the AFGA; and G. Keltie continued as president of the NAGFPL. At the Jan. 9 meeting, Dr. Rooney, by this time a long-standing chairman of the vermin control committee, urged that the bounty on eagles be increased, as a result of the marked decline in mountain sheep; that [domestic] cats be classed as predators; leagues [local AFGA clubs] be more active in "magpie control" in the winter. The big-game chairman reported that timber wolves and cougars were a serious menace, and continuance of protests was advocated. [It should be noted that science has never related deaths of mountain sheep (either lambs or adults) to eagles or any other birds of prey.]

> *A*t a Jan. 21 general meeting, R.B. Mackenzie, on behalf of fellow sportsmen, made the statement that "THIS LEAGUE, DUCKS UNLIMITED, and OUR FISH AND GAME DEPARTMENT, are to be commended in their efforts toward PREDATOR CONTROL, for as a result this past season showed noticeable increase in Game Birds."

Correspondence was read at the Nov. 21 meeting that "Jasper Park proposed Fish Hatcheries… Sum of $10,000.00 appropriated for JASPER PARK announced. SENSATIONAL!!"

During an interview with the Fish and Game commissioner, Eric Huestis, about the government conducting a predator campaign, the president reported that the new game director, superintendent Forsland, was "Enthusiastic about conducting WINTER PREDATOR CAMPAIGN thru his Wardens."

COURTESY OF DUCKS UNLIMITED CANADA

Gordon Lake Cabin, 1940.

The president reported for the membership chairman that the total membership was a record: 812. This was the first official membership report up to this point in time.

1942 Dr. R.A. Rooney became president of the AFGA. The NAGFPL president was Dr. T.F. Macdonald. For the first time since the resignation of G.M. Spargo as secretary of the NAGFPL in 1937, reference is made to a new secretary, V. Whitaker.

There was a special resolution to hire a full-time paid secretary of the provincial association. However, a counter-position was also proposed to abolish the resolution because "funds too limited to allow of per capita tax being used to pay for secretary." Senior members of the executive opposed this counter-position, arguing that "it was to the discredit of the Local Leagues that the man they depended on to do the secretary work of SIXTY LEAGUES had to pay for his own Salary by sale of STAMPS." It appears that the agenda for many of the AFGA meetings during 1942 centred on finances and the need for an increase in revenue from local clubs to support the hiring of a paid secretary treasurer.

Dr. Rooney reported that the government was prepared to spend $1,200 on magpie control by poisoning during the winter.

There was a discussion regarding whether there should be a proposed provincial association convention in 1943. Ottawa had requested that all unnecessary conventions be postponed for the duration of World War II; and this request was supported by the league.

1943 Dr. R.A. Rooney and Dr. T.F. Macdonald continued as presidents of the AFGA and the NAGFPL, respectively. Dan Carrigan was chosen as secretary of the NAGFPL.

Business items seemed to be curtailed during 1943, possibly due to the impact of World War II, even though membership apparently remained high.

At a May 27 Edmonton executive club meeting of the NAGF-PL, the president is recorded as saying, "Now we are beginning to SEE THE POWER VALUE OF A FINANCIALLY STRENGTHENED CENTRAL PROVINCIAL ASSOCIATION, and the wisdom of every Local League doing everything in its power to bring about this IDEAL CONDITION." Local leagues would be called local AFGA "clubs" today.

The usual predator campaigns against crows and magpies are recorded in the AFGA meeting minutes. Ducks Unlimited granted the AFGA a sum of $1,500 toward the crow and magpie campaign. The Alberta government came through with a grant of $2,500, with an additional $500 to handle the transfer of pheasants to selected areas, from the Brooks hatchery.

The annual provincial convention was held in Calgary, with a note that it would be held in Edmonton the following year.

Of interest is a record in the Calgary Fish and Game Association archives regarding the number of big game and fish licences sold, as follows:

	1941-42	1943-44
Big game	6,942	7,949
Fish	1,968	3,512

Correspondence from R.A. Rooney, president of the AFGA, to Mr. M.R. Christie of the Calgary Fish and Game Association, dated Jan. 27, 1943 advised, "The game commissioner and I are both greatly disappointed over the flop of the magpie poisoning campaign." Rooney added, "After much discussion, the commissioner went ahead, got a priority on some strychnine and bought quite a lot of it, had pamphlets mimeographed describing the best and safest means of setting out the bait and had a considerable amount of the poison mixed when the attorney general's department stepped into the picture saying that there were a number of provincial as well as federal statutes which would prevent any such plan as having members of our associations set out poison bait of any kind." Apparently there was a loophole in the legislation whereby "residents" could apply poison on their own premises. So Rooney concluded his letter by stating, "If you have any landowner who wishes to poison he can do so, the joker being that strychnine is very hard to get but some physician, dentist or veterinary might be persuaded to get some for you."

1944 J.A. McGhee became president of the AFGA in 1944. The NAGFPL president was R.B. MacKenzie. Upon acceptance of a motion from C.E. Brown it was agreed that Dr. Rooney, big-game chair, and others would meet with groups of young people and give advice on the safe handling of guns. It was also agreed that the NAGFPL should forward a letter to the *Edmonton Journal* and local *Bulletin* pointing out the illegality of children under the age of 16 being in possession of guns. In March the president welcomed a large gathering of scouts, girl guides, school patrol and young people in general during a presentation on the safe handling of firearms.

Jim Kerr's car with a two-day bag of pheasants, 1942.

Membership remained an issue with concerns expressed about the need to involve other outdoorsmen in the affairs of the league.

Rationing of ammunition was still in force, as a result of the war effort.

Interestingly, there was a motion that the league institute a request that British Columbia Angling Licence Fee to Albertans be equalized with the Alberta Angling Licence Fee to B.C. anglers. [This same sort of reciprocal arrangement was recommended in 2005 during discussions at the Provincial Fisheries Management Round Table meeting.]

The idea of a sportsmen's stamp to raise money for fish and game conservation was not approved unless it applied to fishing licences as well as hunting licences.

1945 President J. A. (Jim) McGhee of Brooks wrote an eloquent 1944 annual report for AFGA's 16th annual convention held in the Macdonald Hotel in Edmonton on Jan. 8-9, 1945. McGhee's passion for Alberta's fish and wildlife, tempered by his grave concern about the crisis of World War II, are notable highlights from this document, being the first year for which the president's report was available for the annual conference. The hot-button item of the day was finance, a lack of which was seen as a major impediment to the growth and development of the organization.

1945

Sportsman's Stamp	The Sportsman's Stamp involved a petition by the AFGA that was presented to the Alberta government in 1945 to make it lawful and compulsory for each sportsman who purchased a game licence to be surcharged an additional $1 to be earmarked for the association to provide operating revenue.
Resolution No. 17	Resolved that whereas many of our hunters for lack of shells have had to leave wounded game in the hills, therefore this local recommends to this convention the release of ammunition to each big-game licence holder. Delegates deferred this resolution to be dealt with by the incoming executive.

The only sources of money to operate the AFGA were a small per capita levy, small grants from the provincial government and from Ducks Unlimited, and revenue from the sale of a few game birds.

In order to raise revenues the association considered three solutions:

1. A sportsman's stamp
2. Increase in the per capita assessment
3. Tax on the sale of ammunition

McGhee reported that Sunday hunting was an issue, as well as the need for an AFGA five year plan, the crow and magpie control campaign, propagation of game birds, bird-game farms, the need for additional fish hatchery and rearing ponds capacity, additional supervision by wardens and a fur tax on wild fur.

COURTESY OF VERN MCINTOSH

Brothers Merv (L), Vern and Ken McIntosh and with Vern's dog Turk and their Daisy repeater BB guns used for grouse, near Anselmo in January 1942.

Despite the Sunday hunting prohibition over the entire province, it appears this law was widely disregarded in the countryside, as there was lax enforcement away from towns and cities.

Concerns regarding the propagation of game birds focused mainly on wild pheasants and Hungarian partridge – the mainstay of upland bird hunters during this decade. Concerns were expressed about late hatches of pheasants. Many of the young birds were not in full plumage by the season opening date of Oct 9. Other concerns were flooding of countless nests due to early flood irrigation brought on by drought, and increased hunting pressure. Also of interest were the government's early attempts to propagate pheasants by experimental releases of eggs and day-old chicks. In all, 11,570 eggs were distributed to 37 affiliated clubs from the American border to as far north as Barrhead. It was noted that the trapping and transplanting of adult birds met with some early success.

McGhee advised in his 1945 annual report, "Your executive officers are greatly perturbed at the situation both as regards the extreme numbers of magpies and crows, as well as the increase in wolves and coyotes during the past few years." He went on to boast, "You will observe that by the united efforts of this Association and its affiliated groups we succeeded in destroying legs [sic] and eggs in excess of ONE HUNDRED THOUSAND CROWS AND MAGPIES. Incidentally, the cost almost bankrupted our Association."

Considerable progress was reported to develop fish-rearing ponds at a number of locations throughout Alberta. There were reports of a large number of fingerlings from these ponds having been planted in streams.

Arrangements were made by the provincial fish and game commissioner to take over from the department of Agriculture the old Oliver Fur Farm and to operate it as a game-bird farm.

One cannot help but be impressed by the cordial relations that existed at this time between the executive of the AFGA and members of government of the day, along with their officials. A harmonious relationship and signs of goodwill are evident in all the proceedings and records. McGhee reports that "if these happy relations continue I am certain we will accomplish much for the cause we represent." This has not always been the case in the history of relations between the AFGA and the Alberta government. There have been disagreements over the years regarding the most suitable approach to address issues and concerns, with some members of the association opting for diplomacy while others called for a hard-line approach. In the end, more often than not, the "sportsman" approach usually prevailed, probably because of the near monopolistic one-party government that has characterized Alberta for so long, and the seemingly futile approach to be too critical of such governments.

The AFGA representatives on the advisory council of the day pressed the government to hire experts to make a survey of fish and game conditions that existed throughout the province. They suggested Dr. Ian McTaggart Cowan of the University of British Columbia for game, and Dr. Miller of the University of Alberta for fish. As it turned out, both Cowan and Miller were already engaged by the federal government for the season. This is an interesting development in its day, and something that is taken for granted by today's sportsmen, that there be surveys of fish and wildlife by qualified officials. Such surveys were virtually non-existent prior to the mid-1940s.

There had been no formal publication to keep members informed of the AFGA activities and the president felt that the time was "...ripe for a regular publication to disseminate items of interest," (President's Report for 1945).

COURTESY OF THE AFGA

GEORGE M. SPARGO
Secretary treasurer (1930-62).

Some remarkable progress was made in the growth of the AFGA under the leadership of J.H. McGhee and the capable administration of his vice president, G.E. Watt, who organized 15 new local clubs and revitalized two existing clubs, adding 17 new groups to the organization. The membership increased from little over 4,000 in 1943 to over 6,000 in 1944. McGhee was firmly convinced the AFGA could have a local organization in every town and village throughout Alberta—a grand vision which fell far short of his expectations—as time would tell.

Rationing of ammunition was still a fact of life as World War II drew to a close, and local clubs offered a box of shells for every 10 pairs of crows' or magpies' feet turned in to the AFGA. There was a lengthy report from the shotgun shell committee on issues related to the output of shotgun shells, in particular. Resolution No. 17 was submitted by the Bellevue Rod and Gun Club (the home town of co-author/editor Duane Radford) in the Crowsnest Pass area of southwestern Alberta.

In 1945 the officers of the association consisted of a president, four vice presidents, a secretary treasurer and an executive committee composed of the chairman of each section of the association, which formed a council to transact business when the association was not in session. In addition to the preceding officers, under the constitution and bylaws there was an elected chairman for each of the following committees or sections: angling, legislative, finance and membership, upland game birds, migratory birds, big game, constitutional and bylaws, scientific and predatory animals and birds.

The secretary treasurer's report from G.M. Spargo for 1944 was very detailed, crammed with minutiae down to how much correspondence was transmitted [Spargo had resigned his position as fisheries director with the provincial government and returned as a paid employee of the AFGA, its first secretary treasurer]: "...2,322 letters were dispatched and 810 additional circulars, a total of 3,132." Spargo practically glowed in his report on the crow and magpie campaign: "We have now, since 1938, destroyed over six hundred thousand (600,000) crows and magpies by united effort." Spargo concluded his report with a civility rarely seen today: "In conclusion, may I please tender my most grateful appreciation and thank you, to our most energetic president, Mr. McGhee, the executive officers, and to all our locals throughout the Province for their co-operation, kindness, and confidence during the past productive year, and to wish them happy days of hunting and fishing in 1945."

At the conclusion of 1944, the association was broke, as their expenses exceeded their revenue by some one thousand dollars and they were looking to find ways to address this shortfall at the 16th annual convention.

Note that in 1945, the annual meeting was called a "convention" which would later be designated as a "conference" starting in 1973.

There was a disturbing report from W.C. Fisher, the big game committee chair, regarding antelope in the 16th annual convention

COURTESY OF TRAVEL ALBERTA

Abraham Lake, along the David Thompson Highway near Nordegg.

1945

Resolution

In 1945 the AFGA mounted a vociferous lobby to allow Sunday shooting, with resolutions submitted from the locals at Stettler, Claresholm, Bellevue, Viking, Innisfail and Hillcrest. The Bellevue resolution read: "Whereas the miners work eight hours or more underground for six days, leaving only the seventh day on which to enjoy the mountain air, scenery and shooting, be it therefore resolved that Sunday shooting be allowable to all sportsmen of the Province."

report: "We had plenty of antelope this year, but our method of hunting them by allowing the shooting of does and bucks is deplorable. A herd of antelope were surrounded by hunters this year who shot the whole herd, using all sorts of weapons. One animal examined by the RCMP had six bullets in it, and the flesh was ruined. We can never hope to have our antelope herds kept in shape until we regulate the hunting of them." The report got worse, "I am advised that the antelope were chased by aeroplanes and jeeps, and that machine guns were used from the jeep to annihilate them."

> *There were a couple of notable motions in the minutes of the AFGA executive meeting held on Sunday, May 13, 1945.*
> *One such motion approved of the formation of the Western Canada – Yukon Fish and Game Council which would become a long-standing advisory council of importance to conservationists in the region.*
> *A second rather bizarre motion dealt with registration of rifles: "Moved by Mr. T. Evans and seconded by Mr. J. K. Webb that the association approaches [sic] the other western associations with a view of an unified front for the continuance of the registration of rifles, especially because of:*
> > *"1. The fact that guns were dangerous weapons.*
> > *"2. The foreign element.*
> > *"3. For statistical purposes registration [was] necessary or in the event of the Federal Government refusing to consider that the matter be brought before all provincial legislators asking that the province undertake such registration. Carried."*

1946 In his annual report for 1945, president J. A. McGhee expressed the AFGA concerns with "...the deluge of hunters and fishermen who will now visit our 'shores,'" as a result of the conclusion of World War II, and how that might compromise the association's goal to build up natural resources of fish and wildlife.

The 17th annual convention of the association was held at the Marquis Hotel Lethbridge in 1946 when the number of clubs in the association reached 55. New clubs were organized at Carbon, Sedgewick, Coleman, Rimbey, Blairmore, Raymond and Bashaw with total membership of 6,489.

McGhee reported that members of the government and opposition alike were all anxious to help the AFGA and "...were governed by a wholehearted interest in the fish and game resources of this province."

> *Editor's Note: This level of political interest in Alberta's fish and wildlife stands in marked contrast to a story related to co-author/editor Duane Radford by Dennis Surrendi, former Assistant Deputy Minister of the Fish and Wildlife Division. In 1982, Surrendi accompanied the Hon. J.E. (Bud) Miller, Associate Minister of Public Lands and Wildlife, during a presentation concerning the proposed Fish and Wildlife Policy for Alberta to the Progressive Conservative Party caucus. Surrendi was shaken when roughly half of the ruling government MLAs got up and walked out of the caucus meeting before the presentation even started. He asked Bud Miller what was going on, to which Miller replied that Surrendi shouldn't worry because the people who left were MLAs from the cities who didn't think fish and wildlife was of any interest to their constituents. He assured Surrendi that he was confident the remaining MLAs would endorse the proposed policy.*

One of the business items of 1945 was discussion and approval of a new game act at the annual advisory council meeting for submission to the upcoming legislative session.

The ongoing crow and magpie reduction program was marked by McGhee as the "...greatest endeavor on record," with $7,332.40 granted by the provincial government for the payment of feet and disbursed to the local AFGA clubs undertaking this summer

Canada Geese on Island Lake.

campaign. Ducks Unlimited provided an annual grant of $2,000 and monthly grants of $25 per month for $300. Over 146,000 pairs of crows' and magpies' feet were collected in 1945, apparently by far the greatest number ever taken since the AFGA started the program. Crows and magpies weren't the only predators on the hit list as the fish and game branch paid out over $40,000 in the extermination of over 8,000 coyotes. Predator control was done almost evangelically, with McGhee proudly stating, "This is the greatest exhibition of control ever accorded in this province, and deserves the commendation and approval of all our sportsmen without qualification."

> Secretary manager G.M. Spargo submitted a three-page crow and magpie campaign report for the 1945 convention yearbook with a breakdown of the number of pairs of crows' and magpies' feet and eggs turned in by all of the local Alberta fish and game clubs, with a footnote that the approximate cost per crow or magpie since 1938 was 3.68 cents per bird. The grand totals were as follows: crows – 49,789; magpies – 97,138; eggs – 19,900.

The magpie eradication program was extended to the winter of 1945, with several hawks and owls also being targeted. The Alberta government gave their support and approval for the AFGA to kill goshawks, prairie falcons, horned and snowy owls which were added to the bounty column.

COURTESY OF THE AFGA

Bighorn sheep.

1946

Resolution No. 46

The Turner Valley Fish and Game Association submitted Resolution No. 46 – Whereas many of our game animals are wounded and left to die at the hands of inexperienced hunters equipped with borrowed guns or guns that have not been shot [sighted] in, or guns of insufficient killing power to do the job: Be it resolved that every person making application for a license to hunt big game must satisfy the Fish and Game Association membership on the following points before the application for a license is approved:
(a) That the applicant has a knowledge of game regulations.
(b) That the applicant has a knowledge of fire hazards.
(c) That the applicant is familiar with the weapon he or she intends to use.
(d) That the applicant is a reasonably good shot and a fair judge of distance.
This resolution was handled by means of a code for rifles which was made available to convention delegates and to the locals following the convention.

Resolution No. 49

Whereas Eagles and Timber Wolves are bad, and on the increase all over the west country; therefore be it resolved that the two Governments (Dominion and Provincial) unite and pay bounties for same both in and out of national parks. This resolution was not carried.

Resolution No. 50

Resolved that the Government make monies available to the parent organization for distribution to the local groups for the purpose of destroying magpies at all times of the year, and that no limit be placed on that amount. This resolution was not carried.

Resolution No. 58

The Lethbridge Fish and Game Association submitted Resolution No. 58 – Resolved that this Association urge the parent organization to petition Ducks Unlimited for the purposes of enlisting American sportsmen to kill off crows during the winter season on their roosting quarters. The resolution carried.

A continuing priority was the new Game Rearing (pheasant) Farm at Brooks. Government officials were engaged in trapping wild birds to collect eggs and rear chicks. It's actually quite amazing that the rearing and release of pheasants has been ongoing for over 50 years and remains a priority to this day, being one of the most popular of all the AFGA programs.

The AFGA executive were strong believers in the value of publicity and encouraged their members to use radio and newspaper at every opportunity to advance the interests of their organization, even at this time in their history. They were also concerned about the importance of gun safety and the need for courses to teach new hunters about safe handling of guns. Concerns were also being expressed about reports regarding paid hunting and the need for restrictions on this menace to the AFGA, as well as the prevention of drainage of wetlands and waterfowl crop damage.

Writing-on-Stone Provincial Park near Milk River.

First MLA Game Dinner

The first game dinner for members of the government was held in the Macdonald Hotel in Edmonton on March 15, 1945. The dinner was reported as one of the highlights of the year, marking a new era of dialogue between officials in the AFGA and their elected representatives. The Edmonton, Calgary, Lethbridge and Turner Valley clubs paid in full the expenses for the dinner.

President J.A. McGhee reported on the dinner in the 17th annual convention yearbook. The report was addressed to the Honourable Ernest Manning, Alberta's premier and members of the cabinet and members of the legislature. McGhee said in the report, "Our purpose in arranging this gathering was to create an opportunity to present you with a picture of Fish and Game conditions as they presently exist in Alberta and to point out the necessity and urgency of instituting a well-planned program, if Alberta is going to regain and maintain its position as the Premier Province in the Dominion for those who love hunting and fishing." In his address, the president provided a snapshot of conditions related to fish and fishing, fish hatcheries, big game, prairie chicken and ruffed grouse, Hungarian partridge, pheasants, ducks, ammunition and finances. He appealed to the government for their co-operation and assistance in managing Alberta's fish and wildlife resources.

The NAGFPL (which would henceforth be called the Edmonton Fish and Game Association) voiced opposition to the draining of Beaverhill Lake in a letter to the game branch.

Big game chair William C. Fisher reported that predators were pretty well out of control. "Wolves are so hard to shoot or trap that they go almost unmolested, and coyotes are so numerous they will ruin our whole game picture unless we do something about it. We must congratulate Mr. Heustis, our Game Commissioner, on the excellent results of the coyote campaign." Fisher also reported that poaching was bad: "There are certain people, both Indians and white men, who are selling game meat and also hides. The whole Forest Reserve is being over-run by lumber and oil men and their crews."

Following the conclusion of the 17th annual convention at Lethbridge, a Summary of Disposition of Resolutions document

1947

Resolution No. 88   As early as 1947, some Alberta sportsmen were of the opinion an American–style system of fish and game management was called for, regarding the following resolution - Resolution No. 88 submitted by the Rimbey, Alder Flats and Wetaskiwin Fish and Game Associations: Be it resolved that we recommend that the Fish and Game Branch of the Department of Lands and Mines be administered under an independent commission and that all receipts for licenses and taxes in connection with the administration thereof be segregated and used to advance conservation of fish and game.

This sort of proposed administration has cropped up periodically over the years to try and take the politics out of fish and game management in Alberta.

was prepared by G.E. Watt, incoming president. This document provided a detailed report regarding the status of each resolution, whether it was defeated, and if carried, what actions resulted.

1947 The 18th annual convention was held at the Phelan and Buffalo Hotels in Red Deer in 1947. In his conference report, president G.E. Watt of Calgary wrote about what he perceived to be a failure of the AFGA as stewards of Alberta's fish and wildlife, following the end of hostilities after World War II.

At the time, the Alberta government matched the AFGA dollar for dollar with a grant to help them reach their goals and objectives, based on the per capita fees paid by local clubs. The AFGA also received financial support from Ducks Unlimited in 1946 and although the total annual revenue was still quite small, at about $7,500, the organization was actually considered to be very sound financially.

Watt reported that the second annual game dinner for the members of the Alberta legislature was even more successful than the first. It "...had all the aspects of a family gathering and the brief presented complimented the Government on the work that it had done."

President Watt practically beamed regarding his comments about crows and magpies: "Our crow and magpie reduction program was a wonderful success, netting over 146,000 destroyed." On coyotes: "The Government is to be congratulated in that they reduced the coyote menace by over 8,000 of these predators, which was a good break for the wild game and also for the farmers of the province who benefited materially."

Watt noted, "We have not gone into the sport fishing operations with a clear and concise plan. There is not at present at the Government's command enough qualified biologists with the proper qualifications and experience to study our fish problems, and to provide the quick and accurate information necessary, that the situation requires. We need a plan now." He also recommended that the government should have separate commercial and sport fishing sections, and that the latter be responsible for a new fish culture program. At the time there were no provincial fish hatcheries and Watt pointed out this disparity by way of comparisons with government fish-stocking programs in British Columbia, Montana and Colorado, all of which were stocking millions of trout annually. The president advised the government that "the fish we believe most desirable for our Trout streams are our own Native Cutthroat Trout and the Rainbow."

On the big-game situation, Watt quoted Dr. Ian McTaggart Cowan, University of British Columbia professor, who chaired the AFGA scientific committee: "Dr. Cowan told us:

" '(a) There is too much disease—lung worm and lump-jaw—in our big game.
" '(b) Parks such as Jasper are over-grazed with horses, which in time will turn it into a desert unless rectified.
" '(c) The same applies to Southern Alberta, where we have allowed sheep to seriously over-graze the area.' "

Few people appreciate just how serious an issue domestic grazing was in the forest reserves of southern Alberta at the time, especially by domestic sheep. It was the AFGA which brought this concern to the attention of the government and eventually grazing of domestic sheep was eliminated in the forest reserves.

Interestingly, Watt and members of the executive continued to visit local clubs throughout the year, a tradition started by his predecessor, Jim McGhee, to establish good relations between his

St. Mary River.

office and local AFGA members. In the section of his conference report on predatory animals and birds, Watt reported, "I wish to say, gentlemen, that we have a long way to go, and it is going to mean the expenditure of more money than ever, before we even start to control these pests." Early AFGA members were dogmatic in their predator control convictions and took it upon themselves to do everything in their power to subvert predators in an effort to increase game populations. Watt added, "It is quite apparent to me that if we want our sport to continue that it is going to cost more and more as the years go by." Another issue was the poaching of hen pheasants, reported to be in the range of 10,000 hens in 1946. Watt insisted in his report, "It has got to stop. We need more respect for the game laws and more law enforcement. Sportsmen themselves will have to take a hand in this matter and do some educational work."

Remarkably, the AFGA claimed as an accomplishment in 1946 that "fishing and hunting rights in the province [are] now protected," enshrined in law. That protection has been lost over the years and is high on the sportsmen's agenda of 2008.

The AFGA also reported that the Alberta Legislative Assembly defeated by only four votes an amendment to the *Game Act* that would have allowed Sunday hunting of big game. However, licence tags were now required to be placed on all big game animals killed.

At the annual conference, the president laid out what the AFGA should try to accomplish in 1946. Some of the highlights were to urge the government to employ more game guardians; that all government law-enforcement officers be in uniform; more publicity; more education; increase the predator control program; more members.

At the end of 1945, locals [clubs] in good standing numbered 55, and during 1946 the AFGA totaled 68 locals with the official membership over 8,160.

COURTESY OF DUANE RADFORD
The badlands of the Red Deer River.

COURTESY OF DON MEREDITH

The Pembina River.

Secretary G.M. Spargo reported: "Junior Fish and Game Associations are functioning at Calgary, Turner Valley, Innisfail, Rimbey, Red Deer, and the groups at Brooks and Castor have suggested they will have Junior Fish and Game organizations underway this winter."

William G. Fisher, big game chair, made a strong recommendation that the government undertake a census of big game in Alberta so they could be properly managed. Fisher reported on what he termed "bush" tragedies in 1946, which saw the killing of a large number of cow elk until almost the end of April in the Castle-Carbondale river area of southwestern Alberta, where no apparent damage could be done to agricultural crops. After a public outcry from local sportsmen the slaughter was stopped. "We still see the same slaughter going on in the Pincher Creek-Waterton Lakes sector this year." Fisher alleged that local ranchers were over-grazing big game winter ranges, which forced local elk populations to fringe areas, to the detriment of the populations. He addressed the need for proper management of wildlife habitat based on science and concluded with the following recommendations: "We should be glad to recognize that the Provincial and Federal Governments are now engaged in conserving our forest coverage in this Province for the good, not only of Alberta, but the other Western Provinces, as has been suggested recently by Robson Black. I would like in conclusion to suggest the following:

"(a) An immediate census of all wild game in our province;
"(b) Licenses issued based on the crop each year;
"(c) That literature inviting hunters and fishermen should be revised and a true proportion of things based on actual census be issued for the future;
"(d) A new grazing policy that will conserve our vegetative coverage in the Forest Reserves and Game Preserves;
"(e) Predatory control;
"(f) Stricter supervision."

In his fish report, chairman K.J. Webb was critical of the government for their lack of a plan to manage Alberta's sport fishery: "Ultimately this unfortunate state of affairs is bound to right itself, either through the medium of a Fish and Game Commission or by the Government coming out into the open and letting us know their program for the future of sport fishing in the Province." Webb commented on the general improvement of stream fishing in 1946, compared with 1945, noting "Surely it is apparent by now that the most essential requisite for good fishing is the restocking of streams. Compare the restocking of streams in Montana or British Columbia with that of Alberta – there lies the difference between good fishing and poor fishing. Our hatchery and rearing ponds are excellent. The hatchery capacity is around 4,000,000—rearing pond capacity is around 1,000,000—yet only 216,400 fingerlings were released in fishing streams in 1946, and these mostly in September and October which is too late and may mean an actual waste, as the peak of natural food conditions in streams has passed."

Of interest is the number of fish resolutions put forward at the convention, Resolutions No. 34-57, compared with recent conferences where only a handful might be submitted.

A total of 109 resolutions were submitted at the 18th annual convention of the AFGA in 1947, indicative of the number of issues and concerns related to fish and game in the province following the end of World War II.

COURTESY OF LILLA PFERSCHY

A busy groundhog.

O U T   F I S H I N'

A feller isn't mean,
  Out fishin';
His thoughts are mostly good and clean,
  Out fishin';
He doesn't knock his fellow men,
Or harbor any grudges then;
A feller's at his finest, when
  Out fishin'.

A feller's glad to have a friend,
  Out fishin';
A helpin' hand he'll always lend,
  Out fishin';
The brotherhood of rod an' line
An' sky an' stream is always fine;
Men come real close to God's design,
  Out fishin'.

A feller isn't plottin' schemes,
  Out fishin';
He's only busy with his dreams,
  Out fishin';
His livery's a coat of tan;
His creed — To do the best he can;
A feller's almost mostly man,
  Out fishin'.

COURTESY OF GORDON KERR
Bill Kerr with Crowsnest River rainbow trout, 1949.

1948-1957

Summary

Major issues: Near extinction of woodland caribou; bighorn sheep threatened; deleterious impact of over-grazing and timber cutting on Alberta trout streams; pollution of lakes and streams; predator control; shortage of big game; Sunday hunting of big game; moose season closure; closure of antelope season; continued loss of waterfowl habitat; need for more game wardens; closure of private property to hunting; farmer-sportsmen relations; length of pheasant season; antelope poaching; grizzly bear hunting season; heavy fishing pressure on central Alberta lakes.

Highlights:
1950 - President George E. Watt advised the Alberta Fish and Game Association (AFGA) members that their policy was "conservation" not "prohibition" of fishing and hunting; preservation of habitat (as a priority) was raised by president for the first time; trained biologists were first hired; first convention report on pollution.
1951 - Alberta Agriculture started use of controversial 1080 bait for coyote control, which also Indiscriminately killed non-target wildlife.
1952 - Start of open-and-closed stream management.
1953 - Over two million crows and magpies had been destroyed by 1953.
1956 - Social Credit government withdrew proposed secretive paid hunting legislation; provincial government created the first hunting zones; "famed" AFGA picnic held at the Raven fish hatchery in early '50s; and highly popular angler's night and hunter's night in Calgary in mid-'50s.

Presidents: George E. Watt (1948-50), C.E. Brown (1950-52), Floyd E. Mitchell (1952-54), Curt P. Smith (1954-56), J.E. (Erle) Carr (1956-57).

Membership: 10,746-1948; 11,346-1950; 11,774-1952; 14,840-1955; 13,252-1957.

After the war, industrial production in Canada quickly turned to the making of consumer goods. Unemployment remained low and for the next 25 years there was an immense expansion of the Canadian economy. This wealth affected Canadian fish and wildlife in several ways, both positively and negatively. On the positive side, it allowed the science of fisheries and wildlife management to develop and prosper in universities and governments, enabling managers to use scientifically derived information to make decisions. On the negative side, the influx of immigrants, mainly from war-torn Europe in the early years, increased demands on resources, including fish and wildlife. Alberta's population in 1951 was about 940,000 people; and the U.S. dollar was worth $7.98 in 2007 USD.

Louis Saint-Laurent of the Liberals replaced Mackenzie King as prime minister in 1948. Saint-Laurent held office until defeated by John Diefenbaker's Progressive Conservatives in 1957. In Alberta, Premier Ernest Manning of the Social Credit party held power throughout this decade.

COURTESY OF JACK GRAHAM
Jack Graham with best buddy Rusty, 1948.

1948 The 19th annual Alberta Fish and Game Association (AFGA) convention was held at the Palliser Hotel in Calgary in 1948. President George E. Watt provided a sobering commentary in the introduction of his report for 1947: "Have we to admit that we find in 1947 our game [is] in a more precarious position than it ever was." He goes on to lament the need for more dollars to manage fish and game in Alberta and asks the membership whether they are prepared for sportsmen to foot the bill. He added, "Our province has only a very small population and we have not got the millions of dollars to bring back our wildlife." On a more positive note, Watt noted that the AFGA had 70 locals in good standing in 1947 with a total membership of 9,226. He added that he visited 15 locals during the 1947 season while G.M. Spargo, the AFGA secretary, visited 48, quite an accomplishment, especially in 1947. At the time of this conference, Spargo had been secretary of the association for 17 consecutive years.

The game dinner for the members of the legislature was held for the third time, again a "huge" success according to Watt. In his report on the advisory committee, Watt said, "While we have not obtained everything we recommended, still every year shows progress and we must remember that most of our requests call for the expenditure of moneys and can only be affected from the moneys supplied by sportsmen through their licence fees." For the first time, a president acknowledged the lack of success regarding predator control, admitting, "I am afraid, gentlemen, that as far as my own personal opinion is concerned, we are not getting anywhere in our predator control. I do not think we are even harvesting the crop." He leaves the delegates with the suggestion that the Fish and Game Branch give consideration to some means of poisoning, if it could be done safely.

Secretary George Spargo reported that the association forwarded a questionnaire to all affiliated groups in order to obtain a cross-section of their activities. This is the first record of the association having polled its membership.

> In his third game dinner report for the 19th annual convention, president Watt reported that the government "safeguarded our heritage of hunting and fishing by having written into the *Game Act* one of the most democratic of all regulations, a provision which has gained considerable advertisement throughout the Dominion, whereby the inalienable right of its citizens to hunting and fishing may not be reduced by the selling of these rights to wealthy individuals and groups of men."

In his annual report on big game, chairman H.F. Herron noted that, generally speaking, the situation throughout Alberta was not good. North of the Bow River there was a marked decrease of big game with the possible exception of deer and elk, and a marked increase in predators, particularly wolves and coyotes. "Every report stresses the shortage of moose and the virtual non-existence of caribou."

Bob Forbes (L), Walter Scott and Vern McIntosh at Coal Branch (Robb), 1949.

Apparently, sheep, goats and grizzly bear were also decreasing in numbers. South of the Bow River the situation was apparently a great deal better and all types of game, except grizzly bear, appeared to be on the increase.

1948

Motion

With the foregoing big-game report in mind, one can only wonder about the following Resolution No. 3 from the Medicine Hat Fish and Game Association: "Whereas reports would indicate that there are large herds of Antelope in the southeastern part of the Province and, Whereas it is admitted that these animals migrate across the International border in winter, where an open season exists, and Whereas these animals are raised on Canadian soil and should be primarily for the benefit of our own citizens, Therefore be it resolved that an open season on Antelope in this area permitting the taking of one of either sex in the fall of 1948 unless circumstances change the situation in the meantime."

Resolution

Another resolution from the Medicine Hat Fish and Game Association moved to open the deer season locally by stating the following: "Whereas deer are very plentiful in southeastern Alberta from the International border in the south to the Red Deer River in the north, and whereas no open season has been allowed since 1928…" It is remarkable that the deer season had been closed for 20 years at the time in such a large area.

COURTESY OF JAMES R. KERR

The dam on the west branch of Allison Creek was built largely by Crowsnest Pass area fish and game members with equipment help from the Coleman Collieries, 1949.

extinction. Predators are particularly prevalent and are the chief cause of the depletion and we should heartily endorse an all-out campaign to exterminate them. We must urge the government to employ full-time hunters, raise bounties, use poison bait, snares or scientific methods or do anything else within its power to get rid of them. It is our belief that as the predators decrease our game will increase."

All of the concerns regarding the big-game situation in Alberta at the time were at variance with a government advertising campaign in the United States of America encouraging tourism, which skeptics claimed was based on misleading information. To this effect, Resolution No. 21 came from the Claresholm Fish and Game Association: "Resolved that the Provincial Government be asked to curtail their advertising of Alberta as a 'Hunter's and Fisherman's Paradise', due to the shortage of fish and game, at least until greater assistance is given to increase the numbers of said fish and game."

Herron reported, "On the prairies our antelope suffered very heavy losses during the very severe winter of 1946-47. Heavy crusted snow made foraging virtually impossible. Many starved, large numbers migrated to the southward into Montana and not all migrated back, and many more in their weakened condition through starvation were killed by coyotes." He noted that in a summer of 1947 game-branch survey there were only 20-30 percent of antelope present on the range compared with the previous year, resulting in a closed season in 1947. "In conclusion," he stated, "game is becoming scarcer year by year in the Province and this Association must do everything within its power to prevent

Poaching was also seen as a serious issue and there were calls for more game guardians from many locals and the need for them to be in uniform. The government was repeatedly asked to appoint volunteer game wardens from the ranks of local clubs.

1949 The 20th annual convention was held in the Palliser Hotel in Calgary in 1949.

While earlier presidents cast a gloomy outlook on the abundance of fish and game in their conference reports, president G.E. Watt was practically glowing in his findings for 1948, advising

1949

Resolution No. 12   Reports of pollution were widespread and the Red Deer Fish and Game Association submitted the following Resolution No. 12: Be it resolved that the Alberta Fish and Game Association appoint a committee to study the pollution of Alberta's streams and lakes.

Resolution No. 12(a)   Similarly, the Bow Valley Fish and Game Association put forward Resolution No.12 (a): Be it resolved, this Association requests the Department of Lands and Mines, Fisheries Branch, to immediately institute action against offenders polluting the Bow River system and with special reference to those committing offences by the release of raw sewage, oil and other deleterious substances injurious to fish life and contrary to the Federal Fisheries Act.
Both of these resolutions were carried.

Resolutions No. 31-41   Dealing with predators had a common theme to eradicate crows and magpies, increase bounties on coyotes, wolves, wolverines and cougars, goshawks and other birds of prey. All of the resolutions were carried except No. 36 which called for "...competent predator control hunters to be employed." Resolution No. 38 from the Coleman Fish and Game Association was typical: Resolved that this Association endorse, and assist by all means within its power an all-out campaign for the extermination of predators. This particular resolution was lost on a standing vote in the General Assembly.

Resolution No. 65   Nine different clubs submitted Resolution No. 65 in support of legalizing Sunday shooting of big game. Without any doubt, the resolution in support of Sunday hunting is the longest-standing in the records of the association and the one the government has most resisted, granting few concessions over time.

Government hatchery truck planting fish in the Crowsnest River, circa 1950.

"However, I feel very happy that 1948 has seen the things we have hoped for become realities." Watt also praised University of Alberta professor William Rowan for his help and advice which enabled the AFGA to make decisions in the best interests of wild fowl and sportsmen.

Watt likewise painted a more positive picture regarding fishing, and commended J.B. Cross for his assistance in establishing a fish hatchery and rearing ponds at his Calgary Brewing Company and Westmount Fish Rearing Ponds in Calgary. The reared fish were being raised to stock streams, which evidently must have had low stocks if this was the purpose. The hatchery was capable of

producing three-million fry, along with the rearing ponds which were positioned to produce 1.5 million fingerlings. Mr. Cross was seen as a great benefactor of the AFGA for coming to its aid and providing financial assistance whereby the Fish Rearing Ponds at Westmount were doubled in capacity.

For the first time, mention is made of the work that Dr. Richard. B. Miller, of the University of Alberta, would do on behalf of the government "...so that our streams can be improved and that we also have accurate knowledge of what streams will support the plantings of additional fingerlings," (president's report for 1948). Watt acknowledged that while deer and elk were plentiful, wood-

1950

Resolution No. 19   It wasn't just coyotes that drew the attention of predator control enthusiasts. The Red Deer Fish and Game Association submitted Resolution No. 19: Whereas, owing to the fact that predators have become so prevalent in the National Parks and Forest Reserves that game animals are being driven to the more settled areas for survival; and Whereas marauding grizzly bear are following the game into the foothills and back settlements commonly used as sport fishing areas, Be it therefore resolved that a bounty of $50.00 be placed on any grizzly bear killed outside the National Parks at any time. This resolution was defeated.

The Medicine Hat Fish and Game Association went so far as to submit a resolution that each applicant for a deer-hunting permit must first turn in to the issuer of the permit, one pair of coyote ears before he or she could obtain their hunting permit.
This resolution was also defeated.

land caribou were almost extinct and moose were headed in that direction, with bighorn sheep being in a precarious position.

The AFGA continued its growth as membership reached 10,746. There were 72 local clubs and junior fish and game local clubs had grown to six in number.

Of interest was a report about the "famed" picnic (first referenced in the 1948 president's report) held during the summer at the Raven River. It was sponsored by local clubs from Didsbury, Olds and Innisfail. There were over 3,000 people at this event which George E. Watt jokingly called the largest political rally ever held in Alberta because there were so many MLAs in attendance. At this time, the government of the day had great respect for the AFGA. Government members seemed to be front and centre at many AFGA events.

The AFGA members endorsed the idea of increasing hunting and fishing licences so that additional revenues could be used to manage these resources. The year 1948 marked the first reference in the records for the AFGA to spend money on stream improvement. Members of the executive continued to attend meetings of the Western Canada-Yukon Fish and Game Council where they addressed regionally important issues. This organization was established in 1945.

There is a reference in the 1948 report to an angler's night and a hunter's night held in Calgary. Some 1,600 people were present at the angler's night and 1,400 at the hunter's night.

Secretary G.M. Spargo noted that the AFGA had succeeded in reaching the 10,000 mark in membership, actually surpassing it by more than one thousand. He beamed: "Like Topsy, we have not just grown, but have reached this astonishing record through the keen interest, co-operation and aggressive oversee ship of our many presidents, secretaries and individuals within the ranks of affiliated groups. Nowhere in America can such enthusiasm be found." ["Like Topsy, I just growed" is a phrase from a quote by Topsy in "Uncle Tom's Cabin; or Life Among the Lowly" by Harriet Beecher Stowe.]

> In the fourth game dinner report, president G.E. Watt reported: "First of all let me say, that we, as an Association, feel that our Government during the last four or five years has shown more interest and done more for Fish and Game than any previous government in the history of Alberta. What has been accomplished reflects the keen interest taken by the members of the legislature; therefore, we take this opportunity of thanking you all for what you have done."

Migratory bird chair J.A. Williams advised, "The zoning of the open seasons was of great advantage to our locally raised geese as they were joined by thousands from the North before the shooting started and this made it difficult for the hunters to concentrate on them during the opening days of the season as in the past." Williams continued, "The fall of 1948 was a very satisfactory season in Central Alberta and I believe the hunters are being educated

to the fact if these conditions are to continue they must respect the laws and be good sportsmen."

Over the years prior to 1950, the AFGA fish chairs registered complaints about the deleterious impact of siltation that arose from over-grazing of domestic livestock and indiscriminate cutting of timber on Alberta's trout streams, conditions which are still of concern to the present time. Williams noted in his report that Dr. R. Miller had initiated biological surveys of some Alberta waters, citing a report on the Sheep River Survey, 1947, dealing with the north branch of Coal Creek which is a tributary to the Sheep: "One mile from the junction are six abandoned beaver dams, now filling with mud." Fish populations appear to have been meager in many streams along the eastern slopes at the time and the AFGA response was to have the government stock them with trout, a practice that would later prove to be unsound.

In his annual report of the big game committee, committee chair H.F. Herron advised that reports from all over Alberta indicated a shortage of big game. On the other hand, reports of numerous wolves and coyotes were widespread. Herron stated, "This committee recommends very strongly that the Game Branch of the Alberta Government be again exhorted very strongly to use every possible means to reduce the number of wolves, cougars, coyotes and eagles in our forest reserves."

Co-author/editor Duane Radford recalls the anti-predator campaign at the time in southwestern Alberta: it was not uncommon for outdoorsmen to carry firearms at all times of the year in their vehicles and upon sighting any predator to bail out and start firing, particularly at hawks, owls and eagles. Magpies and crows were hunted down and shot evangelically, and no coyote was safe. Nests of magpies and crows were destroyed. At the time, very few foxes were present in this area and the few that were present would be considered an oddity, which is unusual because foxes are generally present where coyotes are rare.

There was the usual report on the provincial crow and magpie campaign for 1948 with the record showing 1,032,013 feet and 299,065 eggs being collected since 1938. In 1948 the grand total was: 571 for hawks and owls; 40,333 for crows; 68,763 for magpies [feet].

1950 The 21st annual convention was held at the Palliser Hotel in Calgary.

George E. Watt presided over the AFGA as president for a fourth and last term of office during 1949. As the result of a resolution submitted in 1948 to close a season on big game, Watt advised members in his convention report that the policy of the association was "CONSERVATION," and that members should not become over zealous and turn conservation into "PROHIBITION." The long-standing motto of the AFGA, dating back to 1947, was that "Game Is A Crop" with the proviso that sportsmen should get their fair share of this bounty.

The government commissioned report in 1949 on the abundance of game was very pessimistic, with the exception of elk and deer. Consequently, the Advisory Committee recommended that only one animal per licence be allowed in 1949 and that with such a drastic reduction that the season be open all over the province. This proposal didn't sit well with guides and outfitters and a compromise was reached: the bag limit was set at one horned animal and one antlered animal.

> *The fish and game commissioner's office estimated that the number of big-game licences sold would be in the neighbourhood of 14,000 and the number of bird-game licences some 35,000.*

While reports on fishing were positive there was another reference for the second straight year on the need for stream improvements if fishing conditions were to be improved. The president continued to express concerns about the impact of domestic grazing in Alberta's forest reserves along the eastern slopes.

The membership numbers remained much the same as in 1948 even though there had been a marked increase in the number of big-game and bird-game licences.

The ever-popular game dinner for members of the Alberta legislature was held once again at the Macdonald Hotel on March 9, 1949. In attendance were 90 percent of the cabinet and MLAs.

The Calgary angler's night and hunter's night once again drew big crowds, in excess of 1,600 at each event.

Transportation for the secretary, George Spargo, received full-page coverage in the president's conference report for 1949. Paying for the transportation of the AFGA staff and officials is something that is taken for granted in the 21st century. However, it was obviously an issue of concern in 1950. Spargo had no means of travel, short of asking favours of members to drive him around by car, or travelling by train and bus. The president went into great detail about why the association should purchase a vehicle for its secretary and described a fundraising campaign designed to

achieve this goal. He lambasted lax locals who did not contribute funds toward the purchase of a station wagon so that the secretary could carry his paraphernalia on trips to clubs throughout Alberta. Spargo later reported that the largest single contribution towards the car fund came from Mr. Emil Sick of Seattle who donated $500 - an astounding amount, at the time. Each and every donor was listed in the 21st annual convention report, even those who only contributed 25 cents.

IN MEMORIAM – 1950

Frank L. Farley, past president .... Camrose
A. Y. McCorquodale .... High River
A. J. Hilliker .... Calgary

Secretary G.M. Spargo reported that the number of affiliated clubs in 1950 was 67 compared with 77 the previous year. Membership numbered 10,298 compared with 11,194. Spargo remarked, "This is, however, the second greatest number in our history but far from being a satisfactory one when over 35,000 bird licenses alone were sold in the province in 1949. It is extraordinary that so many hunters will accept the vital work which your organization accomplishes for conservation without so much as a thank you."

> *There was a report appended to the 21st annual convention regarding "Alberta Fish and Game Association League Membership by Years to Date," as follows:*
>
> | | | | |
> |---|---|---|---|
> | 1930 .... 1,100 | | 1940 .... n/a |
> | 1931 .... 1,205 | | 1941 .... 3,105 |
> | 1932 .... 1,700 | | 1942 .... 3,900 |
> | 1933 .... 1,756 | | 1943 .... 4,151 |
> | 1934 .... 1,640 | | 1944 .... 6,178 |
> | 1935 .... 1,921 | | 1945 .... 6,506 |
> | 1936 .... n/a | | 1946 .... 8,160 |
> | 1937 .... n/a | | 1947 .... 9,558 |
> | 1938 .... n/a | | 1948 .... 11,194 |
> | 1939 .... n/a | | 1949 .... 10,548 |

Predators chairman William Hedley commented on a new phase of predator control—organized coyote hunts—with a caution: "Like everything else, I regret to have to say, some of those who offer their services have acted in a reprehensible manner. For instance, I am glad to observe that two men from Alhambra were heavily fined for having deer in their possession after one of these hunts. To take advantage of the opportunity presented, to do good by an evil act thoroughly deserves condemnation of all citizens. Whether the number of predators killed will make a difference to the known population of the 'little wolf' is debatable, but, by the very fact that the thousands of farmers and sportsmen's friends get together on these occasions broods well for the future farmer-sportsmen relationship."

COURTESY OF JIM KERR

Bill Kerr senior (L), Harold McBurnie and Bill Cole of the Crowsnest Pass with one day's pheasant bag from the Brooks area. There were five in the party, but the limit was seven cocks per day during the period of 1947-50. Now that was pheasant hunting!

Big game chairman H.F. Herron reported on an aerial survey of antelope finding only 2,329 in Alberta.

1951 C.E. (Buster) Brown took over the reins as the AFGA president in 1950. He described his frustration over setting seasons and bag limits based on sketchy information, and federal government intervention in waterfowl seasons. He also criticized locals for their lack of co-operation in not submitting timely questionnaires regarding game-bird populations which were necessary to properly assess population levels as an aid in the season-setting process.

The 22nd annual convention was held at the Palliser Hotel in Calgary in 1951.

In Memoriam: Two minutes of silence was accorded in memory of Dr. W.A. Wilson, past president, C. Craddock, vice president, Archie Chiswell and G.B. Watson.

Certificates of Merit were awarded to: Joe Kovach, H. Thomson, W. Wolley-Dod, H. Farthing, G. T. Loney, Morris Ferrie, G. Fanset and J. Bond.

There were additional references to the continued loss of waterfowl habitat due to drought even in 1950, a trend which continues to this day with ongoing global warming.

For the first time, a president acknowledged issues related to fish and wildlife habitat. Brown stated, "This question of habitat must become our number one objective, I feel this is the prime answer to most of our problems. Not only waterfowl, but fish, upland game birds and big game are all dependent on suitable habitat. With intensive logging, grazing and agricultural activities playing havoc with our natural streams and covers, it is essential that a real aggressive policy of restoration must be devised if we are to succeed at all in maintaining any semblance of our present depleted stocks of wild game."

1950

For the first time in a convention report, there is a record concerning pollution – 1950 Pollution Report

Submitted by a committee (evidently not a standing committee), chaired by R. B. Mackenzie of Edmonton. In that record, officials from the association made complaints to the government "...of the terrific pollution of Crowsnest Lake." The Calgary association also complained about pollution of the Bow River, likewise the Red Deer league over the Red Deer River. The Cardston league was involved with clean-up of Lees Creek.

Spargo reported: "We have had the greatest amount of action ever during 1950, and not only are the known pollutive (sic) agencies being attacked, but, sugar beet and packing plant wastes are being investigated."

Members of the association would go on to have a long history of being a thorn in the side of government as pollution watchdogs. They were often the first to call incidences of pollution to the attention of government and their officials and demand corrective action, sometimes at the risk of losing their jobs.

Alberta's streams were sometimes badly polluted in the early 1950s by coal mines and their tipples, often blatantly so with little or no regard for their fish populations. The famed Crowsnest River was a good example and often ran black with slack coal which lead to the following resolution.

Resolution No. 53(A) (Bellevue Rod and Gun Club) Whereas our Crowsnest River has changed from a beautiful river to a river flowing with black coal much of the time and whereas the government knows about this and has curtailed court action against those breaking the law regarding pollution; be it resolved that immediate action of some kind be taken to enlighten or remedy the situation. This resolution carried.

Resolution No. 9 The AFGA locals have a history of occasionally submitting rather peculiar resolutions; one from the 1951 convention stands out in this regard: Resolution No. 9 (from the Red Deer Fish and Game Association): "Whereas under our present system of distress signals for Big Game Hunters, much needed ammunition is rapidly expended by the lost hunters by shooting three shots in a group. Be it resolved that in future, any Big Game Hunter lost in the woods after dark, fire only single shots in five-minute intervals, to be answered by three shots from camp."

The year 1950 also marked the beginning of new era in game management with the hiring of trained biologists by the Department of Lands and Forests to undertake fish and game surveys – Dr. William Rowan and Dr. R.B. Miller from the University of Alberta.

Predator control remained an issue, with complaints there were "...far too many wolves." The moose season was closed throughout the province, as was the season for antelope. The latter closure corresponded with season closures for antelope in neighbouring Saskatchewan and Montana.

While announcing a grant of $5,000 from the government in 1950, the president expressed concerns regarding membership numbers, seemingly a chronic issue. He observed that while there had been an improvement in membership, it was not in line with the 35,000 bird game licences sold in 1950. Like many presidents who would come after him, he felt it should be possible to double the AFGA membership. On a happy note, the president triumphantly reported that thanks to the "grand efforts" of the past president, George E. Watt, the car that was so badly needed for their secretary, George Spargo, had finally been purchased.

The annual game dinner for the members of the legislature was another success with 90 percent of the MLAs in attendance. J. B. Cross and his organization (The Calgary Brewery Company) were singled out again for their "very generous assistance" in hosting the dinner.

This ongoing high level of attendance at the annual MLA dinner contrasts quite remarkably with conditions today. As the province urbanized since the 1950s, the MLA dinner became less and less popular with sitting MLAs. The ever-increasing number of urban MLAs began to think of the AFGA as mainly a rural outfit with rural concerns about rural fish and wildlife, ignoring the fact that the fish and wildlife resource belonged to everyone and that many users of the resource came from urban as well as rural areas. Today, the AFGA only garners the attendance of the sitting minister at

COURTESY OF VERN MCINTOSH

Al Taylor and friends, 1951.

its annual conference. He delivers a carefully orchestrated, brief presentation usually followed by an even shorter question-and-answer period, which is sometimes cancelled.

On a controversial note, the president reported on complaints that Indians had slaughtered big game animals west of Edmonton, and the charges had been dismissed at a trial in Edson. J.B. Cross was again singled out as a great benefactor to Alberta's sportsmen by C. E. Brown "...for so many things, particularly the fish ponds, hatchery [at the Calgary Brewing Company] and many other efforts supported so wholeheartedly throughout the years." The provincial hatchery was a tourist attraction in its own right during the 1950s and featured immense brood trout on display for the public at the front of the brewery where the hatchery was located.

Secretary G.M. Spargo commented that the past year had been a "harvest year" as far as wildlife was concerned. He advised, "Therefore as our motto suggests that 'Game is a Crop,' our Leagues recommend we should gather it when the time is ripe. Our Migratory birds, and our Upland Game reserves are as good,

1951

Motion

Members of the association didn't just confine their concerns about predators to crows, magpies, hawks and owls, coyotes and wolves. They also targeted bull trout, which were not protected at the time. Indeed, as a result of requests from previous conventions the government had removed bull trout from protection. This led to a bit of a dilemma regarding the following resolution at the 22nd annual convention.

Resolution No. 48

(Crossfield, Carstairs, Didsbury, Olds and Innisfail Fish and Game Associations) "Whereas Dolly Varden or bull trout are not considered as a game fish, with no season or limit imposed in Alberta: Therefore be it resolved that Dolly Varden or bull trout be included as a game fish in our fishing regulations."
This resolution was carried with 31 delegates for and 11 against.

It was not until the 1990s that bull trout were actually recognized as a species of concern in Alberta. They were designated as Alberta's provincial fish in 1995.

and in many cases better, than for the year previous; therefore recommendations for more liberal bag limits and longer seasons were asked for and obtained. This is but one instance where the organized sportsmen assist in serving all sportsmen alike with regard for their sporting values."

Spargo also noted that for the second time in the existence of the association of over 22 years (at the time), membership exceeded the 11,000 mark. Spargo went into great detail about new associations that had been established and ones that dropped out of the organization; from all appearances the membership continued to have a strong grassroots foundation. The number of leagues (clubs) increased from 66 to 74, a new high for the AFGA. The membership totaled 11,346 in 1950, an increase of 798 over 1949. There were also approximately 400 junior fish and game association members at the time.

The secretary attended many meetings with various clubs throughout the year: Medicine Hat, Lethbridge, Brooks, Cranford, Pincher Creek, Claresholm, Stavely, High River, Turner Valley, Calgary, Drumheller, Olds, Carstairs, Didsbury, Ponoka, Wetaskiwin, Strathmore, Edmonton, Viking, Red Deer, Leslieville, Haynes, Eckville, Rocky Mountain House, Innisfail, Vermillion and Lloydminster, an increase of eight over the previous year. He reported on volunteers from the association providing assistance to the fisheries branch with trout stockings from rearing ponds at Pincher Creek and Big Hill Springs near Cochrane.

Spargo advised, "It is with pleasure I report the acquiring of a Mercury station wagon, and I tender my appreciation to Mr. George E. Watt, past president who is primarily responsible for this useful acquisition." Once again, he listed all the 1950 contributors to the car fund in the annual report, with the following highlights:

Total 1950 contributions....................................$1,008.70
Previously acknowledged $3,059.53
GRAND TOTAL $4,068.23

In several previous convention reports various officials reported on plans to relocate wildlife, none of which materialized. However, in the 22nd annual convention report, Spargo reports on successful transfers of 50 elk from "...the over-grazed area of the Kananaskis Game Reserve to the headwaters of the Elbow River. It was also possible to transfer two loads of elk from Elk Island Park to the Whitecourt district."

As usual, there was a running tally of the crow and magpie campaign regarding the total number of feet and eggs collected since 1938:

Feet 1,322,355
Eggs 299,065
Total...1,621,420

Similarly, there were records tallied for the number of goshawks and horned owls exterminated – 906.

The annual grand total was dully recorded:

Hawks and Owls...906
Crows.. 53,356
Magpies 97,069

Big game chair J.E. Carr of Lethbridge reported, "Our government saw fit to close the moose season throughout the Province this year which was a very wise move. All you moose hunters know our moose have decreased at an alarming rate the last few years in all areas north of the Bow River."

Carr also noted, "The antelope situation is very poor. Their habitat is decreasing and they were hunted very hard in 1949. The winter of 1949 and 1950 was very severe and took a heavy toll." The antelope season was closed in 1950. On another note, Carr reported, "There were several poachers arrested and fined quite heavily which will help, but, it is extremely hard to catch antelope poachers since most of the hunting is done from cars; consequently they can make a quick getaway." Carr reported that the game wardens had been doing a good job but they all had territories much too large to cover and there was a need for more officers. He stated that several lumber camps were heavily fined for killing moose and deer to feed their crews.

Posting of private property was on the increase in the early 1950s. The good and welfare chair [the equivalent of the program chair in today's AFGA] H.C. Farthing had a lengthy report on this issue in

COURTESY OF DUANE RADFORD

the 22nd annual convention report, in addition to having concerns about the need for additional membership to increase the clout of the association with the Alberta government. Farthing urged members to be good sportsmen to stem the tide of an increase in "No Hunting" signs.

There was an interesting Resolution No. 14 from the Medicine Hat Fish and Game Association calling for a special $1 game-bird licence for juveniles under the age of 16.

In his predator report, chair Harry N. Cornwell as much as admitted the association was beating its head against the wall regarding the crow and magpie campaign: "Game Trails Shield will be presented this year to Viking at our annual convention. The records indicate that this year's total exceeded that of last year. It may be safely stated I believe that crows were down, but, that magpies still are holding their own. It cannot be gainsaid that we merely are keeping magpies down only by the most persistent means possible to our limited resources." This is the first concrete sign of admission about the futility of the crow and magpie campaign by an official of the association. Cornwell went on to advise "Coyotes have become our number one menace. These predators are so dangerously on the increase that a very big campaign by every method possible to reduce their numbers is most urgently required."

The annual convention was the business and social highlight of the year for members of the AFGA. It was structured very formally with much pomp and ceremony. The 22nd annual convention was typical of conventions of the day. On the opening morning, following registration, the president made his introductory remarks and welcomed delegates and guests. This was followed by discussion of the minutes of the previous convention, which in turn was followed by a report from the president, secretary and treasurer. Next, committee members would be formally appointed and the various committees would break for discussions. The Fish and Game Commissioner for Alberta would give a formal address prior to lunch. All the resolutions and chairmen's reports would be covered during the first afternoon of the convention, with a follow-up on the second morning and afternoon (if necessary). Late in the agenda would be a finance report, followed by a welcome to out-of-town guests and government officials, prior to an address by the out-of-town guests. New business would be at the tail end of the agenda.

COURTESY OF TRAVEL ALBERTA

Carson Pegasus Provincial Park.

On Saturday night there was a big game dinner with delegates and guests being piped into the banquet hall. A note on the agenda advised that guests and delegates were to refrain from entering the hall during the playing of "O Canada." There was a sing-song with a Hammond organ and singing of "God Save The King" at the end of the formal dinner after presentation of awards. The dinner included fresh Alberta trout or rolled barbecued elk (supplied by National Parks). There were 180 delegates at the meeting, along with 17 guests and officials including members of the Western Canada Council, and 44 ladies in attendance.

1952 The 23rd annual convention was held at the Palliser Hotel in Calgary. Of note is the large number of ads in the annual yearbook, the start of a trend that would continue for many years.

> *O*n page 1 of the annual convention document was a full-page "Thank You Sportsmen!" advertisement from the Hon. N.E. Tanner, Minister, and E.S. Huestis, Fish and Game Commissioner of the Department of Lands and Forests, respectively. [Similar ads would also be featured front and centre—on page 1—in several upcoming convention handbooks.]
>
> The ad was a message from the Alberta government thanking sportsmen, noting that "1951 was another year of co-operation. By working together we have been able to draw up both seasonal and long-term policies aimed at protecting and improving your hunting and fishing. We are looking forward to further years of successful co-operation."

In his 1952 President's Annual Report, C.E. Brown makes the first significant reference as a president to the problem of farmer-sportsmen relations, without any real elaboration other than to say that the Red Deer league had been active on this file with a recommendation that other locals take up the cause. This reference must be associated with issues related to trespass and access on private property, and the need for hunters to ask for permission to hunt, which had been raised by committee chairs at previous conventions.

C.E. Brown noted there were reports that the moose population was on the rebound but "...in the interests of conserving the remnants..." of the antelope herds, the closed season established in 1951 was extended in both Alberta and Saskatchewan. Apparently, a disastrous wet spring in 1951 also decimated pheasant populations in southern Alberta, especially in the Eastern Irrigation District.

> *S*pecial certificates of meritorious service were awarded by Mr. Floyd E. Mitchell, incoming president of the AFGA, as follows: A. Blocksom, S. Hopkins, John Anderson, J. Speakman, G. T. Loney, W.B. MacGillivray, G. Philpott, C.B. Cheeseman, G.J. Cummings, W.R. Fulton, Herman Hennig, A. McRae, K.J. Webb, Dr. B. Banks, J. B. Cross, R.R. Fuller, Them Kjar, Mike Nolan and Chas Hodges.

Secretary G.M. Spargo reported: "The annual game dinner to members of the Cabinet and Legislature is in the form of a thank you or appreciation for their continued interest in a specialized form of services rendered and to come. There can be no doubt whatever that this is a cooperative venture of great value to all concerned. Where in Canada is this to be found outside Alberta? It is a form of democracy that needs no questioning as to its value or merits." Many old-time fish and gamers still speak highly of this bygone dinner occasion and its political value to the organization.

Membership totaled 10,506 with an additional 200 junior fish and game association members for a grand total of 10,706 (a decrease of 240 over 1950).

Big game chair J. Erle Carr described the ups and downs of big-game populations in 1951 with moose very scarce but elk on the rise. Carr noted that "Eighty head [of elk] were rounded up at the Canmore Ranger Station and planted west of Calgary, and West of Crossfield and Olds. This work was carried out by the Calgary

COURTESY OF TRAVEL ALBERTA
Pine cones and needles.

Association and the Crossfield and Carstairs Associations." The antelope season remained closed; Carr reported, "Their habitat grows smaller every year and poaching is very prevalent." He also advised that the bear population seemed to be holding its own, advising "I do not agree with the policy of open season on grizzly the year round, in the Pincher Creek area. I am sure the bear is not actually responsible for a great deal of killing for which he is blamed, and he is a very valuable trophy. Our friend, Mr. Cunningham, the B.C. Game Commissioner, says they are worth $1,000.00 each in British Columbia, and I heartily agree." He also advised that caribou were very scarce and that there was no open season, except in the restricted area of the Athabasca forest reserve.

Carr had an interesting footnote in his big-game report regarding the number of licences and harvest of animals.

"We issued in 1950, 12,953 big-game licences, made up as follows:

12,731	Resident
98	Non-resident
60	Resident, Special
63	Non-resident, Special

We killed:

1,578	Elk
2,810	Deer
140	Sheep
108	Goats
41	Grizzly
58	Black bear

Total 4,735 Head of big game

"This is not a very large number for an area the size of our Province. In a great many States more elk or deer than this were killed. In my opinion these figures provide additional proof that our predator control is most inadequate."

1952

Resolution No. 5 (Bellevue Rod and Gun Club) "Whereby too many grizzly are shot: Be it resolved that they be taken off the predator list."
This resolution was defeated.

Resolution No. 18 (Calgary Fish and Game Association) "Resolve that an open season be declared on Sandhill Cranes during their southern migration through the province."
This resolution was defeated.

Two well-meaning but misguided resolutions were submitted at the annual conference:

Resolution No. 54 (High River Fish and Game Association) "Be it resolved that there should be a registration box at all main entrances to the forest reserve."

Resolution No. 54 (A) (Hillcrest Fish and Game Association) "Whereas the forest rangers be enabled to keep a closer check on entries and exits to forest reserves: Be it resolved that rangers keep all entrances to forest reserves supplied with necessary permits. These to be placed in appropriate pigeon-holed boxes."
Both resolutions carried.

COURTESY OF THE AFGA

24th Annual AFGA Convention in Edmonton, Feb. 6-7, 1953.

K. J. Webb submitted his fish report in which he noted that the committee previously urged the Fish and Game Commissioner and the Superintendent of Fisheries to bring in a policy covering stream improvement, erosion, restocking, reforestation, pollution and an overall program to provide continued good sport fishing in Alberta. At the previous convention in Calgary in 1951, the fish committee was split into two factions – those in favour of abolishing the legal size limit on trout [10 inches at the time] and opening the Elbow and the Bow River below the Louise Bridge in Calgary and opening the Macleod River drainage year round. Webb noted the association was bewildered. "Remember we are the committee who requested the Department of Fisheries to conduct biological surveys of our sport-fish waters, to advise us of their findings and above all to bring in a management policy on sport fish, and sport-fish waters which was based on fact. Individually and collectively we were fed up with trial-and-error methods; we wanted something concrete, a management plan based on fact." He added that most of the members had by this time received a copy of a departmental report "A Plan for the Management of the East Slope Trout Streams" prepared by Messrs. Watkins, Miller and McDonald at the request of the fish committee. This report represented the first comprehensive fisheries management plan for Alberta trout streams in the eastern slopes of the Alberta Rockies and foothills.

Pollution chair Walter Boote reported, "I regret to say, that in spite of a definite request that pollution of Crowsnest River and its tributaries cease, the Department has not seen fit to take action. This same condition applies to the Bow River in Calgary in regard to waste oil from refineries." Boote did, however, note that "A definite clean up of Lees Creek and pollution from the town of Cardston has been affected, also the pollution of the Red Deer River by the Canadian Pacific Railroad has been discontinued; this is being closely watched by the Red Deer association."

H. Cornwell, predator chair, noted, "It must be said that the Department of Agriculture has certainly gone to town with regard to control of coyotes by: (1) Training interested farmers in the use of cyanide go-getters [a type of cyanide explosive gun that discharged a cyanide pellet into the mouth of a coyote at a bait station]. (2) Educating the general public as to the need for care in the use of the poison, and generally doing a good job under close supervision of district agriculturists." Mr. W. Lobay, supervisor of crop protection service for the department of agriculture, had advised Cornwell that his department had distributed 3,000 coyote go-getters, with about 500 guns being set and about 200 coyotes killed. Alberta Agriculture had also started use of the highly controversial 1080 bait, which was an indiscriminate killer of many non-target species of wildlife in addition to coyotes, in the Municipal Districts of Pincher Creek and Cochrane. [1080 is a poison used for the purpose of vertebrate pest control. The chemical name for 1080 is sodium monofluoroacetate.] Despite all of the concerted efforts of the association in their ongoing crow and magpie campaign, Cornwell concluded his report by advising, "Crows are down, but magpies still remain a major problem."

There were several resolutions that the government pay a bounty on coyotes and that the government also make a greater effort to control wolves and cougars. The Vilna Fish and Game Association declared the coyote situation to have reached a crisis. The Calgary Fish and Game Association declared cougars and wolves a menace. Other associations put forward similar concerns.

Upland bird chair G. T. Loney reported, "There is one matter of importance that I believe is wanting. We have seasons and bag limits set out before us, we as members of the association help to see that these regulations are enforced, we work from an educational angle, and certainly I can see that many so-called sportsmen have become real sportsmen, but, there are large areas that have no such thing as a Fish and Game Association, where before season, on Sundays, as well as week days, shooting upland birds is the order of the day. We need more Game Guardians in the Province of Alberta, to spearhead a drive toward enforcing game laws."

The 23rd annual AFGA convention was the largest in the association's history to that point in time: 172 delegates, 55 guests and officials, 53 ladies. Many distinguished guests attended the convention: Mr. J.R.B. Coleman, acting superintendent of Banff National Park; Mr. F. Bryant, chief warden of Banff; Dr. Bamfield, Mr. Gallop, Mr. Dewey Soper all from the wildlife branch of the Dominion Service; Mr. J.G. Cunningham, B.C. Game Commissioner; Mr. E.L. Paynter, game commissioner from Regina; Mr. Them Kjar, game commissioner of Whitehorse, Yukon; Mr. R.M. Ferrie, president Western Canada Yukon Fish and Game Council from North Battleford; Mr. J. Wilson, President Saskatchewan Fish and Game Association from Saskatoon; Mr. Ben Cartwright, chief naturalist of Ducks Unlimited from Winnipeg; Mr. B. Caldwell of Ducks Unlimited from Saskatchewan and Mr. Fred Sharpe of Tilley. Secretary G.M. Spargo noted, "These introductions were received with great applause."

There is an interesting footnote in the convention minutes regarding a question-and-answer session following an address by E.S. Huestis, Alberta's Fish and Game Commissioner. He spoke on "... such matters as predators, yearly fishing of streams, sportsman-farmer relationship, increasing the numbers of Fish and Game Guardians, wolf menace, the Indian problem and so

forth..." The discussion included an appeal by Henry Stelfox "... always the great advocate for better treatment of Indians..." who strongly urged the delegates "...not to forget to help the native population whenever and wherever the organization could." Stelfox reportedly received an ovation at the close of his appeal.

In addition to the official guests, the Hon. N. E. Tanner, Minister of Lands and Forests, attended the convention, along with four members of the legislature: O.B. Moore (Ponoka), William Kovach (Pincher Creek-Crowsnest), H.G. Hammell (Didsbury) and Mrs. R. Wilkinson (Calgary). At today's annual conferences it would be rare to have any MLAs in attendance during the working sessions.

In Memoriam: Past president C.E. Brown asked for two minutes of silence at the conference for those who had passed away and had unselfishly given a great deal towards the welfare of sportsmen: C. de la Vergne, E. Wiggins, Dr. W.A. Wilson, Frank Farley, Walter Ratcliff and Metro Shapka.

In an interesting development, some criticism was apparently leveled by William Kovach, the locally popular MLA for the Pincher Creek Crowsnest constituency, with regard to the lack of action by the AFGA in connection with the continued pollution of the Crow's Nest River. Spargo advised the convention that the association had offered to provide (1) evidence of the pollution and (2) offered to appear at any prosecution against the offenders provided members so appearing would be protected from any consequences arising from that appearance—that is being sued by the companies if the charges could not be proven in court.

1953

Resolution No. 36   (Red Deer Fish and Game Association) "Be it resolved: that the hunting of antelope be carried out by a draw for the privilege to hunt, or that an antelope be included with the big-game license, for the taking of one only big game head."
This resolution was defeated.

This is the first mention of a "draw" [lottery] for a big-game animal in the annual resolutions submitted by the association.

Resolutions No. 41-54(A)
Dealt with various proposed predator control measures – three pages in total - particularly wolves, cougars and coyotes which were still seen as a major limiting factor on big game by members of the association. Typical was Resolution No. 53 – (Nordegg Fish and Game Association) "Be it resolved: that full-time hunters be employed year-round to kill timber wolves and cougars, and other predators." This resolution was carried.

However, a break in party ranks with respect to predator control occurred with the following two resolutions:

Resolution No. 54   (Calgary Fish and Game Association) "Resolved: That the bounty on all hawks and owls be eliminated."

Resolution No. 54 (A)   (High River Fish and Game Association) "Whereas there are a large number of beneficial owls and hawks killed in the belief that there is a bounty on them, Be it therefore resolved: that owls and hawks should be removed from the bounty list."

Regarding Resolutions No. 54 and 54(A), an amendment was carried: "That all hawks and owls with the exception of horned owls and snowy owls be removed from the list."

Officials of the provincial fisheries branch did not prosecute the coal companies in Bellevue, Blairmore and Coleman because of concerns it might not be possible to charge the companies if they did knowingly permit the deposit of a deleterious substance in the river (i.e. cause siltation in the river arising from slack piles of waste coal beside the river and dumping slurry). Co-author/editor Duane Radford lived in Bellevue at the time, beside the mine site, and recalls trucks dumping slurry directly into the river on occasion and also the erosion of waste coal slack into the river which caused it to run black for weeks on end during the spring runoff. The same problems were also occurring at the same time upstream at Blairmore and Coleman, next to mine sites.

There was an interesting speech by J.G. Cunningham, B.C. Game Commissioner from Vancouver, in which he chided the AFGA for "pussyfooting" with the Alberta government about Sunday shooting. "I cannot understand why you fellows will go cap in hand asking for something which is your right," he said. Apparently, his remarks brought the house down. As well, Cunningham opined that the Indian should stand on his own feet. Such a comment would not be "politically correct" in the 21st century, but was a testament to the deplorable treatment of Canada's Indians at that time. They were not allowed to vote and were generally treated as second-class citizens in the province.

At the time, forest rangers enforced fish and game legislation in Alberta. They were perceived by many as being all-powerful in their districts within the forest reserves. Resolutions No. 54 and 54(a) are good examples of why organizations should be careful what they ask for because they just might get it. In due course, the government implemented such registration systems, much to the eventual consternation of hunters. The result was that on opening day of a hunting season there would be long lineups of vehicles packed with hunters at the unmanned entrance to the forest reserves. Each hunter had to fill out individual registration forms with his name, address, vehicle licence plate number, and the make, model and serial number of his firearms—in the dark, in all manner of weather. Often, there would be no pen or pencil at the registration point—sometimes because previous registrants had intentionally removed them to give the early birds an even better head start on their fellow hunters—the latter often having to search for something to write with in their vehicles, sometimes resorting to using the lead tips of their bullets. It was often pure mayhem, and one of the most frustrating, ill-conceived ventures ever instituted by the Alberta government, based on the good intentions of some members of the AFGA.

1953 Floyd E. Mitchell took over as president of the AFGA in 1952. Mitchell reported philosophically that "although much has been accomplished, there is still a great deal more to be done; in fact our problems will never end which is just as well, for when they do, the need for our association will also end (President's Annual Report, 1953)."

The 24th annual conference was held at the Macdonald Hotel in Edmonton in 1953. Over 240 delegates registered at the convention, which was the largest ever to that point in time.

Certificates of Merit were presented to the following members at the annual convention: John McAfee, James McAfee, Roland Wood, W. Crawford, George Cyr, Pierre Gauvreau, T.C. Williams, Bernard Hamm, C.E. Lofgren, C.W. Johnson, J.A. McGhee, L. Kalbfleisch, H.O. Scragg, Art Allen and George Roth.

Secretary treasurer George Spargo noted, "The splendid representation in uniform of nearly 50 forestry, game and fisheries officials from the department helped to establish the fact that we certainly have a fine-looking intelligent personnel."

Of note is the amount of travel reported by president Mitchell who attended conventions and meetings on behalf of the AFGA throughout Canada and to Seattle, Washington. This signalled the beginning of a new era for the AFGA – attendance of the president and members of the executive at national and international meetings to represent the interests of Alberta's sportsmen. Spargo, likewise, noted his attendance at a large number of meetings in Alberta and elsewhere. In Spargo's 23 years of service to the association up to this time, he had attended meetings in the Yukon, New York, Portland, Seattle, Montreal, Great Falls, Helena and all the principal cities from Winnipeg west to Vancouver.

Membership concerns were again flagged as an ongoing issue, although overall membership had increased. Strangely, as did his immediate predecessor, Mitchell tended to blame the local clubs for declines in membership, not head office.

The annual game dinner for the premier, members of cabinet and the legislature was held on March 10, 1953 and only three members of the legislature were absent, a truly remarkable turnout of provincial politicians at this social function.

1953

Resolution   There was some controversy at the conference about the health of the AFGA provincial secretary, George Spargo. In a resolution, the Red Deer Fish and Game Association moved that "the provincial executive of the AFGA take steps to retire Mr. Spargo on pension, and to replace him with a younger, more robust man, capable of handling the duties of secretary of the association." An amended resolution regarding the retirement of secretary G. Spargo was referred to the executive council.

As usual, the AGFA pheasant propagation program had a high profile, as well as government rearing efforts. Sportsmen of the day were avid bird-game hunters and they were keenly interested in boosting pheasant numbers through propagation measures. Understandably, the president referred to them as "grand game birds." Co-author/editor Duane Radford recalls his early pheasant hunts in the area north of Lethbridge around Barons and Nobleford in the 1950s as being a rite of passage for young hunters. An annual pilgrimage would take place to enjoy a pheasant hunt for residents from all over Alberta. The countryside was bursting with hunters. Non-residents, particularly from British Columbia, also enjoyed hunting pheasants and were very common hunters in those days, often spending several days in pursuit of these sporting birds.

> The Calgary local club had a pheasant farm that released 4,770 birds, more than the government hatchery which produced 4,530 pheasants in 1951.

Secretary treasurer George Spargo had a rather lengthy report in the convention yearbook; he commented on an interesting meeting with officials from the British Columbia Fish and Game Council regarding reciprocal angling licences. "We were unable to convince the members present not to increase angling fees from $3.50 to $5.00, although the vote was very close," he reported. "The Game Commissioners promised a review of the situation the following year. All these matters are of importance to EVERY ALBERTA MAN THAT TAKES OUT A FISHING LICENSE to fish in B.C. We have already by our insistence saved anglers thousands of dollars through the fact that a reduction has been made from the original fee imposed of $10.00 to an aforementioned figure of $3.50 and $5.00." Eventually, hard-won reciprocal angling licence fees between various western provinces were disbanded during hard economic times in the 1990s.

The membership of the association totaled 11,774, with no change in the number of 78 associations affiliated in 1952. Notwithstanding the overall stability of the association, Spargo had a disparaging report on the junior conservation program. "It would seem, however," he wrote, "to our dismay that the junior movement has practically collapsed. I suggest this may have been because too many activities of one sort or another are in effect. Both boys and girls are saturated with 'junior functions' of one thing or another from juvenile age to high school, and one wonders how our youths get time enough to study. Our outdoor program does not seem attractive enough when numerous clubs offer everything on a platter for nothing. I fear that the sturdiness of pioneering has departed from our midst."

Spargo advised that "through the courtesy of the Rock City Tobacco Company of Quebec, 7,500 posters to improve Farmer-Sportsmen relations – 2,000 of which were distributed from Headquarters," had been affected. The Rock City Tobacco Company manufactured Sportsman cigarettes. The signs stated "Shooting by permission, apply at House." The association sent 5,500 directly to local clubs for distribution. He also noted, "You will discover that we now have both Fish [Martin J. Paetz] and Game [George J. Mitchell] biologists in the Provincial employment. This was urged for some considerable time by resolutions brought on the floor of the house."

Big-game chair J. Erle Carr advised, "I am sorry to have to inform you that the overall picture is none too good." He reported on what he perceived as wolf and cougar depredation on bighorn sheep and diseased moose, and an all-time low in deer numbers. Carr noted, "We have only a few caribou left in the Northwestern part of the province, and I do not think there should have been an open season on them this year, if they are not protected then soon this beautiful animal will disappear." He also advised "The antelope season was again kept closed this year, which I considered a wise thing to do, they seem to grow scarcer each year. I drove for two days in the Brooks, Tilly, Scandia and Vauxhall area, this past summer, and I only saw three; others have reported the same condition to me, poaching, and the fact that their habitat grows smaller each year is largely responsible for this."

On the bright side, Carr reported, "Elk are in plentiful supply, and are increasing in numbers, they are by far our most plentiful big-game animal, they seem to stand hunting and the predators far better than the moose or the deer." Carr did not have figures from the Game Department on big game killed in 1951 but advised, "I am sure the number is much less than in 1950." He closed his report by comparing the paltry budget for game management in Alberta with other jurisdictions. "Montana spends about 1½ million dollars on Game work, and Washington about 3 million, what is the matter with us in this wealthy province, we should be heartily ashamed."

H.R. Brooke, migratory birds committee chair, noted, "The season throughout has been very favorable for the propagation of all types of waterfowl." Brooke also commented on the ongoing issue

---

1954

For the first time there were resolutions calling on the government to accurately survey big-game populations.

Resolution No. 22 (Edmonton, Pincher Creek, Luscar clubs.) "Whereas the big-game population of Alberta is subject to increased hunting pressure; THEREFORE BE IT RESOLVED: that the provincial government take immediate steps to commence aerial and ground surveys of our big-game population in order that more accurate information is available to ascertain whether the trend of the game population is up or down from one season to the other." The resolution was carried unanimously.

related to waterfowl crop depredation, a long-standing issue with farmers. "The warm, dry fall also assisted in minimizing the duck damage. In many areas where the duck hatch was heavy, it was feared the damage would also be heavy, but in most cases the crops were taken out of the fields before any great damage was done."

> The AFGA established a committee called the Farmer Sportsmen Relations Committee in 1952 to investigate duck damage to farmers' grain crops and what could be done about protecting farmers in terms of crop insurance, with the Alberta Hail Insurance Board as the agent.

Good and welfare committee chair Gordon J. Cummings reported on progress by the committee. "In conclusion, we wish to re-state our belief that if a suitable plan of insurance can be worked out and put into effect, the federal government, the provincial government and every sportsman who takes out a bird game hunting license, should contribute; the farmers should not be called upon to bear the entire cost." This is a good example of an unheralded policy decision by the AFGA that would be of great benefit to Alberta's waterfowl and farmers alike for years to come, as well as birdwatchers.

> The year 1952 marked the start of an open-and-closed stream fishing regulation for eastern slope streams, which would remain in effect until the mid-1980s when it was rather arbitrarily closed by the fisheries branch.

Angling and fish chair C.S. Buchanan commented on the recently adopted alternate open-and-closed stream management program for eastern slope streams. He expressed concerns about the government not taking advantage of the closed streams to stock those streams with trout and give them a chance to survive and grow before the streams were opened again.

Buchanan noted that stockings from the Pincher Creek rearing ponds had been ongoing for about 10 years to that point in time and had greatly improved fishing in the Pincher Creek dis-

trict. Buchanan advised that a site for some new trout-rearing ponds on the Hunter Brothers Ranch west of Fort Macleod was under investigation to replace the abandoned pond at Pincher Creek. The Cardston Rod and Gun Club had apparently successfully operated a rearing pond on Lees Creek, according to Buchanan. At the time, the government hatchery capacity in Calgary was three million fry, but Buchanan reported they only stocked 120,000 fingerlings in 1951.

Predator chair G. Riach reported, "Our wolf situation is serious from all over the game areas, and there is undoubted evidence of inroads into our game wealth. Take a look at the map: see how we are squeezed by national parks on our entire boundary on the west, and by Buffalo Park on the N.W.T. in the North. These vast areas are breeding places of wolves and predators, and it's a wonder we have any worthwhile game left. We must insist on controls immediately. It's practically of no use to poison, trap or kill cougars and wolves if the balance of nature theorists are permitted to govern."

COURTESY OF TRAVEL ALBERTA

A full harvest moon hangs over Grande Prairie.

1954

Resolution No. 1
"Be it resolved: that there be an open season throughout the Province in 1955 on: (a) deer, (b) moose, (e) elk and the limit shall be ONE MALE animal only, except where special conditions exist."
The motion carried, indicating a perceived recovery of game populations.

Resolution No. 16
(Magrath Association) "Whereas the use of horses and cattle used as a walking blind results in an unwarranted number of wounded and lost geese from pot shooting; BE IT RESOLVED: that the government request that the *Migratory Birds Convention Act* be changed so as to prohibit this needless waste."
This resolution was carried; however, it was never acted upon by government and remains a popular way of getting within range of Canada geese on the Blood Indian Reserve, where the practice likely originated. Historically, the Blood Indian band grazed a large number of horses near St. Mary Reservoir, the main waterfowl staging area in the region, and horse silhouettes were used to disguise hunters so they could close the range on feeding Canada geese.

*P*redator control was a hotly debated issue in and outside wildlife management circles in the mid-20th century. In the early days of the development of the science of wildlife management, several attempts had been made to eradicate predators from certain areas in hope of increasing the numbers of game animals such as deer (e.g., Kaibab Plateau Deer, 1920s). These often ended with the prey species growing in numbers beyond the carrying capacities of their habitats and doing significant damage to that habitat. If allowed to continue, the result could be a sudden crash in the number of game animals. As a result of these studies, wildlife biologists began to change their thinking about predator control, recognizing that predators have their place in the so-called "balance of nature." However, sportsmen and women, who had grown up during times when game was scarce, were hard to convince that predator removal was not an important aspect of game management. This debate continued into the 21st century, as many hunters believe they are competing with increasing populations of predators and wildlife biologists continue to learn about the intricacies of ecosystem biology.

1954 Floyd E. Mitchell continued as president of the AFGA in 1953. He presided over the 25th Silver Jubilee convention of the AFGA, held at the Palliser Hotel in Calgary in 1954. By all accounts, it was a classy convention, judged as "The Best Ever" by members of the executive. A silver sticker featuring a cock pheasant in flight with the notation "25 Years Service - Alberta Fish and Game Association" was featured on the Silver Jubilee convention yearbook. Likewise, an embossed "Silver Jubilee" banner was spread across the program with the numerals 25 overlaid in silver on each page of the agenda.

Mr. Eric Huestis, Alberta's Fish and Game Commissioner, addressed the delegates during the opening session of the convention, as he had done at every convention since 1941. The Saturday night convention banquet featured roast Alberta elk (kindness of the Department of Natural Resources) and roast Yukon Arctic caribou (kindness of Mr. Them Kjar, director of publicity and game commissioner for the Yukon, Whitehorse, Yukon Territory).

Following dinner, Mr. Guy Blake, president of the Calgary Fish and Game Association, introduced the top table personalities. Mr. J.B. Cross, president of the Calgary Brewing and Malting Co., was awarded the Fulton Trophy in 1953; Mr. Sandy Cross, on behalf of the company accepted the award in the absence of J.B. Cross. George Spargo reported, "It is undoubtedly true that NO SINGLE person or business firm have through the years been more generous in assisting worthwhile measures for conservation than this old and excellent company. One has only to view the gardens and fish pools in east Calgary, the Fingerling pools at Westmount, the fish hatchery (one of the most modern in Canada), to understand how well deserving is the Company for such an honour, and of course with it being our SILVER JUBILEE year it is all the more fitting."

A life membership was awarded to Walt Disney of Hollywood, California. This award was accepted by Mr. Irvin Verity of the Walt Disney Studios of Burbank, California. There is no record why Walt Disney was awarded a life membership, presumably because of Disney's coverage of the great outdoors and wild animals.

COURTESY OF DUANE RADFORD

The guest speaker at the evening dinner banquet was the new minister of lands and forest, the Honourable Ivan Casey. In the minutes of the 25th annual convention, Spargo noted, "Mr. Casey stressed two important factors that had a bearing on present-day conditions, one that the organization must always be the voice of hunters and fishermen in dealings with his Department. No other means of obtaining concerted requirements could be recognized by any Government. He urged the 400 persons attending to put membership in the forefront of future programmes. The second was the urgency of better relations with ranchers and farmers."

President Mitchell advised that big-game hunting opportunities were not very abundant after World War II. Restrictions were still in place to protect and grow populations in the early 1950s. For these reasons, waterfowl and upland birds were very important to the sport hunters and likely one of the main reasons the AFGA members were fervent in their predator control campaign. Mitchell reported that the government rabies control program would produce "… a bumper crop of moose, elk and deer calves." The antelope situation remained unchanged, the season remaining closed, as it had been since 1951.

Several interesting highlights were reported by president Mitchell in his annual report:

"The passing of the TWO MILLION MARK in the destruction of crows and magpies with an expenditure of over $100,000.

"The increase in membership to over TWELVE THOUSAND (the first time in the history of the association);

"Start-up in getting better farmer-sportsmen relations underway, by way of distribution of posters, a survey for crop damage by waterfowl insurance and obtaining better permit regulations for crop damage control by waterfowl."

Having survived a vote of non-confidence at the previous convention, now secretary manager, George Spargo presented his 23rd consecutive convention report, noting, "This Jubilee year of our Silver Anniversary will, I believe, establish the fact, that we have truly and rightfully earned a paramount position of trust and confidence seldom achieved in the minds of those who run our province and community." He spoke highly of the calibre of volunteers in the association and that the government invited them to sit on its fish and game advisory council, as well as the long-established Western Canada-Yukon Fish and Game Council. Officials from the association were also invited to attend meetings with Ducks Unlimited, scientific bodies and some federal meetings pertaining to the *Migratory Birds Convention Act*. They also consulted with officials from Alberta's Western Livestock Association and the Farmers' Association.

Spargo noted that the membership was 12,652, with 78 local groups. The top five clubs were Calgary (1,730), Edmonton (1,112), Lethbridge (700), Red Deer (644) and Medicine Hat (600). Four locals were tied for the smallest membership, 10 each (Bawlf-Kelsey, Bassano, Spring Coulee and Coleman). Regarding the annual MLA game dinner, Spargo reported, "I must also pay a very sincere tribute indeed to the one man who has long been responsible for the management of these game dinners and who in and out of office provides much of the game and that is, our valued friend and worker, past president Bill Fisher. Bill's fame in this regard is well known, and his continued interest has proven a most valuable service to this association."

Spargo presented a memoriam for Messrs. Cunningham and Cheeseman: "Two great and helpful friends of our association who for many years back have always been with us, in the persons of Jim Cunningham of Vancouver and Charles Cheeseman of Cardston 'will not tread their ways towards us again', so we say SAYONARA friends, we touch our lips, we touch our hands, and we touch our hearts to you both." [G.J. Cunningham held the position of game commissioner for B.C.; C. (Charles) B. Cheeseman had been a long-standing regional representative of the AFGA for the Foothills Region (south).

Big-game chair J. E. Carr gave an optimistic report, attributing much of the improved conditions to the predator-control program, noting, "The Game Branch, and the men in the field deserve a great deal of credit for a good job well done, there is a better crop of young animals this year than we have had in the past 10 or 12 years." Carr reported the calf moose population up "80 or 90 percent," which contrasted with past years when only "10 or 15 percent of the young survived their first summer."

Carr further stated, "If we are to really have good deer hunting again in Alberta, I think we should plant several small herds of white-tail deer in our Foothills country." At the time, white-tailed deer were relatively scarce in southern Alberta, and even sighting one was quite an event. The Lethbridge association presented a resolution at the conference, calling for the government to study the establishment of white-tailed deer in Alberta, and to proceed with stocking this species "…at the earliest possible time if found suitable." As time would tell, such introductions were not necessary. Over the next few decades, the white-tailed deer invaded Alberta, displacing mule deer from much of their former range. The white-tails were better adapted to agricultural conditions than mule deer, and followed the development of agriculture across the continent from east to west.

Carr also commented that elk were increasing and that an open season on cows would likely be necessary "…in the not too distant future." Many sportsmen were loath to shoot female big game animals in the 1950s as they had been brought up to hunt males only, not as trophies, but as a way of protecting the brood stock. "A large number of us do not like the idea of shooting female elk," noted Carr, "but there comes a time when it is good game management to do so, a fact which has been proven in the U.S."

On another front, Carr reported, "Our caribou population is very low," reported Carr. "While this association has favoured a closed season on these animals for several years now, nothing has been done about it, and if some action is not taken soon, these beautiful animals are going to disappear entirely from Alberta. A closed season on these animals is a must." The antelope season remained closed again in 1953.

Migratory bird chair R. Brooke noted that game commissioner Eric Huestis and members of the Western Canada-Yukon Fish and Game Council had persuaded federal officials to permit at least a workable pre-season control on ducks where damage was being done. "It should help to overcome some of the antagonism which has been developing amongst the farmers towards the propagation of same." Waterfowl management was the ultimate responsibility of the federal government under the Migratory Birds Convention Act. Consequently, crop damage control was a shared responsibility.

Brooke also advised, "Our 1953 bird game licenses still state in large red letters that 'Sunday Shooting is Prohibited.' Where can you go in the country during the hunting season on a Sunday that you do not hear shotgun blasts all around you? Is this another un-enforceable regulation or does it mean anything? It is quite discouraging to those sportsmen who abide by our regulations

and are trying to persuade others to do likewise to see such a total disregard to the enforcement of our existing regulations."

Colin Buchanan, fish chair, reported that the Pincher Creek fish rearing ponds had been decommissioned by "…the Department of Game and Fisheries," and that negotiations were still underway regarding use of springs on the Hunter Brothers acreage near Fort Macleod as alternate rearing ponds.

Predator chair Soren Norre advised "It is a pleasure to report a red letter year in predator control, and I am convinced that a marked impression has been made on wolf and coyote populations especially through government action and the rabies program. Much has been accomplished by farmers, trappers, and our own fish and game associations, some of whom have taken definite action and report marvelous success in poisoning of wolves and coyotes."

The chair of the farmers-sportsmen relations committee, Gordon Cummings, reported pre-season damage shoots for waterfowl had minimized crop damage with very few complaints being reported. On another note, Cummings advised "One local is hoping to improve their farmer-sportsmen relations by issuing a membership card which requires the member to pledge himself to obey Fishing and Hunting Regulations and Laws, and to respect the rights and property of the farmer. In addition, on the same membership card

1955

Resolution No. 6	(Edmonton, Lethbridge, Medicine Hat) "Whereas legalizing of big game bow hunting in 49 States in U.S.A. and most of the provinces in Canada has resulted in conservation of big game, in that many gun hunters are turning to bow hunting with fewer animals taken, Resolved that the provincial game branch be urged to permit bow hunting of big game, resolve that a two week pre-season period with special license be set aside for Bow Hunting, Resolved that only bows capable of casting arrows with at least 7/8 broad head (a broad head is sharpened several times, this being the reason we suggest a larger broad head) this is at a distance of 150 yards to be classed as lethal weapons, resolved that big game bow hunting be governed by the existing big game regulations now in force." This resolution was referred to the executive.
Resolution No. 14	(Lethbridge) "Due to the fact that it is hard and inconvenient for game officers to check a man for his license, be it resolved, that the game branch issue a badge of some kind to every license holder to wear in a conspicuous place when hunting and fishing." The resolution was defeated in committee and on the floor, with a note that this suggestion had met with the same defeat on three previous occasions.
Resolution No. 21	(Red Deer) "Whereas a lost hunter after dark needs to conserve his ammunition therefore be it resolved that the distress signal shall be one shot to be answered by three shots from men in camp." The resolution carried.
Resolution No. 44	(Calgary) "Whereas fishing regulations at present call for the rod to be held in the hands at all times, or it is subject to confiscation and Whereas this works a considerable hardship on many of our old citizens who love fishing, Therefore be it resolved that the Act be amended making all fishermen over the age of 60 years exempt from this particular clause." The resolution was defeated.

Front row : G.J. Cummings (L), C.E. Brown, G.E. Watt and K.J. Webb. Back row: G.J. Keltie (L), J.E. Wiggins, G.M. Spargo, H.H. Bateman and C. Craddock.

the farmer is advised that the bearer of the card has pledged himself to respect the farmer's rights and asking him to allow the bearer to hunt or fish on his land. The card is numbered and the farmer can read it when the card is shown to him previous to permission being given to hunt or fish. If the member's conduct is not satisfactory, the farmer can report same to the local Association when suitable action will be taken. In that way the local hopes to be able to at least control the actions of its members." This item represents the first report of self-policing by members of the AFGA.

1955 Curt P. (Paul) Smith took over as president of the AFGA in 1954. His president's report for 1954-55 signaled a time of change in the organization.

The 26th annual convention was held in 1955 at the Palliser Hotel in Calgary. The year 1955 marked the 50th anniversary of Alberta as a province and in recognition of this milestone the cover of the convention yearbook was gold. In the minutes for the convention, Smith commented, "The association is at its apex in so far as numbers, influence, and community enterprise are concerned, and possibly one of the most important associations in the whole of Canada." The new B.C. game commissioner, Frank Butler, attended the convention. He replaced the late Jim Cunningham.

Certificates of Merit for outstanding work and distinguished service were presented at the annual convention to Dr. R.F. Falconer, Reg. Jarvis, Guy Blake, Wm. Rowan, Urban Young, A.M. Van Ostrand, J.E. Jefferies, Dick Bishop and Les Biscoe.

Smith drew attention to the need for changes in trout stocking in the settled areas of Alberta; to rationalize the biological considerations regarding the shooting of cock pheasants; to study game management practices based on happenings in the Carbondale area of southwestern Alberta which had been set aside as a game preserve and where the season had been re-opened after a lengthy closure to restore local game herds. (There was an open season on both male and female elk in the area south of Highway 3 in 1954.) Big-game chair J. Erle Carr subsequently reported on contradictory reports on this particular hunt: "No doubt there were animals left to rot, and others killed that should not have been killed, but I still think that the idea of thinning them out was good conservation, as their winter range was becoming depleted, and there was a definite sign of disease among this herd."

Smith's other concerns were related to the need to educate sportsmen to improve farmer-hunter relations – an ongoing issue. Smith also chaired the farmer-sportsmen relations committee. For the first time in many years, the slogan of the AFGA underwent a change: "The Voice of the Organized Sportsman" instead of "Game Is A Crop" (although the latter was still featured on the bottom of each page in the convention yearbook).

> Secretary manager George Spargo beamed in his annual report, "Your total membership for 1953-54 has risen to the greatest number in our existence, a magnificent total of 13,394 as against 12,652 for the previous year. This is an increase of 742 fully paid up members contained in 81 organizations as compared with 78 last year or a gain of three."

In 1954 the top five clubs were Calgary (2,000), Edmonton (1,055), Red Deer (1,000), Medicine Hat (623) and Wetaskiwin (500). The Tilley local was the smallest (16). Spargo was a hustler in trying to drum up membership and create new locals. "During the spring your secretary motored around 4,000 miles throughout the Peace River district and northern B.C. lecturing to some 14 organizations during that period. The result is that we have reorganized some of our local groups which for lack of interest had more or less collapsed. We hope that we shall form two new organizations at Hines Crossing and Fort Vermillion."

Spargo described another successful annual game dinner with MLAs, with 95 percent attendance by legislative members. He reported that the St. Paul, Viking, Vilna and northeastern prairie clubs devoted much time and money in the transfer of over 100 elk into that area of the North Saskatchewan River. These animals were obtained through the assistance of the Alberta game commissioner E.S. Huestis and the National Parks Branch in Ottawa.

Big-game chair J. Earle Carr had an optimistic report, "The results of the Rabies Campaign have certainly shown how important it is to have good predator control, and if this good work is kept up, I can see a bright future for your big game." Although the season was closed, Carr noted that moose were coming back rapidly and the deer population was on the increase. On a more pessimistic note, he advised, "The antelope herds are increasing very slowly, the great reduction in the number of coyotes is helping some, but we still have another menace in the number of poachers, who are still taking their toll."

The AFGA had embarked on a massive campaign to maintain good relations between sportsmen and landowners as a result of a trend towards increased posting of private land against trespassers.

The good and welfare committee had an extensive report on this issue in the convention yearbook. The chair advised, "This program became a must because of the deterioration of good will between the man with the gun or fishing rod, and the man whose property contains game and fish." The association put priority on an education program through "Hunting By Permission Cards or Posters" procured from Sportsman's Cigarettes – some 10,000 posters were distributed. Secondly, the association lobbied for an extensive pre-season damage control permitting system to keep waterfowl from damaging farmer's crops. Additionally, a major campaign was sponsored by local associations throughout the province petitioning sportsmen to:

1. Ask for permission to shoot or fish.
2. Shut all gates.
3. Not shoot near farmer's livestock or buildings.
4. Not drive over crops or swathed grain.
5. Fill in goose pits or duck blinds.
6. Be careful with fires at all times and in all places.
7. Respect the rights and property of the farmer or landowners and treat him as a friend.

This campaign was publicized in newspapers, magazines and over radio throughout Alberta.

The government responded by altering the *Game Act* under Section 7 to read as follows: "It is unlawful to hunt or trap over any enclosed land that is posted with 'NO SHOOTING' signs without first having obtained permission and consent of the owner or occupant thereof."

Migratory bird chair G.K. Watts also reported, "As was to be expected, there were early reports of damage to crops in the south but the prompt action of the Game Commissioner in issuing blanket permits for pre-season shooting to farmers in those areas seemed to have taken care of the problem." Damage control permits were used at the time (and still are) to scare waterfowl from swathed grain.

In his upland game bird report, chairman R. Arlt chided hunters for putting their guns away just because the game-hunting season was over when they could be predator hunting, "in the interest of conservation." He noted that in the Cardston-Pincher Creek area, where 1080 poison had been used on coyotes, sharptail and ruffed grouse were increasing every year. [1080 is a poison used for the purpose of vertebrate pest control. The chemical name for 1080 is sodium monofluoroacetate, and its problem as a predator control agent is that it poisons any vertebrate animal that eats it, not just targeted predators.]

1956

Resolution No. 41   (Red Deer, Edmonton, Carmangay, Two Hills, Eastern Prairie Associations, Central Alberta Associations) "RESOLVED: that the Fisheries Branch should be commended for their program of 'pothole' planting and encouraged to continue this good work."
The resolution carried.

Predator chair Soren Norre reported that he regretted the federal government had placed "harmful" raptors "such as goshawks, horned and snowy owls" on the protected list. He suggested the association must actively campaign to get these birds back on the bounty list.

George Hinde, the incoming fish chair, noted, "It cannot be gainsaid that as a whole the stocking of such barren lakes as Cavan, Armstrong and Severn, and the pothole lakes near Cardston have been an enormous success. With continued biological examinations of these dry land waters, I believe that many people are going to have trout fishing right at their back doors for the first time. I heartily commend the Fisheries Branch and the Department of Lands and Forests under Mr. Huestis for this happy augury of better things to come."

Notable in their attendance at the conference were G.J. Mitchell (game bird biologist), R. Webb (government biologist), M.J. Paetz (fish biologist) and R.C. Thomas (government biologist), the nucleus of a new crop of game and fish biologists, as well as E. McCarthy, C.W. Dougherty, B.D. Freeman, H.F. Aastrup and F. L. Foy (game wardens).

1956 The 27th annual convention of the AFGA was held in the Memorial Centre in Red Deer in 1956.

In his president's report for 1955-56, Curt P. Smith reported, "At present our membership stands at 14,840, representing 91 locals," the highest number of members and clubs to date. The top five clubs were Calgary (1,658), Red Deer (1,100), Edmonton (1,000), Lethbridge (900) and Medicine Hat (700) in 1956; the smallest club was the Dickson Ladies Fish and Game Association (10).

It should be understood that in 1956 the population of the province was about 1.1 million people. If you compare the above figures to those the AFGA reported in 1998 when Alberta's population was about 2.8 million—over 15,000 members in over 120 clubs—you see how strong public support for the association was in the 1950s.

Smith continued to express concerns about an imbalance in hen-cock pheasant ratios, and the need to harvest surplus cocks. He also mentioned the widely successful prairie trout stocking program, actually complaining about the abundance of hard-to-catch lunkers and possibly the need to "poison" them out as many were deemed uncatchable! The success of this program can be attributed to Alberta's pioneer fisheries managers: Dr. R.B. Miller, who conducted Alberta's first biological surveys, and Martin J. Paetz, who was hired as Alberta's first fish biologist. The first biological research station in Alberta was established by Dr. Miller at Gorge Creek in the eastern slopes in 1950.

1957

Resolution No. 16	(Calgary, Edmonton) "Whereas more Alberta streams, lakes and pot holes have been stocked and some of these waters have subsequently become inaccessible to anglers for devious reasons; RESOLVED: that the Provincial Fisheries Branch make certain that there be and remain public access to all planted waters for the purpose of fishing." This particular resolution lead to a government policy that waters would not be stocked unless there was public access. The resolution carried.
Resolution No. 38	(Eastern Prairie groups, Alder Flats, Rimbey, Calgary, etc.) "RESOLVED: that we petition the Government to enlarge still further the staff of Game and Fish wardens by additional appointments with special recognition of the district of Vegreville, Tofield to Viking east and north thereof, Alder Flats and the Peace River areas." The resolution carried.
Resolution No. 40	(Calgary, Drumheller) "WHEREAS there is some bad feeling towards hunters due to a certain number of livestock being wounded or killed each year and the farmer or rancher being forced to stand the entire loss; RESOLVED: that the Provincial Government be requested to set up a 'Livestock Indemnity Fund' to take care of all such proven losses, and that all hunters, big game, bird game and migratory bird license holders be required to contribute either by the purchase of a special license or as may be otherwise decided." There was a close vote on this resolution: it carried by 44 to 38 against.
Resolution No. 43	(Stavely, Lethbridge) "WHEREAS the Advisory Council has proven ineffective and WHEREAS it does not seem to have served any purpose; RESOLVED: that the Advisory Fish and Game Council be abolished." This resolution signaled a major change in the confidence the membership of the AFGA had in government at the time. However, it was voted down in committee and was not carried to the convention. In fact, president Carr is recorded to have appealed for a "…wholehearted vote of confidence in the Advisory Council."

"Miller replaced Dr. William Rowan after his untimely death, and became the chairman of the zoology department at the University of Alberta. Martin Paetz was a student of R.B. Miller, and worked closely with him on fish studies at Gorge Creek. Miller was particularly influential in changing government policies on the use of hatchery fish to stock streams. His research showed that the hatchery fish did not survive well for a variety of reasons. Miller was also influential in convincing the government of the need to hire staff biologists, of which Martin Paetz became the first one for fisheries (Innovation Alberta Online, 2006)."

As usual, predators were singled out for control by president Smith, especially magpies, which were perceived the greatest threat to healthy game-bird populations. Smith encouraged clubs to undertake local projects of interest to their members, and promote good farmer-hunter relations.

Mr. Norman Willmore, the new minister of lands and forests, was the principal speaker at the annual banquet.

Certificates of Merit were presented at the annual convention to Dr. L.H. Mason, Fred Sharpe, A. Terry, Dr. F. H. Sutherland, G. Hinde, S. Henders, E.L. Paynter, A.C. Pearson, G. Pigeon, K. Kure and Ed Guinn.

Secretary manager George Spargo reported on the work undertaken by the association to promote farmer-sportsmen relations, including the release of 10,000 folders promoting the program. He reported "Thanks to the Rock City Tobacco Co. (Sportsman's Cigarettes), 'Hunting with Permission' posters were mailed and the assistance given by many of our elevator friends in the distribution of same is most appreciated."

In the minutes of the 27th annual convention, there is a report that arrangements would be made to pay the secretary manager on his retirement the sum of $40 per month until age 70. His contract was to be extended to 3½ years from Jan. 1, 1956 until his 65th birthday. The record indicates "The secretary expressed his deep appreciation of this action accruing from the 27th annual convention, and promised he would continue to do his best for the sake of the association and its conservation policy."

COURTESY OF DUANE RADFORD

Brent Markham shooting waterfowl at Therien Lake.

Gordon Cummings reported on the findings of the farmer-sportsmen relations committee, which surveyed all local clubs by means of a questionnaire the previous November. Sixty percent of the clubs replied with the following results:

1. 41 percent of the clubs reported landowner-sportsman relations were better in their districts in 1955 than 1954; 51 percent reported relations were the same, and only eight percent reported they were poorer.

2. 72 percent reported good relations between landowners and sportsmen. 20 percent reported fair relations. Eight percent reported poor relations.

COURTESY OF THE AFGA
STAN HENDERS

Big game chair J.E. (Erle) Carr reported, "It is my privilege once again to give you a fairly optimistic report on our big game since better predator control is paying dividends." Carr noted that for once the moose had not been plagued by tick infestations (resulting in an excellent calf crop) and had come through the winter in good shape, but he expressed concerns about the lengthy two month season the previous year. He reported much the same situation for deer, but again questioned the lengthy two-month season.

Carr commented, "I don't know why we are so afraid of zoning this Province; it is much too large to make a blanket regulation." He added, "In my report last year, I said that some effort should be made to plant a few small herds of white-tail deer in the lower areas of the province, and I am still of the opinion that they would do well here since they have been successful in both Manitoba and Saskatchewan."

Regarding the lack of many trophy bighorn sheep rams, he recommended, "I believe the only remedy for this predicament is to put a size limit on the rams' horns – an opinion shared by most of the guides and outfitters as well as the experienced sheep hunters. However, this will be brought up for discussion at our annual convention." Carr was really starting to sound like a broken record by this time with regard to Alberta's caribou: "The caribou population is very low. While this association has favoured a closed season on these animals for several years now, nothing has been done about it and if some action is not taken soon the caribou are going to disappear entirely from Alberta."

The antelope season remained closed. Once again Carr expressed concerns about the poaching of antelope. "We will never have an open season on them until we put a stop to them being poached." Carr also heaped praise on the game officers and the impossible odds they had trying to curb poaching.

Acting predator chairman Stan Henders noted that as a result of lobbying on the part of locals at High River, Calgary, Cochrane, Carstairs, Olds, Sundre, Dickson and the Waterloo Stock and Game Association, they now had a solid line along the foothills from Rocky Mountain House to the U.S. boundary with 1080 legally being used in every municipality and improvement district. He added, "Since the coverage within these areas still leaves plenty

of room for improvement, let's all get busy; the Dept. of Agriculture welcomes our help although reluctant to get aggressive themselves."

For the first time there appeared to be a break in the government party line regarding predator control. Henders reported that the Department of Lands and Forests had agreed with a brief presented to it, which in part argued for the protection of birds of prey for so-called esthetic values, and "promptly placed ads in our leading newspapers stating that all hawks and owls were now protected by law. These men are NOT game men but strictly forestry officers." Henders lamented that these same officials were working to rule when it came to culling predators in the forest reserves and resisting the use of 1080 poison for predator control. At the same time, many of these same forest officers killed practically every porcupine they encountered, because the animals barked trees, affecting forest production. This particular practice went against the belief of hunters who were brought up to leave porcupines unharmed because they could be a source of food for lost woodsmen. Such were the competing norms of the day.

Upland bird chair R. Arlt noted that sportsmen from the northern and central areas of the province had to travel south to hunt upland birds. Again, he blamed predators for the reduction of game birds in these areas.

Ken Watts, migratory bird chair, noted, "We still have areas that are not adequately patrolled by game wardens and cannot be looked after until more men are on the job therefore, we must ask for an increase in staff in the game branch until all areas of the Province are covered. However, I have nothing but praise for the manner in which our fish and game guardians carry out their duties and have earned the gratitude of all true sportsmen."

The fish and pollution chairman, George Hind, reported spotty fishing with a note that lakes in central Alberta were being heavily fished and that poorer catches prevailed. He noted, "Certainly the day when people are permitted to take wash tubs full only to lose most of them before getting home is over and past." He added "Pothole fishing in newly stocked lakes in the irrigation districts and on the prairies has taken the brunt of the increasing trout fishermen providing good fishing as a whole."

The fish and game commissioner for Alberta, E.S. Huestis, reported that the Calgary Brewing and Malting Co. had donated the largest hatchery of its kind in Canada to the government and his branch was now operating it without any strings attached whatsoever. He also advised that reports from the last hunting season indicated 65 percent of the big-game kill consisted of moose, 20-25 percent consisted of deer and 10-20 percent consisted of elk.

As usual, there was the routine AFGA crow and magpie campaign report in the annual convention document, with a tally of the number of crows and magpies destroyed by each local association:

37,542 crows and 75,187 magpies with a grand total of 112,729 of these birds killed by members of the association, for a grand total estimated cost of predator bounties of $10,836.45 in 1955. The total of feet and eggs destroyed since 1938 came to 2,202,199 crows and magpies at a cost of $115,278.18 from 1939-54.

1957 J.E. (Erle) Carr became president in 1956. The 28th annual AFGA convention was held at the Palliser Hotel in Calgary in 1957.

In his president's report at the conference, Carr commented on the defeat of legislation that would have created European-style hunting in Alberta by amending the Game Act. Unfortunately, the records of the AFGA do not elaborate on the details. However, it appears the Social Credit government of the day tried to sneak legislation by the AFGA without tabling it before its own fish and wildlife advisory council, which would have been customary. If by "European style," Carr meant that wildlife on privately held land would become property of the landowner, then this represents the first of many attempts by government to place Crown-owned wildlife into private hands.

> *In Memoriam: President J.E. Carr asked for a standing moment of silence in memory of those members who had passed away during 1956, as was customary when good sportsmen gathered. Those commemorated were: J.A. McGhee (past president), Roland Wood (past vice president), Lester Shaw (fish inspector) and Wm. Scott (past secretary treasure, Magrath Fish and Game Association)*

Carr noted that membership was down and, as had so many presidents before, urged the AFGA clubs to double their membership. For the first time in many years, there was no record of membership numbers in the annual convention report.

> **The following members received a certificate of merit for distinguished overall service to conservation over the years at the annual convention: C.T. Lee, Fred Hargreaves, Bruce Stewart, Bill Ross, Len Blades, Harry Hillmer and Jack Pike.**

Carr reiterated a long-standing complaint that local club secretaries do not regularly read head office notices and progress reports at local meetings. This was symptomatic of an ongoing communication issue within the organization, likely a function of its volunteer nature. Carr also signalled trouble with the government over their reluctance to continue financing the crow and magpie control program, which the executive was attempting to maintain. There were also signs of strained relations with the government over budgets for the game branch with the suggestion the executive would make an end run around the minister and go directly to cabinet to voice their displeasure.

Perhaps as an indication of how much relations had become strained between the AFGA and the Social Credit government, there was no reference in the president's report about the success of the annual game dinner for the legislative assembly members in 1956.

Secretary manager George Spargo noted in his convention report, "We have been given approval by the Minister [Hon. N.E. Willmore] to approach the Cabinet, when and if we require to do so, over and above the usual procedure of going with our requests through the Advisory Council." This would be a highly irregular "accomplishment" for a secretary manager to report in a public document, and it could only signal that the minister was giving tacit approval for the association to approach the cabinet on issues beyond his control. Up to this point in time the association had been on reasonably good terms with the Social Credit government and was very strict in maintaining proper protocol with elected officials. Spargo was a gentleman and a stickler for detail. To have the association run counter to a government minister would have been totally out of character for him or members of the executive.

Urban Young, the new big-game chair reported on the impending breakup of the province into several hunting zones as requested at earlier conferences. Also, mountain sheep could not be taken unless they had horns of at least three-quarter-inch curl. "This was a regulation your association has been requesting since 1953."

Young also advised, "Alberta hunters were given an opportunity to hunt antelope for the first time in several years, but once again denied the opportunity to hunt deer east of Highway #2 and north of the North Saskatchewan River." Young observed that the moose population appeared stable, while elk and deer numbers were on the rise. Reports indicated a slight increase in caribou in the area north of Jasper National Park, and a few still remaining in the Swan Hills south of Lesser Slave Lake.

"Winter range must be preserved even to the extent of reducing herds if necessary," said Young. "In this matter we cannot afford to be sentimentalists."

Upland bird game chair Bob Arlt noted, "Sharptail and ruffed grouse were the only species to show an increase this past year which was quite noticeable in the southern part of the Province, and I give the credit to the coyote poisoning campaign in this area." Arlt also reported, "I have heard rumours that the Game Branch is seriously thinking of discontinuing the bounty on

Burrowing owls.

crows and magpies. If this should happen, it would be a slap in the face of some 60,000 game bird hunters in Alberta. It is true that the destruction of some 100,000 crows and magpies each year by members of Fish and Game Associations has not depleted these predators, but, it certainly has helped to keep them under control. Imagine what the situation would be like if they were to go unchecked for two years."

The winter of 1956 was very severe and apparently caused widespread winterkill of trout in many Alberta pothole lakes. Fish and pollution chair George Hinde reported on generally good stream fishing but noted that although fishing on the whole was very good in most parts of Alberta, the association could not rest on its laurels due to the "…terrific increase of fishing pressure on our streams and lakes, etc."

On pollution, Hinde noted, "Now we come to the most distressing part of this report. As you know the new pulpwood industry in the Athabasca drainage is almost complete and ready for operation. This means that at least 250 miles of the last remaining pure watershed is ruined, as I have been told on very good authority that for at least this distance downstream from this plant [at Hinton], it will be completely ruined. Why is it that in spite of warnings from our biologists, the Government allows this company to carry out its operations without insisting on every possible precaution being taken to insure that fish life would be protected downstream from the plant?" He also commented, "On a happier note, I am pleased to report that Edmonton has seen fit to install secondary sewage treatment for its water system and again we can thank our biologists."

Stan Henders reported on cracks that appeared in the provincial predator-control program in 1956. There was an apparent lack of a co-ordinated effort in the green zone by forest rangers and a breakdown in widespread control measures in the settled areas. "As to our magpie and crow campaign unless we can really plan some concerted effort in the contacting of our MLAs, it appears the game department is about to take one of the greatest backward steps in game conservation that has ever been taken in this province." Resolutions No. 26(a)–32 called on the government to step up its predator-control program for all manner of predators, to maintain funding for the magpie and crow campaign, and to increase the 1080 poisoning program. The battle lines were being drawn between the association and the Alberta government!

Migratory bird chair Ken Watts reported, "Our game branch are to be congratulated for their 'workable' regulations this year, but, we still hear of a lot of violations of the Game Act in areas not regularly patrolled by wardens. We still need MORE game guardians."

Public relations chair Gordon Cummings noted that relations between landowners and hunters in 1956 were much better than in 1955. Cummings noted, "At this convention a resolution will be introduced asking the provincial government to set up a Livestock Indemnity Fund to pay farmers and ranchers for livestock losses caused by shooting during the hunting season. All purchasers of hunting licenses both bird game and big game would be required to contribute towards this fund." Cummings stated that the committee believed this was one of the most important resolutions to come before the association and hoped it would be passed by a unanimous vote.

*D*r. R.B. Miller, PhD, professor of zoology at the University of Alberta, scientific advisor to the Alberta government, and a member of the National Research Council, wrote an article "Do Hatchery Trout Die of Fatigue?" in the Fish & Game magazine, convention issue, January 1957. At the time, the association had advocated widespread stocking of trout in eastern slope streams, which they thought were largely barren. Dr. Miller carried out research on the fate of hatchery-reared trout planted in streams at the Alberta Biological Station at Gorge Creek. Sections of the stream were fenced off, one-half to three-quarters of a mile long. Hatchery fish were released into these sections. There were about 300 resident wild trout in each section and hatchery trout of similar (or larger) size were stocked on top of these wild fish. The hatchery fish started dying on the first or second day, and by 10 days 50 to 60 percent of them were dead. The survivors initially lost weight for 30-40 days, then began to gain weight until, finally, by late fall they reached the same weight as when they were planted. Subsequent experiments determined that the weight loss was not the result of handling or treatment. Hatchery-reared fish could not compete with wild fish. They were forced into marginal habitat where they perished because the wild fish occupied the most suitable habitat which they defended. In later experiments, lactic acid levels were substantially higher in the blood of trout that had competed with wild fish (lactic acid indicates muscle fatigue). Dr. Miller concluded that the hatchery fish died of fatigue when planted on top of wild trout in streams.

Whistler Mountain in Jasper on a fall evening.

COURTESY OF VERN MCINTOSH
Goose hunter Charlie Smith in blind, circa 1978.

Fly-fishing on the upper Pembina River.

1958-1967
Summary

Major issues: Woodland caribou near extirpation; poor trout fishing in central Alberta; destruction of Alford Creek riparian areas; shot dead livestock; coyote predation on mule deer and pronghorns; public relations and education; lack of systematic hunter surveys or harvest questionnaires; reports of careless shooting, vandalism and killing of livestock; pothole lake fishing good, stream fishing poor; brush and weed spraying harmful to songbirds and upland game birds; waterfowl crop damage compensation; lack of predator control; priority draw for antelope licences; scarcity of upland birds; access on private land; relocation of the Alberta Fish and game Association (AFGA) head office from Calgary to Edmonton; hunting closure in eastern irrigation district; water pollution; need for stream improvement projects; grazing of sheep in forest reserves; indiscriminate hunting by Indians; continued loss of wildlife habitat.

Highlights:
1958 - The first year a special event was organized for women at an AFGA convention; executive meets with the premier and cabinet; call for revised game commission; big-game populations and hunting pressure increase; separate fish and wildlife division finally established; briefs in support of wildlife and conservation education in schools submitted to government.

1959 - Women attend conferences as voting delegates; creation of Alberta's first wilderness area (Willmore Wilderness Park).

1960 - Protection of grizzly bears urged.

1961 - Minimum stream flows recommended for Alberta rivers; resolutions submitted to enshrine hunting and fishing rights in Alberta; opposition to private shooting preserves in Alberta; wildlife crop damage insurance legislation.

1962 - George M. Spargo honoured for 38 years of service; formation of Canadian Wildlife Federation; Merriam's turkeys released in Cypress Hills; improvement in farmer and sportsmen relations.

1963 - Government adopts AFGA hunter training program.

1964 - Elk transplants to Spirit River area.

1965 - Annual crow and magpie campaign report omitted from convention report, for the first time in the AFGA records.

1966 - Livestock Indemnity Fund established; government orders installation of secondary sewage treatment facilities on Bow River.

1967 - The AFGA zoning system proposed.

Presidents: J.E. (Erle) Carr (1958), Elmer Kure (1958-60), Gordon Cummings (1960-62), Ben Rosnau (1962-64), Henry Lembicz (1964-66), Joe Balla (1966-67).

Membership: 13,252-1957; 14,483-1958; 14,528-1959; 15,183-1960; 17,202-1961; 17,228-1962; 17,233-1963; 17,561-1964; 16,549-1965; 17,044-1966; 18,170-1967.

The expansion of the Canadian economy continued into the 1960s. Unemployment remained low, birth rates were high and immigration continued. In 1961 the population of Alberta was about 1.33 million people; and the U.S. dollar was worth $6.93 in 2007 USD. With the increasing worldwide human population came increasing concerns about pollution and the environment. Rachel Carson's *Silent Spring*, published in 1962, helped create environmental awareness and started a movement to protect the environment.

The Canadian economy became ever more closely integrated with that of the United States through trade agreements and the elimination of trade barriers. As a result of its experience in the Great Depression and along with many other western democracies, Canada became a welfare state with the introduction of such programs as unemployment insurance (now employment insurance), the Canada Pension Plan and publicly funded health care. The result was the spread of some of the increasing wealth down to middle and lower economic-class Canadians.

Federally, Diefenbaker's Progressive Conservative government held power until it was defeated by Lester Pearson's Liberals in 1963. In Alberta, Ernest Manning continued as premier throughout the decade.

In 1958, the government divided the province into 18 big-game management zones where hunting seasons were set to specific areas of the province. In 1961 "party" hunting was prohibited, each hunter having to fill his or her own tag. Wildlife management units in each big-game zone were created in 1964 to further refine management within the zones. Wildlife certificate sales in 1964 (first year of certificates, issued to each hunter) were 118,843; fishing licence sales in 1963-64 were 129,244 (not issued to youths and seniors).

1958 The 29th annual convention of the Alberta Fish and game Association (AFGA) was held at the Marquis Hotel in Lethbridge. Richard Osterberg, president of the Lethbridge Fish and Game Association, welcomed the delegates. He paid a tribute to John Bobinec for the unique identification cards with a hand-tied fish fly attached for everyone attending. Two hundred and twenty-one (221) delegates attended the convention. On the gold-coloured convention handbook was a "50 Golden Years in Conservation" banner, marking 50 years since what became the AFGA began in 1908.

President J.E. (Erle) Carr noted in his convention report that a meeting between the AFGA and cabinet in January 1957 had "...borne considerable fruit". [Such meetings between the association and the Alberta government cabinet would be unheard of today, although the AFGA executive does enjoy regular one-on-one meetings with the sitting minister responsible for the fish and wildlife division and other MLAs.]

Carr noted that the government had allotted approximately $100,000 more money to the game branch. He commended the local clubs for their continued crow and magpie campaign. It appears the closed-door meetings with the cabinet had the desired impact: no cutback in funding for the AFGA predator-control program and additional budget dollars for the game branch. For the first time in years, the president reported that the overall game picture was good, with "lots of game in most districts with the exception of Huns [Hungarian partridge], which were very spotty. The big-game picture was also very good." The antelope season had finally re-opened. Carr stated optimistically that "...a membership of 25,000 is quite possible if we work for it."

1958

Resolution No. 13	(Piyami [Picture Butte], Stavely, Carmangay, Taber, Macleod, Del Bonita, Magrath, Lethbridge and District). "BE IT RESOLVED: that a separate Game Commission be appointed with power to act without political interference." This resolution carried. It was a move to separate game department business from the operations of the Alberta Forest Service. Relations had been rocky between officials in the AFGA and forest rangers who did not have the overall confidence of the association. In a convention speech, the Hon. N. Willmore, Minister of Lands and Forests, advised, "We are absolutely opposed to the question of an independent game commission. We feel that as a government elected to represent the people of the Province we should take responsibility for our own actions. We should take the blame where blame is due and where we have made mistakes and probably we have made lots of them. We think also we should have the credit where credit is due and where we have adopted wise policies." The minister also advised, "The government remains unalterably opposed to private hunting rights and fishing rights on Crown lands and Crown water."
Resolution No. 14	(Red Deer) "Whereas many experts state that the colour yellow is more readily seen than red, RESOLVED: that the executive of the AFGA consider asking the game department to require big game hunters to wear canary yellow or red hunting coats and hats. This clothing to be checked by wardens when a hunter's equipment is checked." The resolution was defeated in committee but carried by a vote of 41 to 37 on the floor. At the time, resolutions were first debated in select committees before being voted on by the delegates at large.
Resolution No. 14	(Piyami, Stavely, Carmangay, Taber, Macleod, Del Bonita, Magrath, Devon, Lethbridge and District). "BE IT RESOLVED: that all violators of the Game Act lose all hunting and fishing privileges for that year." The resolution was defeated – 49 against, 31 in favour.
Resolution No. 18	(High River). "BE IT RESOLVED: that it be an offense punishable by fine or imprisonment to litter any road, trail, highway, campground, riverbank or private land in Alberta." The resolution carried. It represented the first formal acknowledgement of littering as an issue in Alberta by the AFGA.
Resolution No. 23A	(Eastern Prairie Groups, Lacombe, Viking, etc.) "RESOLVED: that we petition the Dept. of Education to provide older school children and high school children with a course of studies and/or lectures dealing with: (a) the nature and habits of wildlife and the propagation and conservation of same; (b) the prevention and control of prairie and forest fire." The resolution carried.

Wildlife Meeting

It's Time To Teach Indians Conservation

The Alberta Fish and Game Association has shot down another long-time belief — that the Indians are great conservationists.

"It's high time," declared president Ben Rosnau at the group's 35th annual convention Friday, "that we teach the Indians conservation."

Rosnau, the outspoken sportsman from Bruderheim, said that while such a statement would come as a complete shock to most Albertans, he has found the Indian reserves almost devoid of wildlife.

"It is deplorable," he told the more than 300 delegates. "But, I am blaming myself.

"We must respect the treaty rights, and it is our job as a conservation club to teach the Indians to conserve wildlife."

Four resolutions (one alleging indiscriminate killing of big game animals) asking legislation to force Indians to conform with normal hunting regulations were presented at the meeting. All met with unquestioned opposition.

RAPS GROUP

Phil Thompson, a native of Spirit River, the director of the Native Friendship Centre in Edmonton and speaking for the Indian Association of Alberta, criticized the F&G for proposing the resolutions.

"I am surprised that a group as intelligent as the Fish and Game should come through the back door on this rather than meet with the people involved," he said.

The Indian spokesman was loudly applauded for his presentation and for his talk in which he reminded sportsmen the Indians feel hunting is their "inherited right." He added that many Indians must still rely on hunting to survive.

In an interview after the discussion, Thompson admitted the Indians need to be taught conservation practices.

"We must learn conservation which, after all is something we cannot see. Indians live in a small area. We can't see the overall picture of conservation."

NO WASTE

He took issue with statements the Indian people kill big game indiscriminately and waste meat. "Indian people are aroused when they see the white hunter take the horn and leave the carcass to rot. We are the opposite. We take the meat and leave the horns."

Edmonton Fish and Game delegate Slim Layley wrapped it up with an eloquent line. Referring to earlier statements from Bill Bowthorpe of Round Hill that duck hunters on Rush Lake have been shooting indiscriminately and have been selecting only the best birds killed to take home, Layley declared:

"In view of this and from our own personal experiences, I fail to see how any of us here could have the neck to point a finger at the Indians for wasting meat."

The resolutions were tabled by unanimous vote to allow the executive to meet with Indian authorities on conservation problems.

Thompson added in an interview: "These regulations were disturbing to us in that if the Indians asked legislation to restrict white hunters, this group would holler to high heaven."

CLOSES TERM

Rosnau is finishing off his two year term today in the final sessions of the two-day convention at the Sportex. And he is going out just as strongly in his comments as when he took the post.

In his president's report, the Bruderheim farmer-sportsman charged that the Fish and Game-sponsored Inglewood Bird Sanctuary committee "has failed in its obligations."

He recommended the committee be abolished and its files and funds be turned over to Alberta. He also proposed that Calgary property be administered by the board of directors.

Following heated argument in which the sanctuary was, at one point, said to be "doing more harm than good" and in which Rosnau was charged with making the issue a "red herring" for personal differences with the Inglewood committee, a vote of confidence in Rosnau was called. The president won. But, opposition increased to 20.

REPORT PASSED

The president's report was favored by an identical margin, thus approving the recommendation.

Rosnau charged that the committee failed in that it did not raise money for the association during its two years of operation.

Under discussion today will be the equally controversial resolution proposing Sunday big game hunting in Alberta. The convention ends today with guest speakers, election of officers, trophy presentations and a banquet.

COURTESY OF HENRY LEMBICZ

Newspaper article, circa mid-1960s.

For the first time, a ladies night was held at the convention with "Mesdames Carr and Osterberg" as hostesses. Nearly 40 women attended.

Certificates of merit awarded for meritorious service in the cause of conservation were presented by president Carr at the annual convention, as follows: Mrs. B. McLeod, Mrs. J. E. Carr, Mrs. Dorothy Knechtel, Andy Russell, Frank Butler, Angus Gavin, H. Ronnenberg, Joe Balla, William Kovach (MLA), Ken Watts, Kai Hansen, Otto Polzin, H.H. West, Ben Rosnau, W.D. Geldert, G. Bursnstad, J. Fedechko, W.T. Davis and Bill Masson.

Secretary manager George Spargo reported, "We have succeeded in approaching the government by the consent of the Minister of Lands and Forests, the Hon. Norman Willmore and now meet on a higher level with the Premier and his cabinet. That is by all consensus definite progress." Spargo also reported that the former farmer-sportsmen relations committee was now called the public relations committee and had been actively working with newspapers and the general membership, as well as farmers. "Our crow and magpie campaign was again sponsored by the Dept. of Lands and Forests, Ducks Unlimited and some municipalities and was very successful indeed," Spargo advised. "This phase of our work was undertaken by some 53 local groups, an increase of three over the year previous and our total bag was 110,883 pairs of feet."

The public relations committee reported in the conference proceedings about a survey the committee had conducted of the local clubs. The survey showed that the majority of the clubs believed that on the whole relations with the "general public, the press, and the farmer and land owner" were good. Committee chair Gordon Cummings commented that it was alarming the total membership in the AFGA had dropped from 14,840 in 1955 to 13,252 in 1957. Cummings noted that the loss in membership meant the association had $1,500 less to spend on its work, a considerable sum of money in 1957.

At the annual conference, the Hon. Norman Willmore, Minister of Lands and Wildlife, addressed complaints about lack of publicity in his department. "We are endeavoring to overcome that,"

COURTESY OF JACK GRAHAM

Orville Welch (L) and Joe Graham on elk (wapiti) hunt, 1958.

he said. "We do now have a publicity officer in the department and we hope that by April we will have our first publication out – that we will have a very modest publication publicizing the rules and regulations of the Game Department, some of the principles we think to be in the interests of good sportsmanship, and they will be free to anyone who cares to get themselves on the mailing list."

As illustrated above, it was the AFGA that often pushed and prodded the government to take action on fish and wildlife conservation. In a personal communication, Ernie J. Psikla (former Fish and Wildlife Division staff member) stated, "Prior to the creation of the fish and wildlife division, the AFGA took the lead role on behalf of fish and wildlife in the province. If you look at the history of fisheries and wildlife within government, it clearly was never a major part of government policy. In 1937 it was housed in the Department of Agriculture and over the years it was moved from department to department always as an appendage and never the primary focus. During those early years had it not been for the AFGA and people of vision who appreciated and realized the inherent value of the fish and wildlife resource to the province, as a priority in government, it would have remained a non-issue and of little political significance."

Big-game chair Urban Young reported, "Generally speaking our big-game situation continues to show a very marked improvement throughout the province." He also noted, "Hunting pressure continues to mount on our big-game herds and therefore we must co-operate with our government in their efforts to carry out efficient game management. A record number of big-game licences were issued during 1957, and will likely continue to increase in the future."

The deer season remained closed east of Highway 2. Young noted, "I am of the firm opinion that we will never be permitted to hunt deer in this section unless we all press our individual MLAs for an open season." Several resolutions were put forward at the conference calling for a big-game survey in the area and declaration of an open season.

The antelope season had been open for the previous two years and Young advised that the hunter success rate had been 70-80 percent each season, and "…yet the population remains about the same or possibly shows a slight increase."

Fish chair G. Hinde argued in his report that allowing large numbers of cattle and stock on watersheds was causing the warming of streams and the loss of fish and fish habitat through the breaking down of banks and removal of vegetation. He argued for "systematic reduction of the big cannibal fish" in stocked pothole lakes because the fish were eating the more numerous smaller size fish. Hinde applauded the resolutions committee for refusing to accept resolutions calling for the stocking of live minnows into lakes. Hinde warned Such stockings would lead to disasters such as carp in lakes at the expense of game fish.

A special fisheries representative, Andy Dow of Coleman, was elected by the convention to be called by the president when matters pertaining to fish resolutions or fish programs were discussed. There is a notation that he would be asked to attend any

COURTESY OF HENRY LEMBICZ

Hunting and fishing fee increases were considered, according to this mid-1960s newspaper article.

meetings with government officials with regard to Resolution No. 40 in particular.

Migratory bird chair Ken Watts noted, "The Game Branch amended their regulations this year to allow shooting closer than 100 yards to certain rivers for the last 10 days of the season in an endeavour to drive out those ducks that tried to winter here and usually were destroyed by predators or died before spring." A resolution to this effect had been passed at the last AFGA convention and was another sign that the association supported concerns raised by farmers with regard to waterfowl crop damage.

Upland game bird chair, Bob Arlt, reported "I was very pleased indeed to learn that our government had reconsidered and decided to continue with the crow and magpie campaign again this year. Ten thousand dollars each year does amount to a large sum over a period of years, but it is a trivial amount compared to the total spent by other Departments and farmers in the control of carnivorous, noxious and insectile [sic] predators."

> A membership table was published in the conference yearbook. The total membership was 13,252 with 83 affiliated clubs. The top five clubs were: Calgary (1,300), Red Deer (1,027), Edmonton (900), Lethbridge (900) and Camrose (603); the smallest club was at Empress (10).

Stan Henders related in his predator report about one particular committee meeting where considerable time was spent discussing the criticism offered by both the "game department" and the Department of Agriculture concerning a predator newsletter apparently issued by the AFGA in the spring. Henders noted many municipalities operated their own predator control program, separate and independent from the Agriculture Department's

1080 poison program. "If Elmer Kure's dream of a central Predator Division is ever realized," Henders said, then the problem of separate programs "would no longer exist and we could really get overall coverage as well as perhaps some much needed help on our magpie and crow campaign."

The nature and tone of the resolutions at the 1958 convention seemed to signal a shift in the association's culture toward a need for a more thoughtful environmental management program by government, and a much better-funded fish and game management program than had existed in the past.

1959 Elmer Kure became president of the AFGA in 1958. Kure would become known as "Mr. Fish-and-Gamer," akin to long-standing secretary manager G.M. Spargo, and was regarded as one of the associations most articulate and respected members. In his President's Report for 1958 he noted that this year marked their 30th annual convention, which was held at the Jubilee Auditorium in Edmonton in 1959.

ELMER KURE President: 1958-59

I was born in Henry, Illinois U.S.A. on Nov. 30, 1921 and immigrated to Dickson, Alberta with my parents in 1924. I was educated in a one-room school in Dickson where I later met Helga Hindbo who became my wife. We had three children; a son Colin and two daughters Jane and Michele.

I chose a career in farming which I did for 30 years, just a few miles north of Dickson near Spruce View. During my farming years, I was active in local agricultural groups and served on the boards of the FUA & UGG associations. I also served as the Ad Hoc Committee member for Canadian Rural Development Council and the Canada Grain Standards Committee for the Canada Grain Commission. I was nominated for the Master Farmer Award in recognition of my farming practices.

COURTESY OF THE AFGA

ELMER KURE

In March 1973, I accepted a position with the AFGA as director of public relations, which I held until June 1986.

I recognized the importance of education and community service and as a result became very active providing leadership in many schools and community organizations, instructing wildlife and hunter education training courses in the schools.

I learned to hunt and appreciate wildlife and the environment from my father Art Kure and developed a strong passion for conservation. As a boy, I supplied gophers and rabbits to a local fur farm. I became an active member of the Dickson Fish and Game Association in 1948. I served one term as president and have been an executive member numerous times. I was elected president of the AFGA in 1958 and served on the executive until commencing employment as Director of the Environmental Public Relations. During my tenure with the AFGA, I was recognized for my service and received numerous awards. I received the Distinguished Service Award in 1957, was given the Life Member Award in 1971, received the Fulton Trophy in 1964 and again in 1988, and was recognized with the "Alberta Big Horn Award" in 1989.

I helped to promote development and the transition of the Canadian Wildlife Federation and served as a director of the federation in its formative years. For my contributions I was presented the Roland Michener Conservation Award in 1990 and then in 1993 I received the Emerald Award and the Commemorative Medal of Canada 125.

As an active hunter and fisherman, I promoted a balanced approach to wildlife management by preserving habitats for all species and supporting a sustained harvest of both game and fur species, including long-haired carnivores. As a supporter and promoter of species management, I was active in predator control in the early 1950s before the rabies outbreak in Alberta.

As a land user and farmer, I recognized the importance of promoting the retention of natural areas in farming country and the preservation of critical wildlife areas. I was instrumental in getting the Landowners Habitat Program established in the County of Red Deer in 1978. As a firm supporter of ethical conduct by all resource users, I was also instrumental in convincing the provincial government to establish the Hunter Training and Conservation Program which came to fruition in 1964.

As a promoter of wilderness preservation, I was instrumental in the establishment of the present Wilderness Areas Act for Alberta.

I held a number of advisory positions in the Alberta government including 12 years on the Game Advisory Council, hunter training instructor since 1964 and service on the Wilderness Areas Committee to define boundaries for the three wilderness areas. I also served on the Legislative Committee for Commercial Fisheries in Alberta.

Under the Minister of Environment, I served on a number of advisory committees. This work included a study of the Environmental Impact Assessment System and the Dickson Dam Project as well as the Public Shore Lands Committee for the Dickson Reservoir. For seven years, I spent time serving on the Public Advisory committee to the Environment Conservation Authority. Other services to the government included a stint on the Block Area Outfitting committee and on various landowner wildlife projects, such as Beaverhill Lake and the North Raven Stream Rehabilitation, two of the very first Buck for Wildlife projects. I served on the task force for Grazing Land, Conversion and Access Committee and on the Livestock Indemnity program, adjudicating claims for losses of livestock to predation. I held a position on the Board of the Environmental Law Centre as well as the Board of Wildlife Habitat Canada, the steering committee for a provincial Conservation Strategy and the Trans Alta Advisory Committee.

I participated in other interesting projects with the AFGA by assisting in the development of a 25-minute film called "Land - A Question of Values" and the gathering and co-ordination of the contents of the book "To Conserve a Heritage" by Margaret Lewis which was created for the association's 50th anniversary.

Most of my public relations work focused on the co-ordination of executive efforts, acting as a liaison with government and other groups and making presentations to public hearings.

My latest activities included efforts to purchase the Ward Ranch and serving on the management committee for the Integrated Agriculture Wildlife Project near Brooks, Alberta and on the World Wildlife Fund, Wild West Committee.

In recent years, I have made presentations to Alberta's Economic Strategy for the Constitution Reform Panel and Integrated Resource Plan for the Central Regions. I continue to promote the Ya-Ha-Tinda Ranch trade for alternate horse ranching and an alternate source of peak power with Trans Alta Utilities Corporation.

[Biography compiled by Elmer Kure.]

Notable in attendance at the annual convention were three lady delegates: Barbara Carr of Lethbridge, Mrs. Wirda from Rocky Mountain House and Mrs. Hindbo from Dickson, all of them most active according to the convention minutes.

COURTESY OF DAVE POWELL

Fred (L) and Dave Powell in 1959 during a goose hunt.

diplomacy and his eloquence as a speaker; he set a fine example for others to follow. Many would say he was one of the most influential of all fish-and-gamers in the history of the association.

The following people received certificates of merit from the president at the annual convention: O. Polzin, Nils Kvisle, Alex Hirsch, Elmer Schielke, Gordon Christensen, Jack Munro, Darwin Cronkhite, Gordon Melary, A. Rutz, Wm. Bauer, Frank Crutchfield, Harry Cornwell, Ken Dezall, Al Strilchuk, Ben Farhham, Ted Omand, Wm. Fish, Ted Burkett, Mike Tomyn and Mel Reed.

Big-game chair Ovar Uggen noted, "The brightening up of the overall big-game picture in Alberta is in no small measure due to the zoning of the province into separate management areas." Uggen mentioned that there had been protests regarding the antlerless deer season in southwestern Alberta, and commented, "This shows a lack of confidence in our biologists, and also in the game management program we have been asking the government to institute. Since the game branch started to follow the biologists advice a couple of years ago our big game and our hunting has improved. He reported, "Ten years ago there were around 7,500 big-game hunters in Alberta, today it is how many? 30,000 to 40,000?" Because of this increase in numbers he suggested that all big-game habitat "…must be made to produce an annual near maximum crop of animals so the hunting pressure will be distributed over the whole province and not concentrated so it over-taxes certain areas."

Uggen advised of a new trend among association members: "The interest in good trophies is growing among big game hunters and I urge all locals or districts to institute big-game trophy competitions in their respective areas, in order to bring to light the outstanding trophies Alberta produces, and to enter their champions with us for the provincial championship competition." He added that in the last Boone and Crockett competition in New York, Alberta hunters took first and second place in bighorn sheep, moose and elk.

Secretary manager George Spargo reported in the minutes of the 30th annual convention on the sudden passing of Dr. R.B. Miller, shortly after that convention.

Kure reported on the number of advisory committee meetings he attended during the previous year and on how valuable these meetings were to the advancement of the interests of the organization. He stated, "I feel that much has been accomplished and co-operation between the organized sportsman and the farmer is at an all time high, certainly working together we can realize the ultimate in harmony and affect things which will be for our common good." Always a gentleman, Kure's trademark was, and is, his

1959

Resolution No. 19	(North Central Alberta Associations) "RESOLVED: that the provincial government be asked to take steps for the preservation of the natural cover on 66 feet on either side of any river, stream or permanent body of water in the Province of Alberta." The resolution carried.
Resolution No. 20	(Pincher Creek and Claresholm) "As the streams are being depleted of fish of spawning age; BE IT RESOLVED: that the season be closed from November 1st to May 31st." The resolution carried.
Resolution No. 40	(Calgary, Lacombe) "BE IT RESOLVED: that the government undertake a comprehensive program of stream improvement throughout the Province spending at least one million dollars a year in this field." The resolution carried. It was a sign of the resolve of the AFGA to address issues related to Alberta's deteriorating riparian ecosystems.
Resolution No.56	(Red Deer). "RESOLVED: that the executive of the Fish and Game Association study ways and means of assisting students who enter biology courses and on completion work in the Province of Alberta." The resolution carried.

Populations of moose, deer and elk were all reported to be on the increase. "Another good example of what sensible game management with proper harvesting will accomplish is our pronghorn herd today," said Uggen. "With either sex, all age hunting, a harvest of 2,500 animals can, under present conditions, be carried on indefinitely. Three years ago when the season was opened again, the 'protect' em' people predicted that our pronghorn was doomed – they would be exterminated. Today our herds are larger and healthier than they have been for a long time with hunter success about 90 percent." He added, "One thing should be severely punished and that is chasing the animals [pronghorns] with cars or trucks to get within range. The sportsmanship of this type of hunting is nil, and there is lots of it going on." Uggen advised "The caribou as a game animal has almost disappeared from Alberta and they should be protected until a thorough survey and study can be undertaken and a solution is found to bring them back."

Program vice chair B.W. MacGillivray noted in the convention report that while good fishing was enjoyed in the area around Edmonton it was a different situation in central Alberta, where

Alberta Legislature To Hear Plea For Private Reserves

By HENRY LEMBICZ
(President of Alberta Fish and Game Association)

Once again we are confronted with the problem of Private Hunting Preserves in Alberta, as I understand there is to be a bill presented at the next sitting of the Alberta Legislature.

The sensible approach to such matters is to consider the advantages and disadvantages of Private Hunting Preserves. I would say the advantages would be: it would give the man who could afford the price and was only interested in going shooting, an easy way of getting a few birds. If he was the kind of a man who must have a sure thing because he cannot face the thought of returning without birds, Private Hunting Preserves could help him. They could also help a man who was so timid or disagreeable that he could not approach a landowner to get permission to hunt on his land. The big business man with a client who likes to shoot birds would take advantage of a private game farm, to impress his client to secure the deal.

Private Game Preserves could relieve a little pressure from men who would be attracted by this type of shooting, but the percentage would be small and this would only support a few preserves. On the overall situation the relief would be negligible.

Private Hunting Preserves would have no attraction for sportsmen.

The disadvantages are: in order to give these few shooters their desires we would have to break down a tradition and law that has always been in Alberta, prohititing the sale, trade, barter or offer for sale the hunting, shooting, killing or trapping rights over any lands for wild game. This law has served well in the past and still is a good law for the future. By licensing Private Hunting Preserves we will break down this principle. It has been hard enough to keep that principle in the past, but once you grant a privilege to one, then others can rightfully expect the same.

In my opinion the establishment of Private Hunting Preserves may satisfy the desires of a few shooters but will open up a large avenue of new problems, such as the desire of any landowner to sell hunting rights, without knowing his responsibilities. The breakdown of law enforcement on private lands could be expected.

The disruption of a game management programme and the curtailment of study and research in the field would follow.

Our Fish and Game Association proposed and assisted in the establishment of the Ring-necked Pheasant and Hungarian Partridge and are investigating the possibilities of establishing other exotic Game Birds to fit into a changing environment. Such conditions would discourage these efforts.

With the establishment of Hunting Preserves would come pressure for cocktail lounges and gambling concessions in connection with the enterprize.

This would be an unfortunate time to make such a change, when we are in a period of adjustment. There has been a need of a change and that change is taking place now with the establishment of the Hunter Education and Training Plan. In a few years there will be more sportsmen in the field knowing the responsibility that goes along with a hunting license. At that time, consideration should be given to only issuing licenses to qualified hunters.

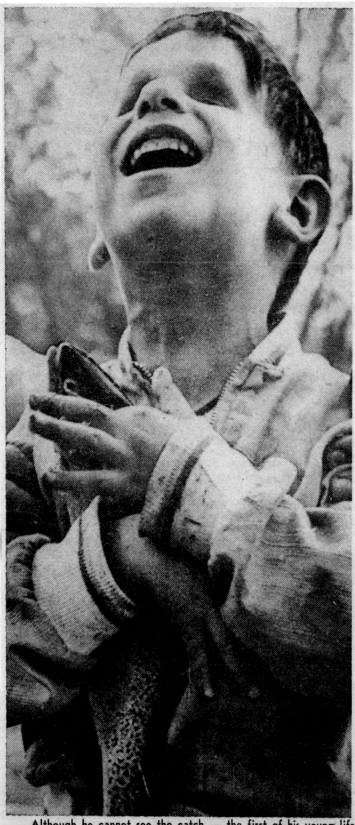

Although he cannot see the catch — the first of his young life — five-year-old Michael Gordon's hands explore the shape and size of a fish he just pulled from a pond. The lad was one of a group of Philadelphia area blind children that spent a day in the country fishing under the guidance of adults. They used conventional line and poles.

COURTESY OF HENRY LEMBICZ

Michael Gordon is blind, but gets to feel the size of his first fish, circa mid-60s.

"trout fishing is the worst in the history of man, white or red." He reported on a request from southern Alberta that the trout season on foothill streams be closed from Nov. 1 to June 1 to protect over-wintering fish.

MacGillivray also reported, "The owners of the land along the middle portions of Alford Creek are ruining the creek for fishing by destroying the brush and timber down to the waters edge. Eventually the beaver will go and most of the trout will go with them unless there are pools for the protection of the fish." He stated there were places where it was impossible to wade because of the brush and trees that were bulldozed into the stream. "It seems a shame to see this creek ruined by land owners who have no interest in conservation."

Migratory bird chair Ken Watts noted that reports of crop damage by waterfowl were rare. The crop in southern Alberta had been harvested under almost ideal conditions, and the ducks did not move south, due to mild weather in northern Alberta, until late in the autumn.

In closing, Watts noted, "Finally, I should like to pass on to this convention a suggestion of my very good friend, Jack McAfee of Edmonton who suggests that a committee be set up by the AFGA to investigate all reports of stock being shot by hunters to determine if these reports are true or fake. We have had many of these reports this fall, and we know that quite often they are rumours but still do a lot of harm to hunter-farmer relations." These sorts of rumours were rampant at the time, and practically every farmer had a report of a neighbour who had cattle shot by hunters. Such stories were to persist for many years and were a source of considerable consternation on the part of Alberta's sportsmen.

Stan Henders, predator chair, provided information from biological reports from Utah, Montana and Saskatchewan, all of which substantiated the concerns of the association regarding coyote predation on mule deer fawns. He also cited similar reports regarding pronghorn fawn predation supplied by the U.S. Wildlife Service. Henders related how these studies were being ignored by bureaucrats as well as school teachers, and how "one half of our potential deer crop is each year fed to the coyotes not to mention our upland bird and antelope losses. In other words the coyote takes a far greater harvest of these two game animals than all our licenced hunters combined."

In order to increase the amount of 1080 poisoning done provincially by the Department of Agriculture, Henders suggested that members of the association provide assistance to Joe Gurba (who took over from his predecessor, Mr. Lobay, as the department's head of predator control) by distributing cards in the local community.

When a dozen or so of these cards were completed they were to be taken to the local reeve or service board chairman, to initiate 1080 poisoning at the local level.

Public relations chair Gordon Cummings reported, "I believe 1958 will go down in history as a most important year in our association's public relations work." He related the appointment of W.H. (Bill) MacDonald as publicity officer for the Department of Lands and Forests, followed by the decision of the department to publish a bi-monthly magazine called *Land, Forest, Wildlife*. He also reported the appointment of a full-time director of fish and wildlife, Curt P. Smith. Smith succeeded Eric S. Huestis, the former fish and game commissioner. As well, a new position of director of forestry had been created, thereby separating the forestry and fish and wildlife

divisions, long recommended by the association. The AFGA could take full credit for the government decision to create a separate and independent fish and wildlife division in 1958, which, according to *Fish, Fur and Feathers* (2005), became established in 1959.

In a personal communication, former fish and wildlife division employee Ernie J. Psikla advised, "Without question had it not been for the persistence of the AFGA, the Fish and Wildlife Division, per se, would not likely have been recognized in legislation, albeit falling short of becoming even a junior ministry. Clearly the appointment of Curt P. Smith, a past president of the AFGA, as the division's first director is evidence of the AFGA role in the creation of the Fish and Wildlife Division and its enshrinement in law. Moreover, the appointment of Curt P. Smith demonstrated the government's desire to ensure the new entity developed within the framework envisioned by the AFGA. Again, the idea and eventual creation of the fish and wildlife division did not originate within government, demonstrating once more the fish and wildlife resources were not a priority."

Total membership for 1958 was 14,483, as compared to 13,252 for 1957, an increase of 1,231. The number of active associations was 80 as compared to 83 for 1957. The top five clubs were Calgary (1,581), Lethbridge (1,250), Edmonton (1,167), Red Deer (1,000) and Stettler (712).

1960 Elmer Kure continued as president in 1959. Noting in his president's report that the AFGA had passed the half-century mark, he questioned whether the organization had met the challenge of the times. He wrote, "It must be stated here that our problem is one of public relations and education with our rising population if our wildlife resources are to maintain their rightful place in modern society with all its demands and advances. It must be

1960

Resolution No. 22	(Lethbridge and District Associations, Red Deer and Huxley) "RESOLVED: that the first two weeks of the upland Bird Season be reserved for Alberta hunters." The resolution was defeated by a vote of 24 to 17. This anti non-resident hunter resolution was in response to early season hunting pressure on pheasants in southern Alberta.
Resolution No. 28	(Calgary) "RESOLVED: that the government be asked to consider the possibility of protecting the grizzly bear when deemed necessary in order to maintain its numbers as a prized trophy animal in the following manner: (a) Restricting seasons when found necessary. (b) No season non-licensed shooting of grizzly bears in forest reserves. (c) The government to take steps to make a study on the grizzly to ascertain any feasible methods that can be taken to increase the population." Amendment moved by S. Burrill of Sundre and seconded by Dave Simpson (d) That the minister only be allowed to issue permits to kill grizzly bears out of season in the forest reserve." The resolution carried.
Resolution No. 35	(Central Alberta associations, Calgary, Eastern Division associations) "RESOLVED: that the hunting of Big Game with steel jacketed or Military ammunition be prohibited." The resolution carried unanimously.

noted that co-operation with government, farm organizations and our own clubs has been excellent yet our problem remains."

Kure noted that he and his wife had attended, as invited guests, a garden party to meet Queen Elizabeth II and Prince Phillip on the legislature grounds in Edmonton, along with past president Earle Carr and his wife. He remarked that this was a signal honour for the AFGA, indicating how high the association was regarded in government circles.

The 31st annual convention was held at the Corona Hotel in Medicine Hat in 1960. Mr. Bob Monkman, president of the Medicine Hat Fish and Game Association, welcomed the delegates. A souvenir plate of the wildlife of Alberta was given to the delegates on behalf of the Medicine Hat club. As well, the *Medicine Hat News* printed a special edition of its paper, highlighting the convention, and delivered it free to each delegate in attendance.

The Honourable Norman Willmore, Minister of Lands and Forests, was the guest speaker at the annual banquet. Spargo reported in the minutes of the convention that "over three hundred sportsmen and their wives and lady friends heard a first rate eloquent address." Pulling no punches, Mr. Willmore expressed his opinion that some of the resolutions were far out of line and that delegates could not nor any association receive action when it

was against public opinion and in some cases, actually detrimental according to the best scientific information available.

Secretary manager George Spargo reported about a brief the AFGA submitted to the Cameron Royal Commission on education with regard to the teaching of wildlife conservation in the classroom. The first brief was prepared by a committee, consisting of "Mr. Sig Lefsrud of Viking, Mr. John Gow of Edmonton, and the secretary-manager", and presented to the commission in May of 1959. "However, the petition was not enthusiastically accepted and the results negative." As a result the committee drafted a second brief and with this they met with the premier and his cabinet. Spargo concluded, "a most cordial and friendly discussion followed."

The membership of the AFGA was at 14,528 and the locals numbered 82 in 1959, as compared with 14,483 members and 80 locals in 1958. At the time, locals in the Yukon and Northwest Territories were affiliated with the association.

Ovar Uggen, big-game chair, noted that the big-game harvest throughout the province in 1959 was moderate to light, and that a large part of Alberta's antelope herd had migrated into Montana. In 1959 the fish and wildlife division did not use hunter questionnaires as it does today through telephone surveys. In those days, to get an indication of how many game animals were being harvested

1960

Resolution No. 7(A) (Calgary, Lethbridge and district, Central Alberta Fish and Game Association, Didsbury Fish and Game, Red Deer, Rocky Mountain House):

"Whereas the stream management program of the past five years has not provided anglers of Alberta with angling as good as it was before this management policy was instituted; and
"Whereas the population of trout in our streams has deteriorated in the past five years; and
"Whereas the population of coarse fish has increased in our streams over the past five years; and
"Whereas many streams are reverting back to their native fish, and Dolly Vardens [bull trout], and
"Whereas the present stream management policy is falling far behind the needs of present angling pressure; and "Whereas the raising of fish at the one hatchery in the province is almost exclusively for stocking of pot holes, and Whereas the need is urgent in order to restore streams to their former productivity of producing enough fish to supply the needs of present day anglers;
"RESOLVED: that the Fisheries branch immediately dispense with their present stream management policy and formulate a new policy encompassing the following features:

(1) Regular stocking of streams.
(2) The building of at least two more hatcheries, and adequate rearing pond facilities, immediately in order to permit the raising of enough fish to get this next program well started.
(3) Institute a regular program of reclamation and replanting of streams in order to eliminate the great population of suckers and other coarse fish presently taking over our streams and to also repopulate these streams with the desired population of trout. This whole reclamation and replanting program on our streams to begin immediately and take no longer than five years to complete.
(4) Investigation of all streams west of No. 2 Highway that presently contain coarse fish and possibly reclaim and replant with superior Game fish and Montana grayling.
(5) Investigation and stocking of Arctic Grayling in Alberta streams."
The resolution carried unanimously. It was submitted annually until the 34th annual convention in 1963, when it was defeated in committee (after being passed almost unanimously during subsequent conventions) but subsequently carried on the floor of the convention.

they relied on statistics from various checking stations strategically located throughout the province. Uggen reported that only 200 animals were checked out during the month of November at the Red Deer checking station and only 116 animals had been checked out from the start of the season to Nov. 21 at the Ghost River station, including at the latter station, 27 bull elk, 12 cow elk, 47 deer, 19 moose, three rams, one goat and seven black bear had been taken. Said Uggen, "This is a very low hunter success percentage and indicates that a satisfactory harvest was not obtained."

Uggen further reported, "In order to prevent the Banff Park's winter horse pasture from being destroyed by the elk, the either sex season on elk was extended to the end of January on the Ya-Ha-Tinda Ranch." The Ya-Ha-Tinda ranch was the winter pasture for Parks Canada horses at the time. "Our game branch officials and biologists maintain that as long as the hunters do not take an adequate harvest of Big Game, we need the rapidly increasing wolf and the cougar to keep the game herds in control," noted Uggen. "If such is the case, why continue to restrict the season and bag limit?"

Members of the association were concerned that the deer season continued to remain closed in zone 21 (east of Highway 2 to the Saskatchewan border, and south of the North Saskatchewan River to the Red Deer River, in eastern Alberta). Uggen reported that game branch officials seemed to not be looking at the situation where "...we have nearly ideal habitat for deer; there is an abundance of feed, lots of shelter and no predators outside of a few coyotes and the area hasn't been open to legal hunting for decades." He speculated that the officials were keeping the area closed for political reasons.

Uggen related several stories of hunters not being able to correctly identify big-game animals, or care for them after they'd been shot, and others displaying ignorance and poor sportsmanship. "Isn't is about time we insisted that the government set up a system by which a hunter has to show proof of his qualifications before he can obtain his license?" He noted, "The usual reports of careless shooting, vandalism, killing of livestock, etc., following

COURTESY OF RAY MAKOWECKI

Magpie hunting in the 1960s was still popular. Ion Campbell (L) and Ray Makowecki, June 1964.

each hunting season are growing in proportion to the increasing number of hunters going out each fall. No matter if the reports are exaggerated, the adverse publicity connected with such claims is affecting each and every one who goes hunting and helps to widen the breach between hunter and landowner."

Fish committee chair Dave Gibson reported that pothole fishing had been good but stream fishing was poor throughout most of Alberta. "We have gained much from the planting of potholes and lakes but the hope that it would relieve the pressure on our trout streams does not seem to be working out too well. Somewhere there must be an answer but it would seem our present plan of stream management is not the answer, according to the opinion of most fishermen. There seems to be just too many fishermen on the streams which are open. The opening of more streams to spread the fishermen out could be an answer. Opinions vary greatly as to how much is gained by the closing of a stream for one or two years. Generally speaking, fishing is good when a stream is first opened but in most cases, tapers off very rapidly with the heavy pressure."

1960

Resolution No. 11	(Lethbridge and District) "Whereas several raccoons have been killed in southern Alberta in the past two years and are one of the worst pheasant predators; RESOLVED: that the raccoon be placed on the predator list." The resolution carried.
Resolution No. 17	(Red Deer) "Whereas there is extensive damage to crops in some areas of the Province each year by ducks (Mallards and Pintails); BE IT RESOLVED: that the government (provincial) institute a crop insurance program for damage done by migratory birds." The resolution carried.
Resolution No. 23	(Red Deer) "RESOLVED: that the Game Branch of the Dept. of Lands and Forests institute further investigations in 1960 into the harmful effects of brush and weed killing sprays on our bird life populations and publicize the results as soon as possible." The resolution carried unanimously.

Gibson's assessment was accurate and studies undertaken in the early 1970s on east slope streams indicated 75-80 percent of the catchable-size trout were caught during the open season, many shortly after the season opened. By the end of the open season, practically no catchable-size trout remained in the streams.

Bob Arlt, bird-game chair, noted, "The reduction in the daily bag limit of pheasant seemed to put more hunting pressure on the sharptail, and this they need. Ever since the use of 1080 has almost eradicated the coyotes, these birds have never ceased to increase, so much so, that here in the south where the sharptail is supposed to be at the bottom of the cycle the hunter had no trouble getting his bag limit."

Migratory bird chair Joseph Fedenchko advised that crop damage was very heavy in nearly all parts of the province as a result of very bad harvest weather leaving a lot of grain in the fields. "The ducks stayed till very late in the season, mainly on larger lakes and protected lakes, which did not help the situation any."

Predator chair Stan Henders described what he perceived as inertia in the Department of Agriculture regarding a provincial crow and magpie poisoning campaign. He went on at length to describe

COURTESY OF THE AFGA
GORDON CUMMINGS

how department staff were letting the program die, probably as a result of negative reaction from the public. He was describing the beginning of the end of uncontrolled, broadcast poisoning as a predator-control method.

Regardless of whether you agree with Henders' views concerning predator control, he deserves a large measure of respect. He came across in the records as one of the most diligent and fervent chairs of a standing committee in the history of the association. He provided excellent reports, interesting commentary and a good understanding of the politics related to the predator-control issues of the day. He could see through government double standards and how one department was played off against another, often resulting in a stalemate. He also understood the need for diligence if control measures were to have any significant impact.

In hindsight, it's easy to be critical of the AFGA's sometimes comic predator-control program. However, in those days many hunters identified with much of what Henders and the predator chairs before him had to say, especially in southern Alberta. In that portion of the province the natural landscape had been impacted so much by agricultural practices that the so-called "balance of nature" (if it ever existed) was largely just an urban

1961

Resolution No. 6 (Edmonton) "RESOLVED: that the government (provincial) give study and in turn, undertake development of pheasant rearing at provincial jails, provincial mental hospitals and at provincial reform schools."
The motion carried.

Resolution No. 16 (Lethbridge and District) "WHEREAS the riparian or downstream rights of water users call for the allowing of a minimum of only 25 cubic feet of water per second past the St. Mary Dam blocking, the St. Mary River in Southwestern Alberta, and WHEREAS for the most part only the minimum amount has been allowed past the St. Mary Dam during the summer and fall months in recent years, RESOLVED: that the minimum flow of water in the St. Mary, Belly, Waterton and Oldman River for riparian or downstream rights, be increased to 100 cubic feet per second as a safeguard to both game fish habitat and human health and welfare. (It should be noted that, while the government of Alberta is supposed to have jurisdiction over streams within the province, the dams are built by the federal government)."
The motion carried. This is a notable resolution. The provincial government had set the minimum flow below these dams and diversions at 25 cubic feet per second by Order in Council. Consequently, it became the legal flow required to be passed by the authorities responsible for these works. The St. Mary River Irrigation District and Lethbridge Northern Irrigation District and officials in Alberta's Water Resources Division in Alberta Agriculture were not obligated to divert any more than the 25 cubic feet per second flows stipulated which basically dried the riverbed of water below the dams and diversions and decimated local fish populations.

Resolution No. 19 (Lethbridge and District) "RESOLVED: that the Government of Alberta issue free Hunting and Fishing Licenses to resident old age pensioners."
The motion carried.

Pictured above from left to right: Gordon Cummings, Past President, G. M. Spargo, Mr Fish & Game, Bruce Stewart, Secty. Manager A F & G, and Ben Rosnau, President A F & G

COURTESY OF HENRY LEMBICZ

Gordon Cummings L), past president; George Spargo; Bruce Stewart, receiving his life membership; Ben Rosnau, the AFGA president, 1962.

myth. Land use changes gave predators a large advantage. There were few natural places left in the landscape, and what little was left was badly fragmented. Prey species had few places they could safely hide or travel between secure habitats without being exposed to predation.

As usual, there were several resolutions calling for a continuation and increase in the predator-control program by the Alberta government, including the following twist:

In his public relations and membership report, Gordon Cummings stated that relations between hunters and landowners "have been reasonably well maintained during the past year." However, he also reported that there had been an increasing number of livestock reported being accidentally shot, with the owners having to bear the cost of the loss. This resulted in more and more land being posted against hunting. It was this critical situation that prompted the AFGA to demand the government establish a livestock compensation program to reimburse farmers for losses due to accidental shooting of livestock where the shooter could not be apprehended and made to pay for his action.

1961 Gordon J. Cummings became president of the AFGA in 1960. In his inaugural president's report during the 32nd annual convention, Cummings made the following remarks about the organization: "Our association is a strong, vigorous organization because it is built on a broad base – it has the support of people everywhere – in cities, in towns, and in the country. Its members have enthusiasm and ideas to burn and I have a feeling that it is growing greatly in strength and public respect because it is accepting its responsibilities seriously without evasion and is sincerely trying to do a big job in conservation. It is an association we can all be proud to belong to and serve."

1961

Resolution No. 27	(Calgary) "WHEREAS from time to time it is suggested that hunting and fishing are a privilege rather than a right; and WHEREAS this association wishes to make its position very clear; RESOLVED: that this association wishes to reiterate its belief that it is the right of every citizen of this province to enjoy the sports of hunting and fishing." This resolution was tabled because of concerns relating to perceived rights on private property.
Resolution No. 49	(Lethbridge and District, Medicine Hat, Red Deer) "WHEREAS water pollution in Alberta is becoming a serious and pressing problem. RESOLVED: that infractions against the Alberta Fish and Wildlife Services (sic) water pollution laws be punishable by much more severe penalties, and further that individuals, organizations, firms, industries and civic bodies all be subject to the same regulations." This motion was carried with an amendment that the wording be changed from "Alberta Fish and Wildlife Services water pollution laws" to "Federal Water Pollution Laws."
Resolution No. 58	(Stettler, Edmonton) "WHEREAS some antelope hunters are successfully obtaining licenses every year, others may never obtain the same privilege, RESOLVED: that the lottery system of distributing antelope permits be replaced by a rotating system, preference being given to previous unsuccessful applicants." The resolution carried by a large majority.
Resolution No. 61	(Calgary) "RESOLVED: that the government take positive steps to eliminate illegal destruction of grizzlies by holders of grazing permits in Forest Reserves." The resolution carried.
Resolution No. 63	(Claresholm) "RESOLVED: that a closer check be made by Forestry Officers on the slaughter of grizzly bears inside the green area." The resolution carried unanimously.

The 32nd annual convention was held at the Banff School of Fine Arts. The cover page of the annual convention guide boasted "Over 15,000 Organized Sportsmen." At the time, the headquarters of the AFGA was at the Inglewood Bird Sanctuary in Calgary, where it had been located for several years. In 1955 a Mr. Ed Jefferies had made a gift to the AFGA of 1.6 acres of land, to be known as the Jefferies Bird Sanctuary. The office of the association was located on this property and the property was managed by a committee of six members, called the Ed Jefferies Inglewood Bird Sanctuary Committee. The committee was chaired by the president of the AFGA.

Membership of the AFGA had reached the highest level in its history to date: 15,183 members in 1960, over 600 more than 1959. There were 86 local clubs, an increase of two. The top five clubs were Lethbridge (1,800), Edmonton (1,230), Calgary (1,200), Medicine Hat (934) and Red Deer (774). The two smallest clubs were the Waterton Lakes Fish and Game Association (19) and Bruderheim Junior Conservation of Wildlife Protective Association (12).

Cummings was encouraged by what he perceived to be an improvement in farmer-sportsmen relations at the time. The AFGA had one special meeting with the premier and cabinet in 1960. Cummings was very flattering about the working relationship between the AFGA and the government, as well as with government officials. He commended the Honourable Norman Willmore, Minister of Lands and Forests, and Curt P. Smith, director of fish and wildlife, "...for their unfailing courtesy and co-operation during the year."

The creation of the first wilderness area in 1959 (Willmore Wilderness Park) was seen as a milestone, and Cummings congratulated the government on their actions in this regard. The new park allowed hunting and fishing but restricted the use of vehicles. Unfortunately, this concept of a wilderness area would be the last of its kind. Future wilderness areas would be very small and hunting would be prohibited, perceived by many to almost smite the AFGA.

A special award for distinguished services was presented to Herman Hennig of Bruderheim. Hennig had been one of the most active conservationists in Alberta over the years and a well-beloved sportsman.

In memoriam: George E. Watt, past president of the AFGA and life member; Hugh C. Farthing, past secretary treasurer, Red Deer Fish and Game Association and regional representative, AFGA; James (Jim) Speakman, Alder Flats Fish and Game Association; Lou A. Brodeur, past secretary treasurer, Pembina Oil Fields Fish and Game Association; Ed Borg of Disdbury; and Bud Davis of the High River Association. A minute of silence was observed at the convention in memory of these former members.

Hunting Proposal Twisted: Manning

Page 2 - ALBERTAN - March 18/65

EDMONTON (Staff)—Premier E. C. Manning Wednesday said the proposed legalization of private hunting preserves has been distorted completely out of context.

Speaking at the 21st annual game dinner sponsored by Calgary Breweries and the Alberta Fish and Game Association, he said no one could tolerate a system in which hunting rights were determined by the ability to pay.

"No thoughts of that kind exist in the house", Mr. Manning said.

"There isn't one member on either side of this House who would tolerate the right to hunt being determined by the ability to pay."

Earlier, Henry Lembicz, president of the Fish and Game Association, said if any changes were made in the present procedure, this would open the door for more changes in the future.

"In the past, the right to shoot game birds was sold by the Crown", he said. "If this resolution passes, the right to shoot game birds will also be sold by the individual.

"If this comes about it will be because of pressure, and it will be because of pressure that other changes will follow once the door is open."

Mr. Lembiciz said it is the desire of his organization to work constructively with the government to bring more outdoor recreation for all Albertans.

One of the first things to be done, he said, is to establish a system of wind breaks throughout the province for the protection of people, livestock, game birds and animals.

Mr. Lembicz also called for control measures to meet increasing water pollution.

"Some rivers are carrying enough pollution to make fish unfit for human consumption," he said. "Pollution can be removed by stricter enforcement of outlaws."

He added streams should be rehabilitated by acquiring land along the stream bank and establishing cover to protect the stream from silting pollution and rising temperatures.

Mr. Lembicz called for greater conservation of the forest reserves on the eastern slopes of the Rockies.

"Consideration should also be given to the gradual removal of the 20,000 head of cattle pasturing in that area as they do not compliment good water conservation practices."

Bruce Stewart was appointed general manager of the AFGA in 1960. George Spargo stayed on as secretary of the association.

In the 32nd annual convention yearbook, a summary is published of a special brief the AFGA presented to the premier and members of cabinet on Nov. 15, 1960 with regard to conservation education in schools. The introduction of the brief stated, "A comprehensive plan to promote conservation education in our schools and to bring about a better understanding between sportsmen and landowners, was presented to you at this past legislative session. These plans were to be financed by requiring all hunters to pay a small increase in their licenses and the monies so collected were to be used by our association to accomplish these above objects."

The brief outlined the following:
We believe there are two great needs at the present time:
1. The education of our children in:
    (1) Conservation and wise use of our wildlife resources.
    (2) The safe use of firearms.
    (3) Principles of good sportsmanship – to know and obey game laws and respect the rights of the landowner.
2. Better farmer hunter relations

We believe our association can do a great deal to help the government meet these needs and we suggest:
1. Education of children
    (a) Formation of junior fish and game conservation clubs.
    (b) Junior hunter safety training programs.
    (c) Conservation essay contests in schools province-wide.
2. Farmer hunter relations
    (a) Hunter education: meetings and literature.
    (b) Meetings with farm organizations.
    (c) Distribution of shooting signs.

"We have 84 associations in Alberta, and very nearly 15,000 members. We are eager and willing to expand our work and activities in fish and game but we have reached the limit of our financial ability. We need your help. We ask that you make us a yearly grant of $10,000.00 over and above our present per capita grant and with this increased help we pledge ourselves to do all we can along the plans outlined." This brief represents a major milestone in the history of the AFGA in terms of its belief about the importance of including conservation and hunter education as part of Alberta's school curriculum.

Bruce Stewart provided his inaugural report for the year 1959-60 as the new general manager of the association. Stewart spoke of the remarkable increase in membership numbers despite a near depression or at least economic recession during the previous year. "Much of the credit is due to our membership and public relations chairman Mr. C.W. Johnson of Calgary whose zeal and management has been outstanding."

Migratory bird chair Joe Fedechko noted that migratory birds were on the decline due to a lack of rain to maintain suitable bodies of water in 1960 and again in 1961. "As to Farmer-Sportsmen relations," he reported, "I believe the situation is improving all along. I ask you to get behind this essential phase of our work, and carry it through to the best possible advantage for all concerned."

Tom (L) and Ray Makowecki enjoy upland bird hunting in the Edmonton area, 1963.

Fish chair Fred Hargreaves noted, "In the central area fishing in accessible areas has been pitiful for the last few years, and this condition grows increasingly worse each year. Calgary and the Lethbridge area's reports the same conditions as the central section. One bright spot in this area is a report from Coleman where there has been some improvement."

Predator chair Stan Henders provided an historical perspective on predator control in his report to the conference. He related how in the early years government had been actively involved in controlling predators. However, over the years this support has waned, and now, "sportsmen are told by top government officers that for any hunter to kill a predatory species for the purpose of increasing the game supply" is being selfish. Henders must have been very frustrated after getting such a classic run-around for many years and from so many different quarters. He called upon someone else in the organization to step forward as predator chair, stating it was time for him to step down.

The number of clubs involved with the crow and magpie campaign had fallen dramatically and the number of crows and magpies killed dropped to 7,107 and 16,643 respectively, for a total of 23,760. Bounties totalled $3,376 for 1960. The grand total from 1938 to 1960 was 1,996,663 crows and 2,483,324 magpies killed with the total amount paid $172,151.48.

Ken Dezall, big-game chair, reported, "The present picture for big game seems fairly bright but with the added hunting pressure and the extra long seasons and also the slaughter of our female population are making serious inroads in our big game which if it continues at its present rate will be very serious in the next few years." He added, "Goats are disappearing fast as they are easy to locate and because our so-called sportsmen are shooting the females and kids. This practice is fast clearing our goat population." Dezall also noted that deer in most parts of Alberta were not plentiful and the caribou were few in numbers.

1962 Gordon Cummings continued as president. The 33rd annual AFGA convention was held at the Capri Motor Hotel in Red Deer in 1962. It was hosted by the Red Deer Fish and Game Association and the surrounding locals. Following an official welcome from the mayor of Red Deer Mr. E. Newman, the president of the Red Deer club, Cec Head, welcomed the delegates. A banner, boasting "Over 17,000 Organized Sportsmen and Over 100 Affiliated Clubs" adorned the cover page of the convention yearbook. A header on that cover page noted that the 33rd annual convention was dedicated to G.M. Spargo.

Cummings also announced in his president's report that the convention was "The George Spargo Convention" in honour of the former secretary manager for his past 38 years of service. Cummings noted, "Our association has grown mightily through his enthusiasm, his devotion, his wise guidance, and until it is now the second largest in Canada. Upon the eve of his retirement, I ask you to pause and pay tribute to him. The measure of our association is very largely the measure of his work."

Spargo had immigrated to Canada from Wales when he was 20 years old and had served the AFGA since 1930, shortly after its formation in 1928. In a tribute to Spargo, president Cummings spoke of Spargo having worked all day and travelled all night on many occasions to visit outlying local clubs. His contribution to conservation had also been recognized by the Western Canada – Yukon Fish and Game Council, and by Ducks Unlimited, both of whom had conferred life memberships on Spargo. As well at the conference, individual presentations were made to Spargo by several clubs, including Sylvan Lake, Alder Flats, Raymond and Vegreville. David Cooper, of the Del Bonita local, said Mr. Spargo would be greatly missed, and mentioned that the little community of Del Bonita, with a population of 100, often had 110 members in its club. Cooper presented a life membership in the Del Bonita club to Mr. Spargo, and also appointed him "Marshall of Whiskey Gap." In recognition of his long service to the AFGA, Spargo was awarded a life membership at this convention.

The AFGA membership continued to increase to a new high of 17,202, a gain of over 2,000 from 1960, and the greatest yearly increase over the previous 10 years. In addition, the AFGA reached another all-time high of over 101 affiliated clubs, an increase of 15 over 1960. The early 1960s did indeed appear to be the golden years of the AFGA.

In the July/August 1961 Fish & Game *magazine, Joe Balla reported "One of the biggest steps in fish and game and conservation circles was taken in the southern part of this province during the later part of June when the Southern Alberta Fish and Game Council was formed.*

"With Fels Balderson of Magrath at the helm, the council has two main purposes for existence:

1. To co-ordinate thinking at resolution time and thus facilitate proceedings provincially, especially at convention time.

2. To co-ordinate fish and game project activity in southern Alberta."

Membership was on the climb in the association and exceeded the 17,000 mark; statistics were as follows:

	1960	1961
Total membership	17,207	15,183
No. of locals	101	86
No. of new or re-organized locals	18	10

The top five clubs in Alberta were Edmonton (2,300), Lethbridge (1,702), Calgary (930), Red Deer (600) and Lacombe (600).

Chuck Johnson, general chairman of the membership committee, was again singled out for praise as well as the district membership chairmen "...who worked so hard to achieve this new membership record."

1962

Resolution No. 1 (North Central Zone) "BE IT RESOLVED: that golden eagles be put on the protected list." There was a lengthy discussion regarding this motion and Elmer Kure expressed surprise that the committee had approved this resolution, "...after the years the association had spent in getting the present provision put into effect. He believed a great deal of thought should be given to the proposed resolution, as he questioned whether the committee was familiar with the life of the golden eagle." Kure advised that the resolution should not be approved. Other officials spoke in favour of the resolution, and the records indicate "Archie Hogg, High River, also supported the resolution, adding that the golden eagle is a beautiful sight. While some of them undoubtedly would be shot in the rare cases when they do damage to stock, he thought the Committee's decision should be approved." The motion was amended by the addition of the words "in prairie areas." The amendment to the motion was approved by a majority of 43 to 30, and the chairman declared the motion as amended, carried.

The AFGA vigorously opposed the introduction of legislation in 1961 that would have allowed private shooting preserves in Alberta. This was consistent with the association's policy of being strongly opposed to any form of paid hunting.

For the first time, the AFGA started publishing a monthly newsletter in 1961, as "…a step forward in improving understanding and co-operation between member associations."

Premier To Discuss Problems With Fish And Game Officials

Damage By Hunters Not On Increase: Game Chief Says

Reported increases in damage to farm property by hunters are largely incorrect, according to Alberta Fish and Game Association president Henry Lembicz of Lacombe.

Such damage is not increasing, he feels, but this impression is created because of widespread publicity given to isolated examples. He also feels the impression that farm damage by hunters is increasing stems from a tendency on the part of the public to blame hunters for every incident noted.

"They get blamed for many incidents wrongly," he says. As an example, Mr. Lembicz suggests such damage as the shooting of livestock could be done by "someone who has a grudge."

"They wait until the hunting season and the hunters get the blame."

He says such hoodlum acts are one of the most serious problems faced by the Alberta Fish and Game Association.

Officials of the organization do not suggest hunters are entirely blameless where farm damage is concerned, however. They have a continuing campaign designed to reduce the problem.

"We want to educate the hunter to be a more responsible man when he is in the field with a gun."

Meanwhile, officials of the Farmers' Union of Alberta contend hunter damage is increasing.

William Harper, publicity director of the FUA, says the organization has received complaints from various parts of the province about hunters who damage crops and fences. There have also been complaints about farm animals being shot and he said it is a fair assumption that hunters were responsible.

The FUA, the Western Stock Growers and the Alberta Fish and Game Association have suggested that crop insurance, now paid by a $1 fee included in the price of hunting licences, be extended to cover damage done on farmland during the hunting season.

This insurance now covers damage done to crops by wildlife, but Mr. Lembicz says the fund which supports it is steadily increasing and his organization has attempted to have it expanded to cover hunter damage.

Mr. Lembicz also reported on an executive meeting of the Alberta Fish and Game Association held Sunday at the Capri Motor Hotel in Red Deer. It was attended by 32 directors from throughout the province.

Plans for the 1965 provincial convention, to be held in Red Deer Feb. 4, 5 and 6, were discussed. Mr. Lembicz said approximately 300 delegates are expected to attend the three-day meet, slated for the Capri Hotel.

The association plans a strenuous membership drive in the near future to bolster finances, he said.

Nov. 9 Meeting Slated On Conservation Topics

[Herald Correspondent]

RED DEER — Henry Lembiez, Lacombe, Alberta Fish and Game Association president, accompanied by committee chairman, will meet Premier E. C. Manning and provincial cabinet members Nov. 9 to discuss wildlife conservation problems.

The announcement of the meeting was made Sunday at an executive association meeting.

Twenty-eight members attended.

Robert Hobbs, Calgary, big game committee chairman, reported the new zone management has been "generally and favorably" accepted by sportsmen.

MORE OUTLETS

He said, however, they would like to see more outlets for the sale of hunting licences, particularly on Saturdays.

Frank Pickering said lack of sufficient outlets was an acute problem in the Edmonton area this fall.

Jack Munro, Red Deer, association vice-president and predator committee chairman, reported the provincial magpie population is at a record high.

He said a recommendation to the government about control of these predators is expected.

It is planned to ask the bounty system be re-instituted.

LARGE INCREASE

Mr. Munro said there has been a large increase in the number of timber wolves in the Edson area.

Association membership is 15,000.

The 1965 annual convention will be held here Feb. 4-6.

Two newspaper articles from the mid-60s.

An AFGA newsletter from 1964.

Another first was the Alberta government creating a Wildlife Crop Damage Insurance program in 1961. It was financed by a $1 surcharge on hunting licences to cover waterfowl crop damage claims. This legislation had been long advocated by the AFGA and was the subject of several annual resolutions.

At the national level, the Canadian Wildlife Federation was formed in 1962. The AFGA president Cummings heralded the new organization as "…a dream come true." This federation was seen by Cummings "…as a means of being able to deal with conservation and wildlife problems on a national basis and to speak for every sportsman in Canada."

In memoriam: Guy Blake, Calgary, vice president, the AFGA; Dr. R.A. Rooney, Edmonton, past president, the AFGA; Lee White, Medicine Hat Fish and Game Association; Hamlen Fahr, Drayton Valley, Pembina Oilfield Fish and Game Association.

"They passed as sportsmen do
To live in hallowed places,
O'r rivers, forests, fields and plains,
Their footprints show their traces."

The members observed a minute of silence in memory of the deceased members, and also any others whose names might not be known to the executive.

Long-serving predator chair Stan Henders forecast a gloomy future for Alberta's game in his annual report. He once again lamented the lack of a predator-control policy and wondered how any game management program could exist without one. He stated, "I don't believe the predator committee has had a single resolution acted on since the days of Mr. Huestis, not one. And have any of your other committees done much better?" He went on to describe the good relations the association had with elected officials when pleading their case, only to be stonewalled by the civil servants. What Henders and many other hunters of the day were fighting were the studies in wildlife biology that were indicating that predators played an important role in the ecosystem, and that large-scale predator control was often counter-productive. This clashed with the views of hunters who had been brought up during times when game was scarce and who believed predators had to be controlled to bring the game back.

The AFGA crow and magpie campaign continued its downward spiral, with 20,929 pairs of feet submitted in 1961, compared with 23,760 in 1960, a decline of 2,831. The total number of pairs of feet taken since 1938 was 4,500,916 at the time.

Henders added, "Boys, we have lost contact with the members of the House so badly that I'm told when one does try to support us the rest sit in total silence for lack of background of his subject. He quickly becomes discouraged, and we are lost. In this my last report to you as your predator committee chairman, I beseech you and I plead with you to stop this chasing the civil servants about with your resolutions passed this day and insist on a Cabinet hearing, or at least a hearing before a group of MLAs selected to hear you and be satisfied with nothing less, before it is too late, if it is not already so."

Migratory bird chair Joe Fedechko noted, "My report for this year will be a very brief one because there were not many ducks around. From Highway 16 south there were hardly any ducks because of the very dry year. From Highway 16 north the ducks were more plentiful, but there was a very definite decrease from last year." He added "Farmer and sportsmen relations are not what we would like to have. Instead of sportsmen we have hunters who violate laws affecting different groups of people, especially the farmer.

Fish & Game Assoc. Seeks Immediate Pollution Study

An immediate survey of water pollution in Alberta is being sought by the Alberta Fish and Game Association.

In a brief presented to the provincial cabinet the association described water pollution in the province as "disturbing" and suggested that new legislation may be required to control the situation.

The request for the survey was included in a list of requests and suggestions contained in the association briefs. Among others were:

● A suggestion that the new method of selling hunting licences through a restricted number of outlets was creating difficulty and inconvenience to hunters.

● A request for a change in the special wildlife damage fund program to allow landowners who have livestock shot during the hunting season to be reimbursed.

● A suggestion that the provincial government form a special department, with a full-time minister, to control outdoor recreation and tourism.

● A request that a special commission be formed to set out public right-of-ways in the province and be responsible for their maintenance.

Edmonton will face a smog problem unless tighter controls are placed on sources of air pollution, reports the provincial department of health.

A department study of air pollution sources and their effects in the Edmonton area states pollution levels are considered higher than normal for a city of this size.

Petrochemical and food processing industries, automobile exhaust fumes and domestic incinerators are major sources of pollution, the report states. More than 11,000 tons of solid matter are spewed into city air annually

The report recommends adequate pollution control device for industry; installation of equipment to reduce carbon monoxide fumes from automobiles; a ban on open fires and small domestic incinerators and expansion of the department's existing air monitoring pollution control network.

Newspaper article from 1964.

COURTESY OF HENRY LEMBICZ

One point that I would like to stress strongly is that all local fish and game associations should watch for these lawbreakers and troublemakers and report them to the proper authorities. Localities where this was done showed a marked improvement in public relations."

COURTESY OF THE AFGA

BEN ROSNAU

Upland bird chair Darwin Cronkhite reported concerns about declines in the numbers of Hungarian partridge and the sharp-tail grouse in southern Alberta. He blamed the drop on "the almost complete fizzle of the government crow and magpie campaign which has resulted in an over-population of these predators." He also blamed the government for increasing great horned owl, snowy owl, goshawk and falcon populations with the result there being less game for the hunter and closed seasons.

On another note, Cronkhite expressed concern for the lackadaisical attitude the government had toward noxious sprays and wholesale destruction of cover on the prairies. "The sportsmen feel that it is high time the government enact legislation which will produce sprays of a type that are not noxious to birds even though they produce the desired results on insects."

Jack Chesney, fish committee vice chair, reported highly variable fishing success in Alberta and also commented on the coarse fish situation: "Sucker population is steadily increasing along with silt on most streams and before long we are going to have to start and reclaim these waters and give them back the rock bottoms if we are going to get our old-time fishing back." He added, "The picture was brighter from the Pass area. Good trout fishing reported but as the case in most places you have got to get off the beaten path to find a good day's fishing."

Big-game chair Ken Dezall noted, "The big-game situation in our Province still looks bright." He did note, however, "Our bear are definitely getting scarce, especially the grizzly and unless the

1963

Resolution No. 10B   (Southern Alberta Zone) "BE IT RESOLVED: that open season for trout fishing in Alberta be restricted to the period June 15 to Oct. 31 of each year."
The resolution was defeated.

Resolution No. 19   (Olds, Calgary, High River and Southern Alberta Zone) "BE IT RESOLVED: that due to the scarcity in general of upland game birds, we have a closed season in 1963, on certain species in areas of known scarcity."
The resolution carried.

Resolution No. 66   (Calgary association) resolved that the government create a separate department of recreation and wildlife conservation. It was the result of perceived conflicts with other interests in the Department of Lands and Forests. The resolution carried.

senseless killing by some of our stockmen is controlled they will rapidly become extinct in our province."

C.W. Johnson, chair of the public relations, good and welfare, and membership committee, noted, "It is our opinion that the excellent work done by various groups combined with the increasing number of farmer members is gradually improving public relations. To our many clubs who have extended their efforts in establishing fishing ponds, beaches, shelters and opening access roads, we can only commend you for your good work and state that good public relations will always be in existence if these projects are continued."

1963 Ben Rosnau became president in 1962. He was a keen member of the AFGA, always very sincere and determined.

The 34th annual convention was held at the Exhibition Pavilion in Lethbridge and was sponsored by the Lethbridge Fish and Game Association. The total registration for the convention was 430 including guests, a new record at the time. The president of the Lethbridge club, Dave Hunt, welcomed the delegates after the convention was officially opened by the mayor of Lethbridge, Cleave Hill. Most of the delegates stayed at the locally popular Marquis Hotel and El Rancho Motor Inn, with buses being provided for those in need of transportation to and from the hotels and the Exhibition Pavilion. Hunt noted that a full-course meal (lunch) would cost $1.50 for delegates.

Carling's Conservation Club was the host club on the first evening of the convention, where "lunch and refreshments were served to all who attended this get-acquainted evening." It was not uncommon at the time for local breweries to host an annual AFGA convention.

The Hon. Norman Willmore, Minister of Lands and Forests, was the guest speaker on the opening day of the conference. Willmore commented that the wildlife crop damage insurance program had been rather disappointing during its first two years of operation. Participants were required to insure their crops against damage the same way they would against hail.

Willmore also spoke about the association's request for a livestock indemnity fund. He stated he was unable to understand the need for such a program. For years he had been telling his colleagues in government that "although cows are often shot, it is not done by hunters but instead by criminals, bandits and no-good-niks." He said he couldn't understand why an organization would want to pay into a fund to pay for damage committed by people who were breaking the law. Addressing the need for education to maintain good relations between hunters and farmers, he said, "The one danger seems to be that the association tends to be labelled as an organization of conservation cranks or nature nuts."

In his report, Rosnau noted, "During the spring we became involved in a land deal that increased our acreage at Inglewood [bird sanctuary in Calgary] from 1.6 acres to 2.42, which made it a neat rectangular block, with no expense to the fish and game association. This was done by doing some trading with Bill Fisher being the broker, lawyer and real estate agent."

The AFGA was successful in saving the waters of Ferguson Lake in the Grande Prairie country from flowing into the Peace River, and thereby preserving the home of the threatened trumpeter swan.

Publicity chairman Norman Shaddock and his committee were singled out for praise by Rosnau for feeding out 120 papers as news releases, and getting the publicity they hoped to receive. Rosnau also noted, "Radio and television also gave us their co-operation." On an administrative note, the president reported that the AFGA "...office equipment has been kept up by acquiring a new electric typewriter. This has greatly improved the quality of our mimeographed material."

Alberta manager Bruce Stewart reported, "In July it was decided that we should look into an insurance plan for the smaller associations. In November it was decided to take the insurance policy out. In the past few weeks it looks like a number of the associations will take the insurance." This marked the beginning of a universal insurance program for members of the AFGA, which currently provides $2,000,000 accidental death and dismemberment coverage for each member.

Membership chair C.W. (Chuck) Johnson noted that the AFGA had fallen far short of its target of 20,000 memberships for 1962. The final membership total reached only 17,228. Johnson provided an interesting commentary on the make-up of the association at that point in time and its relationship to membership recruitment. "In our Alberta organization we have a president, an immediate past president, two honorary vice presidents, eight vice presidents, a manager, a secretary, 60 regional representatives, 108 local presidents, 108 local secretaries." He asked whether it would be a reasonable assumption that 290 people working on memberships would be able to increase membership to 20,000. He closed his report, "So, I now say unto you: Get off your asses, light up your enthusiasm, get out and sell some memberships, before all forms of wildlife and recreational areas have vanished from 'our' promised land."

The top five clubs in membership numbers were Edmonton (2,650), Calgary (1,566), Lethbridge (1,510), Willingdon and District (491) and Red Deer (436).

Big-game chair Ross A. Laycock reported that big game in general were in good numbers in the south and central areas of the province. However, there was a downward trend in northern areas around the Peace River district. He advised, "The major threats to all big-game are still commercial grazing, predators and habitat destruction." He claimed, "Predators in the northern areas are accounting for more than three times the hunter kill on the moose population. With no other big-game animal to be found in this large area, and with no control measures being taken, we shall soon be faced with a closed season in this sparsely hunted area." In support of this latter statement, Laycock reported on a survey in the Peace River-Grande Prairie areas: "During a survey of this area by both plane and on the ground covering 2,000 miles in length, not one moose was observed while coyotes and lynx were seen by the dozens and reports of wolves from all areas." Regarding woodland caribou, Laycock reported "From all reports received, there should be no open season on woodland caribou." He lamented, "The only reason that we have an open season is because of pressure from outfitters to provide an extra animal while hunting sheep and goats."

Laycock also advised that black bear were in poor supply in all south and central areas, and "nothing in the population calls for the present limit of four bears per year; this animal should be classed as a trophy animal and seasons and limits will have to be reduced if the species is to survive." This damning report was superior to many others in the annual convention yearbooks. It covered the whole province and basically all of the big-game species. Considering the nature of this report, there were surprisingly few big-game committee resolutions in 1963 and those few were mainly housekeeping in nature.

The fish committee report was no better. Chair Jack Chesney opened his address as follows: "Fellow sportsmen: all Trout fishing reports which I've had from around the province for the season of 1962 have been consistent; consistently poor." He added, "Now we all realize that stocking of yearling trout last year was practically NIL, around 8,000 to 10,000 yearlings only being available. These

were released mostly for potholes, in small allotments, so that every locality received its fair share." He did advise that a brighter picture was in store for fishermen in 1963 because the enlargement of the rearing ponds at the raven hatchery had been completed and all 37 ponds were full of fingerlings. Chesney went on to note, "But gentlemen, we are not the only ones concerned with the gradual depletion of our fishing. The Alberta Tourist Association and the Beach Manager's Association are deeply concerned and have informed us that they are in accord with any endeavors that we make in this connection. Fishing is and always will be, a main tourist attraction to Alberta."

It wasn't just a lack of stocking that Chesney blamed on the poor fishing. He also singled out pollution as a culprit, especially the insidious siltation of foothill trout streams. He advised, "I would like to see a start made next year on some chosen stream, or part of same, to remove this silt, and then carry on from there over the years until we have this problem beat." He recommended that the Fish and Wildlife Division should create a budget for this purpose and undertake a pilot project, accordingly.

1963

For the second time, there was a resolution to move the headquarters of the AFGA from Calgary to Edmonton.

Resolution No. 41 (Northeast Prairie Zone) "WHEREAS it is desirable that the AFGA work in close contact with the Alberta Wildlife Division (sic) and other government agencies and personnel, and thus be more fully and currently informed of their plans; and WHEREAS it is our opinion that the desires of sportsmen are not made known in the Legislature at times when changes are being contemplated concerning the *Game Act*, or when the annual budgets are being presented, and WHEREAS the offices of the AFGA are too far removed from the capital, which results in less effective and less opportune lobbying on behalf of sportsmen, therefore BE IT RESOLVED: that the offices of the AFGA be transferred to the city of Edmonton." The resolution had been tabled at the previous year's convention with the proviso that it be brought back again before the convention with a recommendation from the executive. The executive could not arrive at a decision so it was moved by them that it be brought back to the general meeting. Elmer Kure moved an amendment that the association maintain a public relations officer fulltime in Edmonton as soon as possible which was seconded by Darwin Cronkhite. The resolution as amended carried and the association once again put off a decision to move its headquarters to the provincial capital.

Resolution No. 51 (Sarcee) "BE IT RESOLVED: that the Government of Alberta recognize the colour of blaze-orange in addition to scarlet for hunters' clothing." The resolution carried.

Resolution No. 55 (Northeast Prairie Zone) "WHEREAS 'No Trespassing' signs are being posted on more and more property every year, in some places for no reason at all, and in other places for the purpose of charging hunters to enter upon their property, BE IT RESOLVED: that drastic measures be taken by the provincial government to check this practice." The resolution carried.

Resolution No. 59 (Southern Alberta Zone) "BE IT RESOLVED: that the Eastern Irrigation District be opened to the hunting of antelope and deer." The resolution carried.
The Eastern Irrigation District (EID) maintains its administration offices in the City of Brooks, Alberta. The administrative jurisdiction of the EID encompasses an area of 600,000 hectares (1,500,000 acres), and is bounded by the Red Deer River to the northeast, and the Bow River to the southwest, making the EID the largest private landowner in Alberta. At various times the board of directors had closed the irrigation district grazing association lands to hunting.

COURTESY OF THE AFGA

Toni and Ben Rosnau, both life members.

Darwin Cronkhite, upland bird chair, added to the litany of concerns expressed by the other committee chairs. He stated there was a general scarcity of upland birds throughout the province. He called for close seasons on "certain species in various areas throughout the province." He also reported that the Fish and Wildlife Division intended to import and release pinnated grouse as soon as the drought cycle improves.

In 1962, 21 Merriam's turkeys from South Dakota were released on the north side of the Cypress Hills; by the summer of 1963 the population was estimated at almost 70 birds.

Jack Munro took over from Stan Henders as the predator committee chair. He reported that the manager of the AFGA had sent out forms to nearly 100 clubs for a status report on the predator situation and programs in their areas. No forms were returned. Consequently, he advised that his report could not provide a true picture of the predator situation in Alberta. He did, however, report on the usual litany of complaints about predators killing game. In the conference, the various predator resolutions called for a more vigorous predator control campaign, that the golden eagle be taken off the protected list in the Green Zone, that the province fund the AFGA crow and magpie campaign, that there be an open season on the horned owl, snowy owl, arctic blue hawk and sharp-shinned hawk. However, perhaps the lack of response Henders reported from the local clubs on the status of predators was an indication of the fatigue the membership was feeling with regard to the issue and the lack of significant government response.

1964

Resolution No. 28   (Southern Alberta Fish and Game Association) "BE IT RESOLVED: that the Alberta Wildlife Service experiment with the stocking of bighorn sheep in the Elkwater Lake area."
The resolution carried.

Resolution No. 32   (Southern Alberta Fish and Game Council) "BE IT RESOLVED: that the appropriate government conduct a province-wide survey immediately on water pollution in Alberta, with the findings of study made public immediately on publication."
The resolution carried.

Resolution No. 38   (Southern Alberta Fish and Game Council) "BE IT RESOLVED: that the practice of grazing domestic sheep in the forest reserve areas of Alberta be abolished." An amended motion carried: "that the practice of grazing domestic sheep in the forest reserve areas of Alberta be 'restricted.'"

Resolution No. 74   (Southern Alberta Fish and Game Council) "BE IT RESOLVED: that the Alberta Fish and Game Branch set up a stream improvement program for the province whereby the fish and game branch will take the initiative in carrying out specific projects and further that such a program be set up in a manner that fish and game and other conservation organizations throughout the province be able to participate in carrying out the work; such a program to be set up immediately."
The resolution carried.

1964

Resolution No. 39   (Southern Alberta Fish and Game Council) "BE IT RESOLVED: that the south branch of the Castle River area in southwestern Alberta be declared a wilderness area as laid out by the Province of Alberta." An amended motion was carried: "that the south branch of the Castle River area in southwestern Alberta be declared a wilderness area as defined by the province of Alberta, and that all islands in lakes and rivers be made wilderness areas."

Resolution No. 44   (Sarcee Fish and Game Association) "WHEREAS the problem of Indians abusing the hunting rights extended to them under 'treaties' has been steadily growing worse in the past few years, therefore BE IT RESOLVED: that the Government of Canada be approached through the provincial government and the Canadian Wildlife Federation to expedite their investigation and solution to this problem."

> *The AFGA crow and magpie campaign experienced an additional downturn with 13,408 pairs of feet submitted in 1962, compared with 20,929 in 1961, a reduction of 7,521. The total number of pairs of feet taken since 1938 was 4,514,324.*

Elmer Kure was the chair of the newly appointed wilderness, access and grazing committee. On the subject of access Kure noted "During the period of my appointment to this committee, it has become apparent to me that access [to private land] is possibly the most contentious question of the day." He felt that an educational program was required, in part, to address this problem, as well as a recreational land use committee (possibly under the Fish and Wildlife Division). "I feel a full-time public relations officer of such a committee could visit our hot-spot areas and acquire or arrange for public access where there is a need."

In terms of grazing Kure noted, "Now, more than ever before in Alberta, grazing land is at a premium, and it may appear as selfish to suggest curtailment of grazing domestic livestock in the forest reserve. However, if by practicing full utilization of east slopes range, problems are actually being created, then I feel grazing of certain areas should be discontinued."

Kure also reported on a recommendation from the AFGA representatives on the Fish and Wildlife advisory council that "a limited number of hunters be allowed in [Banff National Park]

COURTESY OF RAY MAKOWECKI

Primrose Lake near Cold Lake.

PRO. PRESIDENT SPEAKS OUT ON
GAME FARMS IN ALBERTA

A message to <u>YOU</u> from Henry Lembicz, President of the Alberta Fish and Game Association.

Once again we are confronted with the problem of Private Hunting Preserves in Alberta, as I understand there is to be a bill presented at the next sitting of the Alberta Legislature.

The sensible approach to such matters is to consider the advantages and dis-advantages of Private Hunting Preserves. I would say the <u>advantages</u> would be: it would give the men who could afford the price and was only interested in going shooting, an easy way of getting a few birds. If he was the kind of a man who must have a sure thing because he cannot face the thought of returning without birds, Private Hunting Preserves could help him. They could also help a man who was so timid or disagreeable that he could not approach a landowner to get permission to hunt on his land. The big business man with a client who likes to shoot birds would take advantage of a private game farm, to impress his client to secure the deal.

Private Game Preserves could relieve a little pressure from men who would be attracted by this type of shooting, but the percentage would be small and this would only support a few preserves. On the overall situation the relief would be negligible.

Private Hunting Preserves would have no attraction for sportsmen.

The <u>disadvantages</u> are: in order to give these few shooters their desires we would have to break down a tradition and law that has always been in Alberta, prohibiting the sale, trade, barter, or offer for sale the hunting, shooting, killing or trapping rights over any lands for wild game. This law has served well in the past and still is a good law for the future. By licensing Private Hunting Preserves we will break down this principle. It has been hard enough to keep that principle in the past, but once you grant a privilege to one, then others can rightfully expect the same.

July-August, 1964   Page 11

In my opinion the establishment of Private Hunting Preserves may satisfy the desires of a few shooters but will open up a large avenue of new problems, such as the desire of any landowner to sell hunting rights, without knowing his responsibilities. The breakdown of law enforcement on private lands could be expected.

Th_____me management program and the curtailment of study and _____ow.

_____sociation proposed and assisted in the establishment of the _____rian Partridge and are investigating the possibilities of _____irds to fit into a changing environment. Such conditions

_____f Hunting Preserves would come pressure for cocktail _____in connection with the enterprise.

_____ate time to make such a change, when we are in a period _____need of a change and that change is taking place now with _____ucation and Training Plan. In a few years there will be _____g the responsibility that goes along with a hunting license. _____be given to only issuing licenses to qualified hunters. The _____is a privilege to hunt on privately owned land is taking _____blish a fund to compensate a landowner for retaining, _____e habitat for Wild Game. It will be through these _____shall find our solution

Signed: HENRY LEMBICZ, President
ALBERA FISH & GAME ASSCCIATION

COURTESY OF HENRY LEMBICZ

to harvest elk in the Panther River area." It was the first time such a recommendation had been put forward by the association supporting hunting in a national park.

Good and welfare, and public relations chair Norm Shaddock advised, "My predecessor, Chuck Johnson, stated in his report last year that relations between the farmers and the sportsmen were as good as could be reasonably be expected, and I am happy to report that these good relations exist now. To be sure, there are individual cases of strained relations, but overall the situation is excellent." However, the need to create a livestock indemnity fund, recommended earlier by the association and shunned by Minister Willmore, was still extant.

Shaddock also reported, "Never in the recent history of our association have our relations with the press been so good. We were able to make many news releases during the year to the more than 100 newspapers, daily and weekly, and to radio and TV newscasters."

In addition to the following resolutions from the good and welfare, and public relations committee, there were additional resolutions calling on the government to undertake province-wide surveys of pollution, singling out Bow River pollution concerns.

1964 Ben Rosnau remained president of the AFGA in 1963. The 35th annual convention was held at the Edmonton Exhibition Grounds in 1964. The conference was hosted by the Edmonton Fish and Game Association with assistance from other clubs in the Edmonton area. The total registration was 352 including guests.

Once again, the other host club for the first evening of the convention was the Carling Conservation Club, which introduced "Mabel Around The Table." [The "Hey Mabel, Black Label" advertising phrase popularized this brand of beer from the Carling Brewing Company Ltd. At the time it was illegal to advertise alcohol in Alberta.] Later on in the evening the Willingdon Fish and Game Association marched in with their fish and game band. The ladies and sportsmen were dressed in green jackets and hats, with pheasant tails in the hats.

At the start of the convention, Edmonton Fish and Game Association president Frank Pickering welcomed the guests and delegates to Edmonton. Edmonton mayor William Hawrelak also extended his welcome to the delegates to the capital city of Alberta, and the oil centre and "gateway to the north."

Rosnau commented, "Blaze Orange is still on the fire, and the Canadian Research Council is still testing various dyes and fabrics. They have, as yet, not come up with a desirable fabric or dye. However, I am assured that when a favorable material is available it will be adopted by the game branch." The association had a long history of hunter jacket colour preferences for safety purposes: red, scarlet, canary yellow and blaze orange.

The AFGA hunter training program had been adopted by the game branch, Rosnau reported. Forestry access roads were opened to sportsmen for the first time in many years, ending what Rosnau saw as an era of private hunting for a privileged few. Pheasant stocking was proceeding according to the AFGA

recommendations. Rosnau stated that the public image of the AFGA had shown considerable improvement. He noted, "We are accepted by the government as an association that does things for ourselves rather than cry on their shoulders. The farm organizations have found that we are on their side, and we are deeply concerned with problems of mutual interest."

"The Inglewood committee has failed in its obligations," reported Rosnau, "and I recommend it be abolished and their files and funds be turned over to the AFGA, and the property be administered by the board of directors."

Alberta manager Bruce Stewart noted that the insurance program was underway and there were two accidents, both of them property damage which involved the shooting of cars – they were settled with no problems. Secondly, Stewart advised, "In one area, this insurance opened up land to the sportsmen, which had been posted 'no hunting' for the past six years. But, on entering, insured membership has to be shown to the landowner." Stewart advised, "Your headquarters also had to winter some five thousand ducks last winter, and we are doing the same this winter. Grain was purchased when grain donations ran out. Some grain was even sent by truck to other parts of the province." Apparently, these birds had lost their migratory instinct and stayed at the Inglewood Bird Sanctuary on the banks of the Bow River rather than migrate south.

Membership chair C.W. (Chuck) Johnson advised that once again the membership objective of 20,000 was not reached. Membership for the year only reached 17,233. The top five clubs were Edmonton (2,660), Calgary (1,806), Lethbridge (1,574), Lloydminster (494) and Vulcan and District (360).

In 1964, the upland and migratory bird committees were amalgamated into one, henceforth to be known as the bird-game committee. Chair Darwin Cronkhite reported an incident concern-

ELK MOVED TO SPIRIT RIVER

COURTESY OF HENRY LEMBICZ

En route to new stamping grounds in the Spirit River area in the Peace River region, these 14 elk were trapped north of Banff in 1953. Fish and game associations succeeded in obtaining the transfer of the animals to help ease the overcrowding in the elk population in the Banff area.

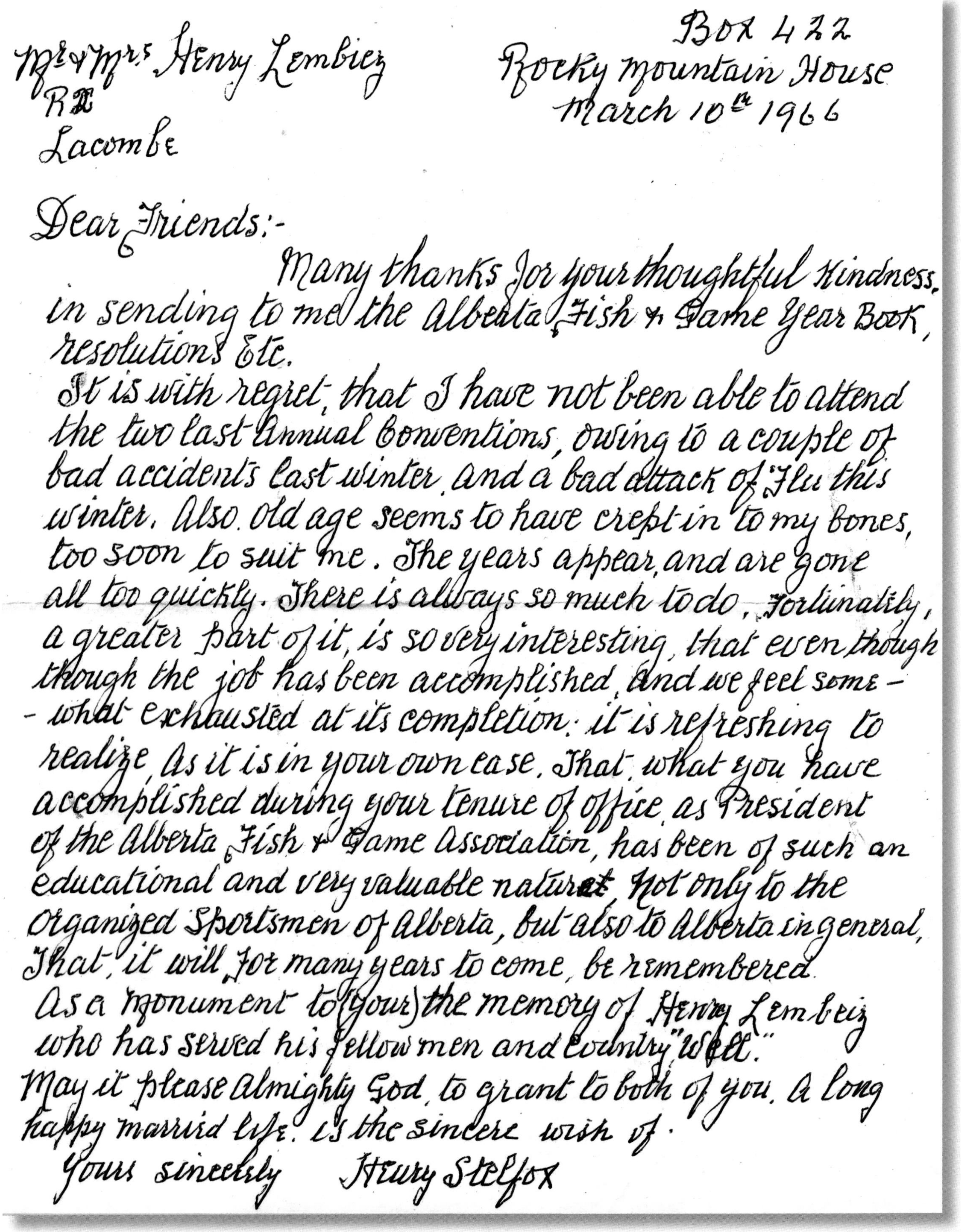

Mr & Mrs Henry Lembicz
R2
Lacombe

Box 422
Rocky Mountain House
March 10th 1966

Dear Friends:-

Many thanks for your thoughtful kindness, in sending to me the Alberta Fish & Game Year Book, resolutions Etc.

It is with regret, that I have not been able to attend the two last Annual Conventions, owing to a couple of bad accidents last winter, and a bad attack of Flu this winter. Also, old age seems to have crept in to my bones, too soon to suit me. The years appear, and are gone all too quickly. There is always so much to do, fortunately, a greater part of it, is so very interesting, that even though though the job has been accomplished, and we feel some — — what exhausted at its completion. it is refreshing to realize, as it is in your own case. That, what you have accomplished during your tenure of office, as President of the Alberta Fish & Game Association, has been of such an educational and very valuable nature. Not only to the organized Sportsmen of Alberta, but also to Alberta in general, That, it will, for many years to come, be remembered. As a monument to (your) the memory of Henry Lembeiz who has served his fellow men and country "well." May it please Almighty God, to grant to both of you. a long happy married life. is the sincere wish of.

Yours sincerely   Henry Stelfox

ing the paid hunting issue. "...It is with mixed feelings I must report an incident which occurred on our good friend Ted Peck's weekly [radio?] program, 'Tides and Trails,' in which he appeared to favour paid hunting shooting preserves. Obviously Mr. Peck did not go out to offend anyone but it did appear that he had not checked with the attitude of the AFGA and other clubs such as the Kennel and Field Trials Club before he put this show on. To put the entire matter into a nutshell, the sportsmen throughout Alberta reacted to that episode like vinegar does to soda and Mr. Peck apologized on his next program. Furthermore, that episode has been withdrawn from circulation. It is too bad this incident happened because many of us consider Ted a pretty good sportsman."

Cronkhite advised that the proposed stocking of pinnated grouse had been delayed yet again due to a drought in the proposed re-stocking areas. He also noted that wild turkeys in the Cypress Hills area

COURTESY OF HENRY LEMBICZ
A letter to Henry Lembicz from his mother.

continued to show an increase in numbers and that the Department of Lands and Forests had been commended for allowing the shooting of Canada lynx in the yellow and white areas to control predators.

Fish committee chair J. Chesney reported fishing had improved greatly from last year over much of the province, especially the pothole and small-lake fishing—thanks to increased stocking. Lakes near Edmonton apparently produced "...some wonderful sport fishing."

Chesney also reported on what must have been one of Alberta's earliest steam enhancement projects. "I did receive some good news from Lethbridge Fish and Game Association. These hard-working boys are experimenting on a stream reclamation program, along with the help of Martin Paetz and his staff headed by Buck Cunningham, biologist. Must mention that Bob Woodward, warden at Pincher, was also invaluable in his assistance. Yarrow Creek

1965

Resolution No. 1
(Southern Alberta Fish and Game Council) "WHEREAS the present stream management policy is falling far behind the needs of the present angling pressure, therefore BE IT RESOLVED: that the AFGA co-operate with the Fish and Wildlife Division and embark upon an extensive stream rehabilitation program, incorporating the following features:
1. Fencing of stream banks where necessary to help prevent erosion and to protect vegetation.
2. Planting trees and shrubs along stream banks to shade the water and to help keep the water temperature as low as possible and to protect fish.
3. Encourage a beaver management policy on all streams for the express benefit of fish culture.
4. Install and maintain obstructions in some streams to form pools and living areas for fish.
5. If advisable, poison stream populations and replant with the most suitable species for the area.
6. Use every means possible to stop pollution of streams."
The resolution carried.

Resolution No. 12
(North West District) "BE IT RESOLVED: that this association re-affirm its stand as being opposed to legislation endorsing shooting preserves in any form."
The resolution carried.

Resolution No. 15
(North West District) "WHEREAS there is a considerable amount of jack-lighting and poaching going on throughout our back roads, Sundays included, therefore BE IT RESOLVED: that the government take immediate action to correct this situation by putting more game wardens in the field, and BE IT FURTHER RESOLVED: that heavier penalties be imposed on those offenders."
The resolution carried unanimously.

Resolution No. 47
(Southern Alberta Fish and Game Council) "WHEREAS bear traps are presently located in several areas of our foothills and WHEREAS many bears are killed by permit holders, therefore BE IT RESOLVED: that killing bears be limited to licensed hunters during the hunting season and to officers of the game branch in the case of dangerous or destructive bears in the green areas."
The resolution carried.

and Drywood Creek were selected for this trial. Cables were interwoven through hog wire and dead-manned to shore. Steel pegs were also driven in the creek bottoms. The mesh was so enclosed to form a cup-shape in the middle of the stream, catching debris, forming a small dam, causing a rise in water and holding place for fish. The water is then forced through the centre of the mesh, causing a pool down stream. Three of these catchers were installed to date." He added, "We'll all be watching this experiment with great interest, as the need for stream improvement has been one of the main topics of conversation with Alberta fishermen for the past several years." This is the first record concerning installation of structures in streams in Alberta to create fish habitat.

The big-game report from Ross A. Laycock noted, "In general the information received and my own observations do not indicate that our big-game is as numerous as last year. One of the most noteworthy changes is in the elk herds with very poor results noted in the area south of the Bow River in all zones." This information was apparently in direct contradiction to government reports. Laycock noted that increased access had resulted in a greater harvest of borderline trophy sheep in the mountains, for example the upper Elbow River area, the Ghost River and Panther River. "Should this type of hunting be substantiated during our committee discussion, then I for one will immediately ask for a closed season for non-resident hunters in the area south of the North Saskatchewan River in the province of Alberta." Laycock's reports on elk, moose, deer, bighorn sheep and goats, caribou and bear were very similar to the year previous.

COURTESY OF HENRY LEMBICZ

Congratulations card from Henry Lembicz's mother.

COURTESY OF VERN MCINTOSH

Vern McIntosh at Wawa Creek northeast of Nordegg, 1967.

... THEY DON'T STAY AT HOME WHILE HUSBANDS HUNT
... Mrs. R. M. Hobbs (left) and Mrs Ross Laycock

Mrs. R.M. Hobbs and Mrs. Ross Laycock, lady hunters circa 1965.

> *R*egarding antelope, Laycock noted they were "in good to excellent condition south of the Red Deer River in the province. Good hunter success was again noted this year. The antelope are in good condition, further opening of closed areas are needed to properly harvest the antelope."

Laycock noted that since the previous convention the association had been able to receive permission to transplant elk from Banff and Waterton Lakes national parks and move 60 head to Spirit River, but due to the economics of the move did not want to proceed until 60 elk were available from government traps, and not a lesser number.

Access, grazing and wilderness chair Elmer Kure noted, "Grazing of domestic stock on the east slopes has in past years been abused and poorly supervised and as a result has been very contentious." However, he said much had been accomplished in terms of better range habits and supervision. "Thus the department has received no apparent justifiable complaints in the past two or three years." The grazing patrons had by this time hired range riders to keep tabs on range use, and employed drift fences and distributed salt blocks to better distribute cattle and try to prevent them from congregating in favoured pastures and over-grazing such areas. Kure also noted that no progress had been made to create de-facto wilderness areas although three mountain areas had been named (Ghost, White Goat and Siffleur).

Norman Shaddock, good and welfare chair, had only positive comments regarding affairs with the media and relations with farmers, ranchers and other landowners. Regarding relations with the government, he advised, "I feel that here a great improvement has been made. In my opinion, relations with the government are at their highest level in years, both in the legislature and with the wildlife division." The exhibits of the wildlife division at the major sportsmen shows were apparently very well received by the sporting public.

On a sour note, Shaddock commented about the maintenance of the residency of George Spargo at Inglewood. Apparently, the AFGA had endorsed Mr. Spargo's residency there, but there were people who were opposed to Spargo living there. Shaddock said he stood behind his old friend Spargo, and that there were a great many advantages to having him reside at the Inglewood Bird Sanctuary. Poor Spargo must have been very dispirited by the undercurrent of minority dissent over his residency at the sanctuary, especially after his many years of loyal service to the association.

Following many years of quiet, the "Indian" issue again surfaced during the 35th annual convention. Several resolutions were presented. All were tabled for discussion by the executive. Resolution No. 44 represents the basic concern.

Predator chair J.D. Munro reported, "The year has rolled by and the predator situation looks anything but bright." He again listed problems with getting the government to act on predators. He advised that the wolf was on the increase and chances of relieving the situation were nil.

1966

Resolution No. 3   (North Central and Northwest Prairie Districts, Edmonton FGA and Dunvegan FGA) "WHEREAS the destruction of wildlife habitat, particularly that of upland game birds, through land clearing for agricultural purposes, much of the time indiscriminately, particularly in the north central part of the province, and WHEREAS this problem is reaching a critical point in many areas, therefore BE IT RESOLVED: that the provincial government institute a study whereby the yearly disappearance of habitat can be accurately determined, and BE IT FURTHER RESOLVED: that the necessary steps be taken to prevent further loss of habitat in areas that are already at a critically low level." The resolution carried.

Resolution No. 4   (Southern Alberta Fish and Game Council) "BE IT RESOLVED: that the Southern Alberta Fish and Game Council urge the AFGA to be in favour of and support a federal duck stamp, provided funds derived from the sale of such stamps be used for the reclamation of wetlands and other waterfowl habitat." The resolution carried by a wide margin.

Munro mentioned that Ducks Unlimited again helped with a substantial predator grant in 1963 and that there were plans for a stepped-up crow and magpie campaign in 1964. The financial statement indicated that Ducks Unlimited provided an annual grant of $2,000 as well as a monthly grant of $300.

1965 Henry Lembicz became president of the AFGA in 1964.

In a personal communication, former fish and wildlife employee Ernie J. Psikla noted, "What impressed me at that time was Henry's global perspective about pollution and that it was well beyond the detrimental effect on wildlife or fisheries. The effect of pollution on wildlife and fish to him was a symptom of a far more widespread problem that required a macro approach within government to address. The AFGA role in the eventual creation of the department of the Environment should not be forgotten nor go unrecognized in Alberta's history. The AFGA brought forward public concern about pollution and the environment decades before it became popular in the news media in general. It saddens me to see the role and function of the AFGA is often portrayed and reported as simply a hunting and fishing advocacy organization. Had it not been for the AFGA, many programs and management initiatives might not be in place today."

HENRY LEMBICZ President: 1964-66

COURTESY OF THE AFGA

HENRY LEMBICZ

Henry Lembicz was a well-known farmer of the Canyon district southeast of Lacombe, and a former president of the Red Deer Fish and Game Association. In 1964 the 58-year-old farmer succeeded Ben Rosnau of Bruderheim as the new president of the provincial association at the annual conference in Edmonton. At the time he was elected president of the AFGA he was also a member of the Parkland Toastmasters Club of Red Deer. Lembicz had been actively involved in fish and game work for some two decades at the time of his election to the most senior position in the AFGA executive. He had served on the AFGA executive for the previous five years.

Lembicz was the first man from the Red Deer district to hold the honour of being president of the AFGA. According to newspaper reports of the day, Lembicz said in a short address to the annual convention that the association must stand ready to fight pollution of lakes and streams along the eastern slopes of the Rocky Mountains. He said the streams and lakes must be kept free of pollution so that fish and water birds have clean surroundings in which to live. "We get more enjoyment from our waters than from any other natural

segment of our province," he said. Lembicz was also elected to the Canadian Wildlife Federation for a two-year term at the annual conference.

In an undated, hand-written note, his mother sent her congratulations to Henry, writing, "I believe you have reached a goal you cherish and I do you hope you enjoy it. I know you accept a lot of responsibility gracefully. This will really tax your patience, I imagine, but knowing your ability to get things done and at a rapid rate, I am sure you will make good although a lot will be expected of you. Keep peace within your ranks as much as possible. 'Many men have many minds' is a favorite saying of my father's and one that has to be often considered when 'politickin.'

Lembicz had been touted as a tireless worker for countless years in promoting the conservation and preservation of Alberta's outdoor resources at the time of his election as president.

At the conclusion of his term as president, Lembicz was presented with the Fulton trophy, the association's highest award for conservation and dedication to the causes of wildlife. He was also awarded the Archie Hogg trophy, given for the greatest contribution to publicity to promote the aims and objectives of the association, as well as a hand-carved buffalo presented for long and faithful service to the AFGA, of which he had been a member for over 20 years at the time.

He served six years as a director of the Farmer's Union of Alberta and also on the board of the Alberta Federation of Agriculture. He joined the Red Deer Fish and Game Association "to find out where the fishing was," and twice served as its president and for many years as chairman of the pollution control committee.

Mr. R.H. (Bob) Scammell, of the Red Deer Fish and Game Association, presented Lembicz with its Sportsman of the Year Award for his outstanding work against pollution in 1970 at the annual Red Deer Sportsmen's Show.

The AFGA established the Henry Lembicz Clean Air, Clean Land, and Clean Water Award. *In honour of Mr. Lembicz, this is awarded to the club or individual that has done the most outstanding job towards pollution control or cleanup of Alberta's environment.*

Help needed

AND while we're speaking of accolades, how about three cheers for the 50 or so hardy souls who gave up a Sunday of leisure to clean a winter's accumulation of litter from our river banks.

Led by Mr. Henry Lembicz, this group of 50, mostly students, collected six truckloads of garbage from the Red Deer River, Waskasoo and Piper's Creeks.

That's a lot of junk and it's really only the beginning. There's lots more where that came from. Thus, it's a shame that Mr. Lembicz had only 50 helpers. He could have used twice that number. In fact, 150 would have been even better. Sunday, Camille J. Lerouge Collegiate displayed the finest sense of civic pride with 27 students from that school pitching in.

But you can still do your bit. The anti-litter and clean-up campaign continues all this week. Why not give up an hour or so of your time sometime this week and do some sprucing up around the yard, your neighborhood streets and lanes, parks and playgrounds. Or how about that attic? Anything there that hasn't been used in years and could be donated to some charity or organization?

Mr. Lembicz and his group have made an admirable start, why not carry it through to a successful conclusion and make Red Deer the cleanest city in Alberta.

COURTESY OF HENRY LEMBICZ

A newspaper article reporting on the pioneering work on pollution done by Lembicz.

In a May 1970 Red Deer Advocate *article, Bob Scammell wrote, "He was fighting pollution back when it was just another two-dollar word." Scammell praised him for being what stands as an ultimate tribute: "he was years ahead of his time." He noted, "A lot of us owe more than we can repay to men like Henry Lembicz, just for starting all the talk we now hear about pollution."*

[Biography prepared by Duane Radford from archival records supplied by Dave Powell, past president of the AFGA.]

The 36th annual convention was held at the Capri Motor Hotel in Red Deer in 1965. The convention started in tragedy. As the main business got underway at 9 a.m., it was reported to the convention that the Hon. Norman Willmore [Minister of Lands and Forests] had been killed in a car accident. The convention opened with the singing of O Canada, then a one-minute silence for the late Norman Willmore. Each day seemed to start with a minute of silence. The minutes recorded, "On Friday the 5th of February, Dr. Langenegger died of a heart attack. He was a delegate for the Wainwright Club."

Lembicz reported on the successful launch of the hunter training program and the wildlife crop damage Insurance program. The president and his executive again met with the Premier and his cabinet in 1964. An important offshoot of this meeting was a subsequent meeting they held with delegates from the Farmers Union of Alberta and Norman Willmore, Minister of Lands and Forests, to create an indemnity fund to compensate landowners for

1966

Resolution No. 18 (South Central Zone and Calgary FGA) "WHEREAS the present stream management policy is falling far behind the needs of the present angling pressure, therefore BE IT RESOLVED: that the AFGA request the Fish and Wildlife Division to embark upon an extensive stream rehabilitation program, incorporating the following features:

1. Fencing of stream banks where necessary to help prevent erosion and to protect vegetation.
2. Planting trees and shrubs along stream banks to shade the water and to help keep the water temperature as low as possible and to protect fish.
3. Encourage a beaver management policy on all streams for the express benefit of fish culture.
4. Install and maintain obstructions in some streams to form pools and living areas for fish.
5. If advisable, poison stream populations and replant with the most suitable species for the area.
6. Use every means possible to stop pollution of streams.
7. Approach the Government of Alberta in regards to acquiring a margin of land along fishing streams for access and to stop silting, and for preservation of cover."
The resolution carried.

Resolution No. 20 (Southern Alberta Fish and Game Council) "WHEREAS there is little or no real protection afforded wild trout while attempting to spawn in Alberta waters, therefore BE IT RESOLVED: that trout spawning streams be closed to all angling from Oct. 31 to June 15."
This resolution was tabled and referred to the executive. It is interesting that this potentially beneficial resolution which had been brought forward at earlier conferences did not have the support of the members.

Resolution No. 40 (Southern Alberta Fish and Game Council) "BE IT RESOLVED: that every affiliate club of the Alberta Fish and Game Association subscribe to an extra 10 cents per capita fee through the AFGA during 1966. BE IT FURTHER RESOLVED: that all fees so subscribed be set aside into a special fund by the AFGA for the express purpose of a Centennial expenditure in 1967 [the year of Canada's centennial] and BE IT FURTHER RESOLVED: that the president of the AFGA name a special committee in 1996 to study and recommend a suitable centennial project on which the money is to be spent."
Following an inordinate amount of time spent debating the merits of this resolution, it was passed on to the executive as a recommendation from the good and welfare committee. It appears as though no action was ever taken regarding this resolution as no further mention is made of any developments in the records.

Resolution No. 47 (Northeast Prairie District and Wasketenau, Warspite and Smoky Lake FGA) "BE IT RESOLVED: that the AFGA make application to proper authorities to have a reward offered to any person who will furnish information leading to the conviction of a poacher."
The resolution was defeated in committee by a vote of 5 to 18, and lost on the floor.

the accidental shooting of livestock during the hunting season, with reference to cases where there was no other means of reimbursement. This must have been a considerable accomplishment given what the minister had said about such a program at a past conference.

Lembicz reported that a hunter-training and a pollution committee were both established for the first time in 1964. As well, he reported that the Canadian Wildlife Federation sponsored National Wildlife Week for the first time in 1964. Another highlight was the successful transplant of 26 elk from Banff National Park to the Spirit River area.

Paul Presidente, who was the head of the fledgling hunter training program for the Fish and Wildlife Division, made a presentation during the convention. He reported, "We think the program is being met with much interest and enthusiasm." Presidente advised that there were over 200 instructors already certified through qualification courses.

A prominent advertisement was displayed in the yearbook, proclaiming that the new hunter education and training program, sponsored by the Fish and Wildlife Division was underway. The ad noted that the program included: elements of game knowledge, hunting courtesy and ethics, outdoor survival, firearm care and safe handling, laws and licences, first aid, care of meat and trophy and many miscellaneous hunting tips.

The key elements of a hunter education program long recommended by the AFGA had been incorporated as part of the government program content. The minister of the day when the program was launched was the Hon. Norman Willmore, and E.S. Huestis was the deputy minister, both whose names were also featured in the advertisement.

Membership chair C.W. (Chuck) Johnson reported that the new low-cost public liability and property damage insurance plan should help increase and stabilize membership in the AFGA. In 1964 total membership in the association was 17,561, with a total of 99 clubs, and a membership increase of 328. The top five clubs were Edmonton (2,450), Calgary (1,940), Lethbridge and District (1,680), Lloydminster and District (479), Medicine Hat and Vulcan and District (400 each). There were 8,808 members insured under the AFGA personal public liability and property damage policy in 1964.

Fish chair W. H. (Bill) Hamilton could not provide a complete report on fishing conditions because ill health prevented him from doing so. He had been asked to commend the fish and wildlife branch for the continued program of stocking pickerel [walleye] eggs in the lakes within 100 miles of Edmonton. Hamilton also noted that the Calgary Hook and Hackle Club installed debris catchers on Jumping Pound Creek; the Lethbridge and district club had already installed seven debris catchers on foothill streams in southwest Alberta. As a sign of high fishing pressure in 1964, he noted, "In spite of the fact that most of the reports say fishing is good, they end up by stating that fishing is not as good as it has been in the past, and most agree that the re-stocking program has not kept pace with the increased pressure. A fine example of

this is given by our good friend Archie Hogg, from High River: 'The total number of 2,450 fishermen registered at Archie Hogg's access gate to one little spot on the Highwood River.' When was the river re-stocked?" At the time, stocking was seen as a panacea to poor catches of trout in foothill steams, which had earlier been proven as a fallacy by Dr. R.B. Miller.

Indian affairs chair Ben Rosnau noted, "A study of Indian Treaties No. 6, 7 and 8, which pretty well cover all of Alberta, showed that conservation for the preservation [of fish and game] is definitely part of these treaties. However, no organization previously has taken any action to teach the Indians anything in this field. I found all parties that I contacted receptive to our idea in regards to teaching conservation to the Indians. The enthusiasm displayed by the Indians was most heartening. One comment by a leading chief was, 'Why is this so late in coming?'" Rosnau felt the answer was to include them in the new hunter training program, an idea which had been endorsed by the Department of Lands and Forests. On another note, he suggested where fish and game associations had access to Indian reserves, they should invite Indians to join their local clubs. If there was a chance of forming an association on the reserves, Rosnau noted this would be most welcome.

COURTESY OF RAY MAKOWECKI

Ray (L), Dmytro and Tom Makowecki with some of the rainbow trout caught at Wildhorse Lake near Hinton, August 1964.

Predator chair J.D. Munro noted, "The year has rolled by and the predator situation remains about the same. The wolf packs are on the increase, probably due to them all but being put on the protected list last year." On a more humorous note, Munro reported, "The cougar seems to remain about the same but every year the settled areas are losing more domestic animals. In a recent report from New Zealand, they are thinking of importing cougars to control their deer population. I would like to see the Alberta government supply about 500 before they find out our Alberta biologists have our cougars trained to only take the weak and the sick, because they have other thoughts in mind." He also noted that the coyotes were far too plentiful in both the settled and forested areas, while he added, "Today our greatest enemy to game birds are magpies, and they will continue to increase until we get a more forceful program from the Department of Agriculture." There was the usual petition for the government to pay bounties on crows and magpies.

Public relations and publicity chair Norm Shaddock noted "Seldom in the history of the Alberta fish and game movement has our association's public image been so high. Our relations with the press in the province continue also at a high level." Shaddock congratulated the *Calgary Albertan* and the *Lethbridge Herald* for the special hunting editions put out by both papers and commended local associations for an upsurge in publicity at a local level. All this publicity translated into good public relations, according to Shaddock.

G.S. Frizzell, access, grazing and wilderness chair, noted, for the first time, impending problems related to road allowances fenced and closed. "There are also a few and these are on the increase. We have some work to do in this area. This is an MD [municipal district] road that has been leased to a farmer or rancher and he will close this road and post it with a 'No Trespassing' sign." On another note, Frizzell reported that access roads in the forest reserves previously closed to motorized vehicles had been opened to public access and this was no longer a significant issue, with few exceptions. There was still a resolution (No. 32 which was carried unanimously) calling for the suspension of grazing of domestic sheep in the forest reserves, a long-standing contentious issue with the association in southern Alberta.

SUPPLIED
Goose hunters.

Game-bird chair Darwin Cronkhite reported that early November snows and blizzard conditions later during that month and on into December, coupled with severe temperatures over a prolonged period of time, dealt "...a disastrous blow to the pheasant and Hungarian partridge populations in the prairie regions." Cronkhite noted, "Alerted by the plight of our wildlife, the Southern Alberta Fish and Game Council, the Calgary Fish and Game Association, the Red Deer Fish and Game Association, the South Central Fish and Game Association, the Edmonton Fish and Game Association and others combined in a gigantic undertaking to feed the starving birds. Head office co-ordinated many of the grain distributions and organized a fund-raising campaign. The fish and wildlife service co-operated in every way possible and we owe the service a special 'thank you.'" He concluded, "Due to the disaster, I think we should take a long look at how the boys over in Saskatchewan manage their pheasant hatchery. We might learn a lot. Who knows, we might get into the hatchery business ourselves."

On a more positive note, Cronkhite forecast that with the heavy winter snowfall there should be a good crop of waterfowl in the coming year. He also advised, "A couple of years ago we received assurance that pinnated grouse would be restocked in Alberta. However, at this late date nothing has transpired. Perhaps we should apply for a permit and raise them through the association."

Big-game chair Bob Hobbs reported "The past year produced an average big-game harvest relative to the previous fine bountiful seasons. Antlered species which most big-game hunters pursue provided good hunter success. The game management unit concept permitted harvest of a record number of antelope, about 5,000. Special tags for mule and white-tailed deer diverted pressure from the larger animals as hunters spent a greater

1967

Resolution No. 2

(South Central Zone) "BE IT RESOLVED: that an experimental season on sage grouse by opened during the 1967 bird game season. BRIEF: there seems to be an over population of sage grouse as evidenced by an overflow of birds into areas not of natural and suitable habitat."
The resolution carried.

Resolution No. 7

(Executive Resolution) "BE IT RESOLVED: that the AFGA request the Minister of Lands and Forests to designate an area in the Kananaskis and the South Castle River and a prairie area as wilderness areas in our centennial year. BE IT FURTHER RESOLVED: that the minister be requested to enact a long-term-use policy for these and already named wilderness areas, so that their future values may be ascertained."
The resolution carried.

Resolution No. 28

(Southern Alberta Council - Claresholm) "BE IT RESOLVED: that the government be urged to initiate an antelope draw program whereby some preference would be given to applicants who have been unsuccessful in previous draws."
The resolution carried.

proportion of their available time hunting deer." Hobbs felt that big game was being "...utilized in an enlightened manner with improvements each year." He also noted, for the first time, concerns with game tags: "Reports have been received indicating certain unscrupulous hunters have perfected methods of unsealing the metal game tags. An improved tag would seem to be indicated, which I hope does not have a big knob on the end to wear holes in one's wallet." At the time, the tags were of the type used to seal cargo containers. Hobbs also noted a number of immature grizzlies were taken the previous fall in the Kananaskis area, "While hunting is not the principal factor in declining grizzly populations, this animal is in greater danger of extinction than any other big-game animal in our province. If fall hunting is to be permitted then I would suggest a five-dollar fee be required to take grizzly [bears] to avoid small bears from being taken on an opportunity basis simply because they are included in the license." This proposal was not supported by the delegates. Resolution No. 47 is an example of the association's early concerns regarding indiscriminate killing of grizzlies.

Hobbs advised, "I am pleased to report that the long awaited elk transplant from Banff to Spirit River took place shortly before Christmas. Only half of the 65 elk permitted by the Department of Fish and Wildlife were accommodated in the first load, the balance to go forward when a sufficiently large number can be trapped." The transplant was fully financed by the AFGA. In a personal communication with former fish and wildlife staff member, Ernie J. Psikla, he noted, "The introduction of elk to the Spirit River area was totally an undertaking by the AFGA. Bruce Stewart was the person who took the lead role in that program for the AFGA. As I recall the elk were trapped at the Ya Ha Tinda ranch and moved by road transport to the Spirit River country. I think it is important to note in the record that the AFGA did a thorough survey of the land owners in that area before the first elk was moved and had gained the support of the local farming community to do the undertaking. In later years when the elk population started to increase and the issue of crop damage arose and the predictable complaints began to come in, the pre-transplant work and local support seemingly were forgotten and preoccupation with farm aid took front and centre as usual in this province."

1966 Henry Lembicz remained as president of the AFGA in 1965.

The 37th annual convention was held at the Banff School of Fine Arts in Banff in 1966. A banner on the yearbook for the convention boasted that the AFGA had over 16,000 organized sportsmen in over 90 affiliated clubs.

*F*or the first time, in Lembicz's convention report he makes reference to a trend for the president of the association to officially represent the organization to the news media and the public at large. He attended 53 meetings, banquets and hearings in 1965 and made six appearances on TV as well as a number of radio announcements. From this date forward, many presidents were increasingly asked to speak on behalf of the AFGA on matters affecting fish and game conservation, as the prime spokesperson for the organization. Lembicz logged 9,560 miles [15,385 km] during 1965, a bit down from the year prior.

In 1965 the first serious cracks started to show in what had historically been a long-standing good relationship between the AFGA and elected government officials, although this is sugarcoated in many of the reports from the chairs of the various standing committees. Lembicz advised, "We have a problem of there being only a few MLAs who are conscious of the need to conserve our wildlife heritage for the future. Most of them do not want to bother peering through the green haze of the present greenbacks to see into the future." This is the first recorded public statement made by a president of the AFGA against the Alberta government in the AFGA archives, and an ominous sign of the beginnings of stormy relations ahead.

"Following up the publicity of 'Help Stop Water Pollution,'" noted Lembicz, "Our association concentrated its drive on the Calgary area. Much publicity was given in regards to pollution from sewage and oil. We also informed and requested our provincial government to take action on the problem. To the best of my knowledge they are still sitting back and viewing the situation with a political eye." He went on to note, "The upheaval in regards to pollution has brought to light that Banff and Jasper are pouring raw sewage into rivers. The question arises, just how far have we progressed in a civilized way, when we still dump our human excrement into rivers for our brothers to consume downstream,

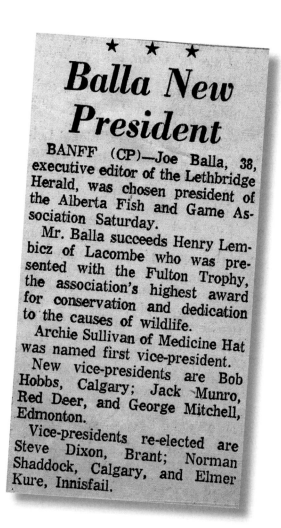

★ ★ ★
Balla New President

BANFF (CP)—Joe Balla, 38, executive editor of the Lethbridge Herald, was chosen president of the Alberta Fish and Game Association Saturday.

Mr. Balla succeeds Henry Lembicz of Lacombe who was presented with the Fulton Trophy, the association's highest award for conservation and dedication to the causes of wildlife.

Archie Sullivan of Medicine Hat was named first vice-president.

New vice-presidents are Bob Hobbs, Calgary; Jack Munro, Red Deer, and George Mitchell, Edmonton.

Vice-presidents re-elected are Steve Dixon, Brant; Norman Shaddock, Calgary, and Elmer Kure, Innisfail.

COURTESY OF HENRY LEMBICZ

instead of properly disposing of it. We can find money to attend cocktail parties, burn costly tobacco, gamble and build beautiful buildings, yet we cannot find money to properly dispose of our human wastes, or stop the dumping of oil into our rivers."

Reference was made to the association entertaining government officials at the annual game dinner on March 17, where they dined on pheasant from Saskatchewan and mountain lion from British Columbia. Apparently the fact that no wild game from Alberta was served at the popular dinner was lost on the government officials.

The AFGA concentrated its drive to curb pollution in the Calgary area in 1965, following up on the National Wildlife Week theme, "Help Stop Water Pollution." The main concern was over the need for Calgary to upgrade its sewage treatment facilities. Lembicz also pointed out issues related to farmer-sportsmen relations and the need to put "...a more educated and responsible hunter in the field," adding, "The sad part of the situation is the small percentage of hunters who belong to our association."

There was another transplant of 28 elk from Banff National Park to the Spirit River area, in two shipments of 14 each in July and November, 1965. [NOTE: Alberta manager Bruce Stewart reported: "I have moved 55 head of Elk to Spirit River from Banff." This must have represented the total number moved to this part of Alberta, although the records are not clear.]

COURTESY OF RAY MAKOWECKI

Moose hunters got their game home any way they could. Clarence Makowecki and hunting crew, 1967.

The Hon. Henry Ruste assumed the position of the late Norman Willmore as Minister of the Department of Lands and Forests in 1965. Fish and wildlife director Curt P. Smith resigned his position as of Sept. 1 when he took a position with the Northern Institute of Technology. Stuart B. Smith filled the latter position on Feb. 1, 1966, transferring from the fish and wildlife branch in British Columbia.

Chuck Johnson, membership chair, titled his report: "A Horror-Scope Without Prejudice," lamenting, "It is astounding and discouraging to have to face the fact that our membership is in round figures, down 1,000 from last year. Now we have to ask why did so many sportsmen neglect to renew their membership this year." Admitting failed membership objectives, he added, "There is however, a very appalling situation within our association that we regret to bring to your attention. A number of clubs are only sending in a token or very small portion of their per capita [dues]. It would seem they wish to have all the privileges of our association but do not wish to support the parent association to the extent of

their true membership. When faith and mutual trust is gone, how can there be success in our united efforts towards conservation."

There were several signs of discontent among the membership and discouraging reports of dissension among members of the association noted in the records. The total membership stood at 16,549, with 91 local associations, a decrease of 1,012 members from the year previous, and a loss of eight locals. The top five clubs were Edmonton (3,040), Lethbridge (1,467), Calgary (1,351), Lloydminster (513) and Red Deer (461). There were 9,035 members insured under the AFGA public liability and property damage insurance policy which did not include the members from associations in Calgary, Edmonton, Medicine Hat or Hinton, which had their own insurance policies.

Game-bird chair Darwin Cronkhite noted "Generally poor hunting conditions were reflected on ring-neck cock pheasant, ruffed grouse, spruce grouse and sharptail grouse. Contributing factors were the extreme cold and blizzard conditions on the prairies, coupled with extensive predation by horned owls, snowy owls, falcons and coyotes on the survivors, occurring during the winter months. Generally unfavourable nesting conditions followed. The department tried to alleviate the situation by opening the season on hawks and owls in the grassland units and they are to be commended for this. Crash feeding programs were operated under the sponsorship of the sportsmen and the Government and this is a step in the right direction."

Cronkhite advised that, generally speaking, the duck and goose populations were satisfactory. Regarding pinnated grouse, he reported "Several sightings of this species were reported by the Lethbridge and District Fish and Game Associations. In view of the hard work the southern Alberta council has done over the years, and the discovery of this species was made in their area, the Darwin Cronkhite Trophy is to be awarded to the council for 1965."

Jack Munro, predator chair, added some humour to the opening line of his report: "Once again we move into a new year and it is my hope to see a very productive one for the association, and a total crop failure for our predators." Munro was of the opinion that predator numbers had remained about the same level as in the previous year, except for magpies and wolves in some areas. Indicative of the mood of the day regarding predators he closed his report on the note: "In closing this report, I would like to give Joe Gurba a long-overdue bouquet for his fight to keep Alberta the only rat-free province in the world, and hope we can come up with a magpie program as effective."

Fish chair Bill Hamilton, noted, "I would suggest that the Honourable Mr. Ruste [Minister of the Department of Lands and Forests] be invited to some of our future fish meetings. I am sure that he would certainly take some cognizance of our position.

It must be that our sport fisheries are now extremely critical. What we need is as follows:

(a) Heavier stocking.
(b) A method of fingerling or adult raised by way of fingerling pools strategically situated from Peace River in the north to Lee Creek in the south (Cardston).
(c) A biological survey which will embrace all our suggestions from a scientific point of view."

"Thanks to Paul Presidente, our provincial training officer," reported Manfred Lukas, hunter training committee chair, "we have the most complete program of all the provinces in Canada. Let us never allow our program to be watered down to safe gun handling only. Today and more so in the future, we have to learn how to manage our wildlife resources wisely to insure that we have a game crop to harvest in the near as well as in the distant future. A well-educated hunter will ensure wise management better than any other single project of ours, no matter how worthwhile it might be." As of Dec. 31, 1965 some 441 instructors had been certified and 1,658 students had passed the hunter-training course.

Big-game chair, Bob Hobbs, noted a drop in big-game populations over the previous year mainly as a result of severe winterkill from the previous year's harsh winter storms. "The main reason for decreases was the severe winter last year which had a marked effect on antelope and deer in the exposed prairie region. Elk appear to have been reduced in numbers throughout their range, whereas moose appear to be doing well, maintaining satisfactory numbers in most areas."

Acting chair of the good and welfare committee, Norm Shaddock, noted that "Farmer-sportsmen relations are as good as they have been at any time in our recent history." He also advised that relations with the government of Alberta had never been better, noting again that they had direct access to the Alberta cabinet. There were a couple of resolutions calling for more staff for the Fish and Wildlife Division and more money for this agency of government.

Ben Rosnau, Indian affairs chair, advised "After two years of negotiations with leaders of the Indian bands of Alberta, I have found the going a bit rougher than I had first anticipated. The chiefs and counselors of the various bands are in general agreement with us, and are aware of the fact that unrestricted hunting by Indians can only lead to disaster for all. However, the rank and file hunters see this as a violation of their treaty rights, and do not realize the gravity of the situation."

1967 Joe Balla of Lethbridge became president in 1966. He was a very popular and colourful president of AFGA.

JOE BALLA President: 1966-69

Joe Balla, 38, executive editor of the Lethbridge Herald *was chosen as president of the Alberta Fish and Game Association at the 37th annual conference in Banff. At the time of his election, Balla had been on the association's executive for six years and a member of the association for the previous 20 years.*

He was a member of the Outdoor Writers of America and the Outdoor Writers of Canada and an ardent angler and hunter. Mr. Balla died in a tragic motor vehicle accident near Kipp, Alberta but it is not known when this occurred.

[Biography prepared from archival records by Duane Radford.]

COURTESY OF HENRY LEMBICZ
JOE BALLA

The 38th annual convention was held at the Macdonald Hotel in Edmonton in 1967, the year of Canada's centennial. At the time, Edmonton had the largest affiliated club in the AFGA, with approximately 3,500 members. Membership in the AFGA increased to over 17,000 in 1966, despite the fact that 17 clubs failed to either organize or to become affiliated with the parent organization that year.

Balla reported, "The Livestock Indemnity Fund, long an objective of this association became a reality in 1966. Approval for this fund came early in the new year. It is an objective that still has to be sold to the farmer and the rancher before it can be described as a measure for improvement in farmer-hunter relations in this province." This was a point well taken; however, the indemnity fund was seen as an important milestone because it demonstrated the sincerity of the AFGA in supporting legitimate compensation claims for shot dead livestock.

Eric Huestis, deputy minister of the Department of Lands and Forests, retired from office in 1965, being replaced by Dr. V.A. Wood, whom Balla reported as "...another friend in fish and game." Mr. Stuart Smith [who later obtained his PhD] initiated "...decentralization of some authority and the establishment of the [wildlife management] zoning system in the province with 'firmness and determination,'" according to Balla.

Smith was a hard-nosed, recently appointed director of the Fish and Wildlife Division who hailed from British Columbia. He was not afraid to make controversial decisions. Smith was also not above chastising officials in the Fish and Wildlife Division if he thought they were falling short of his expectations. He was probably the most outspoken of all directors in the history of the Fish and Wildlife Division, and had a reputation as a tough talking, hard-nosed administrator. Once, when Dr. Smith attended a meeting with fisheries branch biologists, who requested an audience with him over field identity dress so they could be better identified by the public, he gave them a tongue lashing. He said, "All you really need are extra trousers because the only thing you ever wear out are the asses in your pants!" They had a reputation as "windshield biologists" in some quarters. In fact, Dr. Bryant Bidgood, then head of the fisheries research section, even created a trophy called "The Windshield Biologist" award for the regional staff, which was presented on an irregular basis. [Co-author/editor Duane Radford received this dubious award in 1978.] Smith could be very intimidating but was seen as an important benefactor to the AFGA because he would stand up to Alberta's politicians as an advocate for sound management of fish and game in the province.

Dr. George Mitchell, chief game biologist for the Fish and Wildlife Division, who was credited by Balla for Alberta's antelope management program, resigned his position in 1965, taking a position as a professor at the University of Saskatchewan. Balla advised, "I do not believe that liaison and co-operation between our association and the government has been better at any time." He noted, however, that budgets were an issue for the Fish and Wildlife Division. Actually, budgets had been, and have always been, a chronic issue for this agency. Shortfalls in staff and budgets have plagued the division throughout its history and remain a concern to this day. Concerns were also expressed by Balla about impending changes in firearms legislation that were on the horizon, under the Criminal Code of Canada. The government was considering a licensing system program with user fees.

Chukar partridge were stocked in the badlands near Drumheller by the Sarcee Fish and Game Association. An unsuccessful attempt was made by the wildlife branch to bring pinnated grouse (greater prairie chicken) back to Alberta in 1966, after years of planning and deliberation, and Balla noted that another attempt would be made again in 1967.

The government finally acknowledged that the Bow River, downstream of Calgary, was polluted with sewage and ordered the City of Calgary to install secondary treatment facilities within two years. The AFGA deserves a lot of credit for drawing this threat to the attention of the public and eventually getting the government to take action and address the problem. Balla reported on what he perceived as a downhill slide in farmer-hunter relations. He recommended that the AFGA move its head office from Calgary to Edmonton to develop a much closer working relationship with the Farmer's Union of Alberta to address this issue, and also to establish a closer working relationship with government. He urged the membership to support this proposal and undertake the move at the earliest possible opportunity, requesting that the details of the move be left in the hands of the executive.

"I also ask that details regarding the disposition of Inglewood Bird Sanctuary also be left in the hands of the executive, with the provision that all clubs be kept informed about developments as they arise," he reported. "Vital to the betterment of this association will be the establishment of the zone system throughout the province that has already been outlined to you in newsletters," he added. "You will be hearing more about this in convention proceedings. But I ask that this convention give approval to the executive to carry out the zoning program to completion during 1967. Again with the provision that all clubs be kept informed as developments and proceedings arise." He closed his report by

advising that he thought a membership goal of 20,000 was within the grasp of the AFGA in 1967 with a "...little more effort on the part of all concerned."

The long-standing manager of the AFGA, Bruce Stewart, planned to resign in 1966. At the time of the convention details regarding his resignation had not been finalized but the delegates were asked to give the executive authority to hire a consulting firm to accept applications for the position of secretary-manager and report to the executive with their recommendations. "Decision on a new secretary-manager shall be made by committee consisting of past presidents, president and vice president," advised Balla.

Upland bird committee chair Gordon Merrick noted, "The general picture for all upland birds throughout the province is one of complete contrast. Large areas have shown startling declines and other areas have shown tremendous recovery." Merrick reported on very low numbers of pheasants in some areas, to the point there had been outcries for closed seasons for three or four years around Barons, Rosemary, Gem and Calgary, while other areas reported a tremendous recovery, or no birds. He also noted that the sharptail grouse cycle was inconsistent with a large increase in southern Alberta, while north of Claresholm they had practically disappeared. Ruffed grouse were reported in a downward cycle throughout Alberta. Ducks, geese and cranes had a large increase in numbers.

Merrick noted an interesting concept with regard to his committee's stand on pests: "Although we have a pest committee, the bird-game committees have always had something to say about those pests that prey on our game birds. The horned owl and snowy owl have always come in for a lot of scrutiny. In favour of the concept of a harvest, it is time the sportsman and others took a new view of our birds of prey." He asked that the provincial government enact legislation "to allow for the legitimate harvest of surplus birds of prey."

Ken Kultgen, access, grazing and wilderness committee chair, reported no serious access problems in the Green Zone where some logging roads had been previously closed to vehicles.

SUPPLIED

The chukar partridge.

"The establishment of more wilderness areas is imperative if we are to pass along to posterity a small glimpse of our past heritage," he reported. Kultgen suggested a trial wilderness area be set up encompassing badlands and grasslands and the river bottom of the Milk River in southeastern Alberta.

George Mitchell, pollution chair, reported that not much had changed on the pollution problem "for I have not received one written report from any member of the AFGA. I must admit, however," he continued, "that I saw a lot of pollution caused by so-called sportsmen when they threw their empty beer bottles, soft drink bottles, bait cans and fish heads and entrails into the lakes in the Hinton and Jasper Park country."

Mitchell reported, "Again on the credit side is the government's instructions and deadlines for the cities of Edmonton and Calgary to clear up their air and water pollution." He added, "Pollution of the air, land and water will only be kept to a minimum by an aroused public."

Good and welfare chair Dave Hunt noted, "The zoning system, which will be brought up at this convention, is another step towards the easing of district problems in relation with the government and is an important step forward in the operation of the association. When in operation, it should really fill a need that has been long-wanted."

Fish chair Bill Hamilton produced a very detailed report on fishing conditions throughout Alberta, based on information which had been provided by regional contacts throughout the province. He noted that John Anderson submitted a report, "in Pembina field, fishing and bathing abruptly ended in August of each year 1965 and 1966 with the release of waste oil from adjacent wells. Complaints were made to the local forestry officers. It is suggested that lax and dilatory attention by the field superintendents are at fault." In a report from Lorne Wilson of Calgary, Hamilton noted "East Bow still produces rainbow and cutthroat up to eight pounds most of which are unfit for human consumption."

COURTESY OF TRAVEL ALBERTA

Sunset at Footner Lake near High Level.

George Mayberry of Medicine Hat advised, "Local fish and wildlife officer (Bill MacDonald) held in great esteem in these parts thereby revealing a very high tone in relationship between this department and our association." Hamilton also spoke highly of Dr. Stu Smith, as had Dave Hunt in his report.

Big-game chair Vern Arnold reported, "As in the past number of years, it seems that our populations of big-game animals are on the decline, except possibly in remote instances." Arnold noted, "I must compliment the Fish & Wildlife Division for introducing the law whereby a person must be 50 yards from a vehicle before attempting to kill an antelope. It was noticed that this seemed to make more of a sport out of hunting this species, as well as the animals not being as wild and harassed as in previous years." Prior to 1967, it appears as though it was common practice for many hunters to chase antelope in vehicles and discharge firearms at them when they closed the range, a very dangerous, unsporting and unethical practice. There are modern-day opponents to this current law, however, who maintain that it may actually increase antelope wounding mortality for sportsmen who don't use vehicles to chase antelope, rather utilizing them as solid rests for a good shot.

Arnold also reported on a contentious issue regarding deer: "Some slight improvement in populations of mule deer was noticed in the grassland units this fall. However, with a three-day doe season, easily accessible areas were almost virtually cleaned out." This was a common complaint at the time as a result of the vulnerability of mule deer does in the open prairies of southeastern Alberta. The big-game committee did not submit any resolutions at the 1967 convention, although Arnold reported, "A problem definitely exists in Alberta with big-game populations, disease and indiscriminate control measures of some species."

Hunter training chair M.C. Lukas noted, "The hunter training program is praised by all who come in contact with it. Students who have completed the course, and the instructors, are enthusiastic about it."

Bob Hobbs, membership chair, reported, "For this Centennial year, I can think of no better project for this organization than the attainment of a membership of 20,000." Membership standings for the year ending Dec. 31, 1966 were 17,044, an increase of 495 from the total membership of 16,549 in 1965. The number of clubs was 83 in 1966 as compared to 91 in 1965.

The top five clubs in Alberta in 1966 were Edmonton (3,600), Lethbridge (1,515), Calgary (1,200), Medicine Hat (504), Red Deer (366) and Lloydminster (404).

Outgoing manager Bruce Stewart noted that for the first time the Grace Stewart Trophy would be presented to Mrs. Barbara Carr, as the Sports Lady of the Year.

HUNTER ETHICS
"A NEW APPROACH TO ACCESS"

- ALWAYS ASK LANDHOLDERS FOR PERMISSION TO HUNT
- DON'T LITTER
- CLOSE GATES
- DRIVE ON TRAILS ONLY
- RESPECT PRIVATE PROPERTY
- BE CAREFUL WITH FIRES
- OBSERVE ALL HUNTING REGULATIONS

Alberta
ENERGY AND
NATURAL RESOURCES
Fish and Wildlife Division

Fireweed on the Bow River.

1968-1977

Summary

Major issues: Increasing number of hunters and shrinking wildlife habitat; non-resident moose season in northern Alberta; pollution of lakes and streams; stream reclamation; roadside ditch burning; poor communications between clubs and head office; membership numbers; hunting prohibition on Crown grazing leases; Sunday hunting prohibition; predator control; fish hatchery production; change of the Alberta Fish and Game Association (AFGA) name; use of DDT; Bighorn hydroelectric dam on North Saskatchewan River; Swan Hills/Smoke Lake oil pollution; mule deer management in Porcupine Hills; abandoned strip mines; Athabasca River oil spill; use of all-terrain vehicles for hunting; hen pheasant season; poor trout survival in Tyrrell Lake.

Highlights:
1969 - Resolution to create a new political action committee; the AFGA head office moved to Edmonton from Calgary.
1970 - Sale of Inglewood Bird Sanctuary; wilderness act legislation; Cypress Hills Provincial Park gas lease; destruction of Athabasca Delta.
1971 - New AFGA logo; provincial shortfall in fish hatchery production.
1972 - Biological survey of Stauffer Creek [North Raven River].
1973 - Buck For Wildlife program announced; the *Land Surface Conservation Act*; opposition to proposed *Private Land Protection Act*; Outdoor Observer program; Eastern Slopes Policy public hearings.
1975 - Sponsorship of the AFGA wildlife awards.
1976 - Start of construction of Brooks Wildlife Centre; Operation Respect program; opposition to proposed federal firearms legislation, Bill C-83; construction of Red Deer River dam; new AFGA organizational structure.

Presidents: Joe Balla (1968), Gordon Peel (1969-71), Tom O'Keefe (1971-73), R. H. (Bob) Scammell (1973-75), Lewis T. (Budd) Traver (1975-77), A.G. (Tony) Ferguson (1977).

Membership: 22,933 [23,754]-1969; 21,536-1970; 19,847-1971; 19,580-1972; 19,616 [19,600]-1973; 18,599-1974; 22,651-1975; 24,501-1976; 24,494-1977.

The Canadian economy remained strong into the 1970s. The so-called baby boomer generation (those born after WWII, 1946-65) entered the job market, universities and colleges in record numbers. The United States' intervention into an Asian civil war (Vietnam, 1959-75) caused many baby boomers in that country to come to Canada to avoid the military draft.

In 1968 Pierre Trudeau replaced Lester Pearson as federal Liberal leader and prime minister. Trudeau held office through this decade. In Alberta, Ernest Manning of the Social Credit Party resigned as premier in December 1968, and was replaced by Social Credit's Harry Strom. However, Strom, after 36 years of Social Credit rule, lost an election in 1971 to Peter Lougheed of the Progressive Conservatives.

The oil boom in Alberta funded construction of schools, universities, hospitals and infrastructure across the province. Although many were beginning to see the negative effects of the boom on the environment and other renewable resources, governments were slow to react. New environmental organizations came on the scene to give voice to the concerns of the public.

The population of Alberta in 1971 was about 1.6 million; and the U.S. dollar was worth $5.12 in 2007 USD. The number of fishing licences sold in 1971-72 was 132,451; wildlife certificates, 159,934.

COURTESY OF RAY MAKOWECKI

Ray Makowecki (L) and Dan Green fishing for pike and walleye at Wabasca Lake, 1968.

1968 Joe Balla remained president. The 39th convention of the Alberta Fish and Game Association was held in the president's home town of Lethbridge at the El Rancho Motor Inn in 1968. The convention theme was "Aim for Clean Hits or Clean Misses." As was customary for this period of time, the president and secretary of each club affiliated with the parent association was listed in the yearbook; also listed were the various regional representatives, as well as the various newly elected zone officials. The new zones had come into effect in 1967 with the new boundaries corresponding with the regional boundaries of the Alberta Fish and Wildlife Division.

In 1967, the Fish and Wildlife Division issued new non-resident moose licences in northern Alberta, apparently on a first-come-first-served basis. As a result, delegates to the AFGA conference were on the warpath because they saw the licences as an ill-conceived free-for-all and give away to rich American hunters. Always the diplomat, Balla pleaded for the delegates' understanding, "May I ask for your restraint and moderation in dealing with this topic in resolution."

For the first time, a president questioned a resolution to increase the bounty on crows and magpies to 10 cents per pair of feet. Balla asked rhetorically: "Is this type of a resolution in keeping with our thinking today?" His remarks represented the first sign of a change in policy regarding crow and magpie control programs.

There were 67 resolutions at the 39th annual conference, a very heavy agenda. Several resolutions called for greater control over game seasons by biologists. These resolutions reflected concerns about apparent arbitrary decisions made by administrators in the fish and wildlife division, regardless of what the staff recommended, never mind the politicians. Other resolutions included: allowing Sunday shooting in the Green Zone, a long-standing issue within the AFGA; the teaching of wildlife conservation in the school curriculum; over-grazing of domestic stock in forest reserves; building more fish and game-bird hatcheries; and taking a stand against the federal gun-control legislation. Resolution 67 called for the creation of a political action committee, a first for the association and a sign of things to come as the association struggled with a move toward becoming more and more of a political lobby group.

Paul Morck of Sherwood Park was hired as the new manager of the AFGA. He replaced Bruce Stewart, who resigned because of health problems. The head office was finally moved from Calgary to Edmonton in 1968 after many years of debate. A new zoning system had been implemented for the AFGA in 1967, where clubs in certain geographical regions could pool their resources for projects and political action.

The government took action regarding farmer-hunter relations by printing new "Hunting by Permission Only" signs. In his report, Balla felt there appeared to be an improvement in farmer-hunter relations. He closed his report by challenging members to

COURTESY OF GORDON KERR

Dale Jacobson (L) and Lewis Ramstead releasing pheasants.

Resolution No. 41

There was a landmark Resolution No. 41 from the FISH COMMITTEE – "BE IT RESOLVED: that the AFGA asks the Government of Alberta to embark on an extensive stream rehabilitation program incorporating the following features:

1. Purchasing, leasing and fencing of stream banks wherever necessary to prevent erosion and to protect vegetation, especially where livestock are involved.
2. Rehabilitate stream banks to protect and shade water to keep temperatures as low as possible.
3. Encourage a beaver-management policy on all streams for the main purpose of improved fish culture.
4. Install and encourage the installation of approved obstructions in streams for the formation of pools and living areas for fish.
5. Embark on a coarse fish reduction program in certain designated streams, and restock these streams with the most desirable species of fish.
6. Use any and all means possible to stop the pollution of streams.

This resolution marked the beginning of an era that continues to this day regarding Alberta's stream and lake rehabilitation program involving stream bank fencing and riparian management. The fish and wildlife division supported this resolution; with the exception of No. 5; it was not possible to attempt limited control of coarse fish in streams without poisoning the whole stream."

Some of the key Fish and Wildlife Division personnel who pioneered this work were Mel Kraft and Carl Hunt initially working out of Red Deer, and later Rocky Mountain House and Edson, respectively. Ray Makowecki and Floyd Kunnas were also founding fisheries managers and technicians respectively, who spearheaded this work provincially under the formative Buck for Wildlife program out of Edmonton. They would later be joined by fisheries biologist Dave Borutski. They worked under the direction of Dr. Martin Paetz, Alberta's chief fisheries biologist at the time and dean of fisheries management in Alberta. Lorne Fitch, a fisheries biologist and land manager who worked out of Lethbridge, was later instrumental in establishing the award-winning Cows and Fish Program to protect riparian habitat throughout Alberta.

place special emphasis on youth involvement in the association, advising "Let me stress that you can hardly undertake a more worthwhile venture."

For the first time in the history of the AFGA, membership exceeded 18,000 in 1967, with the year end count being 18,170.

Soft-spoken bird-game chair Gordon Merrick advised, "There are several key steps our association must face before we can come of age. First we must handle an increase yearly in the numbers of hunters. Second, we must face the fact that the areas we can hunt are shrinking. Third, much of our wildlife is subject to shrinking habitat." He added, "With our new organization we must either get into the business of providing more habitat for the game we pursue and more areas for the hunters to pursue this game or we will find ourselves eventually as a fish and game movement without fish or game."

Big-game chair Vern Arnold was one of the most outstanding orators in the history of the AFGA. With his booming voice, he spoke about the controversial moose season in northern Alberta. "The department issued a $25.00 come-and-get-them season in the north this year for non-residents who didn't need guides or residents with them providing there were none available. About 10,000 licences were sold, and 30 percent obtained waivers to hunt by themselves. The moose season was critically close to over-population in some areas and it is hoped that the desired harvest was obtained where it was needed." Arnold also spoke about the impossible job of too few staff trying to manage Alberta's wildlife.

Pest-control chair J.D. Munro reported, "It almost seems a lost cause to mention predators today, not that they are becoming extinct but are being classed as trophy animals or beneficial birds. [Munro was referring to animals such as cougars and hawks and owls.] Our biologists lean this way and our head of game branch stated at our last convention he liked magpies. [This kind of remark would verge on blasphemy in 1967.] I cannot see how an introduced bird such as the magpie is required in our balance of nature. However, just keep in mind, fellows and gals, there are good magpies, the ones hanging on the fence wires. So let's put one on every wire and line them up and it's a good off-season sport, too."

David J. Hunt, good and welfare committee chair, reported, "The movement of the head office to Edmonton from the Inglewood property [in Calgary] has not only resulted in a more economic operation, but has also resulted in a more efficient operation of our association's business."

Lands and water conservation chair Henry Lembicz reported on the difficulty of dealing with a complacent government with regard to water and air pollution. "They appear to consider it as just a bad dream when they hear that the Bow River is dead biologically for many miles downstream [of Calgary]. The North Saskatchewan River is nearly dead biologically many miles along the north shore. The Red Deer River could be biologically dead by next spring for many miles downstream. Many miles of our trout streams are lost by the destruction of plant cover along stream banks and the injection of silt and pollutants. Air pollution in the cities of Calgary and Edmonton is a growing menace." At the time, it wasn't just the government that was complacent, it was also a majority of Albertans who didn't seem to think there were any problems with air or water pollution. As it turned out, they were living in a fool's paradise because many rivers were badly polluted, particularly with sewage.

> *N*oteworthy throughout the conference report was a series of slogans on the page bottoms: Alcohol and Gunpowder Don't Mix; Stop Spring Burning [burning of roadside ditches was very common in Alberta at the time, a practice which destroyed nesting habitat for many birds]; Conservation Courtesy Endorses Good Hunting; Stop Air Pollution; Be A Conservationist; The Farmer Is Your Friend; Aim For Clean Hits or Clean Misses; To Stop A Bill, Get It Stopped In Committee; Hunt With, Not For Your Boy; Say You Saw It In The AFGA Yearbook; Fire Destroys Game; Assist With Surveys; Respect The Property Owner; Is Your Partner Insured?; Remove Habitat – Lose Game; Pollution Kills; Leave The Campsite As You Found It; Need A Lesson In Hunting Manners?; Only You Can Prevent Forest Fires; Aim Only To Kill; Conservation Means Wise Use; The Game Hog Is A Thief; The Game Violator Is A Thief; Hunt Like a Gentleman; Take The Hunter Training Program; Game Is A Crop; Support The Advertisers.

1969 As a result of changes in the AFGA boundaries and the zone executive that were made in 1967, Joe Balla remained as president for another term in 1968 during this period of transition. Gordon Peel provided Balla's report (who was absent due to illness) at the 40th annual convention in the Palliser Hotel in Calgary. The theme of the annual convention was "Habitat is the Key."

A major milestone was announced at the conference: the AFGA membership goal of 20,000 was finally reached and surpassed! In 1969 the AFGA had the largest single increase in any single year since the organization was formed, a jump from 18,170 to 23,754 members. Peel noted, "Surely this is a good indication for

the future." The work of Art Miles, membership chairman, and Paul Morck, secretary manager, were singled out for praise in realizing the membership growth. The top five clubs in the AFGA were Edmonton (4,300), Calgary (2,463), Lethbridge (912), Lloydminster and District (468) and CFB Cold Lake (435). Peel noted that the change in the AFGA zones had been implemented and had shown excellent working results. A new committee became active in the AFGA in 1968, a political action committee. It was a harbinger of things to come and a major departure in policy in the AFGA, which had a long history of advocating quiet, back-room diplomacy and "good sportsmanship" in its dealings with government.

> *P*rovincial politics had long been dominated by the Social Credit (Socreds) government that enjoyed strong rural support in Alberta. Ernest Manning led the Socreds to seven consecutive election victories but the party was widely perceived among the populace as arrogant and complacent in the 1960s. Hardly anybody would actually admit they voted for the party, yet they always won big majorities. The 1967 election proved ominous for the party. Despite winning 55 of the 65 seats in the legislature, it won less than 45 percent of the popular vote, its lowest share of the popular vote since 1940. The Progressive Conservative party, led by Peter Lougheed of Calgary won six seats, mostly in Edmonton and Calgary, marking the start of a shift toward urban voters in Alberta politics. The rural-based Social Credit government was slow to adapt to the growing changes in Alberta as its two largest cities gained increasing influence. Premier Manning retired in 1968 and was replaced by Harry Strom, a farmer from southern Alberta. The Social Credit party was soundly defeated in the 1971 election, ending the Socreds 36-year rein on power.

Peel advised convention delegates that "…many people in all walks of life feel that our organization is a negative organization, resisting any and all change as a principle." This perception was totally inaccurate. The AFGA wanted non-renewable and renewable resources used wisely as a matter of principle, and was being unfairly branded as being against industry. The organization wanted to ensure that conservation of the provincial resources was practiced as a matter of policy, and it was certainly not against progress. Peel blasted the government, stating, "We have been and are concerned with some government attitudes. They have been for resource development on a single-purpose basis regardless of the

1969

Resolution No. 16. BE IT RESOLVED: "That the Department of Lands and Forests, wildlife branch, establish a 'habitat stamp.' That the said 'habitat stamp' be compulsory for all purchasers of deer and bird-game licences. That 'habitat stamp' be a minimum of $2. That revenues so derived be specifically directed toward a program of habitat retention and improvement, and that the government match the revenues thus derived. That such a program be so designated that it includes public access payments for land taken out of production, payments for non-productive areas and payment for cultivation of new plantings."
This landmark resolution was the genesis of Alberta's once-renowned Buck for Wildlife program.

long-range costs to other resources or the people of this province." This was one of the strongest public statements from a president of the AFGA recorded up to that point in time.

Secretary manager Paul Morck commented on an age-old AFGA issue: "The Alberta association appears now to have a smooth-flowing communication system, through the newsletter, news releases, minutes of meetings and general correspondence being sent to the clubs, but we have a problem. When requests are made by head office or by committee chairmen asking for replies, the communications system breaks down. The flow does not come back. 'You only get what you put in.' So I plead with our affiliated clubs to please, when you are asked to make reports or return questionnaires, take the time, as the results are for your benefit, your club's benefit and the benefit of the entire association." At the time, circulation of the AFGA's monthly newsletter was nearly 1,400. In addition to being sent to members of the provincial and regional executive, club presidents and secretaries, and affiliated clubs' executives, it was also sent to all newspapers, and radio and TV stations in Alberta.

Membership chair Art Miles commented on increases in membership that far exceeded their provincial targets because the association was perceived to be doing something and in the process was being recognized as an association of real sportsmen, conservationists and defenders of Alberta's outdoor heritage. "People are

COURTESY OF RAY MAKOWECKI

Clarence Makowecki (L) and Mike McCulloch gain access to the high mountain lakes to catch brook trout, 1969.

beginning to realize that, as time goes on, a great number of us are spending more time working to improve our outdoor heritage than we are hunting and fishing. We are becoming recognized as an association, that our aims and objectives and understanding are worthwhile. This, ladies and gentlemen, is something to be proud of."

Game-bird chair John Eisenhauer addressed issues related to enhancement and protection of upland game-bird habitat, noting, "The County of Mountain View is the first county to my knowledge to refuse the application for lease of a road allowance on the grounds 'that it would be better left for wildlife!'"

Access, grazing and wilderness chair Ken Kultgen reported that the province had established three wilderness areas but that more were needed in the Kananaskis and South Castle areas. He also reported on an age-old complaint, the posting of Crown grazing leases, as well as a trend towards a growing number of "No Hunting" and "No Trespassing" signs.

The usual gamut of resolutions was put forward at the annual conference, once again calling on the government to allow Sunday hunting of big game in the Green Zone, addition of outdoor education to the school curriculum, the need to hire more game guardians and biologists, as well as an increase in the bounty on crows and magpies to 10 cents per pair of legs.

Newly appointed pest-control chair Duncan Lloyd reported, "The past year was much the same as previous years, in that our membership was still divided into two schools of thought. One school striving to exterminate all predators; the other recognizing the need for a healthy predator population, but keeping in mind the need for control when necessary." In a significant change in thinking by such a chair, Lloyd subscribed to the latter policy because he claimed that studies had shown that predators had little or no effect on game populations where good habitat was available but that these same predators could reduce populations where the bird or animal was without cover. Lloyd went on to report that there was a large upsurge in the number of clubs entering the crow and magpie contest sponsored by the California Duck Hunter's Association, with members collecting over 30,000 pairs of feet,

Ray Makowecki (L), Barry Latham and Dmytro Makowecki fishing for yellow perch at Moose Lake, 1969.

able to remain at levels which existed 20 years ago. I can't see how it is possible to expect the game to adapt to this changing situation successfully enough to avoid some decrease in their numbers." He went on to suggest that to counter this trend many small wilderness areas be established that would be off-limits to any developments of any kind and closed to vehicular access. He also suggested, "Ideally, hunting would also be prohibited in these areas. If some such action is not taken at once, the game population will decrease." Anderson might well eat his words today, after the government created ecological reserves where hunting and fishing was prohibited, as well as wilderness parks where hunting was not permitted, to the angst of many members of the AFGA.

Fish chair Gene Scully advised, "Pollution is reducing all species in the Oldman River downstream from Fort Macleod. Rocky mountain whitefish, pickerel and goldeye are practically non-existent now at Lethbridge. It has been reported that where pollution has abated, native fish populations have begun to come back. It has been noticeable in the Red Deer River. Pollution control is vital to fishing management." Scully also reported on the lack of hatchery production in Alberta and a pilot project to stock coho salmon in Cold Lake which would later turn out to be a failure.

Pollution-control chair Henry Lembicz painted a bleak picture of polluted waters in various parts of Alberta. Zone 1 pollution chair John Shearer reported sewage entering the Oldman and South Saskatchewan rivers from commercial and private cattle feedlots adjacent to many watercourses, garbage dumps, cans, old cars, dead animals, poultry and refuse from sugar and vegetable processing plants. Zone 2 pol-

GORDON PEEL

lution chair Darwin Cronkhite reported on the newly formed Calgary Fish and Game Junior Conservation Association and how as a project these young people cleared 16 truck loads of garbage, trash and other refuse from six miles of the Elbow River. Overall conditions must have been pretty bad because Lembicz reported that he had prepared and presented a 14-page colour photo documentary on pollution to Prime Minister Pierre Elliot Trudeau.

more than 10 times the number collected the previous year. He had been requested to prepare a policy at a resolutions meeting which he outlined to the conference delegates as follows:

1. "All predator management falls under the jurisdiction of the Department of Lands and Forests. [At the time, Alberta Agriculture was responsible for predator control in the settled areas and the Department of Lands and Forests in the Green Zone.]
2. No organized provincial predator campaigns or bounty systems be initiated by the AFGA.
3. Additional regulations be added to the poison control acts.
4. The establishment of an educational program to enlighten ourselves more fully on predators.
5. The government of Alberta be requested to do more research and study on our predators."

Big-game hunting chair L. Anderson painted a rather gloomy forecast for wildlife in Alberta, lamenting mistakes made by biologists in overestimating elk numbers–issuing too many female permits–and causing "biological difficulties" to the herds; hunters and industrial developers equipping themselves with modern equipment to reach further into the wilderness and invading the back county in "rapidly increasing numbers." [At the time, most hunters used the family car for hunting trips and trucks were uncommon, with 4x4 vehicles being extremely rare and those few in existence being small Jeeps. Snowmobiles and trail bikes were just beginning to appear on the scene.] Anderson advised, "In view of this it would be a miracle if game populations were

One of the AFGA resolutions called for the Alberta government to establish a pollution-control centre to address issues related to air, water and land pollution, as well as a politically independent pollution control authority accompanied by a pollution control act. Such resolutions would be a clear sign that the AFGA officials did not trust the Social Credit government of the day to clean up an ever-growing pollution problem.

Doug Tradewell at Pitchimi Lake in the Caribou Mountains, late 1970.

For the first time, there was an ad in the back of the AFGA conference guide on various merchandise available from the head office in Edmonton: crests, game dishes, windshield stickers, ties, lapel pins, cuff links, etc. These were sold as revenue generators.

1970 Gordon Peel became president in 1969. He was a man of conviction with strong principles, just the sort of person the AFGA probably needed as a leader at the time because the association had virtually declared war on the Alberta government over its dismal environmental record. History would show that Gordon Peel was one of the great leaders of the AFGA in many

different capacities over the years he was involved with the association, despite the fact that he later distanced himself somewhat from the organization.

The 41st annual convention was held at the Macdonald Hotel in Edmonton. The convention theme was "Conservation or Desolation – Challenge of the '70s," a somber note on what possibly lay ahead for the province of Alberta as the provincial economy started to heat up.

Progressive Conservative Leader Peter Lougheed was the guest speaker at the awards banquet, with 375 people in attendance. Within 18 months, Lougheed would become the new premier of the province.

1970

Resolution No. 6   "BE IT RESOLVED: That the government review the policy of alternate opening and closing of streams to fishing, and institute a policy of controlling each stream on its own merit. BRIEF: Winter kill, in most smaller streams, is removing fish that could be harvested. Closing these streams alternate years may be wasting possible sport." This long-standing resolution once again carried.

Clean Up The Rivers And Air And Let Henry Lembicz Retire

"I'm very happy to get this recognition tonight. I would be happier if Red Deer could be called the cleanest city in North America."

This was the wish of the man selected by the Red Deer Fish and Game Association as its sportsman of the year for outstanding work against pollution.

Henry Lembicz of Red Deer received the award Friday during the final day of the two-day Sportsmen's Show from president R. H. Scammell.

In accepting the award in the Kinex Building, Mr. Lembicz said he had been involved in the fish and game association for many years and held most of the offices in the organization. He said he had thought of retiring and getting out but pollution wouldn't let him.

"I wish, somehow, that I would be able to retire from this job. I don't know how to get out. If you would help me get out by cleaning up the messes in our playgrounds and in our streets.

"If you are concerned about the water you use and put back in the stream then I could get out.

"It will be up to us to solve the problem (pollution). It is not they but we."

Mr. Scammell said, in announcing the award, to Mr. Lembicz: "In my opinion and in the opinion of many other people, he is one of the outstanding conservationists in Alberta and Canada."

Mr. Scammell said the award, which has been awarded for the past three years, is presented to an individual who is an outstanding conservationist or an exponent of the Alberta outdoors. He added the award has provincial implications.

Of Mr. Lembicz he added: "He's done a lot for the city and a lot for the country."

Mr. Scammell also presented the association's individual awards. In the hunting section, John Wink collected two awards, one for the white-tail deer and the other for moose. Alvin Arb picked up the mule deer award and Ron Vanson the Elk award.

In the fishing section, N. Larchyk captured the perch and brook trout awards; Bert deGroot, who now lives in Lethbridge, the rainbow trout award; Jerry Wiseman, the Brown trout award; Jim Ming, the Rocky Mountain whitefish award; the goldeye class went to Monty Hilton; the cutthroat trout award to Dale Roth and the Dolly Varden award was picked up by Jim Lodgson.

For the second successive night, large crowds wandered through the Kinex and Arena

LEMBICZ NAMED SPORTSMAN OF YEAR
. . . accepts award from R. H. Scammell, left.

COURTESY OF HENRY LEMBICZ

Mr. R.H. (Bob) Scammell (L) of the Red Deer Fish and Game Association presented Henry Lembicz with the Sportsman of the Year award for his outstanding work against pollution in 1970 at the annual Red Deer Sportsmen's Show.

During his speech, Peel noted that as the delegates started the 1970s they must increase their efforts to meet the challenge of a new decade. "Our affluent society today is making more and more demands on our outdoor environment. Some feel that to retain an affluent society it doesn't matter how much of our land is polluted and desolated," Peel remarked. He added, "We have wilderness areas in Alberta that aren't. They are in fact resource preserves and are fast being eroded." He went on to describe a number of threats to Alberta's great outdoors and the need for proper legislation to protect forest areas and watersheds from destructive activities.

Distinguished service awards were presented to the following members and clubs at the 41st annual convention: Bob Tanghe, Philip Hockhausen, Jim Pollock, Bill Svekla, Thorsby Fish and Game Association, Bob Scammell, Jim Skillen, Mr. and Mrs. E. Knapp and the St. Albert and District Fish and Game Association.

COURTESY OF TRAVEL ALBERTA

Duck at Carson Pegasus Provincial Park near Whitecourt.

For the first time, key policy statements of the AFGA were provided in the 41st annual convention yearbook. The policies had been in effect since the previous convention.

Policy Statement No. 1 – SUNDAY HUNTING
Policy Statement No. 2 - GOOD AND WELFARE
Policy Statement No. 3 - HUNTER TRAINING
Policy Statement No. 4 – MEMBERSHIP TRAINING
Policy Statement No. 5 – GRAZING DOMESTIC LIVESTOCK ON CROWN LANDS
Policy Statement No. 6 – ENFORCEMENT
Policy Statement No. 7 – STREAM REHABILITATION AND FISH HATCHERY
Policy Statement No. 8 – GAME BIRD FARMS
Policy Statement No. 9 – OPEN NUMBER
Policy Statement No. 10 – POLLUTION CONTROL
Policy Statement No. 11 – PEST CONTROL
Policy Statement No. 12 – THE GREATER PRAIRIE CHICKEN
Policy Statement No. 13 – WATER RESOURCES MINISTER
Policy Statement No. 14 – WILD RIVERS

As early as 1970, a resolution was presented to the AFGA to change its name to the Alberta Wildlife Federation, purportedly to encompass the broad aims and objects of the association and perhaps reduce confusion with the government Alberta Fish and Wildlife Division. As well, a new logo was to be developed. The resolution carried almost unanimously with only one opposed; there is no record, however, why the AFGA did not change its name in 1970 to the Alberta Wildlife Federation.

Another resolution called for the Department of Lands and Forests to institute a trout habitat stamp surcharge on fishing licences and the funds be used for the purchase and improvement of the banks and waters of trout streams and for the improvement of access and general habitat; the resolution carried. Conference delegates also addressed controversial resolutions such as a province-wide, limited, open season on female pheasants (carried); a spring trophy season for male sage grouse (defeated); and Sunday hunting of upland game birds in the Green Zone (carried). The delegates also unanimously carried a resolution to dispose of the Inglewood property in Calgary—the location of their former head office—to the city of Calgary for the sum of $15,000, plus an amount sufficient to pay the taxes. A condition of the sale was that the land was to remain as parkland, with a further condition that the association would erect a cairn or other suitable marker to suitably commemorate this land as the Jefferies Inglewood Sanctuary.

A key environmental resolution called for the federal government to ban the use, manufacture and importation of DDT (dichlorodiphenyltrichloroethane) and its metabolites. DDT was first registered in 1946 and used in Canada to control insect pests in crops as well as in domestic and industrial applications. DDT was never manufactured in Canada. In response to environmental and safety concerns, most uses of DDT were phased out by the mid-1970s. Registration of all remaining uses of DDT was discontinued in 1985 with the understanding that existing stocks would be sold, used or disposed of by Dec. 31 1990. After this date, any sale or use of DDT in Canada represented a violation of the *Pest Control Products Act*.

COURTESY OF RAY MAKOWECKI

Ray Makowecki waterfowl hunting in the Vegreville area, 1970.

Secretary manager Paul Morck reported that while membership was down for the second year in a row it still exceeded 20,000; membership was 22,933 in 1969. [Editor's note: This figure differs from other records that the membership was 23,754 in 1969.] Newsletter circulation had increased to 1,500.

Morck also reported, "One objective when I took this job was to find out whether the sportsmen in this province really believed in the multiple use talk that was all the vogue. Whether they did indeed want to turn the AFGA into a comprehensive conservation organization concerned with the total environment." This is the first record of a senior AFGA official mentioning such a change in policy that would be debated many times in the years ahead, as various environmental splinter groups emerged to do battle with the provincial and federal governments. Morck also wisely advised, "There is little point in our dealing solely with the fish and wildlife branch, when, as we constantly stress, all of the key decisions are being made in other resource departments."

Bird-game chair Don Hayden reported, "[The year] 1969 will long be remembered as the year you could not hunt pheasants and Hungarian partridge." Hayden described how Canadian Wildlife Service biologist Richard Fyfe had accidentally discovered mercury in the flesh of hawks, which are at the top of the food chain. The Alberta biologist then tested upland birds, confirmed mercury in their flesh, and recommended the season be closed. However, during subsequent tests it was discovered that the mercury contamination was not as serious as first believed and the pheasant season should not have been closed.

Pollution control chair Henry Lembicz also reported on the mercury issue: "At this time the mercury content in pheasants bombshell exploded with its mysteries. The mysteries are being unravelled with findings of mercury in a larger field and coming from many sources including air pollution." Lembicz advised, "In the year 1969 the exciting *Canada Water Act* was born." He concluded his report, "Let our progress NOT be such that there is nothing worthwhile left to live for." The reference being Alberta's (and Canada's) economic progress which was shifting more into mining and oil and gas after many years of being mainly dependent on agriculture.

Gladys Lembicz was awarded the Grace Stewart Lady of the Year trophy in 1970.

Fish chair Gene Scully continued with the same ominous message: "Under the name of 'progress' many of our formerly good trout fishing areas are being ruined. All along the eastern Rockies pollution of various kinds is taking its toll of fish in our streams. Unfortunately many of the most flagrant polluters are continuing unchecked. In some instances fines have been imposed but they were so light that they almost amounted to a licence to pollute. Some waterways have been visibly ruined for years to come." Scully also lamented: "The allocation of funds for the operation of the Fish and Wildlife Department is very disturbing. Almost no funds are available for research projects and very little for management." He reported on the stocking of 1.5 million rainbow trout in Tyrrell Lake south of Lethbridge near New Dayton, with funds raised by local sportsmen because government hatchery production could not keep up with the demand for stocked fish. Scully noted that "the response to the campaign is very gratifying, but it is a fact that some sportsmen are supplying good fishing for all fishermen."

Pest chair Duncan Lloyd reported: "For the second year in a row we have had a large increase in the number of crows and magpies entered in the contest sponsored by the California Duck Hunters' Association. The final figures show nearly 25,000 eggs and feet were collected. Although this contest is creating recreation for our members I do feel that the $500.00 in prize money could be put to better use. I ask, is this type of expenditure in keeping with our thinking of today?" Lloyd suggested pesticides were the greater enemy and the AFGA should face up to this issue.

Lewis T. (Budd) Traver reported on the introduction of a new hunter training program in 1969 when a new manual became available. At the 40th annual conference in 1969, Red Hasay, Alberta's hunter training and conservation officer, outlined various changes that were to be implemented but the government had been slow to make the necessary changes.

Big-game chair Gordon Cole reported, "There has been a great movement of hunting pressure into the north and central parts of Alberta and I have received many reports from these areas voicing complaints that were common several years ago in the south. Some of these are: too many hunters, not enough game, poor landowner relations and not enough enforcement. These have been common complaints over the years, only now they are being voiced louder and more often and from a much larger portion of the province." Cole said that steps should be taken to reduce hunting pressure and recommended several options: reduce in number of available tags, increase licence fees, implement a draw system and restrict motorized vehicles to built-up [graded] roads only.

Most of Archie Hogg's conference report was devoted to the emotional and controversial road-allowance closures in the Rocky View municipality. Hogg reported that William Lee of Edmonton, a department of highways engineer, found 142 illegally closed roads, 98 legally closed with 68 illegal closures along the Bow River.

---

*T*he AFGA faced many controversial issues in 1969: the Bighorn hydroelectric dam on the North Saskatchewan River, wilderness destruction, road allowance closures, mercury pollution and many others, according to Peel. In a prophetic closing during his conference address, Peel warned the delegates at the annual convention, "We have a challenge for the 70s. We know what the problems are, we know what we face should we fail." Sober words, indeed! The AFGA newsletter, Defending All Outdoors, was rife with content about the sorry state of pollution in Alberta at the time: coal strip mine scars at Forestburg and Wabamun; sewage in the Bow, Red Deer, Oldman and North Saskatchewan rivers; mercury in fish and wildlife. The AFGA members painted a bleak future for fish and game unless the government cleaned up its act.

Roy Ozanne, head of the AFGA policy committee, told of minimal response from clubs with regard to providing input to association policies in the September 1970 *Defending All Outdoors* newsletter. Ozanne took stock, however, after the failure of the government to follow public input into wilderness area hearings. "I know that considerable work was put into briefs on the wilderness act and I know that all of you must feel as I do. 'What a waste of our time and money' to have hearings all over Alberta and then completely ignore the whole thing."

Zone 6 chair Ivan Mosenko reported in the same newsletter that 14 briefs were presented at the *Grande Prairie Wilderness Act* hearings. The Hon. H.H. Sommerville, deputy minister of mines, was credited with the quote of the month—eligible for the boner of the month award according to the newsletter editor—for the following remarks made in the *Edmonton Journal*, Aug. 19, 1970: "One more look may ensure that no minerals worth extracting in the region exist. After that, the province could choose the next most economic alternative and turn the land into wilderness areas for recreation purposes." He was "thrilled" that the petroleum industry was willing to explore for oil and gas in proposed wilderness areas. The editor reported, "Despite the pleas of conservationists, outdoor enthusiasts, representatives of organized labour, support-

ers of national and provincial parks, farmer's representatives and many laymen to place a moratorium on these areas until the *Alberta Wilderness Act* becomes law next year, the department of mines and minerals went ahead and sold exploration leases on 210,000 acres of potential wilderness regions for a pittance: $28,538."

In the same newsletter, president Gordon Peel advised members of the great many controversial issues that the association had been involved in at the time: an accidental oil spill on the Athabasca River; government approval of a Cypress Hills Provincial Park gas lease for Canadian Montana Gas to enter the park and drill one well; Smoke Lake accidental oil spill; Swan Hills oil disaster area; wilderness hearings – "to name a few," in his words. Peel reported "The [Smoke Lake] culprit was prosecuted and fined $300 for contaminating a lake and killing 20,000 fish!! This type of penalty makes a laughingstock of our laws and is nothing more than a licence to pollute. Smoke Lake was stocked and you and I paid for that stocking, to say nothing of being robbed of the chance to enjoy a destroyed recreational resource."

Bob Scammell, vice president at large, issued a scathing report in the November 1970 *Defending All Outdoors* newsletter regarding Bill 106, *The Wilderness Act*: "Predictions? The next session of the legislature will pass Bill 106 exactly as is. Remember, the hammerheads we elect thought Bill 106 was too tough, and now have been astonished and perhaps frightened to find the public thinks it's not tough enough. Just watch how fast they pass that loophole-ridden piece of legislation now!"

---

*M*any long-time members of the AFGA have never forgiven the Social Credit government for betraying their organization following hearings into Bill 106, The Wilderness Act. The hearings occurred in several centres in the summer of 1970. The cynicism of these members would be reinforced when the government later amended the wilderness act legislation in the 1980s and created ecological reserves where hunting and fishing were banned.

The Social Credit government of 1970, that had been in power for more than 35 years, had grown totally out of touch with the electorate, distant and aloof. It was oblivious to public criticism. For example, Dr. J. Donovan Ross was the minister responsible for the fish and wildlife division at the time and was apparently not too keen about the wilderness bill. Individuals present at a meeting with the minister indicated that when discussion about the act occurred, Dr. Ross simply commented that "they" could have their wilderness areas but "they" [whoever "they" actually were] were not going to hunt in them. When the legislation was passed, it protected a few very small areas in the mountains and prohibited hunting within them. The public perception was that of a monarch standing on high throwing coins to the poor.

Gordon Peel reported in the December 1970 *Defending All Outdoors* newsletter that "Senator E.C. Manning, Alberta's former premier, speaking at the northern development conference, has accused the conservation movement of having a 'nature fetish.'" Talk about waving a red flag in front of the president of the AFGA who reported in this same newsletter, "We have seen the [ecological destruction of the] Athabasca Delta, [and] the Swan Hills, the

Athabasca River oil spill, the Freeman Lake oil spill, the destruction of the Mary Gregg Valley, and many others."

An interesting footnote in this newsletter reported, "In an effort to reduce mule deer herds in the South Porcupine Hills, the government opened all of zone 11 for doe hunting on Nov. 13th. The surplus applied only to the south part and instead of splitting the zone they opened it all, presumably to even out the pressure. In an effort to save what few mule deer does were left west of Claresholm and Nanton, the local ranchers, farmers and Fish and Game members worked together to post and patrol the area. Large yellow signs saying 'NO TRESPASSING NOVEMBER 13, 1970' were all over. This was a needed job well done and illustrates the need of more management by our game department." Old timers will recall the dreaded "doe days" when literally thousands of hunters, many from Lethbridge and Calgary, descended on the Porcupine Hills in what amounted to a veritable slaughter of mule deer does.

The early 1970s marked a beginning of a new era for the association, that of an advocate of environmental protection and better game management. Peel noted, "A fact that has become increasingly apparent is that our organization is being looked to for leadership when environmental damage appears imminent, individuals and other organizations are reporting their concerns to us in the hope that we can get some action."

COURTESY OF CAMROSE AND DISTRICT FISH AND GAME ASSOCIATION

Tom Tomaszewski (L), big-game chair of Camrose and District Fish and Game Association, and Robert Kozack show trophy white-tail scoring 170 7/8 in 1971. The white-tailed buck was taken by Robert.

---

*A*llen H. Bill, outdoor writer for the Calgary Herald, *passed away on Sept. 10, 1970. The editor of* Defending All Outdoors *reported, "Allen was a sincere conservationist and ally of the AFGA. With his passing he will be greatly missed by many. Floyd Stomstedt, President of the Alberta Wilderness Association wrote the following tribute to Bill in a letter to the editor in the* Calgary Herald:
"It is my wish to pay a public tribute to the late Allen Bill.
"Though most keenly felt by the outdoorsmen of Southern Alberta, the passing of this articulate gentleman of words is the loss of everyone, man, woman and child. This was a man with a deep understanding of the ever-growing problems facing mankind and his environment; an understanding which he attempted to convey to an apathetic public and disinterested government. His appreciation of nature and her wonders reached a plateau of respect claimed by too few humans today.
"I do hope that he finds that proverbial 'great fishing hole' and for the work that he did while he was here, I say, 'Thank you, Allen H. Bill.'"
Allen Bill has been credited by many as the venerable dean of Alberta's outdoor writers on a level with the late, great Jack O'Connor, Gun Editor of* Outdoor Life *magazine.*

Lewis T. (Budd) Traver reported in the November 1970 issue of *Defending All Outdoors* that the government had sacked the popular Department of Lands and Forests magazine: *ALBERTA – Lands, Forests, Parks and Wildlife.* According to Traver, "This interesting and informative magazine was first introduced in May 1958 by the late Hon. Norman Willmore who was then Minister of Lands and Forests. It was his desire that future issues of this magazine would enhance the liaison that must exist between the people and the government if an understanding of the department's duties in administering our renewable resources was to be reached." At the time, there were over 5,000 subscribers in the U.S. with a total cir-

culation of 18,000. Despite several attempts by officials in the fish and wildlife division to resurrect a similar magazine, none were successful.

1971   Gordon Peel remained as president of the AFGA. The theme of the 42nd annual convention was "Environment for Survival," a continuation of the concern for Alberta's environment which started in 1969. The convention was held at the Park Lane Hotel in Medicine Hat and hosted by the Medicine Hat Fish and Game Association in 1971. Hank Iwaniki, president of the Medicine Hat Fish and Game Association, opened the convention and welcomed delegates on behalf of the local clubs. Dr. Tag, a councillor for the city of Medicine Hat, gave a speech about pollution, a timely topic of the day. On behalf of the mayor, Dr. Tag welcomed delegates and guests to the convention. He noted that pollution of various sorts was one of the biggest problems of the day—pollution of air, streams and rivers—along the highways, contaminated food and pollution of the mind. He encouraged and congratulated delegates for being concerned about pollution, and in wanting to have a pollution-free society.

In his annual conference report, Peel noted, "The past year has produced many controversial situations and has shown us all what desolation can be created by accidental or careless developments." He cited an oil spill on the Athabasca River which showed how "...widespread and far-reaching an oil leak could become under existing regulations," and the occurrence of other spills "...where thousands of fish were destroyed and other wildlife affected." Peel delivered a hard-hitting address, painting a very bleak picture of environmental concerns, including industrial waste, abandoned car dumps, a lack of recycling in the province, the death of the Athabasca delta in Alberta [as a result of upstream hydroelectric developments at the Bennett Dam on the Peace River in British Columbia], and concerns over abandoned strip mines.

A new logo for the AFGA was created. There was a $100 prize and 60 percent went to Michelle Kure for drawing up the six-sided logo (in recognition of the six provincial zones), and 40 percent to Mike Lee, of Sherwood Park, whose colours were chosen to showcase the new logo.

Secretary manager Paul Morck reported, "Nineteen seventy may go down in history as the year in which we began to settle our account with our environment, the year in which we made our first down payment on our debt to our world." Membership stood at 21,536 in 1970.

Pollution-control chair Henry Lembicz started his address with the comment, "Looking back over the year 1970, it reflects a continual rise in the amount of work to be done in the pollution control field." He announced that during the year he gave presentations at many different service clubs and to students at the Red Deer Junior College on concerns related to pollution in Alberta. Lembicz signalled the start of an environmental awareness movement in Alberta that continues to this day.

The AFGA lobbying was starting to pay dividends. A Department of Environmental Improvement had been established to deal with pollution-control needs. The government passed the *Environment Conservation Act* which embodied the Environment Conservation Authority and a Conservation and Utilization Committee to address land-use policy issues. A new bill had been introduced to set up a Department of Environment in Alberta. Dr. Stuart B. Smith had left his position as director of the Fish and Wildlife Division and was now a member of the newly created

Environment Conservation Authority. Dr. Smith gave a speech at the convention on the role of this authority and their powers as outlined by the Alberta government. Smith reported that the authority had no legislative or statutory power whatsoever. This agency was established on Jan. 1, 1971 under the chair of Dr. Walter Trost.

Fish chair Hugh Scott Douglas reported, "In the south of the province an extremely successful project has been undertaken by the Tyrrell Lake Fishermen's Association, which is sponsored and supported by clubs in the area in stocking Tyrrell Lake with 1,106,800 rainbow trout." This was the first project of its kind in Alberta where the AFGA clubs raised money to pay for the costs of stocking trout, which were obtained from private hatcheries in the United States as a result of a lack of production capability in Alberta. A total of $29,875.80 was raised for the project which was matched by the provincial government. Tyrrell Lake had a reputation for phenomenal trout growth, the best of any lake in North America. Fels Balderson, well-known sportsman from Magrath, deserves a lot of credit for this project. The Magrath Rod and Gun Club spearheaded the project with clubs from Taber, Coaldale, Lethbridge, Fort Macleod, Warner, Milk River, Raymond and other individuals pitching in to help. Interestingly, in zone 2 the Calgary Hook and Hackle Club continued their previous policy of paying for a summer student to assist the Calgary fisheries biologists. Dennis Surrendi was hired to undertake studies on Cataract Creek west of Calgary. He would later become the assistant deputy minister of the Fish and Wildlife Division.

Calgary fisheries biologist Dennis MacDonald was undertaking studies on the potential ecological and recreational impact of a dam under consideration by the Alberta government on the Bow River downstream of Calgary. This was a noteworthy milestone, because up to this point in time no such studies had been done prior to construction of other dams in Alberta. Douglas reported, "Such an evaluation should be the prerequisite for the construction of any dam and should be made available to the public before the proposal reaches the detailed planning stage." Douglas also reported that the coho salmon stocked by the Alberta government in Cold Lake were believed to be doing well, "...and in excess of two pounds. in weight last September." [In the conference handbook the province of Alberta ad stated, "The 90,000 cohos planted in Cold Lake will probably qualify as the success story of the year

1972

Resolution	A resolution was carried at the annual convention that the parent body of the AFGA discontinue the offering of cash prizes for the destruction of pests or predators. This event marked a major turning point in policy for the association.
Resolution No. 40	"BE IT RESOLVED: That the general season on hen pheasants throughout the province be discontinued and that the practice of legal shooting of hens be confined to areas of excellent habitat and high pheasant populations where it can be demonstrated that no harm is done to the pheasant population by the practice of shooting hens, or to areas where there is heavy annual pheasant stocking to replace the losses from hunting." This controversial resolution was defeated.

for sport fishermen. Test netting has shown that they are thriving, so look for five- or six-pounders this summer."] This stocking project was intended to provide a salmon fishery to replace a collapsed lake trout fishery. However, it failed to establish a spawning run in the Medley River as had been hoped.

Big-game chair Gordon Cole reported, "Several changes in regulations last year were quite well accepted by hunters, for instance the MED tag [Moose, Elk, Deer] and a limited amount of snowmobile restrictions. Both of these changes have in part relieved pressure and saved wildlife." The MED tag allowed hunters to take one only moose, elk or deer and if it saved wildlife it did so because most hunters opted to try to shoot a moose or an elk (first) and waited until the last minute before they shot a deer, oftentimes getting skunked.

Parks, access, wilderness and grazing chair Archie Hogg reported that 800 people attended a public meeting in Calgary regarding commercial operations in designated wilderness areas; such was the level of public concern regarding wilderness areas legislation at the time.

It appeared as though lobbying by environmentalists had caught the attention of the government. In the January 1971 issue of *Defending All Outdoors*, the AFGA president Gordon Peel reported, "The federal and Alberta governments have become so concerned with environmental damage, they have both finally seen fit to recognize the fact that a problem exists and the trends of the past many years must be reversed. The announcements from both levels of government that Departments of Environmental Improvement are to be set up, is the most far reaching and encouraging news for conservationists in my memory." The president expressed concerns about an oil spill on the Athabasca River, oil and gas exploration activities near Kinuso and the death of the Athabasca delta. The AFGA representatives also attended public hearings regarding proposed wilderness area legislation, but as time would tell were to be double-crossed by a callous government over hunting and fishing prohibitions in these areas. Peel painted a picture of gloom and doom regarding the future of Alberta's environment but also made note that the governments of Alberta and Canada had recognized the problems and were finally taking steps to address concerns expressed by the AFGA. The decade was to see a proliferation of public hearings on all manner of activities that might impact Alberta's Fish and Wildlife and the environment.

COURTESY OF LILLA PFERSCHY

Lily pads on Island Lake.

In the April 1971 issue of Defending All Outdoors *newsletter, Bob Tanghe wrote a blistering letter to the editor, in which he stated, "After talking to several delegates, this has been a very confusing convention. The association wants resolutions but the delegates, which you never have seen before and will likely never see again, combined with the biologists to shoot them down.*

"We are supposed to be a conservation group, yet we encourage young people to shoot crows and magpies and also pay a bounty. Everything was rushed through, hardly any time for debate."

In the same newsletter, vice president at large Bob Scammell wrote: "The 42nd Annual Convention seems to me to have been one of the best. Congratulations are due those responsible for organizing the convention and congratulations are due all the delegates for making our new resolution procedure work so well in its first year. To hear the government officials at our convention tell it, they have adopted our ideas of the past five-odd years so completely that we might as well disband as a conservation group and take up talking about hunting and fishing again."

On Oct. 17, 1971 a cairn was unveiled in memory of the late G. M. (Marshall) Spargo, former secretary manager of the AFGA, 1925-62. [Editor's note: The years of Spargo's tenure in this position vary in the records, being reported as 1925-62 and 1930-62.] About 30 friends of Spargo attended the dedication ceremony. Representatives from the Department of Lands and Forests were Gordon Kerr, director, Fish and Wildlife Division, and Martin Paetz, chief fishery biologist. The cairn was erected at the Raven fish rearing ponds near Caroline, along the footpath at the top of the hill overlooking the large spring that supplies water for the rearing ponds. The cairn was made by Bruce Stewart who became secretary manager following the resignation of Spargo; Stewart also attended the unveiling date. The cairn was erected by Jack Munro, chairman zone 3, and Henry Lembicz.

COURTESY OF GORDON KERR

GORDON KERR

Road allowance closures in the municipality of Rocky View, west of Calgary, were a major bone of contention with members of the AFGA in the early 1970s. In the October 1971 *Defending All Outdoors* newsletter, past president Gordon Peel blasted municipal officials stating, "The age-old excuse that fishermen are littering adjacent land with refuse and beer bottles, shooting up machinery and buildings, is again being used. Again sportsmen are being made the scapegoat for vandals." Peel painted a dismal picture. "The fish and game clubs in the Calgary-Rocky View areas are fighting to prevent these closures. They are also supported by Archie Hogg, the Wildlife Division, the *Calgary Herald* and our old friend Allen Bill. [Bill was an outdoors columnist with the *Calgary Herald*.] If they don't win their fight, fishing on the Bow River west of Calgary will be a thing of the past. If it happens there it will happen all over the province."

In the same newsletter vice president Bob Scammell noted, "It is a rule of groups such as ours that pressure must be brought to bear on the government. Pressure groups can ill afford to engage in partisan politics for fear of guessing wrong. For reasons such as this, the AFGA has never—to my knowledge—favoured one party over another. Indeed, to do so would be ill-advised from an internal point of view as our 23,000 members must come from every possible part of the political spectrum."

In the November 1971 issue of *Defending All Outdoors*, newly elected vice president Tom O'Keefe lamented, "Sometime in the near future we are going to have to take a good look at our membership and make up our minds about whether or not many thousands of members are of value. How many of them are there just because a friend asked them for two bucks? How many are interested in insurance?"

1972 Tom J. O'Keefe became president of the AFGA in 1971.

THOMAS J. O'KEEFE: President 1971-73

Tom O'Keefe, one of the older of its living past presidents, is well-remembered to this day in the AFGA as a distinct character in an organization in which mavericks and characters are not unknown. In his active days with the organization, Tom was shrewd, practical, tough, and habitually said exactly what he meant in a booming voice, always with an edge to it.

Tom was born in Calgary on April 29, 1928 and went hunting as a kid with his lawyer father. Gordon Cummings, one of the AFGA's distinguished past presidents, took O'Keefe to his first Calgary Fish and Game

COURTESY OF JACK GRAHAM
TOM O'KEEFE

Association meeting. From there the story is similar to that of virtually anyone who has served as the AFGA president: working hard and holding many positions in the local club and ultimately serving as its president; also often, serving on the zone executive; then up and into many positions on the AFGA executive, then onward through the vice presidencies to the AFGA presidency.

O'Keefe's strong personality and character served the organization well during what were its golden years in terms of number of affiliated clubs and a total membership of around 25,000. "May you live in interesting times," goes the ominous proverb, and O'Keefe served as president in very interesting times indeed, during the dying days of the Social Credit government in Alberta and the rise of the Conservative government that persists to this day.

These were times of change, bringing immense challenges and opportunities for the AFGA, not the least of which was the establishment of the Fish and Wildlife Trust Fund, long on the organization's wish – and lobbying lists, and the Buck for Wildlife program, which achievements that are documented elsewhere in this history book, particularly in the Epilogue.

Tom travelled frequently between Calgary and Edmonton during his term as president, often stopping off at my house overnight en route, coming or going, sometimes both. The job took a great deal of time away from Tom's freelance

work in bankruptcy security, inventory and liquidation. He was concerned that the AFGA presidency was becoming so time-consuming that most of its members would never be able even to consider holding the job. One of Tom's major achievements was to convince the executive to retain Elmer Kure, himself a past president, in the capacity of executive assistant to future presidents.

Busy as he was, Tom O'Keefe could always find time to hunt. He was among the most ardent and dedicated hunters of all the AFGA presidents. His family verified for me the story I first heard years ago that Tom did not hold a job, just went hunting for the first two years of his marriage. Now that's ardour and dedication! He was never much of an angler, but was game. Once, after he and I attended a Federal-Provincial Wildlife Conference in St. John's, Newfoundland, we took a post-conference Atlantic salmon fishing trip on the Grand Codroy River. Fly fishing only was permitted on Newfoundland's salmon rivers. Tom had never fly fished, but actually cast himself into a hernia that had to be repaired on his return home.

It is hard to understand how I had forgotten, but many of the AFGA old-timers reminded me that Tom was a Cokeaholic, one of only two I have known, the other being Joe Clark, our former prime minister. Clarke kept his stash of Coke right under his bed in the rooming house he and I inhabited years ago in Edmonton while we attended U of A. O'Keefe would establish Coke caches along the trails he loved to hike and hunt in southwest Alberta. Tom actually took on Air Canada by phone and mail for serving only Pepsi on the many flights he had to take to discharge his duties to the AFGA and the Canadian Wildlife Federation.

In talking to the AFGA people about Tom, I would hear various versions of a story about how, at an annual conference, feisty Ann Morck, spouse of then-secretary manager Paul Morck, broke two of Tom's ribs with a Gordie Howe elbow, for referring either to her or another woman in the vicinity as a "broad." Here is the gospel according to Paul Morck: "Ann and I went to the Foremost club's banquet and were in our room with Tom. The Foremost boys sent a bottle of Lamb's rum (Tom's favourite) to the room for Ann and I. Tom reached over Ann's back and tried to grab the bottle. Ann backed up and pinned Tom to the wall. The Foremost hotel did not collapse, but did rattle. When they hit the wall, I guess Ann's shoulder got Tom in the ribs." Oh, those good old days and those Foremost boys and their band!

Age and ill health have now slowed and quieted Tom O'Keefe somewhat. He currently resides in Fountains of Mission seniors' home in southwest Calgary. He maintains a keen interest in current outdoors issues. When I last heard that voice, quieter now, but still with that edge, Tom was telling that it appeared to him that "they" were trying to make hunting so expensive, hard and complicated with too many regulations, etc., that everyone will just give it up and the government will not have to bother with it anymore.

[Biography prepared by Bob Scammell.]

Headlines in the February 1971 *Defending All Outdoors* newsletter typified concerns of the day: "Environmental Damage Recognized; Wilderness Threatened; Habitat is the Key; So Long Savanna Creek." It wasn't just the AFGA that had labelled the government as being incompetent. A district court judge found the government surface reclamation council "incompetent, careless or indifferent" in issuing three certificates in the Drumheller area. In the same issue of this newsletter there was a center fold photo spread of open sewers on the Bow River, iron tailings from the Coleman Collieries coal mine running into McGillivray Creek, air pollution from an asphalt plant north of Ellerslie, oil flaring west of Leduc, municipal garbage dumped at High Prairie and air pollution at Northwest Pulp and Power in Hinton.

SOCRED HOT-SEAT — These were the main participants in the provincial Social Credit League hot-seat panel at the Capri Motor Hotel last night. From the left, Anna Parkinson; Douglas Ure, representative of college interests; Henry Lembicz, for conservation; Frank Hazlett, for Unifarm and Socred leader Werner Schmidt, describing his plans for the party. Report is on Page 1.

Photo by Gary Kuiken

The AFGA had once again considered changing the name of their organization in 1970 to try to appeal to a broader range of members and attract them to their cause. They were concerned that the proliferation of new environmental groups might divide the ranks of the conservation movement and by division the AFGA would lose strength. However, past president Gordon Peel urged the delegates to retain the name of the AFGA and to bear the name with pride. In the February 1971 *Defending All Outdoors* newsletter, he reported: "Let us not again lose sight of what we are. The leopard cannot change his spots. But let us remain proud to represent the original conservationists in Alberta, the fishermen and hunters, and let our name remain the Alberta Fish and Game Association."

The 43rd annual convention was held at the Palliser Hotel in Calgary in 1972. The theme of the convention was "Conservation Education," a continuation of a trend started in 1970 due to concerns about the future of Alberta's environment. Mr. Bill Percy, president of the Calgary Fish and Game Association, opened the convention and welcomed delegates on behalf of the local clubs. Alderman Barbara Carr, on behalf of the mayor of Calgary, gave a welcoming address, noting that long before the general public became interested in conservation, the AFGA had worked to preserve natural areas and battled against the indiscriminate use of pesticides out of concern over their impact on wildlife.

Two cabinet ministers from the new Progressive Conservative government addressed the convention: Dr. Allan Warrack, Minister of Lands and Wildlife, and William Yurko, Minister of the Environment. Dr. Warrack noted that the water resources division had been transferred from the Department of Agriculture to the Department of Environment, and that the *Wilderness Areas Act* legislation would be finalized in the 1972 session of the legislature.

Mr. Yurko reported that the government planned to centralize the responsibility for pollution control and environmental management within the government itself. He also advised that a number of hearings were being scheduled through the Environmental Conservation Authority.

Distinguished service awards were presented at the convention to C.E. (Buster) Brown, Henry Lembicz, Camille Ethier (posthumously), Dwayne Erickson and Sulpetro Canada, as well as an honorary life membership to John Bobinec (posthumously).

Incoming president O'Keefe began where immediate past-president Gordon Peel left off, as a hard-nosed advocate for the protection of Alberta's environment who was not afraid to challenge members of the AFGA to get with the times. O'Keefe admonished the conference delegates saying, "The time is long past when all we had to be concerned about was whether the season opened on Friday or Saturday." The AFGA members were being caught up in the environmental protection movement whether they liked it or not; they really had no choice because of the rapid pace of industrial activity in Alberta and its impact on fish and game. O'Keefe predicted, "There are a number of specific problems that are going to have to be faced head-on during the next two or three years if we are even going to be able to hunt or fish."

The question of road closures and blanket prohibitions of hunting by municipal bodies was a major problem; the right to close public roads rested with the minister of Highways not the minister of Lands and Forests.

A well-organized "paid hunting" campaign had been launched by the Western Stock Growers' Association.

The government was organizing public hearings on various matters such as wilderness areas, strip mining, national parks and ski hills, which meant that more time had to be devoted to conservation issues by the AFGA executive to ensure their voice was heard.

These matters were all very real threats to the future of fish and game in Alberta. The members were being asked to voice their concerns, and not just rely on their executive to carry the message forward.

Secretary manager Paul Morck advised the AFGA delegates at the annual conference, "We are at a critical point in the fight for the survival of our environment and ecological existence, and the fish and game associations of this province and other provinces, must of necessity come to life as a unified body to protect our greatest natural resources, MAN AND HIS FUTURE!" Morck added, "During this past year we have made some gigantic steps towards developing a public awareness of environmental and wildlife issues, and the results are beginning to show. Government and industry are moving towards better managing of resources, towards legislation for the control of pollution, towards a greater awareness of the need to manage the environment on a much broader base than has been done previously." Membership stood at 19,847 in 1971.

Pollution-control chair Henry Lembicz was beginning to sound like a broken record in his annual conference reports. He reported aquatic life in the Red Deer River was dead downstream of Red Deer due to sewage pollution. On a discouraging note, he said he seldom received feedback from his zone counterparts.

Something was wrong with the AFGA in the early 1970s. Based on various records, the membership at large appeared apathetic and uncommunicative. When they did respond, they were overly critical of head office officials. For example, secretary manager Paul Morck reported that returns of a questionnaire included as part of the November 1971 newsletter were less than one percent.

Hunter training chair Don Chapman reported, "Participation in the hunter training program by fish and game clubs in 1971 may be summed up in two or three words. NOT VERY GOOD (DAMN POOR). We have some 116 affiliated clubs in Alberta. Twelve clubs held classes this year with 861 successful students. There were also six other clubs who were not able to conduct classes but still reported their participation. This means 18 clubs have an interest in the hunter training program, 15 percent of our total affiliation, with 10 percent of all the clubs doing instruction."

Hunting chair Gordon Cole reported, "You will notice again resolutions dealing with snowmobiles and other all-terrain vehicles. This has been and will continue to be one of the most apparent pressure factors on our big-game herds. It is our responsibility to police ourselves on these matters and come forward with some constructive suggestions on this situation." It was a sign of the times, and the use of ATVs for hunting remains an issue to this day.

Fish chair Hugh Scott Douglas had some bad news about Tyrrell Lake. "The stocking of Tyrrell Lake appears to have been largely unsuccessful. During a survey this year, 261 trout were netted, marked and released. A census was taken between May 22 and Sept. 30 when 1,411 trout were taken by 3,744 anglers averaging 11.9 hours per fish caught. The proportion of marked to unmarked fish would indicate that there are only about 6,000 trout in the lake, so that the vast majority of the fish stocked have disappeared – or there is an error in the census. However, fishing has been undoubtedly poor." Tyrrell Lake alkalinity was increasing due to a drought and lack of fresh water inflow, which appeared to be affecting survival of the stocked trout. The issue would be partially resolved in 1986 when the Tyrrell-Rush Lake Wetland for Tomorrow project was completed. The project allowed diversion of fresh water back into the lake, and stabilized lake levels. Douglas also reported, "In zone 2 the new sewage treatment plant in Calgary has had a very noticeable effect upon the Bow below the city and the river this year looks—and smells—better than I have seen it in the five years I have been fishing there."

New policy statements were introduced at the annual conference dealing with: water export; flooding across borders; wildlife control; feedlots; habitat retention; compensation to farmers and rancher landowners qualified hunters; and citizens' action. All were carried. Policy statements on snowmobiles and motorized vehicles were to be rewritten for the 1973 conference.

1973 Tom O'Keefe remained as president of the AFGA in 1972. Membership stood at 19,580 in 1972. In his president's report to the 44th annual convention held at the El Rancho Motor Hotel in Lethbridge in 1973, O'Keefe again took a hard line and advised the delegates, "The time has now arrived when we must make a fundamental decision and either change our aims and objects or else confine ourselves more closely to the subject that is the reason for our existence, that is fish and game." In an effort to make his point, he advised that while pollution and environmental problems were important, he felt that in future these problems should be of major concern to the AFGA only as they related specifically to the resources that were of concern to the organization.

The theme of the 44th annual conference was "Man and Resources." Mr. Gerry Pittman of the Lethbridge Fish and Game Association opened the conference and welcomed the delegates on behalf of his club and all of zone 1. [The 1973 event marked the first time it was called a "conference" as compared with the term "convention" used earlier.]

O'Keefe cited the divide and conquer rule of politics as an example of a failing of the AFGA to represent some of their fundamental needs to the government. He concluded, "Over the past few years hunters and fishermen have become the endangered species because of changes in public opinion and our lack of response to this change." The AFGA executive were able to arrange two meetings with the provincial cabinet in 1972, something that was to become less and less frequent in the years ahead as the political landscape changed in Alberta. O'Keefe cited a number of other issues with which members of the AFGA had to concern themselves: the proposed paving of the forestry trunk road, the spectre of paid hunting again rearing its head, access to Crown leased land, closing of road allowances, destruction of habitat, and draining and diversion of watercourses.

C. Burghardt, vice chair for habitat, presented a lengthy bird-game report on behalf of chairman Berg who was otherwise engaged in university studies. Burghardt reported on all manner of bird-game affairs, including the release of Merriam's turkeys by the Fort Macleod Fish and Game Association problems associated with a hen pheasant season.

Fish chair Hugh Scott Douglas reported, "The most important activity within the sphere of influence of the fish committee during the past year has been the study of Stauffer Creek [North Raven River] for which the association contributed $4,000." Douglas praised Dennis McDonald who had transferred from Calgary to Edmonton: "While in Calgary as a regional fisheries biologist, Dennis's influence was dominant, particularly in demolishing the pet theories of amateur biologists in the fish and game association and also complacency in government officials. I am sure that we are all delighted that the whole province will now have the benefit of Dennis' outspoken voice."

In a personal email to co-author/editor, Duane Radford, McDonald commented on the Stauffer Creek study: "Regarding Hugh's [Scott Douglas] remarks about the Stauffer Creek study being financed by the AFGA, members of the AFGA, most notably Bob Scammell, have indicated that this was the first time in Alberta that any sportsmen's organization had helped to finance

the hiring of technical support staff to assist the Fish and Wildlife Division in carrying out its work. To my knowledge, the first conservation organization in Alberta to do this was the Calgary Hook and Hackle Club who in 1970 provided funding to allow me to hire Dennis Surrendi to help conduct a preliminary biological investigation of Cataract Creek in the Highwood River drainage. This study was subsequently reported in *Preliminary Biological Investigation of Cataract Creek, Alberta with Special Reference to Its Wild and Scenic River Potential*, published in February 1974.

"Members of the AFGA approached me in 1971 and offered to finance a technical assistant to help with another study in the Calgary area but, as I was tied up with my MSc research on the Bow River, I suggested they contact Mel Kraft with their offer of support. I believe this resulted in the Stauffer Creek study."

McDonald thought he might get in hot water with the Social Credit government about comments he made concerning the government ruining Island Lake in the Crowsnest Pass by re-aligning Highway 3 through the middle of the lake to shave off a few yards of highway distance between Alberta and British Columbia. In the email message, referenced above, McDonald stated, "Regarding the affair of my criticizing the Socred government about several of their land-use activities including the Crowsnest Lake highway re-routing, I was a guest speaker in a symposium organized by the Bio-Sciences Society at the University of Alberta in 1970. Six months earlier in June 1969, the Government of Alberta published and widely distributed a glossy booklet titled *Alberta: A Land for Living*. In my presentation, I outlined quite a few government activities which were totally contradictory to making Alberta *A Land for Living* I pointed out if the government's present course didn't change dramatically in the years ahead, then the province would surely become 'Alberta: A Land for Leaving.' At the time I made my remarks, I was on educational leave from the government pursuing my MSc work. Nevertheless, the day after several Alberta papers ran a headline citing my remark, I was summoned by the Minister of Lands and Forests, Hon. J. Donovan Ross, to come to have a chat with him.

"As the Social Credit government was getting pretty worried about their chances for re-election, most Cabinet ministers seemed to be getting pretty sensitive about criticism of their track record. As I entered my meeting with the minister, I was pretty apprehensive about the outcome. I was met by a man who was one of the most understanding and caring politicians I have ever dealt with. Instead of immediately criticizing my actions and threatening to terminate my employment with the government (which I thought would be the case), he welcomed me into his office and asked me to explain the environmental concerns that prompted my comment about 'Alberta: A Land for Leaving.'

"He clearly wanted to gain a full appreciation of the context in which I made this remark. I outlined the concerns I had expressed in my presentation at the symposium which underpinned my fear about the province's future state of the environment. I was both shocked and delighted when he told me he understood and appreciated why I had said what I did. He said in his capacity as a Cabinet minister and as one who shared my concerns about Alberta's future, he intended to do all that was within his power

....and is this ever a super-fantastic book

COURTESY OF HENRY LEMBICZ

Jack Graham with the first AFGA trophy book.

In the September 1972 *Defending All Outdoors*, past president J.E. (Erle) Carr wrote about the anti-hunting movement that was developing in the United States with a warning about the implications for Canada. He stated, "Our license fees do not nearly cover the expense that is so necessary. Hence we have to ask for money from the government. Part of this money comes from people who do not hunt. Hence we are not paying our way. We are asking the non-hunter and the anti-hunter to pay part of the shot. Not quite fair or sportsmanlike, when you look at it, is it?" Carr subsequently elaborated on the 11 percent tax on sporting arms and ammunition that the United States enacted in 1937 (Pittman Robertson Federal Aid in Wildlife Restoration Bill), where the proceeds go to approved wildlife restoration programs. He suggested this sort of program could benefit Albertans and Canada's wildlife.

Gordon Kerr, then director of the Fish and Wildlife Division, gave a presentation at the annual conference, noting that in 1972 a five-man team had been formed to do habitat work, the first team of its kind in Alberta. Some of the items this team had been working on were eastern slopes hearings, mineral sales review, new technologies in measuring habitat and base line data on streams, experimental labs for pheasants and a trout stream habitat study on Stauffer Creek [North Raven River].

The 1970s were productive and formative years for the Fish and Wildlife Division as the organization flexed its muscles for the first time to protect and maintain habitat. However, in some ways the decade was seen as the beginning of a long decline. Governments (municipal and provincial) perceived the division to be opposed to economic progress, especially in terms of protecting and enhancing habitats. This came to a head in the 1990s when the Klein government ensured that government got out of the way of business removing many regulatory impediments.

In his presidential pre-nomination speech to the delegates entitled "Good Old Days at the last frontier," R.H. (Bob) Scammell (never one to mince words) advised, "In the past five years or so, my growing concern has been this: that at time when our membership is stuck at 20-odd thousand, and at a time when our executive seems to have only a fuzzy idea of what the priorities of the AFGA should be, the very existence of the sport of hunting is endangered." He lamented the decline in numbers of hunters and the growing specter of the anti-hunting movement. He then chastised the delegates, advising that the major reason for bad landowner-hunter relations was because "...90 percent – and, no, I will not be a hypocrite; I shall include many people in this room – 90 percent of

to change the course of where the province was headed environmentally. He sincerely thanked me for giving him 'a wake-up call.' I left his office elated at the experience I'd just gone through and renewed in my determination to use my career to make whatever difference I could to help ensure that Alberta would truly become 'a land for living.' There was no mention by the minister or my superiors about any disciplinary action being warranted nor was any taken!"

Long-time hunting chair Gordon Cole of Etzikom resigned his position in the spring of 1973 due to domestic and business pressures.

Dr. Allan Warrack remained as minister of the Department of Lands and Forests in 1973 and attended the annual the AFGA conference. Warrack was one of the most respected ministers responsible for fish and wildlife in Alberta. He had a keen and genuine interest in his portfolio. The atmosphere was absolutely electric when he announced that he would support a long-standing AFGA resolution at the annual conference in Lethbridge to tax anglers and hunters to pay for important fish and wildlife habitat protection, enhancement and development. Warrack coined the new initiative "Buck for Wildlife" program in keeping with the initial $1 surcharge on fishing and hunting licences. The program would become a major success story in fish and wildlife management that would endure until the Alberta Conservation Association (ACA) was established in 1997.

all hunters never ever ask permission [to hunt]." In his wisdom, he admonished the delegates to reverse the declining trend in hunters and fishers by taking direct action at the local level. "Ladies and gentlemen, our clubs are going to have to stop grunting and groaning to beat each other at spending their money on more and more obscure projects and get back to hunting and fishing and promoting and propagating the skills involved." He went on to say "…we must build a better hunter from scratch and put thousands of his like in the field. Should I be your president, my aim would be to turn the considerable power of this organization to the goal of ensuring that now and in the future people will be able to hunt and fish in an honourable, sportsmanlike manner and be respected for it here, in Alberta, and not on some far-flung frontier."

Mr. Harold Rhodes, new vice president at large, was presented with a distinguished service recognition certificate by past president Gordon Peel at the conference. Other AFGA members presented with distinguished services awards: Gary Cooper, Dave Simpson, John Shearer, Douglas Belyea, Bill Derkach, Jim Roberts, Lorne Johnson, William Lang, Henry Hodgins, Jim Heather and Marcel Droessaert.

Of interest was the release of 30 wild turkeys in the valley of the Milk River in the autumn of 1972, through the combined efforts of the Southern Alberta Outdoorsmen club (from Milk River, Warner and Coutts) and the Foremost Fish and Game Association, in the hopes of establishing this species to add to the game birds in the area.

1974 R.H. (Bob) Scammell, a witty and affable lawyer from Red Deer, became president of the AFGA in 1973; Scammell was born in Edmonton and moved to Brooks at age two.

R.H. (BOB) SCAMMELL Q.C. President: 1973-74

I was all but born into the AFGA. We lived in Brooks, perhaps Alberta's greatest beneficiary of the pheasant and Hungarian partridge stocking initiatives of our pioneers of the sportsmen's movement, the ancestors of the AFGA.

When World War II ended and we were seeing the bountiful results of those early stockings, I was seven or eight and J.A. (Jim) McGhee, CPR station-master in Brooks, was also the AFGA president in 1945–46. McGhee was a poker-playing and hunting buddy of my dad who, over the years, served on the executive of the Brooks Fish and Game Association. Without straining too hard I could eavesdrop important stuff about the good and welfare of fish and game in Alberta and how one went about achieving action and results.

When I returned from Dalhousie Law School in Halifax in 1962 and started my articles with a law firm in Red Deer, one of the senior partners all but

COURTESY OF BOB SCAMMELL
BOB SCAMMELL

ordered me to join and work for a club as a way to meet people and clients. Considering my background, it was more than natural that I should choose the Red Deer Fish and Game Association which had far more members—few that were lawyers—than any service club in the city. By 1970 I was club president and sometime in there served as zone 3 chairman.

My first AFGA convention was in Banff, in 1966 as I recall, and I have never missed one since. Fairly quickly I was elected to the AFGA executive, particularly as chairman of that wonderful catch-all good and welfare committee we don't have any more. In the late 60s or early 70s I took a run at one of the two AFGA vice president positions. But apparently the delegates wanted someone older than I was and from the north, so I was defeated.

It took less than a year for my opponent—one of those flashes in the pan with which the association was afflicted more in those days than now—to fizzle out. I stayed the course, worked hard, and at the next convention was elected a vice president. In 1973 I was elected president, at 36 the youngest president we had ever had, and was re-elected at the 1974 convention.

Two AFGA achievements during my two years as president stand out: our work in getting the Buck For Wildlife program up and running and the wide influence and good public relations we achieved through the hiring of Elmer Kure as our first and only presidential executive assistant. We even "rented," or seconded Elmer to fish and wildlife and his careful work with the landowners went a long way to the achievement of the first Buck For Wildlife project, the North Raven River rehabilitation, to this day a North American model for trout stream reclamations on private land.

During my presidential term we worked toward and helped to achieve the end of the municipality and county no-shooting bylaws and achieved the defeat and end of the so-called Private Land Protection Act, which really intended to convert public into private land and permit the leaseholders to charge fees to hunters and anglers.

We worked hard at the land use forum and the old Environment Conservation Authority's east slopes hearings and contributed substantially to a hunter training course that could eventually become mandatory for first-time hunters. Considerable travelling and hard work went into the reorganization and refinancing of the Canadian Wildlife Federation. In our spare time, and with the hard work of our secretary manager, Paul Morck, we also made a lot of money back then from our annual conservation lottery.

The 2007 conference was my 41st straight. At that conference, I continued my practice of giving my contact numbers to each new president and inviting them to call if they ever needed to talk. I offered to do anything for the AFGA that didn't involve going to meetings.

Many presidents called. The one I remember most was when Vern McIntosh called wondering what we could do about the plan of the government to convert the $12 million or so of hunters' and anglers' money in the wildlife habitat trust fund into (the government's) general revenue (account). "Tell them we'll sue them for breach of trust," I advised. Apparently the government lawyers knew we had a "slam dunk" case, because the Alberta Conservation Authority (ACA) resulted. Whether or not you consider the ACA a good thing, "our" money is not in General Revenue at the tender mercies of politicians.

Three years ago I made one exception, and have been attending many meetings with some other past presidents and life members on the "Heritage 100" Committee.

[Biography prepared by R. H. (Bob) Scammell.]

The 45th annual conference was held at the Edmonton Inn in Edmonton in 1974. The conference theme was "Conservation and Politics… Wildlife Never Votes." The Edmonton area clubs helped organize the conference, chaired by Jack Graham of the Edmonton Fish and Game Association. Jack's wife Phyllis Graham was chairwoman of the Ladies Day Program.

The host clubs were: Edmonton Fish and Game Association, Sherwood Park, Edmonton City Police Fish and Game Association, Communications Employees Fish and Game Association (Edmonton), St. Albert and District, Leduc, Griesbach-Namao, Devon, Stony Plain and Fort Saskatchewan associations. Attending the 45th annual conference were 232 delegates and guests, 16 observers and four members of the media for a grand total of 252. Acting deputy mayor Terry Kavanagh welcomed the delegates to Edmonton and stressed that the city as well as the AFGA must have concern for the environment.

Distinguished service recognition awards were presented at the conference to the Vegreville Fish and Game Association, Les and Gertie Rhodes, Sam Smolyk, Jack MacIntosh, Lois Brown, John MacLeod, Garnet Anthony, the Edmonton Real Estate Board and J.O. Smith.

The Golden Egg award was presented to Dr. Allan Warrack for politically closing the pheasant season. The Reminder Award was presented to Gordon Kerr, director of the Fish and Wildlife Division, to remind him to remind the minister that he shouldn't close the pheasant season because of chain reactions.

Scammell's term as president was characterized by a business-like, no-nonsense approach where the AFGA made considerable progress. Never one to suffer fools gladly, he had no time for non-sense. In his conference address in 1974 he noted that the Buck for Wildlife program was off the ground with $280,000 appropriated by the Alberta government as seed money from general revenue for the first year of operation, and approximately $220,000 worth of projects already underway.

The pressures on Alberta's fish and wildlife continued to increase during the mid 70s. An important piece of government legislation came into force in 1973: *The Land Surface Conservation Act* to address mining operations and reclamation in Alberta. It was hailed as a model for its day and the AFGA took credit for being one of the first organizations to recommend just such legislation to the Alberta government. The AFGA fought a private member's bill, *Private Land Protection Act*, sponsored by the Honourable Gordon Stromberg, MLA for Camrose. The act purported to give grazing lease holders the right to prevent people from trespassing upon such Crown land, and further, to charge people a fee for trespassing on that Crown land. The bill fortunately died on the legislative order paper. Scammell cautioned the AFGA members

COURTESY OF GORDON KERR

David (L) and Gordon Kerr at Winefred Lake with a catch of northern pike, 1975.

to keep their guard up for similar legislation in the future which would almost certainly arise again.

Another success story was the launch of a government program called the Outdoor Observer program to curtail poaching. It was an offshoot of a civilian wildlife patrol program, recommended by the AFGA. Scammell noted that two former AFGA presidents had gone on to become president of the national Canadian Wildlife Federation, a tribute to the respect for such AFGA past presidents on the national scene. Of considerable interest was the number of the AFGA representatives on various government committees: advisory council to the Minister of Land and Forests,

1975

Resolution No. 29   "BE IT RESOLVED: That the Fish and Wildlife Division of the Department of Lands and Forests consider the licensing of party hunters. BRIEF: The practice of party hunting is a recognized fact although it is presently illegal."
The resolution was defeated.

Carson Pegasus Provincial Park near Whitecourt.

public advisory council of the Environmental Conservation Authority, Alberta government committee on snowmobile regulations, Alberta environmental research trust, Cooking Lake management committee and the public advisory committee on the Red Deer River dam. Scammell also noted the many other situations where the AFGA representatives met with government officials on matters dealing with no-shooting bylaws.

At hearings concerning commercial fishing in Alberta, Scammell advised that the AFGA was accused "...by various other persons present as simply having too much influence," a back-handed compliment about the lobby power of the AFGA. Apparently many people commented that they had never seen the AFGA getting such good press as it received during 1973. The AFGA representatives made submissions at every hearing of the Eastern Slopes Policy in 1973; these were often very stormy and heated deliberations. Public hearings were a hallmark of the early Progressive Conservative government of Premier Peter Lougheed, which used them to good effect, encouraging the public to become part of the decision-making process.

Elmer Kure, the AFGA public relations director, was singled out for praise by Scammell for an outstanding job during the previous year and for being able to not only react to ongoing issues but actually get ahead of many emerging issues. He made a strong pitch that Kure's job be made a paid position. Scammell also noted that the AFGA membership was "stuck" at the same level as it had been before. He recommended the organization consider a full-time paid employee as membership services director "...to assist the clubs in putting their membership on an organized basis." Scammell had an even bigger agenda when it came to challenging the members to embark on a hunter training program at the provincial level. He closed his report by advising "...I would have to say that the past year has been a thundering success for our association..."

Curt P. Smith passed away suddenly in 1973. Smith was a conservationist, farmer, administrator and teacher. He served as president of the AFGA, 17 years as a farmer and 10 years as administrator of Elk Island National Park and as director of fish and wildlife for the province of Alberta. He was a life member of the AFGA.

Secretary manager Paul Morck reported "The six issues of *Defending All Outdoors* during 1973 averaged 9,100 circulation. During the year many complimentary remarks have been received

Big Horn Falls near Nordegg.

on how the newsletter has greatly improved." The clubs purchased the newsletter for their members. The AFGA membership stood at 19,616 in 1973.

Newly appointed hunting chair John Eglinski reported, "With the association's support I've arranged to put some of our own fish and game members on big-game surveys and game counts this winter (December, January, February). In this way we'll be able to observe first-hand just what our big-game situation is." This was a first for the AFGA, which didn't always trust the game-count results obtained from the wildlife branch. Fly surveys would be an important learning experience for many.

Pollution chair Cecil Ross reported on a chronic issue experienced by many provincial chairs, the lack of feedback from clubs. He sent out two letters to clubs asking for co-operation to make newsletter contributions but never received any replies. He also reported on the successful cleanup of litter along the Bow River by the Calgary Fish and Game Association

Hunter-farmer relations chair Elmer Schulz advised, "A compulsory hunter training program with emphasis on the recognition of land owners rights, as part of the course, is certainly needed. The old hunter training course lacked much in this regard."

Zone 4 chair Bob Tanghe reported, "Now that the decision has been made to split zone 4-5 into separate zones, it is time for some of the zone 4 clubs to rejuvenate and re-activate themselves; to name a few, Fox Creek, Whitecourt, Hinton, Grande Cache. We hardly ever hear from them or see any delegates at zone meetings."

Zone 6 chair D. Keith Moran advised, "In 1973, Operation Elk Transplant moved 55 animals from Jasper National Park to the Clear Hills, an area north of Fairview and west of Manning."

Gene Scully, fish chair, carried on with the poor communications theme mentioned by other members of the executive. "It is difficult to give a comprehensive report on fishing in Alberta because of the lack of information from chairmen of clubs and zones. All was quiet, outside of a report from the Alder Flats Fish and Game Association and some correspondence and talks with Tim Rutter, vice chairman."

Parks and wilderness chair Nils Kvisle advised, "Under the *Wilderness Act* of 1971 and as amended in 1972, three wilderness areas have been set up: Ghost River, 59 square miles; Siffleur, 159 square miles; and White Goat, 172 square miles. The maximum size of any given wilderness area was arbitrarily set at 144 square miles. [Note: This arbitrary size mentioned by Kvisle is less than the area of two wilderness areas.] At present, fishing and hunting are not permitted in wilderness areas. The Willmore Wilderness Area has somehow escaped classification. As exploration, mining and hunting are permitted, it neither a park nor a wilderness."

Scammell's presidential diary for 1973 bears testament to his meticulous nature and business-like approach. Entries are typed for each day he was engaged in important business, noting the particulars of phone calls, meetings and correspondence throughout the year. Among the notations, on March 21, 1973 he wrote: "A black day. Gordon Peel's written resignation received, and the spokesman of the Jasper Club advises Jasper is doing just fine without the AFGA notwithstanding that the delegates at our annual convention voted to scrap the policy, written or otherwise, that the AFGA would not hold a major function in a national park. The trouble with democracy is that nobody believes it should apply to them, and in their own personal interests the right way is to have their own way. So we get into disputes over 'unwritten' policy and lose a valuable man and a valuable club. Somehow everyone—the AFGA included—loses." Scammell would later write in *Defending All Outdoors* (1973) that Gordon Peel (past president) stomped out of a meeting where this matter was on the agenda, and neither he nor the Jasper club had been seen around the AFGA conferences since. On May 14, 1973 Scammell wrote in his diary, "Wrote a letter refusing the Jasper Fish and Game Association permission to incorporate under that name and received with regret the resignation of Gordon Cole as chairman of the big game committee."

Scammell wrote about the nature of provincial fish and game associations in *Defending All Outdoors* (1973): "Externally, provincial fish and game associations are and must be non-partisan pressure groups, skilled in the arts of political judo, of persuading and working with the government in power, whatever its stripes; internally these groups are a seething brew of intrigue, factionalism and local and regional power plays. It is an unwise president or aspirant to the position of president of one of these groups who ever forgets the distinction."

In the same newsletter he noted: "One day in particular is worth recounting. There had been a long siege of cleaning up odds and ends for the AFGA and on Oct. 22, 1973, I went into my office full of determination to accomplish many things long neglected for many clients. Then, as they say in stage directions, the phone rang. And rang and rang. For about an hour I talked with three high-ranking officials in the Department of Lands and Forests who were frantic they would all soon have no jobs as they had convinced themselves that a private member's bill then before the house [legislature], the *Private Land Protection Act*, was going to pass. This odious little bill, the hobby-horse of the Western Stockgrower's Association and one MLA, had as its main gimmick the turning of public land into private and permitting ranchers and farmers to charge people fees to hunt, not only on their deeded land but on land they only rented from the Crown."

After spending the rest of the working day drafting letters to Dr. Allan Warrack, Minister of Lands and Forests, a general letter to all MLAs, and Bob Clark, leader of the opposition, Scammell worked on his clients' affairs until midnight. Scammell never got as much as a word of thanks from the government officials who implored him to "do something" that October day. He philosophized, "But I took the job and expected no thanks."

1975 R. H. (Bob) Scammell remained as president of the AFGA in 1974. In his farewell address at the 1975 conference, he said of his two years as president of the AFGA, "Being your president is an experience I would not have wished on my worst enemy, but I would not have missed it for the world." He received a standing ovation.

COURTESY OF THE AFGA

Fishing derby for the physically disabled. Edmonton Police Department Fish and Game Association project started in 1977 and is still in effect today.

Scammell began his president's report on a sour note, "I might as well deal first with the depressing aspect of the past year in the hopes that all of you will have forgotten by the time I get to the end of the report. When I first became president of the association I said that membership is stuck at around 20,000 and I would have to say that, at best, the membership is still stuck and that probably what it is really doing is slipping." The membership for 1973 was 19,600. Had the executive been able to recruit a qualified full-time membership chair they would have done so, but none were apparently deemed suitable. The association was in good shape financially, however, and some clubs exceeded their membership target goals.

The theme of the 46th annual conference, which was held at the Memorial Centre in Red Deer in 1975, was "Stop the Strippers," a reference to the spectre of strip mining for coal. Mr. Lloyd Graff of the Red Deer Fish and Game Association and chairman of this conference welcomed all delegates and guests. Mayor McGregor of Red Deer welcomed everyone to the city of Red Deer.

Distinguished service recognition awards were presented to the following at the conference: Harold Janecke, Lorna Smith, Doug Belyea, Gwen Horning, Russell Forster, Derk Lundy, Vic Scheurman, Bob McPhee, Penny Ross, Don Appleby, Bruce Thomas, Ed Tully, Sam and Brenda Lachman, Jack and Phyllis Graham, Jim Robison, Orest Schur, Jack Mohr, Keith Moran, Clarke Jensen, Pat Bradley, Fred Walker, Irna and William Hrycyk, Environment Conservation Authority, Wendy MacLeod (secretary).

Gordon Kerr, director of the Fish and Wildlife Division, once again made a presentation at the annual conference. He spoke about the start-up phase of the Buck for Wildlife program: "Up till now most projects have been generated through the Fish and Wildlife Division. The division is now requesting the help of sportsmen. All sportsmen should take their suggestions for projects to regional Fish and Wildlife personnel for consideration." On behalf of the AFGA, lottery fund disposition committee chairman Jim Robison presented Gordon Kerr with a cheque for $2,000 toward the Highwood elk study which was being conducted by the Fish and Wildlife Division by Harold Carr, Calgary regional wildlife biologist.

Minister of the Department of Lands and Forests Dr. Allan Warrack congratulated Bob Scammell for the terrific job he did as president and extended best wishes and congratulations to Budd Traver, the new president. Warrack spoke of increased penalties for violations under the *Wildlife Act*, and also noted that the Buck for Wildlife program had already collected $750,000 to that point in time. He also noted that the crop depredation program had originally been financed completely by the sportsmen through additional costs to the wildlife certificates. However, the provincial government had entered into a five-year agreement with the federal government (recognizing that government's responsibility for migratory birds), and now one-third of the costs would be paid by the sportsmen, one-third by the Alberta government and one- third by the federal government. Warrack stated that the Fish and Wildlife Division had hired specialists to handle habitat programs such as Save Habitat and Restore Pheasants (SHARP) in southern Alberta. [Former senior head of wildlife management Gerry Kemp coined another acronym in this regard – FART (Foxes are the Real Trouble)!] Also noteworthy was an announcement that the Alberta government would commence construction of a new, major pheasant-rearing facility near Brooks, the Brooks Wildlife Centre.

Scammell noted that "in the area of our general activities, the year has been a year of triumphs." County and municipal no-shooting bylaws came to an end and would not be permitted in the future without the prior approval of the minister of Municipal Affairs and the minister of Lands and Forests. Also of note was the production of a government brochure, entitled "Where to Hunt in Alberta," which promoted good farmer-hunter relations. The foregoing accomplishments are probably long-forgotten or overlooked by current AFGA members and hunters in general. They do, however, point out the tremendous importance of the organization in lobbying the provincial government to correct local government practices that impinged on hunting.

The AFGA continued to have its hands in the government pockets, something they didn't always publicize. It obtained a government grant of $6,000 in the previous year, which was split equally among three clubs (Red Deer, St. Albert and Olds) for the purpose of expanding club facilities for raising pheasants.

Good public relations continued as a hallmark of Scammell's presidency with a low noise level regarding the behavior of hunters. Elmer Kure's name comes up once more as being extremely busy in the field of environmental concerns, especially with regard to public hearings on land use in the eastern slopes. The Environmental Conservation Authority was to accept many of the AFGA views on matters of concern about the eastern slopes, as well as recognize the public service effort of the AFGA. Scammell went on to recommend that Kure's contract with the AFGA be extended for another year in view of the importance of this position to the organization.

Scammell also praised Paul Morck, the AFGA secretary manager, as being "amazingly competent" and for his tremendous contribution, as well as that of past president, Tom O'Keefe. Morck

COURTESY OF TRAVEL ALBERTA

Dinosaur Provincial Park near Brooks.

reported on a study, "Public Perceptions of Alberta Lands and Forests," that had been just released and dealt with the confusion of fish and wildlife agencies in Alberta. Only 19 percent of those questioned could correctly identify the Alberta Fish and Game Association. Morck advised: "All club members now have factual proof that we must make ourselves more widely known." Membership stood at 18,599 in 1974.

> The keeping of fish and game records was started in 1962 by the Edmonton Fish and Game Association. It kept them until 1975, when the provincial AFGA took over. Also in 1975, sponsorship of the individual awards changed from commercial sponsors to local AFGA clubs.

Game-bird chair C. Burghardt reported, "The removal of ideal bird cover has not diminished either, and having continually seen pheasant groups wiped out by this method along with our extreme winter conditions, it certainly leaves the future of good pheasant hunting in doubt. I would consider 1974 as the lowest point ever in our pheasant population especially in the northern part of the province." [The year 1974 was marked by record snowfall especially in areas in central and northern Alberta.]

Archie Hogg, access and grazing chair advised, "Several municipalities or counties, by pressure from their ratepayers, at annual meetings, implemented 'no shooting' on any road allowances, used or not, within their area. This bylaw soon spread to seven counties or municipalities; with objections by the AFGA and some foresight by wildlife management this was modified to allow 'shotgun shooting only' and this to be confined to undeveloped road allowances."

1976 Lewis T. (Budd) Traver, a dignified and soft-spoken gentleman, became president of the AFGA in 1975.

LEWIS T. (BUDD) TRAVER: President (1975-77)

COURTESY OF JACK GRAHAM
LEWIS T. (BUDD) TRAVER

Lewis "Budd" Traver was born in 1916 and raised in Lougheed, Alberta. Because his mother was ill and his father had a fatal fascination for gates and anything else in the way, Budd was issued a driver's licence at the tender age of 11. When he finished his schooling, he worked in the Lougheed area for a couple of years and then moved to Jasper, where he took on odd jobs, from pounding fence posts to driving a tour bus, and later, even tending bar. After a short time he moved to Mount Robson Ranch where he became a big-game guide in the summer. He met many famous people, including Tex Ritter, Bing Crosby, and various American businessmen. In the winter he had a trap line and played in a dance band.

When World War II broke out, he joined the Royal Canadian Air Force and was stationed in eastern Canada, teaching flight engineering. Because the Air Force wouldn't send him oversees, he transferred to an elite group known as Para search and rescue. Unfortunately, this group was disbanded before they were sent overseas because the war ended.

After the end of World War II, he went to work in a sawmill in the Croyden, B.C. area. Because his younger daughter required constant medical attention, he and his family moved to Edmonton. It was at this time that he began his electrical trade, working with Colin-Allen Co., where he became foreman. He switched over to Edmonton Power while working on a job at the plant after hearing that Colin-Allen was going out of business. He received his Master Electrician certificate in 1958.

Budd was an ardent sheep and goat hunter, and fisherman, and became interested in the AFGA as a result of these activities. He worked his way up in the organization from hunter training instructor to president of the Edmonton Fish and Game Association, and subsequently to the presidency of the AFGA. During this time he became involved in the Canadian Wildlife Federation, the national conservation body. He served as treasurer of this organization. Along with his wife Yvonne, who was a paraplegic, they travelled in a Winnebago across Canada and down to Florida as part of his term. Budd had married Yvonne in 1973. He had many interests: hunting, fishing, boat building, painting, travel and music.

After retirement as an electrical foreman, just one month short of 25 years of service, he hoped to spend a great deal of time on his new boat and in travels across Canada. After retirement, Budd took up oil painting, mostly wildlife. He also worked for some time as a layout artist for a sign-painting company.

He moved to Sooke, B.C. in 1984 and lived for two years on a houseboat he had built especially to accommodate Yvonne and her wheelchair. He devoted much of his time to caring for Yvonne.

Budd was instrumental in founding the Sooke Coast Guard Auxiliary Search and Rescue group, and also was the first president of the Sooke Power and Sail Squadron. He worked as an instructor and mentor of the squadron until poor health forced him to step aside.

He spent his free time fishing, travelling, painting, playing his accordion, working on model airplanes and doing volunteer work for his church.

Yvonne passed away in 1999. Budd married Margaret in 2000 and shortly thereafter passed away from cancer in 2001.

[Biography prepared by Budd's wife, Margaret.]

The 47th annual conference was held at the Highlander Motor Hotel in Calgary in 1976. The conference chair was Ron Goodfellow, who welcomed everyone on behalf of the association, followed by Don Fowler, zone 2 vice president, who spoke briefly about the team effort to make the conference a success. The theme of the conference was "Land – A Question of Values."

In his annual conference report, Traver advised, "For years I think that our association has been fighting a strong defensive battle, always throwing counter punches at whoever threatened our outdoors. However, in the past year I think that our association has begun to emerge in a new perspective, one in which we have begun to take the offensive." There was a lot of truth to

COURTESY OF JACK GRAHAM
Jamie (L) and Jack Graham with whitefish catch from Lake Wabamun.

1977

Resolution No. 35   "BE IT RESOLVED: That the established system of 'ecological reserves' and natural areas throughout the province be re-activated and expanded. BRIEF: The dramatic increase in agricultural, industrial, and municipal impacts on natural communities in many areas of Alberta necessitate an ecological reserve system to preserve native flora and fauna for future generations."
The resolution carried.

this perspective, as quite often the AFGA has had to take a reactive position in response to government actions and legislation that were not in its best interests. For the first time, the AFGA requested $1 million be spent by government on an effective and co-operative pheasant-stocking program. Also for the first time, the AFGA asked the government to invest $1 million a year for five years on a habitat retention and improvement program.

The AFGA continued to oppose compulsory registration of sporting firearms and other senseless firearms legislation, while at the same time they pressed for a safe firearms training course and competency training program. They also introduced the Operation Respect program, which later evolved into the Use Respect program to improve farmer-sportsmen relations. This was primarily a signage program encouraging hunters to always ask for permission to hunt and for landowners to meet them halfway with instructions on how to contact them to obtain permission. There were also radio ads and other publicity associated with the Operation Respect program. The AFGA produced their first professional conservation program film, "Land – A Question of Values." Traver advised, "I doubt if anything has ever given us more credit or recognition in government circles, or has done more to support our conservation programs."

Mr. Allan (Boomer) Adair, Minister of the new Department of Recreation, Parks and Wildlife, replaced Dr. Allan Warrack as the minister responsible for fish and wildlife. The Department of Recreation, Parks and Wildlife was a combination of sections from the former departments of Lands and Forests (Fish and Wildlife Division) and the parks division and included culture and youth sections of the former Department of Culture, Youth and Recreation. Adair reported that construction of the Brooks

COURTESY OF RAY MAKOWECKI

Access to the moose camp in 1977.

Wildlife Centre was slated for 1976, with pheasant production planned for 1977.

The AFGA established their own political action program to help motivate club activity and maintain political contact with individual MLAs. Traver recommended that a political action committee be established in each provincial zone. Traver also recommended that Elmer Kure's probationary period now be ended and that he be retained on a permanent basis. Notable in Traver's report were references to the growing need for paid staff to be engaged in various roles and responsibilities: environmental public relations, political lobbyists, newsletter editor and membership director.

Distinguished service recognition certificates were presented at the annual conference to the following: Fern and Bill Dunn, McDonald's and Burger King, Garry Hrycyk, Harold Watters, LeRoy Peterson, E. Kew, Jack Towle, Steve and Helen Witiuk, Winchester Canada, Don Miller, Eric McDougall, Wade Lundy, Maloney Steel Crafts employees, Janet Hogg and communications employees (Edmonton).

Secretary manager Paul Morck reported: "In 1973 we introduced the membership quota program, with 31 clubs breaking their quota; in 1974 there were 37. In 1975 we added to the program, Quota Buster caps and jackets resulting in 54 clubs breaking their quotas. Membership showed an increase of 3,800 to 22,400 as of Feb. 11, 1976." Membership stood at 22,651 in 1975.

H.M. Rhodes, habitat chair, reported: "We have now adopted in the County of Red Deer a printed policy which states 'that the surveyed right-of-ways in the county are the property of the people of Alberta and should be retained to provide access to lakes and streams and also provide valuable habitat for big-game animals and upland birds.' Apparently, at the time, this was the only county or municipality in Alberta to have adopted such a policy. Rhodes also reported, "The highly emotional hearings on the Red Deer River Dam issue were probably the highlight of the year. I would expect that proceedings on the construction of the dam on the Red Deer River will be postponed for quite some time pending more studies."

COURTESY OF TRAVEL ALBERTA

Bird blind at Crane Lake nature trail near Fort McMurray.

Hunter training chair John Dickinson advised, "In summarizing the activities of the hunter training program for 1975, I must admit I am disappointed in the support this program receives from you, the organized sportsmen of Alberta." Dickinson went on to say that while members insist that the hunter training course be made mandatory (at least for some classes of hunters), most of the AFGA members refused to take the course themselves and that of the 12,000 students who took the course in 1975, only a handful participated in courses run by fish and game association clubs. Most took the course in public schools. Dickinson, consequently, suggested that the AFGA members serve as volunteers to the school programs. He added, "On the positive side, 1975 has seen the formation of a hunter training newsletter which is circulated to the 1,500 active instructors across Alberta." At the time, there were two "survival" camps operating, Alford Lake and Narrow Lake.

> *J*ohn Arthur Hugh Dickinson passed away April 17, 2007 in St. Albert. His favourite pastimes were hunting, fishing, fly-tying and reciting cowboy poetry. John was an RCMP officer from 1963-90, specializing in forensics and firearms who went by the nickname "Cowboy John."

Membership chairwoman Eve Ozanne reported, "Last year I asked for a special effort to get our membership out of a rut. I am pleased to report that I received a tremendous amount of co-operation in this area. The results speak for themselves. Our membership is once again on the rise and for the first time in four years we have topped the 21,000 mark." At least part of the credit for the rise in membership was related to the Quota Buster Club program, started in 1973.

Lloyd Shea, fish chair, advised "When I see what has happened over the past years, I find it hard to be optimistic about the future of sport fishing in our province. Water quality and quantity are the keys to fishing and both of these are declining under farming, mining, drilling and industrial activities." Shea spoke of potholes becoming eutrophic (overly productive in algae), silted streams and destruction of fish habitat in the settled parts of Alberta.

COURTESY OF JACK GRAHAM

Fishing on God's Lake, September 1977.

Part of the problem was related to government priorities for water with the following preferential use: domestic, municipal, industrial, irrigation, water power and other uses. [You can guess where "fish and wildlife resources" fit into the list of overall priorities: at the very bottom!] Shea wrapped up his address by advising that he had tried to put more "fish" into the AFGA, in the form of articles for all issues of *Defending All Outdoors* and by attending zone and executive meetings. Shea was a bulldog of a man who held high principles and wouldn't back down from a fight.

Hunting chair John Eglinski blasted the government over what he saw as poor game management.

- On seasons: In many areas he felt the seasons were too early.
- On elk: "Not too many years ago, we had an elk population of 60 to 70,000; what have we got today, 30,000 or better. We need better management, cut back on seasons, areas closed off for time to replenish again."
- On enforcement: "Another point and area is our law enforcement and game infractions. There are not enough officers in the field to cut down on poaching."

Dave Neave, chief wildlife biologist, spoke on behalf of Gordon Kerr, Fish and Wildlife Division director. He gave a rather sobering speech to the conference delegates. While praising the association's work to curtail poaching, he advised, "However, it's each individual whose attitude must change, and I feel most importantly, every hunter and with enthusiasm. All sports are played by established rules and procedures. Participants who break these rules, particularly for unsporting behaviour, are penalized and often thrown out. Hunting should be no different as a sport, requiring good conduct, special skills, sportsmanship and allowing the advantage to stay with the opponent. Fish and wildlife officers can protect the resource but cannot act as referees. Hunters must keep with his [sic] own rules – code of ethics. Most of us recognize this but few change their rules, their ethics with new developments – the ATV and the snowmobile. In Alberta I sometimes wonder if the days of non-regulated market hunting may merely have faded into days of mechanized, 'no-sweat, kill-'em-and-take-'em-home hunting,' without any set of ethics developing in between."

Archie Hogg, access and grazing chair, addressed the AFGA concerns over plans to allow cattle grazing in CFB Suffield and Vicary Creek (in the Crowsnest Forest Reserve, which had been grazed by domestic sheep before the allotment was cancelled). Hogg, and many other members of the AFGA, believed these areas needed rest from cattle to provide better big-game forage. He also reported on a move by ranchers in the Porcupine Hills, south of Calgary, to open up their land to hunting by foot or on horseback if hunters asked for permission and kept their vehicles off their land except to bring out dead game. At the time, this was a very contentious issue between ranchers and hunters.

In the November/December 1975 *Defending All Outdoors*, Traver reported that "His Honour Lt.-Gov. Ralph Steinhauer, honoured us with his presence at our MLA social evening. It is almost incredible that we should have such honour bestowed upon us." In the same newsletter, Lloyd Shea, fish chair, painted a bleak picture regarding future fishing in Jasper National Park. He stated, "In the past couple of years there has been a phasing out of the fishing in our mountain national parks and Jasper appears to be the most affected by the policy. The hatchery has been closed, the yearly stocking reduced by over 90 percent, the license fees increased and most of the waters closed to fishing on Labour Day." In his column, Elmer Kure, in charge of environmental public relations, philosophized, "The question in the minds of most sportsmen and conservation-conscious Albertans is whether this government will maintain a balance of values in its development policies so as to preserve our nature heritage and the freedom to enjoy it." Many members of the association would argue the Progressive Conservative government did not meet this challenge.

COURTESY OF TRAVEL ALBERTA

Abraham Lake near Nordegg.

*B*ill Bowthorpe passed away on Dec. 5, 1975 on his beloved Diamond E Ranch. Bowthorpe was a recipient of the Fulton Trophy for his work with Canada geese and his educational efforts over a period of more than 20 years.

1977 Lewis T. (Budd) Traver continued as the AFGA president. He hailed his president's report as "Looking Back into the Future."

The 48th annual conference was held at the Highwayman Motor Inn in Edmonton. Steve chaired the conference which was hosted by the Sherwood Park Fish and Game Association. The theme of the annual conference was "Responsible Resource Management." General conference chairman, Tony Ferguson, welcomed delegates on behalf of the association. This was the first year that the conference had opened on a Thursday afternoon, and general attendance was reported as very good.

*O*n a special note, there was a "bouquet" in the annual conference minutes: "Conference Chairman Steve Witiuk and his wife Helen and Ladies' Day co-ordinator Marion van der Merwe and her husband Chris and their respective committees are to be commended for the excellent execution of duties they provided for the 48th Annual Conference of the AFGA."

Traver reflected that in looking back he experienced a "...feeling of newborn respect for those who have served before me..." as president. During his term of office, the AFGA had spent considerable time making presentations at public hearing with respect to various developments along Alberta's eastern slopes. He also felt that the year 1975 marked the emergence of the AFGA as a new and stronger non-partisan but politically oriented association. In 1975 the AFGA started campaigns to exert pressure on various levels of government, for example at meetings with cabinet, with the Minister of Recreation, Parks and Wildlife, and at their MLA hospitality evening. Their revived political action committee also made their positions known not only to various cabinet ministers, but also to all MLAs through local club contacts. As the old saying goes, "The squeaky wheel gets the grease," and the AFGA lobby effort was apparently paying big dividends politically.

A running battle continued with the federal government over proposed firearms legislation, under Bill C-83, costing much in terms of time and money, as the AFGA made its views known by sending various delegations to Ottawa. This is just another example of how the association represented the interests of all Alberta hunters, regardless of whether they were affiliated with the organization. It also illustrates, however, just how much of a distraction these sorts of legislative bills have been to the AFGA over the years because, they took away so much of their resources that might have been allocated elsewhere in their role as a public interest intervener.

There were other issues that the AFGA had to contend with in 1977: the construction of the Red Deer River dam (which would later be called the Dickson Dam); the impending construction of the Three Rivers Dam on the Oldman River (that the government would name the Oldman River Dam); gas drilling in Cypress Hills Provincial Park; issues related to oil and gas activities in CFB Suffield; expansion of Sunshine Village in Banff National Park; public grazing and sale of Crown lands, as well as provincial parks classification.

The AFGA hired Muskeg Productions Limited to work with Elmer Kure to correlate the history of the AFGA and to produce its first book, *Alberta's Early Conservation Movement.*

Further on the communications front, an agreement was achieved with the Saskatchewan Wildlife Federation whereby the regular AFGA newsletter would be sent to all regular members at no extra cost. Paul Morck, secretary manager, reported this would be a different type of

COURTESY OF CAROLE ROMANIUK
STEVE WITIUK

newsletter, called *Western Canada Outdoors*. Morck must have been ready to pull his hair out because a lot of members were not receiving the newsletter since many clubs did not submit their membership lists. As of Feb. 4, 1977, only 39 clubs had submitted names; Morck claimed "...that means there are 74 clubs that are still not reading their mail, or don't care, or haven't got on the ball." Poor communications, usually from the clubs to head office, was often an issue within the association.

Traver reported, "On a note of mixed concern and appreciation, our membership reached 23,000 this year, the same figure we attained nine years ago!" He lamented "Our membership, however, is still far from what it should be and presents a real challenge for the right person."

The theme for the conference in 1977 was "Responsible Resource Management." Traver singled out several AFGA members for their great contributions to the association in his report: Elmer Kure, Paul Morck, the AFGA secretary Gwen Wahlstrom and incoming president Tony Ferguson.

In his senior vice president at large report, Ferguson admonished delegates, advising them that "Lack of communication within our own organization is a problem. We cannot expect proper representation at government levels unless there is greater co-operation within our ranks."

Distinguished service recognition certificates were presented at the annual conference to the following: Cold Lake District Fish and Game Association, Calgary Power, Roy Ozanne, Lloyd Graff, Lloyd Shea, George Ford, Harold Peterson, Don Hayden, Neville Lindsay, Vic Krankowski, Joe Evasiw, Clayben Hood, Ray Albert, Arnold Toeppner and John Stelfox.

The deputy minister of Recreation, Parks and Wildlife, Tom Drinkwater, took a jab at the conference delegates by advising, "There have been many battles within your association and between your association and others, as well as with various areas of government, and it is apparent that these conflicts often confused and clouded the real issues." He urged the delegates to be positive, concluding, "We are in this together and I think this can be said fairly that we are all attempting to get to the same place and with your help we will do it." Drinkwater's stance could be interpreted as a backlash with regard to intense AFGA lobbying over the previous year; it had captured the government's attention if nothing else. As an example, he noted, "The present Livingston fish hatchery, perhaps, was long in coming but is now in place and largely in response to fish and game efforts." This is yet another example of the association representing the interests of all anglers and hunters and successfully lobbying on their behalf, regardless of whether they belonged to the association. Drinkwater concluded "I think you have championed your cause of conservation of fish, wildlife, forests, clean air, clean water, scenic beauty and the total environment. I draw to mind your efforts in all of these areas and I note the conclusions. Some of these conclusions may not appear to you to be reactions to your demands but I think you can take a good share of credit for it." The deputy minister had paid the association

one of the highest of compliments. This was not to be taken lightly, as Drinkwater was a very capable and astute government official.

The Hon. Allen "Boomer" Adair, Minister of Recreation, Parks and Wildlife, praised the association for its annual conference theme, "Responsible Resource Management." He noted, "It gives me confidence in, and admiration for, the Alberta Fish and Game Association for choosing such an important theme for your 48th annual conference." He added, "Your efforts as AFGA members also promote responsible fish and wildlife resource management. Not only have your philosophies improved the taking of fish and game by your members, and by those who are not, but suggestions received from you also assisted the government in the formation of legislation, policies and programs which, in turn, aid all Albertans."

Gordon Kerr, assistant deputy minister of the Fish and Wildlife Division, painted a bright future for fish and wildlife management in Alberta in his speech to the delegates. The pheasant hatchery at the Brooks Wildlife Centre was under construction and Kerr forecast that birds would be reared in the spring and chicks would be released in 1978. He noted, "In the near future, this should mean larger quantities of pheasants being released in the province." The Sam Livingston Fish Hatchery was in full production and plans were being made to develop brood fish to raise eggs and become self-sufficient, free of dependency on outside egg supplies. Kerr noted that a kidney disease had developed in the Raven Rearing Station near Caroline, necessitating destruction of the stock to rid the facilities of the disease.

Secretary manager Paul Morck reported: "At last year's conference, the authority was granted to pursue a different type of newsletter. By now you have all received the first edition of the new *Western Canada Outdoors*." He also noted, "The membership Quota Buster program is still producing results. At the time of writing, we have exceeded the membership of our highest year of 1968 of 23,754. The load is being carried by many hard workers. Our 1976 membership is up by 1,000 over 1975." Membership stood at 24,501 in 1976.

COURTESY OF VERN MCINTOSH

Gary Cumming after a successful shoot, 1978.

In the president's report, reference was made to promoting Morck from secretary manager to executive director of the AFGA. Morck commented, "An executive director speaks and politics for the association, so more of my time would be spent outside."

There was a notice of motion amending the by-laws outlined in the minutes of the annual conference with the following proposed changes:

1. The executive of the association shall be comprised of:

> *president*
> *vice presidents at large*
> *vice presidents of zones*
> *active past-presidents*
> *chairmen of standing committees*
> *chairmen of ad hoc committees*
> *active life members*

2. Chairmen of the standing committees shall be elected by each committee at each annual conference and the following shall be the standing committees:

> *environmental quality*   *legislation*
> *finance*   *non-renewable resources*
> *fishing*   *renewable resources*
> *hunting*   *trophy*
> *information*

And such other ad hoc committees and standing committees found necessary by the president, by the executive, or by the association, to deal with current issues and problems as they arise, such ad hoc committees and standing committees to be disbanded after the expiry of one (1) year following appointment or after the problem or issue for which they were formed to deal with had been resolved, whichever is sooner.

3. A vice president of zone and a zone secretary shall be elected by each zone at its annual meeting which shall be held every year prior to the association's annual conference.

4. Zone secretaries shall become members of the executive of the association when vice presidents of zone are unable to act in that capacity.

Hunter-training chair John Dickinson advised, "I am pleased to report increased interest in hunter training this year. This is probably a result of the concern many of us felt regarding Bill C-83 and the gun control issue." Dickinson reported not only an increase in participation of local clubs, but also club members at schools as resource people to assist school teachers. He was also encouraged by the increase in the number of instructors' courses. While the hunter-training program may have had its early critics, it became a very popular and highly successful program over the years, in no small way due to the efforts of members of the AFGA.

Policy chair Lloyd Graff reported good progress in policy development, the platform of any successful organization.

Trophy chair Jack Graham advised, "A year ago the 13th annual provincial trophy ball climaxed the end of the 1975 trophy season with a new concept in trophy sponsorship. Thirty-one fish and game clubs sponsored the different fish, bird and

COURTESY OF TRAVEL ALBERTA

Cold Lake at sunset, from the shores of Cold Lake Provincial Park.

big-game categories for the Alberta trophy competition. It all proved a complete success and most of the clubs who sponsored were represented in Edmonton to hand out their club trophy to the winner."

The Lady Conservationist of the Year award was presented to Phyllis Graham in 1977 for her support and help to her husband Jack in his years of service to the AFGA trophy records and awards dinners, and for her continued interest in the association.

Elmer Schultz, landowner-sportsmen relationships chair, reported, "The highlight for 1976 was the introduction of the Operation Respect program. With this program it was our endeavour to help make sportsmen aware of their most important resource, which is the landowner. Like any other resources, they must be managed properly or it will not reward us with the proper returns. It seems that a new awareness, not only of the landowner's rights, but the friendly and co-operative sportsman, has been established."

Anti-pollution chair Ron Gladish advised, "I see a renewed interest in the environmental interest of the late 1960s." He also mentioned, "Zone 3 has been quite active over the past year working on the Red Deer River dam project and trying to ensure that our interests in fish and wildlife habitat are being protected. Now we have another dam project in the Oldman River basin that will need our attention and is getting our attention to ensure that the development has had a full environmental impact assessment." This is the first reference to the term "environmental impact assessment" in the AFGA records, a term that would become commonplace in the years ahead.

Archie Hogg, access and grazing chair, reported on the government's move to reduce the size of some Crown grazing leases. "A 260,000-acre lease southeast of Medicine Hat has been divided into four family units with a grazing capability of 600 cattle each. It seems just too bad that after all this land has been split up, no provision has been made for any area reserved for wildlife habitat; this is some of the last and best antelope and sage grouse country left in Alberta. On a few Crown grazing leases, terms have been reduced from 21 years to five years, but of course all are renewable."

Fish chair Lloyd Shea once again painted a bleak future regarding Alberta's fisheries. "Those of you who have read the articles I have written for *Defending All Outdoors* will be aware of my concerns about destruction of our fish habitat and the management of the trout fishery in Alberta and the national parks. Conditions continue to deteriorate and I finish my second term as your fish chairman frustrated and pessimistic about the future of trout fishing in our province."

Shea addressed the problems associated with trying to resolve issues related to fishing by a volunteer organization. He advised, "To be more effective I feel we must establish priorities at each level of our organization. Local issues should be handled by the affected clubs; regional ones by zone and the provincial executive [should] look after those of province-wide concern which are basic to fish and wildlife management." He concluded, "In short, let's quit flock shooting, take dead aim on what we are convinced needs to be done, and keep firing until we see results." Shea's message was not reinforced by what he said next. "At our conference a year ago, we had 13 resolutions dealing with fishing. This year there is only one. I am at a loss to know whether the fishermen in our organization have no concerns, are fully satisfied with present conditions, are simply apathetic, or hope vaguely that someone will do the job for them."

COURTESY OF TRAVEL ALBERTA

Red Rock Coulee Natural Area south of Medicine Hat.

A summer storm heading over the North Saskatchewan River.

1978-1987

Summary

Major issues: Proposed development in Willmore Wilderness Park; Red Deer River dam; Oldman River dam; first-time hunter testing; access to grazing leases on Crown land; elk relocation; the selling of Crown land; amendment to East Slope policy allowing more development on Crown lands, government guiding and outfitting policy.

Highlights:

1978 - Alberta Fish and Game Association (AFGA) protests the Alberta government closing the Environmental Conservation Authority; AFGA urges government to implement first-time hunter competency test; AFGA promotes new Fish and Wildlife Division anti-poacher program, the Outdoor Observer; "Fun Fishing Day for the Physically Disabled" begins; government implements the AFGA-backed east slopes policy.

1979 - Alberta government threatens Willmore Wilderness with roads and tourism development, AFGA launches protest; *To Conserve a Heritage* published.

1980 - Fish and wildlife regional offices and directors created; trappers compensation program begins; first junior conservation camp held.

1981 - Resolution passed to develop an AFGA fish and wildlife habitat-enhancement program, the precursor to the Wildlife Trust Fund.

1982 - Government establishes Order of the Bighorn Award and the AFGA is first organization to receive the award, along with members Archie Hogg and Emma and Bill Bowthorpe; fish and wildlife policy for Alberta approved.

1983 - AFGA Wildlife Trust Fund established; government introduces AFGA-sponsored Use Respect program to improve sportsmen/landowner relations; AFGA opposes Mt. Allan as Olympic ski hill site.

1984 - Government announces site for Oldman River dam, despite AFGA protests over flooding of prime fish and wildlife habitat; the AFGA withdraws conditional support for game ranching; Lyle Fullerton appointed first AFGA Buck for Wildlife co-ordinator; government passes new *Alberta Wildlife Act*; Alberta hunter education instructor association established; east slopes policy revised.

1985- AFGA issues position statement opposing game ranching; government rescinds regulation requiring hunters to wear bright-coloured clothing.

1986 - AFGA publishes *Alberta Wildlife Trophy* book, 1963-85.

1987 - Government announces Antelope Creek Habitat Management Area, purchased, in part, from the AFGA Wildlife Trust Fund; eastern slopes fishing regulations revised; the AFGA initiates hide collection program with funds going to the Wildlife Trust Fund.

Presidents: A.G. (Tony) Ferguson (1977-79), Don Hayden (1979-81), Roy Ozanne (1981-83), Ron Gladish (1983-85), Jack Shaver (1985-86), Nestor Romaniuk (1986-88).

Membership: 24,457-1978, 23,070-1979, 20,850-1980, 22,751-1981, 23,356-1982, 23,784-1983, 23,386-1984, 23,135-1985, 22,574-1986, 19,482-1987.

On the federal scene, the eighth decade of the AFGA was a tumultuous time, politically. In 1978, Pierre Trudeau was entering his eleventh straight year as prime minister of Canada at the head of the Liberal Party. In 1979, however, he lost an election to the Progressive Conservatives, who formed a minority government under Joseph Clark, an Albertan. This government was short-lived, falling to Trudeau's Liberals in March 1980. Trudeau held rein until June 1984, when he retired in favour of new Liberal leader John Turner. Turner only lasted three months as prime minister before he lost an election to Brian Mulroney of the Progressive Conservatives.

It was during Trudeau's last term that his government introduced the infamous National Energy Program (NEP) in 1980. Among several measures, the program levied an additional tax on oil and gas production. Many people in Alberta blamed the NEP for the downturn in the economy that occurred during the 1980s. In reality, the downturn was the result of several factors, including the NEP and a world-wide drop in petroleum prices.

Provincially, politics were a bit more stable. Peter Lougheed of the Progressive Conservatives continued as premier until November 1985, when he retired and Don Getty replaced him as premier and leader of the PCs. Lougheed had a sensitivity for the environment and culture in Alberta and was responsible for many wide-ranging and forward-looking programs and policies. However, the economic downturn that occurred during this time meant cutbacks in government funding for many programs that people had come to expect, including conservation of fish and wildlife.

The population of Alberta in 1981 was about 2.2 million people, or about nine percent of Canada's population. In 1981-82, 330,996 fishing licences and 164,527 wildlife certificates were sold. The value of the U.S. dollar in 1981 was $2.28 in 2007 USD.

1978 A.G. (Tony) Ferguson became president of the Alberta Fish and Game Association (AFGA) in 1977. Ferguson was a strong-willed president who called a spade a spade, and although he was not afraid to tackle controversial issues, he was always very fair. He wore his heart on his sleeve when it came time to represent the interests of the AFGA and does so to this day. Ferguson was well-spoken, and could always be counted on to cut quickly to the chase when dealing with issues.

A.G. (TONY) FERGUSON: President 1977-79

Tony Ferguson was born in Moose Jaw, Saskatchewan in May 1933, the son of a doctor who worked for the Canadian National Railway out of a private railcar. Tony married his wife, Pat, in 1958. He has three daughters: Jane, Catherine and Judy.

He joined the Canadian Armed Forces in 1955 and was posted to Germany later that year. In 1957 he returned to Canada as an officer candidate in training. His military career took him to Victoria and Chilliwack in British Columbia, Calgary and Edmonton and Moose Jaw, Saskatchewan. He returned for a four-year tour in Germany and also spent a year working with the United Nations in Damascus, Syria and another year in Vietnam. He retired from the military in 1983 and started a consulting business dealing with handling and shipping dangerous goods, later operating a fishing camp along the border between the Yukon and British Columbia from the mid-1980s to the mid-'90s.

COURTESY OF THE AFGA
A.G. (TONY) FERGUSON

Ferguson joined the Wainwright Fish and Game Association in 1961 while stationed at CFB Wainwright, which was a game preserve at the time. While attending the annual AFGA conference in Banff, he met Bill Wishart, a biologist with the Alberta government, and together with some other interested parties they hatched the idea of a controlled hunt in the Wainwright military base, which was over-populated with deer at the time. With Tony's military connections and biological background, they were able to convince the base commander that a controlled hunt was advisable. The hunting seasons that Albertans enjoy today in CFB Wainwright are a result of Tony's work. He also became a hunter training instructor while a member of the Wainwright Fish and Game Association and was instrumental in the implementation of game surveys on the military base; he participated in the actual surveys on several occasions by both fixed wing and helicopter.

He started a fish and game association while within the Canadian military establishment posted in Germany. They teamed up with American and German hunting associations and were able to provide fishing and hunting opportunities for Canadian servicemen while they were posted in Germany. According to Pat, this was no easy feat, as there were limited opportunities for Germany's own citizens. Regardless, he was able to convince the hunt master of the benefits of the program. As a result, opportunities were opened for Canadian servicemen to enjoy the outdoors.

In 1971 Tony was stationed at CFB Edmonton and joined the Namao Fish and Game Association. As a club member he attended the AFGA annual conference in Medicine Hat and was elected to the provincial executive as vice president. One of his accomplishments as a member of the executive was to develop the AFGA zoning system to coincide with those in place for the Fish and Wildlife Division at the time. Other issues involved preliminary firearms legislation work and proposed construction of a dam on the Peace River.

As president of the AFGA, Tony continued his involvement with the protection of the environment and hunting and fishing rights of Albertans. He, along with Elmer Kure, Don Appleby and Martha Kostuch, were involved with the Cold Lake heavy oil public hearings. He was also involved with federal firearms legislation, changes in female mule deer harvest regimes and woodland caribou being put on the endangered species list. He was a director of the Canadian Wildlife Federation and the first non-government chair for the provincial Wildlife Advisory Council. During his presidency, Tony, along with members of the Saskatchewan Wildlife Federation, helped establish the Western Canada Outdoors magazine, the predecessor of the current Outdoor Edge magazine. He was also involved with the Namao Fish and Game Association during his term as the AFGA president and helped with development of their skeet ranges and the building of their clubhouse.

During the 1980s and '90s, he continued to be involved with the AFGA and the protection and enhancement of wildlife habitat, along with many other issues of the day. He took part in the Alberta Government Telephones (which later became Telus) peregrine falcon recovery program in both Edmonton and Wainwright.

Because of Tony's background in waste management, he was able to bring his expertise to Edmonton's elementary classrooms, where he taught Grade 4 and 5 students the importance of garbage management. This same expertise came in handy when Tony worked on a committee with the Edmonton Fish and Game Association, the City of Edmonton Waste Management Department, and a citizen action group in the development of a blue box recycling program in the city of Edmonton. Likewise, he was a member of a committee that looked into the feasibility of the Swan Hills waste management plants, which recommended it not be built.

As of this writing, Ferguson is the zone 5 political action chair and sits on the provincial executive as a life member's representative. In this capacity he has assisted various clubs develop their constitutions, helped them address shooting ranges issues, etc. He is also a member of the AFGA Heritage 100 Committee responsible for overseeing production of the organization's 100-year centennial book. He also represents the AFGA on the Chauvin Public Advisory Committee on chronic wasting disease. He remains active at the provincial, zone and club levels of the AFGA.

[Biography prepared by Duane Radford based on information supplied by Tony's wife, Pat.]

The 49th annual conference of the Alberta Fish and Game Association was held at the Westlander Hotel in Medicine Hat in 1978. President Tony Ferguson welcomed delegates on behalf of the association. Conference chairman, John Rhodes, welcomed delegates on behalf of the host club, the Medicine Hat Fish and Game Association. The theme of the conference was "Co-ordinated Resource Management." Some 228 delegates, guests and media attended the 49th annual conference.

COURTESY OF THE AFGA

Jack (L) and Phyllis Graham with president Tony Ferguson (1977-79).

In his first annual president's report at the annual conference, Ferguson noted that the organizational changes of the provincial committees made during the previous conference had been fully implemented and in most cases were starting to grow in stature and in activity accomplishments. Starting in 1978, delegates would be asked to elect the provincial committee chairs for the first time. The zone vice presidents had been delegated more authority and fully integrated into the executive decision-making process. These changes were all signs of an organization well connected with its grassroots. Ferguson asked the delegates at the annual conference to consider hiring a full-time fundraiser for the AFGA. Delegates would also be asked to approve a new educational policy. While the AFGA had maintained "an excellent dialogue" with the minister of Recreation, Parks and Wildlife according to Ferguson, such was not the case with the environment minister where they had differences regarding the Environment Conservation Authority, the Red Deer dam and the Oldman River dam. Some progress had been made in constituting the hunter-training program. An experimental habitat retention program had been put in place through the efforts of Elmer Kure and others. The federal government was criticized for not meeting its obligations to provide adequate funding for wildlife (waterfowl) depredation compensation, a federal responsibility. Membership did not grow appreciably in 1978 and zones 2 and 6 were singled out as not meeting acceptable membership levels. A new membership brochure was produced and was made available at the conference. Ferguson closed his address to conference delegates by stating "The Alberta association is second to none in Canada. It takes dedicated people to make such an organization and I am proud to be associated with all of you."

The Minister of the department of Recreation, Parks and Wildlife, the Hon. Allen "Boomer" Adair, reported to the conference delegates, "To deal with the wide variety of demands being made upon Alberta's natural resources, we are into a new area and that's a practice we hope will be integrated very shortly, co-ordinated resource management, taking into account all the concerns of the interest groups. We have made some very significant strides in this direction just." Adair also noted that the government had been evaluating the need for mandatory hunter testing and certification in Alberta for some time, with deference to Resolution No. 6 that had been carried by the association at their annual conference.

BOUQUET: Conference chairman John Rhodes and his wife Esther and Ladies Day co-ordinator Dot Ish and her committee were commended for the excellent execution of their duties for the 49th annual conference.

1978

Notice of Motion No.1(a) Article VI – Meetings: All affiliated organizations in good standing, having paid minimum affiliation of 20 members for the current year by Jan. 31, shall be entitled to representation and voting privileges at the annual conference or at any special general meetings of the association as follows: Two votes for the first 100 members or fraction thereof, plus one vote for each additional 100 members or fraction thereof, up to 500 members, plus one vote for each additional 500 members or fraction thereof to a maximum of 10 votes. This motion carried.

Resolution No.6 BE IT RESOLVED THAT: The AFGA urges the provincial cabinet to cease its procrastinating and immediately put in place a program whereby first-time hunters and Wildlife Act violators in Alberta be required to pass competency tests in the following before they are issued a wildlife certificate:
- firearms handling and safety
- game identification
- first aid
- conservation and courtesy attitudes
- hunting ethics and landowner's rights

This resolution was carried and marked the beginning of a long battle to legislate a requirement that first-time hunters be properly trained and educated.

Moments of Silence: In respect to the memory of the late Erle Carr, a moment of silence was observed at the annual conference. Mr. Carr, longtime member of the association and recipient of the Fulton Trophy (1975), passed away in February 1977. As well, a moment of silence was observed for the late Mrs. Barbara Carr. Mrs. Carr was often called "Mrs. Fish and Game" for her tireless efforts on work pertaining to the association. In 1976 she was the recipient of the Lady Conservationist of the Year trophy.

Secretary manager Paul Morck reported the publication of a club manual in 1977 and advised that the membership quota buster program was still producing good results with 41 clubs breaking their quota in 1977. A new brochure about the AFGA was made available to conference delegates to promote the association and attract new members. Morck also reported that Conservation Lottery No. 7 sold over 105,000 tickets. Membership stood at 24,494 in 1977.

Elmer Kure, environmental public relations director, provided his first summary report in the conference handbook since being hired four years earlier. He reported on the completion of the east slopes policy and zoning for the mountains and the foothills which he advised (at that point) reflected on the major efforts made by the AFGA during earlier public hearings. This was a landmark document that would later be amended under the administration of Don Sparrow, Minister of Public Lands and Wildlife, much to the chagrin of the AFGA.

Don Hayden, senior vice president at large, commented that Fred Peacock, in all his years as an MLA, had never been contacted by a member of the AFGA. Hayden suggested that all locals have a group of three to five members who would contact their MLA to make them aware of what the association stands for and their expectations.

Vice president at large Lloyd Graff reported, "During this past year, two particular issues stand out: gun control (supposedly), in the form of a federal Bill C-51, and the gutting of the Environment Conservation Authority, by way of provincial Bill 74."

Neville Lindsay, legislation chair, also reported that Bill 74, the *Environmental Conservation Amendments Act* "...provides for the demise of the environmental conservation authority, and leaves a void in the area of protecting our environment from being ravaged by expanding industry and growing population and the problems that arise from the combination of the two." The Environment Conservation Authority was a thorn in the side of the Alberta government because it was perceived to overstep its authority

in recommending controversial policies to the Progressive Conservative government, which was sensitive to public scrutiny and wanted control of the environmental agenda in Alberta.

Nils Kvisle, renewable resources chair, presented a brief on behalf of the AFGA for the public hearings on the environmental effects of forestry operations in Alberta conducted by the new Environmental Council of Alberta. Kvisle had a full agenda, and was involved with numerous other issues: wildlife habitat improvement in Alberta's forests; Moose Creek habitat improvement project; reclamation of disturbed lands; presentation of a brief opposing the construction of a dam at Site 7 on the Red Deer River as a result of its ecological impacts on the fishery; presentation of a brief at a meeting organized by the Cattle Commission at Caroline to discuss grazing reserves.

Bird-game chair Phil Ficht reported that there were nine AFGA clubs participating in the pheasant-rearing program. This was a popular club activity at the time.

COURTESY OF JACK GRAHAM

The AFGA conference, 1978.

Jim Jensen, outdoor observer , advised, "Now we have an Outdoor Observer program. Thanks to Ernie Psikla, Jim Struthers, Dennis McDonald and many more of the staff of the Alberta Fish and Wildlife Division, who have worked for many months on the slide presentation." [This program to encourage the public to report poachers was first introduced at the annual conference in Medicine Hat, Feb. 23-25, 1978.] Jensen reported, "The responsibilities of the AFGA will be to promote the program. We will have to work with fish and wildlife officers to set up dates for the public presentation of 'The Outdoor Observer program.' It is expected that each club in the province will show the presentation at least once in their area."

Information chair Gary Hrycyk reported that "membership for 1977 reached 24,303 [24,501 in the AFGA's official year book records] nearly as good as our record year of 1976. Not bad. There were 41 Quota Buster clubs. Projected 1978 membership is 25,000 plus."

New fish chair Don Appleby took a shot at the provincial fisheries program. He addressed shortfalls in fish hatchery production; issues related to the commercial fishing by-catch and the "same old, same old, government response." He noted, "Perhaps as a change in the format of their speeches, Recreation, Parks and Wildlife officials will explain some of the things we can expect which will enhance Alberta's fisheries, rather than the long standing replies of 'lack of funds' and 'lack of personnel' we have almost begun to accept."

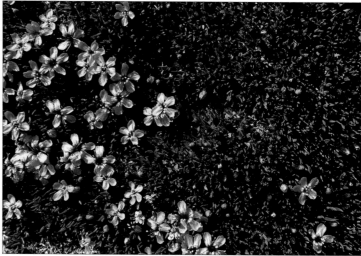

Moss campion in Jasper National Park.

FUN FISHING DAY FOR THE PHYSICALLY DISABLED

In 1977 a Canadian television celebrity by the name of Ted Peck came into the offices of the AFGA along with manager Don Miller of Rothmans Tobacco Products, looking for a provincial club that would organize a "Fun Fishing Day for the Physically Disabled," a program he had been involved with in the B.C. lower mainland for some years that he wanted to expand to the three Prairie provinces. The winners would then be flown to Vancouver for a salmon fish off. Paul Morck, executive director of the AFGA at the time, referred them to the Edmonton Police Fish and Game Association, as he felt this club would do a good job in getting the program off the ground in Alberta. For the next two years, Sportsman's Tobacco Products, a subsidiary of Rothmans of Canada - would sponsor this program in the three prairie provinces.

Ted Peck and Don Miller convinced Nestor Romaniuk and his club to organize a "Fun Fishing Day for the Physically Disabled" event, to be held on the first Sunday in June. With the help of the AFGA president at the time Tony Ferguson and Al "Boomer" Adair, Minister of Forestry, Lands and Wildlife, the first "Fun Fishing Day for the Physically Disabled" was successfully launched at Camp He Ho Ha on Lake Isle west of Edmonton.

Two years later, Sportsman Tobacco Products discontinued their sponsorship of this program on the Prairies. However, because so many "fish-and-gamers" thought this was a good program, the parent body was persuaded to help sponsor and continue on with this positive initiative. The program soon spread to zones 1, 2, 3 and 6, even if it meant just taking one or two physically disabled people fishing for a day.

Nestor and Carole Romaniuk planned and organized this successful program for the next 17 years until 1994. Under the guidance of Randy Collins, past president of the AFGA, the "Fun Fishing Day for the Physically Disabled" event still flourishes and is as popular today as when it was first launched in 1977. Collins, representing the St. Albert and District Fish and Game Association, has co-ordinated the event since 1994.

In recognition of the community benefits associated with this annual event, the St. Albert and District Fish and Game Association received a National Recreational Fishing Award in 2008.

[The above information was provided by Carole Romaniuk.]

Gordon Kerr, assistant deputy minister of the Fish and Wildlife Division, admonished the AFGA delegates at the 49th annual conference in his speech, as he reflected on his involvement with the organization since 1961: "I know there's a group of people in Alberta working very hard towards the improved situations on fish and wildlife resources and general outdoor situations. I think I detect though a decrease in effectiveness of that work over those years. It seems to me in the early meetings of fish and game more was accomplished through co-operative working with government than is now being accomplished. I don't think the dedication has

declined, I don't think you people out there are working any less and I don't think the government is working any less or listening any less to what you are saying, but I think we are missing the boat on what the issues really are."

Gordon Kerr, who had a long history with the AFGA as a member and a government biologist and administrator, was not afraid to call a spade a spade. It can be argued that the AFGA had such dressing down coming. Relations between the association and the Fish and Wildlife Division had been rather stormy at times during Kerr's term as assistant deputy minister. Kerr admonished the delegates in his speech, saying "I think the AFGA has very little credibility. Very little credibility with non-members and the public. There are two million Albertans in the province. There are 24,000 fish and game members and I think there is a great number of the uninvolved public who look on (the AFGA) as being a self-centred fish organization. I don't think that's a fair appraisal but I think that is their appraisal."

Dmytro Makowecki (L) and Jennifer, Natalie, Geoff and Michele with white-tailed deer in the St. Paul area, 1978.

Kerr didn't stop there, slamming the AFGA members who were game-law violators, alleging there was no difference in the violation rate of people who are members of organized sportsmen's clubs, or had been in the past, and the rest of the people. "There is another area that concerns me, if I can be a little blunt," he added. "I think in many quarters the Fish and Game Association is used as a 'bitch' session and an anti-anything group. They aren't, I know they're not, and you know they're not but I think the people who are listening on the other end of things don't see the objective. They put it into perspective of people wanting more fishing for their personal gain, more hunting, and they're saying don't build the dams, don't produce irrigation systems, don't cut the forest, don't drill for oil because you are destroying fish and wildlife, because *you* want it."

It was a very hard-hitting address, one of the bluntest on record from an official of the Alberta government. However, such a speech would never be seen again at an annual AFGA conference. In fact, the culture of the conferences was forever changed after this particular meeting, which subsequently seldom had speeches from the head of the Fish and Wildlife Division. Those few presentations that were made by the division heads were non-political for the most part and shied away from controversial issues.

Kerr continued on in his speech to encourage the delegates to be positive, imaginative and creative. He did single out several members for praise, for example Tom O'Keefe as "...one of the guys who follows through," adding "I'd like to mention a couple of other people, Elmer Kure and Tony Ferguson, who make a point of contacting various department personnel and beat the drum and make their thoughts known." Co-author/editor Duane Radford attended this annual conference as an official working for the Alberta government at the time; he recalls that you could have heard a pin drop during Kerr's speech, the atmosphere in the banquet room was somber and deathly calm. It was a bitterly cold winter in 1978 with deep snow throughout southern Alberta, even in Medicine Hat, and the chill in the conference room was palpable.

THE AFGA AND ALBERTA ANGLERS AND HUNTERS AT LARGE

It has been common practice for critics of the AFGA to allege that the organization does not truly represent Alberta's sportsmen and women because only a relatively small number of hunters and anglers actually belong to the association, compared with total provincial angling and hunting licence sales. This perceived shortfall seems to give these critics licence to undermine the AFGA resolutions, policies and platforms, both in government circles and among the general public.

However, an examination of the options concerned hunters and anglers have in Alberta to become involved in shaping conservation policies and programs quickly concludes that the AFGA is truly the only provincial organization that represents those interests. Other related organizations, such as Ducks Unlimited (Canada), the Federation of Alberta Naturalists or Trout Unlimited (Canada), have common interests with anglers and hunters but do not share all interests.

Increasing membership has always been a concern of the organization. For example, in his 2004 annual conference report, senior vice president Randy Collins stated, "More members will mean more clout, and with more clout comes the respect and recognition we already have and deserve."

People do not belong to the AFGA just because they enjoy hunting and fishing and having a meal of fish or wild game. They belong because they are concerned about the future of fish and wildlife and their habitats in Alberta. In reality, the number of AFGA members in any particular year represents anywhere from five to 10 percent of the total hunting and angling population in the province, which is typical of organized sportsmen and women in jurisdictions throughout North America. As in most recreational activities, only a small portion of the participants become concerned enough to take an active part in determining the future of the activity. Many either do not have the time, motivation or interest in joining others. That does not mean they do not agree with what the organized participants seek to do.

The AFGA represents the interests of anglers and hunters throughout the province. Indeed, its democratic structure has evolved to ensure that all viewpoints are heard and considered. Of course, there is disagreement on specific issues, but overall the concerns of the AFGA are the concerns of Alberta's anglers and hunters.

1979

Resolution No. 8 BE IT RESOLVED THAT: The Government of Alberta postpone its decision to build a dam on the Oldman River until proposed Stage I of integrated irrigation and water development is completed. This resolution was carried.

Resolution No. 29 Environmental Quality Resolution #29. BE IT RESOLVED THAT: There be no spring burning of grass along roadway ditches or rights-of-way in the province of Alberta. BRIEF: The practice of spring burning of roadways, ditches, and railway rights-of-way has played a large role in the decline of nesting area for song and game birds.
The resolution was carried, in an attempt to counteract this pervasive practice in the settled areas of Alberta which devastated wildlife cover in roadside ditches.

1979 A.G. (Tony) Ferguson continued as president of the AFGA in 1978 and presided over the 50th annual conference held in 1979 at the Mayfield Inn in Edmonton; 297 delegates, guests and media attended the conference. The conference theme, "Wildlife Needs You" was very appropriate for the time. The keynote speaker was Lester McCann, author of *A New Day for Wildlife* who spoke about the wrong messages being broadcast concerning wildlife—not about the need to protect habitat, but critical of hunters and hunting—with his advice: "Our opponents are a belligerent lot; we have to take on a little more starch so they will take us seriously."

D istinguished service recognition certificates were presented at the annual conference to Jean Appleby, Emma Bowthorpe, Don Cameron, Sharon Dutchak, Don Fowler, Bob Hallam, Dennis Hindbo, Ken Monson, Carol Romaniuk, Norm Shaddock, Rita Smolyk, George Stern, Bob Vair and Ken Yank.

COURTESY OF DUANE RADFORD

Buck for Wildlife signage.

President Ferguson provided a philosophical address to the delegates and came out swinging in his report: "Our governments have so divorced the environmental fields into so many departments that communications in many cases is non-existent. Why, for instance: is Willmore Park managed by Energy and Mines; Tourism calling for resort development; and the Parks and Wildlife Branch unable to say anything let alone control the very things they were established for? Why is the Department of Environment building flood control on Lesser Slave Lake without consultation with wildlife managers? And so the tale goes." Ferguson was never one to mince words and would go down as one of the most colourful and outspoken AFGA presidents; he didn't pull any punches and was well known for his hard-hitting speeches. He didn't let the AFGA off the hook either, asking a rhetorical question "What constitutes the current day fish-and-gamer? As in any organization we have those that belong in name only, those that criticize, and we have those who provide the backbone of the association. The fourth group is those who are not members. My concern is with those who provide little input to their clubs and to the association, and I am concerned that all of us who are members are not getting our message to the public and to those users of renewable resources." It was a sobering address and food for thought with regard to the next 50 years that lay ahead of the AFGA.

Paul Morck, still calling himself secretary manager, not executive director, was upbeat in his conference address as he reflected on his own past 12 years of employment with the association: "The newsletter is now going to 20,000 regular members rather than 200 affiliated club executive. The conservation lottery has raised nearly $500,000 for conservation projects. The budget is now eight times greater than what it was in 1967. Two to three times as many delegates attend the annual conference. Many new programs have been instituted. The association has also been successful in lobbying for many changes in the laws and regulations that affect us as fishers and hunters." On the downside, he noted: "Yet, I see many worthwhile programs, like Operation Respect, Hunter Training, Outdoor Observer, Acres for Wildlife and Junior Conservation becoming non-existent. Programs like firearm safety and fish-

ing and hunting classes never really got off the ground" It was typical Morck "philosophizing"—questioning the very existence of the AFGA—challenging the members to answer some tough questions! His address called for some soul searching: "People who are concerned about their sport want to become involved, and it is becoming patently obvious that many of our fish and game clubs are not providing a creative outlet for these people to become involved in problems."

It was one of Morck's best-ever addresses to the delegates. He concluded: "I am convinced that unless the clubs throughout the province are prepared to broaden their area of activities, and cater to the total interest in hunting and fishing awareness, we as the Alberta organized sportsmen will not be meeting the challenges that we are being posed. Why? Because our shareholders became spectators instead of participants! Conservation and sportsmanship requires the participation and support of everyone. It is not enough to sit back and root or cheer once in a while. We are a team in a very tough league, and it's the teamwork we display that will decide the outcome of the game. Are you sitting on the bench?" Morck also reported, "The membership Quota Buster program is still producing results. Membership for 1978 was 24,440." Membership was officially recorded at 24,457 for 1978.

True to form, environmental public relations director Elmer Kure heaped praise on others for a job well done, staying clear of the limelight despite his many accomplishments: "I mention some of these because of the major effort made, first your president, Tony [Ferguson] and Don Appleby, their ambition and hard work accounted for the intervention and brief to the ERCB [Energy Resources Conservation Board] relative to the heavy oil application at Cold Lake. Gordon Peel and his committee effort in preparing a major paper relative to native hunting and fishing and providing an alternative for politicians to reflect on. I would also like to mention Horst Fauser and his zone 1 group efforts in presenting at the public hearings on the Oldman River proposal. Also, Bob Tanghe and his committee's efforts in responding to the Willmore Wilderness Park proposal."

Senior vice president Don Hayden described an action-packed year on top of his being president of the Calgary Fish and Game Association. He was president of this local in 1978 and was re-elected in 1979. Hayden noted, "For the first time in seven years the membership increased over the previous year in 1978. Uncovering good quality active people is the greatest challenge." Some of his activities were as follows:

Preparation of a brief for the environmental effects of forestry operations in Alberta.
Attended 41st Annual Ducks Unlimited convention in Winnipeg.
Attended Alberta Wilderness Association conference in Calgary.
Attended Environmental Advisory conference in Ottawa
Presented AFGA comments on Parks Canada policy discussion paper on behalf of AFGA in Calgary.
Attended British Columbia Wildlife Federation executive meeting in Vancouver.

> *There was an interesting quote at the bottom of Hayden's report: "Conservation begins when a man realizes there will be a tomorrow."*

Lloyd Graff, vice president at large, advised he was happy to report that some of his contributions to the association produced some results. "At Red Deer there was a significant advance made in changing both municipal and provincial government opinion on the desirability and feasibility of disposing sewage effluent to the land instead of discharging that effluent into the nearest handy surface water body. Red Deer city council resolved to obtain a pilot project and Alberta Environment has been drafting guidelines that would be a major improvement on allowing such land disposal schemes in Alberta."

Fish chair Don Appleby reported on a government study of licensed and unlicensed anglers, noting that for the first time fishery managers recognized that the resource was being utilized by many more people than licence sales would indicate. Appleby also noted, "The Buck for Wildlife program report indicated a number of fishery enhancement programs and I do get the feeling this program is a solid attempt by the Department of Fisheries and Wildlife to do what they can within the political and financial restrictions their budget poses." Appleby always had that happy-go-lucky hangdog appearance and reflected: "After two years as Fish Committee chairman there is a disappointment in having no real positive report on the numerous resolutions submitted on your behalf. Fish hatchery production of rainbow trout seems to be our only real capability, the commercial fishery licensing still requires up-to-date legislation, the involvement of Indians in the fish management scheme, management of inter-provincial lakes with respect to limits, seasons, etc., the protection of fish during spawning seasons are a few." In retrospect, it would take almost two additional decades for most of these fisheries management issues to be resolved by the Alberta government and their officials.

Non-renewable resources chair Horst Fauser had a busy year, working on forestry briefs, the Oldman River dam water manage-

A nice catch of lake whitefish from ice fishing.

ment studies and environmental impact studies related to the Cold Lake heavy oil sands plant proposal while attending several public advisory council meetings of the recently created Environment Council of Alberta. Fauser reported "The good news from 1978 was (a) the rejection by our provincial government of Livingstone Mines proposal to build a rubidium mine in the Livingstone Range; (b) the ongoing land reclamation from the Department of the Environment." The rubidium mine proposal was widely seen as a farce in terms of its cost benefit and environmental impact assessment analysis.

For the first time zone chair reports were included in the annual pre-conference handbooks.

Zone 2 chair Jim Jensen advised, "Other objectives for 1979 are: Promoting Alberta Fish and Game merchandise, a booth at the Calgary Stampede, and river cleanups for the Bow River and the Highwood River."

Zone 5 chair Jim Owens reported, "Thanks have to go to Roy Ozanne for his two years as vice-president of zone 5. Roy ensured that commitments were kept and that work was done, by keeping in contact. Much of that time was spent travelling to clubs, phoning, writing letters, as well as keeping tabs on what the government bodies have been doing." He also advised, "Roy and Nestor Romaniuk of Edmonton City Police Fish and Game were the driving forces that made the Handicap Fish Derby at Camp He Ho Ha the success it was. They made sure that member volunteers were there and everything ran smoothly."

Zone 3 chair Martha Kostuch advised, "After the government's decision to go ahead with the Red Deer River dam, even though the majority of the public opposed the dam site, people in this area are very wary of public hearings or of any request for public input. After all, if the decisions have already been made, why waste our time and money participating in hearings. Although this might be the case, we must continue to participate in the hope that the government may change its attitude and may in the future consider public opinion prior to making the decisions." Unfortunately, Kostuch might have been looking through rose-coloured glasses because the elected government rarely changed its mind based on public hearings.

Outgoing hunting chair John Eglinski lamented, "I think this association and the wildlife division better take a hard look at the bird predators, such as crows and magpies; there's just getting to be too many. Our songbirds, upland birds, migratory birds, etc., have their eggs destroyed by bird predators when nesting and the young are killed after they hatch. At one time we had some incentives within this association and the Wildlife Division that promoted some controls – today there is nothing. Take a good look around you and think about it."

Eglinski went on to remark about how the government people with whom the AFGA members worked used to be in the Department of Lands and Forests, but over the years (with a proliferation of government departments and agencies) the Fish and Wildlife Division seemed to be shuffled about and usually ended up at the bottom of the pile in terms of budgets and program priority.

It was a point well-taken and shared by many members of the Fish and Wildlife Division who have always had concerns about insufficient staff and budgets to do the job—a perception that remains to this day.

Trophy chair Jack Graham advised "Last April the first edition of the *Alberta Trophy Book* was introduced and due to its popularity and success it will be updated and available again this year."

In the February 1979 Alberta edition of *Western Canada Outdoors* there was an editorial written by Norman Flaherty entitled, "Encroachment on Willmore Park." It outlined a move by the Alberta government to commission a consultant study into the feasibility of opening up the Willmore Wilderness Park to motorized tourism. The reason provided was "...to possibly help the sagging economy of the town of Grande Cache. Some of the suggested priorities are: to build a trunk road from Rock Lake to Grande Cache, an access road from Grande Cache up Smoky and Jackpine rivers to Ptarmigan Lake deep inside the park, alpine villages, ski resorts and golf courses." The editor lamented "Willmore Wilderness Park today is a wilderness in trouble." The Willmore Wilderness Park was (and still is) Alberta's last great mountain wilderness and it had already been reduced in size since its inception in 1959.

Bob Tanghe chaired the Save the Willmore Wilderness Committee of the AFGA and had this to say in the same issue of *Western Canada Outdoors*: "Because some industries and individuals only see the short-term dollar value of the area, it is not surprising that greed will take over from common sense. How does one place a dollar value on the recreational resources of the Willmore, its diverse land forms, unique vegetation types, endangered wildlife, pristine landscapes and wilderness aesthetics? Alberta's recreational demands and needs are obviously increasing, at the same time our recreational resources become fewer, both in terms of supply and quality." There was a strong movement afoot to preserve the Willmore in its natural state but Tanghe put his own spin on the prospects: "Regardless of the government saying that a study does not mean that any development will occur, too often they tell us one thing and then do another. We can't help remembering the Environmental Conservation Authority, which was so effectively emasculated by the government, the Red Deer River dam, a dam on the Paddle River, which are going ahead regardless of strong public opposition."

1980 D.J. (Don) Hayden, an Imperial Oil Company executive from Calgary, became president of the AFGA in 1979. While president of the AFGA he was manager of the company's Computer Production Control Department which maintained computerized control of 80 percent of Imperial Oil's oil production as well as most of their pipelines, including detection of pipeline leaks. Hayden was no stranger to the business world and knew full well how decisions were made in industry and government. He was also an astute manager who understood the dynamics of an organization and knew how to get the best out of its members. Teamwork, accountability and co-operation were the hallmarks of his term of office; he insisted on running business-like conferences with the executive at the head table with visible leadership.

DON HAYDEN President: 1979-81

COURTESY OF THE AFGA
DON HAYDEN

I was born and raised on a farm near High Prairie, in Alberta's Peace River Country. I can't remember when I didn't prefer to be outside enjoying nature.

I first became officially involved with Alberta's conservation movement when I helped form the St. Albert and District Fish and Game Association about 1967. I was the second president of that club, whose fight against the Dixon Dam on the Red Deer River led to a rarely used legislative hearing. The dam still went ahead, as we all know. While in St. Albert I initiated the first 4-H pheasant-rearing project in Alberta. The local fish and game club provided all the building materials plus the pheasants.

I have held various positions on the AFGA executive including: zone 4 chairman for two years; bird-game chairman of the AFGA for three years; senior vice president for two years, then president of the AFGA from 1979 to 1981.

I was elected as president of the AFGA at their 50th annual conference, held in Edmonton. Interestingly, the president of the AFGA at the first annual conference was a man from Calgary, who was the publisher of the Calgary Herald, Charles Hayden, no relation. I was president during the period when the AFGA had more than 24,000 members. One of my most vivid memories of being president was working with the excellent and motivated staff of the Fish and Wildlife Division. Many lifetime friendships were established during this period.

The last MLA wild game dinner that was hosted by the AFGA, which I organized, was held in Edmonton at the Old Timers Log Cabin in November 1980.

I obtained the assistance of Senator Reale Belisle to successfully secure charitable status for the AFGA in 1981. In the same year clubs were encouraged to "take their MLAs to lunch" and discuss the issues of the day. The AFGA paid $50 to each club that submitted their invoices for this action. I developed the first club manual for the AFGA in 1976.

I relocated to Calgary in 1977 and was elected as president of the Calgary Fish and Game Association; at the same time I was the senior vice president of the AFGA.

I drafted the terms of reference, which were adopted by the wildlife advisory committee in 1980 that resulted in the first non-government chairman being elected. Also in 1980, I was named to the steering committee of a study carried out by the Sage Institute, a consulting firm, to examine the entire delivery system of big-game hunting licenses in the Fish and Wildlife Division.

The AFGA had tried unsuccessfully to get the Alberta government to implement mandatory hunter training for first time hunters for over 20 years. In 1979, I sent a letter to each MLA outlining the need for this training and why it was a good idea to make it mandatory. One of the government's reasons for not implementing mandatory hunter qualification was the fact that it was mandatory. I reminded the Honourable Bud Miller, the minister of the day, that blaze orange or scarlet clothing was at that time mandatory for all hunters. Enough MLAs were convinced that mandatory hunter training was the right thing to do, and the government finally implemented this requirement in 1982. Some years later the requirement to wear blaze orange or scarlet clothing while hunting for big game was dropped.

I was a board member of the Canadian Wildlife Federation (CWF) from 1979 to 1983. I was elected to the executive of the Canadian Wildlife Federation in 1983 and served as president from 1985 to 1987. In 1986, the CWF hosted the World Sustainable Development conference in Ottawa with 114 countries in attendance. I received the Canadian Outdoorsman of the Year award from the CWF in 1999.

I served as parliamentarian for two years at the AFGA annual conference in the 1970s, and another five years in the 1990s.

I represented the AFGA on the Alberta Conservation Association (ACA) board of directors in 1999 and 2000; I was elected as chairman of the ACA board of directors in 2000.

I'm still very active in conservation. On behalf of the AFGA and the CWF, I have vigorously pursued the restoration of Lac Magloire from 1999 to 2003. This 2000-acre lake, located 42 kilometers south of Peace River, is listed in the North American Waterfowl Management Plan as a significant waterfowl rearing and staging area. A farmer owning property on the shore - with close ties to the Progressive Conservative Party - began draining the lake in 1983. In 1998, the lake completely dried up. The various ministers of Alberta Environment had steadfastly refused to resolve the situation, until January 2003 when a Ministerial Order was finally issued to the land owners to fill the drainage ditch. The lake is now fully restored and attracting many thousands of migratory waterfowl annually.

I'm still an active fisherman and hunter. I hunt waterfowl, upland game and big game. In 2001, I retired for the third time, having flunked the previous two tries, and plan on building a retirement home with my wife Joanne on a quarter section of land near Waterton Lakes National Park.

[Biography prepared by Don Hayden.]

The 51st annual conference was held at the El Rancho Motor Hotel in Lethbridge in 1980; the theme of the conference was "Hunting: Past and Future." Some 254 delegates, guests and media attended the conference at which Andy Russell gave a keynote address. Russell's address was entitled "Hunting – Past and Present" and it was about the history of game and hunting in Alberta. In characteristic form, he didn't pull any punches and gave a sobering snapshot about the dark side of game management and hunting. One part of his speech hit home particularly hard, in terms of the impact of access roads constructed by industry outside of the national parks, after World War II. "Hunters turned to road hunting – a most unethical and non-selective procedure denying what real hunting is all about. Where hunting should be an outdoor recreation, tuning the senses, sharpening the eyes and toning up the muscles with the accent on sport rather than killing, it degenerated into a kind of mechanical bingo game. It became a kind of macho-ego feeding game about as far removed from real sport as it can get."

Distinguished service recognition certificates were presented to the following individuals at the 1980 conference: Hugh Bossert, Bill Brennan, Norman Ferguson, Phil Ficht, Ron Gladish, Neil Goeson, Jim Jensen, Dai Jones, Martha Kostuch, Mike Lamb, Darlene Levoir, Terry Psaltis, Sam Richards, Steve Stephens and Vern Truxler. Eve Ozanne, the first lady president of a fish and game club in Alberta, who had worked for years as a chairperson of the membership committee of the Edmonton club, and had been active in provincial affairs, was awarded a life membership, along with John Eglinski, long-serving chair of the hunting committee for many years, and Tony Ferguson, the immediate past president of the AFGA, who remained active on the executive of the Canadian Wildlife Federation.

The kid is about to get his first pheasant.

Special Presentation: C.G. (Grant) Campbell, director of administration for the Fish and Wildlife Division, received a special presentation on behalf of the AFGA at the annual conference: "Grant has been a member of the department since 1955. He has been the regulations co-ordinator and critic, designer of mechanics of license draw systems and computer programs, co-ordinator and provider of budgets and facilities which keep the division going. Because of this position he, naturally, has been the absorber of criticism when things don't work. Grant is an ardent trophy hunter and fisherman, as well as an outdoor enthusiast."

One of the highlights of the annual conference was an announcement about a book *To Conserve a Heritage*, written by Margaret Lewis for the AFGA from information compiled by Elmer Kure, about the history of the conservation movement in Alberta in commemoration of the 50th anniversary conference in 1979.

Hayden reported that "[the year] 1979 proved to be a year of challenge for your rookie president," as he described the business-like manner in which he worked with the AFGA paid staff – setting out their objectives and appraising their performance. He heaped praise on the staff, in particular Elmer Kure, Paul Morck and Gwen Wahlstrom, whose performance exceeded his expectations. Kure remained as the director of environmental relations, Morck as the manager and Wahlstrom as secretary. Hayden joked that "if we ever lost Elmer Kure as our director of environmental

relations, the impact on our effectiveness would be enormous. We not only get his services at a bargain-basement price, but I work him as hard as two ordinary people." He also chided the rank and file members to be specific if they wanted the executive to work on matters of concern, advising, "The AFGA is most successful when our issues are fought at two levels – provincial and local."

There were many issues tackled by the AFGA executive and members in 1979, with the following being of major concern: Cold Lake hearings, Energy Resources Conservation Board hearings on Calgary Power's application for a transmission line into southern B.C., Oldman River dam public hearings, Berland-Fox Creek timber allotment hearings, native hunting issues, co-ordinated resource planning, hunter training and press releases (i.e. publicity on the AFGA conservation lottery problems), Lesser Slave Lake water level stabilization, *Western Canada Outdoors* as the voice of the AFGA and the Saskatchewan Wildlife Federation, reorganization of the Fish and Wildlife Advisory Council and the Select Committee on (Commercial) Fishing in Alberta. Hayden advised the delegates that the biggest issue facing the association was access to Crown land.

Also noted was a reference to the MLA dinner, which had not even been mentioned in any of the president's reports for several years prior to 1979. It appeared that this dinner had vastly diminished in importance by this point in time as it received virtually no hype by any members of the executive in the AFGA records.

COURTESY OF RAY MAKOWECKI

Dmytro (L), Tom and Clarence Makowecki duck hunting in Ranfurly area, fall 1980.

Secretary manager Paul Morck reported a revision of the club manual and the sale of the AFGA merchandise, netting $20,367 in 1979, which he said was "...not bad for the first year." Membership in 1979 was 23,070 and 32 clubs broke their member recruitment quotas at the time of the conference.

The year 1980 marked the 10th anniversary of the province-wide conservation lottery of the AFGA.

Environmental public relations director Elmer Kure reported, "1979 also saw our association test its wings at ERCB [Energy Resources Conservation Board] hearings in January at Cold Lake and in Calgary in October. In both cases, our provincial and local executive members carried the ball in an outstanding fashion. Hearings on the Oldman water management, and efforts to save the Willmore were other examples where our executive members carried a big load and did us proud. Alberta can thank them for

Hayden stated, "Our relations with the Alberta government are currently very positive." He singled out for praise Fred McDougall, deputy minister to Bud Miller, associate minister of Public Lands and Wildlife, who had made a significant contribution to the reorganization of the Fish and Wildlife Division. Hayden commented, "He is not only a man with excellent principles, but the conviction, courage and drive to carry them out."

McDougall was a hard-nosed deputy minister who could put the fear of life in his staff. He was one of the very few deputy ministers who made it a point to attend the AFGA annual conference to address the delegates and listen to their concerns, often staying for the entire proceedings. McDougall was most likely the Fish and Wildlife Division's most outspoken advocate ever in the ranks of government officials. Similarly, Miller also seemed to have the best interests of the AFGA at heart and could be counted on to be a true steward of the fish and wildlife resources of Alberta, a job he took very seriously. Hayden commented, "In Bud, I see a genuine concerns and agreement on many of our issues." Miller and McDougall were a formidable team, unlike no other minister and deputy minister in the history of the AFGA, because they were both highly committed to the interests of Alberta's fish and wildlife resources and were both hard-working, strong-twilled individuals.

COURTESY OF DUANE RADFORD

Andy Russell, an icon of Alberta conservation.

1981

Resolution No. 16 BE IT RESOLVED THAT: Crossbow hunting be made legal in Alberta with the same seasons and legal areas as bow hunting. This resolution was defeated, the first such resolution presented to AFGA.

Resolution No. 6 BE IT RESOLVED THAT: Developments which require an environmental impact assessment and where that assessment shows a major loss to fish and wildlife habitats, mitigation for such losses be "a requirement for replacement in kind or by dollar." This resolution was carried and marked an important milestone in public philosophy regarding environmental losses in Alberta because prior to this time compensation for loss of fish and wildlife habitat was not supported as a matter of policy by government.

helping mold big decisions." Characteristically modest, Kure stated, "It was my privilege to be involved in part of these efforts, but only in a supportive way." Where he did carry the ball was in representing the AFGA in various government committees (public advisor to the Environment Council of Alberta, the Livestock Indemnity and Losses Committee, the Block Areas Outfitting Committee and the Environmental Impact Assessment Review Committee) and at meetings with other stakeholders.

Senior vice president Roy Ozanne listed the various meetings that he attended on behalf of the AFGA during 1979. The list covered two-and-a-half pages, a typical year in the life of a member of the AFGA executive spent working with members of local clubs and officials at the zone and provincial executives throughout Alberta, not to mention Ozanne's trips elsewhere in Canada such as Regina and Ottawa to attend various interprovincial meetings.

Junior vice president at large Chris van der Merwe reported, "Our action to date to prevent or minimize the commercial and tourist development in Willmore [Wilderness Park] has been good. Excellent response to the petition, public support and media coverage, and some hot discussions within the provincial government arose. Strong support also came from the NDP [New Democratic Party] and Social Credit parties." Van der Merwe also advised that compulsory hunter training would have to be supported politically and would not come forward from the Fish and Wildlife Division – the message: get political support for compulsory hunter training.

Hunting chair Les Yaceyko reported, "Deteriorating habitat for upland birds and big game is one of the primary concerns

throughout the province. Increasing land forest development with little reclamation is resulting in rapid decline of adequate habitat." He also reported another concern about increasing numbers of scavenger birds such as crows and magpies. Yaceyko advised that compulsory hunter testing for game regulation violators would finally be enacted in the coming year.

Zone 1 chair Norm Ferguson reported, "The magpie problem is very big within most areas in zone 1. Two clubs have reported taking steps in trying to control this problem. I encourage other clubs to take an active part in this. Those desiring to do so may see me for a design for a very effective trap." Ferguson stepped down as zone 1 chair after the conference, having served five years in this capacity.

COURTESY OF GORDON KERR
David Kerr with a mule deer buck from Antelope Butte, 1981.

Zone 3 chair Martha Kostuch advised, "I was glad to see so many Fish and Game members present at the meeting of the Select Special Committee on Recreational and Commercial Fishing. I hope that your interest pays off with a higher priority being placed on fishing by the Government of Alberta." This committee held meetings throughout Alberta and made recommendations to the government; unfortunately, most of them were not implemented until many years following the conclusion of the hearings due to budget and staffing shortfalls.

Non-renewable resources chair Horst Fauser represented the AFGA at meetings to establish minimum instream flow levels for Willow Creek and the Little Bow River to maintain healthy fish populations. He also attended ERCB [Energy Resource Conservation Board] meetings on Calgary Power [later to be re-named TransAlta Utilities Corporation] to build a 500 kV

1981

Resolution No. 8 BE IT RESOLVED THAT: Additional revenue from hunting and fishing licences be directed to the Buck for Wildlife Fund and designated for wildlife habitat. This resolution was carried; at the time $2 from the sale of each wildlife certificate was earmarked for this purpose (an increase from $1 originally), which was seen as insufficient for fish and wildlife programs in the form of new or improved habitat.

Resolution No. 9 BE IT RESOLVED THAT: The AFGA develop a fish and wildlife habitat enhancement program for Alberta at the earliest possible date, to be financed by donations from outside the Association. This resolution was carried and would become the genesis of the AFGA Wildlife Trust Fund.

Max Bradshaw (L), Fred McDougall, Kim Hanson and Bud Miller.

transmission line connecting with B.C. Hydro in southwest Alberta. In the January-February 1980 Alberta edition of the *Western Canada Outdoors* newsletter, Fauser noted: "With great regret, I do have to report that critical wildlife zones are of no importance to Calgary Power, or the ERCB, but instead rank last on the list of impacts worth considering when building a power line." In his conference report, Fauser advised, "I was pleased to note that the ECA [Environmental Council of Alberta] panel on water management in the Oldman River Basin incorporated all my recommendations in their report to the Government of Alberta and recommended against a dam on the Oldman River." The government later over-ruled the recommendation not to build the dam (with taxpayer's dollars), against the advice of their experts, blindsiding Fauser in the process.

Fish chair Gene Scully also reported on the Willow Creek instream flow needs meeting, "The first-ever meeting to set a minimum flow on a stream being diverted for irrigation purposes was held at Claresholm last spring. Representation by Fish and Game was in support of Fish and Wildlife and the Department of Environment to maintain a minimum flow of 40 cfs [cubic feet per second] on Willow Creek. Forty cfs is the compromised minimum flow needed to preserve a viable sport fishery." Scully concluded his report by advising, "The need for an increased budget for our fishery department is mandatory. To manage a renewable resource without an inventory and survey of needs and services is stupid and our politicians have kept it this way, probably through ignorance. Our job is to educate these people. How, is the secret? To inform them with a flood of letters would do wonders, for such a flood could bring positive results. Four hundred thousand anglers in the province would get one good diamond anniversary present!"

Phil Ficht, pheasant-rearing co-ordinator, reported, "Since 1977, there have been 23 clubs that have become involved in the project. These clubs started pheasant-rearing projects utilizing funds provided under government grants and some who began in 1977 have expanded the capacity of their facilities each year." Some 10,000 pheasants were being raised by the AFGA clubs at the time.

1981 D.J. (Don) Hayden remained as president of the AFGA in 1980. He noted in the 52nd annual conference report that the year 1980 was the first of AFGA with a new executive council in place and fully functioning zone vice presidents. The 52nd annual conference was held at the Black Knight Inn in Red Deer in 1981. The conference theme was "Responsible Use of Fish and Wildlife – Our Heritage"; some 285 delegates, guests and media attended the annual conference. Dr. Valerius Geist, a professor of Environmental Sciences at the University of Calgary, gave the keynote address on "The Responsible Use of our Fish and Wildlife" which he noted had its roots in the Germanic tradition of land ownership and wildlife ownership. He spoke out against the commercialization of wildlife and game ranching, in particular, and the importance of public ownership of wildlife.

The Hon. Bud Miller, Associate Minister of Public Lands and Wildlife, gave a presentation at the annual conference on behalf of the Alberta government. Miller noted "Regional offices have been established [in 1980] and they are effectively coordinating enforcement, biological and habitat divisions in local areas. There is closer co-operation between other departments of government on

Dennis Surrendi showing off a "classic" tee shirt.

the regional bases [sic]." The newly hired regional directors were: Duane Radford (Southern), Tom Smith (Central), Gerry [Gerald] Thompson (East Slopes), Ray Makowecki (Northeast) and Frank Cardinal (Peace River). [The regional director positions responsible for co-ordinating and overseeing fish and wildlife management at the regional level were eventually phased out in 2002 under the department of Sustainable Resource Development.]

Miller spoke about access problems on the Bow River. These would be addressed by Tom Smith, regional director for the Central Region, after many meetings and negotiations with local landowners, resulting in new fishing access sites eventually being created at Policeman Flats, McKinnon Flats and Carseland. Miller also noted that the Trappers Compensation Program had been established whereby it was possible to reimburse trappers whose lines had been damaged by resource development activities. A major announcement was the creation of a provincial Advisory Council on Integrated Resource Planning – one of many steps the government would take to address competing land uses on Crown lands throughout the province.

> *B*OW RIVER FISHERIES ACCESS – T.W. (Tom) Smith
> In 1980 the Alberta Fish and Wildlife Division included an item in its budget estimates to develop fisheries access to the Bow River near Calgary. The Bow River is a world-renowned trout fishery. Although fishers have stood on the bank and fished the river for years, one of the best methods is to float down the river. Access would have to be downstream from the Western Irrigation District weir on the Bow River in the middle of Calgary.
>
> The Bow River banks below Calgary are mainly on private land all the way to the Carseland Dam. A review of possible Crown land parcels with vehicle access that could be used to develop access for boats was undertaken by map and by onsite inspection. There appeared to be two possibilities. One at a site locally known as Policeman Flats on the south bank and another on a road allowance on the north bank near Carseland. The road allowance involved a long, steep climb dragging a boat from the river. This site was considered marginal for boat access but good for a "park and walk" site.
>
> Policeman Flats was vociferously opposed by one nearby landowner who objected to the anticipated traffic volumes disturbing his privacy. Because of this opposition, the Department of the Environment required all issues to be settled before a permit could be issued. Despite repeated efforts, the objection to traffic remained and the project had to be carried over to the next two fiscal years. The ministers of the departments of both Environment and Forestry, Lands and Wildlife visited the site to familiarize themselves with the problem. Finally, the Department of the Environment granted a permit and construction of a parking lot and boat launch was undertaken.
>
> In the meantime, the Alberta Fish and Wildlife Division was able to purchase the 1896 homestead of Lachlan McKinnon from the McKinnon family. This ranch, on the north bank of the Bow River, known as McKinnon Flats, was ideal as a fisheries access site and was quickly developed for this purpose with parking and boat launch facilities. The June 2005 Bow River floods destroyed the Policeman Flats site but McKinnon Flats and the road allowance were still operational as of this writing. Repairs were undertaken at Policeman Flats in 2007.

> *M*any of the employees of the Fish and Wildlife Division would fondly remember the 1980s as the end of the golden years of that organization, an era that started in the 1970s. That era ended in the early 1990s with the gutting that took place during the Klein revolution as government staff and budgets were slashed to eliminate the provincial deficit. Many outdoorsmen lament that the Fish and Wildlife Division was practically invisible in the public eye during the decade prior to 2007 and was a shadow of its former self.

> *D*istinguished service awards were presented at the annual conference to Herb Cobb, Eugene Deford, Elmer Driver, Stella Ferguson, Niels Kloppenborg, Steve Kubasek, Boyd Loyst, Sam McGee, Gordon Merrick, Lorne Plante, Carole and Nestor Romaniuk, Bruce Thomas and Paul Zukwiski.

Hayden advised the conference delegates, "The most outstanding achievement is in the area of credibility. Your association is well respected in industry, government and particularly by other organized groups." Hayden also noted that, "Rapport with all levels of Alberta civil servants is outstanding," singling out deputy minister Fred McDougall [incorrectly called "McDonald" in the official report] and associate minister Bud Miller's executive director, Brent Shervy. He also advised about the good working relationship with Miller, who "…kept his door open to me throughout his time as minister." Hayden reported that "Outstanding financial support for our habitat enhancement pilot project has come from Gulf Canada and Petro Canada," a signal of significant industry co-operation due the high credibility of the AFGA. "Due to the pressure we put on government about the big-game hunting authorizations implemented during 1980, they have hired the Sage Institute consulting firm to examine the entire delivery system of big-game hunting licences," he reported. "The study began in late December and will be completed around our conference time in late February. I am on the steering committee of this study." The AFGA continued to press the government for a requirement that all first-time hunters be qualified, noting that the premier did not support this concept along with very few MLAs. Hayden closed his address by stating, "The last shot has not been fired in this struggle."

The AFGA volunteers had been appointed to many of the Integrated Resource Management planning processes – a job that would stretch through the 1980s and take a considerable amount of time and effort to complete.

The AFGA Junior Conservation School held at Camp Goldeye Lake was reported as an outstanding success. Dr. Martha Kostuch agreed to chair this venture once again in 1981. Kostuch, a veterinarian out of Rocky Mountain House, was an avid member of the AFGA at the time who was later to have a fallout over a matter of principle related to a position taken by the AFGA on the Oldman River dam. During her tenure, she made a very significant contribution to the association and her leaving was seen by many as a major loss to the association.

COURTESY OF JACK GRAHAM

Jack Graham with locked deer antlers, 1981.

Hayden also reported that over two-thirds of the AFGA clubs were actively involved in raising pheasants a–testament to the love affair association members had with this outstanding game bird. He also noted the very close working relationship the AFGA enjoyed with the Canadian Wildlife Federation, along with the Saskatchewan and B.C. Wildlife Federations. The AFGA delegates would be asked to approve a proposed habitat enhancement program at the 1980 conference, hailed by Hayden as representative of the "...threshold of a new era in conservation programs sponsored by the sportsmen of Alberta." As he stepped down as president he advised the new president "...will take over the reins of a smooth functioning and financially stable organization."

Secretary manager Paul Morck reported that sales of Lottery 10 tickets were down from a high of 105,000 to 66,000, "a $23,000 loss of proceeds to the AFGA." He advised that membership in 1980 was 20,730 and made a recommendation that the minimum affiliation for 1982 be raised to 50 members and that all clubs under 50 who wish to continue affiliation have their application approved by the executive. Morck noted that in 1980 there were 10 clubs with fewer than 25 members and that these clubs cost the AFGA money and speculated they wanted cheap insurance for their club and rifle or pistol range. The official membership for 1980 was 20,850.

Vice president at large Chris van der Merwe reported, "I had the opportunity to visit several clubs and zones in the province during 1980. Problems and concerns are the same all over. Poor communications with their zone executive and with the provincial executive and the lack of communications within the clubs themselves." Similar to a question raised earlier by secretary manager Paul Morck, van der Merwe asked: "Who loses? Our members of the Association in the long run, as in the clubs, zones and provincial executives, too many of the elected people have been around for years, have become stale and inactive and are not willing to step down and let some new blood in with fresh ideas and a willingness to work." He reported that the first junior conservation camp in 1980 proved to be a great success, and that plans were underway for a second camp in 1981 at the Goldeye Lake Centre. He also advised that membership in the AFGA was down (but gave no figures) apparently "...as it is in all other volunteer organizations in Alberta."

Les Yaceyko, the new hunting chair, advised that transplants of elk were underway from Elk Island National Park to the Hinton and Clearwater River areas, as well as the Athabasca area. He also noted that 1980 was the first year of large-scale authorization draws in Alberta, which would become a fixture in the future.

Trophy chair Jack Graham reminded the conference delegates that clubs who had their competitions in December had not taken the mandatory 60-day shrinkage period into account, as most big-game seasons did not end until the end of November. He also

1982

Resolution No. 6   BE IT RESOLVED THAT: The AFGA policy does not approve interbasin transfer of water. However, in the event of government approval for such projects, the Alberta government be asked to confirm that as part of the study of interbasin water transfer for agricultural enhancement and industrial expansion, an environmental impact study be incorporated and, in the event that interbasin transfer is made, that an equal allocation of funds be made to reduce negative impacts plus the creation of enhancement of wildlife and recreational opportunities. The resolution was carried to strengthen the government's commitment to mitigation of fish and game losses associated with water management projects.

advised that again there would be a trophy workshop at the annual conference. Graham also reported that two new categories were added to the competition in 1980: the photography and the largest big game taken with black powder.

National Wildlife Week chair Gordon Stretch advised that of the 100 AFGA volunteers who received resource kits, including pre-addressed return envelopes, only eight responded. These volunteers reached some 30 school groups and over 1,000 students during National Wildlife Week.

> *D*ee Aumuller, fish chair, attended the official opening of the Raven Brood Trout Station near Caroline, which would supply the Sam Livingston Fish Hatchery in Calgary with eight to 10 million eggs annually, mainly rainbow trout.

Environmental quality chair Ron Gladish reported on several new developments:

1. The federal government banned chlorofluorocarbons as spray propellants for hairspray, deodorants and antiperspirants to protect the ozone layer in the atmosphere.
2. The provincial government started to set up disposal sites for pesticide containers.
3. There was an increased level of public awareness about acid rain.
4. The Environment Council of Alberta conducted public hearings on the management of hazardous wastes.

Zone 1 chair Horst Fauser reported on various activities, notably the anticipated input from the AFGA into integrated management plans being developed for the Castle River and Livingstone-Porcupine Hills areas.

Jack Easterbrook, information chair, advised that the new hunter training manual was in its final form and should be completed in 1981 under the direction of Bob Stevenson, head of the extension services branch in the fish and wildlife division.

Easterbrook had words of praise for the junior conservation camp at Goldeye: "Sam Smolyk did an excellent job of organizing and setting up the program. Instruction and coaching were done by Lionel Dunn and Tom Bateman of Fish and Wildlife. Both are NRA [National Rifle Association] coaches and did first-class work with the boys and girls, particularly with the shotgun. Martha Kostuch [zone 3 chair] and her instructors have set a standard that will be difficult to surpass at future camps."

Newly appointed zone 2 chair Ken Yank reported that it was no secret there were a lot of problems in his zone:

1. The closing of access roads, the restrictions on hunting and the size of Kananaskis Country.
2. The closing of access roads to hunting and fishing south of Kananaskis Country.
3. Ranchers wanting to reduce the elk herds.
4. Government indifference toward hunters and anglers.

COURTESY OF THE AFGA

Roy (L) and Eve Ozanne, life members.

Renewable resource chair George Chronik advised: "The provincial government has committed itself to dam the Oldman River, quite possibly at the Three Rivers site. I realize this is a blow to Horst Fauser, who worked very hard in the fight against the dam. However, I believe in the necessity of a dam on the Oldman River, and tend to look for possible benefits with water management. Now it should be possible to get a guaranteed minimum flow capable of keeping a viable, healthy watercourse, as well as supplying water for irrigation and urban growth." Chronik also reported on the tremendous loss of wildlife habitat associated with rehabilitation of the irrigation systems in southern Alberta.

1982 Roy H. Ozanne became president of the AFGA in 1981. Ozanne was a fun-loving person and a proud member of the organization, a stickler for protocol at the AFGA conferences. He was a straight shooter and a gentleman; his wife, Eve, also an avid "fish-and-gamer" and life member, was never far from Roy's side.

ROY OZANNE President: 1981-82

Roy Ozanne was born in Davidson, Saskatchewan and as a youngster, moved to British Columbia where he completed his education. Upon graduation from school he enlisted in the Royal Canadian Army and served until the end of World War II. He later joined the Royal Canadian Air Force and completed 26 years of service before retiring to the Edmonton area, where he resided while president of the AFGA.

He was married to his wife, Eve, in Ottawa on June 24, 1950 and had three sons: Paul, Dean and Mark.

Mr. Ozanne was a qualified business accounting instructor. Throughout his service career he was active in youth organizations and held several

COURTESY OF THE AFGA
ROY OZANNE

appointments including: district commissioner of Boy Scouts – Canadian NATO Forces Europe; commanding officer – Lord Byng Air Cadet Squadron; coach – Little League baseball.

He first joined the AFGA in Claresholm in 1954. He subsequently was a member of various associations at Cold Lake, Griesbach-Namao and lastly the Edmonton Fish and Game Association. At each club he was active in club affairs and served on many committees – newsletter editor; treasurer and membership. At the zone level he was zone 4 education chair and later zone 5 vice president. At the provincial executive level he was policy chairman, vice president at large as well as president.

Mr. Ozanne was a member of the game advisory committee, the Grazing Lease Improvement Board, the Land Use Planning Board and the Canadian Wildlife Federation.

[Biography prepared by Duane Radford from Mr. Ozanne's personal history on file in the Provincial Archives of Alberta.]

In his president's report at the 53rd annual conference in 1982, Ozanne advised, "During 1981, we continued to work closely and harmoniously with other groups, on a provincial and national level." Willingness to be a team player has been a hallmark of the AFGA, a tradition that goes back to its founding members. The annual conference was held in Edmonton in 1982 and hosted by the Sherwood Park Fish and Game Association. The theme of the annual conference was "The Value of Wildlife." The keynote speaker was Mr. Dennis Pattinson, president of the Canadian Wildlife Federation, who had held various positions in the Saskatchewan Wildlife Federation, including president, prior to his affiliation with the Canadian Wildlife Federation. Some 245 delegates, guests and media attended the conference, with 66 affiliated clubs represented.

Lady Conservationist of the Year was awarded to Carole Romaniuk, who was first elected to the executive of the Edmonton City Police Fish and Game Association in 1972. She organized and co-ordinated participation of volunteers at the annual sportsmen show booth and was also attributed as being the right-hand lady in the organization of the fishing derby for the physically disabled, known as the "Fun Fishing Day for the Physically Disabled" in its formative years.

Access to hunting and fishing areas continued to be a priority of the AFGA. A new proposed policy crafted by the Wildlife Advisory Council, as well as the proposed sale of over two million acres of land in the special areas of eastern Alberta, would take up a lot of the organization's time. The special areas are tax-recovery lands expropriated by the government dating back to the 1930s. As well, elk transplants from Bob Creek in southwest Alberta to the Amadou Lake near Athabasca were underway, a controversial project at the start which pitted the AFGA members from different parts of Alberta against each other, fairly typical of north/south bickering in the province.

Ozanne acknowledged the Recreation, Parks and Wildlife Foundation for awarding two grants to the AFGA, one in the amount of $20,000 to assist in addressing a deficit accumulated in the pheasant-rearing program. The AFGA was also awarded another $56,298 grant for an experimental stream-enhancement project, to be conducted by Dr. Stuart Smith. This latter project was very controversial among government circles; it involved fertilization (and supposedly nutrient enrichment) of streams with barley, an unproven technique. The Recreation, Parks and Wildlife Foundation had a rich history of supporting worthy projects of benefit to Alberta's fish and wildlife resources.

The long-standing fish derby for the physically disabled continued and Ozanne reported that it was as usual a great success, as was the Goldeye conservation camp, presently named the Goldeye Centre, near Nordegg. Without going into details, Ozanne reported that 1981 saw an increase of about 2,000 members in the AFGA.

Bud Miller, associate minister of Public Lands and Wildlife, gave a presentation to the AFGA conference delegates, noting that the pheasant-raising program had one of the most successful years the province had ever experienced, with some 100,000 birds being released during 1981 in various parts of the province. Miller also noted that upgrades to the Raven brood trout station had been completed and that Allison Creek brood station was being completed, with plans underway to build the Cold Lake fish hatchery. Regarding decentralization of the department, Miller reported the program had been effective in bringing the department down to the grassroots level, and that he was going to look at opening some new field offices throughout the province so that people did not have to travel great distances for their licences. He was the architect behind elk transplants to the Athabasca area and also to the Blackstone Gap, west of Rocky Mountain House in the early 1980s.

Dennis Surrendi replaced Gordon Kerr as assistant deputy minister of the Fish and Wildlife Division in 1981. Surrendi had worked for the Ministry of Natural Resources in Manitoba prior to coming to Alberta, having been previously employed by the Canadian Wildlife Service. Surrendi was widely perceived as a workaholic, almost always starting work early in the morning and working until late into the night. He seemed to have no end of ideas on how to run the Fish and Wildlife Division. Upon commencing his job, he labelled his directors as a bunch of Wayne Gretzkys in need of a coach because he felt they seemed to be going in different directions at times.

Secretary manager Paul Morck advised that the Membership Quota Buster Program of the past nine years had, over the time, lost its impact. As a result, he announced a new membership incentive bonus plan that gave clubs prizes for increased membership. Morck noted that lottery no. 11 had sales of 91,500 tickets, "...a respectable increase of 25,000 over lottery no. 10." Membership stood at 22,751 in 1981.

Environmental public relations director Elmer Kure reported, "Some days I find working for you a bit difficult as it seems we are asked to oppose many of the things our government or developers think are in the provincial interest. In each of these circumstances every effort is made to look at the positive as well as the negative impacts and with advice of your president and executive members, a decision is made to act or not to react. Hopefully our reaction and follow-up actions are as constructive, and seen to be so, as they are intended to be." Kure concluded his report, "As a final note, let us remind ourselves that we will have the kind of government we deserve – that's the democratic way – you either tell your MLA what you want in our society or someone will tell you what's good for you."

COURTESY OF BLAIR RIPPIN

Athabasca Fish and Game Association volunteers doing an elk transplant in the Pelican Mountains, 1982.

1983

Resolution No. 1 BE IT RESOLVED THAT: The Alberta government establish minimum flow regulations on all rivers and streams in the province consistent with the survival and well-being of all native species of fish and wildlife and that no new diversions from a stream or river be authorized until a minimum flow has been established. This resolution was carried, indicative of the wide-ranging environmental policies of the AFGA.

Resolution No. 33 RECOMMENDED EXECUTIVE RESOLUTION #33 BE IT RESOLVED THAT: The Government of Alberta appoint a special select committee of the Legislature to publicly review all matters related to acid-forming emissions in the province of Alberta. This resolution was carried, also indicative of the broad-minded philosophy of members of the association, long before such matters became public issues among the general populace.

Vice president Ron Gladish hopped on the membership bandwagon, a perennial issue with the AFGA: "The only weak spot in our association is our lack of numbers. We lack in total membership and in the number of people who are directly involved in the AFGA, its zones and member clubs. If we could only get every hunter and fisher in Alberta to donate time to our association or belong to a club. Imagine if you will, our association having 300,000 members. Further, imagine if of those 300,000 members, half donated 100 hours a year to conservation projects."

> *The AFGA stood by its principles in 1981 when the Fish and Wildlife Division announced it was making plans to authorize damage permits for ranchers to shoot elk that were guilty of raiding haystacks in southern Alberta. The ranchers would have to field dress the shot elk and turn them over to the department, who in turn would give them to needy people. This was seen as a last resort to ward off property damage.*
>
> *When assistant deputy minister Gordon Kerr appealed to Roy Ozanne for support, he was curtly told the only support the association could provide would be "silence" at the official level. AFGA members subsequently picketed the Fish and Wildlife Division regional headquarters in Lethbridge carrying "Stop the Cow Elk Slaughter" placards in protest, causing a major media black eye for the division. They also contacted the wife of Dick Johnston, Lethbridge MLA and provincial treasurer, and complained that pregnant females would be slaughtered. Shortly thereafter, government officials announced they were cancelling plans to provide damage permits and would instead work on other means of controlling the depredating elk.*
>
> *As an interesting side note, retired veteran fish and wildlife officer and problem wildlife specialist Dennis Weisser often jokingly said, "The Americans can put a man on the moon, but we can't figure out how to keep elk out of haystacks!"*

National Wildlife Week chair Jack Easterbrook reported on the AFGA activities which ran into a number of obstacles; he advised that feedback from the clubs was very disappointing. However, in the list of participating clubs that he provided there were some positive results but it was apparent that much more planning and co-ordination were required to make the program-delivery effective. Easterbrook advised: "Three names figure prominently in this report: Norm Ray of High River, who spoke to 264 pupils in 11 presentations; Jim Agnew of Cold Lake, who spoke to over 900 pupils; and Yvonne Traver, who repeated 1980 by phoning each of the elementary schools in Edmonton. There were more responses than we could handle." In the area of Alberta hunter education, the province started to make plans to include a section on fish in the training manual, as a result of persistence on the part of the AFGA to have this as part of the study material.

COURTESY OF BLAIR RIPPIN

Elk release at the Pelican Mountains, 1982.

1983

Resolution No. 20

BE IT RESOLVED THAT: Hunting and fishing regulations apply equally to all residents of Alberta, including the native people. BRIEF: Native people seemingly have the right to hunt and kill game anywhere in the province and at any time. This defeats the purpose of game management, as there is no way of determining how many animals have been taken. But through licensing and questionnaires, etc. it is possible to obtain some indication. In addition, to suggest that one segment or race within a population has or does not have more or less rights than some other segment or race does not say very much for our civilization. The resolution was carried, a sign of frustration over what was perceived as wantonly unregulated native harvesting of fish and game in Alberta.

Resolution No. 35

RECOMMENDED EXECUTIVE RESOLUTION #35 BE IT RESOLVED THAT: The government of Alberta remove that section of the game hunting regulations which requires hunters to wear a long-sleeved outer garment, completely scarlet or blaze orange in colour, and a cap or other head-dress, completely scarlet or blaze orange in colour, while hunting big game, fur-bearing animals or furbearing carnivores at a time and place that is lawful to hunt big game or upland game birds in certain wildlife management units.
This resolution was defeated but it was a sign of changing times, contrary to earlier resolutions calling for hunters to wear highly visible clothing as a matter of public safety.

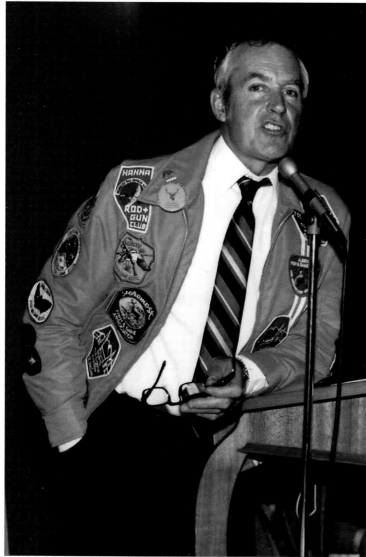
COURTESY OF THE AFGA

Jack Graham, trophy chairman and MC at the wildlife awards banquet in 1982.

Zone 1 vice president Horst Fauser reported on a multitude of regionally important AFGA activities. He advised, "I am looking forward to some strong lobbying in 1982 for habitat improvement for elk wintering ranges in the forestry [reserves], and some compensation for lost bird habitat due to irrigation upgrading." The latter request was a lost cause as he was given the run-around by Alberta Environment, who wouldn't accept any responsibility for the loss of wildlife habitat associated with their multi-million dollar irrigation rehabilitation program underway in southern Alberta. As the various irrigation canals were upgraded, seepage areas were eliminated along with the shrubs and bushes that thrived in such locations; escape cover and over-wintering habitat for upland birds, in particular, were destroyed in the process.

It appeared as though Ken Yank, zone 2 vice president, took secretary manager Paul Morck's suggestion to get some new blood into the organization to heart: "Another year has slipped by, and a lot of time spent, but I wonder if we really have accomplished anything worthwhile. Some opinions were to let the younger generation take over. In some cases I tried that. Either their self-starters are broken or they need a crank."

Newly appointed zone 3 vice president Doug Rumsey reported "One of the biggest disappointments I have found is the lack of participation and communications that some of the clubs are showing. Too many clubs are segregating themselves away from the AFGA. If the AFGA is to be strong in its decisions and dealings with government and other outside pressure organizations, then we must communicate better with each other in order to achieve the aims and objectives of the organization." Rumsey added, "With the regionalization of the provincial Fish and Wildlife department, communications and co-operation have been extremely good in zone 3 and I hope that they remain so in the future."

Zone 4 vice president Bob Tanghe painted a bleak picture for his region. Several new strip mines for coal had been announced for west central Alberta and although they had not yet been approved it was a foregone conclusion in Tanghe's opinion that the outcome was grim: "More mines mean of course more destruction of habitat of our fish and wildlife, and although the destruction may be temporary, it's destruction we cannot afford. Furthermore, the influx of additional people will put still more pressure on our dwindling fish and wildlife populations." He also advised that the sport fishery in the zone was declining each year, except for the government-stocked lakes and ponds, which were then providing some of the better fishing in the area. Tanghe made it known that he intended to resign from the AFGA executive in the spring of 1982. He had served eight years off and on as zone chair, one year as senior vice president at large and held positions as various committee chairs during his 20-year tenure with the association.

Don Appleby, zone 5 vice president, gave a prophetic report on what the future held for northeastern Alberta in view of impending large-scale development of the area's rich oil sands. One of the more profound questions he raised was "For example, how many times have we heard a community or region expounding on the merit and economic value of tourism, good fishing, campsite development and outdoor recreation after the downturn of the non-renewable resource boom cycle. Is there any reason why these cannot be fully considered in the beginning?" This would turn out to be somewhat of a moot question under the Klein government, which announced in 2006 that priority for the area would be economic development of the oil sands at the expense of other resource interests which would be of the lowest priority.

Zone 6 vice president Percy Hunkin reported, "We still have dissatisfaction with having only one Fish and Game association representative on the Grazing Lease Advisory Council." During the early 1980s the government funded large-scale range improvement projects on Alberta's provincial grazing leases, many of which would be later privatized. This resulted in the loss of much wildlife habitat.

Environment chair Gordon Merrick reported, "The state of our rivers continues to deteriorate because of pollution. The Crowsnest can now be added to our endangered rivers list. Although we have brought specific cases to the attention of Alberta Fish and Wildlife, no charges have been laid." At the time, the nation's strongest environmental legislation was the Canada Fisheries Act [federal law that Alberta's Fish and Wildlife Division officers were empowered to enforce] and charges likely would have fallen under the section dealing with prohibition of adding deleterious substances to fish-bearing

COURTESY OF TRAVEL ALBERTA

The mesmerizing stare of an owl.

waters. Merrick concluded his report by advising, "In the following 12 months I would like to see a start on the province's hazardous waste plant, a true commitment by the government to clean up the rivers; the Clean Air Act enforced; a ban on 1080 poison [for coyotes and wolves]; and each club take an MLA fishing below town."

Fish chair Nestor Romaniuk reported, "Last year, being the International Year of the Physically Disabled Person, high on my priority list was to have the most successful fishing derby for the physically disabled. I am very pleased to report that last year's derby was in fact one of the highlights for our organization." Romaniuk also reported on budget shortfalls in the fisheries branch and the economic benefits related to sport fishing.

Trophy chair Jack Graham advised that a new trophy book would be produced in 1982 with updated information. He also advised "The first-ever Alberta Measuring School was held in April, 1981 which proved to be very popular and great club interest was shown." Graham traveled to Champaign, Illinois, at the invitation of the Boone and Crockett Club to attend a Measurer's Training Workshop on Oct. 11, 1982. The AFGA sponsored his trip and he was subsequently appointed an official Boone and Crockett Measurer for the Boone and Crockett Club's North American Big Game Records.

Hunting chair Les Yaceyko reported, "Most of the time and effort was directed towards the elk issue. Extended seasons in the south, transplants in the north, proposals for future projects, and the keen interest in all these by many, have kept elk a primary topic. As new programs and developments germinate, this issue will continue near the top of the list."

The Alberta Order of the Bighorn Awards was established by the Honourable Bud Miller, associate minister of Public Lands and Wildlife in 1982. The awards became Alberta's most prestigious award for fish and wildlife conservation.

The AFGA was the first-ever organization awarded the Alberta Order of the Bighorn Award by the Alberta government in 1982. Roy Ozanne, president of the AFGA, accepted the award on behalf of fish and gamers throughout the province.

The AFGA citation, read by the minister, said, "The devotion and direction the AFGA has given to innumerable projects, in conjunction with the Fish and Wildlife Division, has contributed to the conservation of fish and wildlife resources, for the benefit of all Albertans."

Archie Hogg, long-time member of the AFGA, also received an Order of the Bighorn Award in 1982, along with AFGA members Emma and Bill Bowthorpe. Hogg, a long-time active naturalist, had devoted a lifetime to the conservation of Canada geese and other waterfowl. His conservation work with the geese, his waterfowl sanctuary and public campsite have given much to all Albertans, but particularly those in the High River area.

Emma Bowthorpe and her late husband Bill devoted 40 acres of productive farmland and 30 years of loving care to the conservation of Canada geese and other Alberta wildlife. They established the Big E Wildlife Paradise near Round Hill as a sanctuary for Alberta wildlife.

Distinguished service certificate awards were presented at the annual conference to Horst Fauser, Clay Hood, Martha Kostuch, Bob Loewen, Gwen Wahlstrom and Les Yaceyko.

The fish and wildlife policy for Alberta was approved by the Alberta government on Oct. 14, 1982. At the time, this policy represented the only comprehensive commitment of any government, federal or provincial, in Canadian history toward fisheries and wildlife resources. It is important to recognize that this policy represents a position of the Alberta government as a whole and not just the Department of Public Lands and Wildlife who drafted the document.

All AFGA clubs were sent a copy of the policy which was reprinted in its entirety in the November-December 1982 issue of Western Canada Outdoors newsletter. Les Yaceyko, hunting chair, advised in the newsletter that "the development of the policy has been a long, gruelling task involving a committee involving fish and wildlife and provincial associations. AFGA was one of these organizations involved in the committee."

Don Hayden, past president of the AFGA, was instrumental in preparing the new policy on behalf of the association.

1983

Resolution No. 8   BE IT RESOLVED THAT: The government of Alberta select a site, other than Mount Allan, for the venue of the Winter Olympics Alpine Skiing events for 1988. This resolution was carried unanimously by conference delegates.

1983 Roy Ozanne remained as president of the AFGA in 1982. That year, the 54th annual conference was held for the first time in Grande Prairie in the Peace River country, hosted by zone 6. The theme of the conference was "Reserve a Place for Wildlife." Some 254 delegates, guests and media attended the conference which would be remembered as one of the best-ever in the history of the AFGA.

At the annual conference Fred McDougall, deputy minister of the Department of Public Lands and Wildlife, reported that the regionalization of the department, implemented in 1980, was working well, helping to develop a harmonious working relationship both with municipal governments and within the Department of Energy and Natural Resources and with other departments. This is a point well taken because concerned members of the AFGA could work with local regional managers who had decision-making authority to address their concerns without having to work with officials in Edmonton or resort to taking political action. There was also a report from Ernie Psikla, executive director of operations for the Fish and Wildlife Division, on regional operations and implementation of the new Wildlife Policy for Alberta. The various regional directors (Frank Cardinal, Ray Makowecki, Gerry Thompson, Tom Smith and Duane Radford) also provided a summary of their activities.

Don Sparrow, newly appointed Minister of Public Lands and Wildlife, who replaced Bud Miller, gave a conference address on three general subjects: (1) Implementation of the 1982 fish and wildlife policy for Alberta, (2) Public access to private and public lands, and (3) Hunter training. Sparrow advised, "I am not pre-pared, at this point in time, to endorse compulsory hunter training as a policy position of this government."

Although he was no longer with the Fish and Wildlife Division, Gordon Kerr, regional director for the Canadian Wildlife Service for the western and northern regions, once again made a presentation at an annual conference and addressed the various functions of this agency.

Distinguished service recognition certificates were presented to Herb Cobb, Vince Durda, Terry Ferster, Cecil Fowler, Bob Little, Jack McIntosh, Norman Ray, the Royal Canadian Legion (Ogden Branch – Calgary) and Robert H. (Bob) Scammell.

Special plaques were awarded to Garry Allison of the *Lethbridge Herald* for his continued co-operation with clubs in southern Alberta; Ed Struzik of the *Edmonton Journal* for his efforts in reporting environmental issues of importance to the AFGA; Fred Kazakoff of CFRN Radio for providing coverage of environmental issues in which the association had input and Wayne Brown, St. Paul fish and wildlife officer, for actively promoting hunter education and conservation in the various districts where he had been stationed.

Ozanne advised that the controversial stream enhancement project being conducted by Dr. Stuart Smith, who at the time was working as a private biological consultant, "…has been progressing satisfactorily and the first phase of the project is now completed." Lynx Creek was the study stream, and a progress report was made available to delegates.

Eve Ozanne was honoured as the Lady Conservationist of the Year for her support and help during her husband Roy's term of office as president and for her continued interest in the association. This was the second time she had been so honoured.

The AFGA Wildlife Trust Fund became operational and started to receive donations from Mrs. Dianne Loewen, Denis Pattinson and Archie and Janet Hogg. Issues related to toxic chemicals in the environment were of concern to members of the AFGA and Gordon Merrick of Lethbridge made presentations at the hazardous waste public hearings, being singled out by Ozanne for his outstanding contribution. In his closing address, Ozanne thanked the many members of the AFGA for their help and support, and in particular his wife, Eve, and family. Ozanne was a class act; he closed his address by saying, "How do you thank a family like ours who are always supportive without reservation in everything we do?" This is a point well taken because the AFGA president's office is very demanding on family members, who seldom receive the recognition they so richly deserve.

Secretary manager Paul Morck reported that head office licence sales revenues were about $10,000, compared with $1,500 in 1979. Lottery 12 had sales of $92,300, a small increase of $800 over

Canada geese at lakeside.

COURTESY OF TRAVEL ALBERTA

COURTESY OF LILLA PFERSCHY

Bird nest in a tree.

Lottery 11. Over the years, the AFGA clubs had raised $750,000 from the sale of lottery tickets. Membership had increased from 22,751 in 1981 to 23,356 in 1982.

Environment chair Gordon Merrick reported on open and frank discussions during meetings with Alberta government officials regarding the need for a hazardous waste site. On the other hand, he advised: "The same cannot be said of the government's attitude and secrecy involving water in the province. Last spring was to be the beginning of a brainwashing attempt by the Provincial government to convince us that inter-basin transfer was necessary. This is in the form of a program called 'On The Waterfront'. This sleek television show was run without commercial breaks for half an hour on prime time over CBC stations at taxpayer's expense. It has since been used at one meeting I attended to demonstrate government stupidity and secrecy."

On a more positive note, Merrick advised: "We now have new spill legislation in the province and another tool in our fight for clean air and water. Again it is at the local level where the action is. If you come across an environmental emergency (such as a spill) promptly report it to Alberta Environment." Merrick also supported a landmark resolution at the 1983 conference dealing with minimum flow. "It suggests that what we require for a minimum flow in our rivers and streams is such that native fish and wildlife will continue to thrive in a healthy condition."

Vice president Ron Gladish announced that the Wildlife Trust Fund had commenced. "We have had some donations and hope this conference will be the kick-off of the fund. The aim is to acquire lands that are important from a wildlife point of view. Our major thrust will be to enable hunters and fishers to make any size donation to the trust in either money or land, or even long term leases."

Gladish congratulated the Fish and Wildlife Division for completing the 1982 Fish and Wildlife Policy for Alberta. "I think one of the most important parts of the policy is that the Minister must give periodic declaration on the status of the wildlife resource in Alberta." Critics have subsequently complained this is akin to arranging deck chairs on the Titanic, in the absence of concrete action to preserve fish and wildlife habitat, however, this is seen as a fundamental requirement to manage Alberta's fish and game resources. Former assistant deputy minister Dennis Surrendi deserves full credit for initiating this ongoing monitoring program. [At present, the Fish and Wildlife Division is undertaking such status reports on a five-year basis.] Gladish also reported: "It is really gratifying to see some of our zone directors taking the bull by the horns and solving problems in their own zones. We truly need our zone directors to act on their own and deal with the resolutions in their own areas as they can be just as effective as your senior executives."

Junior vice president Jack Shaver advised, "The life blood of our association is the local club. Their activities in the community do much to form an opinion of our association by the general public. Those clubs active with projects that benefit everyone are to be congratulated."

National Wildlife Week chair Jack Easterbrook beamed: "In 1982 the music began to come in. At the conference, 24 clubs took 305 Wildlife Week kits. Reports were received from eight clubs. These eight clubs reached over 5,000 students. This is very encouraging and represents a lot of hard work by a few dedicated people. In fact it is an incredible performance. The northeast region of the Department of Energy and Natural Resources [under Ray Makowecki, Regional director] reported contacting over 10,000 people during National Wildlife Week."

Environmental public relations chair Elmer Kure was uncharacteristically blunt in his conference report: "As president Roy [Ozanne] has put it many times, it gets downright irritating to have to continue to update new ministers and new management personnel on fish and game positions and policies, as if our values had changed, or were no longer worth defending. We have staked our claim on most issues like the east slopes policy, and protection of Alpine areas, like the Willmore and prime protection lands. We have made our position very well known on air and water quality Standards and there would be no better heritage to pass on to the next generations than clean air, water and unspoiled land. We are challenged to continue to re-state our position on access to public lands, and a qualification system for those who go afield to hunt and harvest wildlife. But we are hampered in achieving some of these goals by unconcerned civil servants and misguided politicians who somehow think freedoms can be best protected without any rules for accountability." Kure wound up his address: "And, despite my criticism of some civil servants and politicians who seem uncaring, thanks to those who do care and work with us."

Elmer Kure may not have realized what he was on to. There was change in the wind, including the commercialization of wildlife and the de-regulation of industry to spur economic development of Alberta. Privatization was the mantra of the Progressive Conservative government – a stated party policy. Government was laying the groundwork to step aside as a regulator, passing the buck to industry to be its own watchdog in the years ahead and to create private-sector opportunities to profit from Alberta's fish and wildlife.

The culture of the civil service was also changing from being more or less impartial to the party in power to that of being an obedient servant of the government. For example, the Bureau of Public Affairs was largely perceived as an extension of the ruling party, being responsible for disseminating political messages as well as government policy. The next couple of decades saw the Fish and Wildlife Division transferred from one department to another in a series of seemingly never-ending government re-organizations, under a multitude of different ministers - most of them of a junior portfolio - who used the department as a stepping stone up the ladder of power. Regional boundaries were forever changing and divisional staff were kept off balance. Files often moved from one office to another, some being misplaced in the process. A great deal of continuity and productivity were lost. As more and more services were privatized the public became disconnected from the staff in the Fish and Wildlife Division.

One example was the privatization of sales of fishing and hunting licences in the 1990s, in which private businesses were provided equipment to issue licences. After this occurred many members of the public no longer had a reason to visit an office of the Fish and Wildlife Division, and gradually lost contact with the staff. Many staff in the Fish and Wildlife Division were left demoralized and frustrated. Some left the organization for more meaningful work. This was a marked contrast to the 1970s and 1980s, the glory years of the Fish and Wildlife Division, when staff such as Frank Bishop, veteran Peace River and Lethbridge regional fisheries biologist, joked he was having so much fun he didn't even like to take holidays.

Fish chair Nestor Romaniuk reported, "It would appear that 1982 will go on record as not being a very good year. It was a year where our environment suffered tremendously due to pollution. We have rivers polluted to the extent that the fish were not edible. As your fish chairman, I find it very difficult to report to you that I have accomplished anything significant that will resolve the problems that have been decades in the making." Fish in the Athabasca River near Fort Chipewyan were heavily contaminated with an unknown chemical prompting the closure of the commercial fish-ery. Grande Prairie's new water supply weir on the Beaverlodge River blocked the spring migration of Arctic grayling spawners – no fish ladder had been installed on the weir. Romaniuk also reported on the provincial walleye enhancement program being in full swing. Design of the Cold Lake fish hatchery construction was on schedule with production planned for the spring of 1994. He advised, "I'm pleased to report to you that in 1982, the Alberta government had the best year ever in reference to fish stocking: 5,790,000. There were 4.8 million rainbow trout; 250,000 lake trout; 93,000 cutthroat trout; 266,000 brook trout; 8,000 brown trout; 17,000 pike; 140,000 perch and 150,000 walleye."

Both Romaniuk and information chair Norm Ferguson once again addressed the lack of communication between clubs and zones and zones and head office, a seemingly chronic issue.

Romaniuk advised, "It would appear many members feel the best way to solve a problem is to wait and present it at conference, but we can't solve too many [problems] on short notice." Ferguson reported he "received no response as to your thoughts on a national hunting and fishing day."

Renewable resource chair Martha Kostuch advised, "A major change has taken place during the past five years. No longer do fish-and-gamers react negatively to spending time (and money) protecting the environment. Most members now realize that quality hunting and fishing depend on clean air, clean water, and good habitat." She also reported, "The Lodgepole Blowout [sour gas well west of Edmonton] brought concerns about sour gas emissions to a head. The AFGA added its support to recommendations calling for a health study, a full investigation of the environmental effects, and a public inquiry." Kostuch also advised that water quality, especially in the South and North Saskatchewan and Athabasca rivers, was and would continue to be a major concern until Alberta adopted and implemented a policy of zero pollution (point source). This was just another example of the slow progress of the Alberta government to clean up Alberta's waterways.

Hunting chair Les Yaceyko reported, "In 1982, we have seen significant progress in terms of wildlife management. The introduction of the [fish and wildlife] policy statement has set the direction for other government departments as well as all Albertans for future game management. The decentralization program of the Fish and Wildlife Department is showing positive effects in several ways. Response to important regional issues has shown a marked improvement and the establishment of new district offices has helped to fill the gap in enforcement distribution." Yaceyko

1984

Resolution No. 8   BE IT RESOLVED THAT: The AFGA petition the government to add an additional $5 stamp to our wildlife certificates each year, and such funds from these monies be turned over to the AFGA "Wildlife Trust" to be [used] solely for the purchase of wildlife habitat. This resolution was defeated.

Resolution No. 10   BE IT RESOLVED THAT: Fish and Wildlife [Division] enforcement officers be given the right to bear sidearms in the interest of officer safety and improved enforcement. This resolution was defeated.

COURTESY OF JACK GRAHAM

Jack Graham on a cougar hunt, January 1984.

stated that the elk transplant to the Athabasca area in 1981 was more successful than the previous year and that there was some reproduction in the herd. He also advised, "Reduction of the caribou herds in Alberta continued at an alarming rate even though a hunting moratorium on the species has been imposed. An estimated 30 percent of the population in the Berland-Willmore herd was lost during 1982 to carnivores and other natural causes."

Pheasant-rearing program co-ordinator Phil Ficht reported on the steady growth of this program among affiliated clubs. "Last year we had five new clubs entering the program. These were Vulcan, Thorsby, Devon, Onoway and Picture Butte. These clubs completed rearing pens and released approximately 800 pheasants to the wild." There were 10 clubs already involved in the program: Leduc, Calgary, Iron Creek, Claresholm, West Buffalo Lake, Cold Lake, St. Albert and District, Fox Creek, Vegreville and Sylvan Lake. [note: zone 1 chair Horst Fauser reported that the following clubs in his zone also had rearing projects: Medicine Hat, Fort Macleod and Lethbridge.] Ficht stated the purpose of raising and releasing pheasants. "I believe this project serves a three-fold purpose:

1. It increases the population of pheasants in our province.
2. It keeps the membership of participating clubs actively working for their association.
3. The projects promote: a public awareness of habitat retention and enhancement for wildlife; an image of Fish and Game Associations as more than groups of hunters and fishermen; co-operation between landowners, organized sportsmen and our government."

Zone 1 chair Horst Fauser provided a lengthy regional report with several notable highlights: the South Saskatchewan River basin planning program to develop long-term strategies for water allocation and management had started; work was underway on the Castle River and Livingstone-Porcupine Hills co-ordinated land management policies. Fauser advised: "Ecological reserves: the act is a joke. The least damaging activities on these reserves, like hunting and fishing, are prohibited outright. Mining, lumbering, grazing, seismographic trails if presently in operation are allowed to continue and licences might be renewed. Eight are planned for

southern Alberta." These reserves were a very controversial issue among members of the AFGA, especially in southern Alberta. The AFGA members appeared at public meetings hosted by the provincial parks division, which spearheaded the proposed legislation. However, the input of these members was largely ignored.

While zone 2 chair Ken Yank reported poor participation of clubs in zone meetings (only eight people showed up of 1,700 regional members), zone 3 chair Doug Rumsey reported "Communication and co-operation of club to club and club to zone has improved dramatically. The involvement of clubs in zone 3 doing hunter training courses, building rifle ranges, raising pheasants, goose-nesting projects, National Wildlife Week, and the conservation camp participation has also increased to a level of zone recognition."

Zone 5 chair Don Appleby advised, "The zone 5 spring and fall meetings continue to be well attended. Club reports indicated pheasant projects, hunter training, elk transplants, wild game suppers and fish derbies are high on the list of accomplishments and interest in club operations." Appleby also reported, "The St. Paul regional fish and wildlife office continue to cooperate by sending staff members to make presentations and engage in open discussion during a question period."

1984 Ron Gladish became president of the AFGA in 1983. Gladish was a very popular president who always seemed to have a smile on his face, and was well respected by members of the AFGA and government. He was a very obliging person, easy to work with and a master of compromise.

RON GLADISH President: 1983-85

I was born in Princeton, B.C., in 1948. My dad worked in a gold mine at Hedley, along Highway 3 between Keremeos and Princeton. We moved to Victoria briefly and to Calgary in 1953 and Edmonton in 1956. As a youngster, I spent my summers in Penticton and started to understand my love and appreciation of the outdoors. My maternal grandparents were avid outdoors people and I spent most weekends either camping, fishing or hunting.

COURTESY OF THE AFGA
RON GLADISH

I think I was around 20 when I went to my first Edmonton Fish and Game Association (EFGA) meeting; I was hooked. I met other outdoor enthusiasts of all ages and from every walk of life. It was gratifying to be involved with a group of people who shared my passion. Over the next 17 years, activities included the Uncles at Large fishing weekend, pollution committee, hunter training, Edmonton sportsmen's show, EFGA magazine, rifle range and goose bale nest sites, to name a few.

There were also many controversial political issues and briefs on Jasper National Park development, urban land use and pollution in the North Saskatchewan River to which I had to attend. My first AFGA conference was in Edmonton, I think in 1969. My keenness for anti-pollution issues earned me a chairmanship. The first time I addressed some 300 delegates was one of the hardest things I had ever done in my life to that point in time.

Upon reflection, being involved with the fish and game clubs and provincial executive was not a hobby, a pastime, or even numerous events. Being part of the fish and game association was a lifestyle. Most activities were family oriented and a great way to teach your own children the values that you held so close.

I hosted the 50th AFGA conference in Edmonton for the EFGA. After that meeting, I became more involved in provincial issues. I was appointed to the provincial committee to develop integrated resource management plans and spent numerous hours reviewing the planning process and providing a fish and game perspective to the provincial government.

Looking back, there were many personally rewarding programs that I was involved in. The Fishing Derby for the Physically Disabled is one of the best. My wife Linda and I fished with different people over the years including Ben and Bev. Ben was totally blind and Bev had about 10 percent vision. They were phenomenal. After trolling for a while without much success we decided to try casting in this little cove. I showed Ben how to swing his fishing rod back, and touch the outboard motor with the tip to get the right distance. From then on he never did touch the motor, he brought the rod back to within an inch and then made his cast. He even bragged to Bev that he could cast further; he listened to the button on the reel being released and the splash of the lure and timed the distance between. Yes, Bev and Ben caught lots of fish, but I learned all the lessons.

The issues of the day were no different than they are today. Hunter ethics, access to land for hunting and fishing were paramount when I was president. It is hard to look back and measure our successes because we seemed to lose more battles than we won. However, if we were not there, if our voice was not part of the many divergent views, just imagine how our province would have developed or evolved.

Many provincial government programs started with the AFGA. What began as Hunter Ethics by Linda Hirsche and the Southern Alberta Outdoorsmen became Operation Respect. The Wildlife Trust, which Roy Ozanne and I spearheaded, became Habitat Trust. It is with great pride that I look back at being instrumental in the hiring of our first co-ordinator for the Buck for Wildlife program to liaise with the local clubs. The working relationship with the then -minister Hon. Don Sparrow enabled us to develop a system to get our clubs funding for many worthwhile programs.

I served on the steering committee for the provincial government to establish integrated resource management plans across the province. While the system was not perfect, we were a major partner in participating with other stakeholders in developing plans that attempted to consider all resource users in the planning areas.

During my term we developed a new club manual that informed local clubs, zone executives and provincial committee chairs of the multitude of programs the AFGA offered and how to be more effective in their local areas. I was privileged to attend meetings at some 70 local clubs and all of the zones in the province.

After my term on the provincial executive, I served on the board of directors for the Canadian Wildlife Federation (CWF) and was their president from 1993-95. My involvement in the AFGA over the years gave me a multitude of skills, and a conservation perspective that has served me well in my involvement with the CWF and in my business dealings over the years. I still am an active sheep and deer hunter and angler who enjoys the out of doors as much as when I was 20. I am sure that without the continued involvement of the thousands of Fish-and-Gamers my pastime would be quite different.

[Biography prepared by Ron Gladish.]

The 55th annual conference was held in Edmonton in 1984; the theme of the conference was "Natural Resources and Law Enforcement." Some 278 delegates attended the conference which was hosted by the Leduc Fish and Game Association.

Dock at Crimson Lake.

COURTESY OF TRAVEL ALBERTA

Distinguished service recognition certificates were awarded to: John M. (Jack) Graham, Ron Pittman, Ed Tremblay, Doug Hodgins, Percy Hunkin, Darrel Skinner, Lyle Fullerton, Harold Rhodes, Bill Nummi and family and the Edmonton Activettes.

Fred McDougall, deputy minister of Energy and Natural Resources, summarized the highlights of departmental relations with the association, noting that vice president Jack Shaver worked effectively on a subcommittee to simplify the hunting regulations. He also spoke of departmental co-operation with the association to develop shooting facilities on Crown land and the Use Respect program that was introduced in 1983, noting that it seemed to have worked very well. McDougall summed up matters by advising that both the department and the AFGA were working for the same goal, which was better hunting and fishing in the province of Alberta.

The assistant deputy minister of the Fish and Wildlife Division, Dennis Surrendi, deviated from presentations given by his predecessor Gordon Kerr and presented a non-political, non-controversial, philosophical dissertation about the importance of hunting at the annual conference. It is notable that after Gordon Kerr resigned from the Fish and Wildlife Division, his successor, Surrendi, gave the last presentation by an assistant deputy minister at the 1984 annual conference, and it was not about divisional activities, goals or objectives.

Gordon Kerr, however, did attend the conference as regional director for the Canadian Wildlife Service and reported that the swift fox had been reintroduced into Alberta. He also spoke about a new five-year waterfowl crop-damage agreement between the federal government and Alberta, and announced the formation of Wildlife Habitat Canada as a non-profit corporation in support of wildlife habitat protection and development across Canada.

Don Sparrow, associate minister of Public Lands and Wildlife, provided an overview of his portfolio and departmental operations, with regard to *Wildlife Act* revisions, a status report on fish and wildlife in Alberta, the Mount Allen ski site and the department's public information program regarding access to public land. Sparrow was never one to shy away from controversy and met it head-on at the annual conferences. He spoke highly of the good working relationship he enjoyed with officials from the association, singling out vice president Jack Shaver, who had been elected as chairman of the Fish and Wildlife Advisory Council in 1983.

Sparrow announced that the Allison Creek Brood Trout Station in the Crowsnest Pass opened in 1983 and was in production. Sparrow provided one of the most comprehensive and detailed reports ever presented at an annual conference by the minister responsible for fish and game in Alberta.

*A*nother major announcement the minister made at the 1984 conference concerned the Alberta Fish and Wildlife Division introducing a new and innovative wildlife education program called "Project WILD." Project WILD (Wildlife In Living Design) is an American program the Canadian Wildlife Federation (CWF) adapted and modified for use in Canada. In 1982, the CWF seconded Norm Gaelick from the Alberta Fish and Wildlife Division and hired Alberta writer and biologist Don Meredith to adapt and implement the program. Project WILD introduced wildlife topics to school classrooms using activities that did not detract from regular curriculum subjects. It was designed to help teachers use wildlife as a motivator to learn—"why count oranges and apples when you can count deer and ducks?" For example, while learning a math lesson through Project WILD, students would also come to understand something about population biology and the need to harvest a surplus. It was a very popular program with both teachers and students. As of this writing, Project WILD is alive and well in many jurisdictions across North America and is still sponsored by the CWF in Canada.

Gladish reported that "the zone system has never worked so well since our directors began working directly with their counterparts in government," yet another kudo in support of the regionalization of the Fish and Wildlife Division in 1980. This view was re-enforced by environmental public relations director Elmer Kure who reported: "We are also getting more co-operation from the Fish and Wildlife Division. There is also optimism on the political horizon, as land and water-use plans unfold as a result of past studies and public involvement in these important areas."

Senior vice president Jack Shaver advised: "I represented our association on a 'simplification of legislation' subcommittee of the [Fish and Wildlife] advisory council last year. One very positive offshoot of the committee was that for the first time our zone directors met with Fish & Wildlife personnel to review a draft proposal for the 1984 hunting season covering season dates and limits for various species of big-game and game-birds. Our zone directors were thus able to present club suggestions directly to fish and wildlife." [Editors note: This was the first time a non-government official was elected to chair the advisory committee. A new terms of reference, drafted by Don Hayden, past president, approved by the advisory council, was put in place just before the election of Shaver.]

*A*fter the 1980 re-organization of the Fish and Wildlife Division, creating five administrative regions, there was a major shift in decision-making from headquarters to the regions. A further decentralization of program delivery occurred in 1982 when additional authority in the Fish and Wildlife Division shifted to the regions from headquarters. In hindsight, it seems odd that this very positive regional structure was eliminated in 2002, phasing out the regional director positions, after such a decentralized system had received so many accolades from both elected officials and senior members of the AFGA.

The provincial government adopted one of the AFGA farmer-sportsman relations programs, "Operation Respect," and coined it the "Use Respect" program in 1983, a highly popular move. The Use Respect program featured radio and TV ads with NHL celebrity Lanny McDonald, the wildly popular Calgary Flames hockey player and Glen Sather, then Edmonton Oilers' coach and general manager. The government had finally taken direct intervention in matters of access after participating in workshops orchestrated by Alva Bair, one of Alberta's most well-respected sportsmen and a farmer from the Milk River area. The most common complaint of landowners was that hunters did not ask for permission to hunt, and this lack of courtesy was a real concern, especially in southern Alberta. Gladish reported that implementation of the Use Respect program "...has been a major factor in reducing conflicts between hunters, fishers, and landowners." Much of the formative work on the Use Respect program was done by the AFGA Southern Alberta Outdoorsmen out of Milk River as well as fish and game clubs at Foremost, Medicine Hat and Lethbridge.

Gladish urged the AFGA delegates to make their concerns known with regard to the drafting of a new *Wildlife Act*.

*T*he AFGA purchased its first computer in 1984 and was experimenting with word processor and the machine's programming capabilities.

The AFGA senior vice president, Jack Shaver, became chairman of the Fish and Wildlife Advisory Council, an advisory committee to the minister responsible for fish and wildlife management in Alberta—a sounding board for all new policies and programs. The Fish and Wildlife Advisory Council would be enlarged to 22 organizations in 1984. The Western Stock Growers' Association and the AFGA were represented by two members each. So-called "white papers" (researched discussion documents) were to be brought forward, including fish management, game farming/ranching, and fur management. At the time, the council was working on several other items: protection of hunters from harassment, authorized hunting equipment, baiting of black bears, firearm restrictions relative to roadways, disposition of seizures, and shotgun restrictions.

Many members of the AFGA were active with the integrated resource planning program, as these plans were being developed throughout Alberta.

The minister of Public Lands and Wildlife recognized the value of the AFGA junior education programs and embarked on a process to assemble land in each zone for zone recreation camp sites. A controversy arose between the AFGA and Alberta government plans to build ski facilities for the 1988 Winter Olympics on Mount Allan in Kananaskis Country. The area in question was an important bighorn sheep winter range.

Secretary manager Paul Morck reported that membership at the end of 1983 was 23,784 up slightly (400) up from 1982. Morck commented, "The Olympic skiing on Mount Allan appears to be going ahead at any expense, including resident sheep herd."

Vice president Nestor Romaniak reported: "I was very pleased to see the government recognize the Athabasca Fish and Game Association for their elk transplant efforts at the Annual Order of the Bighorn dinner. This recognition proves that our affiliated clubs are doing a commendable job and are, in fact, being rewarded for their efforts."

In the May 1984 issue of Western Canada Outdoors magazine, Irwin McIntosh paid tribute to three Alberta women who had distinguished themselves as active leaders in the association: Eve Ozanne, Bibiane Foisy and Dr. Martha Kostuch.

Mr. McIntosh reported that when Eve Ozanne was president of the Edmonton Fish and Game Association in 1976 and 1977, membership rose to more than 2,700; she spent her apprenticeship as a membership chairperson and editor of the club's newsletter, before becoming president.

Bibiane Foisy had been recently elected as president of the 329-member St. Paul Fish and Game Association. McIntosh noted: "She took the job in January because no one else wanted it. She's glad she did." Bibiane enjoyed hunting and took a trophy white-tailed deer that was big enough to rate an article in the Western Sportsman magazine, entitled "Feminine Intuition Pays Off." Foisy was chair of the St. Paul AFGA's social committee for 10 years, prior to becoming president. She also served as a hunter education and firearms safety Instructor, as well as being a committee member of her zone's conservation camp.

Mr. McIntosh reported that Dr. Martha Kostuch was "a gal with a mind of her own." She was a doctor of veterinary medicine who refused to accept the AFGA "Women's Conservation of the Year Award" in 1981 because she did not believe in special awards based on gender. She and her husband, Tom, came to Alberta from Minnesota in 1975; both were practicing veterinarians at the time at Rocky Mountain House. Kostuch was a past president of the Rocky Mountain House AFGA club, and at the time was chair of the renewable resources committee. Despite being a mild-mannered person she had the heart of a lion and was not afraid to tackle the government or big corporations on environmental issues.

Bighorn sheep along the highway.

Fishing chair Lloyd Shea reported: "The fishing picture is at the very best spotty. The stream fishermen of the eastern slopes face an increasingly gloomy future. I started fishing in the western part of central Alberta just after World War II. Since that time I would estimate we have lost 75-80 percent of our most productive trout water – the meadow streams. Unfortunately, only those who fished the area seem to realize or care about what was lost."

Hunter education chair Keith Baker reported there were two conservation camps in 1983, one at Goldeye Lake near Nordegg, and one at Lac Bellevue near St. Paul in zone 5, with the possibility of a third camp in 1984. Baker also noted that Dan Merills had founded the hunter education tournament as an affiliate of the newly formed Hunter Education Association. Baker advised: "A major step for hunter education in this province was the statement in the discussion paper for the proposed *Wildlife Act* (Nov. 1983), which reads, 'it is proposed that all first-time hunters be required to pass a test before becoming eligible for a hunting licence.'"

COURTESY OF LILLA PFERSCHY

Calming view of the sky against Canadian Rockies.

Zone 4 director Bob Tanghe reported: "In my visits to the clubs I have become aware that quite a bit of parochialism is being practiced by some of the clubs. By that I mean they are only interested in what goes on within their own sphere of influence. This is not good. We have to adopt the attitude of one for all and all for one; work together for the good of the organization and forget about feeding our own ego. We must be just as interested in what goes on in other areas of the province, and give whatever help we can, as what goes on in our neck of the woods, because at some point in future time we might have to deal with a similar problem in our own area and will be looking for help."

Linda Hirsche, hunter ethics chair, sent samples of posters and bumper stickers to all clubs to help promote hunter ethics; her vision was to reverse the trend of posting land and to continually educate all hunters to practice proper hunting behaviour. Hirsche also suggested that clubs should use billboards in prominent locations to get the message to hunters about hunter ethics, a popular program started by clubs in Foremost, Warner and Milk River.

In the May-June 1984 *Western Canada Outdoors*, physically disabled fishing derby chair Carole Romaniuk rallied the membership around the June 3 derby "I am of the opinion that all members of the fish and game clubs will get involved and make this derby the best ever. This is a great opportunity for us, as members of fish and game, to get publicity in the positive, as we endeavor to help people who may not be as fortunate as most of us. There are times when fish and game members unintentionally receive negative publicity; be it from farmers, ranchers or individuals who want guns done away with completely. Let's show the people of Alberta that we care by getting together as a group and helping others who too often are left out, and let's help them enjoy the wonderful outdoors for at least one day in a year."

1985

Resolution No. 10 **BE IT RESOLVED THAT:** Fish and Wildlife [Division] enforcement officers be given the right to bear sidearms in the interest of officer safety and improved enforcement. This resolution was defeated.

Resolution No. 18 **BE IT RESOLVED THAT:** The AFGA petition the government to add an additional $5 stamp to our wildlife certificates each year, and such funds from these monies be turned over to the AFGA "Wildlife Trust" to be [used] solely for the purchase of wildlife habitat. This resolution was defeated.

In the same newsletter, renewable resource chair Martha Kostuch reported the AFGA was one of six organizations that won a court appeal on March 14 against the proposed Odyssey development. "The Odyssey is a convention centre-resort complex for 500 people proposed for development at the junction of the Cline River and the David Thompson Highway," reported Kostuch.

Don Bate reported that one of the most notable changes in bird-game regulations in store for sportsmen was the introduction of a $10 pheasant stamp in addition to the regular $5 upland bird-game licence for pheasant hunters. The extra revenue was

COURTESY OF THE FISH AND WILDLIFE DIVISION

Hon. Don Sparrow (L) and Garnet Anthony, 1985 Order of the Bighorn award recipient.

COURTESY OF THE FISH AND WILDLIFE DIVISION

Fish and Wildlife Division representative Norm Gaelick (L) and Hon. Bud Miller at the 1985 Order of the Bighorn awards.

to be earmarked to aid in the rehabilitation of pheasant habitat. In the Alberta edition of the July-August 1984 *Western Canada Outdoors* newsletter Bate worried "…I can foresee the extra pheasant stamp revenue being lost in the shuffle;" as it turned out, an accurate assessment of the situation.

In the July-August 1984 *Western Canada Outdoors*, Bob Scammell reported: "For starters, the message should be simply that changing the concept upon which our wildlife management is founded—that the game is public, not private, property—is unacceptable and so is the concept of game ranching. Throw in, if you wish, a plug for public access to public land." Also in the same issue of *Western Canada Outdoors*, Bruce Masterman reported on the success of a 1973 introduction of Merriam's turkeys in the Porcupine Hills, 11 years after introducing them into the Cypress Hills in southeastern Alberta. An April report from the Fish and Wildlife Division estimated the Porcupine Hills turkey population at 125-175 birds. [A status report prepared by the division in April 1983 said landowner sighting reports indicated 175-215 turkeys in and around Cypress Hills Provincial Park in the winter of 1982-83.]

In the September-October 1984 *Western Canada Outdoors* Bruce Masterman reported: "Aug. 9, 1984 will go down in history books as a dark day for southern Alberta outdoors groups. That was the day Premier Peter Lougheed and Environment Minister Fred Bradley sat together at a Lethbridge press conference and announced what amounts to be the pending execution of cold-water fisheries on three scenic rivers." Construction of the Oldman River Dam was slated to begin in 1986. Masterman quoted Ross MacDonald, Coleman Fish and Game Association secretary and local outdoor writer, who called the decision "lousy" and "strictly political."

A hot-button issue of the day was the revised east slopes policy 1984, an offshoot of the 1977 east slopes policy, which was touted by the AFGA as an excellent framework for use of Alberta's eastern slopes area. Under the revised policy, which was pro-recreation and tourism, integrated regional management plans would be utilized to set the pace for development and forest-land-use zones would be used to enforce regulatory issues related to access.

Another highly controversial issue was the proposed ecological reserve legislation, which would prohibit hunting and fishing in designated areas. Members of the AFGA from southern Alberta, in particular, were opposed to such measures, and at least some of the local MLAs complained they had not been properly briefed on the implications of this legislation by provincial parks division officials.

The new Minister of Public Lands and Wildlife, Don Sparrow, issued the AFGA clubs a challenge at the 1984 conference to apply for a $10,000 grant under the Buck for Wildlife program for a fish or wildlife project; many clubs took up the challenge. Because of some administrative problems, AFGA decided to hire a co-ordinator to assist clubs in developing proposals. Lyle Fullerton was hired as the co-ordinator in 1984 and spearheaded the preparation of projects.

Pauline (L) and Lewis Ramstead, with Hon. Allan Adair at the 1986 Order of the Bighorn awards.

In 1984 a new *Wildlife Act* replaced Alberta's former *Wildlife Act* which was Chapter W-9 of the Revised Statutes of Alberta 1980. The old *Wildlife Act*, in section 32(1), prohibited hunting of big game and game birds on Sunday. Sub-section (2) of the new act made special provisions to hunt on Sunday in much of what is termed the Green Zone, primarily unsettled Crown lands in northern Alberta.

1985 Ron Gladish remained as president of the AFGA in 1984.

The Hon. Don Sparrow, associate minister of Public Lands and Wildlife, and Stephen Stiles, MLA Olds-Didsbury and Chairman of the Alberta Integrated Planning Advisory Committee, announced the advisory groups' unanimous support of the 1984 revision of the eastern slopes policy in the January-February 1985 *Western Canada Outdoors*, just prior to the annual conference of the AFGA. The Alberta Integrated Planning Advisory Committee was created in 1981 to provide the advice of resource user groups to the associate minister on the integrated resource planning program for Alberta's public lands.

In taking stock of events during his term of office, Gladish stated in his conference report, "We have come a long ways in two years, with so many things happening especially within the Fish and Wildlife Division." The 56th annual conference was held at the El Rancho Motor Hotel in Lethbridge in 1985. The theme of the

conference was "Water - What Is Its Worth?" Norm Ferguson, a veritable institution in the ranks of the AFGA, was the host conference chairman.

Gladish reported that consultants were working on over 20 integrated Resource Management Plans; Ed Wildman was the government official responsible for this program. Public input was a big part of the planning process and Gladish advised "One thing the plans accomplish is that we can finally see what all government agencies have in mind for the planning area. The planning exercise forces all government agencies to state their objectives in the plan. So finally, a fish and game member can

Phyllis (L) and Jack Graham at the 1986 Order of the Bighorn awards.

look in one book and see what the government intends to do." Gladish also advised, "I have seen a vast improvement over the past couple of years," regarding the AFGA relationship with government, with meetings with key officials at least once every two months. Membership stood at 23,386 in 1984. Finally, a hunter-training program proposal had been drafted for first-time hunters and the AFGA members were directly involved in providing information for hunting season changes.

Many provisions in the new Alberta *Wildlife Act* were supported by the AFGA, with the exception of sections dealing with trust funds and game ranching. In particular, the AFGA had long advocated provisions concerning:

COURTESY OF THE FISH AND WILDLIFE DIVISION
Ernie Psikla (L) and Vic Scheuerman, 1985 Order of the Bighorn award recipient.

COURTESY OF THE FISH AND WILDLIFE DIVISION
Lloyd Shea at the Order of the Bighorn awards, 1985.

1. Provision for mandatory hunter training for first-time hunters.
2. Heavier fines and penalties.
3. Anti-harassment protection for hunters.
4. Interest-bearing trust funds.
5. Ability for the AFGA to institute a hide collection programs for fundraising.
6. Prohibition against hunting on game ranches.
7. Prohibition against using Crown lands for game ranches.
8. Provision for the sale of seized items due to *Wildlife Act* offences.

Gladish closed his report by pointing out the influence of the AFGA in government circles because the organization was effective, influential and well respected.

The AFGA issued a position statement on game ranching which was presented at the 56th annual conference.

1986

Resolution

The Spruce Grove Fish and Game Association made an extraordinary resolution at the annual conference, BE IT RESOLVED THAT: whereas a press release was issued by associate minister of Public Lands and Wildlife, Don Sparrow, on Aug. 1, 1985 and this press release announced a major change in public land policies whereby current grazing lease holders are given the option to convert their lease to development for cultivation without competition from other applicants, be it resolved that the AFGA categorically oppose the Alberta government's proposal to sell any public lands, grazing leases and community pastures. And be it further resolved that the government reverse this new policy for the sake of future generations and that this public land remain public land in perpetuity. The resolution was carried.

Senior vice president Jack Shaver reported, "Our association has two representatives on the Alberta Fish and Wildlife Advisory council. In December 1983 I was elected chairman of this council by members for a two year term." He went on to explain, "The primary interest of the council is to ensure that government policies, programs and legislation to manage the fish and wildlife resources of Alberta recognize the needs and sensitivities of all resource users."

Shaver also mentioned, "As I have said on many occasions, the lifeblood of our association will always be the local club. Their activities in the community do so much to form public opinion as to the value of our association and the need for membership." He added, "Our conservation camps were most successful, thanks to Martha Kostuch and zone directors Doug Rumsey and Don Appleby." Shaver's vision was to eventually have a conservation camp in each zone.

Jack Shaver presided over a ribbon-cutting ceremony for the new AFGA head office on Nov. 29, 1985 as the association officially opened its new provincial headquarters at 6924-104 St. in Edmonton. At 3:30 p.m., the AFGA president Shaver and past president Ben Rosnau cut the ribbon, signifying the opening, with Alderman Ron Hayter representing the City of Edmonton and Don Sparrow, associate minister of Public Lands and Wildlife, representing the Alberta government.

Vice president Nestor Romaniuk reported, "Looking into the future, I feel that the executive of this organization must submit to the Fish and Wildlife Division a list of our priorities. All energies must be expounded to see that these priorities are accomplished." Romaniuk also explained, "This past year, I was afforded the opportunity to serve as a member of the Fish and Wildlife Advisory Council representing our organization. I would like to take this opportunity to explain to the membership that our representatives on the council have only two votes out of 26. The democratic system applies: if we are not in favour of the issue, we are certainly given the opportunity to express our views on behalf of the association and try to convince the others. However, in the final vote, we only get two votes. Some we win, but we can't win them all." Critics within the AFGA accused Don Sparrow, associate minister of Public Lands and Wildlife, of rigging the council by continually adding members until he tipped the vote the government ostensibly wanted.

COURTESY OF JACK GRAHAM

Lyle Fullerton, 1986 past executive director.

Newly appointed Buck for Wildlife co-ordinator Lyle Fullerton reported on the challenge issued by Don Sparrow, in 1984 for the AFGA clubs to undertake habitat development and enhancement projects using the Buck for Wildlife Fund, and place a further emphasis on the need for more and better quality habitat. Fullerton reported, "In the first eight months, over 60 project proposals have been generated. Of these, 30 are now active programs being undertaken by clubs." He went on to advise, "Club participation in the habitat program will develop and enhance over 5,000 acres of wetland and upland habitation, stabilize 60 beaver ponds, enhance three lakes and provincially important trout streams, develop two ponds and in addition make available over 600 nest sites for geese, cavity nesting waterfowl and non-game birds." This was quite a remarkable beginning in response to Sparrow's challenge!

Zone 1 director Horst Fauser reported that 10 acres of land had been secured for a zone 1 conservation camp. Fauser also advised, "Clubs throughout the province are picking up the campaign started by Milk River Outdoorsmen and Foremost to improve farmer/hunter relations. Posters, bumper stickers, advertising, radio and highway signs are working in this direction." On a negative note he reported "We lost one-third of our pheasant habitat in southern Alberta due to irrigation upgrading. Only 25 percent of upgrading is completed. At present rate, after completion of these projects, we can kiss our pheasants goodbye."

Zone 3 director Doug Rumsey, in his third and final year as a zone director advised, "The most successful item that zone 3 can be proud of since last year's annual report is the first annual conservation camp that was held at Lake Pofianga, under the direction of Gary Hrycyk and the Ponoka Fish and Game Club."

Zone 4 director Phil Ficht echoed concerns raised by other AFGA members regarding changes in the eastern slopes land-use policy under Minister Don Sparrow. "The original policy afforded protection to critical habitat areas, which does not seem to have been carried into the revision. We must continue our efforts for intelligent development of this area..." Sparrow would enjoy a love-hate relationship with the AFGA during his tenure as associate minster of Public Lands and Wildlife, primarily because of his enthusiasm to mingle with club officials and involve the AFGA clubs with hands-on projects versus his zeal to commercialize wildlife and open Crown lands to private developments.

Popular zone 5 director Don Appleby reported that the junior conservation camp held at Narrow Lake had been very successful and that "the contents of the critiques from all those taking part indicate that the demand for this program will continue."

Hunter education chair Keith Baker reported, "The Hunter Education Instructors Association [of Alberta] has been formally established and has approximately 100 members. The association held its first conference Jan. 25-26, 1985 in Calgary." By 2006, one million students had taken the hunter education

course – quite an achievement! Baker also reported, "A new program, Project WILD, sponsored by Alberta Fish and Wildlife, is being introduced into Alberta schools on a trial basis and seems to have a great potential as an introductory conservation course."

Fish chair Lloyd Shea advised, "The new hatchery for Cold Lake came in over estimate and is being re-tendered; however, this will delay it for a least one year." Shea went on to say, "While the success of the hatchery programs is welcome and laudable it is not without its negative aspects. To many it gives a false sense that now all is well and the future of fishing in Alberta is secure. They, like some of the politicians, think that as long as it's wet and you add fish you have it made. Much of our good fish habitat has been destroyed and now we are faced with more major dams, accelerated land clearing and an open-door eastern slopes policy. In addition, there are more people, more leisure time and dwindling resources. What it means, of course, is that there is less to share and new regulations are forthcoming. It is doubtful that they will be in effect in 1985, but look for shorter seasons, size limits and lower catch limits on many of our waters in the near future." Shea's prophecies would prove correct as the fisheries branch instituted what many called draconian regulations throughout the late 1980s and on into the 1990s.

Trophy chair Steve Witiuk reported, "The North American average is that one buck in 1.5 million qualifies for Boone and Crockett, while in Alberta we produce 12 to 20 [white-tailed bucks] that qualify each year."

On a sad environmental note, environmental quality chair Gordon Merrick of Lethbridge advised, "The provincial government chose the Three Rivers site as the next great environmental tragedy for Albertans. To say it like Bob Scammell, 'Only in Alberta would they flood three river valleys and number-1 world-class streams at the same time." The government had announced its decision to site and proceed with construction of a $200-million (estimate) dam at the Three Rivers site on the Oldman River in 1984, to be built at taxpayer's expense.

Renewable resources chair Martha Kostuch reported "The associate minister of Public Lands and Wildlife released a new "revised"

COURTESY OF DUANE RADFORD

Jack Shaver (L), Don Sparrow, Elmer Kure and Stewart Morrison. Antelope Creek Ranch opening ceremony, October 1986.

COURTESY OF DUANE RADFORD

Gene Scully (L) and Norm Ferguson. Tyrrell Lake opening ceremony in October 1986.

policy for the resource management of the eastern slopes in August. The emphasis in the new policy is on development and not protection or conservation. The new policy is so flexible and open it allows for almost anything. The worst that could happen under the new policy is that the public land would all be sold."

Hunter ethics chair Linda Hirsche reported on the very successful start-up phase of the hunter ethics program in the Foremost and Southern Alberta Outdoorsmen Fish and Game Associations over the previous several years and how this success had really blossomed as the program expanded throughout Alberta. Hirsche took the bull by the horns and actively promoted the benefits of improved relations between landowners and hunters throughout Alberta. She remarked, "Even nonhunters have been very vocal in applauding the efforts of those involved in promoting hunter ethics." Radio ads, mall displays, bumper stickers, posters and newspaper coverage were all used as methods to promote good hunter ethics.

Fishing derby for the physically disabled chair Carole Romaniuk advised, "Once again, in 1984, a major project of the AFGA province wide, namely, the Fishing Derby for the Physically Disabled, has been rated as highly successful." Romaniuk singled out Al Schroeder of Calgary and Earl Langille of Lethbridge, in particular, for praise in making derbies a success on the Amico Pond and Nicholas Sheran Lake, respectively.

The annual conference yearbook acknowledges two individual members of the AFGA and one club which received the Order of the Bighorn Award in 1985. The ceremonies were presided over by the Hon. Don Sparrow, associate minister of Public Lands and Wildlife. A special guest was the Hon. Don Getty, Premier of Alberta. The following information regarding these awards was taken from the 1985 AFGA yearbook.

COURTESY OF CAROLE ROMANIUK

Carole (L) and Nestor Romaniuk cooking up a storm at Camp Pofianga, 1987.

Lloyd Shea received an Order of the Bighorn Award for over 25 years of work to improve trout populations and trout fishing in Alberta. He was instrumental in focusing the attention of the public, as well as the government, on the unique and precious east slopes streams and on native fish populations in the province. Mr. Shea had personally been a force in influencing the policies and programs of the Fish and Wildlife Division in a broad range of fisheries management areas, including stream bank restoration, brown trout management and habitat enhancement.

Vic Scheuerman received an Order of the Bighorn Award for over 20 years of dedicated participation in the hunter training program and the conservation and hunter education program. He was one of the first volunteer instructors when the Fish and Wildlife Division commenced hunter training courses in 1964. Later, he assisted in expanding this course into the internationally acclaimed conservation and hunter education program. Mr. Scheuerman conducted course sessions for hundreds of students of all ages. At the time, he was assisting other instructors in presenting the program to handicapped Albertans.

The Stony Plain Fish and Game Association received an Order of the Bighorn Award for contributing thousands of volunteer hours toward the enhancement of wildlife habitat at the Wabamun TransAlta Utilities property, a reclaimed portion of TransAlta's Whitewood Mine. With the co-operation of TransAlta Utilities, the Stony Plain Fish and Game Association planted thousands of trees and shrubs. It also established a monitoring program to evaluate the effectiveness of the habitat-enhancement project on different wildlife species in the area. The program also evaluated the growth and survival rates of different species of trees and shrubs in the enhancement project. The Wabamun habitat improvement project was reported as a resounding success, and included a trout pond – East Pit Lake.

In the June-July 1985 *Western Canada Outdoors*, fishing chair Lloyd Shea addressed the subject of fish derbies: "One subject that comes up year after year is fish derbies and what our policy is towards them." Shea added, "I know that many may not agree with me but I feel most strongly that fishing should not be made a competitive sport. Our dwindling fish stocks can ill afford the severe pressure that large derbies can create however there are a few places where the impact is not damaging. Stocked trout lakes that have a winter-kill history are an exception and also at times the removal of large trout can benefit future plantings. Some derbies do feature catch-and-release but I feel we are promoting a wrong principle."

Hunting chair Darrel Skinner noted in his hunting report in the foregoing newsletter that "a one-year moratorium placed on game ranching by Don Sparrow gives us more opportunity to make the general public aware of the ramifications of game ranching. This 'economic opportunity' can in no way benefit our wildlife and will in the long term lead to reduced values compared to the existing high regard Albertans have for wildlife."

Don Hayden of Calgary, past president of the AFGA, was elected president of the Canadian Wildlife Federation (CWF) at its annual meeting, held in Calgary May 31-June 1, 1985. Hayden had previously held posts of treasurer and secretary with the CWF.

1986 Jack Shaver became president of the AFGA in 1985. He took the unprecedented step of not running for a second term. Shaver was a former employee of the Canadian Wildlife Service, responsible for enforcement of provisions related to the *Migratory Birds Conventions Act*. He was a business-like person, with a good understanding of the workings of government and the importance of dialogue to advance the AFGA interests. Shaver admitted in his report at the 57th annual conference held at the Carriage House in Calgary in 1986 that "some clubs and individuals have been critical of myself in two particular areas – not sending enough news releases out of central office and not meeting enough with government; presenting our position on programs we feel are detrimental to Alberta's natural resources and/ or wildlife habitat: essential for its survival now and in the future. I can assure you that I have done my best in both of these areas and devoted as much time to Association business as was possible for one person."

The theme of the annual conference was "Conservation: Management or Politics?" based on the rhetorical question: Is Alberta's game being administered for the improvement of game management, or are some decisions made on political grounds? The conference was hosted by the Sarcee Fish and Game Association; in excess of 280 delegates, guests and media attended the 57th annual conference.

COURTESY OF DUANE RADFORD
Jack Shaver, past president 1985-86, at the Antelope Creek Ranch opening ceremony in October 1986.

Distinguished Service Awards were presented to Douglas Hodgins, Ken Yank, Dave Shepherd, Dave Powell, Doug Rumsey, Gary Hrycyk, Jack Easterbrook, Dennis Grover, Terry Ferster, James Graham, AMACO Petroleum and the Royal Canadian Legion – Ogden Branch.

For the first time, a president reported on the AFGA "Five Year Plan," which had been prepared by the executive and sent to all clubs. The 1980s were characterized by all sorts of soul searching by organizations; strategic planning initiatives were immensely popular with intense navel-gazing being rampant. Organizations laid out their mission, goals and objectives and deliverables on a regular basis – an axiom of the day was that "if it isn't broken, break it," contrary to an earlier adage, "If it ain't broken don't fix it." You can well imagine the conundrum these conflicting messages created among the membership of various organizations.

The AFGA membership experienced a decline under Shaver; however, the number of clubs increased and the association was reported as being on a solid basis. Shaver commented, "Those of you who attended our conference in 1985 will recall that I was critical of people who used the '2x4' method of communicating with government. I was, and still am, a firm believer of the following: when we have issues, we must meet these issues in an orderly manner." He went on to describe the number of times he met with the media and the number of press releases issued by the AFGA on matters of concern to the organization.

Good progress was reported in terms of the hunter education and Buck for Wildlife programs, with 55 percent of the AFGA clubs involved with local habitat projects. The executive was also heavily involved in the new *Wildlife Act* and draft regulations. Shaver also reported on the Fish and Wildlife Advisory Council which by now had 24 organizations and two members at large. He reported that the council was working well and gave the AFGA input into wildlife matters. This view was not shared by all the AFGA members, however, many of whom continued to complain that Minister Don Sparrow kept adding new members to tip the vote in favour of the government's inclination.

Concerns remained regarding crop spraying for grasshoppers in southern Alberta with a pesticide that was harmful to wildlife. Game ranching was also seen as a serious issue and the minister agreed to postpone any legislation concerning game ranching for another year. The massive irrigation rehabilitation program that was underway in southern Alberta was also seen as a disaster for local wildlife, as key wildlife habitat was obliterated by the irrigation canal improvement program. Finally, the sale of Crown lands under Don Sparrow was another major concern that might result in the loss of much critical wildlife habitat. While he was a very likeable person, probably no other minister had the propensity to make more unpopular decisions than Don Sparrow. The Métis Association of Alberta also publicly expressed a demand for aboriginal hunting rights, an ominous sign of future problems for Alberta's fish and wildlife.

Shaver didn't pull any punches in his closing statements, admonishing the delegates: "We are the largest conservation organization in Alberta. We are no longer a hobby – we are a business. How we move will be up to the delegates at this conference."

Members of the AFGA continued their love-hate relationship with Don Sparrow because he seemed to be preoccupied with commercializing wildlife. Several past presidents spoke very highly of him as being approachable and easy to work with, while others had less complimentary remarks. Sparrow was a rookie MLA with a cabinet post in Premier Don Getty's government which was coming under increasing pressure to diversify Alberta's economy and to scale back the growing provincial deficit. In what some critics claim was a move to impress the premier, it was Sparrow who actually initiated budget cuts in his department, allegedly to demonstrate that it was possible to reduce government spending without a loss of public services. Consequently, annual budget cuts were already being implemented when Sparrow was minister, long before it became government policy under the later Klein administration. By the time Klein's cuts were implemented (on a provincial scale in the 1990s), the Fish and Wildlife Division had already had its budget trimmed of what might be termed non-core program dollars, which really compromised their program delivery capabilities. In the February-March 1986 *Western Canada Outdoors*, Bob Scammell commented: "As the year waned, some wags were discussing presenting Mr. Sparrow with a crystal replica of an athletic supporter, emblematic of the imaginary and transparent support he is fond of claiming for his many pet schemes."

Senior vice president Nestor Romaniuk reported: "[The year] 1985 can best be described as a turbulent year for the hunting and

COURTESY OF TRAVEL ALBERTA

Cypress Hills Interprovincial Park.

fishing enthusiast of Alberta." Romaniuk noted, "A very positive statistic for 1985 would certainly have to refer to this fact: 'not one' hunter in Alberta was fatally wounded because of the mandatory blaze orange clothing dress restriction change. I know many hunters continued to wear their blaze orange and I hope this practice continues. However, it is an improvement to not be regulated as to what colour we hunters must wear when other outdoor enthusiasts groups who utilize the same outdoors at the same time of year, are not." Historically, rifle hunters in Alberta had been required to wear scarlet red or blaze orange, allegedly for their own safety, until 1985, when this regulation was rescinded.

COURTESY OF RAY MAKOWECKI

Pheasant releases were popular in the 1980s.

Romaniuk gave the membership a bit of a lecture with his closing remarks. "I am hoping that in 1986 the AFGA membership realize we are one group, with the same common goals. There is no north and south; there is NO 'you guys in head office; there is no you guys in Edmonton.' What we all are is a cohesive group with the same common goals. The people elected to co-ordinate (lead) this organization are peers to the people who elected them; they are 'non-paid volunteers,' endeavouring to project your image to the public-at-large and to bring forth your problems to the government."

In the April-May 1986 *Western Canada Outdoors*, Romaniuk noted the discussion draft on guides and outfitting presented by the Alberta government was the AFGA's first order of concern. Darrel Skinner was delegated to appear at public hearings scheduled for Athabasca, Rocky Mountain House, Grande Prairie, Calgary and Edmonton. There was such a strong public backlash over the initial proposal that it was scrapped. Romaniuk singled out the following AFGA members for their efficient input on behalf of the association: Daryl Skinner, Roy Ozanne, George Page, Steve Witiuk and Martha Kostuch.

Vice president Jack Graham also reported on the frustrations of being a full-time volunteer subjected to a lot of criticism from the AFGA members in the form of letters, phone calls and at meetings, etcetera. He also addressed the large amount of work required to serve in the office of a vice president of the AFGA.

COURTESY OF THE AFGA

Carole Romaniuk. Lady Conservationist and life member, 1987.

In the February-March 1986 *Western Canada Outdoors* Kure reported: "Last week I had a call from an 80-year-old senior who lives in a seniors' lodge. He said he had read of the provincial government's plan to sell off public lands to leaseholders. Frankly, he said, 'What the hell's going on with this government?' He then went on to explain that he didn't know who to call but knew I was working for Alberta Fish and Game and wanted us to know his view and how upset he was over the matter." Mild-mannered Kure added, "Well, I find it very difficult to defend our government when they pull these stunts, and quite frankly I get some upset when I have to tell our pioneers that our government is not consulting with conservationists in Alberta." This unpopular policy was put on the back burner by Premier Don Getty, who declared a moratorium on the sale of Crown land initiated in August 1985.

All the zone directors shared similar zone reports, reflecting that the major issues of the day were game ranching, the sale of Crown grazing leases and the continuing threat of paid hunting. Doug Rumsey, zone 3 director, reported, "Several zone 3 clubs are now becoming involved with family-oriented programs. Thus getting away from the 'male-only' image." Many clubs were also actively involved with local integrated resource management plans and various Buck for Wildlife projects.

In his last annual report to the AFGA, environmental public relations chair Elmer Kure reminisced about bygone days after having served the association for 38 years. He was blessed with a lot of wisdom and reflected on a companion's remark that he must get tired beating the same issues year after year, although he was a patient man. "I had to admit though; there were times when I did get impatient. But the older I became, the more I realized that some things do not change. Governments come and go, but as long as we have resource demands and people with conflicting priorities, there will always be problems." Amen, and therein lays the very reason for the existence of the AFGA.

---

*Zone 1 director Horst Fauser paid a special tribute to Nyal dee Hirsche in the August-September 1986 **Western Canada Outdoors**. Hirsche died in a tragic plane crash while crop-spraying on his farm near Warner on June 23, 1986. He served the Foremost Fish and Game Association in many capacities, being a past president and was also a director of the club, as well as serving the Southern Alberta Outdoorsmen, in addition to being the political action chair for Zone 1. He received a distinguished service award from the AFGA for his many years of volunteer service. Hirsche was an obliging and popular member of the AFGA, and his sudden passing hit members of the conservation community in southern Alberta hard.*

Kure went on to state, "Actually, one should get tired of hearing much the same issues rehashed conference after conference for 38 consecutive years as I have. However, I've concluded that this is also a form of strength. We do not give up on issues that are right and proper, and if it is right, we will eventually succeed through these persistent efforts." When Kure took this position in 1973 he reported there was a great need to harmonize the AFGA objectives with industry, other conservation groups, and municipal authorities. "Naturalists were promoting anti-hunting, seven counties passed 'no shooting' bylaws, and industry was running roughshod over the land." At the end of his term, he claimed there was no fighting between Alberta environmental groups, the Association of Municipalities had revoked the no-shooting bylaws and most industries were more receptive to the AFGA objectives than government.

Carole Romaniuk, chair of the Fishing Derby for the Physically Disabled, asserted, "I'm still convinced that one of the most favourable public-relations motivated projects, sponsored by the AFGA, is the Fishing Derby for the Physically Disabled. I am very pleased to report that we have increased our participation to four locations – besides Lethbridge, Calgary and Edmonton we welcome Peace River." Romaniuk noted that in 1986 the AFGA celebrated the 10th year of the Fishing Derby for the Physically Disabled program.

Environment chair Gordon Merrick reported on the government circus act related to the eastern slopes land use policy, and that the AFGA executive advised the government that they did not agree with changes in the revised east slopes policy and they requested that the 1984 policy be rescinded and that the government return

Sir Winston Churchill Provincial Park near Lac La Biche.

to the 1977 policy until new public input could be incorporated into any proposed changes. Merrick also reported on new legislation passed by the Alberta government called the *Westcastle Development Authority Act*, which turned 1,600 acres of Crown land in the West Castle River area over to this authority with the intent to permit the sale of 7,000 acres of the land for condominium and cottage development (to help finance a proposed four-seasons resort).

Merrick's report read like the description of an environmental holocaust: the government's changing policy on the sale of grazing leases; government funding of up to $6.5 million for pesticides with no strings or controls attached and little monitoring; the government also permitted the pumping dry of the Oldman River for approximately 30 miles in violation of the federal *Fisheries Act*. Merrick was one of the better environment chairs and he concluded his report "This has been a hard report to put together. We have not protected our resources from the greedy and we have a slogan of privatization that we must get rid of. This is going to take place at the club level or not at all. In closing, I must pay tribute to Martha Kostuch and Elmer Kure. These two have devoted their lives to the cause of conservation. They have both left a legacy for future generations of both people and wildlife, and have been a source of inspiration to me."

The feisty fish chair Lloyd Shea advised, "The Buck for Wildlife fisheries projects, (sponsored) by clubs, is very disappointing. There are a total of five, one of which was building a trout pond; a use with which I entirely disagree. The stream bank fencing program has slowed due to some landowner opposition and, all in all, I feel fish habitat work is being left behind. One way or another, this should be corrected." Shea also reported that the new fish hatchery

in Cold Lake would start operations in 1986. In the February-March *Western Canada Outdoors* newsletter, Shea had a scathing report regarding the Buck for Wildlife program. "A recent release from the department convinces me that our priorities are becoming confused and our money is either being spent to get public attention or in response to political pressure. Three of the projects headlined are for the construction of artificial trout ponds. I'm about as ardent a fisherman as there is but filling even an existing hole with water and planting it with fish each year is not my idea of acquiring, maintaining or preserving fish habitat."

The hunter education chair Terry Ferster reported, "The Alberta government has upgraded and put new emphasis on the Outdoor Observer program. Now, anyone that may witness a fish or wildlife violation may report it immediately by calling [a toll-free number], 24 hours a day." He also reported that the First Time Hunter program was underway in Alberta, although not a lot of clubs were involved. This program was developed by the Southern Alberta Outdoorsmen Association out of Milk River to get novice hunters in the field. Ferster singled out Dale Halmrast of Warner for all his efforts in promoting this program, as well as the Use Respect program. Dale is the son of Lawrence D. Halmrast, noted southern Alberta conservationist and gun collector, who was awarded an Order of the Bighorn in 1986.

Hunter ethics chair Linda Hirsche reported on yet another highly successful year, thanking the AFGA and the Fish and Wildlife Division, both of which donated $2,000 to support this worthy program and promote hunter ethics.

Darrel Skinner, hunting chair, reported, "At a time when our provincial government is bent on privatizing everything from our wildlife to the public lands we hunt them on, we must stand firm to protect our hunting heritage. It seems that in this day and age, just maintaining the status quo is a step forward. Shrinking habitat; competition from other forms of recreation; a greedy, uncontrolled guiding industry; and people with hunting licences constantly abusing access privileges all add up to tougher times ahead for the hunter." Skinner went on to report, "The major challenge for this chair in 1986 will be to work to ensure that hunting regulations are impacted less by political decisions and more by sound biological conclusions and recommendations."

In the February-March 1986 *Western Canada Outdoors* Skinner tore a strip off road hunters: "...when Don Bate and I hunted deer on the Prairies in November, we faced total frustration day after day, hunting coulees on foot only to find jerks driving from one coulee to another along the top, often three of four 'hunters' to a vehicle drinking coffee and waiting for deer to be pushed up so they could roll out and open up. It's no damn wonder hunters have such a poor image in the public eye."

COURTESY OF TRAVEL ALBERTA

Lodgepole pine nestled among the Rockies.

Continuing with the message of doom, upland bird chair Donald Bate reported, "It [1985] will unceremoniously go down into the record books as being the second least productive year since we started hunting these birds [pheasants] some 40 years ago." Bate advised that 45 different AFGA clubs participated in the six-week long pheasant raise-and-release program, with a total of 13,706 birds distributed. He lamented, "There were some clubs involved in habitat retention/improvement projects and the rear-and-release program does have its usefulness in bolstering sagging populations. These two efforts, while encouraging, do little to alleviate the fact that we are rapidly headed towards a largely sterile prairie landscape, and an unrewarding put and take pheasant hunting situation." In the February-March 1986 *Western Canada Outdoors*, Bate lamented on what was fast becoming a put-and-take pheasant-hunting experience in Alberta. "Many echoed a particular distaste for the highly publicized and over used release sites like Bigalow Dam, Buffalo Lake and Millicent. Too many times I've been told that these areas attract a breed of hunter (I use the term loosely) more interested in procuring a limit of birds so that he or she may be the first ones back to town to brag of their quick success."

Information chair Dave Powell reported, "Our promotional tape has been the highlight of the year for me personally. It has taken two years to get this project completed."

The AFGA appointed Lyle Fullerton as their executive director on March 19, 1986. He had been the Buck for Wildlife co-ordinator for the previous two years and had also served as game ranching and hunting committee chairmen for the association. Grant Nieman was hired as the new AFGA Buck for Wildlife co-ordinator, replacing Lyle Fullerton. Nieman had more than 10 years of habitat development and management experience.

President Romaniuk reported in the May-June 1986 *Western Canada Outdoors* that Minister Sparrow announced that due to concerns expressed by the public and the AFGA, the province would reject a highly controversial forest-spraying plan for Champion Forest Products in the Hinton area. In the August-September 1986 *Western Canada Outdoors*, Romaniuk said that Sparrow assured him there would be no regulations regarding game ranching in 1986 and there would be a moratorium on game ranching for another year. Romaniuk reported that the AFGA had sent every MLA in Alberta a letter of opposition to game ranching.

1987 Nestor Romaniuk became president of the AFGA in 1986. A native of Lamont, Alberta, he was as tough as nails but fair; he had a charm all of his own and was a very likable person. Romaniuk was a very strong leader of the AFGA, and a highly committed and motivated president. He joined the Edmonton city police in 1963 and held the rank of Sergeant in 1986. His wife Carole was also an officer in the Edmonton police service for 26 years. She had been very active as a member of the AFGA and was chairperson of the fishing derby for the physically disabled. Carole was awarded the Lady Conservationist of the Year Award trophy by the AFGA in 1987.

Advisory Council, 1987.
Back row: Dave Ealey, Federation of Alberta Naturalists (L); Cleve Wershler, Alberta Wilderness Association; Paul Rebkowich, Alberta Game Growers' Association; Peter Armstrong, Western Stock Growers Association; Joe Smith, Alberta Association of Municipal Districts and Counties; Tom O'Keefe, Canadian Wildlife Federation; Herman Schwenk, Unifarm Association; Ken Steinhauer, Indian Association of Alberta; George Amato, Métis Association of Alberta; Jim Struthers, Fish and Wildlife Division.
Middle row: Dr. Roy Crowther, Alberta Chamber of Commerce (L), Terry Bocock, Alberta Motor Association; Hank Peterson, Alberta Outfitting/Guiding; David R. Coupland, Alberta Bowhunters and Archers Association; Rod Roth, Tourist Industry Association of Alberta; Jack Graham (AFGA); Edmund Pawluski, Improvement Districts Association of Alberta; Erik Butters, Alberta Cattle Commission; Jim Findlay, Métis Association of Alberta; E. Millard Wright, oil and gas industry; Gerald Labrie, Alberta Trappers Association; Rod Fowler, Ducks Unlimited Canada.
Front row: Dave McArthur, Alberta Commercial Fishermen's Association (L); Lewis Ramstead, co-ordinator, Fish and Wildlife Division), Helen Curr, secretary; Roy Brassard, MLA, Olds-Didsbury constituency; Dr. Steve West, MLA, Vermilion-Viking constituency; Jack Shaver, chairman/citizen at large), Hon. Don Sparrow, minister-Forestry, Lands and Wildlife; Dave Simpson, vice-chairman; Fred McDougall, deputy minister-Forestry, Lands and Wildlife; Dennis Surrendi, assistant deputy minister-Fish and Wildlife Division.
Missing: Nestor Romaniuk.

Queen Elizabeth Provincial Park on Lac Cardinal near Grimshaw.

Athabasca River at Moberly Falls near Fort McMurray.

NESTOR ROMANIUK: President 1986-87

COURTESY OF THE AFGA
NESTOR ROMANIUK

Nestor first became involved in the AFGA through the Edmonton Police Service Fish and Game Association. His first taste of the parent body came in 1977, when the Edmonton Police Service Fish and Game Association was selected to organize a fun fishing day for the physically disabled.

At the annual general meeting of the AFGA in Grande Prairie in 1983, when elected as second vice president, he had no idea what was in store for him for the next 21 years. Under the guidance of president Ron Gladish and vice president Jack Shaver, he was well trained and was able to step in as president of the AFGA a year earlier than planned, as Jack Shaver served only one term as president. Nestor met a lot of challenges that first year as president, the first being to hire an executive director. Lyle Fullerton, who was the Buck for Wildlife coordinator at the time, was hired.

Some of the issues at the time were big-game outfitting and guiding; Crown land sales; designated routes; eastern slopes land use zoning changes; fishing derbies; forestry developments; game ranching; grizzly hunting; gun control; fish and wildlife habitat loss; native hunting and fishing; landowner big-game hunting permits; provincial parks policy and senior citizen's licensing.

Some of the programs included the Antelope Creek Ranch habitat development area; Buck for Wildlife; fun fishing day for the physically disabled; hide collection; trophy measuring school; trophy awards; Wildlife Trust Fund; and conservation camps in zones 1,3,4,5 and 6.

During his tenure as president, the organization lacked funds. The executive decided to hold a casino to help fund some of the projects. Initially, the AFGA application to operate a casino was turned down by the Alberta Gaming Commission; they felt that the AFGA was not a charitable organization. The executive appealed the commission's decision and were subsequently granted a licence to operate a casino, and have not looked back since. Nestor was well known for "Romaniuk Math;" he brought the organization from the red into the black financially.

While president of the AFGA, Nestor was a representative on the board of directors of the Canadian Wildlife Federation (CWF). In 1988 he became a director at large on that board and became the CWF president in 1999. He was awarded the CWF Stan Hodgkiss Canadian Outdoorsman of the Year Award in 2000 for outstanding conservation achievement. "Romaniuk Math" also came into play with the CWF.

In 1991 he became the CWF representative on the board of directors of Wildlife Habitat Canada, and served as chairman of the board from 1993-95. He returned to the board of Wildlife Habitat Canada in 2003 as the CWF representative until he passed away on Sept. 26, 2004.

To this day, you can still hear his name mentioned with regard to some of his accomplishments during his time with the various organizations that he was previously involved with.

Nestor, and his wife Carole were awarded the AFGA's highest award, the Fulton Trophy, in 1993, for promoting the objectives of the AFGA; it was often said they were "Mr. and Mrs. Fish and Game" at the time.

[Biography prepared by Nestor's wife Carole.]

The 58th AFGA annual conference was held in Edmonton in 1987 at the Edmonton Inn, hosted by the Edmonton Police Department Fish and Game Association; the conference theme was "Wildlife '87 – Participating In Its Future." The conference was chaired by Carole Romaniuk, Nestor's wife. The president of the host club was Allan Bohachyk, a long-serving member of the association. Alan Herscovici, noted Canadian author of the book *Second Nature-Animal Rights Controversy*, was the keynote speaker at the annual conference; he gave a stirring address on the dark side of the anti-hunting movement and how the AFGA members should oppose the activities of the animal-rights activists, most of whom were seen as self-serving, profit-oriented philosophers.

In his first annual report, Romaniuk outlined the role of the president, as given in the club manual: "The president will be the leader and goodwill ambassador of the association. It also says that he will be responsible for all the general administration of the association." Later on in his report, he joked: "Let me tell you here and now that I soon learned what that club manual meant when it said 'responsible for all general administration of the association.'" It would take a strong-willed person like Romaniuk to deal with all the issues facing the AFGA in 1986, which he reported on as "…our problems as a conservation fraternity is [sic] in the crisis situation."

The first priority after Romaniuk's election was to hire an executive director for the AFGA. Lyle Fullerton was selected from a short list of candidates to fill a gap left by the recently departed Paul Morck. Membership numbers were 22,594 in 1986.

A time-consuming issue, which was high on the agenda, was the draft government policy on guiding and outfitting that was to set off a firestorm of controversy in rural Alberta and took several long years to settle down. Romaniuk reflected that a

COURTESY OF TRAVEL ALBERTA
The wild rose, Alberta's official flower.

great many issues came to a head when he took over as president, issues that had been simmering for the previous few years. New *Wildlife Act* regulations were released in 1986. The Lesser Slave Lake Commercial Fishery Management Plan was formulated and implemented in 1986. The Guide and Outfitting Policy was released with the new *Wildlife Act* regulations, along with a game-ranching discussion paper. On top of all these initiatives, grazing lease public hearings took place in 1986. There was also a Caribou Restoration Plan and grizzly bear issues that Romaniuk had to contend with.

Don Sparrow, Minister of Forestry, Lands and Wildlife, announced the appointment of a task force to review public concerns regarding the unpopular grazing lease conversion policy.

The committee consisted of seven members and was chaired by Jack Campbell, MLA for Rocky Mountain House. Greg Stevens, MLA, Banff-Cochrane was the vice chair. Other members: Elmer Kure (AFGA); Herman Schwenk (Unifarm); Dr. Steven West, Janet Koper and Roy Brassard (MLAs for Vermillion-Viking, Calgary Foothills and Olds-Didsbury, respectively).

Under the policy, the holders of a grazing lease could apply to purchase or convert "suitable" land to a lease that permits cultivation.

The task force was charged with holding public hearings at the following locations: Edmonton, Red Deer, Lethbridge, Medicine Hat, Calgary and Peace River.

The AFGA submitted an executive resolution at the 1987 conference to endorse the Crown Land Conversion Task Force Report on the August 1985 Grazing Lease Conversion Policy, urging the provincial government to follow through with the recommendations as presented by the task force.

Don Sparrow, announced that the Antelope Creek Habitat Management Area, commonly known as the Antelope Creek Ranch, would be developed and maintained through the co-operative efforts of the Alberta Fish and Wildlife Division, the AFGA, Ducks Unlimited Canada (DUC) and Wildlife Habitat Canada (WHC). This 2,255-hectare (5,500-acre) area – formerly the Ward Ranch, located west of Brooks – was the largest conservation property purchased to this date in Alberta. Elmer Kure played a key role for the AFGA in the purchase of the Ward Ranch. This purchase was one of Sparrow's key initiatives during his term of office, along with his announcement of a new three-year "Buck for Wildlife" project to commit $1.5 million of the Alberta Fish and Wildlife Trust Fund to develop and enhance critical wetland habitat in the eastern irrigation district.

Funds were provided by WHC, the AFGA, DUC and the Alberta government to purchase the ranch. A management committee was established in 1986 to oversee overall ranch operations with the following representatives: WHC – Elmer Kure; Alberta government – Ken Ambrock; DUC – Garry Stewart; AFGA – Jack Shaver. A technical committee was created to address day-to-day ranch operations, with the following representatives: Fish and Wildlife Division – Lorne Fitch; DUC – Kim Schmitt; AFGA – Gordon Peel.

Romaniuk attended numerous meetings during his first year of office, lamenting, "The most difficult task that I see is to properly measure the success or failure in attending all these meetings." Additionally, the executive faced many administrative issues with regard to the value of the conservation lottery, the need to evaluate the AFGA merchandising, club mailings, etcetera. Notwithstanding all the demands on his time, Romaniuk also held down a responsible job with the Edmonton City Police service and had a family to care for; including his daughter's wedding to plan. He remained philosophical, thanking all the AFGA staff and executive for their help, advising the delegates, "I have never been turned down. I ask you all to get involved. Let's get together. Only together will we be successful."

Senior vice president Jack Graham reported, "Many new things are taking place in our outdoors and your concerns are our concerns. So to be effective, you as an individual should write your MLA with a copy sent to the Fish and Wildlife minister and the Alberta Fish and Game office. With your issues being presented through the right channels they will be dealt with through caucus and your MLA will vote those recommendations into law. Your personal letters are the best tool to show your concerns or pleasures. Remember, we are volunteers too, and as your elected representative we can only be effective with the help of your input. Be involved."

COURTESY OF TRAVEL ALBERTA

Muskeg Creek Park in Athabasca.

Don Appleby, the colourful and entertaining zone 5 director, wrote a scathing report in the 1987 conference yearbook about the double standards and contradictory positions of government and some government officials regarding allocation of fish stocks and public access to grazing leases. Appleby noted, "For years, fish-and-gamers, trappers and other users have questioned the policy of public access to public lands held under grazing lease. It looks like the answer to this problem is to sell the leases to the lessee and the problem of access disappears." He also ranted about other illogical government policies. "Surveys indicate that elk populations in Alberta are about half of what they should be. The answer here is to give anyone who wants to start a game farm (game ranch) some elk." Appleby continued to lambaste the government, "Perhaps the most confusing part of the whole thing is the Fish and Wildlife department cutbacks. The reason given is the poor economic times. Correct me if I'm wrong, but it seems to me that even when Alberta was rolling in money and the price projected for a barrel of oil was up to 95 dollars, the management of fish and wildlife resources was never very high on the government list of priorities. This prompts the question, if they did not manage these resources when they were rich, and they can't manage them when they are poor, when do they intend to manage them?" Where would members of the AFGA be without their sense of humour!

Hunting chair Darrel Skinner stepped down in 1987, reporting the major issues were the Kananaskis grizzly bear hunt, a proposed wolf reduction program in the Willmore wilderness area and the guiding and outfitting discussion paper. There had been numerous meetings during the year between officials in the AFGA with Minister Don Sparrow, deputy minister Fred McDougall and assistant deputy minister Dennis Surrendi of the Fish and Wildlife Division regarding implementation of the guide and outfitting policy. Incoming hunting chair George Page, Jack Graham and Nestor Romaniuk represented the AFGA at most of these meetings.

There is a tribute in the 1987 AFGA yearbook to Nyal dee Hirsche, who died in a tragic plane accident June 23, 1986 on his farm near Warner: "In November of 1986, Mr. Nyal dee Hirsche received an Order of the Bighorn Award posthumously for his outstanding efforts toward the conservation of Alberta's wildlife.

"Nyal devoted 21 years as an active member of the Foremost Fish and Game Association and 17 years with the Boy Scouts of Canada; working to increase people's awareness of themselves, their responsibilities to each other and to the environment.

"Remembered by all fish and gamers, Nyal's endeavours, on behalf of wildlife, exemplify the genuine sportsman. Together with his wife Linda, the Outdoor User Ethics program became a major component of the provincial association and will serve as a model in achieving harmony with hunters and landowners.

"The presentation ceremony of the Alberta Bighorn Awards was attended by Mr. Alan Hyland, MLA Cypress, Red Cliff, Linda and Sonda Hirsche, Hon. Don Sparrow, Minister of Alberta Forestry, Lands and Wildlife and Justin and Tania Hirsche."

This presentation was the only time such an award was presented posthumously to a member of the AFGA.

Nyal's wife, Linda K. Hirsche, outdoor ethics chairperson, stepped down in 1987 due to changes in her personal life. She was a driving force behind the AFGA rejuvenated Use Respect program that featured radio ads, hats, posters, signs, placemats and other promotional and marketing tools.

Trophy chair Steve Witiuk reported that the *Alberta Wildlife Trophy Book* was finally completed; it contained a list of all species records taken in Alberta as well as all the AFGA records from 1963-85. Also included were records of trophy bird game and fish, along with information about big-game, bird-game and fish written by outdoor writers, in addition to information about the history of the AFGA, fishing and hunting ethics, gun control, the value of habitat, field care of trophies and a list of official Alberta trophy measurers.

Fishing chair Lloyd Shea reported, "I have spent a busy year as your fish chairman, much of the work stemming from the on-going struggle to protect the walleye from the commercial fishery. Lesser Slave Lake, with the resurgence of the walleye combined with the low value of the whitefish, has become a management, enforcement and political problem." Shea also reported, "The Cold Lake hatchery is now in operation, with about 400,000 lake trout eggs hatched. The rearing ponds at the hatchery were used for walleye this year and had an astounding success rate of about 80 percent. About 8.9 million walleye fry and fingerlings were stocked in 1986, with about two-thirds going into Wabamun Lake. Much greater success was reported with the Arctic grayling this year, a total of 76,000, one third of which

COURTESY OF TRAVEL ALBERTA
The convergence of the Peace and Smoky Rivers near Peace River.

were fingerlings, were stocked in the NW part of the province." He concluded his report with his assessment of major changes in fishing regulations implemented in Alberta's eastern slopes. "The new regulations are going to need some fine-tuning as time goes by and I have been assured that it will be done. The stream fishery on the Eastern Slopes has deteriorated and one of the reasons has been over-fishing. Our organization has asked for many of these changes and, while I feel sure that not all members will agree with each and every one of them, I ask that we give Fish and Wildlife our full support in this matter." The conference yearbook featured a full-page ad from the Department of Forestry, Lands and Wildlife on the 1987 changes in regulations in Alberta, and, in particular, the eastern slopes streams. These changes were not without controversy, as the AFGA officials in the Crowsnest Pass area voiced concerns that they had not been properly consulted, with the result that the local MLA for Pincher Creek-Crowsnest, Fred Bradley, insisted on a public meeting with his constituents before they were implemented.

Carole Romaniuk, co-ordinator of the "Fun Fishing Day for the Physically Disabled" program, reported on a very successful year of activities. Participating clubs were at Lethbridge, Calgary, Sarcee, zone 2, Edmonton and the Peace River area.

Gordon Merrick, environment chair, reported, "One of the highlights of 1986 was the official dedication of the Tyrrell-Rush Lake water management project. Special recognition must be made to the Hon. Don Sparrow and the Hon. Ken Kowalski for the very difficult task that they were given to secure this habitat, including a fishery that was nearly lost for good. As our country turns slowly to desert, this oasis will be a legacy to future generations." The Tyrrell-Rush Lake Wetland for Tomorrow project was a key fish and wildlife conservation project near New Dayton.

Martha Kostuch, renewable resources chair, reported "Few issues have raised as much concern as the sale of Crown grazing leases. After a considerable amount of pressure, the government finally agreed to review their policy for the conversion of Crown grazing leases. Many fish and game clubs have made their positions known at these public meetings."

> The AFGA initiated a hide collection program in 1987 to raise money for their Wildlife Trust Fund for the purchase of habitat. The program operated in conjunction with Halford Hide and Leather in Edmonton.

In November 1987 Bryce Chase, a member of the Sarcee Fish and Game Association and the Brooks and District Fish and Game Association received the Order of the Bighorn Awards; the following information regarding these awards is taken from the 1988 AFGA conference yearbook.

> An Order of the Bighorn Award was presented to Bryce Chase for his dedicated involvement in fish and wildlife habitat work through the Sarcee Fish and Game Association. Not only had Chase been responsible for the initiation, organization and implementation of major habitat projects, but he had also actively participated in their construction. His achievements included the Gap Lake Habitat Enhancement project that involved placing artificial cover on the lake bottom for fish; the Wolf Lake Habitat Enhancement program that entailed planting shrubs on 12 islands for waterfowl nesting; the Fish Creek Trout Enhancement work that required beaver dam removal to aid the movement of Bow River trout upstream to spawning grounds; and upland game bird habitat project to benefit partridges and other wildlife.

Various AFGA officials such as information chair Dave Powell and zone 3 director Venny Chocholacek expressed concerns about the impact of budget cuts on the Fish and Wildlife Division; the impact of these cuts on the Fish and Wildlife Division district officer staff, in particular, was immediate as over-winter patrols were basically eliminated. Ironically, Minister Don Sparrow announced in the June-July 1987 *Western Canada Outdoors*: "Introduction of the Outdoor Observer hotline by Alberta's Fish and Wildlife Division has increased the success rate in apprehending fish and wildlife offenders to 38 percent. This increase is credited to a better informed public which in turn provides better information concerning violations to assist enforcement officers in protecting the fish and wildlife resource. The program is promoted by Use Respect/Outdoor Observer signage and other advertising activity."

COURTESY OF TRAVEL ALBERTA

Crane Lake nature trail near Fort McMurray.

COURTESY OF LILLA PFERSCHY
Canola field near Athabasca.

A majestic bald eagle in the Rocky Mountains.

1988-1997
Summary

Major issues: Game ranching; tuberculosis in game-ranched elk; local clubs leaving the Alberta Fish and Game Association (AFGA); outfitter-guide policy; forest management agreements and forest conservation strategy; carbon dioxide emission reduction; Oldman River Dam; in fish hatcheries; government cutbacks; Brooks pheasant hatchery; Alberta Conservation Association; federal firearms control, bills C-17 and C-68; Cheviot coal mine.

Highlights:
1987 - Cold Lake fish hatchery opens; government initiates first-time hunter testing.
1988 - Government introduces fishing education program; first annual Pheasant Festival and auction dinner held at Brooks; Zone 1 holds first conservation camp; IPN (infectious pancreatic necrosis) reported infecting Cold Lake fish hatchery.
1989 - The AFGA encourages government to reduce carbon dioxide emissions to reduce impact on climate; government introduces outfitter-guide policy; 25th anniversary of hunter education in Alberta celebrated.
1990 - Oldman River Dam issue threatens to divide the AFGA.
1991 - The AFGA switches position and supports construction of Oldman River Dam; reduced finances threaten the AFGA, staff laid off.
1993 - Government initiates northern moose management program; downsizing of government fish and wildlife programs begins under the 'Klein Revolution.'
1994 - Government implements WIN [wildlife identification number] and priority draw system.
1995 - WISE Foundation created, separate from government, to fund hunter and fishing education programs; federal government passes Bill C-68 to control licensing and owning of firearms; provincial government proceeds to privatize Brooks pheasant hatchery; Special Places 2000 discussions begin; the AFGA launches website.
1996 - The AFGA proposal to run Brooks pheasant hatchery rejected.
1997 - Alberta Conservation Association (ACA) created; the AFGA joins provincial government in court challenge of federal firearms act, Bill C-68; Becoming an Outdoor Woman (BOW) program initiated in Alberta.

Presidents: John M. (Jack) Graham (1988-90), Doug Rumsey (1990-90), Dr. Niels Damgaard (1990-93), Horst Fauser (1993-95), Vern McIntosh (1995-97).

Membership: 19,296-1987; 17,675-1988.

During the late 1980s, Canada was experiencing a deep recession. Governments both federally and provincially responded by running up deficits to maintain some programs while at the same time cutting back on others. In 1988 the federal Mulroney government negotiated a free-trade agreement with the United States. That agreement was expanded to include Mexico in 1992 as the North American Free Trade Agreement (NAFTA). Thus began the first steps in the globalization of the Canadian economy. Soon governments were reacting to the needs of multinational corporations, cutting government programs to reduce costs. Much of this cutting had to do with the privatization of some of what governments used to provide.

Brian Mulroney continued as prime minister of Canada until June 1993, when he retired and new Progressive Conservative leader Kim Campbell took over. However, she could not stem the tide of change the people felt was necessary; she held office for only four months before her party lost in a landslide election to the federal Liberals under Jean Chrétien.

Alberta was not immune to the perceived need for change. After losing his own seat in his government's re-election to power in 1989, Premier Don Getty was forced to enter and win a by-election for a "safe" seat in the legislature in order to remain premier. Before the next general election, Getty resigned as leader of the PCs and turned over the premiership to new PC leader Ralph Klein. Klein went to the polls in 1993, promising to balance the budget and eliminate government debt. He won in a landslide, and soon more government programs were on the cutting block. Alberta's population in 1991 was about 2.5 million people. Fishing licence sales in 1991-92 were 253,963; and wildlife certificate sales were 114,208. One U.S. dollar in 1991 was worth 1.52 in 2007 USD.

With all the cutbacks and downsizing, the 1980s and '90s were also the era of the management consultant, where organizations both in and out of government spent considerable time in "navel gazing" exercises to develop visions, missions, goals and objectives that were rarely referenced because of more pressing concerns of budgets and fulfilling mandates.

1988 Nestor Romaniuk remained as president of the Alberta Fish and Game Association (AFGA) in 1987. He reflected on what had been a very busy two-year term of office in his year-end report as president, remarking that "I have certainly learned to appreciate the term 'time marches on,' since becoming president."

The 59th annual conference was held at the Edmonton Convention Centre in 1988; the conference theme was "Management Today For Wildlife Tomorrow."

The guiding and outfitting policy—a very divisive but necessary government move to regulate guiding and outfitting in Alberta—was one of the most serious issues Romaniuk had to deal with as president. Town hall meetings called to address the proposed policy by government officials were packed with outdoorsmen throughout Alberta; discussions were often heated over the controversial draft policy which pitted residents against non-resident hunters over proposed assignable licences for various big-game species. Romaniuk advised that "The guiding and outfitting policy absorbed more man hours than any of the other 139 issues [he had to address]." Two of the foremost AFGA concerns about the draft policy were that it did not address conservation of the resource as being the top priority, and the needs of the resident hunter, secondarily. Members of the AFGA were concerned the outfitters would receive special treatment at the expense of the resident hunter.

LeRoy Fjordbotten had been appointed as the new Minister of the Department of Forestry, Lands and Wildlife, replacing Don Sparrow. Fjordbotten, a farmer from the Claresholm area in southern Alberta, told his staff that he wanted to be remembered as the "conservation minister" but had inherited several bombshell draft policies left over by his predecessor. His mandate would be blackened by government approval of game ranching, arguably one of the worst decisions ever made by the Alberta government respecting Alberta's wildlife resources. Initially, Fjordbotten announced that he would support his predecessor, Don Sparrow, and also, personally oppose game farming (Bob Scammell, January/February *1988 Western Canada Outdoors*).

Another contentious issue was an ongoing long-fought battle with the government over conversion of grazing leases to private ownership. Grazing leases were seen as being very important as

wildlife habitat, especially in the settled areas of Alberta; the government was prepared to offer them for sale to leaseholders. Jack Campbell, MLA for Rocky Mountain House, had chaired a task force to address this matter and released their report "Grazing Lease Conversion Policy" in November 1987.

Membership numbers were 19,296 in 1987.

COURTESY OF DUANE RADFORD

Proud Mathew McNichol holds up his first yellow perch.

| Motion | There was an executive resolution at the AFGA conference—that the AFGA endorses the Crown Land Conversion Task Force Report—on the August 1985 Grazing Lease Conversion Policy and urges the provincial government to follow through with the recommendations as presented by the task force. |

Alberta Fish and Wildlife Advisory Committee (chaired by past president Jack Shaver), the Alberta Forestry and Natural Resources Caucus Committee (chaired by Jack Campbell), and Fish and Wildlife Division staff taken in 1988 at a Government House meeting. Top row: Jay Litke (L), Arden Rytz, Herman Schwenk, Joe Smith, Dave Ealey, Tom O'Keefe, E. Millard Wright, Eric Musgreave, Garry Helfrick, Edmund Pawluski, George Amato, Wm. (Bill) Barnett, Mike Sterling, Terry Bocock, Dr. Roy Crowther, Rod E. Fowler, David R. Coupland, Chuck Lacy, David J. McArthur, Dr. Steve West, Rod Roth, Gerald Labrie, Clay E. Chattaway, Henry (Hank) Peterson. Middle row: Nestor Romaniuk (L), Jack Graham, Dianne Mirosh, Jack Shaver, Jack Campbell, Peter Armstrong, Harry Alger, Dave Simpson, Roy Brassard. Bottom Row: Grant Campbell (L), Lewis Ramstead, Dennis C. Surrendi, Jim Struthers, Ernie Psikla, Harold Sellers, Ken Crutchfield.

Sergeant Nestor Romaniuk was presented with the Oil Capital Kiwanis Award on Oct. 20, 1987. The award recognized a police member who has devoted outstanding volunteer service to the community. It highlights the fact that police officers not only protect society, but are concerned, contributing members of the community. Romaniuk was recognized for his contribution from 1977 to 1983 to Camp He Ho Ha on Lake Isle. As provincial co-ordinator, he was the driving force behind the camp's annual Fun Fishing Day. Nestor Romaniuk joined the Police Department in 1963 and had served in a variety of positions. He was promoted to sergeant in 1980 and planned to retire in July 1988.

Senior vice president Jack Graham reported "The 1988 convention is being held with a totally new concept. It will be hosted by the AFGA and is going to involve the public and general membership being invited to attend our display exhibition. In past years the hosting of our annual conference has posed a large financial burden to our clubs so we are hoping this year the new concept will show the way for future conventions. We also hope that in the future hosting of the conference will be taken over by our zones."

Junior vice president Doug Rumsey took a shot at the AFGA membership. "I, also, strongly believe that if some of our members spent as much effort and time participating as they did criticizing, we could probably have one of the best organizations in the world to protect our wildlife resources." He urged the members to go back to their clubs and sign up at least one new member, and to ask themselves: "What can I do for the fish and game association or my club, and not, what is the club going to do for me?"

Zone 1 director Dwayne Johnson reported, "As we all know, the eastern irrigation district [EID] had planned on closing their leased land to hunting due to poor hunter-landowner relations. With the help of fish and wildlife, the Brooks and District Fish and Game and the Tilley and Rolling Hills Fish and Game, meetings were organized with the EID These meetings developed a hunter ethics program which was very helpful in keeping these grazing leases open to hunters." Johnson also remarked, "As usual there have been many controversies."

Zone 4 acting director Carole Romaniuk reported "The issues in zone 4 are no different than the issues facing our overall organization. We in zone 4 are gravely concerned about the tremendous forestry expansion proposals. We are not against forestry; however, our first concern is wildlife and its habitat." Romaniuk became acting director due to the resignation of Bob Tanghe.

Zone 5 director Charlotte Drake (who took over from former zone director Don Appleby in October 1987) initiated a zone newsletter to improve communications at the zone level. Drake reported on the opening of the Cold Lake fish hatchery in May, 1987 which she advised "...will be a boon to the fisheries of this province." She also reported, "Cold Lake was also the target of a joint-use agreement with the Saskatchewan government. A more equitable allocation of the fisheries has been reached, along with the one fishing licence, either Alberta or Saskatchewan, being required for the lake." Long in the planning, Drake advised that zone 5 would be opening their Youth Camp at Marie Lake in the summer of 1988.

Zone 6 director Dave Ridgeway reported on a number of positive club projects being undertaken throughout northwestern Alberta, advising, "This year the big 'Atta Boy' goes to the High Prairie Club. They not only held their own in membership sales, but surpassed last year, which 'outguns' every club in the zone."

Fishing chair Lloyd Shea reported on what he called the long-delayed changes to the fishing regulations for Alberta's east slopes streams. Unfortunately, these changes were rammed through by officials from the head office in the fisheries branch with little or no public consultation at the local or regional level, resulting in a public relations backlash in southern Alberta, in particular. Furthermore, they weren't particularly scientifically sound and had to be revisited in the 1990s, and basically overhauled to get them right. It was a typical example of how some changes were implemented by officials in head office at the time without adequate public consultation with local clubs to obtain their comments and support. This represented a clash between the cultures of head office staff and regional staff, who had to implement the changes in the face of controversy.

Shea reported that he was shocked when he learned of an outbreak of IPN [infectious pancreatic necrosis, a viral disease of fish] at the recently constructed Cold Lake fish hatchery in November 1987, which resulted in the destruction of the entire stock of 300,000 rainbow trout and about one million lake trout eggs and fry. No shrinking violet, Shea also advised, "There is some controversy in our organization regarding involvement of the AFGA in commercial or fundraising fishing derbies. My strong personal feelings are that we, as Alberta's largest and oldest conservation organization, should not be involved in an endeavour that turns the sport of fishing into a commercial competition. Some large derbies do impact the resource and, if it continues, regulations and controls will have to come. Let us put the AFGA on side right now and keep fishing a sport."

COURTESY OF BOB SCAMMELL

Elmer Kure receiving the Order of the Bighorn, 1989.

The Alberta Fish and Wildlife Division announced the launch of a new fishing education program designed to help anglers, both new and old, get more enjoyment from the sport. Top-notch instruction was to be delivered by volunteers. The course included information on fish management and identification, fishing ethics, legal responsibilities and even tips on cooking fish.

Provincial "Fun Fishing Day for the Physically Disabled" coordinator Carole Romaniuk reported, "The 1987 Fun Fishing Day for the Physically Disabled had the most participants since its inception in 1977, totalling close to 300." Events took place at Milk River Ridge near Lethbridge, at the Amoco Pond in Calgary, Sylvan Lake near Red Deer and out of Edmonton at Camp He Ho Ha on Lake Isle. Romaniuk singled out the following sponsors: IGA, Ogden Legion, Canada Dry, Labatts and the Edmonton Activettes.

Hunting chair George Page blasted the government in his report: "After a year of meetings and discussions, I have formulated some opinions that the politicians are not going to like hearing. The first thing I am sure is that all direction and policy sent down to our wildlife managers are politically motivated. Politicians don't give a hoot about the wildlife or the resource. They only care how the most people will regard their moves and try to avoid controversial issues at all costs. Now, with a large and vocal anti-hunting element at work this has had the following result: WE DO NOT HAVE WILDLIFE MANAGEMENT, WE HAVE ONLY HUNTER MANAGEMENT."

Page was especially concerned about the impact of wolf predation in Alberta's Rockies and foothills on goats, moose and elk, which he estimated were killing 70,000 big-game animals a year! He spat, "What the hell is going on? Let's manage all wildlife, not just manage hunters." It was one of the most stinging reports against the government from a hunting chair in the records of the AFGA.

Upland bird chair Don Bate provided a much more positive report regarding upland birds than usual, and singled out the Lethbridge Fish and Game Association for praise. "When it comes to 'turkey talk' there is no one more talkative or on top of the situation, if you prefer, than the Lethbridge Fish and Game Association. Were it not for their continuing efforts, the Merriam's turkey would have long ago been forgotten in this province. They have been funding and providing the manpower for a winter feeding program since 1984. In conjunction with the Fish and Wildlife Division, they were undertaking a transplant project of two groups of 15 birds this winter, in an attempt to broaden the turkey's range." Alberta's upland bird hunters are indebted to the Lethbridge Fish and Game Association for the Merriam's turkey hunting they enjoy today, which blossomed after a successful transplant in the Lees Lake area near the Crowsnest Pass, in particular; this is yet another example of how projects undertaken by the AFGA benefit all Albertans, not just members of the association.

Outgoing trophy chair Steve Witiuk commented he would be spending more time on the second edition of the Alberta wildlife trophies book, as well as the Sherwood Park Fish and Game Association and, "In addition, we must do something to increase the membership of the AFGA, along with changing the present name of our organization to something like Alberta Wildlife Federation," so as not to be confused with the Alberta government's Fish and Wildlife Division.

Renewable resources chair Martha Kostuch highlighted the three major issues she had dealt with during the past year: The Oldman Dam, Sour Gas and Forestry Developments. She painted a very bleak picture regarding the impact of the Oldman Dam on fish and wildlife. Kostuch's counterpart, non-renewable chair Hank Holowaychuk, reported, "I would like to thank the little lady with the big heart, Martha Kostuch, for her help and encouragement throughout the year. I couldn't have harrowed in a day what you plow." It was a nice compliment about Kostuch, a dedicated conservationist who would soon quit the organization over a point of principle, primarily related to the Oldman Dam.

1989 John M. (Jack) Graham became president of the AFGA in 1988. Graham was a likeable and highly respected president, an ardent angler and big-game hunter and an official scorer of the Boone and Crockett Club. He was an eternal optimist, a high-energy person noted for his positive attitude.

In an interview, Graham said he originally became a member of the Edmonton Fish and Game Association because he saw an opportunity to join a group of sportsmen who shared his interests. He got involved in 1962-63 with the first trophy measuring competitions at the club level and then moved to the provincial level. "Since then I've travelled to every corner of North America, almost… and one of the things that comes out of every meeting I've ever been to, is 'Oh, you're from Alberta. I'm going to go there some day. And I want to go there because of either the hunting or the fishing, or the scenery.' You kind of felt like a hero when you went to these meetings," Graham said. "I was very proud to be a part of that. Plus, I was able blow our horn in lots of cases when it came to the biggest moose, the biggest antelope, and whatever."

JOHN M. (JACK) GRAHAM: President (1988-90)

COURTESY OF DUANE RADFORD
JACK GRAHAM
Past president and all-around AFGA super volunteer for 50 years.

I was born and raised in south Edmonton, as was my father, and had the pleasure of fishing and hunting with him at an early age; consequently, enjoying and respecting the outdoors was always a part of my life. After graduating from high school I became a licensed journeyman mechanic and in 1956 became service manager for an automotive dealership for three years. I then spent 21 years as fleet manager for a large oil equipment company, and a further eight years as fleet supervisor for Canada Dry, after which time I went into business for myself.

I married my wife Phyllis in 1954 and we have four children – two daughters and two sons, the youngest of whom died in an accident at age 21. We now have five grandchildren and two great grandchildren who keep us young and committed to looking after our environment and wildlife so that they can enjoy the same camping and outdoor experiences that we have.

I first became involved with the AFGA as a member of the Edmonton Fish and Game Association in the late 1950s, serving on many committees as well as being the junior rifle training instructor. In 1962 I became involved in a fish and game trophy committee and subsequently became involved in setting up the

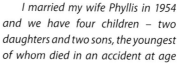

1989

Resolution   Of note is a conference resolution that the Government of Alberta establish a goal to reduce carbon dioxide emissions in Alberta by at least 20 percent of 1989 by the year 2005. This was the first time the AFGA made such a motion regarding the impending threat of global warming, first brought to the membership's attention by their renewable resources chair, Martha Kostuch.
There were the usual resolutions to increase the budget of the Fish and Wildlife Division; that the present complement of Fish and Wildlife Division field officers was inadequate and should be increased substantially. There was also a resolution that the Alberta government adhere more to wildlife biologists' recommendations and suggestions; the government did not always adhere to staff recommendations and this became more and more of an issue in the years ahead as the staff became increasing politicized.

provincial wildlife awards program. I became president of the Edmonton Fish and Game Association in 1973 and was awarded a life membership in 1975.

The fish and game trophy competition was originally sponsored commercially and administered by the Edmonton Fish and Game Association. In 1975 I organized and ran the competition and had the responsibility of records keeping for the AFGA; from its inception I organized and set up the sponsorship to involve the affiliated clubs as sponsors of all award categories. This was well received by then-president Lewis T. (Budd) Traver and the AFGA executive. At this time a trophy committee was formed under the provincial AFGA and I was appointed chairman. I single-handedly researched all available records information and compiled the data for the first Alberta Fish & Wildlife Records Book 1978, with updates every two to three years, thereafter. For all my work setting up the trophy records and awards competition, I was given a life membership in 1984 by then-president Ron Gladish.

I became an official Boone and Crockett Club scorer in 1982 by attending a workshop and seminar in Chicago, Illinois to receive my official measurer certificate. I have since been invited six consecutive times to be a judge on their awards panel, which meets every three years. In 1995 I became the only Canadian in the history of this organization chosen as chairman of the awards committee which met in Dallas, Texas. In 1981 I initiated a measuring school for the AFGA affiliates, recognizing the need for qualified scorers, using the Boone and Crockett Club measuring system. To date I have instructed more than 800 students from across Alberta and am still involved in instructing these classes.

I taught wildlife identification and measuring to hunter training students at the Hinton Forestry School from 1985-89. I am also an official measurer for the Pope and Young Club and the Longhunters Society.

I have been a delegate at AFGA annual conferences since 1960 and was conference chairman in 1974 in Edmonton.

While my wife, Phyllis, was chairwoman of the ladies program, I assisted with the fishing outings for the physically challenged from its beginning in 1976 up to 1988, at which time I was involved in the Canadian Wildlife Federation (CWF), whose annual conferences were held at the same time.

In 1975 I, along with Phyllis, received distinguished service awards at the 45th annual conference for our duties.

I was elected vice president of the AFGA in 1985 (for three years) and subsequently became president from 1988-90. During my term as president, I served on the provincial wildlife advisory council for five years (1986-91), during which time I presented briefs at forestry hearings with Daishowa and Sunpine Forest Products and also at Alberta-Pacific Forest Industries Inc. (Al-Pac); at the Alberta Tourism, Parks and Recreation Steering Committee; at the Alberta Professional Outfitters Association appeals board and on game ranching issues. I was the AFGA representative on the Report-a-Poacher rewards committee from its start to the present. I was also the AFGA representative on the rewrite of the provincial Wildlife Act.

In 1992 I received the Fulton Award, the highest AFGA award given for outstanding and unrewarded contributions to conservation.

I attended the CWF general meetings and conferences from 1986-91 as the AFGA representative, and then became a director at large from 1991-2001 during which time I served on the federal fisheries committee, publicity committee, and the native affairs committee. As chair of the affiliates committee I headed the meetings with all other provincial representatives.

In 2002 I received the Canadian Outdoorsman of the Year award, presented to the individual who has demonstrated an active commitment to wildlife conservation in Canada.

As past president I represented the AFGA on the guide and outfitting advisory council, as well as being the AFGA life member's representative from 1993 to 2003, attending all executive meetings and conferences as their voice, reporting all concerns and the health of past presidents and life members to the senior executive.

During my term on the AFGA executive I was present in head office most days dealing with general issues, one of which was the ongoing search for an executive director after the loss of Paul Morck (who had 17 years service, from 1967-84) then Lyle Fullerton (three years) until the hiring of Ron Hauser who did a very diligent job for nine years. I was actively involved in the search for and purchasing of our head office building in 1985, and in the fundraising by going to affiliate clubs and zone meetings to impress upon them the advantage of owning our own office space and the hope for a historical museum as part of this purchase. I was also involved in the early fundraising casinos as assistant general manager for many years.

In 1996 I became involved with the Edmonton Old Timers Fishing Club on the board of directors and then as program chair. I was elected vice president of this organization in 2000 and became president from 2002-04. I am still on the executive of this club as a board member; I'm also a life member and their representative to the AFGA.

I remain involved with the AFGA to this day and have attended every annual conference since 1973 as a delegate; I continue to travel throughout Alberta teaching the Boone and Crockett Club measuring system to affiliated members and I still administer the provincial wildlife awards competition. I am an avid outdoorsman and appreciate and enjoy all of nature's resources and always work to encourage conservation and respect to promote projects that will enhance the interests of club members.

[Biography prepared by Jack Graham.]

Graham began his opening address at the 60th annual conference at the Westin Hotel in Calgary in 1989 with the remark: "I think 1989 will be another banner year for the AFGA." Financially, it was one of the best years ever, a direct result of the increased affiliation dues and adjusted administration costs that were long overdue. The theme of the annual conference was "Take Pride In Our Wildlife And Our Fish." Ralph Klein was the

Astotin Lake in Elk Island National Park.

Jack Graham (centre) elected president March 5, 1988. Doug Rumsey (L) and Niels Damgaard.

Membership records from 1961 to 1988			
1961-17,202	1968-23,754	1975-22,651	1982-23,356
1962-17,228	1969-22,933	1976-24,501	1983-23,784
1963-17,233	1970-21,536	1977-24,494	1984-23,386
1964-17,561	1971-19,847	1978-24,457	1985-23,135
1965-16,549	1972-19,580	1979-23,070	1986-22,574
1966-17,044	1973-19,616	1980-20,850	1987-19,482
1967-18,170	1974-18,599	1981-22,751	1988-17,675

**EDITORIAL NOTE: Membership records exclusive
of this time period are incomplete.**

mayor of Calgary in 1989 at the time of the conference and extended greetings to the conference delegates; Klein would later serve as Alberta's minister of environment after being elected as an MLA in 1989 and was premier from 1992 to 2006. In his welcoming letter Klein commented on the conference theme: "We are now realizing the importance of preserving our environment and the AFGA has played a significant role in focusing public attention on this vital issue."

Some of Graham's objectives for the coming year were to improve communications between head office and the affiliated clubs using new technology. The AFGA had already outgrown its two-year-old photocopier and had purchased a new computer to produce its own membership lists; they also purchased a facsimile machine, a new dictating machine and updated their phone system. Graham also spoke of greater involvement between members of the AFGA and other organizations, citing the first-ever meeting held with the president of the Indian Association of Alberta, Mr. Roy Louis, to address issues of mutual concern. Graham addressed the massive forest management agreements signed between the government and Alberta's forest industries in 1989 – so much for the desire of Minister LeRoy Fjordbotten to be remembered as Alberta's conservation minister; he would also be the architect of the ill-fated game ranching industry, a chronic nemesis of the AFGA.

"Nearly every stick of wood is now designated to this [forest] industry," Graham remarked in his conference report. He was a pragmatic president, however, who advised, "Now that these announcements have been made, it is up to us and our government representatives to speak out for the resource and the environment. Our first plan is to meet soon with the developing companies to find out what is in store for Alberta's wildlife and how we can help to oversee the habitat for the wildlife that will be immediately affected, for instance native birds, such as the pileated woodpecker, and the beaver." This vision represents yet another example of how the AFGA represented the broadest interests of all Albertans to conserve fish and wildlife resources.

He also spoke of membership concerns, seemingly a perennial issue, and the need to grow the AFGA membership, candidly advising, "In order to achieve our goals we need members. As you know, the larger the group, the more impressive you appear."

Senior vice president Doug Rumsey reported, "Congratulations also go out to the Pheasant Festival committee [at Brooks] who worked hard at making their first annual dinner auction a super success. A net revenue of approximately $13,000 was gained. These funds will be used for pheasant-habitat retention and improvement." Rumsey also noted, "This year will see the AFGA sponsor its second casino, to be held in Edmonton on Sept. 29 and 30. Your help will be needed again. The monies generated from this casino are earmarked for the building fund." He also advised, "This past year we saw for the first time, the Indian Association of Alberta and the AFGA meet together to discuss problems that seriously affect both user groups. We realize that we may never agree on every issue but for those that we do agree on, we can cooperatively endeavour to resolve."

Zone 1 director Norman Ferguson reported, "Zone 1 held its first conservation camp last summer, just north of Coleman [McGillivray Creek Youth Camp]. Seventeen youths attended and all seemed to enjoy themselves. Horst Fauser has been working very hard to get capital funds which are needed to establish this camp as a permanent base."

Zone 5 director Steve Witiuk reported, "On a positive note, I would like to acknowledge the Sherwood Park Fish and Game Association's involvement in the project of relocating elk. This has been funded by the Sherwood Park Fish and Game, The [Rocky] Mountain Elk Foundation, The Foundation for North American Big Game, Buck for Wildlife, and Alberta Sport, Recreation, Parks and Wildlife. To date, we have relocated 128 elk in the northeast part of Alberta. The project has had some problems with wolf predation and illegal hunting but, overall, should be successful."

Zone 6 director Darryl Smith advised, "In April of this year, because of the rapid and often detrimental changes that are occurring to our landscape, I took on the task of zone director. Ten years ago, when I left Edmonton to settle in the Peace River region, a prime motivator in choosing this area was the abundance of wilderness and the fish and wildlife it contained. Suddenly, a new industry, forestry, has arrived on the block and that will profoundly alter the region unlike any other time, except when white men first plowed the region's soil during the first half of this century. Man's greed for the resources of the region's forest, soil and water, without regard for the wildlife, fish and wildlands they harbour, may leave a legacy that will make issues such as the Oldman Dam and game ranching look small in comparison." Smith went on to praise the local clubs for their work in addressing issues of concern

COURTESY OF JACK GRAHAM

Jack Graham measuring for 1992 video at a Wildlife Awards Competitions banquet.

to fish and wildlife in zone 6, despite the difficulty of covering such a large area. He concluded, "Our children will be glad you cared. Taking pride in our wildlife and fish tomorrow will only be possible if you show your concern today."

Renewable resources chairperson Martha Kostuch reported, "The Oldman Dam, forestry developments galore, sour gas developments and the greenhouse effect are some of the issues which have kept me busy during this past year. Starting with the Oldman Dam, three court cases have been fought over the dam. The first one we won, the next two we lost but we still haven't given up. More fish and wildlife habitat will be destroyed by the Oldman Dam than has been created by all of the Buck for Wildlife projects in the province." Kostuch later went on to describe the consequences of greenhouse gasses on global warming in her address, drawing on her attendance at a conference in Toronto she advised, "Many speakers at the conference stated that the only threat to the survival of the earth, greater than the greenhouse effect, is nuclear war." History bears testament to just how accurate an assessment she made at the time of the 1989 conference, as global warming came to crisis proportions in the new millennium.

Hunter education chairperson Mark Jobson advised, "The first time hunter test, which the government instituted in 1987, has produced some very good statistics for the first and second years. During the first year, there were approximately 3,000 students tested, with a 40 percent failure rate. The average age was 21. The second year was comparable to the first. The best news is that many of the younger people are taking the hunter education course, instead of just trying to write the test. The fishing education program started in 1988. It is a program which can be taught separately or as part of the outdoor conservation and hunter education course."

Information chairperson Dave Powell stated, "The year 1988 has been one of reward for the AFGA. Several issues that were outstanding, such as Crown land sales, have come to a satisfactory conclusion."

1990 Jack Graham remained as president of the AFGA in 1989. The 61st annual conference was held at the Edmonton Inn in Edmonton in 1990. The annual conference theme was "Wildlife And Its Habitat Are Inseparable – Let's Ensure Both." At the conclusion of his two-year term, Graham reflected, "It has been a rewarding and sometimes an exasperating experience as it does not come easily trying to please the concerns of the membership." For the first time, a president makes reference to "the mandate – the resource first and the resident sportsman next – is always in our statements and with that intent we have tried to be the voice on behalf of wildlife."

Graham reported that one of their successes had been to establish the central office as an effective group of dedicated people to serve the members' needs and, under the leadership of executive director Lyle Fullerton, this was accomplished. During the previous three years the AFGA had paid off their head office building completely, purchased office equipment, computers and furnishings, all of which contributed to their membership equity. Graham singled out Fullerton for praise. He also reported that, "Programs are one area on which we are constantly working. The major one is our membership renewal program," acknowledging the newest staff addition, Del Scammell, contributor services representative, for his sincere efforts.

"The issues of the past two years have been ongoing ones; native hunting and fishing, game ranching, guiding and outfitting, poaching, commercial fishing, access to public lands, lease holder compensation and predator management – just to name a few," advised Graham. Sadly, Graham reported that in the AFGA meetings with forestry development companies, they learned that wildlife was not on their list of concerns, "...but in the end picture it shows up at the bottom of their priorities, as economics is always on the top." So much for Minister of Forestry, Lands and Wildlife LeRoy Fjordbotten's wish to be remembered as a conservation minister; the Don Getty government of the time was determined to diversify Alberta's economy and Fjordbotten was one of his foot soldiers, along with his deputy minister and assistant deputy ministers.

Graham acknowledged that Brad Fenson was hired as the new habitat development co-ordinator in 1989, taking over from Grant Neiman. Fenson had worked as the interim AFGA executive director in 1990.

Senior vice president Doug Rumsey reported, "In my 10 years of sitting on the senior executive, I am finding that each year is becoming more challenging. There are increasing numbers of other users of our resources, especially in the agricultural and industrial

Pelican on the Bow River near Calgary.

areas, as well as increased numbers of anti-groups forming across the country. I find it ironic that several issues that we are trying to deal with today were a top priority of concern when I joined The AFGA in 1975 such as; predator control, habitat loss, commercial fishing, native hunting, access, etc." Rumsey reported, "Forestry has been a dominating issue over the past year and will continue to be one for some time. The AFGA put in a lengthy brief to the Al-Pac hearings. I thank Dr. Martha Kostuch and Dr. Wayne Roberts for their efforts in coming up with the brief and their presentation of it. We must also thank Dr. John Stelfox for his effort in leading our forestry committee and leaving us with a list of recommendations on how to proceed in the future." Rumsey had a good sense of humour and reported: "The access issue on Crown grazing leases has certainly been a hot issue. As I write this, the appeal of Judge Robbin's decision has been heard and we now wait for the decision. Will the public finally be able to go on their own land?"

Newly appointed zone 1 director Ron Pittman advised, "I would have to say that game farming and ranching is one of the most contentious issues that we are asked to deal with and, I am sad to say, one that in my opinion, we are losing. However, we will never give up the fight, as I am convinced we are right."

Zone 2 director Ike Johannson reported, "This year, zone 3 hosted another great conservation camp at Pofianga. A thank you goes to Garry Hyryck, organizers and instructors for contributing much time and effort to make it so successful. It is very important to educate our future fishermen and hunters."

Zone 5 director Steve Witiuk advised, "I would also like to thank Ray Makowecki, director, Blair Rippin, and Hugh Norris from the St. Paul Fish and Wildlife Division. These people have supplied the

clubs, at both the spring and fall meetings, with some very useful information." Makowecki, at the time northeast regional director, had set a high standard with the wealth of information in his fish and wildlife division regional operational reports which were well received by members of the AFGA and other user groups. Regrettably, as veteran Lethbridge fish biologist Lorne Fitch was fond of saying, "No good deed will go unpunished." Senior administrators in the Fish and Wildlife Division criticized Makowecki for providing these factual reports. This agency had a reputation for eating its young and was prone to chastise staff who showed initiative, particularly when it came to public outreach activities, due to potential political sensitivities. It wasn't just Makowecki who came under fire for his public education and information initiatives - there were lots of other examples. The southern region under the direction of Duane Radford also produced an excellent summary of the resource status and Radford received similar criticism. Critics perceive that this unfortunate practice continues to this day, stifling initiative, and breeding mediocrity at the lowest common denominator within the Fish and Wildlife Division.

Zone 6 director Darryl Smith reported on the escalating scale of forestry developments and new access in his area. He also advised, "Public involvement in fish and wildlife management will be increasingly important in the next decade. This will lead to a change in many of our clubs from shooting organizations to watchdogs for the wildlife resource. This change has occurred provincially, and most clubs in the north are adapting to this role very well."

Fishing committee chairperson Eileen Christensen reported: "In the 1970s we thought we had problems of over-fishing, inadequate stream protection, lack of management, poor land use practices (e.g. over-clearing and stream damage from livestock use), exces-

Sunflowers in Kalyna Country near Smoky Lake.

sive siltation and loss of prime fish habitat. Now in 1989, we can add a lot more to this list with all the lakes that suffered winter kill last winter, IPN [infectious pancreatic necrosis] virus infecting the hatcheries, unlimited access, newer innovations in fishing methods (hooks, fish finders, etc.), more seismic activity, pulp mills, forestry giants, etc." It didn't sound like a very rosy picture as she went on to advise: "The bottom line of my report is this resource is in a serious decline in both quality and quantity, throughout the whole province. We, as sportsmen and the AFGA members, must demand from the provincial and federal governments that they fulfill their responsibilities in management, reclamation of lost habitat and enforcement of existing legislation of this resource for all future generations. We must realize fishing is now a privilege."

Hunting chair George Page reported, "The government has recently put forward the outfitter-guide policy. This policy has been over five years in the works, and essentially limits the outfitters to 10 percent or less of the available harvest for all species of big game. In some cases it is a lot less than 10 percent. The guides will have to bid on licence allocations in various wildlife management units on a per species basis." Page went on to advise that while there were reservations regarding the proposed policy it was still better than no policy "...that allows uncontrolled numbers of guides to swarm into certain areas."

Hunter education chair Mark Jobson reported, "The year 1989 marked the 25th anniversary of hunter education in Alberta. On April 7 and 8, the Alberta Fish and Wildlife Division and the Alberta Hunter Education Instructors Association cosponsored a 25th anniversary celebration at the Edmonton Convention Centre. Approximately 1,000 instructors gathered for a weekend of information and entertainment." Jobson went on to report, "Those 25 years saw approximately 180,000 students successfully complete the program. In the future we hope to better those figures with more emphasis on ethics and responsibility."

Renewable resources chair Martha Kostuch advised, "The need to protect the environment is finally making the news. In fact, most people now consider the environment at least as important as the economy. The changes that are occurring are exciting." She also reported that construction of the

1991

Resolution

A general resolution was put forward at the annual conference by the Picture Butte Fish and Game Association that the AFGA conditionally support the completion of construction of the Oldman Dam at the Three Rivers site provided that:
1. The provincial government comply with the federal environmental assessment review and recommendations.

2. Mitigation for losses in fish and wildlife habitat provide a net gain of fish and wildlife habitat for the benefit of all Albertans for the life of the project.
This resolution was carried.
The Picture Butte Fish and Game Association was in the heart of the Lethbridge Northern Irrigation District, which would stand to gain the most from construction of the water management storage dam on the Oldman River.

Oldman Dam was continuing, and "the struggle to save the Three Rivers and the fish and wildlife that depend upon them is also continuing." Kostuch added, "A very successful rally was held on the banks of the Oldman River in June. Over 10,000 people came to what turned out to be the largest environmental rally in Alberta's history. A significant amount of money was raised at the event, which featured Ian Tyson and David Suzuki."

A Wildlife Policy for Canada was adopted by the Wildlife Ministers' Council of Canada, the first of its kind in Canada, at its meeting on Sept. 26-27, 1990. This is a national policy, providing a framework for federal, provincial, territorial, and non-governmental policies and programs that affect wildlife. The document expressed the will of Canadians to conserve wildlife for its own sake and for the benefit of present and future generations of Canadians.

Lloyd Shea, AFGA past fisheries chairperson and at the time still a member of the Edmonton Trout Fishing Club, was awarded the 1990 Conservation Award by the Alberta Council of Trout Unlimited Canada. This award was established in 1989 to recognize outstanding contributions to the conservation of Alberta's wild trout by individuals, groups, business or government agencies. Shea had previously received many conservation awards, including the AFGA Archie Hogg Memorial Award as well as the Alberta Order of the Bighorn Award.

Stan Henders passed away in October 1990, from a heart attack while moose hunting at age 77. Henders, a life member of the AFGA, was prominent in forming the Calgary Sportsmen's Show, and was an active member of the Calgary Fish and Game Club, often holding positions on the executive, most notably as a long-standing predator committee chair.

COURTESY OF DUANE RADFORD

Oldman River Dam.

1991 Dr. Niels Damgaard became president of the AFGA in 1990 after the executive appointed him president to fill out the term vacated by Doug Rumsey, who resigned his presidency in September 1990 for personal reasons.

DOUG RUMSEY: President (1990 – six months)

DOUG RUMSEY

In 1975 my family and I moved to Red Deer from Ontario, afterwards which I attended the annual Sportsman Show being hosted by the Red Deer Fish and Game Association. That's when I bought my first club membership and became a member of the AFGA. For the next five years I held various chairman positions within the Red Deer Fish and Game Association.

In 1980 I was elected as zone 3 director, a position I held for six years. This position involved attending two zone meetings annually, which were hosted by a different club each time. Subsequently, I would represent zone 3 at the provincial executive meetings, and then represent the zone at the annual conferences. Also, every spring I would attend 12-14 annual AFGA awards banquets in zone 3. At these banquets, I am sure that I have eaten the meat of every animal known in Alberta. Some were very good tasting; others, once was enough!

In August 1984 Garry Hrycyk and I started the Zone 3 conservation camp at Lake Pofianga, which is owned by the Ponoka Fish and Game Club. This was a co-ed camp of 30 students between the ages of 12-16 years. We taught several topics including wilderness survival, firearms use and safety and canoeing. This camp ran for one week and the students all slept in tents at that time. This camp was a great learning experience for both the students and the leaders. The zone 3 conservation camp continues today, but in a new location.

In 1986, I was elected second vice president of the AFGA. For the next two years, I represented the provincial body at three different zone meetings, both spring and fall. I also tried to represent the AFGA at meetings with both government and non-government agencies regarding problems that had an effect on our natural resources or our wildlife. I also attended the AFGA's executive meetings that were held either at Edmonton or at Elmer Kure's campsite on the Red Deer River. I also represented the AFGA at the British Columbia Wildlife Federation Annual Convention, which was held in Nanaimo, B.C. in 1987.

In 1988 I moved up to the position of first vice president, or senior vice president, where again I represented the AFGA at different zone meetings, both spring and fall, as well as attending meetings with the government and non-government agencies and the AFGA's own executive meetings. I was also a representative on the Canadian Wildlife Federation (CWF) board of directors, where I had the opportunity to travel to Victoria, Halifax and Ottawa, attending their board meetings and annual conventions.

In 1990, I was acclaimed president of the AFGA. Shortly after becoming president, I was invited to speak to the CWF in Quebec at their annual convention. This was the first time a president from another wildlife federation or fish and game association from across Canada had ever talked as a guest speaker at such a convention.

During my years on the executive of the AFGA there were, same as today, many controversial issues. I think two of the main issues at that time were game ranching, which the AFGA was opposed to because of the potential of

disease problems and the potential for paid hunting. The second issue was the construction of the Oldman River Dam. Due to the controversy that was being created between the two vice presidents at that time and me by the media, regarding the Oldman River Dam, reluctantly I decided for the good of the association to resign my position as president six months later.

In 1994 I was given a life membership award at the annual conference. I still pay my annual membership to the Lacombe Fish and Game Club. Unfortunately, I have done very little with the AFGA since resigning. However, I have stayed involved with other wildlife agencies pertaining to wildlife and habitat issues.

As for my years on the AFGA executive, they were a great learning experience, as well as rewarding and memorable. I use the experience that I gained quite frequently, as I will continue to promote and protect our natural resources and wildlife until my last day.

[Biography prepared by Doug Rumsey.]

Damgaard, a family physician, seemingly appeared out of nowhere as a member of the AFGA executive; past president Graham had referred to him as Dr. Niels (Crash) Damgaard in his 1989 conference report. He was an obliging person with an easy smile and seemed to enjoy being in the limelight as president. Damgaard faced some serious financial problems within the association - an accumulated $125,000 deficit with no more previous surpluses to offset the deficit, not unlike the situation facing the Alberta government in the early 1990s.

The 62nd annual conference was held at the Capri Inn in Red Deer in 1991; the theme of the conference was "Countdown to a New Century." The guest speaker was Dr. David Schindler, a world-renowned environmentalist and scientist from the University of Alberta who spoke about the implications of forestry developments in northern Alberta.

Damgaard walked into a major controversy over the Oldman River Dam, which had divided zone 1 from the rest of the association. Immediate past president Doug Rumsey was worried that conflict over the dam might split the 18,000 member group

LeRoy Fjordbotten, Minister of Forestry, Lands and Wildlife, circa 1991.

because zone 1 members had threatened to form their own organization if they didn't receive some support from the provincial body. Ron Pittman, zone 1 director, said that many AFGA members were ranchers or small-town residents who could see the benefit of the Oldman River Dam. He was quoted in *The [Red Deer] Advocate* as saying; "When nobody else seems to understand, it sort of irritates us. There's been thought given to pulling the pin." To placate zone 1, Rumsey issued a press release endorsing a motion from southern clubs that accepted finishing the dam as long as proper mitigation to offset fish and wildlife losses was accommodated. Rumsey was also quoted in *The [Red Deer] Advocate* as saying; "A lot of members have left [the association] because we are getting too environmentally oriented. They joined the organization because they want a group to fight for their hunting and fishing rights." Dr. Martha Kostuch, a Rocky Mountain House veterinarian, countered that debate within the AFGA was healthy and she didn't think zone 1 was united in favour of the dam.

Damgaard philosophized, "Our wonderful but vanishing heritage of wilderness, wildlife and fish resources and public lands are so rapidly disappearing that we are the last generation that can do anything about it. We owe it to future generations to be responsible stewards so that they too can experience some of the outdoor activities we enjoy today, and sometimes take for granted." This is yet another testament to LeRoy Fjordbotten's false hopes to be remembered as a conservation minister. In his conference report, Damgaard stated, "I have always had pride in the AFGA based on our democratic processes," no doubt trying to brace the delegates about the serious financial situation facing the AFGA, and the need to lay off five full-time staff (down from eight full-time positions) to address the budget shortfalls in the past year.

An announcement was made that there would be a new magazine, *The Outdoor Edge*, with the inaugural issue in April 1991 to enable the AFGA "...to better utilize merchandising opportunities to bring in other revenues so that important programs can be delivered to our membership."

As had been predicted all along by members of the AFGA, the game-ranching industry would be plagued by disease problems.

COURTESY OF THE AFGA

The AFGA executive at the Red Deer conference February 1992. Back row: Andy von Busse (L), Ron Pittman. Middle row: Ike Johannson (L), Darryl Smith, Eileen Christensen, Don Norheim, Fred Girdwood. Front row: Don Hayden (L), Horst Fauser, Niels Damgaard, Vern McIntosh, Jack Graham.

Damgaard reported an outbreak of bovine tuberculosis which he said "...was entirely predictable and easily our biggest issue today." He slammed the agriculture department, now responsible for game ranching in Alberta, stating, "The millions of dollars the tax payers of this land have to spend now to bail out diseased game farms are but an example of bureaucratic bungling incompetence and bull-headed attitudes. We told them so! We were right on this one and we are right on other ones too."

The federal government also came in for a tongue lashing by Damgaard, for its failed green plan, stating, "I wrote a very extensive brief to the green plan outlaying the concerns of the association and we, like so many other concerned citizens and groups, were all but ignored." He also railed about problems with ecological reserves, a serious issue of the day for many members of the AFGA. There were no provisions for hunting or fishing in these reserves, and Alberta's weak-kneed clean-air-strategy was considered a joke by many Albertans.

Damgaard described his predicament in his conference address: "The executive appointed me to be your president to fill out the term vacated by Doug Rumsey when he resigned in September.

1992

Resolution — The Calgary Fish and Game Association submitted a resolution that the AFGA seek a legal opinion on the constitutionality of the law that prohibits hunting on Sunday within the boundaries of the Alberta forest reserves. The AFGA had twice in the previous three years passed a resolution that would allow for Sunday hunting in this area, which was denied by the Alberta government. The Calgary club advised it was now time to take more aggressive action to ensure the rights of hunters were protected by law.

Resolution — There was also a resolution that the Alberta government immediately stop all game ranching in the province. This resolution arose as a result of alarms raised when several elk escaped from game farms under quarantine because of an infection of TB [tuberculosis] and the unknown whereabouts of the elk.

This has left me with a lot to do in a minimum of time. Wholesale changes have occurred in the office. It was obvious downsizing had to occur before we proceeded with a new plan and process. It is hard to justify increasing administration with a failing membership, especially with a deficit to clear up. However, these changes will see us better able to adjust to conditions as we near the next century, and I am extremely hopeful and confident you all will see positive results. The AFGA will make you proud!" Damgaard wisely said, "The association is bigger than any one person, club or group of clubs and therefore it will always be there in the future."

COURTESY OF DUANE RADFORD

Adrienne Radford (L) with an Athabasca River walleye and Ray Kohlruss from Reel Angling Adventures.

Newly appointed vice president Martha Kostuch, who had a very brief report in the conference yearbook, advised the conference delegates: "The AFGA, unlike so many of the single species groups, can and does actively lobby the government at all levels to protect fish and wildlife and their habitat and the rights of sportsmen. What other broad-based group in Alberta does that?"

Kostuch was to step down as vice president in 1991. In an interview, she said that she left the AFGA for two reasons. One was personal, her husband left her, and the kids were at home so she had to look after them. The other reason was that the AFGA narrowly voted to support the construction of the Oldman River Dam; this latter situation put Kostuch in a conflict of interest as vice president of both the AFGA and Friends of the Oldman River organization which was opposed to construction of this dam at the time. She felt she couldn't represent both points of view, and decided to resign from the AFGA in 1991. Kostuch said the AFGA was an important part of her life and she still counts many friends in the organization.

Zone 1 director Ron Pittman reported, "It seems that once again the AFGA is going through another crisis, or at least from zone 1's perspective it looks that way. What with the access to lease land, the Oldman River Dam, not to mention the resignation of our president, it is enough to make one want to quit, and that has certainly crossed my mind. However, after lengthy second thought I still believe the good we have done and can do outweighs the bad, and it is far easier to change the organization from the inside than from the outside. Hang in there people, I will!" It was a spirited address from Pittman, never one to sidestep controversy that the AFGA was mired in at the time. He made a pitch that the organization should search its roots for an answer to the dilemma facing the membership – focus on fish and game and short-list the AFGA objectives to enhance their image. His advice: "There are a host of conservation and environmental organizations out there that one can join if that is your interest, but if you are really concerned about fish and game – then join us." Pittman's address was a harbinger of an impending showdown with Martha Kostuch, a very capable member of the AFGA and a staunch environmentalist who claimed, "I see the association's diversity, just like the diversity of nature, as strength, and not a weakness." These philosophical differences would eventually lead to a major rift in the association, which would be followed by the resignation of Kostuch.

Zone 2 director Donald Fowler had an interesting report on the fourth annual Family Fisherama held Aug. 11-12 at Lake McGregor, near Milo. "Over 1,700 entrants attended with their families bringing the number of people at the lake to over 5,500." Fowler said that proceeds from the event supported the zone 2 handicapped fish derby. He also reported: "Thanks to Jim Harvie who worked hard on an alternate plan not to use Highwood River water to fill a proposed on the Little Bow to provide more irrigation for farmers and ranchers. His alternate plan is to take the water out of Travers and build a pipeline to carry the water over to the Little Bow ; more farmers and ranchers can receive their water for irrigation from the pipeline as well as the Little Bow . The cost of doing this is higher, but would save the fish habitat on the Highwood River and if this habitat is not saved the Government of Alberta will eventually destroy a lot of fishing on the Bow River."

Zone 4 director Vern McIntosh reported, "The game ranching issue, which appeared to be a *fait accompli*, has reared its ugly head with the discovery of numerous diseased herds. The clean-up burden will again be borne by the taxpayer regardless of whose responsibility it becomes, federal or provincial. A discrepancy in recorded herd numbers, wherein a rancher is unable to account for missing animals, demonstrates the fallacy of rigid control of the industry that some people would have us believe. This is reinforced by known escapes of other ranched game animals. So much for the eight foot fence, ear tagging and recording procedures that Agriculture says will control the industry. Keep up the fight on this one for after it comes the push for paid hunting!" McIntosh was right on the money regarding his concerns about the waste of taxpayer money and the impending move toward hunt farms that was looming on the horizon because game ranching was built on a pyramid scheme that was about to collapse.

The AFGA summer executive meeting at Elmer Kure's, September 1993. Ivan Johnson (L), Brian Evans, Minister of Environment, Elmer Kure, Jack Graham.

Steve Witiuk resigned his position as zone 5 director but provided an annual report. Eve Ozanne replaced Witiuk, the first woman to hold a zone director position. Witiuk outlined a litany of issues of concern to members of zone 5 one of the most pressing being the lack of aerial surveys of big game because the government had slashed the budgets of the wildlife branch.

Fishing chair Darryl Smith reported, "Most anglers today give only lip service to the issues that face their sport. They complain among their peers, yet seldom become involved, particularly if that puts them in conflict with neighbours and friends. The simple act of joining a conservation organization is a first step few anglers take. A scant handful becomes active by volunteering their time and knowledge." He also advised that governments no longer had the resources to be everything to

*R*on Gladish, past president, was elected president of the Canadian Wildlife Federation at its annual meeting in Edmonton, June 2-4, 1993.

everyone and the money once allocated for wildlife management dried up in the 1980s; consequently, the small group of conservationists in the AFGA would be asked to do more.

Agriculture chair Elmer Kure advised, "The good news is we are getting our act together expanding habitat retention on private lands through the expansion of the North American Waterfowl [Management] Plan first step in Alberta, Buffalo Lake region. We are expanding the Landowner Habitat Program in the settled area, and we are demonstrating how to do it on our own Antelope Creek ranch and stewardship programs." Kure philosophized, "Now if we could just stop this lust to commercialize our wildlife in Alberta, we could give some more credit lines to our legislature for having some guts to preserve the environment and our fish and wildlife resource."

Contributor services representative Del Scammell provided an excellent illustration of just how much Alberta's sportsmen benefited from the good work done by the AFGA in his conference report. The association raised about $22,000 worth of gold, silver and corporate sponsorships from a direct mail-out campaign. Fund raisers in 1990 included dinner/auctions that raised about $40,000. Scammell also reported, "Perhaps the most meaningful and successful program I have ever been involved in is the hunter ethics placemats. Sponsored by Labatts Brewery, the AFGA, and some helpful input from the Alberta Fish and Wildlife Division, approximately 200,000 of these mats were distributed to restaurants in our province. Content of the placemats centred on the 'Use Respect – Ask Permission' program; this received very positive response from the restaurants that used them and the general public."

1992 Dr. Niels Damgaard remained president of the AFGA in 1991. The theme of the 63rd annual conference held at the Capri Inn in Red Deer in 1992 was "Working Together is Better," a theme that was intended to reinforce the value of building positive relationships and reinforcing existing partnerships. Damgaard snickered in his remarks to conference delegates, "As a conciliatory gesture our provincial government has even suggested that the association should be involved in an advisory capacity on game

1993

Resolution	A resolution calling for a change in name of the AFGA to the Alberta Wildlife Federation was again put forward, this time by the Stony Plain Fish and Game Association, because of the supposed confusion with the Fish and Wildlife Division of the Alberta government. The brief noted, "At times, numerous phone calls are directed to AFGA clubs, which were to be directed to the Alberta Fish and Wildlife Division. Also during phone surveys, AFGA volunteers sometimes take, a lot of heat from irate fishermen and hunters." The resolution was defeated.
Resolution	The High River Fish and Game Association again submitted a resolution to discontinue the landowner special licence. The resolution was defeated. The landowner special licence was the result of lobbying by Zone 1 clubs to placate landowners who had to contend with all the problems associated with big-game hunting and yet saw few benefits. The local clubs suggested these people be given special status for a landowner licence if they had applied on a draw and were unsuccessful, as an incentive for them to protect wildlife and maintain good relations with local hunters.

ranching?" Damgaard spoke of the measures taken by the executive to create harmony and make members proud to belong to the AFGA. He also spoke about the importance of the *Outdoor Edge* magazine as a communication vehicle, a partnership with the wildlife federations and fish and game associations in B.C., Manitoba, Saskatchewan, the Northwest Territories and the Yukon.

Ron Hauser was hired as the new executive vice president in 1991, replacing Lyle Fullerton in an open competition.

Damgaard spoke of the recession that had hit Alberta in 1991, contrary to what Premier Don Getty was quoted as saying, "Alberta is booming." The recession had an impact on the AFGA revenue line: donations dried up, government grants were cut back and some clubs lost membership. He also mentioned the "Ayotte" court decision in favour of commercialization of wildlife by natives, rallying the delegates by saying the AFGA simply cannot allow this to happen with the cry, "This is the hill we die on if we have to!"

The federal gun control Bill C-17 became a reality, increasing requirements for acquiring a firearms acquisition certificate and prohibiting certain military and automatic firearms. Damgaard wailed, "Law-abiding gun owners who happen to use firearms for vocation or recreation are once again being penalized to satisfy the anti-crowd."

The AFGA lost some clubs that joined allegiances with the National Firearms Association as fallout of this misguided and ill-conceived legislation, which would turn into a billion-dollar money pit during the years ahead. Damgaard also took aim at the provincial government over game ranching and the disease problems that had been forecast by the AFGA. Clearly, the president was displeased with elected officials in both Ottawa and Edmonton.

COURTESY OF TRAVEL ALBERTA

A stunning view of Maligne Lake near Jasper.

Similarly, he expressed concerns about the divisive nature of the Oldman River Dam within the AFGA. In closing, Damgaard referred to the sacrifices he had made as president, putting in some 2,000 hours of volunteer time and commitment to the association during the previous year, not to mention the impact on his job and family life. He would be remembered as one of the most articulate and outspoken of all the AFGA presidents, and was seen to wear his heart on his sleeve.

Senior vice president Horst Fauser reported, "McGillivray Creek [youth camp] took over 500 hours of my time. Over 450 children were able to use the facility last summer."

Junior vice president Vern McIntosh reported, "1991 has been a crucial year for the AFGA. Many cost-cutting innovations have been put into effect until there is little else that can be done to further cut costs. We are at a critical point in our history and unless finances change in 1992, we may well see the demise of the association as we know it. Unless there is a change for the better in 1992, the only alternative will be to discontinue all services, dismiss all staff and sell off our assets to prevent bankruptcy."

McIntosh went on to comment, "The dissolution of the AFGA will mean the loss of the only multi-interest group that speaks for sportsmen in this province. Hunters and fishermen will be left in small voiceless groups with no united front." He continued ringing the alarm with his closing comments: "In my opinion, the most important issue that faces us in the coming year is the state of this organization. Without a healthy, united association, we are unable to face the many issues confronting us that are so important to us today and for our children in the future. Our advisory capability, as a group, plays a part in wildlife management in this province. Wildlife can ill afford to lose us."

Hunting chair George Page reported progress made respecting outfitter guide allocations for non-resident hunters. He noted that the AFGA executive and the Alberta Professional Outfitters Association (APOS) had reached agreement on a formula that cut down the number of outfitter permits in an area where there was a draw for residents in effect. Page advised, "I can now tell the truth and explain what the policy has really meant… the total number of outfitters has decreased from a high in 1986 of 648 to a low in 1991 of 261 or a reduction of 60 percent." One of the goals of the policy was to reduce the number of guides and outfitters; the policy was obviously very successful in this regard. Page added, "Now for the coming year if we could deal with a predator problem and the unregulated native hunting issue we could have the best hunting in the world. Our biggest problem is the native issue [and] we cannot get our government to do anything. The natives are now selling game, getting huge land claims and lots of money. To fight this real threat we are going to have join other organizations [and] spend a lot of money to combat the natives. They have loads of money and will use it to control your hunting rights."

Fishing chair Darryl Smith was absolutely glowing in his report with respect to being consulted by the provincial fisheries branch officials in a way he had never seen before in the history of the AFGA, praising them for their comanagement policy.

Program chair Nestor Romaniuk (who did not attend the annual conference) painted a sinister picture of the times. "It appears that our country's unity, our country's financial status, our own organization and in particular our environment and wildlife are all in a precarious state. The rivers are being polluted, the forests are being raped and the wildlife decimated, and the organization that can prevent this dreadful happening is strapped for cash. Adding to this dilemma, valuable time is wasted with negativism towards each other, and the elected executive. There are some members in our organization who spend more time criticizing the efforts of others than contributing positive solutions to the issues facing this association." Romaniuk spat "I have always wondered how a person feels when he looks in the mirror and says, "I contributed nothing to our wildlife resource, but I sure did a good number on the elected executive; that's my contribution to wildlife."

On a more cheery note, zone 4 director Andy von Busse advised, "We are the ones who know what affects wildlife positively and negatively, but we do a poor job of communicating our knowledge to even other hunters and fishermen. My challenge to you is to get more members in the door, get them more involved and make your club a more active one than it is now. Direct your activities toward the thing that matters the most, the resource."

Zone 6 director Dave George reported that even though they had a small membership they had some very dedicated and competent members to keep them in the forefront on all issues – George stepped down as zone director in 1991, turning over the reins to John Flynn of Peace River.

Trophy chair Ab England reported two new trophy categories: sauger, sponsored by the Southern Alberta Outdoorsmen; Merriam's turkey, sponsored by the Calgary Sportsman Club. England advised, "From the talk we hear 1991 looks like a record year for big-game animals. We hear of a new record typical mule [deer], two typical white-tails near 200, and a large non-typical white-tailed over 260."

COURTESY OF THE AFGA
NIELS DAMGAARD

1993   Dr. Niels Damgaard remained as president of the AFGA in 1992, completing three years in that post. Damgaard was something of an institution in the AFGA by this time; he maintained his strident position in support of fish and wildlife conservation in Alberta, not afraid to speak out against the government about any ill-conceived programs and laws. Damgaard's charming wife, Penny, was also a driving force in affairs of the AFGA; she chaired the 64th annual conference at the Marlborough Inn in Calgary in 1993. The theme of the conference was "Together We Make The Difference."

Few people realize the amount of time and effort that goes into the job of being president of the AFGA, consequently Damgaard's summary for the 64th annual conference in Calgary bears quoting: "As your president, I gave over 3,000 hours; read over 100,000 pages of mail, briefs and material; had over 5,000 pages go through my fax machine; answered over 4,000 phone calls; wrote over 500 letters; wrote several reports and briefs; attended hundreds of meetings; did over 200 media interview and press conferences; received several threats; strained family relationships to the fullest; drove over 30,000 kilometres; flew many tens of thousands kilometres more; and much, much more; yet somehow all that was willingly done. It was a privilege to be your president."

COURTESY OF MARTIN SHARREN
Kassandra Sharren proudly holds up her first fish, caught at Talbot Lake in 1994.

Saskatoon berries at a U-pick farm.

COURTESY OF TRAVEL ALBERTA

Hunting chair Ike Johannson reported on the controversy surrounding outfitters and guides over northern moose allocations and issues related to public lands, game ranching, access, predator control, native issues and gun legislation.

Fishing chair Darryl R. Smith (in his fourth term of office) advised, "You are by far the most committed generation of anglers this province has ever seen. Compassion and sacrifice would be good adjectives to describe you. You have been disappointed all too often in the past. Times are changing. Attitudes even among ourselves have altered dramatically because we see we are dealing with a finite resource that can disappear forever. Once gone, there are no stewards to protect and make sacrifices for it. Managers have suddenly realized they need us! Not just to share blame with, but to allow for real change. This is the opportunity we have been asking for; it is in our ball park now!"

Environmental chair Andy Boyd spoke highly of Darryl Smith "The contribution Darryl Smith is making to our association on such issues as fishery management is obvious. But as I become more closely involved with executive work, I am amazed at the wide range of issues Darryl is involved in. He continues to make suggestions and bring to my attention concerns related to my role as environment chair. Good solid teamwork like this is what is needed to meet environmental challenges we face today." Smith was a Valleyview dentist who was awarded a national recreational fishing award, as well as an Alberta Order of the Bighorn Award, for his work on the Little Smoky River Arctic grayling fishing regulations and management plan in 1992.

Zone 1 director Ron Pittman, a tireless advocate for fish and wildlife conservation who resigned this chair at the 64th annual conference, reported, "We always seem to be addressing ourselves to the many controversial issues that forever plague the fish and wildlife of our province. Let me assure you that I think our association's credibility and overall profile is in great shape and our rapport with the majority of people in the province and particularly the government is as good as can be expected."

Zone 2 director Fred Girdwood spoke of "tree and shrub planting, waterfowl nest structures and bluebird boxes, along with pheasant rearing and release projects, all combine volunteer hours and Buck for Wildlife funds to promote the well-being of wildlife populations. The promotion of 'use respect' signs particularly in the special areas along with the habitat steward program are highlights for several zone 2 clubs. Many volunteer hours are spent supporting the Wildlife Trust, hide collection plus countless hours by most clubs to collect statistics for Forestry, Lands and Wildlife on the annual [big game harvest] phone survey." Girdwood hit the nail on the head with his accurate description of the rank and file volunteer effort of the AFGA members. A little known fact is that volunteers from the AFGA assisted staff from the Fish and Wildlife Division and Trout Unlimited Canada with the transplant of brown trout from the Bow River to the Red Deer River, below Dickson Dam to help kickstart this fishery.

Zone 4 director Andy von Busse spoke of concerns related to clubs in Jasper, Hinton and Edson not reaffiliating with the association. "Ex-members are also missing out on receiving the

Such are the sacrifices of the position of highest office in the AFGA, and that's just during their term as president, a fraction of the amount of time actually spent on executive duties. Damgaard reported that the membership (which had been falling for several years) had stabilized in 1992, in "…many areas is rising again," and that financial control had returned. Regrettably, he reported that while the AFGA had built many bridges with other organizations they were stabbed in the back by the Ralph Klein government when the Public Lands Division was turned over to Alberta Agriculture. He said, "Premier Klein didn't even seem to know about it at first," typical of the Klein government's sad legacy with respect to the low priority it had for fish and wildlife stewardship. He spoke about the gun-control debacle and its negative impact on the AFGA, and of entering a sad, new era for wildlife in Alberta, an era of privatization.

Damgaard stated, "I still believe today that privatization of wildlife remains the biggest threat to wildlife, a point I made when first elected as a vice president of the AFGA." Damgaard would be remembered as one of the most eloquent of all the AFGA presidents.

Junior vice president Vern McIntosh took a shot from the hip with his remarks: "We are still having clubs disaffiliate for various reasons. Some of them later rejoin. The clubs that leave have lost their opportunity to participate in decision-making in wildlife issues. Government departments want to talk to and negotiate with an organized, unified body, not with a series of individual interest groups." McIntosh's arguments are valid because government ministers, in particular, do not want to deal with splinter groups; they prefer to deal with organizations at the provincial level, leaving the local and regional affairs to departmental officials.

COURTESY OF RAY MAKOWECKI

Jennifer Lamontagne (Makowecki) (L) and Ray Makowecki on a white-tailed deer hunt in the St. Paul area, 1994.

highly acclaimed magazine, the *Outdoor Edge*; are not covered by our $500,000 third party liability insurance; nor are their views being represented when hunting and fishing seasons are being developed in conjunction with the Fish and Wildlife Division. Affiliation is a win-win situation; the AFGA gets the support and input from the clubs and the clubs are able to have some influence on fish and wildlife policies through the AFGA, direct lobbying with government and through resolutions which pass conference." On another note, von Busse advised, "Let's not forget, that before the Progressive Conservative party had their recent leadership election, the AFGA had more paid-up members than the ruling party of Alberta did. If you suspect those numbers carry some clout, you are right."

Zone 6 director Dave Ridgeway advised, "With the announcement of government approval in principle of the Manning Diversified project (sawmill operation in Manning) and the Grande Alberta Paper Project (pulp mill and coated paper mill) the ball is rolling for environmental hearings. I hope that when the time comes that you as members of the hunting and fishing lobby take the time to give your impressions during the review

process. What you think is important, no matter how insignificant you feel it might be." This was sage advice, as all too often individual club members underestimated their influence on government decision-makers.

While documentation is scanty in the AFGA records, Alberta Environmental Protection had a massive, long-range, integrated resource-planning program underway in 1993. Local AFGA clubs played a major role in these planning exercises in support of defining fish and wildlife management goals and objectives for the various plans.

1994 Horst Fauser became president of the AFGA in 1993 and gave one of the shortest reports ever at the 65th annual conference held at the Medicine Hat Lodge in Medicine Hat in 1994. The theme of the annual conference was "Youth – Our Link To The Future." Fauser was a long-standing member of the AFGA from Lethbridge who had immigrated to Canada from his native Germany to work in the dairy industry (originally). He was a highly committed fish and game member who had a knack for being able to crystallize key issues very succinctly and speak passionately about them; he was not a microphone hog and was noted for brief, hard-hitting commentary. Fauser was the first president from Lethbridge since Joe Balla held this position in 1966-67 and knew what he was up against in terms of time and travel with a head office located in Edmonton, some 500 kilometres away.

HORST FAUSER: President (1993-94)

I joined the Lethbridge Fish and Game Association in 1968 and subsequently served as the environmental chairman for this club, shortly after joining the association.

In 1977, I was elected as non-renewable resource chairman for the parent body, the AFGA

Following are the major milestones that I recall, prior to my becoming president of the AFGA, and thereafter:

- Elected zone 1 chairman in 1978.

-Wrote and presented a brief to the Environment Conservation

COURTESY OF THE AFGA

HORST FAUSER

1995

Resolution

The Wetaskiwin Fish and Game Association submitted a resolution that the province of Alberta maintain permanent working field fisheries personnel, wildlife biologists and technicians at or above present staffing levels. The brief noted: "Fish and wildlife are important to us all as Albertans. The time has come to take a firm position on the very future of our Alberta fish and wildlife. Accurate management data is paramount to the resources' general well being."

The resolution reflected a sign of the times as the ruling Progressive Conservative party under Premier Ralph Klein embarked on a major cost-cutting budget exercise, coined the "Klein Revolution" to eliminate the provincial deficit; positions were being abolished throughout government as part of this downsizing exercise and the Fish and Wildlife Division was left reeling from the impact of both staff and budget cuts.

Association (ECA) hearings on the Oldman River Dam; the ACA agreed with my views regarding the preferred dam site location but the provincial government over-ruled their recommendation and selected the Three Rivers Dam site instead.

- Wrote and presented a brief on a 500-kilowatt TransAlta power line right-of-way (against it) in southwestern Alberta through the Whaleback Ridge; unfortunately lost that one.

- Served for 13 years on the public advisory committee to the ECA.

- Served six years on an ecological reserves committee trying to allow hunting as a permitted activity on these reserves; outvoted mostly, except at Bob Creek while Ross Lake was stricken as a candidate site.

- Incorporated zone 1 under the Society Act 1986 as the Southern Alberta Fish and Game Society.

- With financial help ($9,000) from the Lethbridge Fish and Game Association, purchased and installed Swareflex wildlife warning reflectors to reduce highway road kills of deer in southern Alberta, which are now widely used in B.C. and elsewhere in Alberta.

- Got five clubs involved in a winter Merriam's turkey feeding program and made two turkey transplants, one into WMU 302 and the other into WMU 306 which turned out to be very successful.

- Raised $200,000 to construct the McGillivray Creek youth camp which took five years to complete; managed site as director for 10 years when the summers were always fully booked with children.

- Resigned my position as zone director due to the workload associated with the McGillivray Creek youth camp in 1986.

- Obtained charitable taxation status for the McGillivray Creek Youth Camp which took two years to accomplish.

- Elected president of the AFGA in 1993.

- Issues: Bill C 68 [Firearms Act] was established and the AFGA did manage to get the provincial government on side in opposition; game ranching continued to be a major issue as well.

- Started discussions again with the Alberta Cattlemen's Association regarding access to Crown land.

- Stopped an attempt by provincial government to transfer Buck for Wildlife funds into general revenue; supported the Alberta Conservation Association (ACA) to save these funds; regretfully, funds were subsequently not always spent wisely.

- Now serve as treasurer for the Southern Alberta Fish and Game Society.
[Biography prepared by Horst Fauser.]

"In 1968 my neighbours introduced me to fishing," Fauser said in an interview, "and then I said, gosh, I'd like to go big-game hunting. We went duck hunting with them, but I'm from Europe, and Germany, and I haven't got a clue. So they said you join fish and game and they'll teach you about hunting. And I joined and the same year we had a big-game hunt in tents out in Dutch Creek. It snowed like heck; I shot a cow elk way in the bush with a friend and that's how I got into fish and game, due to my neighbour, Bill Elliot."

In his presidential conference report, Fauser reported, "At the time of writing it is not clear if the federal Liberals and/or our provincial government will follow through with their election promises to us to hold public hearings into game ranching." This was a hollow promise, never kept by either level of government – a grand cover-up to sidestep disease and economic issues related to game ranching. He advised the conference delegates, "The challenges for 1994 are to convince our government to maintain their limited sup-

port of our association, to increase our membership, defeat game ranching and resolve the issue of access to public lands." Fauser added, "Our strength and continued efforts are needed to maintain fish and game management under the principle that fish and game belongs to all people of Alberta. Germany has shown what will happen if no one speaks up for wildlife and its wise use."

Senior vice president Vern McIntosh noted: "1993 was a good year for fish and game in Alberta. It brought about a number of new committees on wildlife and the environment to which the AFGA and clubs were invited to participate as a stakeholder. The process of public participation on issues is definitely on the increase. This increases the workload for executive and committee appointees but on the other hand the increase is most welcome. The trend indicates the desire of government and its agencies to cooperate with the public on issues of common concern, joint projects, policy and regulation. Industry has joined many of these committees where their operations affect wildlife, habitat and the environment. We are being heard. 'Working together is better.'"

McIntosh also reported, "Niels [Damgaard] is still fighting game ranching/farming as is evidenced by correspondence from the venison growers association. They are not happy with our group. This is a fight that must be continued because when these businesses become uneconomical there will be pressure exerted by agriculture for shooting farms then, or paid hunting of wild species on any private lands. Texas in the north. I shudder to think of it." While McIntosh was never one to seek the limelight, he was always astute in his forecasts and his analysis of the situation; he would be remembered as a thoughtful president and straight shooter in his own right.

Keith Pugh in a moose-hunting camp in the Slave Lake area, 1995.

COURTESY OF YVONNE KELLER

Sunset over a calm Slave Lake.

After many years of lobbying and countless resolutions from the AFGA, the Alberta government finally implemented a new wildlife identification number (WiN) and a priority draw system.

Junior vice president Andy von Busse said it well in his conference address: "Our membership has been involved with lobbying government at the local, regional and provincial level, for improvements and rationalization of regulations involving wildlife and fisheries management. Some of our members have been recognized nationally for their efforts, as was Dr. Darryl Smith, your retiring fish chairman. We, combined, have had an enormous positive effect on wildlife in this province. A primary reason why we are effective is that we are viewed by many as reasonable, credible and responsible in our endeavours." Von Busse also singled out

highly respected environment chair, Andy Boyd, for his efforts, as well as Sheila Ferguson-Marten, (daughter of Norman and Stella Ferguson of Lethbridge, both long-time members of the AFGA), for her work on the AFGA youth program. Von Busse remarked that it was Ferguson-Martin's idea to have youth delegates at the conference, "...delegates that can help develop the program to fit the needs of the youth, and not of the adult."

Dr. Darryl Smith stepped down as fish chair at the annual conference on a positive note. "Many have asked why we have so few fishery resolutions. The reason is fundamental. Fishery issues are dealt with in a consultative process that extends from a local to a provincial level. Changes in management have the needed broad support with anglers and government. The use of resolutions for fishery issues in the AFGA therefore is reserved as a sounding board for major changes in direction. The wildlife branch and the AFGA hunting committee must develop a similar approach. Most of the hunting resolutions would be needless if a similar system existed."

1996

Resolution

A controversial resolution that senior citizens of Alberta who enjoy the sport of fishing pay a regular licence fee to fish, with the revenue going toward stocking ponds and establishing and/or maintaining ponds, to benefit Alberta's aging anglers was submitted by the Iron Creek Fish and Game Association. There is no record whether this resolution passed or failed.

Programs chair Sheila Ferguson-Martin started her report with the quote: "Tell me – I will forget. Show me – I might remember. But involve me, and I will understand." This was a prelude to her work involving the participation of youth delegates at the annual AFGA conferences, which started the ball rolling to rejuvenate the membership.

Environment chair Andy Boyd spoke of the major issues faced by the AFGA: Draft policy for managing Alberta's peatlands and non-settled area wetlands [Beyond Prairie Potholes Wetland Policy], *Water Resource Act* review, Lakeland Provincial Park and Recreation Area advisory committee participation, Special Places 2000 pending cabinet endorsement, forest conservation strategy and Al Pac Forest Management Task Force.

Zone 1 director Ross MacDonald reported on work done by various clubs to develop the McGillivray youth camp and work to oppose a major four seasons resort in the West Castle River valley.

Zone 2 director Rod Dyck reported, "The Calgary Fish and Game Association along with clubs from High River, Sarcee and Calgary Rod and Rifle as well as the Drumheller Fish and Game Association hosted two separate fish derbies for the disabled this past year. An excellent outing and fun day with fish biting was had by all participants." Dyck also reported on other important projects undertaken by zone 2 clubs, as follows:

- Family Fisherama at Lake McGregor.

COURTESY OF TRAVEL ALBERTA

Aurora borealis (northern lights) over the Athabasca River near Fort McMurray.

COURTESY OF LILLA PFERSCHY

A busy beaver working along the North Saskatchewan riverbank.

- The transporting of 21 mountain goats from Lillooet, B.C. to Picklejar Lakes in Kananaskis Country.
- Tree girdling in WMU 305 to enhance browse and habitat for moose and mule deer.
- Formation of a committee to oversee the proposed re-introduction of the pinnated grouse and work on sharp-tailed grouse habitat.

Zone 5 director Steve Witiuk reported on an ongoing dilemma faced by members of the AFGA, the raising of funds through the auctioning of special wildlife licences. Witiuk reported that the issue had come up three times in the last three years over the raffling and auctioning of big-horn sheep licences as a fund raiser for "making big bucks." He continued, "Is this what hunters want? This will make hunting as commercial as buying stocks and bonds. For example; the auction of an elk licence in Saskatchewan produced approximately $20,000 and went to the North American Elk Foundation. With the bad economy, this has made the politicians recognize the money-making potential that will directly affect the wildlife."

Native affairs chair Andy von Busse advised, "Of course the big issue for 1993 was the moratorium on non-Native hunting of moose in Northern Alberta." He advised the Treaty 8 chiefs present at a meeting in Moberly Lake, B.C., that the AFGA, as an organization, would not and could not stand aside with the request that they had made, and would fight vigorously against any attempt to have it implemented.

The Fish and Wildlife Division initiated a northern moose management program in 1993 to determine the status of moose in northern Alberta and the reasons for declines in populations. The program consisted of (1) A major population survey in late 1993 and early 1994 to determine moose densities and sex and age ratios; (2) Collection and analysis of teeth from hunter-killed moose during the autumn of 1993 to obtain a better understanding of the age structure of various herds; (3) Collection and analysis of reproductive tracts from moose to determine pregnancy rates of yearlings and older age class animals; and (4) Analysis of moose that died during the spring of 1994 to determine the exact causes of deaths of moose that were infected with ticks. At the time, moose populations in west-central Alberta and north-

Founding Board ACA, 1997. Back row: Glen Semenchuk (L), Andy von Busse, Dave Powell, Dave Gursky. Front row: Ed Lakusta (L), Don Pike, Deryl Empson, Brad Stelfox, Sven-Erik Janssen.

ern Alberta were below historic levels and below the carrying capacity for the available habitat. The Minister of Environmental Protection, Brian Evans, advised in a government of Alberta news release dated Sept. 16, 1993: "There is no need for a moratorium on recreational moose hunting in Alberta. Recreational hunting regulations and restrictions have been designed to reduce the moose harvest in the 1993 season."

1995 Horst Fauser remained as president of the AFGA in 1994, reflecting that two years as president—compared to the 70-year history of the AFGA—was a short time. He said that the years went by quickly, with a minimum of "…four hours each and every day were spent on association business." He spoke of all the issues he had to contend with: provincial government budget cuts, an election, MLA changes, department changes, etc. Due to being semi-retired he was able to spend time "…needed to carefully guide our association through these chaotic times." He also advised that he spent a minimum of one full week each month in Edmonton on AFGA business, with as many as three additional trips being needed from time to time, which speaks volumes about the commitment necessary in the role of president of the AFGA.

The 66th annual conference was held at the Coast Terrace Inn at Edmonton; the conference theme was "Conservation Is a Family Affair."

Fauser advised conference delegates of the success he and his vice presidents enjoyed tackling: northern moose management,

native affairs, Special Places 2000, gun control, forestry management, exotic animal policy development, WISE foundation (start-up issues), etc. The WISE foundation was a non-government funding organization in support of hunter education. It was the result of the government privatizing its hunter education program (which was picked up by the Alberta Hunter Education Instructors Association) and laying off all its hunter training staff.

> The Conservation Education WISE Foundation began in 1995 and presently exists largely as a funding tool to assist in the administration and delivery of Alberta's hunter and fishing education programs. The acronym WISE stands for "Wildlife is our motive, In trust our objective, Safekeeping is our goal, Education is our tool." The foundation was created to increase the level of public commitment to the conservation of Alberta's fish and wildlife through the training responsible users of the resource.
>
> In its formative years it provided funding for the following courses: Alberta Conservation and Hunter Education, Alberta Fishing Education program, Project Wild, Outdoor Youth seminars, Outdoor Women's seminars, Outdoor Camp programs, Canadian Firearm Safety, instructor certification and workshops. It was created when the Klein government downsized government departments as part of its deficit-elimination program (eliminating the Fish and Wildlife Division hunter education program); the government provided assistance by way of an annual operating grant to the WISE Foundation. Tom Bateman was the first executive director of this foundation, which was headquartered in Calgary, and his wife Bonnie served as the chief administrator, under the direction of chairperson Bob Gruszecki.

The McGillivray youth camp was built (largely through the personal efforts and drive of Fauser) in southwest Alberta, north of Coleman, as a hunter training camp for zone 1. Fauser was also successful in obtaining funding for the AFGA during a time of government cutbacks, as the Klein government moved to eliminate Alberta's deficit. The cutbacks would see the Fish and Wildlife Division gutted during Klein's term of office.

Fauser said the challenges ahead include "…increasing our membership, maintaining our good working relationship with all levels of government, and recruiting new people into all three executive levels of our association – clubs, zones, provincial." The finances were reported as being "secure" in 1995. He concluded his report by reminding the delegates, "On a final note, do not forget to have fun and good fellowship times throughout your involvement with

1997

Resolution The St. Albert and District Fish and Game Association submitted a resolution that the AFGA actively lobby the Alberta government to require the mandatory licensing of all anglers over the age of 16 years; the motion was carried.

This resolution represented a roundabout way of requiring seniors to purchase a fishing licence, a move that did not have the support of the ruling Progressive Conservative government, which perceived a loss of the senior vote if they were required to purchase angling licences. [The PC government had already angered the seniors in 1993 when it cutback funding to many seniors' programs.]

the AFGA," which is an important aspect of being a member of the organization that should not be lost on it members.

Senior vice president Vern McIntosh reported, "Troubled species like walleye and bull trout will be the subject of intensive management efforts to increase their numbers and restore depleted fisheries. Co-operation of industry, government, and the public is a must for the survival of bull trout." He also advised that gun control continued to be the biggest issue facing the AFGA; challenging the members, "It is important that each gun owner stand up and fight rather than wait for someone else to do it for them."

Junior vice president Andy von Busse reported, "The AFGA members who are on the wildlife advisory and fishery advisory boards of the provincial Wildlife Trust Fund have made a major impact on the manner and the type of decisions that are made in spending the Buck for Wildlife monies that come from hunters and anglers. That fund has assets approaching $10 million, so it is a major improvement that we finally have a real say in how it is to be spent." [All this would change in 1997 when the trust fund revenues would be turned over to a fledgling organization created by the Klein Tories, the Alberta Conservation Association.]

Hunting chair Dave Gibson, who had one year under his belt in this new position, advised that the past year had gone by with "blinding speed" due to the volume and diversity of issues that required his attention. Gibson advised, "The Buck for Wildlife

Fund will have seen a few changes by this time with the formation of regional advisory boards working with fish and wildlife regional staff to develop and make recommendations on projects in each zone. This is a great opportunity to affect change at the grassroots level."

Fishing chair Dr. Darryl Smith waxed philosophical in his year end report, "When it comes to fishery management, we are viewed as one group along with several others, most notably the Western Walleye Council, Walleye Unlimited and Trout Unlimited. Other organizations are poised to set up shop in Alberta as anglers search for a group that represents them." New special-interest groups were emerging in Alberta that catered to species such as walleye and trout only and were competing with the AFGA for the attention of government officials. Smith offered the opinion, "We must learn how to make constructive decisions that look beyond either just the fish or the angler. This will mean anglers and managers must be guided by the same principles and develop an objective and broad decision-making process. Knowledge and education will be the cornerstone to a successful partnership."

Environment chair Andy Boyd spoke of the need to prioritize the environmental issues facing the AFGA and that it was impossible for one person to cover all the bases. He personally devoted much of his energy to the Alberta Forest Conservation Strategy and

COURTESY OF YVONNE KELLER

A parade of goslings paddle across Great Slave Lake.

the Special Places 2000 protected areas program. He advised that other AFGA officials tackled various other issues: "For example, past president Niels Damgaard's excellent handling of the difficult Suffield 'wild' horses issue, Darryl Smith's championing of the Little Smoky Primitive Area, and Elmer Kure's tireless work on a host of issues ranging from the Landowner's Habitat Program to the Environment Councils' Future Environmental Directions Project."

> *L*ife member chair Jack Graham reported, "1994 was again a sad year for our association when we have to report that we lost three of our life members, Gene Scully, Sam Smolyk, and Nils Kvisle. All were active and contributing support to the AFGA. They will be sorely missed. We offer our condolences to their families."

Ross MacDonald stepped down as zone 1 director, turning over the reins to incoming director Gerry Pittman, advising, however, that he had asked the representatives of zone 1 to allow him to retain the land-use chair position. MacDonald advised, "I believe that it is here that I can make the best contribution to the

AFGA. I have been at many hearings by both the NRCB [Natural Resources Conservation Board] and the ERCB [Energy Resources Conservation Board]. I am pleased to say the association has made a considerable impact at these hearings and we have gained a position where we are well thought of by both proponents and opponents in any given situation." He closed his report with the statement: "We are solution people and we have great pride in that."

Zone 2 director Rod Dyck kicked off his address to conference delegates advising, "Here it is, the AFGA's 66th annual conference. That's a long time for any organization to be in operation. It is only through the hard work of dedicated volunteers who care about wildlife, conservation and preserving and enhancing Alberta's many splendours for future generations that this has been made possible." Dyck reported on many activities to engage young people at the club level, as well as the popular High River and Drumheller fish derbies for the disabled. He said, "Keeping our families involved in our club projects is the best way to ensure the future of our wildlife and the AFGA. The clubs in zone 2 have been doing a pretty good job of this but we still must strive to keep our membership numbers up by introducing new families to our clubs and the ideals that we stand for."

Myles Radford (L) and Vic Bergman out on another fly-fishing trip!

Zone 4 director Ralph Leriger reported: "The declining number of angling and hunting licences sold each year in the province and fewer numbers of young people taking up these activities demonstrates the need for us to look at the entire picture when it comes to conservation and not just our own particular area of interest."

Zone 5 director Steve Witiuk advised, "A lot of issues have arisen that the clubs and the AFGA need to work on. At one time we had 24,000 members. We need to assess what has happened to cause the decline in membership and collectively work on some solutions. Some of the issues that have been raised by individual clubs are:
- We need lower per capita [fees].
- More service to the clubs and zones is required.

From the AFGA side of things:
- Need more media attention and respect.
- Get the conservation lottery back so the clubs can get involved again.
- The AFGA cannot charge clubs for everything as they need money to operate as well."

Witiuk also addressed a great many other issues facing the association: the right of access to Crown grazing leases, the need for better inventory of all wildlife, concerns about use of ATVs, the zone 5 objection to using raffles and/or auctioning of wildlife for profit, government plans to shut down the Environmental Council of Alberta, gun control and sale of Crown grazing leases.

1996 Vern McIntosh became president of the AFGA in 1995. A resident of Ardrossan, east of Edmonton, McIntosh worked for the Edmonton city police service; he was a soft-spoken, likeable person with a good sense of humour, and got along well with members of the AFGA, members of government and their officials. He didn't pull any punches when dealing with controversial issues and had the respect of his colleagues with his down-to-earth approach. McIntosh could always be counted on for hard-hitting media quotes, short and to the point.

COURTESY OF THE AFGA
VERN MCINTOSH

COURTESY OF TRAVEL ALBERTA
A moose family grazing in Kananaskis Country.

VERN MCINTOSH: President (1995-97)

At the time of writing, I am a 75-year-old father and grandfather. I am married to a woman (Marlene) who puts up with my absences and antics without complaint. Sometimes I think she is glad to get rid of me for awhile. We have a son and daughter. The son hunts and fishes. My daughter's husband has been converted to a hunter and I am working on the two grandsons. I have been retired from the Edmonton Police Service for the past 19 years.

I am a long-time member of the AFGA, starting with the Edmonton Police Fish and Game Association where I was trophy chairman for years. That club was very active as a group in many endeavours. We charted all the waste water out falls to the Saskatchewan River in the city of Edmonton, did a series of water testing with University of Alberta students to demonstrate the poor mixing of water between Edmonton and the Vinca Bridge (where a government testing station was on the wrong side of the river), as just one of many club projects.

I have been a hunter since age eight, chasing grouse with a slingshot and later a BB gun and a dog. I stalked sharptails and sandhill cranes with a .22 rifle as a food source on an Anselmo-area (a hamlet just outside of Mayerthorpe) farm. I learned to fish there by snaring Arctic grayling in creeks because we had no hooks. To finance Saturday night in town, we sold squirrel skins at Battagins Store in Mayerthorpe. In later years the hunting and angling continued; however, in a more refined manner, according to regulations at the time. I traveled many miles to local lakes in a 1928 Whippet automobile to fish and a 1928 Chev to hunt and fish the foothills. I walked cross-country many miles in a day to reach a trout stream where there were no roads or trails – all great memories!

My involvement in the AFGA began with a two-year term as zone 4 director; then two years as junior vice president; two years as senior vice president; two years as president; two years as immediate past president; two years as financial chair (which was a disaster) and three years as fish chair—which I thoroughly enjoyed—all at the executive level of the AFGA.

My personal life has been extremely busy but old age has relieved me of many responsibilities and given me time to go fishing when the urge strikes. Great!

Some of the things I was involved with as a volunteer member of the AFGA are as follows:
- Five years as provincial fish chair
- Wildlife Ungulate Damage committee
- Alberta Forest Conservation Strategy (four years)
- Northern Pike advisory committee
- Eastern Slopes Regulations review committee
- Walleye task force
- Alberta Conservation Association (ACA) board of directors
- Whirling Disease task force
- Disabled Hunter review committee (five years)
- National-Canadian Coast Guard licensing and boating regulations committee

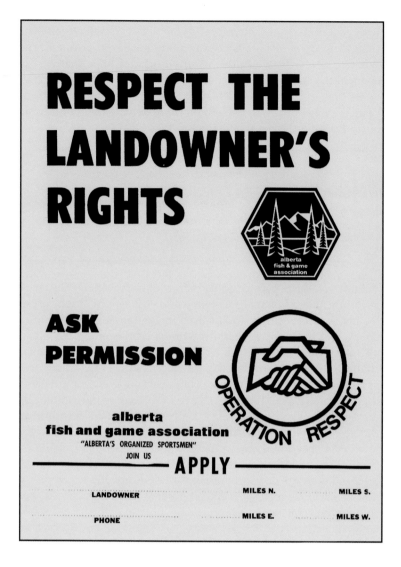

RESPECT THE LANDOWNER'S RIGHTS

ASK PERMISSION

alberta
fish and game association
"ALBERTA'S ORGANIZED SPORTSMEN"
JOIN US — APPLY —

| LANDOWNER | | MILES N. | | MILES S. |
| PHONE | | MILES E. | | MILES W. |

COURTESY OF VERN MCINTOSH
VERN MCINTOSH

- *National – Canadian Wildlife Federation*
- *Captive Exotic Wildlife Policy Development committee*
- *Captive Exotic Animal technical risk assessment team*
- *Competitive Fishing committee (nine years)*
- *Original Caribou committee*
- *Humane trapping animal care committee*

There have been many other fishery and wildlife initiatives that have required my attendance and input. I have continually pushed government for more resources for wildlife management and enforcement personnel. I have volunteered for anything where the AFGA needed my assistance.

During my term as president of the AFGA, we heard a rumour that the surplus in the Buck for Wildlife Trust Fund, amounting to many millions of dollars, was to be transferred to the provincial treasury (general revenue). This caused us great concern as it did other non-government organizations (NGOs). A frantic rush ensued to derail this intention, including direct representation to the premier's office. The result was the eventual transfer of the surplus funds to a partnership of organizations under the name of the ACA. This group took on a life of its own and performed in a manner very different from the old Buck for Wildlife Fund. To this day, I regret my rush to secure the fund. I now believe that the rumour may have originally been started by government in order to cause the events which gave them the opportunity to dispose of a large number of employees which met their downsizing requirements to reach budget levels at the time.

One of the happiest events of my term as president was when I received, on behalf of the AFGA, a $250,000 cheque as a grant from Ty Lund, Minister of Environmental Protection. Subsequently, a grant has been awarded annually to the AFGA in the amount of $150,000 and is appreciated tremendously.

I have spent a good portion of my life as a volunteer in the service of the AFGA and if I had to do it over I would in a minute, and will continue to serve where and whenever I'm able. The efforts of the AFGA and affiliated members have tremendously improved the numbers of wildlife in the province since the lean years of old and added considerably to the quality of life for many Albertans. Bless this organization.

I fondly remember travels all over the province to club projects, dinners, events and meetings, enjoying good times with good people. I appreciate the rapport that developed with wildlife management officials, and the co-operation, help and the advice that they gave me has been a big part of my fish and game direction.

In my 33 years of service as a police officer I learned plenty, but one very important thing was people who spend time fishing and hunting are seldom involved in serious criminal activity.

[Biography prepared by Vern McIntosh.]

In an interview, McIntosh said, "I was a member of the Edmonton Police Fish and Game Club for a number of years and there was an opportunity to get involved as zone 4 chair with the parent association which I took advantage of. Fish and game was a subject that was really dear to me because of all the hunting and fishing I've done since I was eight years old. And that's what got me into it and I just keep on going today."

The 67th annual conference was held at the Capri Centre in Red Deer. The theme of the annual conference was "Hunting and Fishing – Our Cultural Heritage."

McIntosh reported: "1995 was a good year in some respects and a bad year in others." The AFGA linked with groups nationwide in its battle against Bill C-68, the ill-conceived gun control legislation. He also spoke highly of the credibility enjoyed by the AFGA in government circles, and elsewhere. The AFGA Wildlife Trust Fund expanded to acquire and protect habitat by forming partnerships with other organizations – provincial, national and international in scope. McIntosh advised, "Habitat loss and destruction is a major problem facing our wildlife and fisheries which must be addressed if we are to have anything in the future."

In a move to champion the rights of hunter access to grazing leases, the AFGA provided financial support in defense of Wade Patton, charged by the O.H. Ranch in southern Alberta for hunting on their grazing lease without permission. There were repercussions from some landowners who called the AFGA head office and said that the AFGA members would not be allowed to hunt on their lands as a consequence of this action. McIntosh took a hard line in response to this situation, advising, "So be it. We cannot abandon principles because of a narrow biased view taken by a few. Those who think in this manner have few concerns for wildlife, conservation or anything other than their own selfish interest. They will not be capable of rational thought or negotiation on an issue of any kind."

McIntosh reported that membership remained stable. He commented about the pheasant situation being of concern as government cutbacks forced the cancellation of their long-standing raise and release program.

Senior vice president Andy von Busse reported, "Much of my time spent on AFGA business in the past year involved issues surrounding Bill C-68, the federal government's new firearm-control legislation." Despite numerous rallies, speeches and letters to the editor, news releases and radio talk show appearances, the legislation did pass, bringing Canadians some of the strictest and toughest firearm legislation in the western democracies. Von Busse also spent a considerable amount of time as a member of the provincial government's regulatory reform task force; the AFGA was the only non-profit group, other than the Environmental Law Centre, who were given the opportunity to participate in this task force.

The AFGA produced and distributed 100,000 placemats in partnership with the Alberta Cattle Commission and the Report-A-Poacher program in 1995 promoting the Use Respect program which encourages hunters and anglers to ask for permission before accessing private land. Von Busse spoke of a better relationship with government, commenting, "Many of us can well remember a time when we were best known as fighting with government, and as a result, very little positive was transacted. I hope that we can channel the energy and resources that had to be spent on negative issues such as Bill C-68 in a more positive direction in the coming year. We must continue to build on the positives, but not be afraid of confronting the negatives when required."

> In 1996 Jack Graham, himself a past president, advised that the AFGA lost a long-time friend, past president and life member Roy Ozanne. "He will be missed and remembered for his dynamic efforts and outspoken character. As you recall, Roy was a founding member of the AFGA Wildlife Trust Fund."

Andy von Busse painted a rosy picture of improved relations with government decision makers in his conference report. "Many of our members and executive are involved in committees that influence policy, and the scope of that involvement is broadening. As example, I represent the AFGA on the regulatory reform task force, chaired by MLA Garry Friedel, which is looking at the whole issue of regulations that affect all areas of Albertans lives, not just those that are hunting-and-fishing related. We have representation on the forest conservation strategy committee (Vern McIntosh is on the steering committee), Andy Boyd has ably represented us on the rewrite of the *Water Act*, we have numerous members sitting on fisheries and wildlife advisories, both at the regional and provincial level and there are dozens of others." These are all good examples of how the AFGA represents the interests of all Albertans, not just

COURTESY OF TRAVEL ALBERTA

A moose and deer eyeing each other up in Kananaskis country.

A golden eagle stays alert.

hunters and anglers. He also reported, "I spent a considerable amount of time developing and launching an AFGA Internet site. We have our own domain address at www.afga.org."

Junior vice president Dave Powell reported on the government's plans to privatize the Brooks pheasant hatchery in 1995 and 1996, another casualty of the Klein revolution to eliminate Alberta's deficit and pay off the provincial debt. Powell prepared a plan to secure and operate the hatchery at no cost to the AFGA. The first proposal was not accepted by the Alberta government and he advised the organization would work on another proposal.

Hunting chair Dave Gibson reported that the AFGA liaison committee with the Alberta Professional Outfitter's Association was very busy because the five-year review of non-resident alien allocations was up for discussions always a contentious issue.

Programs chair Mary Mitchell advised that the most significant achievement in 1997 was the introduction of the internationally acclaimed BOW program. BOW—short for Becoming an Outdoor Woman—is a unique and highly successful program designed and instituted by Christine Thomas of the University of Wisconsin at Steven's Point. The program was designed to provide an opportunity for women (and men) from 18 to 80-plus years of age to be introduced to outdoor activities in non-threatening surroundings. In August 1997, AFGA became the official sponsor of the BOW Program for Alberta. Mitchell also reported on the resurrection of the *Cold Lake Wild Game Cookbook*, a new and improved version of an old fish and wild game favourite recipes book, with over 800 recipes, which was scheduled to be published in 1997.

Environmental chair Andy Boyd reported, "The Special Places 2000 program is still underway but unfortunately the 'pro-development' stakeholders and the 'protection oriented' stakeholders on the provincial co-ordinating committee, do not share a common vision of what SP 2000 is trying to achieve. In spite of this some progress is being made toward the completion of a protected area network." Boyd provided some sage advice, "Rather than sit on the sidelines and whine, we've proven the most effective way to influence the outcome of the game is to develop a workable plan, team up with like-minded players, and get in the middle of the action."

1997 Vern McIntosh remained as president of the AFGA in 1996. The 68th annual conference was held at the Capri Centre in Red Deer in 1997; the theme of the annual conference was "Private Land - Public Wildlife."

An honest broker, McIntosh advised the conference delegates: "We have accomplished many things in the past year and failed to reach successful conclusion on others." He reported: "Our efforts to isolate the [Fish and Wildlife] trust fund from treasury control have borne fruit and resulted in the formation of a governing organization with broad representation to control the fund and the projects it finances. This makes the fund independent of provincial budget reductions and downsizing." McIntosh was referring to the genesis of the Alberta Conservation Association (ACA), a non-profit, non-government association whose goal was to work collaboratively to conserve, protect and enhance Alberta's fish and wildlife and their habitats. Most of its funding for conservation and enhancement came from levies on fishing and hunting licences, the balance from partners.

The ACA is also a funding agency. Through its Grant Eligible Conservation Fund, it supports other conservation organiza-

Abraham Lake along the David Thompson Highway, near Nordegg.

Lily pads float on a quiet day at Island Lake.

tions and individuals through grants and project funding. The fund distributes about $1 million annually.

The ACA, a child of the Klein revolution, was created in 1997 by Ty Lund, who was then Minister of Environmental Protection. In an interview, Lund said, "The one big reason that we went this route was because of the way the budget system works. We were being required to reduce our expenditures by 20 percent, but at the same time the Trust [Fish and Wildlife Trust Fund] was growing. We were going to have to reduce the expenditures because of consolidated budgeting. That created a real problem. The fund was increasing. At the time, there was a rumour spreading that Treasury was looking at confiscating some of the money, but that was never a worry of mine. I don't know really where that [rumour] started but it wasn't from us." Lund emphasized, "It was an issue when budgets were consolidated and we had to take a cut in our bottom line. So, that meant that if we didn't include the programs under the Trust then we had to reduce by that much more our other spending."

Thus, the ACA emerged as a delegated administrative organization. As such, the revenues from licence sales used to support fish and wildlife management were protected from the eyes of the powerful Treasury Board. Back in the days of the Klein revolution, when administrators' pencils were sharp and paranoia ran rampant, it was perceived that Treasury Board just might re-appropriate those funds for other purposes, like health care and education, or so the rumour went.

A striking butterfly perches at the Devonian Botanic Gardens near Edmonton.

The ACA became a divisive force in Alberta's conservation community as critics complained it siphoned off sportsmen's dollars to non-game programs and frivolous ventures. The mandate of the ACA that was established by the Alberta government and their officials remains a source of consternation to this day among many members of the AFGA and has caused a major strain in relations among the executive and its members.

McIntosh advised delegates that the AFGA had been well represented on environmental issues covering pipelines, mining, forestry, water resources, provincial parks, etc. and thanked Andy Boyd, Ross MacDonald, Dave Scobie, Colin Kure and others who made their concerns known at local public meetings. He lamented that "we have been unsuccessful in attempting to resolve the access issue on public lands (grazing leases)," long a nemesis of the organization. He reported that the AFGA membership was stable and their financial position favourable.

Senior vice president Andy von Busse reported on the many positive aspects of improved communications with members of government and their officials. He took a decidedly different perspective regarding creation of the ACA, reporting: "Much of my time in the past year, along with Dave Gibson and Vern McIntosh, has been involved in working on saving the Wildlife Trust Fund (our Buck for Wildlife Fund) from being a target of the provincial Treasury Board. As a result of our efforts, we have now been able to establish a separate delegated administration organization (DAO), which will take over the administration and ownership of the approximately $14 million in the fund. This has been a major success for us, and will ensure that the money contributed by hunters and anglers is in fact used for the purposes intended."

Junior vice president Dave Powell reported on the privatization of the Brooks pheasant hatchery and a proposal under review for the AFGA to secure and operate the hatchery at no cost to the association; the initial proposal was rejected.

Hunting chair Dave Gibson also made reference to his involvement in creation of the ACA, along with Andy von Busse and Vern McIntosh, and the time and effort put forward to administer the funds. He also noted that the AFGA liaison committee with the Alberta Professional Outfitters Association was very busy during the previous year because the five-year review of non-resident alien allocations was up for discussion.

Fishing chair Jim Clarke stepped down after the annual conference and spoke about several issues of concern to the members: fishing derbies and tournaments, the provincial walleye and bull trout task forces, a proposed ban of lead sinkers and jigs under review by Environment Canada, Alberta's golden trout management plan, fishing regulations in Banff National Park and a plan to try to simplify Alberta's sport fishing regulations.

Zone 4 director Randy Collins noted that he had been involved with the "Alberta Hunters for the Hungry" program that had a successful pilot project in the autumn of 1996, where some deer venison from the CFB Camp Wainwright hunt was donated to the Edmonton Food Bank.

COURTESY OF TRAVEL ALBERTA

Secondary Highway 510 through the Old Man River Reservoir.

Lone wolf roaming Jasper National Park.

1998-2007
Summary

Major issues: Court challenge of federal firearms control act; paid hunting on private land; Cheviot coal mine; volunteer fatigue; Ultimate Whitetail Challenge; ACA use of licence funds; Special Places 2000; ACA funding cutbacks; Northern Pike Management Task Force; oilsands development; access to private land; creation of new provincial parks; closing public land to hunting; chronic wasting disease (CWD); government cutbacks to programs; Cervid Harvest Preserves ('canned hunting' farms); mismanagement of federal gun registry; Interim Métis Harvest Agreement; closure of spring grizzly bear hunt; low water levels in lakes and streams; sale of public lands; decline in number of anglers and hunters; Water for Life program.

Highlights:
1999 - Hunting for Tomorrow Foundation created.
2000 - Resolution passed encouraging Alberta government to create a "Heritage Hunting, Fishing and Trapping Act."
2001 - The Alberta Fish and Game Association (AFGA) Fish Committee established in response to restrictive fish regulations.
2002 - Number of commercial fisherman reduced.
2003 - Provincial act proclaimed to promote co-operation between crown lease holders and recreationists; the AFGA, among others, win Emerald Award for Buffalo Lake Moraine project; the AFGA publishes Alberta Wildlife Records, 1963-2001.
2004 - "No Beef No Hunting" became an international story that placed the AFGA in a position to support farmers and landowners during the Bovine Spongiform Encephalopathy (BSE) border closures to cattle sales; pike regulations were altered and several new harvest opportunities were allowed; walleye harvest opportunities were expanded in a few lakes; the Gordon Leslie bequeathal of six quarter sections of land to the AFGA was a major gift that also brought in revenue from oil wells on the lands.
2005 - The AFGA opposes government Interim Métis Harvest Agreements; Sunday hunting areas increase in white (agricultural) areas; CN train derails along north shore of Wabamun Lake spilling diesel oil into the lake. The AFGA executive updated and re-wrote the policies, position papers and operational procedures for the association.
2006 - Government implements walleye tag licensing system; government suspends grizzly bear hunt.
2007 - More CWD cases found along eastern border of province; government terminates Interim Métis Harvest Agreements.

Presidents: Andy von Busse (1997-98), Dave Powell (1998-2000), Gerry Pittman (2000-01), Rod Dyck (2001-03), Ray Makowecki (2003-05), Randy Collins (2005-07), Maurice Nadeau (2007-08).

The 10th decade of the Alberta Fish and Game Association (AFGA) began at a time when both the Canadian and Albertan economies were in an upswing. Federally, Jean Chrétien's Liberals had balanced the budget and were paying down much of the national debt. Similarly, the Ralph Klein Progressive Conservatives in Alberta had made drastic cuts to budgets in all areas of government spending. As well, increasing oil and gas revenue was putting much cash into the provincial treasury, and the PCs had passed legislation that ensured the provincial debt was paid off as soon as possible. Klein remained in power in Alberta until he retired in December 2006, turning over power to new PC leader Ed Stelmach, who did not go to the polls until early 2008, when he and his party won in a landslide.

On the federal scene, Jean Chrétien served as prime minister until December 2003, when he resigned in favour of new Liberal leader, Paul Martin. Martin went to the polls in 2004 and won a minority government that he headed until it was defeated in 2006 by the newly reformed Conservative Party of Canada, led by Albertan, Stephen Harper. Harper's government was also a minority that kept power through 2007.

Both federally and provincially, the decade was marked by governments cutting back on programs and abrogating much of their responsibilities in the areas of the environment and the sustainability of natural resources. The population of Alberta in 2001 was about 3.0 million or 10 percent of the Canadian population. In 2001-02, 226,449 fishing licences (youth and seniors are not licensed) and 92,465 wildlife certificates were sold. One U.S. dollar in 2001 was worth $1.17 in 2007 USD.

1998 Andy von Busse became president of the AFGA in 1997. Von Busse, a resident of St. Albert, was a giant of a man in stature. He had a forceful personality and strong convictions, never one to shy away from controversial issues, but willing to compromise when necessary.

Zone 2 director Bev Chipchase welcomed the delegates to the 69th annual conference of the AFGA, advising "The decision to host the convention in zone 2 coincides with the 90th anniversary of The Calgary Fish and Game Association's beginning." The annual conference was held at the Coast Plaza Hotel in Calgary in 1998; the theme of the annual conference was "90 Years of Conservation."

Von Busse started his president's report at the annual conference with profound remarks, "The past year has in many ways been an overwhelming one for the AFGA." The firearms control issue, which had been simmering on the back burner of Canada's parliament for the previous three years, culminated in the Alberta government-led constitutional challenge of federal Bill C-68 (passed in 1995). This was one of the few situations where the Alberta government actually represented the concerns of Alberta's sportsmen during the Klein government. Von Busse remarked, "The AFGA took the lead in being the only wildlife group in Canada to have intervener status in this challenge." He also noted that it had cost the AFGA almost $100,000 during the previous year alone (presumably in legal fees), although the association did receive donations in support of the challenge from across Canada.

Von Busse reported that either he, or members of his executive, had met with many provincial politicians during his first year of office: Premier Klein, Justice Minister Havelock, Environment Minister Ty Lund, Municipal Affairs Minister Iris Evans, Public Works Minister Stan Woloshyn, Social Services Minister Lyle Oberg, Agriculture Minister Ed Stelmach, and federal Justice Minister Anne McLellan, a strong supporter of the despised gun-control legislation, under whose watch exorbitant cost overruns occurred.

COURTESY OF THE AFGA
ANDY VON BUSSE

Von Busse made note that "one of the most time-consuming, and at times frustrating, issues I have been involved in is the formation and development of the new Alberta Conservation Association, the group that has taken over the management of the Fish and Wildlife Trust Fund from government." As a harbinger of issues that would arise down the road, he commented, "We see much potential in the new organization, however we, as the AFGA, must ensure that the focus remains on the interests of the people who contribute to its funds, the hunters and anglers of Alberta."

Access to public land under lease remained an issue because the Alberta government was unwilling to concede that the public had such a right of access to public land. A legislative committee on grazing leases travelled throughout the province to receive input from local constituents on this issue. Likewise, officials from the Alberta Cattle Commission continued to lobby the government to allow paid hunting on private land, another issue that would not go away.

With regard to the 90th anniversary of the Calgary Fish and Game Association and the beginnings of the fish and game movement in Alberta, Von Busse noted, "...When I look back at some of the issues that we were concerned about in the 1940s conferences, I am surprised to see that many of those [issues] we are still dealing with today."

Past president Vern McIntosh reported that 1997 brought together stakeholders to formulate a plan to rejuvenate the east slopes fishery which had suffered much from overuse. Recommendations were made to government to create a fishery that provides better angling opportunities for trout in flowing waters to make regulation changes that included bait bans, catch-and-release stream designations and reduced catch limits.

McIntosh also submitted a report on the Wildlife Ungulate Damage Committee, formed in 1997 as a result of serious wildlife damage complaints from the winter of 1996-97. The committee included representatives from the provincial departments of Agriculture and Environment, the AFGA and Alberta Cattle

1998	
Resolution	For the first time the association took steps to enshrine hunting and fishing as a right by law in Alberta, with a resolution that the provincial government legislate and establish as policy that its land management agencies support, promote and enhance hunting and fishing in Alberta. This resolution was carried as submitted by the Red Deer Fish and Game Association.
Resolution	The Lethbridge Fish and Game Association submitted a resolution that the AFGA encourage the Alberta government to establish an annual Family Fishing Weekend on the third weekend in June, where residents and visitors could fish anywhere in Alberta without a licence. The resolution was defeated.

Commission. The group met to develop recommendations to prevent damage and compensate landowners for damage that does occur. McIntosh stated, "All groups involved worked co-operatively to arrive at excellent recommendations that consider both land owners/users and wildlife." This is yet another example of the AFGA officials working quietly behind the scenes to benefit Alberta's wildlife. McIntosh also advised that after three years of work, the ministerial Alberta Forest Conservation Strategy Committee had finished its work and a draft of recommendations was forwarded to the Government Standing Policy Committee, but not without a lot of controversy.

Senior vice president Dave Powell reported that "one of the top time-consumers this year has been the Alberta Conservation Association. The formation and initial direction, the regional committees, revenue loss on licence sales, the U of A Chair, conflict-of-interest guidelines and all those hundreds of incidentals that occur when making a major transition such as this, were all issues that had to be looked at."

Junior vice president Gerry Pittman reported problems with the guide and outfitter allotment under the government's outfitter-guide policy, explaining that current practices that had been in effect for several years were not working in some areas. As a general rule, outfitters in a specific area paid for a number of tags for a specific species, such as pronghorn antelope, up to a limit of 10 percent of the total tags available to residents and non-residents in that area. They held these tags for several years. However, if proper management strategy dictated that the number of those tags should be reduced to conserve the resource, they were not because that would have affected the outfitters' business. Pittman felt that non-resident, alien big-game hunters should enter draws just like the resident hunters. If they were successful in the draw then they could hire an outfitter of their choice. In this way, he felt game numbers could be properly controlled.

Hunting chair Dave Shepherd's report had a common lament, "As is recently seen in all volunteer organizations, people are just volunteered out. We need to look seriously at hiring staff to promote the AFGA strongly in all media factions and to strongly solicit funds to run and support our many programs. Don't jump up and yell it can't be done, as all the so-called bunny and tree hugger groups are doing this very successfully."

Fishing chair Ivan Johnston addressed a litany of issues facing the AFGA: declines in Arctic grayling, reduced catch limits for walleye, pike and perch, the need for spawning closures, compulsory registration of fishing derbies and tournament, lack of enforcement and compliance and the need for harsher penalties for poaching.

Programs chair Mary Mitchell reported, "Sept. 5-7 [1997] marked the first Becoming an Outdoor Woman (BOW) program for Alberta. The workshop had 24 enthusiastic participants, many energetic instructors and one determined photographer. Overall the weekend was a great success with good weather, great food and fabulous instruction. Many of the ladies have declared that they will return in 1998."

Environmental chair Andy Boyd reported on a wildlands category of provincial parks: "Although at times we've had to remind park planners of their commitment to allow hunting in these protected areas, we now have three major wildland parks where hunters are welcome." Boyd reported that the Special Places program was "struggling along" and was disappointed about the way many smaller protected area nominations were being handled. He represented the AFGA at the Cheviot Mine [south of Hinton, near the border with Jasper National Park] hearings; he advised that despite a last-ditch attempt by an environmental coalition to block the mine through court actions, it appeared as though the pilot project would proceed. Boyd advised, "The position of the AFGA was not to oppose Cheviot but to call for greater habitat protection and enhancement. For the most part our concerns were satisfactorily addressed." He also advised, "Pipeline construction activity is still very high around the province. The AFGA participated in the Alliance Pipeline hearings and, thanks to dedicated fish-and-gamers such as Dave Scobie and Ross MacDonald, we've provided effective input on several new pipeline proposals." Boyd stepped down as environment chair after the annual meeting, after serving five years on the executive.

> Jack Graham reported that "we have lost another of our life members with the passing of Henry Lembicz of Lacombe. Henry was past president of our association (1963-66) and will always be remembered for his dedication and devotion to the upkeep and stability of the Red Deer River. His name is on one of the Alberta Fish and Game's prestige awards, the 'Henry Lembicz Clean Air, Clean Land, Clean Water' award – which is awarded to the club or individual who has done the most outstanding job towards pollution control or clean up our environment."

1999 Dave Powell became president in 1998. A very committed member of the AFGA and another giant of a man in stature, Powell came from the Lacombe AFGA. He had strong convictions that would be tested to the fullest; his term of office proved to be a time of turmoil with many changes.

DAVE POWELL: President (1998-2000)

I was raised in east central Alberta in the small town of Hughenden. I was third in a family of four children. Hunting and fishing in those early years sparked great interest and were primarily a matter of feeding the family. Being from a generation deprived of television and most other forms of canned entertainment, we quickly learned to amuse ourselves in other ways, such as being of service to the local community and by developing a lifelong love affair with hunting and fishing. Those pursuits drove us to learn all we could about nature and wildlife and our relation-

COURTESY OF THE AFGA
DAVE POWELL

ship with nature. Most rural Alberta males, in particular, can likely empathize with this culture.

My first AFGA membership was with Iron Creek or Hardisty in 1967 primarily for the trophy competition. By 1973 I had relocated to St. Paul and married my partner of the last 34 years, Bernie. I attended my first AFGA meeting in St. Paul in the spring of 1974 and went home as their president. After serving as president and in many other capacities in St. Paul, I moved to Lacombe in 1980 and joined the Lacombe Fish and Game Association. I served there as membership chair, vice president, president, campsite co-ordinator, newsletter chair and trophy chairman. I have remained on the executive of the Lacombe Fish and Game Association for some 27 years and received a life membership in 2000.

My involvement on the executive of the AFGA began in 1983 when I took the position of information chairman. I was also director of zone 3 and served in several different positions at the zone level. In 1995 I was elected as a vice president of the AFGA, and subsequently served on the senior executive as vice president, president, past president and finance chair until 2005; I received a life membership in the association in 2005.

If I had a single cause to rally behind, it became the need to preserve opportunities to go hunting and fishing for future generations and the natural abundance of fish and game that my generation has enjoyed. I have always felt that youth education and public awareness were key factors in pursuit of these goals.

I was elected president of the AFGA in 1998, immediately after the formation of the Alberta Conservation Association (ACA). I sat on the inaugural board of directors for the ACA but soon realized that this was not a time to be wearing two hats. I subsequently resigned my seat on the ACA to give my full attention to the AFGA. Our first challenge was a wildlife derby called the Ultimate White-tail Challenge. It took about two months for Rod Dyck, junior vice president, and I to have the event withdrawn by the sponsors. That gave us a bit of confidence. We all took on major tasks: I became involved in business associated with the ACA; Jerry Pittman, public access to grazing leases in southern Alberta; Rod Dyck got the really short straw: game ranching. We also became involved in other major activities, which for me involved the creation of the Hunting for Tomorrow Foundation (HFTF), a coalition of major players whose primary mandate was to promote the sport of hunting in Alberta. Funding was more easily gained once the coalition was formed and it opened more doors to sportsmen for meaningful input than we had seen for a quite a while. The controversial grizzly bear hunt was an annual topic at conferences and throughout the year; the AFGA was successful in maintaining the status quo during my terms as president. Partner licences for moose came into being in 2000 as a result of lobbying by the AFGA members. Goat season closures were also a hot topic and a season was eventually re-opened in 2001.

My two years as president was a period of building bridges to other like-minded groups especially the Alberta Hunting Education Instructors Association (AHEIA) and the Alberta Professional Outfitters Association (APOS). The HFTF was the flagship of success in that regard; a catalyst to generate a spirit of co-operation among like-minded organizations. The one place where we were simply unable to gain ground was with the ACA. As long as we spoke of resources and things related to this topic, we agreed with the other organizations involved; but on how to get it done we were light years apart. Trying to correct this shortfall was a serious failure of the AFGA administration of the day and a subject which has dogged each subsequent administration in the same manner. Hopefully we will see an end to the turmoil soon.

I was truly lucky to have had such a cohesive and strong executive to lead. The group was unified and energetic. Vice presidents Pittman and Dyck were both solid individuals and very supportive members of the association. When we were running a little short of horsepower I turned to the past presidents, many of whom took single-task initiatives to a superb completion giving the rest of the volunteers a much-needed helping hand. At one point, seven past presidents or life members were all working on various issues. In many cases they were better suited to the task and provided a better "fit" than any of the rest of us. The association and I owe a debt of gratitude to all those who pitched in and helped the AFGA cause. It's that volunteer effort that sets the AFGA apart from all other organizations. It was indeed a pleasure to have been part of that fraternity.

Epilogue: I have maintained a hand in the fire since leaving the AFGA executive. I currently am a vice president of the Canadian Wildlife Federation. I still remain on the board of directors for the Hunting for Tomorrow Foundation and the WISE Foundation, as well as the ACA. I'm also on the executive and remain active with the Lacombe Fish and Game Association. I retired from my position with the town of Lacombe in 2005, but proved to be a failure as a retiree. Actually, I have been consulting for about 60 percent of the time since I officially retired. As long as there is work to do and I feel healthy, I'll carry on with the worthwhile tasks that need doing to support the AFGA goals and objectives.

Editor's Note: Mr. Powell was awarded the Fulton Trophy in 2001 and the Alberta Order of the Bighorn Award in 2002 in recognition of his long-standing contribution to the conservation of Alberta's fish and wildlife resources.

[Biography prepared by Dave Powell.]

The 70th annual conference was held at the Coast Terrace Inn in Edmonton in 1999. Dave Powell opened his address to the conference by advising, "1999 already promises to be busier and contain more issues than last year. It also must be a year of change. We can't stand still as everything else is leaving us in the dust." Powell observed, "The one thing that has impressed me about my first term as president has been the willingness to work by our members. I have never requested help and not had someone come forward to accept the task. In most cases I had a volunteer before I asked. It's that attitude and that camaraderie that keep our association strong."

Nestor Romaniuk, past president, was elected president of the Canadian Wildlife Federation in Yellowknife on June 11-12, 1999. He had previously been director at large and treasurer of CWF.

COURTESY OF JACK GRAHAM

Jim Robison (L); Les Cooke, assistant deputy minister of the Fish and Wildlife Division; Jack Graham and Joe Smith. Jim Robison, life member, passed away in 1999.

COURTESY OF TRAVEL ALBERTA

Golden mantled ground squirrel in the Rocky Mountains.

the province of Alberta, the Minister of Environmental Protection Advisory as well as assist in any other duties that the president or the executive may ask me to be involved in." Von Busse noted, "Most of my time has been involvement with the ACA and its sub-boards. It is my feeling the relations have improved from this time last year, especially as the ACA has found some direction and is maturing as an entity." As things would turn out, the relationship between the AFGA and the ACA would only get worse in the years ahead.

The Endangered Species Conservation Committee was a new committee established in 1998, pursuant to change in the *Wildlife Act*. Von Busse reported that the committee allows a made-in-Alberta solution to address problems that existed with previous attempts by the federal government "to dictate to Albertans on how to deal with endangered species."

Senior vice president Gerry Pittman had mixed feelings about the outcome of the Agricultural Lease Review Committee hearings. As the committee's final draft stood at the time, the leaseholder had been given total authority as a "gate keeper" and it would be 10 years before the present oil and gas revenues would be diverted to a fund for lease improvement and management. Furthermore, the Alberta government was still proceeding to sell Crown grazing leases they didn't need or want.

In 1998, a group of entrepreneurs decided to offer prize money for the largest white-tailed deer taken that year. Participants had to pay an entry fee, similar to a fish derby. They called the derby the "Ultimate White-tail Challenge." It was just another step along the way to the commercialization of wildlife, and the AFGA opposed it strenuously. It took eight months for the issue to be resolved, and the proponents returned the entry fees, avoiding another black mark on hunting's reputation.

Powell mentioned that, "The ACA [Alberta Conservation Association] and the AFGA continue to iron out wrinkles and try to ensure the safety and effectiveness of our trust funds. We have had a board-to-board meeting and will continue to work towards positive results. By convention time I hope to be in a position to make a major announcement which has the ability to put many of our conflicts behind us." Bob Scammell of Red Deer, past president, had replaced Powell on the ACA board of directors; Scammell advised that he realized he "...could not serve two masters, hence my resignation from the board of the ACA." If you read between the lines, a difference of opinion had already surfaced with regard to the governance and mandate of the ACA that persists to this day.

Past president Andy von Busse reported, "Although I have stepped back in my involvement from last year, I am still extremely active on a number of issues. I represent the AFGA on the boards of the Alberta Conservation Association (ACA), the Canadian Wildlife Federation, the Endangered Species Conservation Committee of

COURTESY OF JACK GRAHAM

Andrew Schoepf (L), Randy Glasspole and Ron Hauser at the AFGA office fishing day, 1999.

1999

Resolution

There was a resolution that the AFGA work in conjunction with the WISE Foundation, the Alberta Hunter Education Instructors Association, and the Department of Natural Resources to implement a hunter mentor program within Alberta; the motion was carried.

There was yet another resolution that Sunday hunting opportunities be increased, which was also carried.

One of the more controversial initiatives the ACA decided to do was create an academic "chair" at the University of Alberta in fisheries and wildlife. Using some of the money that had been accumulated in the old trust fund, the ACA financed the chair in 1999 to ensure that fish and wildlife management studies would always be a priority at the university and that Alberta would produce its own biologists in those fields. Summing up the feelings of many about this initiative, Pittman commented in his report, "Does everyone feel real good and proud about the ACA spending three million dollars to sponsor a university chair? That's three million dollars that was, or will be, collected from hunters and anglers. If you think that was a good idea or that it even should have happened at all then you sure as hell have a different perspective than I do!" The ACA chair in Fisheries and Wildlife was occupied by Dr. Mark Boyce, a highly qualified and respected wildlife biologist and professor. He and his graduate students have since completed several studies, advancing wildlife knowledge and management in the province.

COURTESY OF BOB SCAMMELL

Ben Rosnau (L) with Toni after getting the Bighorn Award, 2000.

The Alberta government had seemingly created a monster when it established the ACA, because it was supposed to be independent of government yet it received most of its revenues from levies on angling and hunting licences. There would be a litany of governance reviews and program agreements to clarify roles of the ACA and the Fish and Wildlife Division in the years to follow, but no clear resolution of the various issues, most of which remain controversial to this day. Interestingly, the ACA started advertising itself in the AFGA conference yearbook in the 70th annual conference, advising, "The ACA is proud to be continuing the many programs originally delivered by the Fish and Wildlife Trust Fund."

Hunting chair Dave Shepperd reported, "Another area of concern is ACCESS and hunters-landowners relationships. We need to help them by reporting all trespass and poaching problems. We also need to take a youth or adult non-hunter out hunting and guide them through the whole process. Let's get others out in the field and show them how to enjoy the experience."

Programs chair Mary Mitchell reported on the following accomplishments:

1. *The AFGA Wild Game Cookbook* – Cold Lake Fish and Game Association, revised edition (1998) was completed and available for purchase.
2. Becoming an Outdoor Woman program was growing in popularity and expanding in Alberta. One successful program was run in 1998 and two were proposed for 1999.
3. The AFGA youth scholarship had the finishing touches made and applications delivered across Alberta. The first scholarship was to be awarded in April 1999.

Quentin Bochar of the Morinville fish and game club took over from Rod Stewart of Cold Lake as the environment chair and reported a very busy year with considerable pipeline activity and forestry development in Alberta. Ross McDonald of the Hillcrest Alberta Fish and Game Protective Association represented the AFGA in four separate pipeline hearings in the Crowsnest Pass area of southwest Alberta. Special Places 2000 ran into some roadblocks with several grassland proposals being rejected at the community level, the main reason apparently being fear of increased public attention and access on existing grazing leases affected by the designation. The Cheviot mine proposal stalled after the Federal Court of Appeals overturned a lower court decision, which allowed interveners another opportunity to present more evidence regarding their objections for environmental reasons.

*J*ack Graham reported, "We have sadly lost two of our life members during 1998 with the passing of Gordon Peel of Edmonton. Gordon was a past president of our association (1969-71) and the recipient of the Fulton Award for his longtime involvement in the Antelope Creek Financial Committee. Gordon was a hard-working and sometimes controversial volunteer in many fish and game issues—Native Affairs and Guiding and Outfitters—and was always willing to help and contribute.

"The second long-time member was Jim Robison of Whitecourt. Jim was a dedicated member who held the record for the most fish and game conventions attended. He was a member of the Alberta Trappers Association, a qualified outdoorsman who sat on many wildlife councils representing the trappers and the fish and game. Both will be sincerely missed."

Zone 1 director Heinz Plontke advised, "Some of the issues and concerns of the clubs that arose at our zone meetings were ACA funding cutbacks for projects in all the regions within Alberta, the Northern Pike Task Force meetings, and the numbers of antelope tags being given to non-resident aliens." Plontke also reported, "At several of our zone meetings we have invited the 'press.' Mr. Garry Allison, an outdoor writer, attends and reports on information from the meetings in *The Lethbridge Herald*, which has an outdoors section in each of its Sunday editions. We have been getting a tremendous amount of publicity through Garry, which overall benefits fish and game as a whole." Garry Allison was one of the most prolific of all Alberta outdoor writers, a great benefactor of the AFGA, a fair and honest reporter who attended many of the AFGA conferences and meetings.

With respect to the pike management meetings held in Edmonton and Calgary, zone 4 director Randy Collins reported "I attended both seminars in Calgary and Edmonton. These meetings are slick, professionally done, but most of all scary! Some of the proposals that they recommend are unacceptable, such as zero limits, or fishing on a draw system. The AFGA has taken these seminars very seriously and I can see recommendations coming out of a drop of limits (three possibly), and maybe some increased spring closures. The problem is there and we understand that there has to be changes, I just think that maybe the solutions they are proposing are a little too drastic."

These were interesting observations, because the Northern Pike Management Task Force, which was chaired by Hugh Norris of the Alberta fisheries branch, was done professionally, with a good data set (actually much better than for any other management plans, for example for bull trout, walleye, the eastern slopes trout streams and the Lower Bow River) and yet they were the most controversial, and remain so to this day.

The golden age of public consultation ended after the Northern Pike Management Task Force completed its mandate and there have been no subsequent, similar species-management planning exercises in Alberta of any significance. During the 1990s and early 2000s, the fisheries branch was involved with several major public consultation exercises: bull trout, walleye, and eastern slopes stream management; Lower Bow River fishing regulations; northern pike and fishing licences fees review.

Collins also reported on the disabled fish derby held at Camp He Ho Ha at Lake Isle on May 30, 1998. "St. Albert hosted this event for the fifth year in a row, and again we couldn't have done it without the generous support of some zone 4 clubs, plus a few clubs from of zone 5, and Leduc of zone 3 in paying for the lunch." This worthy annual event is an example of an excellent local project to help disabled Albertans enjoy the benefits of fishing.

He went on to report that he attended an ACA priority setting meeting in Edmonton on Sept. 19, 1998. "A slick run meeting, the same format as the pike management meetings. ACA priorities and ours are not on the same track. The stakeholders involved are not all on side when it comes to the priorities of fishing/hunting and the way of life we so passionately pursue."

2000 Dave Powell remained as president of the AFGA in 1999. He kicked off his president's report to the 71st annual conference at the Red Deer Lodge in Red Deer on a high note, "As my term as president draws to a close, I must admit that it has been a worthwhile and rewarding two years." The theme of the annual conference was: "The New Millennium – Proud To Be a Fish-and-Gamer."

Powell gave credit to the AFGA paid staff and also remarked "Alberta fish and game volunteers are still alive and well. They took on many habitat projects, they continue to raise pheasants and they participated in the fall fish rescue on the Bow River." The fall fish rescue was inaugurated by Trout Unlimited Canada to rescue fish that were stranded in the large irrigation canals that fed off

2000

Resolution	A milestone resolution was submitted by the zones 2 and 3 Firearms, Environment and Wildlife Club and Provost and District Fish and Game Club that the government of Alberta create a *Heritage Hunting, Fishing and Trapping Act* (Bill of Rights) guaranteeing Albertans the right to exercise ethical and safe hunting, fishing and trapping practices and acknowledging the role anglers, hunters and trappers play in environmental conservation. The resolution passed.
Resolution	The Rocky Mountain House Fish and Game Association once again submitted a resolution that the Alberta Department of Environmental Protection allow Sunday hunting of big-game species in all Green Zones.
Resolution	A fisheries resolution resolved that the provincial government enact legislation that would prohibit paid access for fishing. An additional resolution called for the government's priorities for managing northern pike to be directed towards programs and projects that will enhance habitats and increase northern pike recruitment and production. Yet another resolution called for the provincial government to arrange for an external scientific review of the status on northern pike populations in Alberta and to further assess the need for restrictive size-limit regulations.
Resolutions	There were two resolutions submitted by the St. Paul Fish and Game Association calling (1) for the provincial government, through an external review process, to assess the administrative costs associated with managing the Alberta Conservation Association and determine if such costs might be reduced, and (2) recommending that an external review be conducted by the provincial government to determine if the role of the Alberta Conservation Association in managing fish and wildlife resources duplicates the provincial government's role in Alberta Environment, Natural Resources Service [the name of the Fish and Wildlife Division (and park service) at the time.]

the Bow River (Carseland and Bow River irrigation district) when they were de-watered each October. He also mentioned "Clubs host a myriad of projects from sportsmen shows to trophy balls, to disabled fishing days to conservation camps. And yes, our membership continued to climb over the past two years."

Powell reported on changes in membership of the ACA board of directors, philosophizing "Hopefully this will result in a new direction and put to rest the turmoil of the last two years."

In memoriam: Past president and life member Jack Shaver was born in 1925 and passed away June 14, 2000. He served as president from 1985-86. Life member representative Jack Graham reported, "Jack [Shaver] was a retired conservation officer and educator in firearms training and safety and hunter education."

George and Joan Mitchell died instantly when their truck was hit broadside by a semi-trailer six kilometres south of Entwistle on Aug. 7, 2000. They were always concerned about fish, wildlife and their habitat, being members of several affiliated clubs. George was the founder of the Alberta Fishing Guide annual magazine. They were an inseparable couple who were true, long-time conservationists and devoted to Alberta's outdoors.

Life member representative Jack Graham reported, "In December 2000 Mr. Ben Rosnau of Bruderheim, a long time dedicated member and past president (1962-64) passed away; he remained active in our association until recent years when his health no longer permitted him to champion his objectives. Ben was a recipient of the Order of the Bighorn and was involved in the 1985 official ribbon-cutting of the ownership of our own building."

Graham also reported, "During the past year we lost Mr. Ken Yank of the Sarcee Club in Calgary. Ken was a long-time dedicated worker. I will always remember Ken working on duck and goose nests, cutting and welding oil drums. He will be sadly missed." Yank was a regular fixture at AFGA conferences and a very keen and outspoken conservationist.

In junior vice president Rod Dyck's report, he stated, "Why do we do the things we do? I say it's because I strongly believe in it. The future of wildlife and its habitat depends on what we do now. That is the same future that my daughter and your children will inherit from us. I do it to ensure our heritage and to help make the future brighter and I'm proud to do my small part. I'm a proud member of, and fortunate enough to be on the executive of, the best organization in the country. An organization dedicated to preserving habitat, with strong conservation attitudes and high ideals on ethics and proper game management. The AFGA is that organization and so much more." No shrinking violet, Dyck reported, "In the fall of 1999, the game ranchers lobbied the government to allow hunting on game farms and so I took them on. After numerous press interviews and a lot of public and media support we pretty much shut them down. The high point was getting a commitment from Environment Minister Gary Mar saying that since the government had previously stated there would be no hunting on game ranches, they would stand by that statement. But we all know the game ranchers will try again in the future and we will need to be ready for them. From some of the threats I received, I know I've made some enemies there."

Hunting chair Dave Shepherd commented, "User pay sounds like a good idea but why is it only hunters and fishermen are paying? That's who pays into the trust fund the ACA is milking, but every group conceivable wants a piece of it. The Alberta government seems to think we must pay for all the research and aerial surveys. Remember, the Government of Alberta is responsible for fisheries and wildlife and if they can't pay for its upkeep then why are they not taxing bird watchers, campers, snowmobilers, trail riders, ORVers, [off road 'vehiclers'] mountain bikers, boaters and canoeists for their share of user pay?"

Fishing chair Gilbert Magnan reported on concerns about fish habitat loss at Pigeon Lake due to proposed cottage and marina development, as well as proposed cottage developments at Sylvan Lake. On a more sinister note, Magnan also reported that several Alberta newspapers had run an article about a company from the United States negotiating with landowners to purchase access to selected rivers in southern Alberta.

Environmental chair Quentin Bochar advised that oil and gas activities remained high in Alberta, including pipelines, and that Suncor had an application for the Millennium project in the Athabasca tar sands near Fort McMurray.

COURTESY OF MIRO MICOVSKY

Devonshire Beach at Lesser Slave Lake Provincial Park.

Zone 1 director Heinz Plontke reported on access problems in the Porcupine Hills area, citing liability as a major issue. He stated, "Most (people) do not realize that fish and game members have liability insurance when a membership is purchased from a club that is affiliated with the AFGA." He also remarked that memories were short because just a few years earlier southern Alberta AFGA clubs had raised over $9,000 to help rebuild fences lost to a range fire in the Porcupine Hills. As well these clubs had scraped together funds for a separate monetary compensation for individual ranchers suffering from elk depredation problem as a result of the fire. Finding this discouraging, he closed his address, "I only hope that some day soon all hunters and anglers will join fish and game and become involved in trying to keep our heritage of hunting, fishing and trapping alive."

Zone 5 director Steve Witiuk stepped down, advising, "After three years as trophy chairman and 11 years as director, I felt a new person was needed. It is with great confidence and respect that I introduce you to Maurice Nadeau, the new zone 5 director" for northeast Alberta.

2001 Gerry Pittman became president of the AFGA in 2000. Pittman was a committed and highly respected member of the association who had belonged to the Warner, Picture Butte and Lethbridge AFGA clubs. He had very strong principles and would meet controversy head-on. He was an honest broker and always spoke his mind. As well he also had a great sense of humour, and was well known an incorrigible practical joker. At the time of the AFGA 78th annual conference in 2007 he had been a member of the association for 56 years.

Sandhill crane.

COURTESY OF TRAVEL ALBERTA

GERRY PITTMAN: President 2000

COURTESY OF DUANE RADFORD
GERRY PITTMAN

I first became interested in the AFGA in 1951 because my dad was a member of the Warner Rod and Gun Club, and I joined then and have been a member of the AFGA ever since. I joined the Lethbridge Fish and Game Association in the late 1960s and served on several committees as well as being president in 1971-72. In the early 1970s I was chair of the provincial conference that was held in Lethbridge. In the 1980s, I was president of the Picture Butte Fish and Game Association for a few years and chair of the wild-game dinner from the get-go.

I became a life member of the Lethbridge Fish and Game Association in 2001.

I have also served as zone director on two separate occasions as well as zone secretary and hunting chair. I was elected provincial vice president and served as both junior and senior vice president before becoming president of the AFGA in 2000.

There were many hot issues on the table during my time as president. Chronic wasting disease (CWD) had just reared its ugly head in Saskatchewan on game farms, and since we had long before that lost our battle to have game farms outlawed in Alberta there was concern that it would only be a matter of time before we faced the same problem in Alberta. Struggles with the operation and management of the Alberta Conservation Association (ACA) were on-going but in 1990 the AFGA had four members on the board and one of them was the president, which worked to our advantage.

Near to my heart was the issue of access, especially to public lands. We had many consultations with government and were able to reach somewhat of an agreement whereby hunters, anglers and recreationalists can still gain access to most of that land as a result of Bill 31, the Agricultural Dispositions Statutes Amendment Act.

We had to suffer with the really bad Bill C-68 [federal Firearms Act] as well as considerable renewed effort by the "antis" of every stripe.

During my term we dealt with some major staff re-alignment and re-assigning of positions in the provincial association as well as spending considerable time formulating our mission, goals, long- and short-term plans, and a business plan. All of this was fairly daunting and early into my second year it became apparent that I did not have 100 percent confidence of the Executive Board. So in the best interests of the AFGA, as well as myself, I resigned my position as president.

Since that time I have again accepted some lesser positions with the association. I sit on the Technical Committee of Antelope Creek Ranch, and also as a board member of the Alberta Environmentally Sustainable Agriculture Council. I am also the zone 1 hunting chair.

In 2003 I received a life membership in the AFGA.

[Biography prepared by Gerry Pittman.]

The 72nd annual conference was held at the Lethbridge Lodge Hotel in Lethbridge in 2001; the zone 1 conference co-ordinator was Deb Clarke, daughter of long-standing zone 1 chair, Heinz (Shirley) Plontke, and wife of former zone and provincial fish chair, Jim Clarke.

In 1999 and 2000, Gilbert Magnan and Ray Makowecki, on behalf of the AFGA and affiliated clubs from Thorsby, Wetaskiwin, Millet and Leduc, attempted to stop a marina development on the northwest corner of Pigeon Lake in SW-12-47-02-W5 that further threatened the fish habitat that was quickly diminishing in Pigeon Lake. The debate moved to an Environmental Appeal Board hearing and the following response provided by Mr. Makowecki demonstrates what had happened as the AFGA was discussing the proposed development at the appeal:

On Sept. 21, 2000, the AFGA withdrew from the environmental appeal mediation process and provided the following statement: "Mr. Chairman, at this stage of the mediation and environmental appeal process the AFGA would like to make a statement.

"First, the AFGA is concerned for the long-term well-being of the fish and fish habitat of Pigeon Lake. Our primary goal is associated with the long-term conservation and use of the natural resources, that being fish and wildlife and their habitats.

"Second, the AFGA is largely an organization of volunteers and in so doing, we would acknowledge the efforts of the citizens who have come forward to express their concerns. The concerns are in many ways similar to those of the AFGA. We commend these Albertans for their efforts and expressions of concern and their volunteering.

"Third, the AFGA does not in a wholesale manner oppose all developments and we recognize the entrepreneurial spirit of the developer who has submitted his applications to the government.

"Fourth, the AFGA believes that the land and associated waters of SW12-47-02-W5 are clearly unique and are important to the production of northern pike and other fish species in Pigeon Lake.

"Fifth, the AFGA believes that the land determined to be public land by the Government of Alberta should be re-examined and re-assessed to more accurately reflect what was public land.

"Sixth, the AFGA believes that the Alberta government must better assess developments that are intended for flood plain areas of watercourses (includes lakes). Policy must be clearly defined to address all proposed developments within flood plains.

"Seventh, the AFGA believes that there is significant evidence that establishes the marshland areas north and south of Legerski's Pond as well as Legerski's Pond as fish habitat. Previous court rulings in 1980, on-site investigations, witnesses, anglers, photographs, and biological assessments conclude that such marshland areas and these specific marsh areas were and are important habitats for the spawning and rearing of northern pike. Such areas are unique to Pigeon Lake and the productive capability of northern pike will be diminished by the planned changes and activities with this development at this site-specific location.

"As a result of the discussions on Sept. 19, 2000 and Mr. Sprague's convincing and constructive comments, the AFGA will withdraw from these mediation proceedings. We thank you Mr. Chairman for the opportunity to participate in this process.

"In further assessing the matter of the AFGA appeal with federal and provincial fisheries and environmental personnel, the AFGA determined the following:

- The marsh areas to the north and south of Legerski's Pond (and Legerski's Pond) were not deemed to be fish habitat at the time of the assessment.

- No level surveys were conducted to establish the frequency of flooding nor the elevation of the beds of these marshes in relation to the lake bed.

- No fish sampling was conducted within the areas in question.

- No aquatic vegetation species composition was conducted or requested in the marsh areas or Legerski's Pond.

- The AFGA is unclear as to how the marsh areas were not viewed as fish habitats in 2000, while in 1980 assessments revealed spawning fish, fish habitats and a court conviction of Roger Legerski who had altered 7,000m² of the Pigeon Lake marsh (Alberta government files).

- The surface areas of the marshes that were to be filled in were never calculated.

- Persons who had specific on-site experience with fish, fish habitats were not interviewed in determining the value of these flooded areas as northern pike spawning and rearing habitats.

- Department of Fisheries and Ocean and Alberta Environment personnel believe that they have provided sufficient compensation to address this proposed marina development.

"In taking this information and combining it with the fact that the north and south marshes were filled in while the mediation process was in progress, the AFGA has decided to withdraw from the environmental appeal.

"The mediation and appeal processes seem to have little value as we observe such activities proceeding while discussions were in progress. As volunteers, we became tired and cynical of such time spent to discuss these matters. As the AFGA, we have nothing personal to gain. We only seek to conserve the fish and wildlife resources for future generations. These marsh areas of Pigeon Lake were truly unique and biologists said it, fishermen said it, landowners said it, and the courts have said it.

"Now it is lost and we have all failed. The AFGA withdraws from this appeal."

In his president's report to the annual convention, Pittman reported on gains made by the AFGA Wildlife Trust over the years, mentioning that their hide and shed antler gathering had contributed significantly to this fund and added to the number of acres protected. The executive was involved in negotiations with the Alberta Professional Outfitters Society to review the outfitting and guide policy over allocations for non-residents, long a controversial issue. He advised the delegates, "We have four highly qualified members of the AFGA sitting as directors on the Alberta Conservation Association [ACA] board, and one of them is the chairman of the board. I am confident that we now have the tools to raise the profile of the ACA and guide it to achieve the purposes for which it was created." As time would tell, the ACA was to become the nemesis of the AFGA, primarily because of its spending priorities.

The provincial government had by this time created a Northern Pike Task Force on which the AFGA was represented by Vern McIntosh, fish chairperson. Pittman advised, "We have identified what we believe to be critical problems or deficiencies in the sport fisheries management program, especially as it pertains to pike, and are well on the way with suggestions and recommendations for improvements." During the 1990s, the provincial government had participated in the Bull Trout Task Force, led by non-government organizations, and had established several of its own task forces on walleye, eastern slopes stream management, Lower Bow River regulations, and a review of sport fish licensing (including senior citizens) of which the AFGA was always a lead member. The Bull Trout Task Force received an Alberta Order of the Bighorn Award for its efforts in 1995.

Pittman stated, "Down the road for 2001, and thereafter, there are many things we need to do. We desperately need to convince the provincial government that funding for NRS [natural resources services] has been cut way too far and must be reinstated. We need more fish and wildlife counts and surveys, more enforcement or conservation officers, more biologists, and more tools to do the job."

The 1990s were characterized by the "Klein Revolution," during which time the Ralph Klein Progressive Conservative government slashed government spending to eliminate the provincial deficit. In so doing, they gutted the Fish and Wildlife Division, which saw its budgets cut annually by 10-30 percent most years, and likely lost over half the staff it had in the 1980s. Budgets were so bad that biologists and game wardens parked their vehicles for the tail-end of many fiscal years to stay within budget; things were so bad they practically had to resort to bottle drives to gas up their vehicles and had virtually no discretionary dollars. As a result, staff morale hit rock bottom.

A new provincial park was created in the Spray Lakes area, near Kananaskis Country, where hunting was banned. This was a forerunner of other similar parks that would be created later on where hunting was also prohibited, a major bone of contention with the AFGA to this day.

True to the AFGA prophecies, game farms were turning into wildlife disease cesspools, with a major outbreak of chronic wasting disease in some elk herds in Saskatchewan, forcing the slaughter of 1,700 animals.

On a positive note, Pittman advised that the AFGA membership was increasing and was higher in 2001 than it had been during the previous seven years.

On May 9, 2001, the AFGA and area clubs hosted a partnership appreciation day and media event at a newly acquired Wildlife Trust Fund quarter-section of land on Tide Creek, a tributary to Pigeon Lake. The property would be known as the George and Joan Mitchell Memorial Property in recognition of these longtime AFGA supporters. George Mitchell was the founder of the popular *Alberta Fishing Guide*, which is published today by his son, Barry Mitchell. George's wife, Joan, was never far from his side. This particular property is located adjacent to the Pigeon Lake AFGA property, and together they protect critical spawning habitat for walleye, pike and suckers along Tide Creek as well as important upland habitat.

In his annual conference report, senior vice president Rod Dyck raised an interesting point: "Saskatchewan, with a population of one-third of Alberta's, has 10,000 more members in their association than we have in ours. So what's the problem? Is it because we are against everything and perceived to be negative all the time? Like it or not, I feel that many times we have to be negative in order to achieve positive results. Maybe that attitude keeps people from joining, or maybe too many are complacent and feel that the other guy can do it all."

On a similar note, junior vice president Ray Makowecki advised, "I am most concerned that the interest is dwindling in hunting (from a high of 166,191 wildlife certificates in 1990 to 93,389 in 2000) and in fishing (from a high of 345,809 resident fishing licences in 1986-87 to a projected 203,000 in 2000-01)."

Makowecki had personally been involved with a number of projects during the previous year, which he noted as follows:

- Pigeon Lake fishery
- herbicide use on forested public lands
- alteration of fish habitat on the northwest shore of Pigeon Lake
- the draft government pike management strategy; [he also chaired the AFGA Pike Management Committee]
- increased restrictions in the fishing regulations
- the 2000 AFGA resolutions, and other smaller projects.

COURTESY OF THE AFGA

Elmer Kure receiving the Pintail Award from Jay Bartsch of Ducks Unlimited, Aug. 18, 2001.

Additionally, Makowecki set up a study and arranged funding for Blair Rippin and Brad Stelfox to undertake an assessment regarding the "silviculture use of glyphosate herbicide in Alberta's boreal mixed-wood forest and probable long-term consequences to forest-dwelling wildlife and public wildlife user groups" for the AFGA, which was partially funded by the Alberta Professional Outfitters Association. He also prepared a booklet for the AFGA that described Pigeon Lake fish habitat.

*L*ewis T. (Budd) Traver passed away in July, 2001 at the age of 85. He is remembered as a past AFGA president from 1975-77. Traver spent countless hours involved in hunter training instruction and is credited for instigating the Outdoor Observer program, or the Report A Poacher program, as it is known today. He had retired to Sooke, B.C., "...not far from the salmon fishing he so loved," according to a report by Jack Graham in the annual yearbook.

Makowecki advised in an email, "Pigeon Lake was a major travesty and as I stated at a few conferences, 'All the kings men could not put Pigeon Lake back together again.'"

Past president Dave Powell reported, "The main issues I have been involved with are the ACA [Alberta Conservation Association], the Canadian Wildlife Federation, Hunting for Tomorrow, APOS [Alberta Professional Outfitters Society] Liaisons Committee and the WISE Foundation." He advised, "The ACA has not had an easy time the past year. In April, they were put on a 90-day leash from then-Environment Minister Gary Mar. After a not-so-complimentary auditor general's report in October, a consultant was commissioned by [incoming] Minister Jonson to examine the workings of the ACA and make recommendations on restructuring. Shortly after the annual general meeting of the ACA, at which the members attempted to set themselves up as an approval agency presiding over the board, the AFGA pulled our support for the association as it exists and requested that Minister Jonson rescind the ACA's authority or change its makeup to an elected body. Potential candidates would be required to have been a contributor to the fund for a set period of time. The changes sought by the AFGA are aimed at ensuring that the 'taxed' (fishers and hunters) control the direction of the fund."

Fishing chair Gilbert Magnan reported on the creation of an AFGA fish committee as a result of public consultations the government had conducted with regard to northern pike management. Relations between members of the AFGA and officials in the fisheries branch of the Natural Resources Service (NRS) had become strained over the findings of the Northern Pike Task Force, chaired by Hugh Norris of NRS. Norris was faced with a formidable challenge when called upon to address issues related to the collapse of many of Alberta's pike fisheries and implement measures to recover the populations. Many anglers thought it was virtually impossible that pike could be over-fished. However, the biological evidence was conclusive that pike populations were in trouble in many lakes. That evidence was backed by the perceptions of the general public reported by the Equus Consulting Group.

The Equus Consulting Group had long been the go-to consultant of fisheries branch officials, having worked on several task groups (eastern slopes stream regulations review, Lower Bow River fishing regulations, angling licence review and northern pike management), largely because of their capability to use option-finder technology, as well as a demonstrated track record of commendable public consultation exercises. The option-finder technology involved a hand-held polling instrument which ensured confidentiality of participants in the decision-making process – nobody could know how each participant voted. However, not all the AFGA members trusted Equus Consulting Group, perhaps because the meetings were so well-orchestrated they seemed to create the impression among some participants that they were canned and the outcome a foregone conclusion. This was not the case.

Subsequently, a 12-member AFGA fish committee was established to address the future of pike management in Alberta. This committee was chaired by Ray Makowecki, junior vice president, and included the following members: Jim Clarke, Dave Gibson, Ray Courchesne, Vern McIntosh, Dr. Darryl Smith, Tony Ferguson, Peter Mappleback, Jim Hall, Dave McArthur,

Ray Kohlruss from Reel Angling Adventures with a jet boat on the Athabasca River.

COURTESY OF CAROLE ROMANIUK

"Two trout fishing buddies." Jack Graham and Nestor Romaniuk at Swan Lake, 2001.

is no shame in the enjoyment of hunting. Done with rightful purpose and with respect of rules and ethics, it is a noble sport to be promoted and encouraged."

Zone 1 director Heinz Plontke reported on an interesting elk wintering range enhancement project, in which the Lethbridge club applied for and received funding from the ACA, involving the clearing of brush at higher elevations which was encroaching on important big-game wintering range in the Castle River area. Brush encroachment was seen as a serious issue in the foothills and mountains, spreading at the rate of about 2-plus percent annually in places. Plontke reported, "Originally, it was anticipated that 60-80 acres would be cleared but, with the good working conditions, over 100 acres were successfully done. It will certainly benefit the elk and other wildlife such as deer and moose."

Zone 3 director Andy Hogberg reported on yet another interesting AFGA project. "Some of the great work done by clubs includes Wetaskiwin Fish and Game Clubs painted birdhouse program. They built birdhouses and then, through the schools, had children paint them any colour they wanted. The club then put the birdhouses on poles or streetlights and the children can watch their [bird] house and see what type of bird uses them. This program is good because it educates the children on their environment in the city and forms good working relations with the schools in their area." Hogberg also advised, "Red Deer Fish and Game held a physically disabled fun fishing day. Every year for the past 14 years, the dedicated volunteers take physically handicapped people out fishing on Sylvan Lake. They have purchased one pontoon boat for this event and rent another, as well as many as 12 private boats are used. The club puts on a lunch and evening dinner for the participants and volunteers." Hats off to the Red Deer club and all the other AFGA clubs who organize and conduct fishing derbies for handicapped anglers in Alberta!

Dr. Martin Paetz and Gilbert Magnan. Dr. Bill Mackay and Dr. John Casselman also participated as ex-officio members of the committee. The committee was developed in response to the Alberta government fisheries pike regulation changes in 2000 and consisted of concerned AFGA members and other interested citizens. It reviewed the available scientific information related to pike in Alberta, and requested changes to the restrictive northern pike regulations. This government did not respond favourably at that time. However, over the next several years less restrictive harvest regulations were implemented.

Maurice Nadeau had been elected as hunting chair the year prior to the annual conference and saw his role thusly: "…To promote, enhance, and protect our dear sport of hunting." He noted, "There

Zone 4 director Randy Collins reported, "Since we have been running our casinos, the zone has committed over $10,000 to different programs including land purchases, our Narrow Lake Camp, lake aeration projects, and numerous other youth programs." Collins advised, "The Alberta Hunters Who Care program, which originated in our zone, has grown and has become an invaluable tool in helping out the Edmonton Food Bank and those less fortunate. The donation of deer meat as a nutritious food source is a great help to the food bank and is accepted with great thanks." Members of zone 4 were vocal when issues like gun control or paid hunting arose, and had members on the northern

2002	
Resolution	There was a resolution at the annual conference that the Alberta government should establish an annual checkoff of $1 on each wildlife certificate and angling licence, payable to the AFGA. The resolution carried.
Resolution	A resolution calling for the portion of hunting and fishing licence fees distributed to the Alberta Conservation Association be discontinued and reallocated to a true "trust fund" was narrowly defeated by a count of 83 (opposed) to 68 (in favour).

pike task force, Hunting for Tomorrow Foundation, Special Places 2000 and many other committees and groups that deal with hunting, angling and environmental issues.

Zone 5 director Dave Doonanco advised, "There are a host of other activities that have taken place in the zone, from the various antler-measuring events, suppers, trophy days to fishing events, shooting competitions, and habitat-development projects. The variety and number of events that take place in any given year attest to the dedicated people who are the fish and game association."

Zone 6 director Darryl Smith reported "What the AFGA offers is a way for local concerns to be addressed in a provincial and regional perspective. It brings people together who have common values and concerns. It makes you realize you are part of a family that realizes our outdoor heritage is part of what defines us as Canadians. In this world of the Internet and mass media, many have forgotten our roots. The concerned sportsmen in the north believe a renaissance is on the horizon which will see a renewed focus on hunting and fishing."

Colleen MacDougall was appointed as the chief executive officer/executive vice president of the AFGA on June 15, 2000, replacing Ron Hauser. In a press release, Gerry Pittman advised, "This change is consistent with board strategy to more closely align operations with education, lobbying and program goals established by the board." MacDougall ceased employment with the AFGA within the year.

2002 Rod Dyck became president of the AFGA in 2001. Dyck was a member of the Drumheller FGA. He took over the reins of the AFGA after Gerry Pittman resigned before his term of office expired, at a time when the association was mired in controversy over game farming and the outfitting policy. It also faced some serious internal problems with staff and budgets. Dyck was a tireless worker who would stay the course because of his strong

COURTESY OF THE AFGA
ROD DYCK

beliefs and sound character. Future presidents would be faced with similar problems, and a seemingly never-ending stream of contentious issues that would tax their volunteer capacity.

Dyck had been a hunter and angler for many years before he joined the local club in Drumheller. What attracted him to the club was a seminar the club sponsored with Dr. Valerius Geist, noted environmental biologist from the University of Calgary at the time. Geist spoke against game ranching. "It's been no secret since then that game ranching has been a pretty hot topic with me – whether it's hunt farms or game ranching, or whatever – it's the root-of-all-evil type of thing when it comes to chronic wasting disease, as far as I'm concerned," he said in an interview. "That was the type of thing that attracted me – they put on a seminar with an issue that pertained to me with [regard] to the future of hunting in this province. I wanted to hear what was being said. As soon as that meeting was over I said, 'Where do I sign up.'"

Appropriately, the theme of the 73rd annual conference held at the Delta Edmonton South Hotel in 2002 was "Our Natural Heritage Is Our Future," a telling theme for a new decade that would see immense changes in the Alberta landscape, largely as a result of a hot economy tied to the oil and gas, agricultural and forestry industries, with a major increase in Alberta's population and pressures on fish and wildlife resources. Gerald Foster was the zone 4 conference chair in 2002. He advised the delegates "This year's conference theme is well suited to the objectives of our conference: to share ideas and concerns, support each other's efforts and inspire each other to contribute to land and wildlife preservation in every way possible."

Dyck started his president's address with the comment, "Sure this has been a year with a lot of strife and problems." He later added, "We are now an association that has cleared up many of our internal problems rather than covering them up." The AFGA had experienced some turnover in the executive vice president positions in 2000-01, and was forced to address some major budget issues arising from problems associated with overspending its budget.

Martin Sharren was hired as the new executive vice president, "...who has over the past 10 months helped us clean things up," advised Dyck. There had been a nearly wholesale turnover of office staff as a result of the state of internal affairs in the AFGA over the course of the previous year.

2003

Resolution A resolution drafted by the St. Paul Fish and Game Association calling for the Alberta government to institute a walleye catch record and tag system that would allow anglers to keep a limited number of walleye for consumption was defeated.
A resolution from the Medicine Hat Fish and Game Association that the AFGA petition the provincial government to introduce a fishing licence for seniors was carried.
A resolution from the Willow Valley Fish and Game Association that the government develop a strategy that would allow for the harvest of some bull trout in some Alberta waters was carried; there was a zero limit on bull trout at the time and had been since 1995.

Notwithstanding the association's staffing and budget issues, the AFGA had purchased over 32,000 acres of critical wildlife habitat by the Wildlife Trust Fund over the past 20 years. Furthermore, Dyck advised "Our habitat staff has garnered funding for a variety of projects and helped with protecting endangered species like the burrowing owl and loggerhead shrike." This is a side of the AFGA not well appreciated by the general public, a conservation ethic that went beyond the consumptive side of fish and wildlife management.

Dyck closed his address with the statement, "Ask yourself what would the state of our wildlife, fisheries and habitat be if we didn't have the AFGA to keep things balanced and to keep tabs on government, big businesses, etc. As an organization we are at the forefront in regards to conservation and representation of hunters and anglers interests in Alberta."

As a follow-up to the conference, Dyck sent a message from the president in the April 2000 club bulletin advising the AFGA members, "One such issue that has consumed a lot of time and effort over the past few years has been our association with the Alberta Conservation Association. After much discussion and debate, the delegates decided that at this time it would be in the best interests of the AFGA to continue to work with the ACA. However, the ACA is being put on notice that we expect it to represent, through proper funding and programs, the hunters and anglers that are the main contributors to the ACA coffers. The ACA will no doubt once again be a main topic of discussion at next year's conference."

Past president and long-time volunteer of the AFGA, John M. (Jack) Graham was presented with the Canadian Outdoorsman of the Year award by the Canadian Wildlife Federation for his 35-plus years of involvement with the AFGA, serving on many committees and boards, and for setting up the Alberta Trophy Competition to involve clubs as sponsors and his instructing of 600 members from all over the province as official measurers of big game. In 2002 he was still active in the outdoors as an official scorer and was the president of the Edmonton Old Timers' Fishing Club.

Dyck also advised the members that the Alberta government denied the AFGA a request to meet with the Standing Policy Committee (SPC) over their concerns with the proposed Cervid Harvest Preserves (hunt farms), even though game ranchers were allowed to make a presentation to SPC which smacked of a double standard.

The AFGA lost one of its long-time life members in 2002, Robert (Bob) Tanghe. Tanghe was a dedicated, hard worker for the AFGA and was zone 4 director for many years. He resided in Edson, where he was close to the streams and mountains he loved and spent many hours pursuing his love of the outdoors. Jack Graham, past president, paid Tanghe a fitting tribute, stating, "He gave back as much as he received and will be sadly missed by all who knew him."

Past president Dave Powell reported, "Hunting for Tomorrow has also seen changes. The foundation began as an idea, spent time developing that idea and philosophy of operations and now moved into the area of attaining its goals by positive action. Bob Gruzecki has taken on the role of chairman and Kelly Semple is the manager. Strides are being made in the area of fundraising and deliverables to the general public. I expect nothing but positive in this area for 2002."

The Hunting for Tomorrow Foundation (www.huntingfortomorrow.com) was created in 2002 to foster public understanding, involvement and support of hunting and to ensure opportunities for every Albertan to hunt within a management system that conserves the wildlife resource. The foundation was governed by a board of directors. The functions of the Hunting for Tomorrow Foundation were carried out by an executive director under the direction of the board of directors, various working groups and task force committees. According to their mission: Our efforts are positive, organized and focused. Our coalition of hunting, fishing and trapping organizations includes participation from all major stakeholder groups as indicated below: Alberta Bow Hunters Association; Alberta Conservation Association; Alberta Fish and Game Association; Alberta Hunter Education Instructors' Association; Alberta Professional Outfitters Society; Alberta Sustainable Resources Development Department; Alberta Trapper's Association; Alberta Traditional Bow Hunter Association; Canadian Wildlife Service; Delta Waterfowl Association; Disabled Hunter; Foundation for North American Wild Sheep– Alberta Chapter; National Wild Turkey Federation; Pheasants Forever; Pope and Young Club; Rocky Mountain Elk Foundation; Safari Club International – Alberta chapters; Taxidermist Association.

The foundation was chaired by Bob Gruzecki of Calgary.

Kelly Semple was hired as the first executive director of the Hunting for Tomorrow Foundation.

COURTESY OF TRAVEL ALBERTA

Mountain goat grazing along a glassy water's edge.

Powell also advised, "As the [AFGA] ACA liaison, the year has been one fraught with upheaval and change. The Szumlas report came down bringing with it a significant board change and work on defining the role of the ACA. In August I passed the buck to Ray Makowecki, who now looks after things and is doing an excellent job."

Dave Powell and Andy Russell were both awarded an Order of the Bighorn Award in 2002. Powell received the award for a lifetime of service to Alberta's conservation movement and for his work at the local and provincial level with the AFGA. Powell held a variety of positions at the local, zone and provincial level with the association and was president of the association in 1998-99. Andy Russell received the award for his work to educate Albertans about the plight of Alberta's grizzly bears and public education in support of a healthy environment. Russell was a regional representative from the Waterton district on the AFGA executive and vice chair of the big-game committee during the mid-1950s.

Vice president Ray Makowecki advised, "Blair Rippin and Colin Kure participated in the bison grazing on public lands committee and we contributed to the development of a procedure that restricts such use if it has the potential of harming fish and wildlife habitats, or if it affects wildlife movement, or if it influences access for hunter or anglers. This was important work volunteered by Colin and Blair." Makowecki also blasted the ACA, stating, "the AFGA was particularly interested in narrowing and clarifying the purpose and role of the ACA and in so doing, reducing duplication and confusion with the government function and at the same time clarifying roles with associations such as the AFGA. The AFGA executive believes that significant changes are in order to help all concerned conservationists achieve harmony; and most importantly to achieve effective and efficient use of anglers' and hunters' monies that are used to protect, develop, and manage Alberta's fish and wildlife resources."

Fishing chair Vern McIntosh admonished delegates, stating, "No major government effort will be undertaken without much improved funding and that will not happen unless it becomes a political issue. We are few in numbers so to effect major change in attitude we have to become politically active. That may have to be our major project for the next few years." By 2002, the fisheries branch had been gutted by the government after more than a decade of budget cuts, and downsizing and a lack of fisheries programming was a major concern of the AFGA. Notwithstanding these shortfalls, the AFGA did put pressure on the government to finally take some positive steps to better manage Alberta's fisheries in 2002, including such initiatives as the introduction of an interactive salmonid identification key on the government website; implementation of a policy to downsize the Alberta commercial fishery from 800 to 200 commercial fishermen to better manage the harvest and reduce the commercial by-catch on non-target species such as pike, lake trout and walleye.

Mike Cardinal, Minister of the Department of Sustainable Resource Development, deserves the lion's share of credit for taking the initiative to downsize Alberta's commercial fishery, where previous ministers had failed, by single-handedly moving this initiative forward; this policy was a major achievement of his administration.

A stately moose pauses on a deserted highway near Slave Lake.

2003 Rod Dyck remained as president of the AFGA in 2002. The theme of the annual conference was "Not Just a Voice in the Wilderness, But Your Voice in Conservation." The 74th annual conference marked the 95th birthday (1908-2003) of the AFGA and was chaired by Gerald Foster of zone 4. It was held at the Ramada Hotel and Conference Centre in Edmonton. Dyck advised, "Without a doubt the biggest issue for me was fighting the legalized Cervid Harvest Preserves (CHPs) or shoot farms in Alberta."

The Alberta game-farming industry had been built on a pyramid scheme where those first into the business had made huge profits on the sale of breeding stock to late-comers. As the industry expanded, this lucrative market dried up and operators focused on more traditional markets, such as the sale of antler velvet to Asian interests. [The sale of meat never materialized in a significant way because it was overpriced from the very start and only appealed to a rather small niche market.] With the outbreak of chronic wasting disease in Canada, Asian markets for velvet closed, forcing the game-farm industry to look for other markets, such as selling hunts of farmed game animals. Such a concept was repugnant to most hunters and the AFGA. The Alberta government had earlier prohibited such hunts in the *Wildlife Act*, but there was a strong lobby of game ranchers who pressed to have them legalized.

The AFGA banded together with other like-minded groups and were successful in preventing Cervid Harvest Preserves from being legalized. The term "Cervid Harvest Preserve" was coined by the provincial Department of Agriculture, as they were the government agency responsible for game farms and fronted the concept of hunt farms as a way for game ranchers to stay in business. The whole affair was just another sad story of how successive Progressive Conservative governments had given placid support to an industry that was doomed from the start. Instead of listening to the constituents who understood the value and history of wildlife management in Alberta, they chose to follow their ideology of private is best—once again abrogating their responsibility to protect Alberta's wildlife heritage in the minds of the AFGA members.

On another note regarding the commercialization of wildlife, Dyck reported that he and his vice president Maurice Nadeau had spent much time in negotiations with the Alberta Professional Outfitters Association to complete the allocation review for the upcoming five years. Dyck advised the conference delegates that the AFGA executive had prepared a three-year business plan during his second year of office. Business plans came into vogue in the new millennium on the heels of wide-spread strategic planning exercises during the 1990s, with a new focus on the financial bottom line, more so than mission, goal and objective-setting exercises characterized by earlier strategic planning.

Dyck also reported on the mismanagement of the federal gun registry, cost overruns and the futility of the whole registration system, termed a "billion dollar boondoggle." Interestingly, Dyck reported that he did about 350 media interviews on behalf of the association in 2003, a trend that would escalate in the future as the AFGA would be called on to speak out for wildlife even more often on many different fronts.

COURTESY OF RAY MAKOWECKI

Janice (L) and Ray Makowecki with walleye catch at Pigeon Lake.

2004

Resolution

The ACA continued to be a source of controversy. There were two resolutions on the floor at the annual conference: (1) That the ACA recognizes in all its advertising and promotion materials; audio, video, and print, the anglers and hunters of Alberta who provide the largest percentage of funds to the ACA programs, projects and studies; and (2) that the AFGA withdraw membership from the ACA, the latter resolution being withdrawn at the annual conference.

The Agricultural Dispositions Statues Amendment Act 2003 (Bill 16) was proclaimed in July 2003, introducing new regulations for recreational access to public lands under lease. The new regulations promoted co-operation and respect between lease disposition holders and other users of the land through clear rules and better communications. The AFGA offered to give presentations to local clubs to help members better understand the process for access to public lands for fishing and hunting, or any other recreational pursuit; information was also made available on the AFGA website: www.afga.org by following the links to the recreational access website.

The AFGA, in partnership with the Alberta Conservation Association, Ducks Unlimited Canada, the Alberta Fish and Wildlife Division and the Nature Conservancy of Canada, won the 2003 Emerald Award for environmental excellence in the not-for-profit category for the Buffalo Lake Moraine Conservation Area Project.

The Alberta Foundation for Environmental Excellence, founded in 1991, recognizes outstanding initiatives and leadership that Albertans demonstrate in the face of the many environmental challenges. The Emerald Awards were created by the foundation to celebrate these achievements, and the foundation encouraged all Alberta individuals, organizations and corporations to participate.

This particular project demonstrated a model partnership that influenced other partnership project successes, making the AFGA proud to be involved with such a prestigious achievement.

A long-awaited book, Alberta Wildlife Records, Official Records of the Alberta Fish and Game Association second edition 1963-2001 was published in 2003. The book covers all yearly fish, bird, photography and big game records for the AFGA from 1963-2001. It also includes the all-time records for Alberta's fish and big game and the all-time records of the Alberta Bowhunters Association. In addition to the complete list of records, it contains 30 feature stories of Alberta's top wildlife trophies, including the tales of all of Alberta's number-1 big-game entries.

Dyck was successful in obtaining an annual grant in the amount of $150,000 from the Hon. Mike Cardinal, Minister of Alberta Sustainable Resources Development, after many negotiations with Cardinal and his staff. Dyck advised that the grant was to be used to further the AFGA goal of "conserving our heritage" in relation to habitat and the AFGA projects. For example, in 2003 the AFGA staff were able to acquire matching grants with the seed money granted by Cardinal to the amount of $350,000, which was used for new land purchases and project maintenance. This grant was not without controversy among the membership, as some critics saw it as hush money to keep the AFGA from speaking out against government. However, most members were very grateful to have received these much-needed dollars.

Past president Dave Powell gave a sobering perspective in his conference report about the ACA: "On the ACA front, since taking my position on the board of directors in October, I have come to a realization that any chance of meaningful change is all but a figment of imagination. With the constitution change as of the AGM we boycotted there is no chance of getting a change backward through six of the seven groups involved. The MOU [memorandum of understanding] has changed how the money is dispersed with little left for outside groups to utilize for programs of any sort. All that is left to do is fight over the scraps, which will be few and far between. There is little chance of obtaining funding for the AFGA habitat staff under the current regime." The ACA continued be a thorn in the side of the AFGA with regard to its spending priorities.

Environment chair Quentin Bochar reported, "First and foremost, a study commissioned by Alberta Environment and Sask Water shows the cost of building the Meridian Dam [on the South Saskatchewan River downstream of Medicine Hat] outweighs the economic benefits, without even considering environmental concerns. As a result of the consultant's findings and report, both [provincial] governments agree that economics alone make a dam unfeasible, even before environmental impacts are considered." The Meridian Dam had long been on the drawing board of water management authorities in southern Alberta, and would have represented an unmitigated environmental disaster for local fish and wildlife in the area.

2005

Resolution	The ACA continued to be a source of controversy; there were two resolutions on the floor at the annual conference: (1) that the ACA recognizes in all its advertising and promotion materials; audio, video, and print, the anglers and hunters of Alberta who provide the largest percentage of funds to the ACA programs, projects and studies; and (2) that the AFGA withdraw membership from the ACA, the latter resolution being withdrawn at the annual conference.
Resolution	A resolution at the 2005 conference resolved that the Alberta government should amend the Interim Métis Harvest Agreements with the Métis Nations so that their hunting and fishing rights restrict them to Métis settlement areas.

Past president and fish chair Vern McIntosh lectured the AFGA delegates in his fishing report to the annual conference. "We as anglers must practice conservation in the true form. Practice what we preach. Too often obvious and continuous violations take place on our waters. Many of us witness these incidents, are cavalier about it or just can't be bothered to report to the authorities. The eastern slopes trout fishermen have instituted a watch program that should set an example for the rest of us."

2004 Ray Makowecki became president of the AFGA in 2003. Makowecki was a principal in an Edmonton environmental management consulting company, EnviroMak Inc. and a long-time member of the St. Paul Fish and Game Club. During his career with the Alberta Fish and Wildlife Division, he was responsible for the Fisheries Habitat Enhancement and Protection Program, served as regional director for the northeast region, and as director of the Northern River Basins Study. He initially went to work as a school teacher after graduating from the University of Alberta, where he later returned to complete a master of science degree in zoology. Makowecki was a visionary who wore his heart on his sleeve; he was a caring and compassionate advocate of Alberta's fish and wildlife, a tireless worker for the AFGA who counted many friends in the association. In an interview, Makowecki said what attracted him to become a member of the AFGA "was the obvious thing, just an absolute interest in hunting and fishing. I was a kid in the mid-'60s and the Edmonton Fish and Game Association was active and I became keenly involved with this group who talked hunting and fishing."

RAY MAKOWECKI President: 2003-04

I first joined this great organization in 1964 as a member of the Edmonton Fish and Game Association and was also active in St. Paul club activities such as the crow and magpie shoots.

I was a student in the first Alberta hunter education instructor's course in the 1960s and was a certified instructor while I taught high school for a few years. I taught parts of the hunter training course at various times several years ago.

As a former long-time government fisheries biologist and director, I was unable to actively participate in the AFGA for many years but was fortunate to meet and work with so many

COURTESY OF THE AFGA

RAY MAKOWECKI

of the exceptional people who were part of the association. The dedication of these volunteers through the '60s, '70s, '80s and '90s was truly remarkable. As a government employee I attended many conventions and would participate as much as I was allowed. For many years Duane Radford, southern region director, and I would be the election scrutineers and ballot counters.

When I retired from government and went into the private sector, I decided to become more involved in the AFGA, and in so doing was elected vice-president in 2000. I came with a personal mission and three goals.

First, I wanted to see the AFGA, the voice of hunters and anglers and conservationists, become more independent financially. I wanted the association to obtain a "checkoff" of funds from the sale of every resident hunter and angler licence. I wanted the association to speak for all hunters and anglers.

Second, I was very concerned about the changes to fisheries management. In my deliberations and review of the new government fish management direction I saw too many regulations and too many precautionary actions. I saw a movement away from consumptive use of our publicly owned fisheries resources.

Third, I wanted to promote the AFGA and I wanted to tell people that we do save habitats for all Albertans and that eating a fish, a duck or a moose was good for the conservation of fish and wildlife.

The major issues I faced as president from 2003 to 2005 did not necessarily have to do with my priorities. As president, you have no choice but to address those issues that come before you and the ones that seemed to require considerable time and effort included: the grizzly bear hunt; chronic wasting disease; the Interim Métis Harvesting Agreement; the "No Beef No Hunting" issue connected to BSE [bovine spongiform encephalopathy] and the plight of the farm and ranch communities; the role of the Alberta Conservation Association (ACA) within government and with the AFGA; the sale of public lands; and declining fishing opportunities.

Organizationally, we maintained a positive financial position. We streamlined our communications by focusing on the Outdoor Edge magazine, executive reports and the AFGA website. In so doing, we eliminated the club bulletin. We reviewed and redrafted the operations manual and the AFGA policies for which we sought support from the 2005 convention.

We developed a series of AFGA position papers: sale of public lands, Métis hunting and fishing rights, game farming, use of barbless hooks, use of lead sinkers and jigs, bison grazing on public lands, waterfowl hunting in Alberta and grizzly bear hunting. These papers helped all zones, clubs and members to speak out on issues with the assistance of some supporting background information.

We initiated the development and promotion of the Alberta Fishing, Hunting and Trapping Heritage Act. A draft of this proposed Alberta Natural Heritage Act, the right to hunt, fish and trap (from Quentin Bochar and his committee) was submitted to the provincial government.

We initiated the AFGA Heritage 100 History Book Project for completion in our centennial year of 2008. The Heritage 100 Committee was chaired by Don Hayden.

We developed a new communication system to address fish management and regulations issues with the Government of Alberta.

We continued to reflect our position on game farms, hunt farms and chronic wasting disease (CWD).

We strongly supported our resident hunters in the discussions on the future of waterfowl hunting.

We fought for our concerns during the federal, provincial and municipal elections; thanks go to a strong effort from past president Tony Ferguson in this regard.

We advocated increased funding or re-assigned funding for fish and wildlife management programs and we encouraged clubs and zones to contact their local MLAs.

The wisdom and continued dedication of the past presidents and life members was of tremendous benefit to me as president; they should never be overlooked in their contributions – they are our elders.

Despite all the issues facing Alberta's fish and game resources, we continue to be fortunate to have a diversity and abundance of fish and wildlife that we are able to enjoy. We are also fortunate to be able to share bread and drink and thoughts with people who have such strong convictions and dedication to hunting and fishing, and conservation. Enjoy the bounty of our land and water, and teach the children to enjoy and respect by catching and eating a fish, as it is not bad to eat what the outdoors produces.

I was elected as director-at-large on the board of directors for the Canadian Wildlife Federation and served as a director of the Cumulative Environmental

In his president's report at the 75th annual conference held at the Executive Royal Inn Hotel and Conference Centre in Leduc, Makowecki signalled a change back to the old days when he reported, "Our mission as the AFGA has been to conserve fish and wildlife and protect their habitats and at the same time we want to ensure continued use of those natural resources." [Editor's note: "conservation" should not be confused with "preservation;" rather it should stand for wise use, with "use" being the key word.] He also reported that the association achieved financial stability in 2004. The annual conference was hosted by the Leduc Fish and Game Association and chaired by Gilbert Magnan,. The theme of the conference was "Conserving Our Heritage."

Noteworthy in Makowecki's report was that the AFGA participated in 52 different committees during his first year in office; he praised Andy von Busse and Andy Boyd for their work on endangered species and grizzly bear management committees respectively. Steve Witiuk served on a bighorn sheep committee and Gerry Pittman on sustainable agriculture, with Colin Kure on a sustainable forestry committee. Makowecki told the delegates, "The drafting of the proposed *Alberta Natural Heritage Act* (the right to hunt, fish and trap) [by Quentin Bochar] will be a special piece of legislation that we all seek." He also announced that the Heritage 100 Committee, chaired by past president Don Hayden, would be producing an AFGA history book for the AFGA centennial year in 2008.

Some of the key goals set forth by Makowecki in 2004 were to increase funding for fish and wildlife management; seek opportunities for new openings of Alberta's fisheries that were being managed on a precautionary basis with zero limits; to encourage youth and non-hunters to become active in hunting and fishing; encourage advocacy among all members of the AFGA and openly invite non-members to share in responsibilities and benefits; monitor the sale of public lands still being pursued by the Alberta government [seemingly still hell-bent on privatization]; continue to advocate the removal [elimination] of game farms to prevent the spread of chronic wasting and other diseases and continue to support the provincial grizzly bear hunt.

Makowecki's closing objective was to "Eat fish. We must continue to strongly promote that utilizing fish and wildlife for recreation and human consumption is good. It is not bad to eat a fish!!" This particular goal is consistent with the philosophy of Canada's First Nations peoples and many outdoorsmen who

COURTESY OF THE AFGA

Ray Makowecki with the number one mule deer at the provincial awards in 2004.

do not subscribe to catch-and-release regulations except where required to conserve fish populations. Detractors were quick to pick up on his message and jokingly began to refer to the AFGA as the "Fish and Eat Association."

Past president Rod Dyck made a profound comment in his conference report that bears repeating "Our members continue to realize that Alberta is a unique and diverse province with ever-changing demographics. They realize that our heritage in Alberta, mainly the fish, the wildlife and the land resources that have been passed down to us from previous generations, must be responsibly looked after so we can pass that heritage on intact to the generations that will follow us. The very people that use the resource, namely the hunters and anglers, are also the guiding force in conserving the resource, and the leaders of that group are the members of the AFGA. To be blunt, future generations depend on the decisions that you and I make today."

Senior vice president Randy Collins addressed the importance of marketing the AFGA in his conference report, based on his advertising experience with the *Edmonton Journal*. He advised the delegates "We are here because we have a love for this organiza-

tion and what it stands for. We are all salespeople for the cause. We can get our 'bark' back by being more involved, by not being complacent, by 'doing' rather than reacting. By 'selling' ourselves and the organization that we belong to."

Junior vice president Maurice Nadeau rallied the troops with his conference address. "We are a proud group and as such take pride in our many fine accomplishments. The association's role in all things regarding hunting, fishing and conservation has been an active one and has gained the respect of our peers as well as the government. We should be pleased by the fact that as hunters, anglers and foremost conservationists, we have had a part in shaping the province's landscape. The vision of the 22 founding members, delegates from local fish and game clubs, holds true to this day."

2005 Ray Makowecki remained as president of the AFGA in 2004. Makowecki advised that the AFGA maintained a positive financial position; streamlined communications by using bi-monthly reports in the *Outdoor Edge* magazine and the AFGA website.

Sunrise over Cold Lake Harbour.

The executive reviewed and re-drafted their operations manual and the AFGA policies. They also developed a series of position papers (i.e. sale of public lands, Métis hunting and fishing rights, game farming, use of barbless hooks, use of lead sinkers and jigs, bison grazing on public lands, waterfowl hunting in Alberta, grizzly bear hunting). This project was a major undertaking and several senior executive members were to be commended for their personal contribution to the task: in particular, Makowecki singled out Rod Dyck, Dave Powell, Randy Collins and Martin Sharren, in addition to the time he was personally involved.

Makowecki reiterated the work done on a draft *Alberta Natural Heritage Act* and the AFGA Heritage 100 History Book. There were numerous other issues that the AFGA tackled in 2005.

In closing, Makowecki re-affirmed the AFGA's new goals, in particular to strive for financial independence; to seek greater funding for fish and wildlife management; and to pursue more fishing opportunities through a newly created Fishing in the Future Council. [Editors note: This stakeholder committee, which was the brainchild of the AFGA, would be re-named the Alberta Fisheries Management Round Table by the Hon. David Coutts, Minister of Sustainable Resources Development in 2005.]

During this election year, the president sent letters to all members of the association expressing concern about the increased sale of public lands and the Interim Métis Harvest Agreement; the latter issue began with a change in government ministers from Mike Cardinal to David Coutts.

There were two major issues that arose in 2005 according to Makowecki: the AFGA was expected to be involved with a review of the spring grizzly bear hunt and a proposed checkoff they had requested.

Past president Rod Dyck reported, "This conference will mark the end of my tour of duty on the AFGA senior executive. It's been quite a ride from junior vice president to senior vice president to president and finally to past president. I suppose I could write about our accomplishments over that time period, but someone else can do that. It doesn't matter to me who does the work or takes credit for it, what matters is that the work gets done. The bottom line is that the AFGA is in the conservation business and in the conservation business you don't usually get second chances, you have to do it right the first time as mistakes take a long time to fix. Many other conservation groups do great work and we partner with them on many projects, but unlike other groups the AFGA is volunteer-driven and volunteer-based. That gives us the edge in the conservation business. As volunteers we have the heart and the drive to make sound conservation decisions. Decisions based on our personal experiences and time spent in the field pursuing and enjoying our passions and thinking of ways to enhance them."

Senior vice president Randy Collins gave a pre-election report as part of his conference address. "I have been an outspoken member of the AFGA and the executive for many years now (that's probably why I'm in this position). I've gone through the ranks and have a clear understanding of how the association operates and what our mandates are. That being said, I am always learning something new each and every day. So what does this all mean,

Rocky mountain bighorn sheep.

and what does Randy Collins want to do? Well for a start, I want to continue to keep open communication with our clubs and open the communication back with the other outdoor-minded organizations and our provincial government. I think in the past few years our communication has improved with the clubs but we need to work on our partnerships with the government and our peers in our outdoor-related activities. The AFGA and its members and executive have to become more proactive, not reactive, we have to become the force that we once were and can become again. We have a tradition and a reputation that has stood the test of time. We are respected, listened to and called upon when issues relating to the habitat and fisheries of this province are being compromised. And if I am elected your next president I hope to carry on that tradition and ensure that the AFGA truly is "the voice of angler, hunter and conservationist of this province."

Junior vice president Maurice Nadeau had a way with words, expressing himself quite passionately when writing about Alberta's great outdoors. In his conference report he queried, "How many times have you been out on a lake on an early summer's morning, the water like glass, it's quiet, it's just a little cool and the mist has not yet been burnt off by the coming heat of the sun. As you breathe in the smell of forest and lake, is there anywhere else you would want to be? And then your rod pulls downward and your reel starts to whine…. Thank God for people like you and I, conservationists!

"Conservation is defined as the act of conserving; protection from loss or waste. Conservationist is defined as a person who advocates the conservation of natural resources. I am a conservationist and I am 99.9 percent sure that if you are attending this conference and are reading this or any report in our conference guide that you too are a conservationist. For nearly one hundred years the AFGA has been a part of conservation in this province. We have been conservationists of fish, birds, game and non-game animals as well as conservationists of the land the water and skies. Some of us are hunters, some are not, and some fish, some do not, some fish but never or rarely keep a fish. Birds are the passion for some, waterfowl and upland game birds, other members will spend their winter evenings in the garage building new bird boxes to be put out for the spring arrival of songbirds. Not all fish-and-gamers carry a gun onto the land, preferring a camera or binoculars or a berry-picking pail, maybe a simple walking staff, each venue a way to appreciate all that is nature. Nature that we all strive to conserve. The AFGA is not alone in its conservation efforts; there are many other organizations, groups and individuals that share our concerns, interests and passions. Groups like the Alberta Trappers Association, whom I had the pleasure of addressing last spring. Trappers have, perhaps longer than anyone, been practitioners of conservation. Yes they trap animals for their fur but they do so in a wise and mindful manner, not to upset the natural balance of things, always keeping an eye out to the next season's harvest. Conservation is also important to the Alberta Professional Outfitters; they depend on good conservation of habitat and game-birds and animals for their livelihood. They depend on access to this habitat.

"The Alberta Conservation Association is, by its own definition, a part of conservation in Alberta, and though it is true that the AFGA and other ACA member organizations do have our differences as to how funds (collected almost entirely from WIN

COURTESY OF TRAVEL ALBERTA
Bushy-tailed woodrat in the Rat's Nest Cave at Canmore Caverns.

card holders) are allocated, it stands true that in most all cases it has benefited Albertans and our natural landscape. That said, the AFGA would still like to push for a larger portion of the funds to be distributed toward fish and wildlife-related issues and management, the fish and wildlife we angle and hunt. The benefits of the ACA's conservation efforts in the field or financially should go closer to those who pay into the fund; hunters and anglers."

Nadeau concluded his report by advising that as conservationists there were a few matters the AFGA would be addressing in the coming year:

- the sale of public lands
- Métis hunting and fishing rights
- game ranching and chronic wasting disease (CWD)
- the expenditures of ACA funds
- waterfowl management
- fisheries management

Environment chair Quentin Bochar reported, "Another natural area was proclaimed this year (Garner Orchid Fen) near Lac La Biche, and the Clearwater-Christina Rivers in northeast Alberta are now recognized under the Canadian Heritage Rivers System. This is the first designation in the province." Bochar also advised that over the previous 10 years approximately 81,000 acres of public lands had been sold, most of which was in the White Zone, where areas for recreation are already at a premium.

Program chair Alan Baker reported, "Our first attempt at a province-wide leadership seminar with the youth was a success. Only a handful of youth participated, but they handled themselves very well and most of them are continuing to take an active role in their club. The shooting competition was also a success. Competitors from several clubs met at Genesee for a fun day of shooting. We learn from our interactions with others. I look forward to these programs continuing and expanding. Shooting competitions are scheduled for the Sherwood Park Range and the youth seminar is planned to be held at Narrow Lake."

Baker also advised, "Part of our job is to teach the young people about our role as stewards of the flora, fauna and the environment of the province. Being a steward of the resource also puts us very close to the users of the resource. If the resource is compromised, all users will be affected, from hikers, bird watchers, campers, as well as direct consumers like hunters and fishers. We owe it to the resource to ensure that this stewardship continues and that means involving young people."

Hunting chair Wayne Norstrom painted a rather bleak picture in his annual conference report. "Our sport is taking hits from all sides," he said. "Hunting numbers are declining and the hunting effort is going along with it. Gun laws make us criminals and the media makes us [out as] barbarians. Few of the youth are taking up the sport. What remains is the dedicated hunter and outdoorsman and we are generally stubborn and unwilling to change. It's our nature. It is time to step back and take another look at wildlife management and hunting opportunities." Norstrom proposed the following somewhat controversial ideas for the delegates to consider:

1. Increase the cost of applying for a trophy tag to encourage only those who are really interested in hunting that animal at that time to apply. He suggested the increased fees could be designated to go to the AFGA. He argued the draw system was too "cheap,

easy and quick" and encourages those that are not really interested in the hunt to apply.

2. If a tag is not filled for one of the "primo, hard-to-draw-for animals," such as goats and grizzlies, allow it to be added to the next year's quota for the particular animal. "This management practice is done in other provinces and territories with sheep, goats and grizzlies," he argued. With the few permits allocated it was unlikely such a scheme would affect the population.

3. Place sheep on the draw. Although such an action would limit hunting opportunities, he argued, it also would do a number of good things. "It would take away the curl restriction, no longer would short sheep be left on the mountain or be seized in the wildlife office. It would allow those big, heavy rams that never make legal because of brooming to be shot. It would put some age structure back in the sheep population. And it would spread hunters out, making for a better quality hunt."

Fishing chair Vern McIntosh also painted a bleak picture in his report regarding the state of fishing in Alberta. "The past few years have not been beneficial for the anglers of Alberta. Many areas have been victimized by drought conditions that have assisted in decimating fish populations. Winter and summer kills have taken place caused by low water levels, increased water temperatures and reduced spawning areas. Anglers have not been totally responsible for reduced sport fish numbers. A number of flowing waters in Alberta are below volumes required to maintain instream flow

Living Waters boardwalk at Elk Island National Park.

needs. Weather conditions, industrial, agricultural and domestic use all contribute to water loss and the demand continues to grow with little visible effort being made to conserve this vital resource. Coal-bed methane exploration and drilling will affect our water sources and quality. Continuous expansion of oil sands development will affect both the landscape and water sources in this province. Forest destruction on a massive scale by energy exploration, seismic, etc., continues. Forests are converting to tree farms at an unsustainable rate. All this affects quality and quantity. Until such time as government becomes seriously concerned about water issues and the environment, the future does not bode well for the angler."

McIntosh also advised, "There is a tendency to blame [the Alberta] fisheries management [branch] for all our woes but keep in mind there are many factors that cannot be controlled by the managers. Underfunding and politics add to the problems when managers have to concern themselves with political fallout from any decision they make. Fish and wildlife issues are very low on the priority scale of government in Alberta." He reported, "We can only pray that weather and natural conditions improve, politicians wake up and see the light. In the meantime, take advantage of every opportunity to help out your fisheries managers. They need the information and assistance that anglers can supply. Get to know your local managers or technicians."

For the first time in several years, the Alberta government enriched the budget of the Fish and Wildlife Division in 2005 under the administration of David Coutts, MLA for Livingstone-Macleod, the affable Minister of the Department of Sustainable Resources Development. Mr. Coutts would be remembered as one of Alberta's foremost conservation ministers; unfortunately, he lost his Cabinet position and was relegated to the back benches when Ed Stelmach replaced Ralph Klein as Alberta's new premier in 2006.

Long-standing zone 1 director Heinz Plontke reported, "I am sure disappointed in our provincial government for signing an interim agreement to allow Métis people the right to hunt and fish without a licence at all times of the year in Alberta, with little or no thought on the impact it will have on our wildlife and fish. Most Métis do not need to hunt and fish for subsistence in this day and age. If it was really warranted for food, the Métis should not be targeting the trophy ungulates (bighorn sheep, etc.) that are currently being taken. I only hope that our government will reconsider this decision. Also, our government should not have offered our public lands for sale. It was stated in the Agricultural Lease Review Committee report (which came as a result of the meetings held throughout the province regarding the 'access issue') that the general public was opposed to the sale of any public lands." Plontke also advised, "Again, the Lethbridge, Coaldale, Picture Butte and Cardston fish and game clubs assisted in releasing 2,200 pheasants (from the Canadian Pheasant Company, in Brooks) along the Milk River Ridge area. A staggered release was done over a five-week span, which sure makes a lot of bird hunters happy. Apparently pheasant licence sales have increased over the last couple of years since fish and gamers have been assisting with the release. This program is to continue for another three years, but after that who knows. We should be lobbying our government to continue support for this worthwhile program." Plontke stepped down as zone 1 director after the conference following many years

of exemplary service to the AFGA, and subsequently took a position as zone 1 fish chair.

INTERIM MÉTIS HARVEST AGREEMENTS

In September of 2003, the Supreme Court of Canada upheld lower court rulings in Ontario where charges of hunting moose without a licence were dismissed against Steve and Roddy Powley, two members of a Métis community near Sault Ste. Marie, Ontario. The court ruled that members of the Métis community could hunt without a licence on traditional Métis land associated with Métis settlements.

In September of 2004, ostensibly to satisfy the requirements of the Powley ruling, the Alberta government struck interim agreements with the Métis Nation of Alberta and the Métis Settlements General Council. The agreements allowed Métis people the right to hunt, trap or fish, for subsistence purposes, without licences, year around, on all Crown lands and privately owned lands to which they had permission from the owner to access.

It was the opinion of many people, both Métis and non-Métis, that these agreements went well beyond the intent of the Powley decision and were a threat to the province's fish and wildlife resource. The AFGA spearheaded the opposition to the agreements, partnering with other like-minded groups. After much pressure, the government allowed the interim agreements to lapse in 2007, and expanded the definition of a subsistence licence to include anyone who could prove the need to use fish or game to feed themselves and their families, without reference to native status or culture.

Zone 2 director Cliff Deitz reported, "The Sarcee Fish and Game Association organized their 30th annual disabled fish derby at Crossfield Pond in June, along with High River Fish and Game Association and Calgary Fish and Game Association. There were 90 registered people fishing with 100 volunteers. The largest rainbow caught was four-and-a-half pounds. The Drumheller Fish and Game Association also held a disabled fish derby at Michichi Reservoir with 40 people fishing and 10 volunteers helping. The largest rainbow caught was over two pounds. There were BBQs at both with plenty to eat and drink. The Sarcee group was the fortunate one with a windup social at the Airdrie Legion." The work done by the Sarcee Fish and

COURTESY OF TRAVEL ALBERTA

Willow ptarmigan nestling in for some warmth.

Game Association, in particular, is truly commendable and a testament to the dedication of this organization to promote fishing to physically disabled Albertans.

Zone 3 director George Belter asked a rhetorical question on his conference report: "How many times do you see a father bringing his son or daughter to a meeting, they sit and listen to all the reports, old business, new business, and at the end of the meeting they go home, totally bored, and probably will not come again. Let these teenagers form a group and let them decide what they would like to do. At this point help them along the way with all the support your club can offer, and watch them grow. They will tell their friends, and they will come, then the parents will come and your membership will grow into an active club."

Zone 4 director Gerald Foster reported, "The spring and fall zone meetings were successful with about the same attendance as usual. A lot of topics discussed were the normal things that relate to hunting, fishing and the environment. However, items that developed ample discussions at the fall meeting were the health authorities proposed regulations regarding wild game banquets and dinners put on by clubs throughout the province. With this subject being circulated I decided to invite the Capital Health Authority people to the meeting and get the necessary input so clubs can be prepared and meet the requirements. I do believe we had some input on this matter, maybe not all good, but I guess we will wait and see." This particular policy really irked a lot of long-time AFGA members such as past president Jack Graham, who advised that in Edmonton the club members had to prepare wild game dishes at home and bring them to halls to be served.

2006 Randy Collins became president of the AFGA in February 2005 in Grande Prairie. At the time, he had been a long-standing member of the St. Albert and District Fish and Game Association. Collins was an outspoken advocate of the AFGA who had genuine concerns about Alberta's fish and wildlife and their habitat. He was known for his ability to communicate not only with individual AFGA club members and their concerns,

but also with elected government officials, and treat both with the same consideration and respect that they deserved. Collins, in his own way, would also raise the bar another notch in terms of communications and marketing initiatives. He was known to say numerous times that "the AFGA had to do a better job" at selling itself and becoming a more vocal voice on the Alberta outdoors landscape.

RANDY COLLINS: President 2005-07

Originally from Stoney Creek, Ontario, I moved to Alberta in the spring of 1978 in a job-related work transfer. In 1980 I married my wife, Loretta, and we are the proud parents of two children, Daniel and Vanessa, both of whom are taking career courses at the Northern Alberta Institute of Technology and Grant MacEwan College, respectively.

COURTESY OF THE AFGA
RANDY COLLINS

I've been employed in the newspaper industry (originally as a journeyman compositor) for 36 years. I started at the Hamilton Spectator and in 1978 transferred to the Edmonton Journal where I'm currently employed as a graphic artist.

I am an avid, year-round angler and enjoy camping, boating and all outdoor activities.

I was introduced to the AFGA in 1979 through a member of my wife's family; both my sister and brother-in-law were past presidents of the St. Albert and District Fish and Game Association.

My background with the AFGA is as follows:
- *Joined St. Albert and District Fish and Game Association in 1980; member for the past 28 years.*
- *President, St. Albert and District Fish and Game Association (1993-96)*
- *The AFGA zone 4 director (1996 to 2001)*
- *The AFGA junior vice president (May 2001 - February 2003)*
- *The AFGA senior vice president (February 2003 - February 2005)*
- *The AFGA president (February 2005 - February 2007)*
   Some of my AFGA activities and accomplishments are listed below:
- *The AFGA representative on a Special Places 2000 committee for Big Lake (1997-98).*
- *Original committee member on the Alberta Hunters Who Care Program (1998-2001).*
- *Original committee member on the Hunting for Tomorrow communications committee (1999-2003).*
- *Successfully co-ordinated the Camp He Ho Ha AFGA Physically Challenged Fishing Derby for the past 15 years (1994-present).*
- *As zone 4 director, I instituted a successful resolution to have more zone representation at the annual AFGA conference (1996).*
- *Designed the AFGA award-winning postcard for St. Albert club for a membership drive.*
- *Designed the AFGA zone 4 logo, the AFGA 75th anniversary logo and crest and various other print designs and requests within the AFGA.*
- *Opened up lines of communication between zones 4 and 5 with the zone 5 director including joint raffles, initiatives to help fund and keep the Narrow Lake Camp operable, which is now a reality.*

COURTESY OF DUANE RADFORD
Trevor Patterson (L), Claude Keller and Warren Wallace (upper right) at the weigh-in of his pike entry during the Fun Fishing Weekend at Camp He Ho Ha, 2005.

- Spoke out against the original "fishing on a draw" proposal that was being considered in 1999 on Seibert Lake for northern pike. The proposal was withdrawn later that year by the Alberta Fish and Wildlife Division.

- One of the first zone directors in the 1990s to institute additional meetings held at our annual conference, an activity that many other zones have subsequently adopted.

- Gave reports to the Alberta government's Resources and Environment Standing Policy Committee on Cervid Hunt Farms (2003), Health and Wellness and the Outdoors (2005).

- From 2001 to 2007 was principal signing authority for the AFGA.

- Canadian Wildlife Federation director from 2004 to 2007.

- As a member of the AFGA executive for the past 12 years, I have always been an advocate for the "fish" in the AFGA.

- Instrumental in getting government to initiate round-table meetings with provincial fishing organizations.

- As president of the AFGA from 2005 to 2007, I was extremely vocal on the Interim Métis Harvesting Agreement, Wildland Parks issues, chronic wasting disease (CWD), a new walleye tag initiative, continuing partnerships with like-minded organizations, membership and club activities and promoting the association to the greatest degree possible, province-wide.

I have been an active, vocal and enthusiastic voice for the AFGA for 28 years and am looking forward to 28 more!

[Biography prepared by Randy Collins.]

Collins welcomed delegates and guests to the 77th annual AFGA conference which was held at the Red Deer Lodge Hotel and Conference Centre in Red Deer. The annual conference theme was "Promoting Conservation... Protecting Habitat," which he said was one that "...rings ever so true with the activities, issues and concerns that your AFGA has dealt with this past year. From the Interim Métis Harvest Agreements that struck a nerve throughout the outdoor conservation community to the threats on our wildlife from chronic wasting disease to the disastrous oil spill that occurred at Wabamun Lake in early August, the need for promoting conservation and protecting our fragile resources seems even more of a priority as we reflect on this past year."

COURTESY OF FORT SASKATCHEWAN FISH AND GAME ASSOCIATION

Randy Collins and Alberta Premier Ed Stelmach at the 2008 Fort Saskatchewan wild game awards evening.

Collins reported that the AFGA had numerous meetings with government about the Interim Métis Harvest Agreements (IMHAs). They had also met with the Métis Nation of Alberta in April, mobilized members to undertake a "contact your MLA" campaign, placed ads in 100 weekly Alberta newspapers, conducted a public opinion poll, released its findings to the public, and were instrumental in getting an MLA committee, chaired by Denis Ducharme, to look at the IMHAs that the Klein government had negotiated without public consultation. Several conservation and environmental groups had come together to form a coalition to oppose these ill-conceived agreements. In so doing, many of these groups had used the AFGA material, including the AFGA press release and position paper, to bolster their own arguments.

Chronic wasting disease (CWD) was a major issue in 2005. Collins reported that the government and the concerned hunting public had taken steps to prevent this horrific disease from spreading even farther into Alberta, including culls and quota hunts. The one issue, however, that Collins said must be addressed was the root cause of the problem in the first place—game farms. It was the view of the AFGA that game farms had to be eliminated to prevent further introduction of the disease. However, even scarier was the resurgence of talks on "hunt farms." He questioned why some elected officials were even considering such a move again.

Collins reported on developments with "protected areas" being created throughout the province. While it was the mandate of some government departments to ensure unspoiled areas were protected within Alberta, the AFGA had serious issues when activities such as hunting, angling, trapping or off highway vehicle (OHV) use were going to be curtailed in these areas. He told the delegates that the AFGA was standing firm in voicing its views that these activities can and should continue in these areas. What was disturbing was the notion that some wildlife management plans for these areas would be transferred from the Sustainable Resource Development Department to the Department of Community Development.

Public lands were under attack from other areas, Collins reported, such as bison grazing and leaseholders being able to purchase additional parcels of land in some areas of the province. He questioned, "How many times do we have to say enough is enough, stop selling off our public lands!"

On a positive note, Collins reported that the AFGA Wildlife Trust Fund had a banner year conserving habitat lands and ensuring these would be available for activities such as hunting, angling or just wildlife enjoyment and viewing. Acquisitions during the previous year included the Peigan Creek property south of Medicine Hat, the Murdoch property by Innisfail and the Steinbrenner lease north of Grande Prairie.

Sunday hunting opportunities continued to increase throughout the White Area, Collins advised, as a result of the AFGA and its clubs meeting with various municipalities throughout the province. The AFGA executive met numerous times with officials from the Department of Sustainable Resource Development regarding current and future hunting and angling changes, always looking at how to improve or better the opportunities for residents.

Collins advised that one of his goals as president was to expand partnerships with the AFGA. He attended the Alberta Bowhunters conference and the Alberta Professional Outfitters Association (APOS) convention in 2005. Members of the AFGA executive worked with APOS on their disciplinary committee and both Maurice Nadeau and John Kyndesen started the next five-year outfitter allocation meetings with government officials. Collins met with the Alberta Hunter Education Instructor's Association and Alberta Trappers Association representatives, and attended the ACA annual general meeting. He reported that a new committee would be meeting to look at new membership on the ACA board, and the AFGA would be part of the process.

Collins reported in the *Outdoor Edge* magazine, "The marketing and communications component of the AFGA was and still is a top priority when I became your president back in 2005. In my mind we have met or exceeded our goals in getting the message out on the mandate and activities we as an association have or are involved in." He referred to some of the new initiatives that were integral in the AFGA communications to all Albertans about the association. He saw the "Let's Go Outdoors" radio program, hosted by Edmonton radio broadcaster Michael Short, as an invaluable tool to get information out to all Albertans interested in the outdoors. He also referred to the AFGA website, which had been revamped to create a more user-friendly, information-packed site. The *Outdoor Edge* magazine (sent to each member of the AFGA) continued to provide bi-monthly activity reports from the executive about events and activities, along with timely messaging from the central office to keep the members fully informed. The AFGA also provided a monthly message in the *Alberta Outdoorsmen* magazine. As well, the AFGA placed newspaper articles and timely features about hunting and fishing in major Alberta daily papers, as well as their weekly supplements. Collins summarized communications messaging by stating, "Effective media coverage through print, Web, newspaper and radio has placed us in these positions to effectively communicate."

Past president Ray Makowecki reported "In 2005 the issues included such important matters as the sale of public lands, loss of fish and wildlife habitats, declining numbers of hunt-

COURTESY OF DUANE RADFORD

2007-08 AFGA executive. Back row: John Kyndesen (L), hunting chair; Gord Poirier, fishing chair; George Belter, zone 3 chair; Al Plantinga, zone 6 chair; Fred Stamper, zone 4 chair; Andy Boyd, environment chair; Don Koziol, program chair. Front row: Steve Witiuk (L), zone 5 chair; Martin Sharren, executive vice president, Conrad Fennema, second vice president; Quentin Bochar, first vice president; Carole Romaniuk, life member and past president representative; Maurice Nadeau, 2007-08 president; Randy Collins, past presidents; Wayne Lowry, zone 1 chair/finance chair. Missing Robert MacKenzie, zone 2 chair.

ers and anglers, chronic wasting disease, game farming, need for increased fish harvesting opportunities, too many unnecessary fisheries regulations (e.g. barbless hooks, pike size restrictions, zero limits), Wabamun Lake spill, allocation of resources amongst domestic, recreational and commercial users and more parks and more land use restrictions. Our mission as the AFGA has been to conserve fish and wildlife and to protect their habitats and at the same time we want to ensure our continued use of those natural resources. This mission is etched in the hearts and souls of many of our members and it should be the uniting force of all Alberta hunters and fishermen. What we do and accomplish in meeting this mission will attract Albertans to our membership. This wonderful mission has not changed and our organization has been speaking such words for almost 100 years (2008 is the AFGA Centennial)."

Makowecki outlined the following goals for 2006:

1. Address issues with solid facts and well-constructed positions.
2. Speak out and be visible on all issues that influence the AFGA mission.
3. Simplify fishing and hunting laws.
4. Focus government spending and reduce the duplication between governments and others in managing fish and wildlife.
5. Unite all anglers and hunters to be more effective in achieving the AFGA mission.
6. Work toward the development of a fish and wildlife licence checkoff for the AFGA.
7. Exert more effort in examining and assessing issues associated with fisheries and fish habitats.
8. Encourage our youth and non-hunters and non-anglers to become active in hunting and fishing.
9. Encourage all members to participate and to openly invite non-members to share in responsibilities and benefits, including youth.
10. Promote that utilizing fish and wildlife for recreation and for human consumption is good. "It is not bad to eat a fish!!"

11. Support our fish and wildlife biologists and officers to ensure they continue to play a role in managing the lands and fish and wildlife habitats.

First vice president Maurice Nadeau started his annual address by advising, "The value I place on hunting, fishing and the conservation of habitat is growing year by year. This may be because the number of seasons into the memory bank outnumber those yet to come or maybe because with age and maturity comes a heightened sense of appreciation and responsibility."

He went on to describe how as a kid he enjoyed fishing a local creek, "dragging in pike after pike and occasionally the odd humpbacked perch. ...We'd take home the proverbial washtub full of fish to be frozen or canned." There seemed to be a limitless supply of fish. "Today we are facing the implementation of fishing draws, tags for those who want to keep a fish.

"Alberta is a dynamic place. Our population has doubled in the last 30 years. Large-scale agriculture, resource industries, shoreline development and recreational demands have taken a toll on fish and their habitat." Nadeau illustrated how bag limits and other restrictions, such as size limits and waters closed to angling for some species, have been imposed to gain control and rebuild, enhance and conserve Alberta's fisheries.

"Conservation and management strategies have paid dividends," Nadeau stated. "Game populations are stable or growing, hunting opportunities are being expanded. For hunters, it really has never been better, but dare we take it for granted? Remember the past sacrifices and tremendous efforts to restore moose and mule deer numbers, save our spring bear hunt from the antis and reinstate a goat season. Remember the volunteers, committees and meetings, frustration and more meetings."

Nadeau stated, "Habitat will be as critical in the restoration of some of our fish stocks as it was in restoring waterfowl. We are obliged to conserve habitat for our future generations, for fish and wildlife, those that we pursue and those we don't. To this end the AFGA's flagship, The Wildlife Trust Fund has 26,611 acres

COURTESY OF MAURICE NADEAU
AFGA president (2007-09) Maurice Nadeau shows off a fine Cold Lake trout.

COURTESY OF BOB SCAMMELL
AFGA past president (1979-81) Don Hayden in 2007.

[in 2006] of habitat in our province. We should be proud of our undertakings in this area and know that it would be impossible to boast of such accomplishments if it were not for individuals, fish and game clubs, landowners, corporations and other conservation groups working together."

Second vice president Quentin Bochar reported about the Community Development's Parks branch "god-like complex," whereby staff believe hunting, angling, trapping or OHV access be banned from all Alberta parks and natural areas. "This has been made very evident by their decisions regarding the Caribou Mountains Wildland Park."

"Lastly, a discussion paper regarding the need for Alberta to have a *Heritage Hunting, Angling and Trapping Act* has been sent out to other like-minded organizations as well as some MLAs for comments. Once this process has been completed, then the discussion paper will be forwarded to the Hon. Minister of SRD, Dave Coutts, as requested."

Environment chair Andy Boyd advised: "It's been eight years since I last served as the AFGA environment chair. It is said, 'the more things change, the more they stay the same.' This rings true regarding environmental issues in Alberta. In many ways little has changed since 1998 when I stepped down from this position.

"The Special Places 2000 was well underway back then and there seemed to be some promise the new wildland park category would be exactly what outdoor enthusiasts were looking for; a type of protected area where hunters were welcome. Many wildland parks were established but in most cases we still face considerable resistance in confirming our right to hunt in them. It is essential that local fish and game clubs be directly involved when management plans are being drafted. If we continue to use it, we won't lose it.

"The new *Water Act* was a hot topic during my last term and water issues are still front and centre today. The act cleared the way for basin specific water management plans and, it is hoped, the provincial Water for Life program will deliver these plans. However, it is clear from the plans drafted thus far, finding a balance between water conservation and water withdrawals will be challenging. Anglers and hunters understand the need to ensure enough water remains in our rivers to sustain aquatic environments. Be sure to take every opportunity to actively participate in the water plan development in your area.

"There are a few new issues emerging as well (or at least old issues in a new form). We are keeping an eye on the development of a comprehensive land use framework and some progress is being made on a provincial bio-monitoring program to measure long-term environmental and biotic changes."

Fish chair Vern McIntosh noted, "With an '05 budget increase came an increase in fishery management activity, which we hope continues. Round-table discussions took place amongst many stakeholders in '05, where we aired our concerns and in the future will continue to do so, at lease twice a year.

COURTESY OF DUANE RADFORD

Maurice Nadeau, 2007-08 AFGA president.

"Lake levels increased during the year, which relieved some spawning trauma. If stocking commences in the near future for walleye, '05-'06 could contribute a welcome age-class season for future use.

"Because of our concern for the demands for use of our flowing waters, we have taken the following position on instream flow needs to protect water aquatic environment and the fishery:

"On a first-priority basis, the minimal flow should be based on the annual median flow and should vary in time with the natural seasonal variation. Water withdrawal should not be permitted at water flows that are below the minimum flows (median annual discharge curve).

"To ensure a natural flow regime, water conservation objectives must consider that short-term releases from hydro facilities do not negatively impact the aquatic environment.

"Winter minimum flows must be reviewed to determine if such flows have been altered by human-caused factors. If minimum flows have been reduced below natural levels, adjustments must be factored in to ensure the best representation of minimum is used.

"The AFGA believes that sufficient flows for fish and wildlife must be maintained in all flowing waters in Alberta. The median flow should be developed for various watercourses at specific locations by a committee of knowledgeable scientists using instream flow data calibrated over several years. The data should be available for review by stakeholders. Instream flows must be maintained above a minimal level as the health of the aquatic environment correlates with the health of humans."

Viewing wildlife in Jasper National Park.

Hunting chair John Kyndesen reported that there was no settlement of the Interim Métis Harvest Agreement and that the MLA committee chaired by Dennis Ducharme had yet to submit their report and recommendations. He also advised that chronic wasting disease remained a very serious issue and government officials had yet to announce what steps they had planned to combat this disease. Past presidents Tony Ferguson and Rod Dyck had represented the AFGA at meetings held in Chauvin and Empress, respectively.

Newly appointed zone 1 director Wayne Lowry reported that the clubs in the zone had finalized the deal on the Peigan Creek property near Medicine Hat. The 640-acre parcel contained significant habitat to the area. One of the key issues in zone 1 was the proposed park for the South Castle region. The park would comprise a total of 650 square kilometres of provincial Crown land just north of the northern boundary of Waterton Lakes National Park. The Alberta Wilderness Association was spearheading the proposal with support from Robert Bateman (artist), Sid Marty (poet), Farley Mowat (author), David Schindler (scientist), and former PM Joe Clark. Lowry felt that the AFGA and outdoors people generally should take a strong stance against these parks as they will undoubtedly reduce or eliminate activities associated with hunting and fishing.

Cliff Deitz, zone 2 director, reported a kill of 400 plus deer during the last week of January by the Sustainable Resource Department to curtail the advancement of chronic wasting disease from Saskatchewan.

Gerald Foster, zone 4 director, reported improvements to the zone 4/5 Narrow Lake Conservation Education Centre, including a new trap machine, clearance and enlargement of the range, gravelling the road within the campsite, and levelling, re-blocking and skirting the bunkhouse.

Zone 5 director Steve Witiuk advised, "Our zone has been very busy with the Narrow Lake Conservation Education Centre, southwest of Athabasca, a joint partnership with zone 4. There has been a great deal of improvements completed to date with still much to do. We require interest from groups, clubs, schools and other organizations to book the centre so we may have a cash flow to operate and maintain and run the centre."

2007 Randy Collins remained as president of the AFGA in 2006 and presided over the last conference prior to the centennial of the AFGA. It was held in Medicine Hat in February 2007, at which time Maurice Nadeau took over as the president.

MAURICE NADEAU: President 2007-09

It is my belief that for anyone who has ever served this association as president, it has been a responsibility they took on with great pride, devotion, and purpose. Not all have enjoyed terms without controversy, or have seen their aspirations come to pass, and not one saw a term without issues. Threats to habitat, conservation, hunting and fishing have always been there, and a president has always led the AFGA in their defense. Some presidents faced personal controversy, and for some the toll was great; a lot to endure when you are in a volunteer position. I have not yet spoken to a past president who can claim to have accomplished all his goals as

MAURICE NADEAU

president, but, to a man, they all made a valuable contribution nonetheless.

I trust it was an honour and a privilege for all those who served this association as its president, but to be the president of the AFGA in its 100th year is indeed an overwhelming distinction. I am the president fortunate enough to have this distinction; closing a century of history and amazing accomplishments and setting the course for the next 100 years.

I remember saying to my wife, Nadine, on the way home from my first executive meeting held at past president Elmer Kure's residence on the Red Deer River, "Some day I'd like to be president of this association." It was the experience of that meeting, and the passion and devotion of those in attendance, that fired my strong belief in the conviction and ethics of this association. I had long been voicing my growing concerns about our hunting and fishing resources, and with 100 percent support from my family, decided to put my money where my mouth was.

My first AFGA membership was a requirement for entry to a local walleye tournament hosted by the Beaver River Fish and Game Association. It would be several years before I attended a club meeting at the insistence of a good friend and president of the day Morley Hancock. For the next several years it was rare for me to miss a club meeting; I was elected to vice and then as president of our club. My involvement grew; I wanted to do more, make the club bigger and stronger, and with Nadine's support and often her participation I dedicated more time to see it through.

As vice president and president of Beaver River Fish and Game Association I attended the twice-annual zone 5 meetings. There I saw a bigger picture of the AFGA and a chance to become more active in things of great importance to me; the promotion and education of hunting, fishing and conservation. We were in Athabasca when Steve Witiuk, director of zone 5, approached me with the intent of having me run for vice director. I accepted the opportunity and served in that position for two years.

I had only briefly settled into the zone director's position when I was strongly encouraged to consider running for the AFGA hunting chair by vice president Rod Dyck. For an hour-and-a-half we stood in the parking lot of the Coast Terrace Inn talking about the direction of the association, what would be expected of me, and was I ready? A few months later I was elected hunting chair, a position that I would hold for three years.

About the time that I took this position, the Alberta Professional Outfitters Society (APOS) was starting up their discipline committee; having a sitting member from the AFGA was a requirement. President Dave Powell submitted my name for consideration. I sat on this committee for five years; its longest-serving member. The significance of this committee cannot be understated. I also worked with the outfitting industry, sitting on two allocation review committees. The negotiating process for the first of these reviews occurred over 18 months. As hunting chair I sat with Rod Dyck (the second vice president) and representatives from the outfitting industry and Sustainable Resources Development. In the end, the outfitting industry took substantial cuts to their allocations. It is important to mention that we were always mindful of the impacts our decisions could make on the incomes and livelihoods of families.

I have enjoyed working with APOS. I have met many fine people and consider many to be my friends. I believe that the AFGA and APOS have accomplished good things working together and that our future depends on even more collaboration.

I served my first two years as second vice president under president Ray Makowecki. As first vice president I willingly took on more responsibility; I sat on more committees, attended more meetings. The demand on my time and family was more than it had been in the past, as my work rarely found me near home. A committee that involves relatively little work as a member is the one that gives me the most pride – Wildlife Trust Fund – the gem of the AFGA. There is such satisfaction in knowing that not only are we conserving habitat but we are building a legacy for our children and theirs. It was as first vice president that I first took part in the Canadian Wildlife Federation. I have already been asked to continue on with this organization after my time as the Alberta representative terminates. As always, Nadine remains behind me.

As I write this I have only been president for four months. Since this is supposed to be a past president's biography, I am at some disadvantage because I won't know how the story will turn out. So, I will share with you my aspirations or goals for the AFGA in the coming two years:

- Recruit strong, passionate and dedicated volunteers for our executive.
- Increase our public exposure using magazines, radio and television.
- Increase the information flow to our members
- Start a poll on the AFGA website to survey our membership opinions.
- Reinforce with government (federal and provincial) that the AFGA wants to be part of the decision-making that affects our members, fish, wildlife and habitat. They should want to make use of our expertise.
- Work more often with like-minded groups, coalitions and alliances to bring quicker, more effective resolutions to issues.
- Promote more youth and ladies programs and involvement.
- Find ways of becoming more financially self-sufficient.
- Promote the WTF properties. In these days of global warming concerns,

these properties just may become more valuable.
- Promote the social, economical and personal benefits of hunting, fishing and trapping.
- Promote the adoption of new and innovative fish management strategies with emphasis on the opportunity, sustainability for now and into the future.

The greatest reward of having been part of the AFGA is just knowing that I made a difference. I stood on the front lines defending our fish and wildlife heritage and the privilege to use them now and into the future. I have done so to guard my quality of life and that of my children and theirs. It is with pride and honour that I have served you, Alberta, and its fish and wildlife as the 47th president of the AFGA.

[Biography prepared by Maurice Nadeau.]

"Back in 1908 a group of conservation-minded Alberta residents began a venture that was to become the AFGA," reported Randy Collins in his presidential report to the 78th annual conference. "Since that early time, the Alberta Fish and Game Association has been providing education, awareness and advocacy services to Alberta's hunters, anglers, and outdoor enthusiasts. As outdoor recreational sports, hunting and fishing activities have changed dramatically over the century. No longer are hunters and anglers merely users of our precious natural resources; they are conservationists, managers of wildlife habitat, and dedicated long-term supporters of our environment."

Collins went on to comment about Alberta now being a rich province with people flocking to it to find jobs and prosperity. "So, what are these new and existing Albertans going to do with those higher wages and a more disposable income?" he asked. "Probably invest in new housing, new transportation and some form of recreational activity to enjoy in our great outdoors. Be it a new trailer, camper, motor home, OHV [off highway vehicle] or boat, this will be a choice for many. Nowadays people want to get out and enjoy the outdoors and all it offers. And who can blame them? One of the best drawing cards for Alberta is our mountains, our vast, wide-open spaces and our tremendous scenery and abundant habitat opportunities that attract not only Albertans, but people from all over Canada and around the world.

COURTESY OF LILLA PFERSCHY

Mountain ash berries.

"But with all this good fortune and increased recreational activity comes significantly increased conservation-related responsibilities. Responsibilities we at the AFGA have been promoting and implementing for the past 99 years. Yes, we are the voice of the angler and hunter, but we are another force, first and foremost, and that is conservationists."

He commented on how the AFGA's mission statement, "to promote, through education and programs, the conservation and utilization of fish and wildlife and to protect and enhance the habitat they depend upon," was going to be increasingly harder to uphold in the next few years. "Rapid population growth and with that increased activity in our wild places and spaces will take its toll on these ever diminishing areas throughout the province," he said.

Collins stressed that "education, increased information and promoting activities such as hunting and angling as important management tools for the resource must be top priorities with not only our organization, but our provincial government, its leaders, and all other outdoor stakeholder associations. It is something that has to happen much sooner than later."

Past president Ray Makowecki offered some "rather blunt suggestions for the government and our members" to pursue the mission and goals of the AFGA, including:

1. Protection and enhancement of the fish and wildlife resource base, the habitat.
   - Create legislation that restricts the sale of public land.
   - Support the AFGA for habitat protection and land acquisition as they currently own approximately 30,000 acres of habitat and have landowner stewardship programs that acknowledge another 87,000 acres. Ensure that the AFGA continues to accumulate fish and wildlife habitats through land purchase and landowner recognition programs.
   - Enforce and support the enforcement of the provisions of the federal *Fisheries Act* that protect fish habitat and prohibit pollution.
   - Through legislation, ensure that instream flows for fish and wildlife are protected forever.
   - Establish monitoring that tracks the maintenance of the quantities of fish and wildlife habitat, so as to ensure that they are not lost in a cumulative manner.
   - Regularly report to the people the status of the resource base (habitat) in quantified measures.

2. Secure and enhance the number of resource users.
   - Work towards the principle of equality of resource user opportunity and resource allocation for Alberta residents.
   - Support associations that represent the general resident user. A checkoff from hunter and angler existing license fees should be provided to organizations that represent the general Alberta resident (i.e. AFGA).
   - Establish the *Fishing, Hunting and Trapping Heritage Act* recommended by the AFGA.
   - Establish increased targets for the numbers of new hunters and anglers and ensure that actions and programs that would diminish the numbers of users are discouraged or eliminated. Actions that should be reconsidered or carefully assessed include the grizzly bear hunt closure, wildland park ATV access closures, more restrictive and complicated regulations, increased costs for licensing, overly precautionary management especially when declining user numbers are evident, and improved access for fishing and hunting.

3. Ensure effective and efficient management and spending of taxpayer dollars.
   - Stabilize the Fish and Wildlife Division from frequent changes in structure and function. Reduce middle management. Ensure that fisheries and wildlife biologists are specialized to provide effective services in an ever-increasingly complicated world of fisheries management and wildlife management and enforcement.
   - Reduce confusion and duplication of fish and wildlife management in this province. Focus the spending of hunter and angler licence fees to reflect hunter and angler priorities. Ensure that government managers are responsible for inventory of the fish and wildlife by lump-funding the licence fees and assigning significant funds to the Fish and Wildlife Division. Eliminate duplication of administration, programs and responsibilities. Ensure that the government managers are clearly the people accountable and responsible to the users. Assign a $1-million fund from hunter and angler licence fees for granting some monies to interested Albertans for creating fish and wildlife habitats and for conducting

COURTESY OF DUANE RADFORD

important conservation work. Assign the Fish and Wildlife Division managers and biologists the responsibility for habitat enhancement and protection to create more efficiency. Ensure that strategic plans are results-oriented and have measurable targets, goals and objectives.

- Create the annual checkoff program from existing hunter and angler licence fees (with no increase in licence fees) with those funds going to the AFGA. In so doing, allow the AFGA to be an independent body that serves the interests of the resident Albertan, the fish and wildlife and their habitats.

4. Increase fish harvest opportunities.
- The opportunities for increased consumptive harvest on winterkill lakes, several pike fisheries, some smaller-sized fish, some walleye fisheries, some Arctic grayling fisheries and some mountain whitefish fisheries should be explored and implemented.
- Targets for angler interest (numbers of anglers) should be established and should be higher than the current numbers.
- Create new methods of increasing participation in consumptive harvest of fish (e.g. stocking more put-and-take fisheries and supplemental walleye stocking)

5. Management of chronic wasting disease (CWD) and other diseases.
- Using good science, continue to be firm and diligent in ensuring that CWD does not spread into our wildlife.
- Use the hunters and general public to participate by collecting and harvesting ungulates to allow for an active provincial monitoring program for disease incidence. Ungulate surveys for population size should be systematically conducted on a regular basis.

COURTESY OF LILLA PFERSCHY

Squirrel in trees along North Saskatchewan River valley pathway.

6. Continue use of wildland parks.
- Ensure that wildland parks continue to provide hunting, fishing and trapping opportunities under the direction of the Alberta Fish and Wildlife Division.

7. Increased opportunities.
- Establish increased opportunities for hunting and fishing in urban settings, parks and ecological reserves especially for population management and nuisance wildlife control.

"The future belongs to our children," reported first vice president Maurice Nadeau in his conference report. He noted that a renowned Canadian author once commented, "Hunters and anglers merely hide behind the name of conservation in order to deceive the public into accepting them." "Oh really!" Nadeau disputes. "The AFGA holds title to 26,931 acres of habitat, spread in parcels of varying size throughout the white areas of the province. Funding for these invaluable pieces of habitat came from clubs, members, the AFGA supporters and grant agencies; many of which are funded by the sportsman of Alberta. Some properties were donated and others bequeathed to the association by people who recognized the good we do. Last year (2006) alone our Wildlife Trust Fund properties grew by 656 acres. The AFGA has always recognized that habitat is vital to the conservation of fish and wildlife, large and small. We're putting our money on the ground literally. None of our habitat property is for resale; it will forever be conservation habitat. A heritage of land, wildlife and tradition, secure and protected, for our children and theirs.

"The AFGA has long been acclaimed as the champion of the great out-of-doors, a leader in conservation, the voice for anglers and hunters. This recognition has come not only from our provincial government but from our peers, outdoor enthusiasts. We must work continually to impress upon every scrutineer, that although we are an association that promotes hunting and fishing, our first loyalty is to the conservation of the resource that provides us our game opportunities."

Second vice president, Quentin Bochar reported, "The issue of the Interim Métis Harvesting Agreement is still in the hands of the provincial government. The AFGA was not granted intervener status and the stakeholder groups are no longer part of the process. So we are waiting to hear what the negotiations between the

Alberta Justice Department and the Métis will be and if they will follow the recommendations of Ducharme's report." [Editor's note: SRD Minister Ted Morton advised the conference delegates that this agreement was essentially declared null and void as a result of court rulings during his conference address. The interim agreement was terminated by the Alberta government after being unable to reach a consensus with Alberta's Métis before the 90-day limit on negotiations expired on July 1, 2007.]

Bochar continued on to report that the quality of Alberta fisheries and waterways were starting to gain more attention, especially with the amount of industrial activity that requires the use of water. "The minister of environment has been given a written mandate by the Premier to renew and resource the Water for Life Strategy, and to develop a new environment and resource management regulatory framework to enable sustainable development by addressing the cumulative effects of development on the environment. The Minister of SRD [Sustainable Resource Development] has been given a written mandate to develop a biodiversity strategy and enable sound management of Alberta's natural resources on a sustainable basis."

The minister of SRD was also given a written mandate to complete the Land Use Framework to address conflicts over competing use of land, as well as an aggressive strategy to protect the health of Alberta's forests.

Bochar reported that the AFGA presented the discussion paper, "Need for an Alberta Heritage Hunting, Angling, and Trapping Legislation" to then-SRD Minister Coutts and the association was awaiting the government's response.

Andy Boyd, environment chair, reported, "Through 2006 a number of environmental issues seemed to be in a holding pattern. Grizzly bear management slipped onto a back burner after the hunting season was suspended." As well, efforts on Integrated Land Management and the Water for Life programs were proceeding but with little to show.

He reported that one new issue that will not be afforded the luxury of an undetermined completion date is the management of the mountain pine beetle [MPB] outbreak. "The experience suffered by our neighbors in B.C. has shown action must be taken early and aggressively if we are to have an impact on this insect pest. I represent fish and game on the MPB advisory committee and my primary objective is to ensure efforts to control the beetles through accelerated harvest of mature pine stands consider the non-timber values of our forests."

Alan Baker, program chair, asked in his report, "Why do clubs affiliate with the AFGA? Primarily the reason is insurance. Secondary reasons would be the pooling of knowledge about environmental and wildlife matters. The more people we come in contact with, the more knowledge we gain."

Fish chair Gordon Poirier advised, "I am working on a response to the new provincial five-year Alberta Fish Conservation Strategy with the input of the board of directors of the AFGA. I can tell you we are not pleased. With water quality problems and spawning

habitat degradation and a lack of restocking by fisheries management branch there is lots to work on and more to learn."

Jack Graham reported taking Conrad Fenema of New Sarepta and 9 members of the Leduc Club under his wing in teaching him the ropes to instruct future classes of the AFGA in horn measuring. "Conrad is now a qualified Boone and Crockett Club official measurer."

Wayne Lowry, director zone 1, wrote, "Over the past year the clubs in zone 1 have had some great successes from the work that they have been doing. In particular, the Coaldale and Picture Butte associations have had some great successes with their youth programs. The Fort Macleod club has been involved in some major improvements to their campground and we are planning on having a zone campout at their facility on the May long weekend next year. The Lethbridge AFGA acquired their active status for their gun range after having been closed for a period of time. Their range is very well managed and very well developed.

COURTESY OF TRAVEL ALBERTA

Crescent Falls near Nordegg.

AFGA executive and families at meeting at Narrow Lake by Athabasca, Aug. 2006. Randy Collins, president (2005-07).

"The antelope study in the southeasterly part of the province is continuing and some interesting statistics are being achieved. The range of the antelope was surprising, however the major concern is the low reproductive rates. They are the lowest of all the species found here in the south. Some of the mortality is due to vehicle collisions, some due to feed sources and some due to predation. Personally, I believe that the coyote populations are the largest single factor to the low reproduction/survival rates of young antelope. The study will be wrapping up soon and I hope that some positive results will be forthcoming.

"The bighorn sheep study is completing its third and final year and I also hope that some positive findings will be forthcoming. Some 30 ewes have been collared in order to study their mortality and causes of mortality as well as their reproductive rates and success/failure in raising a lamb to maturity. There were some disappointments early in the study but the final results will be available soon. I have also heard that Shell Canada has commissioned a study of about 70 elk in an area south of Highway 3 to determine what affect, if any, their activities are having on the elk populations in this area. The elk will be collared and their travels mapped to see if there is any disruption to their natural, seasonal movement patterns.

"The pheasant-release program was once again undertaken this past fall by the Lethbridge AFGA as well as some of the other local clubs, namely Cardston, Picture Butte and Coaldale. It was appreciated by those who were out there hunting them. The number of birds released in the area was about the same as in past years (2,500 +/-), however it would still be nice to have more to get the numbers back up to where they were in the past. The AFGA in conjunction with ASRD [Alberta Sustainable Resource Development] entered into a three-year agreement to supply 3,000 hens in the spring of each year to be released in designated locations in an effort to improve the natural reproductive levels. This past year was the first year of the program. T.J. Swanky was instrumental in getting the deal put together; however this would not be possible if it were not for the dedicated individuals from the local clubs that did the placement of the hens."

George Belter, zone 3 director, noted, "[The year] 2006 has been a busy year with the conference hosted in Red Deer, next came the Panther River expansion problem, which will have to be watched in the future. Pigeon Lake [walleye] tag system is another problem, since the large fish for which this was intended are not in the lake anymore. The disappearance of fish in the Red Deer River from the Dickson Dam to the city of Red Deer is probably due to the flood of 2005."

Zone 4 director Fred Stamper wrote about the importance of communication between the clubs and zones. As an example, he offered, "A few years ago, as president of Busby and District Fish and Game Association, we put on a horn-measuring course. I invited the unaffiliated Hinton and Edson fish and game clubs and they sent people to take the course. These types of invitations keep the doors open to possible re-affiliation to the AFGA."

"As far as the clubs go," Stamper continued, "I see the tired executives. A perfect example is the Mayerthorpe Fish and Game Association. Good membership numbers, but no help to run the club. In the end, Mayerthorpe and Wildwood Rod and Gun Club amalgamated. This was the only possible solution."

With regard to CWD, Stamper noted, "the Department of Sustainable Resource Development are doing all they can. However, I feel the Department of Agriculture could stand up and take more responsibility."

On the grizzly bear hunt, he wrote, "While hunting in WMU 524 this fall, I found there is a real bear problem. There are numerous sightings of grizzlies. Problem bears are put to sleep and dropped off between miles 127 and 150 on the Chinchaga Forestry Road, which causes the moose population to suffer. The bears follow a cow moose when she is ready to calf. When she does, the calf is lunch and usually the cow is too. This was addressed at the hunting meeting in December. Hopefully something can be resolved."

COURTESY OF LILLA PFERSCHY

Pussy willow.

Walking dynamo Steven Witiuk, zone 5 director: "Our zone has been very busy with the Narrow Lake Conservation Education Centre southwest of Athabasca, a joint partnership with zone 4. I would like to thank all the volunteers who donated their time to the Narrow Lake Project in 2006. The site has never looked so good in its history, with the grass cut and the weeds under control, a new washroom facility and kitchen unit with a well onsite.

"Our casino, held on May 15 and 16, 2006, has brought us a profit of $84,672.98, which will help us to finish a lot of our club projects and the Narrow Lake Conservation Education Centre."

Allen Plantinga, zone 6 director, reported, "There continues to be many issues that we are working on that affect the northwest part of the province or the "Peace Block" as all you southerners call it. This past year saw the spread of the mountain pine beetle much farther into the province than was expected, with millions of trees being affected all throughout the northwest. The continuing struggles with development of a Caribou Mountains Wildland Park management plan and the closure of the grizzly hunt by SRD to allow for more population study. The mild winters have continued to allow our wild game populations to flourish and the hunting opportunities continue to be excellent. With the heavy snows early this winter we will see how the deer populations make it through the winter but I guess this is just Mother Nature's way of balancing things out. Even with a harsh winter I know that hunting opportunities in the north will be great this next year."

This award-winning photo was taken by Robert Loewen of the Sherwood Park Fish and Game Association, March 2007.

Chapter Two

The Fish and Game Clubs and the Six Zones

The backbone of the Alberta Fish and Game Association (AFGA) is its associated, local clubs. In short, there would be no AFGA without these grassroots organizations. As of 2007, the AFGA was composed of six geographical zones and 93 active clubs. The zones were formed in 1967 to help organize the clubs into effective lobby units to influence the provincial policies of the AFGA. Each club sends a representative to the zone meetings and each zone is represented on the provincial AFGA executive by the zone's elected director.

The geographical boundaries of the zones are largely based on the Alberta Fish and Wildlife Division regional boundaries extant in 1967. In that year, Dr. Stuart Smith, director of the Alberta Fish and Wildlife Division, advised the AFGA that the government was creating six administrative regions and suggested that the AFGA make similar changes to its regional organization. Such a resolution was introduced by the AFGA president Joe Balla and was passed at the 1968 convention, creating the six zones. Although the government zone boundaries have since been redrawn several times over the decades, the AFGA boundaries have remained relatively the same.

At the turn of the 19th to the 20th century, people got together over coffee or a campfire to talk about the lack of wild game in their area and the need for conservation. When the provincial government came into being in 1905, many of these informal groups realized if they were going to create or change provincial resource conservation policy they needed to become a more formal organization with an elected executive and standing in their respective communities. In so doing, they could speak as a group of concerned citizens to their local member of the legislative assembly (MLA) in Edmonton.

Over time, it soon became apparent that a more formal provincial organization was needed, and the AFGA came into being.

Alberta

This chapter of the book, however, is concerned with how the various grassroots organizations were formed and each of their contributions to the conservation of fish and wildlife in their local areas, as well as their influence on the provincial organization.

Since those early days, clubs have formed for a variety of reasons. Some wanted to recognize the outdoor prowess of their members by presenting awards for trophy fish and game. Others wanted to fund and build a shooting range for firearms or archery and hold competitions, or to build and stock a fish pond to increase fishing opportunities for their communities. Still others wanted to fund and initiate a conservation project in their area, or organize a hunter training or firearms course. Of course, once a club formed, other projects and programs were adopted, often after members learned what other clubs were doing. All realized they needed to be organized to fight for and protect their outdoor values.

Some of those outdoor values have changed over the years. In the early days, many clubs formed to organize predator shoots and lobby the government to place bounties on wolves, coyotes, magpies and crows. These animals were perceived to be in competition with hunters and needed to be thinned to increase game populations. Since that time, the science of wildlife biology has shown predators have their place in the natural community, and their numbers are now controlled through less aggressive means. As well, clubs realized the value of other non-game wildlife and sponsored bird counts, blue-bird box trails and the establishment of natural areas that conserve all kinds of wildlife.

The following are histories of each club that chose to submit to this book. The histories are grouped by the AFGA zone. Each zone section begins with a description of that zone and any history of the zone that was submitted.

Zone 1

Zone 1 is in the southernmost part of Alberta, with the U.S. border on the south, zone 2 on the north and British Columbia and Saskatchewan on the west and east, respectively. It has the largest expanse of prairie habitat, along with a portion of the southeastern slopes of the Rocky Mountains.

The 16 clubs in zone 1 are:
- Bow Island Fish and Game Association *
- Brooks and District Fish and Game Association
- Claresholm Fish and Game Association*
- Coaldale and District Fish and Game Association
- Foremost Fish and Game Association*
- Fort Macleod Fish and Game Association
- Hillcrest Fish and Game Association
- Lethbridge Fish and Game Association
- Magrath Fish and Game Association*
- Medicine Hat Fish and Game Association
- Picture Butte Fish and Game Association
- Porcupine Hills Wildlife Association
- Taber Fish and Game Association*
- Vauxhall Fish and Game Association
- Vulcan Fish and Game Association*
- Willow Valley Trophy Club
          * clubs that did not submit histories

Zone History

Zone 1 clubs came together for the following events and activities:

1962   first Merriam's turkey releases (see The Turkey Story)

1970   elk trap built in foothills and used for two winters by Fish and Wildlife Division

1977   extensive antelope feeding program

1980   clubs from Lethbridge, Fort Macleod, Claresholm, Vulcan, Picture Butte, purchased pheasant chicks for raising and releasing in the fall.

1986   the association of zone 1 clubs is formalized into the Southern Alberta Fish and Game Association as registered under the Society Act.

1987/90   fundraising and building of zone 1 conservation camp, McGillivray Creek Youth Camp.

1988   after two years of feeding wild turkeys by the Fort Macleod, Claresholm, Lethbridge and Willow Valley clubs at feeding stations built by the clubs, the Fish and Wildlife Division made two transplants of 15 birds each into wildlife management units 302 and 306.

1989   zone 1 donated $9,223 toward Porcupine Hills fire relief.

2000   zone 1 clubs Cardston, Lethbridge, Fort Macleod, Picture Butte and Coaldale took over pheasant releases during fall hunting season.

2006   above clubs now do spring hen releases to increase wild pheasant production.

Over the years, zone 1 has donated over $20,000 to the Alberta Fish and Game Wildlife Trust Fund.

Zone Directors:

Dave Hunt, 1966; Gerry Pittman, 1970; Bob Vair, 1976; Norm Ferguson, 1977-78; Horst Fauser, 1979-86; Dwayne Johnston, 1986-87; Norm Ferguson, 1989; Ron Pittman, 1990-92; Ross MacDonald, 1993-95; Gerry Pittman, 1995-96; Heinz Plontke, 1997-2005; Wayne Lowry, 2005.

COURTESY OF DUANE RADFORD

Ross McDonald, Horst Fauser, Myles Radford and Ron Pittman at ribbon-cutting ceremony at McGillivray Creek Youth Camp grand opening.

McGillivray Creek Youth Camp

In 1984 Ron Gladish, president of the AFGA, and the Hon. Don Sparrow, Minister of Forests, Lands and Wildlife agreed to give 10 acres of Crown land to each zone of the association to build an outdoor education camp for youth. Don Appleby, zone 5 director, and Horst Fauser, zone 1 director, took advantage of the offer. In zone 1, it took five years to select a site, raise the required funds, build and finally open the camp.

The first site selected was south of Cardston but had to be abandoned because of financial problems obtaining grants in that area. The second site at McGillivray Creek in the Crowsnest Pass was looked upon more favourably. A recreational lease was secured from the Alberta government. Funding was provided by the Alberta government $90,000; various fish and game clubs $5,400; National Sportsmen's Shows $13,000; donated equipment and materials $18,000; and over 20 zone club members donated countless volunteer hours to build and prepare the site.

At first tents were used to accommodate the students. Later, seven zone clubs built and donated seven cabins. Approximately 400 youths used the camp each year. The Alberta Hunter Education and Instructors' Association used the camp for five years.

Horst Fauser served as camp director for 15 years. In 2000 Ron Montgomery took over as camp director. In 2004, as a result of high insurance costs, the camp was turned over to the Crowsnest Pass Bible Camp for their outdoor programs. Zone 1 clubs continue to use the camp annually.

Programs available at the camp include: archery, fishing, canoeing, water safety, trap shooting, .22 rifle shooting, hiking, fitness, wilderness survival and winter camping.

COURTESY OF DUANE RADFORD

Myles Radford at the opening of McGillivray Creek Youth Camp.

The Turkey Story
by Horst Fauser

The following is the story of the role played by the AFGA in introducing Merriam's turkeys to the wild in southern Alberta. As a result of lobbying by the AFGA, the Government of Alberta released 21 Merriam's turkeys from South Dakota in the Cypress Hills, south and east of Medicine Hat in 1962. The birds initially did well in their new home; their population grew to 200 birds by 1965. However, limited habitat and severe winter conditions eventually reduced the population.

SUPPLIED

Merriam's turkey.

In 1967 the government moved 12 of the Cypress Hills turkeys to the Porcupine Hills, west of Claresholm. These were followed in 1973 by the release in the Porcupine Hills of 13 wild turkeys from Nebraska and 75 hatchery-raised birds from the Alberta government's Brooks (Wildlife Centre) pheasant hatchery.

There was also a release of hatchery-raised Merriam's turkeys along the Milk River, which was organized by the Milk River fish and game club, the Southern Alberta Outdoorsmen. About the same time, the Fort Macleod club handled a release of turkeys along the Oldman River.

The Lethbridge Fish and Game club donated $2,000 to the Alberta Fish and Wildlife Division in 1972 for further study of the various flocks of released turkeys. Over the years the wild turkeys in the Porcupine Hills took a liking to cattle feed that was put out by local ranchers during the winter months. One rancher didn't appreciate the turkeys chasing his cattle away from the feed and complained to the Fish and Wildlife Division. Such complaints resulted in Fish and Wildlife abandoning the turkey study in 1975. Fish and Wildlife actually tried to alleviate the turkey-cattle conflict by capturing 80 of the Porcupine Hills population and relocating them to the Brooks Wildlife Centre research facility.

COURTESY OF THE FISH AND WILDLIFE DIVISION

DUANE RADFORD

In 1982 Horst Fauser, a past president of the AFGA, approached Duane Radford, the Fish and Wildlife Division regional director for the Southern Region in Lethbridge, in regard to the status of the wild turkeys still remaining in the Porcupine Hills. Apparently there was no budget allocated for turkeys but it was agreed that feeder stations could be put in place to assist in the turkeys' survival over winter. It was felt that this would slowly bring the turkey population up to the point of establishing a hunting season. The feeders were built and provisioned by the clubs in Fort Macleod, Lethbridge, Willow Valley and Claresholm at a cost of about $500 per club during the winter of 1983-84.

With the help of all these AFGA clubs, the Porcupine Hills turkey population thrived. Fish and Wildlife agreed to the capture and release of some of the established population into Wildlife Management Units (WMUs) 302, 305 and 306. Five gobblers and 10 hens were released in each of the three new sites. Sixty birds were counted in WMU 302 the first year after the release. In 2005 the turkey populations were estimated to be 300 in WMU 302, 200 in the Cypress Hills, and over 300 in WMUs 305 and 306 (the south Porcupine Hills).

The turkey population continues to slowly expand. In 1991 a total of 50 turkey-hunting permits were available on a draw basis. In 2005 the number of hunting licences issued for turkeys reached 200. The Alberta wild Merriam's turkey population is well established and continues to expand. Not bad for a humble start of 12 birds in the Porcupine Hills in 1967.

COURTESY OF DUANE RADFORD

Second annual MLA novice pheasant hunting seminar, sponsored by the Brooks Fish and Game Association, 2005. The "Hunkey Dorey" station is set on a trap range where youth fire shotguns at clay pigeons from a rocking boat.

COURTESY OF DUANE RADFORD

Brooks Fish and Game Association signage.

COURTESY OF DUANE RADFORD

Second annual MLA novice pheasant hunting seminar, sponsored by the Brooks Fish and Game Association, 2005.

COURTESY OF THE AFGA

Brooks youth hunt.

COURTESY OF DUANE RADFORD

Second annual MLA novice pheasant hunting seminar, sponsored by the Brooks Fish and Game Association, 2005.

Club Histories of Zone 1

Brooks and District Fish and Game Association
1918-present

The Brooks area has been well blessed with fish and game. Early settlers of the area realized the importance of maintaining an abundant supply of big game, birds and fish to help provide food in times of need. To aid their cause, a number of interested people banded together to form the Eastern Irrigation District Fish and Game Association sometime in the early 20th century. This club later became the Brooks and District Fish and Game Association. One of the club's earliest projects was the introduction of Chinese ring-necked pheasants to the area.

Beginning about 1910, the Canadian Pacific Railway (CPR) built an irrigation system in the Brooks area in order to provide water for farmers in this very dry area. As a result, farmers were able to produce excellent crops, and in doing so also provided excellent

cover for wildlife. However, this switch in farming methods made the habitat less suitable for some of the native wildlife, such as sharptailed grouse and pinnated grouse.

To fill this void, the CPR, along with the Eastern Irrigation District Fish and Game Association, decided to introduce ring-necked pheasants to the area to see if they were a viable species. One hundred pheasant eggs were brought from California in 1925. The eggs were hatched at the CPR demonstration farm near Brooks, with the birds being raised and released on that site. Thanks to the great support of both time and money from Don Bark (superintendent of the CPR Irrigation Investigation Branch), Gus Griffin (superintendent of operations and maintenance, CPR Irrigation Eastern Section), Ralph Baird (Brooks district agriculturalist), Jack O'Brien (Brooks Hardware), the Williams brothers from Duchess, Dempster Havens from Patricia, and the Duke of Sutherland, the project achieved moderate success.

The Eastern Irrigation District Fish and Game Association was quite involved in the early years with the collection of pheasant eggs for the rearing station as well as the release of pheasants into the wild. The association also organized a number of training programs for bird dogs. These were greatly appreciated by the local dog owners. Crow and magpie derbies were held in various years in an attempt to reduce the destruction of game-bird nests by these predators.

Very little information is recorded about the Brooks Fish and Game Association during the period of 1950-71. Likewise, little information is available about the first Brooks Gun Club, although records indicate it was formed in 1918. However, in 1955 Bob Asher was instrumental in reviving this organization. The two clubs were brought together in 1971 to form the Brooks Fish and Game Association and Gun Club through the efforts of Cecil and Barbara Ray, Tom and Ev McLean, Gordon Anderberg, Don Anderberg, Bob Asher, Jack Orr, Ken Zorn, Ozzie Schalm, Ray Sako, Ray Cole, Jack Ressler, Don Swanson and several others.

Fishing derbies were also held in the area. People were very appreciative of Gus Griffin's persistence in having whitefish eggs introduced into the irrigation waters. This finally occurred in 1932 when he and a fisheries officer personally helped to scatter four to five million eggs in Lake Newell, resulting in an excellent fishery that to this day continues to support commercial and sport fishing.

The Brooks Fish and Game Association and Gun Club was very active during the 1970s, hosting fishing derbies for children, planting shelter for wildlife at the Louisiana #13 and Gun Club lakes, holding the annual trophy and awards nights with the accompanying wild game suppers, as well as attending the provincial fish and game conferences.

In the late 1970s and early 1980s, interest in the fish and game association dwindled so extensively that in 1982 the gun club and the fish and game club parted ways. As a result a new club known as the Brooks and District Fish and Game Association was incorporated.

Education
The club has actively promoted the safe handling and use of firearms, holding numerous firearms safety and hunter education courses, especially for young people. The club has sponsored numerous young people to attend the Southern Alberta Fish and Game Society Youth Conservation Camp in the Crowsnest Pass (McGillivray Creek). Shooting competitions, both competitive and fun, have been an important part of club activities.

Projects
Pheasant numbers have always been a concern to people in Brooks and the surrounding area. In the early years before sprinkler irrigation was introduced in the area, numerous patches of land could not be irrigated because the fields were not level enough. These areas were usually overgrown with wild vegetation, providing excellent cover for game-bird nesting sites. When sprinkler irrigation was introduced, these areas disappeared as farmers could now irrigate them. The result was reduced game-bird habitat and a corresponding reduction in the pheasant population.

Over the years, the various fish and game clubs of the area have helped to improve pheasant habitat in various ways. Much of the funding for these activities came from volunteer organizations involved in the Brooks Pheasant Festival, organized by the Brooks Pheasant Festival committee and the Brooks and District Fish and Game Association. The festival first began in 1988, and has raised approximately $400,000 for pheasant habitat projects within the County of Newell.

The club has also been very active in habitat development for other species of wildlife. Projects included helping plant thorny buffalo berry along the Loggerhead Shrike Trail (an abandoned CPR right-of-way), donating funds to the Alberta Prairie Conservation Action Plan to help conserve the biological diversity of the prairie and parkland of Alberta, tree planting on the numerous fish and game properties purchased with Brooks Pheasant Festival proceeds, aiding in fish stocking projects in the area, the placement of bales for goose nesting sites and placing discarded Christmas trees for trout habitat.

A "Use Respect" program was introduced in conjunction with the Eastern Irrigation District (EID) to allow hunters continued access to private EID land. Through this program, many large signs were placed at key access routes, and radio advertisements were broadcast encouraging hunters to respect the landowner and follow rules when entering private land. The club has also produced the video "Our Changing Land: The Prairie Landscape," showing how farmers can successfully run a farm operation while including the retention and even creation of wildlife habitat.

COURTESY OF DUANE RADFORD

Donna Martin, Lady Conservationist of the Year award recipient.

Annual Events

The annual wildlife dinner and awards night is a much-anticipated event each winter. Along with the excellent supper consisting of many varieties of wild game, annual awards are presented for the largest game-bird, big-game animal and fish of each species legally harvested during the previous seasons. Larry Busse has been instrumental in making the awards program very competitive and successful over the past several decades.

Club Awards

The Brooks and District Fish and Game Association has won the following the AFGA awards: The G.E. Stevens Memorial Award, promoting firearms safety; Outdoor Ethics Award, promoting hunter ethics; and the Guy Blake Memorial Award for wildlife habitat enhancement. The provincial government presented the club with the Order of The Bighorn Award for wildlife habitat enhancement.

Special People

The following people have won AFGA awards for their outstanding service: Donna Martin, Lady Conservationist of The Year; and Kelly Busse and Dennis Hindbo, Predator Trophy.

Coaldale and District Fish and Game Association
1968-present

The Coaldale and District Fish and Game Association was registered under the *Society's Act* in January 1968. The planning and registration for the club began in the early fall of 1967 under the guidance of Joe Balla, who was the club's first president. Founding members were Earl Foxhall, Buck Geldert, Frank Molnar, Jim McQuillan, Duncan Lloyd, Len Steinbrenner, George Begany, Edwin Wiebe, Robert Skiba, Harold Unger, George Murakami and Bob Mainzer. The founding objective of the club was, and remains today, conservation and protection of wildlife habitat.

The majority of the club's membership comes from Coaldale and area; however, supporters reside throughout the province. In 1969 the membership chairman registered 377 paid memberships, a number which has never again been achieved throughout its 39-year history. Membership numbers today range today between 50 and 100.

Education

Many of the club's efforts have been directed towards education, not only for its youth but for life-long learning for all. Countless conservation and hunter education and fishing education courses have been offered over the years by dedicated members. Most recently, members have been learning and becoming informed through the Internet.

Projects

The association's largest undertaking has been the construction of a 30- to 40-acre man-made water impoundment for rainbow trout fishing, Lake McQuillan. Adjacent to Lake McQuillan is the Indian Hill Campground and Recreation area. Again this large undertaking was only achieved through partnerships with the provincial government, County of Lethbridge and the St. Mary River Irrigation District.

Although the club's chief concern is the well-being of fish and wildlife, the organization has been involved in many community projects from raising funds for a sportsplex to annual duck-race activities for the food bank. Most recently, the club has participated with the Family Day committee to hold "go fish" opportunities for youngsters and pellet gun target shooting for over 300 children. Members of the club are developing indoor ranges for youth archery and pellet gun shooting. It is hoped this will increase youth membership. Despite many club activities, a declining membership remains a concern.

Annual Events

On a culinary note, the annual wild game dinners prepared by a Lethbridge College food instructor with the help of his family are worth driving miles and miles for.

Fort Macleod Fish and Game Association
1951-present

It was quite a night, on May 29, 1951, when 125 of the 158 newly signed up members of the fledgling Fort Macleod Fish and Game Association came together to hold their organizational meeting in the Independent Order of Odd Fellows Hall in Fort Macleod. Dignitaries included: William C. Fisher, Q.C., president of Ducks Unlimited Canada and past president of the Calgary Fish and Game Association, and George Spargo, secretary of the AFGA and former director of fisheries for the Alberta Fish and Wildlife Division. Others present included Dick Osterberg, vice president of the AFGA, Bill Masson, president of Lethbridge Fish and Game Association and O.B. Eritsland, chairman of that club's publicity committee. Mayor A.G. Swinarton welcomed the members and guests.

Officers elected that evening included Harry Winchcombe, president; A.A. Neddow, vice president; Dr. R.L. Falconer, secretary; John S. Collins, treasurer; and Joe McNab, Gordon Stewart and Charlie Miller, executive members-at-large.

SUPPLIED

Heinz Plontke and Julius Moltzahn taken in front of antler display at the Fort MacLeod Fish and Game awards night.

Re-roofing camp kitchen at Fort MacLeod fish and game park.

Unfortunately, the early records of this club have been lost. However, it is known that A.A. Neddow and Dr. Falconer were instrumental in keeping the club active in the formative years. The club became inactive around 1957. In 1958 the club was reactivated with Gary O'Sullivan as president and Julius Moltzahn as secretary treasurer. The group flourished for a few years with meetings held in the local Java Shop banquet room.

On or about Nov. 23, 1959 the Fort Macleod Fish and Game Association was awarded a trophy for the largest number of crows and magpies destroyed; 14,793 pairs of crow and magpie feet were turned in, the provincial record for the greatest number of crows and magpies destroyed at the time.

As a result of executive members working out of town or moving away, the club disbanded in 1960. However, in 1968 the club became active again and has continued up to 2007. Annual membership exceeded 300 people during the next 10 years. Through the generosity of local businesses and individuals, a grand display of trophies was awarded to successful sportsmen and photographers at the annual trophy night, held at the beginning of each year.

Education

During the 1970s the club sponsored a chapter of the Junior Forest Wardens, a very active youth group in the outdoors. Club members presented hunter education courses, and the club sponsored students to attend conservation training camps and the provincial fish and game association conference each year.

Projects

In 1968 the club started negotiations with the provincial government to establish a Fort Macleod Fish and Game Association park. The club obtained a lease in 1970 for approximately 33 acres of land along the Oldman River across from the golf course. A group of volunteers and students (hired through a government grant) built fences, and installed or built playground equipment, horseshoe pits, a camp kitchen, outhouses, signs and picnic tables. The park is used by a variety of people throughout the summer for family reunions, church picnics or just to enjoy the outdoors and wildlife that frequent the area.

In the early 1970s the club financed and released two flocks of wild turkeys along the Waterton River under the supervision of the Alberta Fish and Wildlife Division. The club was also involved in the raising and releasing of pheasants in the area; the building of artificial goose nests on Pinder Lake and along the Oldman River; and the building and placing of bluebird houses.

Annual Events

A pioneer picnic and fish derby was held each July during the 1970s and early '80s, for anyone age 65 or older. The event was held at the Beauvais Lake and included fishing, boating and lawn games.

Special People

Some of the club's most active members over the years include: Tenus VanTol, Ed Todd, Bob Moses, Elmer Driver, Gene Koopman, James Vandervalk, Bill Havinga, Pat Wharton, Noel Doherty, Joe Tarnes, Norma VanTol, Brenda Hartness, Larry Zoeteman, Mike and Gloria Flynn, Ken Hedley and Julius Moltzahn.

Hillcrest Fish and Game Protective Association
1924-present

The Hillcrest Fish and Game Protective Association began in 1924. The first president was Alex Warner, and the vice president was Jack Stubbs. Some of the significant members of the club over the years include David Jones, Frank Sickoff, Eli Hurtak, Godfrey Hungar, Ross McDonald and Earl Scott.

The club presently has 140 members. The membership peaked in 1987 at 150 members. The club has a clubhouse in Hillcrest Mines, and sends youth members to the zone 1 McGillivray Creek Youth Camp for outdoor education and firearm training.

Projects

From 1945-60, the club raised pheasants for the provincial stocking program. It has collected hides for the AFGA provincial hide collection program for 15 years. The club has installed wildlife protection signs along roads and highways, and has been involved in the long-term care of Burmis Lake and local area streams and rivers. As well it has been involved in mountain goat relocations, and helped to build bridges, roads and cabins at the zone 1 youth camp.

The club was actively involved in the West Castle ski hill development hearing, and hearings on Special Places 2000 and a Chevron well-site at Bob Creek.

Annual Events

On the first Saturday of each February the club holds a trophy measuring day. A bingo and smoker are held on the second Saturday in February. All are well attended by members and the general public.

COURTESY OF THE LETHBRIDGE FISH AND GAME ASSOCIATION

Heinz Plontke (L) and George Zuffa releasing pheasants at the annual Lethbridge Fish and Game Association pheasant release.

COURTESY OF DUANE RADFORD

Glen Gordon (L), Horst Fauser, Stella and Norm Ferguson, 1986.

Lethbridge Fish and Game Association
1923-present

The Lethbridge Fish and Game Association was founded by a small group of dedicated sportsmen who came together to address concerns about fish, game and various predators. Unfortunately, the keeping of records and reports was not a priority. However, the few early records that do exist indicate that Mr. George Stacey served as the club's first president in 1923.

The club went through many name changes from the Lethbridge District Fish and Game Protective Association to the Lethbridge and District Fish and Game Association and since 1968 has been registered as the Lethbridge Fish and Game Association. By 1959, the club became the second largest fish and game club in Western Canada with a membership of about 1,800.

Projects
- The club lobbied and fought hard to remove domestic livestock from Waterton Lakes National Park.
- In January of 1965, a severe winter storm left wildlife in the area near the point of starvation. The club launched the "Save the Birds" drive where cash, grain and equipment were donated to feed starving pheasants. Also, large areas of snow were cleared in fields and efforts were made to feed antelope and deer.
- Artificial nesting sites and tree planting at Rush Lake.
- Assisted the Fish and Wildlife Division with the Merriam's wild turkey transplant, including maintaining feeding stations.
- Pheasant raise and release program.
- Annual deer classification survey for the Alberta Fish and Wildlife Division.
- Installed "Use Respect" signs in rural areas where this program was used to encourage better landowner/outdoorsmen relationships.
- Canadian Pacific Railroad Reservoir lake habitat project, 332 acres.

COURTESY OF DUANE RADFORD

Horst Fauser (L) and Bruce Thomas.

- Donation of the Lethbridge Fish and Game Association Bob Vair Memorial Scholarship to a second-year student in the Renewable Resource Management program at Lethbridge Community College.
- Junior Forest Wardens began in 1967 under the direction of Bill Nummi.
- Work began in 1958 to develop the Lethbridge Fish and Game Range on land in north Lethbridge, donated by Mr. J.A. Jarvie. A contract with the City of Lethbridge transferred the original range site to the City for present land location in 1988. Today, the Lethbridge Fish and Game Range is considered one of the best ranges in Western Canada.
- In 2001 the club contributed $7,500 to the Alberta Conservation Association for gravel to put walleye spawning beds in the Milk River Ridge Reservoir.

Annual Events

In the early years the club's banquets were wild-game suppers. The first annual banquet was held on March 24, 1932 at the Marquis Hotel. In 1958, the club started holding bingo nights with proceeds going to the club's building fund. Thousands of dollars were raised.

Special People

Over the years, the club has had many active members, one of the most outspoken being Glen Michelson, who served as the political action committee chair for over 20 years and was still active at age 83 in 2007. Mr. Michelson wrote hundreds of letters on behalf of the Lethbridge Fish and Game Association on issues such as game farming, the Gun Control Bill C-68, the closure of the Brooks pheasant hatchery and its privatization, chronic wasting disease, cervid hunt farms, the Stirling Lake Wetland for Tomorrow project (now Michelson's Marsh named in honour of Glen and his late brother, Ralph's family), lack of funds for the Fish and Wildlife Division and budget cutbacks. He was presented with a life membership in February 2000 and won the Archie Hogg Memorial Trophy for the best environmental publicity program in 1998 and again in 2002 as a long-time lobbyist for the AFGA concerns.

Past presidents of the club include George Stacey, 1923; Judge Shepherd, 1926; D.R. Yates, 1927; George Rowe, 1928-29; George Rowe, 1932; L.E. Fairbairn, 1933; George Stacey, 1934; Gelder, 1935; Bob Routledge, 1936; J. Wiebe, 1938; W.P. Davidson, 1942; Bob Routledge, 1943-44; Tom Evans, 1945-46; R. Weiler, 1947; Erle Carr, 1948-49; Tom Evans, 1950; R. Spenser, 1951-52; W.D. Geldert, 1953; Harry Baalim, 1954; Richard "Dick" Osterberg, 1955-57; W. "Bill" Masson, 1958-59; Ken Watts, due to ill health, replaced by John Bobinec, 1960; Dave Hunt, 1961-63; Matt Brooker, 1964-65; Matt Brooker/John McGee, 1966; John McGee, 1967; John McGee/E. Landry, 1968; E. "Frenchy" Landry, 1969-70; Gerry Pittman, 1971-72; Larry Holland, 1973; Bob Vair, 1974-76; Bob Vair/Norm Ferguson, 1977-78; Norm Ferguson, 1979-80; Ron Goodwin, 1981-85; Rollie Stewart, 1986-87; Harold Janecke, 1988-89; Frank Johnston, 1990-91; Chet Kovacs, 1992; Chet Kovacs/Heinz Plontke, 1993-95; Wayne Heighington, 1996-97; Debbie (nee Plontke) Clarke, 1998-99; Ron Pittman/Matt Zazula, 2000; Matt Zazula, 2001-03; Jim Clarke, 2004; Wayne Heighington, 2005; Jack Stewart, 2006; Brian Dingreville, 2007.

COURTESY OF DUANE RADFORD

Shirley and Heinz Plontke.

Medicine Hat Fish and Game Association
1960s-present

The Medicine Hat Fish and Game Association came into being in the mid-1960s according to the club records that remain after a fire destroyed the rest. The club is located within the city of Medicine Hat, tucked away in the southeast corner of the province. Membership numbers have varied over the years, probably averaging over 100; numbers are currently in excess of 100.

Projects

While the club has been involved in many projects in the past, it is currently focused on habitat projects and the gathering of funds necessary to finance these projects. The Sauder Project involves establishing food sources (food-bearing trees) to encourage the return of pheasants to this area. The club provided 25 percent of the funding toward the purchase of the Peigan Creek section of land acquired under the AFGA Wildlife Trust Fund. This is ideal property for upland birds and other wildlife, with plenty of food sources, cover and water. The club is the steward of this property.

The Medicine Hat Fish and Game Association was engaged in the pheasant-raising program and built several pens with attached brooder facilities to raise and release the pheasants in the area. The pens were built on the basis of a five-year agreement with the land owner, so at the end of the five-year term, the pens would automatically become the property of the landowner.

COURTESY OF GLEN MICHELSON

Glen Michelson with mule deer, 1996.

COURTESY OF THE AFGA

Ron Pittman (L) and Duane Radford, Picture Butte trophy night, 1985.

and Adrian Jalbert from Dunmore had access to a number of used washing machines, the tubs from which made excellent nest structures. They stockpiled over 100 tubs of all makes and models for Canada geese nesting platforms.

Another club project was bluebird house construction and installation. Barry Plante advised the club that bluebirds were in trouble. Bluebirds are cavity nesters and good nesting sites were becoming harder to find, hence a decrease in the bluebird population. Barry and Adrian Jalbert donated their time, tools and supplies to build the boxes out of used materials. Numerous members and non-members service the boxes each year. Servicing consists of cleaning out the boxes and repairing them if necessary. The club has at least 800 boxes in operation.

In 1966 Don Boll captured Hank Iwanicki's interest in providing nests for wild Canada geese. The first nests were barrels cut in half and nailed to trees along the South Saskatchewan River. The nests were very popular with the geese, and every nest was used every year. This prompted further installations. One year, Hank

The Medicine Hat Fish and Game Association decided not to continue expanding the goose and bluebird nesting projects any further. However, those boxes already in place will be maintained.

Twenty-six Merriam's turkey chicks were purchased in 2005 and raised by Dennis Reese on his farm south of the Cypress Hills on Thelma Creek. Sixteen turkeys were retained by Dennis Reese and 10 birds were given to P.A. Yeast, who has property beside the Reese farm. The plan was to release the birds at two different

Medicine Hat club signage.

COURTESY OF DUANE RADFORD

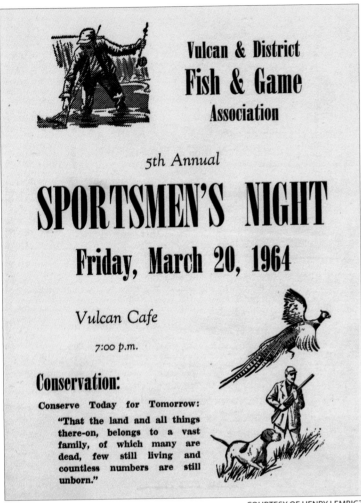

Vulcan & District Fish & Game Association

5th Annual

SPORTSMEN'S NIGHT

Friday, March 20, 1964

Vulcan Cafe

7:00 p.m.

Conservation:

Conserve Today for Tomorrow:

"That the land and all things there-on, belongs to a vast family, of which many are dead, few still living and countless numbers are still unborn."

COURTESY OF HENRY LEMBICZ

From the Vulcan Fish and Game Association.

sites. Several birds disappeared after release and only a few are left. However, the remaining birds seem to be predator wise, so another attempt at raising and releasing is being considered.

Annual Events

The club has an annual awards day, which is usually held in the Cypress Centre, at the exhibition grounds. The day consists of a silent auction of merchandise donated by local merchants. Antlers are scored and winners of the various categories determined. Deb Kopp has spearheaded the operation, while Merv Kopperud has run the silent auction for many years. This event makes about $3,500 profit each year for the club, providing the funding necessary for the general operation of the club. Volunteers provide many hours of their time to make the event a success, including Kane Brandt, Dr. Brian Vest, Howard Gehring, Ted Bowyer, Alf Baldwin, Charles Hellman, Duncan Baldie, Merle Westergreen and Walter Eisenlohr.

The club has operated a casino for several years. The two-day event makes a profit of $21,000-$23,000 every year. The casino funds are earmarked for the club's wildlife habitat projects. Club volunteers for the casino have been Boyne Lewis, Ted Bowyer, Deb Kopp, Walter Eisenlohr, James Foy, Keith Freeman, Howard Gehring, Hank Iwanicki, Colin Jackson, Jim Patrich, Greg Dyck, Rob Young, Charlie Hellman and Wayne Dola.

Picture Butte Fish and Game Association
1952-present

The club was started in 1952 by a few dedicated people who saw the need to develop some policies to conserve and enhance the fish and wildlife of the area while maintaining the right to enjoy and use those resources.

By 1955, with Buck Geldert as president, the club expanded to 100 members and officially became the Piyami Fish and Game Club. Piyami is an aboriginal word that means "steps in the embankment," referring to a prominent coulee near Picture Butte, now known as 12 Mile Coulee.

In the late 1950s the club had an unheard-of membership of 500, with membership fees only $1. The main interest of the club at this time was the lack of fishing opportunities in the area. To address the concern, Takas Pond was stocked with rainbow trout. When this proved to be unsuccessful, the club successfully lobbied for the reservoir behind Lehto's Dam to be stocked with trout. For many years this was an ongoing project and provided great sport fishing and entertainment for all the local population.

In 1961 the club joined the Southern Alberta Fish and Game Council in order to become more involved with fish and wildlife concerns in the area. By 1968 the council disbanded and the club became associated with the AFGA and a member of zone 1 of that association.

Some time in the 1950s the club started an archery division and in the following years counted among its membership some champion archers of Alberta as well as western Canada.

Projects

By the 1970s pheasants became the major concern in the area. To help increase the number of these birds, the club built its first pheasant-rearing pen near Diamond City. It was soon discovered that this large pen did not work well so the club decided to build smaller "fly away" pens around the area. These worked very well and the project continued for many years and helped reintroduce pheasants to this area.

In 1976 the club started a project to address the shortage of geese in the province. Goose nesting sites were built wherever suitable habitat was found.

In the 1980s, the controversial debates and hearings over the proposed Oldman River Dam placed much stress on the 400-strong membership. The club was opposed to the provincial AFGA position against the dam. The club, along with the rest of zone 1, eventually convinced the provincial association to change its stance, and the club believes it was instrumental in getting the proposed dam approved. This episode illustrates how members can come together to influence important decisions in Edmonton.

In 1985 the club purchased the old Picture Butte curling rink for a clubhouse. After raising much money and putting in many hours and days of hard work, an inside archery range was constructed, believed to be one of the best and longest (45-plus yards) in the

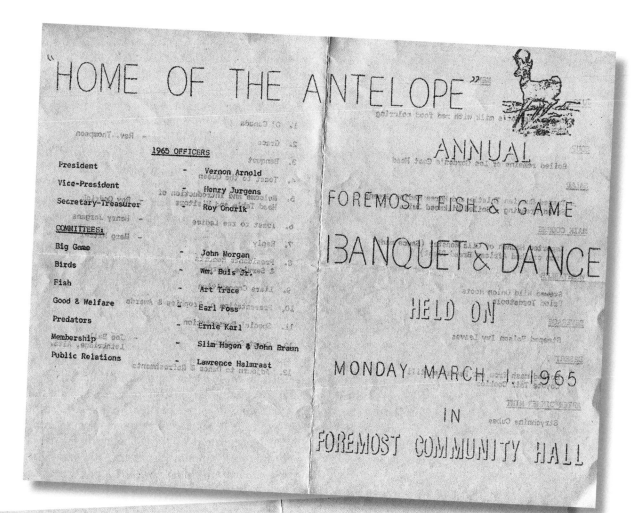

"HOME OF THE ANTELOPE"

1965 OFFICERS

President	-	Vernon Arnold
Vice-President	-	Henry Jurgens
Secretary-Treasurer	-	Roy Ondrik

COMMITTEES:

Big Game	-	John Morgan
Birds	-	Wm. Buis Jr.
Fish	-	Art Trace
Good & Welfare	-	Earl Foss
Predators	-	Ernie Karl
Membership	-	Slim Hagen & John Braun
Public Relations	-	Lawrence Halmrast

ANNUAL

FOREMOST FISH & GAME

BANQUET & DANCE

HELD ON

MONDAY MARCH 1. 1965

IN

FOREMOST COMMUNITY HALL

MENU

JUICE

Curdled Marmot's milk with red food coloring added

SOUP

Boiled remains of Les Gordon's Goat Head

SALAD

Tossed Russian Thistle and Horse Radish Greens - Salad Dressing - Boiled Milkweed Juice

MAIN COURSE

Imported Haunch of Gila Monster (Sauce made from crushed African Bread Plant)

VEGETABLES

Stewed Wild Onion Roots
Fried Toadstools

BEVERAGE

Steeped Poison Ivy Leaves

DESERT

Boiled mash from our Favorite Still
Coyote Tail Cookies

AFTER DINNER MINT

Strychnine Cubes

1.	O' Canada	
2.	Grace	- Rev. Thompson
3.	Banquet	
4.	Toast to the Queen	
5.	Welcome and Introduction of Head Table and Visitors	- Roy Ondrick
6.	Toast to the Ladies	- Henry Jergans
7.	Reply	- Marg Mitzel
8.	Presidents Remarks & Service Awards	
9.	Liars Competition	
10.	Presentation of Trophies & Awards	
11.	Special Presentation	
12.	Guest Speaker	- Joe Balla Lethbridge, Alta.
13.	Adjourn to Dance & Refreshments	

country. The building also provides a place to hold meetings and to teach various courses, such as hunter training, big-game measuring, boating safety, fly tying, and firearms safety.

The club sponsors a Junior Archery Club which currently boasts a membership of 70-plus young people who are instructed about the finer points of archery by certified coaches. The Picture Butte Fish and Game Association also has a Senior Archery Club with a membership of over 40. Between the two clubs the building is used at least three nights a week. The lanes are also used by the local schools and various other clubs, such as scouts.

Annual Events

In 1976 the club started its wild game supper and trophy night. It was an instant success and is still going strong today—tickets are sold-out every year. The club hosts an annual Family Fishing Day at Butte Lake that has proved to be very successful.

Porcupine Hills Wildlife Association
1939-present

The origin of the Porcupine Hills Wildlife Association can be traced back to June 1939 when the Nanton Rifle Club decided that a local chapter of the AFGA was needed to address some of the outdoor needs and issues in the Nanton area.

The Nanton Fish and Game Club was formed in June 1939 with the following executive: J.C. Hiebert, president; C.R. Miller, vice president; R.V. Hallet, secretary treasurer; J.D. Hayden, big-game chair; P.C. Loree, game-bird chair; J.T. Foster, songbird chair; Trond Berger, game-fish chair; and H.C. Armstrong, gun club chair.

The club remained active until the mid-1950s when it went into a period of "hibernation." In the fall of 1964, under the leadership of Pat Bradley, the club was reactivated with Pat elected as president and Ken Eld elected as secretary treasurer.

In 1977 the Nanton Fish and Game Club changed its name to the Porcupine Hills Wildlife Association, a name suggested by Bill Watt. That is the name that remains today.

Education

The association has been sending two to three young people each summer to the zone 1 Junior Conservation Camp at McGillivray Creek, north of Coleman. The camp has been operated by zone 1 of the AFGA since 1990.

Projects

One of the popular activities in the early years was the collection of crow and magpie eggs and legs, for which a bounty was paid.

In the 1970s and '80s the club put a lot of effort into a pheasant raise-and-release program, where young chicks were purchased and raised by members. In the early years, releases were concentrated in the Nanton/Mosquito Creek area and west of Nanton on land owned by the Chattaways and Scarlets.

The association was also involved in a major goose-nesting project on Silver Lake, east of Connamara in the 1970s. The project

COURTESY OF TRAVEL ALBERTA

An alert squirrel perches in a tree, on the lookout for food and predators.

was largely financed by donations of funds from George Reel and gravel from Raffins. Twenty-eight sites were created on the lake, which included tires lined with flax straw. Many successful broods were raised during this time as long as the lake had water.

When the Chain-of-Lakes [Chain Lakes Reservoir] was being developed, the club lobbied long and hard to have the area designated a provincial park. The result was Chain Lakes Provincial Park, which included a stocked children's pond as lobbied by the club. It is at this park that the club held several fishing derbies and ensured young people were always involved.

When sucker fish were becoming a problem on North Willow Creek, the club, in conjunction with the Stan Wilson family, created a trap on the creek. This trap resulted in the demise of thousands of suckers going upstream to spawn. The fish were hauled onto the grasslands to be used as fertilizer.

Another fishing project was the stocking of trout in the Arie Wannop pond southeast of Nanton. Many a young angler had their first fishing success at this pond, leaving with big smiles on their faces.

Gun enthusiasts in the association organized many gun shows at the Community Centre. As well, the association was very active in lobbying against the federal Gun Control Bill C-68, 1995) and the mandatory gun registration included in that legislation. Letters were sent to the government and the association joined forces with other concerned action groups to gather funds and attempt to defeat the bill. Unfortunately, the bill passed parliament, including the registration of all firearms. As predicted, the registration system has since proven to be a total boondoggle, neither reducing crime nor being an effective use of taxpayers' money.

In 1994 the area was experiencing a cougar problem. These large cats were creating a major concern in the west country. The club took the lead and facilitated a meeting between government officials and landowners, resulting in action within the year to assist in resolving these concerns.

The club works with other AFGA clubs to protect critical fish and wildlife habitat throughout Alberta through the AFGA Wildlife Trust Fund. The Porcupine Hills Wildlife Association has contributed several thousand dollars to this fund over the years.

With the interest of the landowner, Harry Dwelle, and the leadership of Irv Gerbrandt, the club has developed a proposal and submitted it to the Alberta Department of Transportation to reclaim Harry Dwelle's gravel pit when the Department of Transportation is finished with it. The club proposes to help reclaim the pit by creating a fishing pond and a small wildlife park.

Annual Events

In 1995 the association began its annual Wolves for Supper evening where landowners and association members get together for a meal and to share information and concerns. Biologists and other informative speakers make presentations about current issues. The association also hosts an annual trophy night to recognize the accomplishments of its members.

Vauxhall and District Fish and Game Association
1963-1967
A personal memoir by Dennis Grover

I became a member of this club in 1963. Membership was about 40 at that time, but had doubled by the time I left the community in 1967. The district encompassed the communities of Hays, Grantham, Retlaw, Enchant and Circle Hill. Soon after I joined the club, past president Jeff Lickiss persuaded me to accept the position of secretary treasurer, which had become vacant. Other members of the executive committee included Bauke Braak, Jeff Lickiss, Wayne Anderson and Jim Garrett.

Finances were a chronic concern. The annual membership fee was $1.25. The biggest bite from this fee was the AFGA affiliation dues. Rent for the Masonic Hall was $8 and meeting notices were rarely sent. We believed that in a community where virtually every man and boy hunted, the membership should have been several hundred. However, memberships were a hard sell. In some cases the $1.25 was an issue. People I had known for years would refuse to join because it was an organization they knew nothing about but more frequently they refused because "you guys never do anything."

The welfare of our members and ultimately our own fortunes were never forgotten. A box of 20 rifle cartridges cost the better part of a day's pay and most of us could ill afford to shoot centre-fires at all. To help his fellow members, Jeff Lickiss let it be known that he would allow members to use his reloading equipment and provide assistance where needed. Over the years dozens of Vauxhall Fish and Game members were introduced to reloading via the Jeff Lickiss apprenticeship program. Jeff worked out a deal with Hoyts Hardware in Lethbridge, which included Norm Ferguson of the Lethbridge Fish and Game Association, to get a 10 percent discount on fish and game club purchases of reloading components.

Aside from membership and finances, we faced the same issues that fish and game clubs face today. One such issue was the proposed introduction of private pheasant-hunting preserves. The Social Credit government of the day was determined to pass this legislation, the thrust of their argument being that pheasants were an introduced species only marginally suited to our climate and that privatization would have no impact on native species. We argued if hunting preserves became a reality, we could expect to see other species of wildlife privatized within a generation. So we fought it to the best of our abilities. We were able to convince our MLA, Ray Speaker, to vote against the legislation. However, private so-called "pheasant shooting grounds" were allowed in the *Wildlife Act* of 1970; these eventually led to the current private game-bird shooting grounds where other types of game-birds are also hunted.

The club pretty much functioned autonomously as far as wildlife issues were concerned. If it affected us we became involved. If not, there were other things to occupy our energies. Occasionally there would be a concern important enough to take to the AFGA conference in the form of a resolution. However, president Braak advised that in the conferences he had attended, resolutions important to southern Alberta hunters were rarely discussed and were frequently dismissed as having only limited relevance.

As a result, we began to scrutinize the AFGA in a more critical light. Disaffiliation with the AFGA was discussed. Eventually, a meeting with Lethbridge Fish and Game Association president, Joe Balla, convinced the Vauxhall executive to stay in the AFGA but help him form the Southern Alberta Fish and Game Council with the objective of dealing effectively (independently of the AFGA if necessary) with southern Alberta issues. This was done and Joe eventually became president of the AFGA.

Other issues included fighting the registration of certain "restrictive firearms" and the prohibition of others, feeding wild pheasants through a difficult winter, and the threat of Inter-basin transfer of water.

Like most clubs, the executive acquired a nucleus of supporters that it came to depend upon, including Max Wendorf, Flory, Roy and Frank Unser, George Forchuk, Bob Waddle and Harold Skretting. The two sporting-goods dealers in the community were both members: Merv Nattress, the town mayor and proprietor of Merv's Clothing and Sporting Goods, and past president Norm Erskine owned the Marshall Wells store. Norm made raffle prizes available at his cost. Marshall Wells kept a good stock of firearms and ammunition. Norm had more than a passing interest in firearms and would go to considerable lengths to obtain gun parts for those who needed them. When the club became involved with pheasant feeding, Corona Hotel owner John Kubasek wrote us a cheque and advised that we should let him know if the amount proved inadequate.

COURTESY OF DON MEREDITH

Trophy measuring at Willow Valley trophy day, 2007.

Willow Valley Trophy Club
1949-present

One of the many reasons people come together to organize a fish and game club is to recognize each other for taking the best fish and game trophies during the year. It is one thing to sit around a table or campfire and tell your stories to friends and acquaintances and quite another to actually have your fish or game trophy officially measured and recognized by your peers. Such recognition was the main reason the Willow Valley Trophy Club came into being.

Back in 1949, a number of ranchers in the Willow Valley area (about 30 miles northwest of Pincher Creek) were sitting around a puffing wood stove, telling stories about their hunting experiences, when Wilbur Pharis and Stan Webber suggested they should organize a trophy club with competitions so "the boys will be able to prove the stories they tell." The idea was an instant hit, and it wasn't long before an organizing meeting was held and work began to establish the first competition. The club sold 69 memberships that first year. Club membership in 2006 was 493.

Anyone may join the Willow Valley Trophy Club, but a member must be a resident of Alberta to compete for trophies in the annual big-game and fish competitions which take place each January at the Willow Valley trophy day. From 1949 to 2006, a total of 5,281 prizes have been awarded for big-game, fish and bird trophies, and photography. Big-game categories include mule deer, white-tailed deer, elk, moose, bighorn sheep, mountain goat, cougar, black bear and grizzly bear. Fish categories include Mackinaw lake trout, brown trout, cutthroat trout, northern pike, rocky mountain whitefish, rainbow trout from river/stream, rainbow trout from lake, and walleye. Bird categories include wild turkey, pheasant, Canada goose, ducks, blue grouse, sharptailed grouse, spruce grouse, ruffed grouse and grey [Hungarian] partridge. The photography competition includes categories for wildlife, scenery, and sportsmen and outdoors women in the field.

COURTESY OF DON MEREDITH

Willow Valley trophy day, 2007.

For big game, the club follows the scoring rules laid out by the Boone and Crockett Club of the United States, one of the oldest conservation organizations in North America. When the Boone and Crockett Club introduced a new system in 1953 to score big-game trophies, the late George Browne of Seebe, who was on the Boone and Crockett scoring committee, trained several Willow Valley Trophy Club members in the scoring system. As a result, the members were accepted as official Boone and Crockett measurers in Alberta and many more have since qualified.

From 1954-94, the club qualified 385 big-game trophies for the Boone and Crockett Club's book, *Records of North American Big Game*, an average of more than nine trophies a year. Since 1994, the club has provided the completed Boone and Crockett Club scoring forms to owners of qualifying heads and they have sent them to the Boone and Crockett Club head office. As the annual trophy day steadily grew in popularity, the club required larger and larger venues. The 1949 trophy day was held at the Willow Valley School; from 1950-61 it was held in the Lundbreck Hall; and from 1962-82 at the Lundbreck Community School. Since then, trophy day has been held at the Pincher Creek Community Hall. Attendance at each event over the last 10 years has consistently approached or exceeded 1,000 people.

Willow Valley trophy day is always held the second Saturday in January. Awards are given for top-ranking current entries (animals taken the previous year) in each category, as well as the Trophy Day Challenge for the largest head present that day for each category, pitting older heads against current heads from members or from non-members who have purchased a membership for the new year.

The names of the winners of each category and species are placed on plaques that are displayed at each trophy day. As well, the winners during the club's first 49 years were listed in the *Willow Valley Trophy Club Book of Records, 50th Anniversary* (1999).

Other projects of the Willow Valley Trophy Club are hunter safety training and wildlife surveys. Gary Hackler, who took over hunter training in 1970, still holds classes, qualifying 25 members in 2006. In June, an annual target shoot is held.

Special People

In 2006 the club membership included five life members: John Sekella, Hilton Pharis, Tenus Van Tol, Russ Rowledge and Charlie Price. The club is pleased to enjoy the company of four charter members: John Sekella, Hilton Pharis, Joe Kubasek and William Hucik. Over the last year, the club was saddened to have lost three charter members: Ralph Michalsky, Jim Price, and Steve Sekella. As a result, the theme for the 58th Willow Valley trophy day, held on Jan. 13, 2007, was "Senior Sportsmen of Yesteryear."

Presidents of the Willow Valley Trophy Club include: Stan Webber, 1949-52; Hilton Pharis, 1953-56; Stan Webber, 1957-59; John Sekella, 1960-61; Stan Webber, 1962-65; John Sekella, 1966-67; Hilton Pharis, 1968-69; Dave Glen, 1970-71; Jack Dezall, 1972-75; Terry Webber, 1976; Ted Smith, 1977-80; Jack Reedman, 1981-82; Dennis Olson, 1983-84; Neil McKellar, 1985; Jack Reedman, 1986-88; Gene Earl, 1989-90; George Reynolds, 1991-92; Rick Evano, 1993-97; John Sekella, 1998; Tenus Van Tol, 1999-2000; Paul Erickson, 2001-02; Wayne Lowery, 2003-04; Keith Smythe, 2005-06; Paul Erickson, 2007.

Bull moose.

COURTESY OF DON MEREDITH

Zone 2

Zone 2 covers an area of southern Alberta from British Columbia to Saskatchewan, north of zone 1 and south of zone 3, including the City of Calgary. Although it includes some prairie landscape, it is largely a transition area from the southern prairie to the parkland. Its eastern slopes of the Rocky Mountains have some of the finest elk and sheep habitat in Alberta.

The eight clubs in zone 2 are:
- Big Horns Club of Standard *
- Calgary Fish and Game Association
- Drumheller and District Fish and Game Association *
- High River Fish and Game Association
- Hussar Fish and Game Club *
- Okotoks and District Fish and Game Association *
- Sarcee Fish and Game Association
- Wheatland Conservation and Wildlife Association
    * clubs that did not submit histories

Club Histories of Zone 2

Calgary Fish and Game Association
1908-2007 (by David Finch, © CFGA 2008)

Calgarians were certainly leaders in the fish and game preservation in Alberta in the early years. According to assistant history professor George Colpitts of the University of Calgary, prominent Calgarian Robert A. Darker deserves credit for starting the first fish and game association in Calgary in 1908. And it appears Darker intended it to be the founding member of a provincial association too.

Darker, an immigrant from Ireland via Quebec, landed in Calgary in 1902 and quickly contributed his considerable organizational skills to the outdoor community. He was described as "seven feet of muscular manhood" in a magazine article.

Who better to call interested parties together in 1907 in Calgary for a three-day meeting? Harrison Young, a Department of Marine and Fisheries inspector, attended the event and reported that it was "composed of all the best settlers in the country and principal men of the towns and villages."

Indeed, though this impressive meeting brought together the sporting types in southern Alberta, they had already been meeting independently for some time. Eighty men attended this founding gathering of the Alberta Fish and Game Protective Association, hosted by the Calgarians who created their own Calgary Fish and Game Protective Association (CFGPA) in 1908 and then provided leadership for a provincial association for twenty years before the founding meeting of the AFGA was held during the Stampede in July 1928.

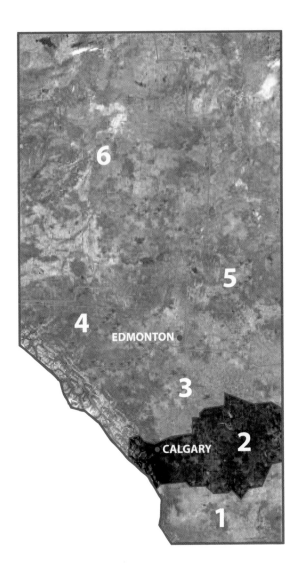

The provincial Minister of Agriculture attended the Calgary meetings and took away the group's suggestions for changes to the Alberta government's game regulations. Issues of the day included changes to some regulations and the minister's actions helped establish the relationship between lawmakers and the fish-and-game community.

But the Calgary group did not sit around to see what was going to happen provincially. Founding members Austin de B. Winter, Fred Green and George Wood had privately financed a release of 15 pair of Virginia quail in 1907.

The infamous winter blizzard of 1907 that killed so many cattle also wiped out the CFGPA's first release of game birds. Henry Stelfox, a recent arrival to the province who became an important CFGPA leader, experienced the harsh conditions on a ranch southwest of Calgary and saw "snow drifted up over fences."

The Calgary group soldiered on. When Darker retired as the CFGPA's first president in 1909, he summarized the accomplishments of the group that was also known as the Calgary branch of the AGFPA. He thanked other founding members including Dr. Sisley, Mr. Green, Mr. de B. Winter and Mr. Adams; the last three for "the splendid work they have done in connection with the introduction of the Hungarian partridge and the Hungarian [sic] pheasant, and I would ask on their behalf a continuation of your loyal support to them." The association to date had raised and spent $1,700 – or well in excess of $35,000 in 2008 currency – for the introduction of these game birds.

Calgarian Austin de B. Winter later recorded that the first 15 pairs of Hungarian partridges were released April 20, 1908 at Dan Patton's place 2.5 miles west of Midnapore, and more were let go that November at five ranches belonging to Robinson, Shannon, Patton, Lloyd and Turnbull. "In liberating these birds in the several places we put them down in localities where there were coveys from the original 15 pairs." They released 10 more pairs on Dec. 10 at John Hamilton's place 18 miles southwest of Calgary.

In the spring of 1909, in 1911 and again in 1914 the CFGPA released birds, for a total of 250 pairs. "Some $3,000 in all was expended on this bid and all but $500 (from the provincial government) was donated by the sportsmen of Calgary and vicinity. They have increased and spread until they are now in Saskatchewan, Manitoba and Montana and in every part of Alberta."

Historian George Colpitts attributes this successful release of birds in the pre-World War I period to the central role played by the Calgary association in the development of Fish and Game Associations in Alberta. Austin de B. Winter, as secretary of the AGFPA, encouraged the "establishment of satellite associations all over southern Alberta."

The CFGPA also lobbied the provincial government during this period, according to Sue Clarke in *Fish, Fur and Feathers* (p. 45). "As early as 1910, the Calgary association provided input to the Alberta government's proposed amendments to the *Game Act* by making suggested changes to hunting regulations in a variety of areas such as licensing, bag limits, the length of hunting seasons, and licensing of market hunters."

In 1911 a Calgary brochure bragged about the area's hunting possibilities. "It is well to remember in this connection that the city has a Fish and Game Protective Association that keeps the mere pot-hunter and trader from spoiling the chances of the genuine sportsman."

CALGARY FISH and GAME ASSOCIATION

HONORARY PRESIDENTS:
Hon. P. J. A. CARDIN,
    Minister of Marine and Fisheries, Ottawa.
Hon. GEO. HOADLEY,
    Minister of Agriculture, Edmonton.
PRESIDENT:
  CHARLES A. HAYDEN
VICE-PRESIDENTS:
  DR. J. N. GUNN
  DAN PATTON
HONORARY TREASURER:
  R. G. CHRISTIE

EXECUTIVE COMMITTEE:
A. G. PLUNKETT
DR. A. H. McLAREN
FRED J. GREEN
A. de B. WINTER
F. N. SANDGATHE
JACK MILLER
OLE KIRKWOLD
CHARLES CRIST
PERCY BARTON
W. CRICHTON
W. NICHOLSON
GEORGE BELL
W. E. UNDERWOOD
FRANK STEWART
DR. J. B. WHITEOAK

CALGARY, ALBERTA
  May 31, 1929.

Crows and magpies met their match when the firepower of the CFGPA took aim in 1912. According to one account by the Alberta Teachers' Association, the CFGPA enlisted the schools in the "mass destruction of crows and magpies. To do this they deemed their easiest access to the younger generation was through the many rural schools. Consequently the task of counting, recording, destroying and reporting the tally to some headquarters was allotted to the school teachers. The destructors were paid a small sum for each egg or pair of feet… Payments were sent to the teacher who apportioned to each their rightful share of the bounties."

In 1917, after badgering the Alberta government for some time, Austin de B. Winter was able to convince C.W. Fisher, the MLA for Cochrane, and Duncan Marshall, Minister of Agriculture, to financially support the fish and game association's cause with a grant. The $100 contribution paled in comparison to earlier government funding, but suggested an ongoing relationship between the association and the provincial government of the day.

Other southern Alberta fish and game associations sprang up during this period too, including groups at Stavely in 1919, Pincher Creek in 1920, High River and Macleod in 1921, Coleman, Okotoks, Banff and Bellevue in 1925, Claresholm in 1926, Cardston in 1927 and Didsbury in 1928.

Although these independent fish and game organizations, and many others further north in Alberta, attempted to deal with the increasing level of hunting and angling activity, according to George Colpitts, it became apparent that something more had to be done.

"By the end of the 1920s," Colpitts wrote in *Alberta History*, "when Charles Hayden began uniting the many independent protective associations and former affiliates of the AGFPA into a single, united body (the present day AFGA), local conservation groups had already made a significant mark on conservation policy and practices in the province."

The year 1928 is celebrated elsewhere in this book as the founding year for the current AFGA. But while the AFGA founders were spending many hours in talks forming the provincial association in Calgary during the Calgary Stampede, Calgary sportsmen were busy walking the walk.

In the July 14, 1928 *Calgary Herald*, it was reported, "'More than 400 ring-necked pheasants were set out Thursday south of Calgary,' said Fred Green, secretary of the Calgary Fish and Game (CFGA), Saturday night. 'Finer types of birds could not be desired. They were lively, strong and healthy, and when we liberated them they obviously took very kingly to their new surroundings…. We have still to set out about 800 birds by our association. These will be arriving in the next couple of weeks, and will be delivered promptly.'"

The co-operative nature of the release program was also reflected in the report. "'The sportsmen of Calgary and district and those from elsewhere who helped in this undertaking are to be congratulated on their generous spirit and on their part of the valuable and constructive enterprise,' concluded Mr. Green."

SMILE YOUR ON CANDID CAMERA: Darwin Cronkhite, President and Helen Hobbs, Secretary d i c u s s Association Minutes. Overseers are: Tom O'Keefe First Vice-President and Bill Hamilton Vice-President (Left to Right).
PHOTO CREDITS: Courtesy The Calgary Herald.

Years later Austin de B. Winter noted in a summary of activities in this most busy year: "During 1928-30 we spent on pheasants and eggs $7,829.21."

In 2008 currency, this investment would be worth over $95,000 and according to a *Calgary Herald* article at the time, 1,800 "hard-flying birds" were to be released in 1928 and these ring-necked pheasants from the Benson pheasant farm in Silverton, Oregon, would help to prove "Alberta a Paradise For Fishermen and Game Bird Hunters."

The CFGA introduced 800 Mongolian pheasants and an additional 250 Chinese pheasants into southern Alberta in 1929 as well as 70 bob white quail, which Austin de B. Winter over-wintered at his home and then released near High River in May.

In 1931 the Calgary association took another initiative. According to federal government records: "A shipment of 20,000 each of cutthroat and rainbow trout were delivered to the retaining ponds of the Calgary Fish and Game Association."

Calgary Fish & Game Association

Complimentary

DIRECTORS and WIVES

ANNUAL BANQUET & DANCE

Sunrise Drive-In Restaurant
1635 - 37th Street S.W.

FRIDAY, JUNE 4th, 1965

BANQUET: 8 P.M. SHARP   DANCE: 9 P.M.

Western or Eastern Cuisine   82   Tickets: $2.50

At the 1954 Western Canadian Sportsmen's Show in Calgary, the CFGA stocked a pool with 300 trout and invited the public to try a hand at fishing. Kids of all ages participated and the event served as another way for the Calgary association to interact with the public.

A Calgary Power radio broadcast in 1956 highlighted the accomplishments of the AFGA and the CFGA and also mentioned an important annual event. "The Calgary association also undertakes a major project each January when it transfers hungry elk and deer from over-cropped southern Alberta areas to the forests of the Rocky Mountain game preserve."

In 1958 the CFGA sponsored a birdhouse-building contest. Cub Scouts from all over Calgary competed in the event and, according to a history of scouting in Calgary, "as a result of Cub efforts 'residents' of the Calgary Bird Sanctuary have had well-built homes to live in for many years."

The sale of public lands to private interests raised the ire of the CFGA membership in 1959. "Calgary Fish and Game Association has protested that leases of cottage lots on the Lower Kananaskis Lake has been approved without giving the people a proper opportunity to protest," reported the *Calgary Albertan*.

The association unsuccessfully opposed the cottages because they would withdraw most of the useable shoreline from public access. The requirement that at least $8,000 – or $60,000 in 2008 currency – be spent on construction also meant "that only those of some means would get leases." The CFGA went on to ask "the government members to assist in preservation of the lakefront for the use of the people and for future generations." "It is contended by the association that the general public loses whenever public land is lost, especially in settings similar to the Kananaskis area where there is a limited amount of land available."

The city began the development of Glenmore Park in 1960, so the CFGA organized and sponsored a tree-planting program around the lake. When a group applied for a lease for a private yacht club, Norman Shaddock led the fight against the plan on behalf of the CFGA and the private yacht club was defeated. In its place the city allowed a sailing school that is jointly operated by sailing group volunteers and the Calgary parks department.

During the 1940s CFGA members continued contributing to provincial initiatives. Calgarian Austin de B. Winter was one of several AGFPA members who spearheaded the idea of bird-game stamps in 1942. Hunters who bought stamps along with their licences helped contribute financially to the solution of wildlife problems.

In 1946 the AFGA leadership registered itself under the societies act in Alberta, a move that the CFGA followed 22 years later.

During 1947 D.S. Rawson did biological investigations on the Bow and Kananaskis rivers. His report was requested by the CFGA, funded by Calgary Power and approved by Alberta Department of Land and Mines as well as the University of Saskatchewan. Rawson presented the results of his findings to these agencies the next year.

And in 1948 W. Boote, who served two years as chairman of the fish committee for the CFGA, provided input to the provincial government. "At the request of Dr. R.B. Miller, I wrote my ideas of the fishing regulations for Alberta. Most of these passed the game convention and became law in time."

Increasing grazing pressure in forestry areas caused the CFGA to file a protest in the late 1940s. Ranchers were asking for more room on Crown land on which to graze their cattle and so in January 1948 the CFGA presented a brief that argued for the conservation of streams and forests on the Bow River watershed. "It was generally believed that cattle and wild ungulates, particularly elk, could not compete evenly for grazing range…"

When a spring snowstorm wiped out 90 percent of the pheasant population in March 1951, the CFGA rose to the challenge. Led by president Floyd E. Mitchell, the Calgary group raised $15,000 from public donations, bought pheasant eggs and chicks and helped restore the game-bird population. More than 10,000 birds were raised and liberated.

In 1953 Ed Jefferies purchased the Inglewood Bird Sanctuary and leased the property to the CFGA. As a result, the CFGA offices were able to reside at the 59-acre Federal Migratory Bird Sanctuary that had been set aside in 1929. The City of Calgary took over the property in 1970.

177 Members!
Dates back to 1911

1965

SPONSORS of
Junior Rifle Club

STAVELY

Fish & Game Assoc.

BANQUET

N. Ohler
PRESIDENT

W. J. Malchow
SECRETARY

The CFGA inaugurated its newsletter, called *Our Vanishing Heritage*, on Feb. 1, 1960 and this publication has informed the CFGA and the public on issues of importance to the association ever since.

In 1962 the CFGA created its Conservationist Of The Year Award. The first recipient was W.R. Wolley-Dod, a long-time CFGA member and member of the executive.

On April 15, 1968 the Alberta legislature read into the record the formal recognition of the CFGA as an incorporated entity in the province of Alberta. Incorporation papers had been signed by the registrar of companies on March 25, 1968 in Edmonton. It is interesting to note that the CFGA had to request permission from the AFGA, which consented "to the use of 'Fish and Game' in the name of your club. This permission is for registering the club under the *Societies Act*." Paul Morck, manager of the AFGA, signed the letter on behalf of the provincial organization.

The CFGA was busy in 1969 with many programs. It decided to hire a secretary manager that year to help with the office work relating to the 2,463 members in the association. Lifetime memberships were offered for the first time in 1969 and membership dues rose from $2 to $5. The CFGA spent $500 on a float for the Stampede, and gave a small prize to Miss Outdoors 1969 and the runners-up.

That year the CFGA opposed strip mining of coal along the Elbow River and sent a letter to the mayor of Calgary that thanked "the city of Calgary for its decision not to use DDT in the future."

The next decade was busy in Alberta as the oil industry boomed. In 1970 the *Calgary Herald* ran a photograph of CFGA member Darwin Cronkhite and Alderman John Kushner collecting samples of pollution beside the CPR's Ogden shops. "Fears are that the oil may seep into the city's water table. Canadian Pacific responded by saying that they were unobliged to act differently, until the city changed its air pollution laws."

That year the CFGA formed a women's committee and it wasted no time in making useful improvements to the association's operations. The women suggested cleaner toilets at campgrounds, a wild game cookbook, and a Christmas tree and party for kids – the directors approved $200 for the event. The women also suggested an annual game dinner for the association, an event that continues to be an important part of the CFGA. They also wondered: "An interesting subject is why do husbands go fishing and we have to live with it?"

In 1972 the CFGA gave its Conservationist of the Year Award to 12-year-old Sandra Crawford for her work starting the river cleanup in Calgary in 1968. The Calgary Pathway and River Cleanup has been an annual event ever since.

Throughout the 1970s the CFGA continued its many and varied programs though membership began to fall. Finances became tight in spite of income from lotteries and other fundraising initiatives.

The last 30 years of the CFGA's history have been trying and the association considered ceasing operations several times. But the faithful managed to keep the key programs alive and these included the annual pheasant-rearing and release, the game dinner, a booth at the sportsmen's show and other initiatives as resources permitted.

In 1990 the association increased its dues to $20, supported the Buck for Wildlife program, promoted a photo contest and held regular slide shows. The CFGA also came out officially against game ranching and became an annual sponsor of Fun Fishing Day For the Physically Handicapped. Members built new pheasant pens on the Bates family property near Strathmore.

By 2002 a small but vibrant membership of about 140 people was busy promoting CFGA issues in many ways. The newsletter started up again; it had been an on-and-off-again proposition over the years. Chronic wasting disease became an issue during this period. Club activities included sponsoring members to take the Alberta Conservation and Hunter Education program or the Fishing Education program and funding the Allan H. Bill Memorial Scholarship, a $1,000 prize.

In early 2005 the CFGA restructured the club, increased communication with its membership through a website and newsletter and revised its bylaws to fit the current situation. The directors also re-registered the association with the Alberta government; it had been struck from the provincial registry in 2001 for failing to file annual returns.

The board of directors grew to 12 members and the club provided financial support for hunter education, wildlife enhancement and habitat projects. The pheasant-rearing project continued, as always, and the CFGA also provided financial aid to the Public Action for Wildlife Society (PAWS), a group that "has had a measured success in helping to take down the misguided Interim Métis Harvest Agreement," according to president Bob Semchuk. This issue was resolved in 2007 when a judge decided against unlimited Métis hunting rights.

As the CFGA celebrates its centennial in 2008, the club consists of more than 100 members and still continues with its key objectives. It hosted the 2007 Alberta Trophy awards banquet on April 26, 2008. Club members raised and released 800 ring-necked pheasants this year. Members participate in shooting events, a photo contest, an awards banquet, trophy measuring and club meetings and other activities. They also receive the CFGA's newsletter, *Our Vanishing Heritage*, and the AFGA's *The Outdoor Edge* magazine and in this way share experiences with other sports and outdoors people.

The CFGA is proud to celebrate its centennial in 2008 and to join with the 17,000 members of the provincial AFGA to celebrate 100 years of activity in support of our sporting heritage.

High River Fish and Game Association
1920-present

The High River Fish and Game Association represents hunters and anglers of all ages in the High River area, including Longview, Okotoks, Black Diamond, Turner Valley, Blackie, Arrowwood, Mossleigh, Cayley and Nanton, plus a large number of members live in Calgary. The club also has members from Spirit River, Grande Prairie and as far away as Prince Edward Island.

The club was formed on March 18, 1920, with the first official meeting held at the local branch of the Bank of Commerce. Bank of Commerce manager W.E. Elliot was elected as president at this meeting, with I.N. McKeage as a strong supporter. The first secretary for the local club was Arthur Bowmen.

The club membership peaked at 220 members and now varies between 125 and 200.

Education

A number of the club members became involved with teaching the Alberta Conservation and Hunter Education program, as well as firearm safety training courses. The club was involved with training more than 120 youth and adults in the area.

Projects

The club strongly supported stocking of trout in streams, and in 1999 stocked 50,000 trout in the Highwood River. The club also lobbied for the protection of owls, migratory hawks and eagles, and a bounty for crow and magpie eggs was paid.

The club built a hockey-rink-sized pen in 1988 for pheasants north of the cemetery in High River. The club can raise 1,000 pheasants per year in the pheasant pens, and has done so for many years. The club also raises Merriam's turkeys in the pheasant pens for release.

During the 1980s the club purchased and set out numerous flax straw bales on many ponds and wetlands in the area as nesting sites for Canada geese. The club wrapped the bales with chicken wire to prevent muskrats from tunnelling into them.

In 1998 the High River Fish and Game Association purchased 39 acres along the Sheep River west of Okotoks. This property has great habitat for white-tailed deer, moose, elk, cougar, grouse, migratory birds as well as a large variety of song birds. A restricted covenant was placed on the property to prevent development and protect the habitat. The club was also instrumental in acquiring the adjacent 55 acres just east of the High River property, which was deeded to the AFGA in 2004.

Annual Events

The club holds a wild game dinner and fundraiser on March 25 (or the Saturday closest to that date). The event is attended by upwards of 300 people who enjoy an evening of great food, silent and live auctions and other fundraising events. The overall big-game, migratory and upland game birds, photography, fish and youth awards are presented at the event.

Every year the club holds two campouts: the first being on the May long weekend at Hogg Park and the final campout of the year being the last weekend of September at Hogg Park.

COURTESY OF THE SARCEE FISH AND GAME ASSOCIATION

Sarcee Fish and Game students releasing mature pheasants behind the Millarville School as part of the Millarville Community-Youth Pheasant Raise and Release Project in 2003. This project was set up by Dean Loewen and Art Yeske of the AFGA and involves 11 families and the school to raise and release 100 pheasants per year.

The Sarcee Fish and Game Association display at the Calgary Sportsmen's Show.

In June, the club holds a handicapped fishing derby at a local trout pond near High River. All participants are awarded and given gifts for their fishing skills and successes. A barbecue is held to feed participants and volunteers.

On the second weekend of August, the club holds its annual fishing derby with a grand prize of $1,500 to the participant with the largest pike. Other prizes are awarded to other successful anglers in different categories.

Special People

One of the founding members of the High River Fish and Game Association was Archie Hogg. He came to Canada in 1904 at the age of five years and from then on enjoyed wildlife and nature and grew up to be a dedicated conservationist. As he acquired his own land, he established a bird sanctuary with his wife, Janet, at East Longview. In 1981 Archie and Janet donated their river frontage land along the Highwood River to the M.D. of Foothills to be used as a park and campground that is still active to this day.

The AFGA presented Archie Hogg with a lifetime membership in 1948 and the Fulton Award in 1973 for his contribution to wildlife preservation. In 1980 Premier Peter Lougheed presented Archie and Janet with an Alberta Achievement Award. Archie received the Order of the Bighorn Award in 1982 from the provincial government.

Archie Hogg passed away at the High River Hospital on June 5, 1984. Honorary pallbearers were mostly long-standing members of the fish and game association from various clubs, including David Morrison, Elmer Kure, Norman White, Ken Yank, Jim Cooper, Dan Fowler, Jim McKidd and Ray Paschal.

The Sarcee club booth at Wild Thing 2002, with a child assembling a bluebird box.

The Sarcee Fish and Game Association display at the Calgary Sportsmen's Show attracts youthful members with various activities.

The Sarcee Fish and Game Association display at the Calgary Sportsmen's Show. The fish tank provides lots of fun for kids.

Sarcee Fish and Game Association
1956-present

The Sarcee Fish and Game Association was formed in 1956 by members of the Canadian Army serving at the Sarcee military base in Calgary. The founding members were Barry Connatty, Percy Faith, Pete Bacon, Ken Mohr, Ken Yank, Vic Johnson, Ken Linge, Ed Swan and Fred Harris. Membership was restricted to Armed Forces service personnel and to civilians in the employ of the military. In 1958 the club affiliated with the AFGA.

Early club membership numbered at about 125. However, in the early 1970s, the club opened its membership to include civilians, and numbers increased considerably. For the past 10 years, membership has ranged from 650 to over 700.

Projects

Shortly after its formation, the club built a skeet range, started a program to teach safe gun handling to Cub Scouts and created a branch of the Junior Forest Wardens. The club assembled a series of trophies to be awarded annually to members for the top game specimens taken each year. An extract from the December 1961 provincial AFGA Newsletter quotes president Gordon Cummings commending the Sarcee club for "being on the ball," and "appearing to be well on the way to having a banner year."

Habitat development has been a major function of the club. It has planted over 100,000 trees and shrubs, built and placed 350 nesting structures for geese, 270 nesting boxes and "hen houses" for ducks and over 3,300 nesting boxes for bluebirds. The club submerged 65 large bundles of brush in Gap Lake to create artificial reefs for fish habitat. In addition, the club assisted in the construction of a large reef project to improve fish habitat in the Ghost Reservoir.

COURTESY OF THE SARCEE FISH AND GAME ASSOCIATION

The Sarcee Fish and Game Association's adopted blind pheasant has been a hit for many years.

Pheasant raising and releasing has been a significant activity of the club for many years. These birds have been raised in as many as five locations, two of which were projects involving school

COURTESY OF THE SARCEE FISH AND GAME ASSOCIATION

George Loades (Order of the Bighorn) second from left, with a group of seniors who monitor the yearly output of 300 bluebird boxes.

Ken Yank, Sarcee Club Projects, preparing a 45-gallon drum for cutting and turning into a goose nest.

Dave McIver (L) and Fred Girdwood from the Sarcee Fish and Game Association early style "duck box" program.

children. In addition, the club involved about 80 children in the Alberta Junior Pheasant program each year for the past four years. These young people have been introduced to hunting through safe gun handling instruction and the guided hunting of pheasants and turkeys on the Dan Radomske farm near Innisfail.

The club has been involved in a variety of other fish and game-related activities. The annual Fishing Derby for the Handicapped has seen up to 100 participants each year since its inception over 30 years ago. The club has been an active participant in the annual Calgary Sportsmen's Show as well as conservation activities aimed

Bryce Chase, recipient of an award from the Alberta government for all his contributions to recreation opportunities in the province, Dec. 8, 2005. Tony Ferguson (L), Jack Graham, Vern McIntosh, Ray Makowecki, Bryce Chase, Don Hayden and Carole Romaniuk.

at youth such as Wild Thing at the Sam Livingston fish hatchery. Over the years, the membership has enjoyed club campouts, fishing derbies, river cleanups, shoots, and the annual banquet and awards night. Recently the club has become the custodian of a stocked pond near Crossfield where the annual fishing derby for the handicapped is held.

Special People

Four club members have been recognized by the Government of Alberta for admission to the Order of the Bighorn. They are Vic Scheuerman for his work in hunter training; Bryce Chase for habitat development; George Freeman for development of waterfowl habitat; and George Loades for his efforts in the successful recovery of the mountain bluebird.

Wheatland Conservation and Wildlife Association
1993-present

In 1993 Larry Olson gathered information on the AFGA, and how to set up a new club in the Wheatland County area. He contacted many local people and in January 1994 an interested group from the area gathered at the Strathmore stockyards to discuss the formation of a local chapter. That evening they elected their executive to head up the new organization: Ed Beaudin, president; Joe McCluskey, vice president; Kelly Frank, secretary; and Craig Cooley, treasurer. After much deliberation, Wheatland Conservation and Wildlife Association was chosen as the official name. Fred Girdwood, zone 2 director at that time, was a very strong supporter and friend of the Wheatland club. The club's membership peaked at 200 in 1995-96 and was 170 in 2007.

Education

Approximately 500 students have completed the club's conservation and hunter education courses and approximately 300 students have completed course work in preparation for the firearms possession and acquisition licence qualification test. The club sends children to a hunter education camp each summer.

Projects

The club's first project was to establish goose-nesting areas by placing round bales in prime nesting locations. Another project involved the purchase of 500 pheasant chicks from the pheasant hatchery at Brooks, which were raised on Larry Olson's property until they were mature and released into areas of prime habitat. This continued for several years. Today, Otto Naggy incubates eggs each spring, then releases adult birds while raising chicks for the next year's stocking. Over the years the club has partnered with 4-H and others to release approximately 5,000 adult birds into prime pheasant habitat.

As such a great percentage of trees and brush have been re-moved for agricultural land use and by irrigation management, Wheatland Conservation has been planting trees and shrubs in privately donated habitat project areas and along irrigation canals. To date it is estimated that 80,000 trees and shrubs have been planted for habitat reclamation.

COURTESY OF THE SARCEE FISH AND GAME ASSOCIATION

Dave Yeske and Dr. Niels Damgaard with some "stream fishing results" at the Sarcee Fish and Game annual family campout and pig roast at the Damgaard farm near Dickson in 1973.

The club has been active with the annual hunter surveys each December since 1995. It has donated to the AFGA Wildlife Trust Fund, youth education fund, and has supported the National Firearms Association in its opposition to the national gun registry program and the local 4-H club (in particular the newly formed shooting club); the local crisis shelter; Ducks Unlimited, Partners in Habitat Program; single mothers and their family Fish for a Day program; and the Sarcee Fish and Game Association handi-capped fishing derby. The club has donated two floating docks to the Kinsmen Lake project in Strathmore; much needed equipment to the local Fish and Wildlife Division for environmental protec-tion; a global positioning system collar for the University of Alberta bear research program; the club's bear is named "Wheatland." The club has also sent delegates to the AFGA annual conference since 1995, providing both member and monetary support.

Annual Events

In 1996 the club hosted the annual AFGA awards banquet in the Carseland Hall. Other annual events include: horn measure-ment competitions, the annual Christmas party, annual land-owner appreciation day, monthly meetings, club fun days, 4-H meetings and training courses.

In March 2007, the club hosted its 13th annual wild game dinner and silent auction at the Strathmore civic centre. The 300 tickets available are usually an early sellout.

For 12 years the club has hosted an annual youth and senior fishing derby at the Strathmore town lake. This derby was named the Rob Rebeyka Memorial Fishing Derby in memory of the departed president in 2000. In 2005 the club hosted its first Landowners Appreciation Day in conjunction with the local Fish and Wildlife Division Report-a-Poacher appreciation event.

Club Awards

The club annually sponsors the white-fronted goose award at the annual AFGA awards banquet. In 1996 and 1997 the Wheatland Conservation and Wildlife Association was the proud winner of the AFGA Guy Blake Memorial Trophy for the best club project award.

Special People

In 1997 president Ed Beaudin was presented with a certificate of merit from the AFGA's executive board of zone 2 by Darwin Cronkhite, director. In 1998 Jack Nielsen won the predator award for magpies and coyote control. This same year, youth members Tanner, Darren and Tammy Blackley won the Camskill Ltd. Trophy for junior conservation with their work on the club's Trees for Habitat and pheasant projects.

The following members have made significant contributions to the club and its projects over the years: Larry and Darriel Olson, Bert Caveny, Ed Beaudin, Daryl Blackley, Craig Cooley, Troy Blackley, Shawn Mullen, Bill Stephenson, Joe McClusky, Mike Vanvervegem, Bill Morion, Jason Lardon, Art Harris, Doris Thompson, Leon Yasinskl, Bob Stanley, Ray Proulx, John Getz, Daneen Olson and Barren Blackley.

Blaine McGrath (L) and Fred Girdwood have just installed a duck and goose nesting platform.

Zone 3

Zone 3 covers an area of south-central Alberta from British Columbia to Saskatchewan, north of zone 2 and south of zones 4 and 5. Zone 3 has the highest percentage of parkland left in the province. There are many fine trout streams in the west along the foothills, much agricultural land and some of the best goose and white-tailed deer country in Alberta.

The 20 clubs in zone 3 are:
- Alberta Falconry Association
- Battle River Fish and Game Association *
- Breton and District Fish and Game Association *
- Camrose and District Fish and Game Association
- Castor Fish and Game Association *
- Dickson Fish and Game Association *
- Innisfail Fish and Game Association
- Iron Creek Fish and Game Association
- Lacombe Fish and Game Association
- Leduc Fish and Game Association
- Millet Fish and Game Association
- Ponoka Fish and Game Association
- Provost and District Fish and Game Association *
- Red Deer Fish and Game Association
- Rimbey Fish and Game Association *
- Rocky Mountain House Fish and Game Association
- Sundre Fish and Game Association
- Sylvan Lake and District Fish and Game Association
- Thorsby and District Fish and Game Association
- Wimborne and District Fish and Game Association
  * clubs that did not submit histories

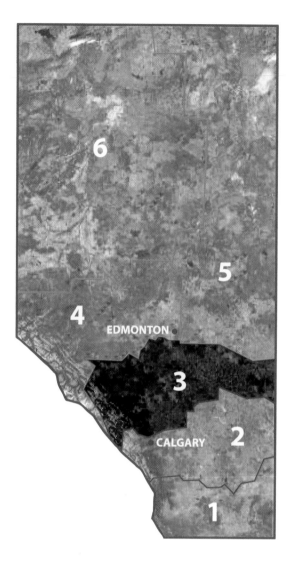

Club Histories of Zone 3

Alberta Falconry Association
1965-present

The Alberta Falconry Association (AFA) was first formed in January 1965 with John Campbell as president and Mike Person as vice president. The first problem that had to be addressed was the legalization of falconry in the province. The club met that year with the Alberta Fish and Wildlife Division's director of wildlife and corresponded with the Minister of the Department of Lands and Forests to lobby for legalization. However, at that time in Alberta there was a large number of unsympathetic naturalists and fish and game club members who opposed legalizing falconry. The club struggled to persuade these groups while at the same time helped the Canadian Wildlife Service with its surveys of the peregrine falcon, whose populations appeared to be in trouble as a result of persistent pesticides in the environment.

In 1978 the falconers of the province reorganized into the Alberta Raptor Association (ARA) that recognized members' broader interest in birds of prey rather than just falconry. However, the ARA continued to lobby for legalized falconry. It was clear that the government was not going to legalize falconry if the province's naturalist groups and the AFGA were opposed to the sport.

Therefore, in 1978 John Campbell and Richard Fyfe of the Canadian Wildlife Service gave a presentation to the Lethbridge Naturalist Club; and John Campbell, Wayne Nelson, and Ross Lein (University of Calgary professor) gave a presentation to the Calgary field naturalists. They focused on falconry, its methods, its long history, its acceptance elsewhere, its benefits to raptors and society, and its non-impact on raptor populations. These meetings, and an article about falconry the group wrote for the *Calgary Field Naturalist* newsletter, changed the minds of people who had previously been opposed to falconry in Alberta. The group also made presentations to the AFGA at the regional level. John Campbell addressed the AFGA annual convention, seeking endorsement of a resolution supporting falconry. The resolution was carried. Subsequently, the minister and the Fish and Wildlife Division agreed to draft falconry legislation. In November 1981, after 17 years of lobbying, falconry was finally legalized in Alberta.

Because the legislation requires permit holders to be members of a registered falconry society, the club once again reorganized itself as the Alberta Falconry Association (AFA), and completed bylaws and formalities so that the AFA could be officially registered as a society and the legislation could take effect. In July 1982 the AFA came into being as a registered society. In August of that year, the AFA held its inaugural meeting, electing John Campbell as its first president. The club soon had 21 members.

Falconry progressed slowly in the 1980s because the harvest of wild raptors was not permitted; even injured birds from rehabilitation facilities were not available to falconers, and captive-bred falcons were extremely expensive. In 1987 the *Wildlife Act* was amended and allowed a limited harvest of wild raptors for falconry purposes. Injured birds also became available to AFA members.

AFA membership has increased to approximately 35 members, of which 25 actively participate in falconry.

Club objectives: to promote the conservation of raptors and their prey species through the application of wise use; to promote and perpetuate the highest standards of falconry practice; to inform and advise members and prospective members about falconry in Alberta; to maintain and promote the association's code of ethics.

The highlight of the year for AFA members is the annual field meet. This informal gathering is held in early October. Members attend from all over the province and often host guests from other provinces and countries.

John A. Campbell, Sr., Founding father of Alberta falconry, 1926–2003
by Dr. R. Wayne Nelson

On Aug. 29, 2003 John Campbell, Sr., died at the age of 77 at the family ranch near Black Diamond after a lengthy battle with cancer. The Alberta Falconry Association lost one of its founding fathers and a very fine gentleman. In large part, John's love for falconry and birds of prey, and his dogged persistence in pursuing certain challenges, were responsible for the existence and quality of the sport of falconry in Alberta today. John also contributed substantially to the return of the peregrine falcon to the province in those frustrating early years of captive breeding and recovery.

DEPARTMENT OF LANDS AND FORESTS
PROVINCE OF ALBERTA

This is to Certify

That

THOMAS TOMASZEWSKI

has attended the

HUNTER TRAINING PROGRAM

STUDENT CANDIDATE COURSE

and

Successfully passed the Examination

19 April 1966

Director of Fish and Wildlife

Instructor

Hunter Training Officer

SPORTSMEN'S EDUCATION TODAY....SAFE HUNTERS AND SPORTSMEN TOMORROW

COURTESY OF THOMAS TOMASZEWSKI

John developed his love for falconry as a boy in his native England. He immigrated to Canada in 1948 and attended Agricultural College at Guelph, Ontario. He married Elizabeth Balfour and they bought their ranch at Black Diamond in 1954; they raised seven sons.

In 1964 John acquired two eyas (nestling) goshawks that brought him back into falconry. As a result, he set out to find others interested in the sport and to get falconry legalized in Alberta.

John and other Alberta falconers regularly helped the Canadian Wildlife Service survey Alberta, the Yukon and the Northwest Territories for peregrine falcons. As a result, John legally acquired peregrine falcons from the Yukon and brought them home for falconry purposes. It was not legal to hold such birds in Alberta. After some legal wrangling, John began operating the provincial government's peregrine breeding project, a job he held until 1985.

In 1973 John fledged the first captive-bred anatum race of peregrines in Canada. Subsequently, in 1974 he and Phillip Glazier, a British falconer and breeder, were the first to successfully breed merlins in captivity. John's success with the breeding and release of falcons was an immeasurably positive factor to the eventual legalization of falconry in Alberta in 1981. He subsequently served several terms as president of the AFA and under his leadership the club evolved in many ways. In 1987 it successfully lobbied changes to the *Wildlife Act* that allowed falconers to take raptors from the wild in Alberta instead of relying on birds from other jurisdictions. Through the 1990s the quality of falconry in Alberta improved dramatically as education, camaraderie and gentle peer pressure from fellow members of the AFA encouraged all falconers to work hard and do well with their birds. For all these works and many more, NAFA bestowed upon John an honorary membership in July 2003.

Alberta falconers sincerely thank Elizabeth and the rest of the Campbell family for sharing this wonderful man with us for all of those years.

Camrose and District Fish and Game Association
1938-present

The Camrose district has always been an attraction to naturalists and outdoorsmen. Although a fish and game club was in existence in the 1920s, unfortunately the records from those days are lost. Today, senior members of the Camrose and District Fish and Game Association remember a fish and game club being organized in 1938 by Len Blades, who was the first president. Some of the first members were Ellsworth Hills, Harry Wilcox, Laurie Byers Charlie McDonald, Stan Bailey, Dave Bowes, Bud Roose, Jim Cowie, Peter Trautman and Gilbert Hoyme.

Fish and game meetings were held in the town hall in Camrose. There was a skeet/trap shooting range on Harry Wilcox's farm just south of town. Many turkey shoots were held there as well. A rifle range was set up south of Camrose and is still in use today.

COURTESY OF THOMAS TOMASZEWSKI
Fifteen magpies were caught in one day in one of the magpie traps built by the Camrose Fish and Game Association.

COURTESY OF THE CAMROSE AND DISTRICT FISH AND GAME ASSOCIATION
Fishing from the wheelchair dock at the pond "Pleasure Island." Al Finley (L) and Jaron Wensley.

COURTESY OF THE CAMROSE AND DISTRICT FISH AND GAME ASSOCIATION
Display at the wild game fundraising supper in Camrose, 1996.

COURTESY OF THE CAMROSE AND DISTRICT FISH AND GAME ASSOCIATION

The Camrose and District Fish and Game Association fish pond signage.

The club became inactive in the late 1950s. It started up again in 1960 with Al Richardson as president. Tom Williams was membership chair and remembers selling 200 memberships that year for $5 each. In the late 1970s, the number of members declined and the club was once again disbanded.

In 1993 the Camrose and District Fish and Game Association was reactivated. Founders of the new club were Tom Tomaszewski, Glen Hand and Bruce Blumhagen. The first president was Bruce Blumhagen. Other members of the executive were Dan McIntyre, Rod Ross, Glen Hand, Tom Tomaszewski, Jun Mah and Bob Adamson. The membership grew and one year surpassed 275. In 2006, it had 181 members.

Education

The club offers hunter education and firearms safety courses. Each July the club sends three youths to the zone 3 youth camp. The club donates $550 each year for a scholarship at Augustana University in Camrose to a local student who is studying in some field associated with resource conservation.

Projects

In 1947 club members planted trout at the Dodd's coal mine pit, now known as Black Nugget Lake. Bert Freeman was the Fish and Wildlife officer in the area at that time and helped with that venture. One of the club members, Garnet Burnstad, remembers he was lucky enough to catch a 10 pound trout there.

In 1949 Bill Bowthorpe, Henry Quail and Garnet Burnstad made three trips to Brooks and brought back truckloads of pheasants to be released. They dropped about 10 birds each at various locations where there was good ground cover and water, including New Norway, Edberg, Meeting Creek and around Camrose, Ohaton, Bawlf, Round Hill and Kingman areas. For many years after that it was easy to go out and get your limit of three pheasants.

In the late 1940s and early '50s, the club played a big part in organizing coyote hunts, usually in the fall or early winter. An ad would be placed in the local paper with the location, time and date of the hunt.

Today the main club project is a trout pond, Pleasure Island, just east of Camrose off Highway 13. Previously known as Twomey's Pond, it is an old reclaimed coal mine site. The club spends hundreds of hours each year developing the pond and the surrounding area, which is owned in partnership with the AFGA and leased by Ducks Unlimited Canada. Rainbow trout are stocked yearly and anyone can fish there; catch and release is encouraged.

The club builds bird feeders and lots of bluebird houses. The club also builds magpie traps and sells or rents them to control the magpie population. The club has built 12 purple martin houses and set them up in Camrose, Bashaw and Bittern Lake. The club also does hunter surveys and hide collection.

Annual Events

Each year, usually the first Saturday in March, the club holds a wild game and beef supper, silent auction and trophy awards. Every June, the club holds a potluck picnic and meeting at the fish pond and also clean a portion of the highway that evening. At Christmas, a casino and fun night is held.

Special People

Bill Bowthorpe, another member, loved Canada geese ever since his childhood. He turned his farm into a wildlife sanctuary in the Round Hill area. Bill was recognized in 1959 for his good work with wildlife and was awarded a distinguished service certificate, followed by the Fulton Trophy in 1963 from the AFGA. His wife, Emma Bowthorpe, was also very active and was awarded the Grace Stewart trophy in 1967 and the award of merit in 1978 from the AFGA. Emma wrote a book, *For the Love of a Goose* (1976), about the Bowthorpe's wildlife history.

COURTESY OF THE CAMROSE AND DISTRICT FISH AND GAME ASSOCIATION

Left to right: Syd Travers, Herman Blatz, Alex Blatz and Tom Tomaszewski, 1968, when wild meat was very much appreciated.

Aeriel view of Pleasure Island, Camrose Fish and Game pond.

The club appreciates the 40 years of assistance member Jun Mah, owner of Jun Mah Studio, has provided. His business has been a gathering place for members, where they can drop something off or pick something up, or just to come and socialize. He has sold many tickets for club events.

Innisfail Fish and Game Association
1929-present

The Innisfail Fish and Game Association started in 1929. However, no written records are available prior to 1973, and much of the following history is based on verbal accounts. The club meetings were held in the Orange Hall, Moose Hall, or Legion boardroom in Innisfail. In 1981 the membership was 717. The club was the third largest fish and game club in Alberta that year.

Education

The club started offering conservation and hunter education courses in 1997. Over 200 students (youths and adults) have graduated from the program. The club pays the membership dues for its instructors in the Alberta Hunter Education Instructors Association. In April 2002 the club gave a course in Bentley for 19 students, as they had no instructors in their area. In 2003 the club expanded its team to include qualified firearms instructors so the club could offer the Canadian Firearms Safety course.

Projects

In 1962 the club leased for 99 years from the Brian Kelly Family 20-plus acres of riverfront land on the Little Red Deer River. The club has looked after the lease and it is enjoyed by many people as a site for picnics, family reunions, birthday parties and weddings. A kitchen, horseshoe pits and a playground have been built, and a permanent campground is in place. The club provides free camping to Scouts, Girl Guides and Junior Forest Wardens in a wilderness area where they practice survival training.

In the 1960s and '70s, club members organized outings for youngsters to hunt crows and magpies. The feet of the birds were collected for a bounty.

The club obtained private donations and a grant to build the Bennett Pond east of Innisfail on land leased from Ron Bennett. The pond has been stocked every year and is very successful, except for winterkill that occurs from time to time.

In 1983 goose nesting bales were put out in several areas to enhance the number of geese in the area. This project continued for several years.

Since 1989 quite a few members have participated in the annual hunter survey questionnaire for the provincial government. The members placed phone calls to hunters for information on hunting activities and success rates.

In 1983 a pheasant project was started at the Dan Radomski farm; a $1,372 grant was obtained to build pheasant-rearing pens. This project also provides youth with training in firearm safety, shotgun skills, dog handling and a chance to bag their first upland game birds. It is believed to be the only program of its kind in Canada. To qualify for this opportunity, the youth must first pass the Alberta Conservation and Hunter Education program, which covers a wide range of topics from game identification to hunting laws and ethics. Dozens of organizations support the junior pheasant program with funding and equipment; the youth participate for free.

Annual Events

Awards banquets were held every spring in the Moose Hall. Large crowds attended and were served a delicious supper. The event was moved to the Legion when the crowd became too large for the Moose Hall.

Special People

Members granted life member status for their service to the club include: Niels Damgaard, Stan Dent, Dick Mountain, Nils Kvisle, Allen and Ethel Smith, Glen and Ella Ferguson, Fred Goldstrum, Syd Quartly, Jim Rich, Morley Mielke, Jim and Barb Scott, Lloyd Moore and Doug Whorrall.

Some of the past presidents of the Innisfail Fish and Game Association are Lynn Kelly, 1973-75; Albert Smith, 1976-77; Bruce Heaton, 1979-80; Gordon Calvert, 1981-82; Glen Ferguson, 1983-84; Fred Goldstrom, 1985-86; Wayne Abrahamson, 1987-88; Ross Calverly, 1989-90; Morley Mielke, 1991-92; Glen Ferguson, 1995; Fred Goldstrom, 1996-2000; Art Holmes, 2001; Ed Tingey, 2002-05; Mel Garland, 2006.

Iron Creek Fish and Game Association
1965-present

A number of sportsmen in the Hardisty, Lougheed, Sedgewick and Killam area had spoken for quite some time of the need for a fish and game club. In 1965, Albert Whitbeck, with the assistance of Bill Bowthorpe and Jack MacArthur, spearheaded the creation of the Iron Creek Fish and Game Association. The name Iron Creek was chosen because interested sportsmen from all four towns were in attendance at the organizational meeting. Instead of choosing the name of any one town, the attendees decided to name the club after a creek that runs just north of the four towns.

Albert Whitbeck was elected the first president of the club, a position he held until 1970. John Wagemaker was elected the first secretary treasurer. A total of 124 members were recruited in the club's first year.

Education

The club formed a Junior Forest Warden club in 1969 for local children under the leadership of Ken and Dianne Clousten. Many club members took the Hunter Training Instructor course in 1970 and taught many courses to local youth throughout the area. In 1980 Iron Creek sponsored two youngsters for the zone 3 conservation camp. Five additional club members attended a Hunter Education Instructors course in 1997. Club volunteers taught two successful fishing clinics in 1999 for youngsters at the Lougheed trout pond.

Projects

In 1966 the club established a trap shooting range on Albert Whitbeck's farm, with Jack MacArthur donating the trap equipment. The club purchased the Valley School property in 1970, including the school and adjacent 2.5 acres, which later became the club's pistol and trap shooting ranges.

The club started setting out large numbers of flax-straw bales for goose nesting sites in 1975. This was the beginning of a large increase in Canada goose numbers locally.

In 1976 the club constructed its first pheasant pen, located on the Yelle farm where the Yelles took on the task of raising the six-week-old birds for release locally for a number of years. An addition to the pheasant pen was built in 1978, doubling its capacity to raise pheasants. In 1980 the club constructed its third pheasant pen on the Vernon Simpson property, and a fourth pheasant pen was constructed at Holmberg's farm in 1982.

Volunteer members spent many winter days constructing bluebird houses in 1977. These were made available to local landowners, free-of-charge to set out on their property.

In 1981 the club assisted with the installation of outhouses and a fish-cleaning table at the Diplomat trout pond. The club assisted with the planting of spruce trees in the parking area of the pond in 1982 and assisted financially with the fencing and gravelling of the access road and parking lot.

In conjunction with Flagstaff County, the club began a tree-planting program in 1984 that would result in the planting of thousands of trees in the next decade, greatly improving habitat and establishing new shelterbelts.

In 1987 the Iron Creek club began its first year collecting game hides with the collection depot at Vernon Simpson's place. Vernon has co-ordinated the program for nearly two decades.

Vernon Simpson was nominated to serve on the Flagstaff Agriculture Advisory Committee in 1988 to help draw up a policy on roadside brushing and spraying. This policy remains in place and has proven to be beneficial to the environment.

Graham Brothers Construction began digging the Iron Creek club's trout pond at Lougheed. When completed it measured 550 feet long, 200 feet wide and 23 feet deep at a cost of $60,000. Phase two of the trout pond construction was completed in 1989 with trout being stocked, access road constructed and gravelled, water-well drilled, campsites and fire pits constructed and playground built. In 1990 the club built a fence around the trout pond. That same year, the club constructed a camp kitchen and wood shed at the Lougheed pond and also purchased gravel for another access road and parking lot at Diplomat trout pond at Forestburg.

The club leased Crown land at Wavy Lake in 1994 near Strome and hired Abalone Construction from Edmonton to construct four nesting islands on this lake at a cost of $7,000. In 1997 following a very severe winter, the club assisted Alberta Fish and Wildlife Division personnel with a deer-feeding program and helped farmers fence feed stacks. Some volunteer members also assisted Fish and Wildlife Division personnel with a deer depredation survey in the spring on property where the deer had yarded up during the severe winter.

Iron Creek Fish and Game sold its gun range property in 2003 and all gun club property as a result of a lack of interest and high insurance costs. In 2005 the club staged a very successful fish derby for children.

Annual Events

The club started its trophy competition and annual trophy dinner in 1967. The club began its annual children's fish derby in 1968.

Club Awards

Iron Creek club won two provincial AFGA awards in 1968: the George E. Watt Memorial Award for the largest financial contribution to fish and wildlife projects, and the Herman Henning Predator Award for the most magpies and crows taken by a club. The club won the Herman Henning Award again in 1969, 1970 and 1971. In 1977 the club won the AFGA Darwin Cronkhite Award for its work in bird rejuvenation. In 1979 the club agreed to sponsor a photography award for the provincial trophy competition. The club won the AFGA's Guy Blake Award in 1985 for the best club project—the building of deer feeders and donating them to farmers to help feed deer starving, as a result of a severe winter and deep snow.

Special People

In 1998 Vernon Simpson won the AFGA's J.B. Cunningham Memorial Award for membership sales, selling nearly 200 memberships during the previous year as well as selling 100 memberships the previous few years. Irene Yelle won Lady Conservationist of the Year Award from the AFGA on two different occasions.

Past presidents of the Iron Creek Fish and Game Association include Albert Whitbeck, 1965-70; Vernon Simpson, 1971-72; Ab Martin, 1973-74; Eber Waite, 1975-76; Francis Bovencamp, 1977-78; Edwin Davidson, 1979-80; Leo Markwart, 1981-82; Erik Holmberg, 1983-84; Lane Parsons, 1985-86; Vernon Simpson, 1987-88; John Sarasin, 1989-90; Brian Lee, 1991-92; Marvin Simmons, 1993-94; Erik Holmberg, 1995-96; Zane Parsons, 1997-98; Eric Davidson, 1999-2000; Ron Tanton, 2001-02; Lane Parsons, 2003; Craig Whitehead, 2004-05.

In summary, the Iron Creek Fish and Game Club has been one of the strongest, most active clubs in Alberta, especially in the 1970s and '80s. Unfortunately, over the last few years, the membership has been getting older and it is becoming more difficult to recruit younger members. With all the changes that are occurring to the fish and wildlife resource and the opportunities to enjoy that resource, ways must be found to attract new, younger and active members.

Lacombe Fish and Game Association
1930s-present

The Lacombe Fish and Game Association is based in the town of Lacombe and serves the surrounding area from Red Deer to Ponoka and Rimbey to Stettler. However, its tentacles of influence, mainly through the help it has provided with land purchases, extend from Edmonton to Castor to Pine Lake, west to the Dixon area and back to Edmonton.

Most old-timers agree the club was officially formed shortly before World War II, likely in the late 1930s. The earliest known president was Earl Scott in 1940-42. The Lacombe AFGA was formally incorporated on Jan. 26, 1971 as a not-for-profit society. The directors at the time were Roger Holteen, Bert Popow, Orest Schur, Carl Ganter, Mrs. R.J. White, Jack Towle and Stu Baird.

Recent membership in the Lacombe club has been approximately 200, but a high of 500-560 members was recorded three times.

Education
Club members have taught Alberta Conservation and Hunter Education and Firearms Safety courses since these programs came into being. They have reached well over 5,000 people directly through these programs and have helped grow the programs, certifying instructors in Stettler, Castor and Ponoka. They have been involved in helping to run more than 20 zone 3 conservation academies since that program began.

COURTESY OF DAVE POWELL

The Powell family of Lacombe, Dave (L), John and Jenny in 2005.

Projects
The first evidence of conservation work supported by volunteers from local sportsmen was a bird sanctuary and upland bird project, which required members to live-trap birds (ruffed and sharp-tailed grouse). This project began in 1938 and was headed up by Alex Bendick. The next evidence of club projects was in the early 1940s and 1950s when one of the club members, Clifford Lee, became a friend and driver for G.M. Spargo, then provincial secretary manager, wearing out a 1950 Mercury station wagon donated to the AFGA by Basil French of Calgary.

In the 1950s and '60s the club ran an active predator bounty program for crows and magpies. In 1940 the club was involved in pheasant stocking and providing chicks to interested members for raise-and-release. After several years of producing pheasants this project was discontinued. In the early 1960s the club reinstated the pheasant-stocking project that ran until the mid-1960s. The club supported Alberta's 4-H program to provide materials to enable 4-H clubs to stock pheasants until the late 1980s.

Construction of the Wilson Beach campsite began in 1967 to provide local residents camping opportunity and access to Gull Lake. By the mid-1980s it had grown into a Municipal Recreation Tourism Area and Fisheries Access Site. The site is enjoyed by countless Albertans annually. Total club investment in the project was over $1.5 million plus labour and still remains one of the largest and most successful club projects on record. The property is leased from the County of Lacombe and was originally donated by the Wilson family for public use.

Closely associated with Wilson Beach was the club's annual fish derby that ran from 1963-94. With the advent of catch-and-release fishing and depletion of fish stocks, the club cancelled all derbies allowing for kill categories and began running youth fishing days focusing on how to fish, how to handle fish allowing release and having fun fishing which continues to this day. In 2007 the club sponsored a very large catch-and-release derby which proved to be quite controversial but profitable for the resource.

Along with the derbies the club has also worked to promote stocking of fish ponds in the area. The club stocked the Lacombe Research Pond in West Lacombe from 1962-82 until summer fish kills forced cancellation. The club was involved with building fish ponds at Tees, and at Bentley in the early 1960s. They also adopted two Lacombe stormwater retention ponds and began stocking them in the early 2000s, planting 2,000 trout annually. Utilization of these stocked ponds by young and old alike has been high.

Lake stabilization projects have also been the focus of club attention. In Lacombe Lake, the project was completed; however, the re-establishment of northern pike did not occur. Perch did show up in the lake as late as 2004, when a minor fish kill was evident. The Gull Lake Stabilization Project was completed in the late 1970s. However, when the pumps were shut off, massive fish kills of trapped fish occurred in the ponds along and in the channel. Years of lobbying resulted in repairs being made to the channel and a fish blockage structure to prevent these kills. In early 2001-02 members helped fence off sections of the Blindman River bank to prevent cattle from destroying the riverbank. Re-planting upland areas also occurred to protect and enhance three miles of riverbank.

Burbank Park was another fisheries access site which was established in 1982. Land was purchased from the Town of Lacombe to provide the general public with access to the junction of the Red Deer and Blindman rivers. Site development required safety fencing of cliffs, a small campsite, a recreation area and outdoor education facility as part of the Municipal Recreation Tourism Area designation. The site was expanded in 1987 with a long-term lease on a county municipal reserve. Club investment of over $1 million has resulted in a stable, permanent family site on the rivers.

The Chain Lakes fishing access site and wildlife habitat site was purchased in the 1990s with the Ponoka and Millet fish and game clubs as partners. The area is the only public access to centre Chain Lakes and the wintering area of many local ungulates. Installation of utilities and a clubhouse/kitchen should help make this area into a permanent youth education facility for the summer months as well as preserve important winter ungulate habitat.

The club has also purchased 60 acres of land on the drain end of the Lincoln Wetlands, providing for a secure wetland for waterfowl for future generations. Other contributions in the order of $10,000 or more have been made to five other sites including Cain, Cain III, Stonehouse and Tide Creek on Pigeon Lake. The club was also active in the Nevis Gas plant donation of 320 acres of habitat that was finalized in 2007.

The club procured the initial grants and started the Parkland Habitat Steward program under president Grant Creasey. The program was eventually turned over to the parent association, where it is still active today.

In either 1984 or 1985 a meeting was held in Lacombe with members of Red Deer and Ponoka fish and game clubs to address the existing organization structures of the AFGA provincial executive. A resolution was put forth to restructure the executive. That resolution was lost on the floor of the Medicine Hat AFGA annual conference by a vote 111 to four. In subsequent years, all of the recommendations in that particular resolution were eventually adopted from resolutions presented by others, resulting in the current organizational structure.

Annual Events

In l961 the Lacombe club initiated wild game suppers, which continued until 2005. The suppers featured wild game, the annual club trophy awards and entertainment. Every fourth year since 1964, the club hosted interclub awards with fish and game clubs in Rimbey, Ponoka and Wetaskiwin.

Club Awards

The club annually sponsors local wildlife awards: the zone 3 trophy for best white-tail and the provincial cutthroat trout trophy.

The club has won the following AFGA provincial awards: Henry Lembicz – Clean Air, Clean Land, Clean Water Award; J.B. Cunningham Award for club membership; G.M. Spargo Award for children's programs; Guy Blake Award for best project; Archie Hogg Award for environmental issues awareness; George Watt Award for financial contributions to projects; Gerry Gibson Award for rural hunter training (and Jack Towle); Outdoor Edge Communication Award; and Neville Lindsay Award for fisheries project.

Special People

At present the club has given out four life memberships: Clifford T. Lee, a 1950s member who chauffeured George M. Spargo around Alberta in the AFGA station wagon; Jack Towle, a long-time member, one of the original hunter education instructors, past club president and a Spargo award winner; Ray Hutchinson, a 50-year member; and Dave Powell, a past president of the AFGA.

Members of the club have won the following awards: Dave Powell, the AFGA Fulton Trophy for outstanding contribution to conservation and the AFGA; Shirley Dobirstien, the AFGA Lady Conservationist; Jen Powell and Kerri-Ann and Kent Heppelhouser, Junior Conservation Award, Nebraska 4-H; Ron Seely, the AFGA Dennis Hindbo Award for predator control; Dave Powell, the AFGA G.E. Stevens Award for firearms safety; Fred Hargreaves, Len Thompson, Ed Tilley, Dave Shepherd, Dave Powell, George Watt and Steve McKenzie, the AFGA Distinguished Service Award. In 2002 Minister Mike Cardinal inducted Dave Powell into the Alberta Order of the Bighorn.

Past presidents include J. Ebeling, Don Moore, R. Kerr, Wally Haines, Fred Hargreaves, Len Thompson, Jim Barr, Cec Pallister, Edgar Todd, Ed Tilley, Jack Malmas, Fred Dobirstien, Orest Schur, Walter Bell, Roice Henderson, Martin Wilson, Dennis

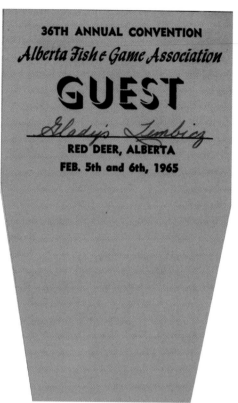

Lea, Jack Towle, Ron Spink, Jim Lembicz, Dick Morris, Chris Thiberge, Art Reitsma, Dave Powell, Dave Shepherd, Bill White, Ron Alexander, Ron Selvas, Grant Creasey, Danny Reitsma and Bob Brown.

Other hard-working members of the club are George Neis, Martin Wilson, Ray Hatchison, Peter Grant, Dave Cookson, Jalayne Towle, Shirley Dobirstien, Bernie Powell, Bobbie Bobinson, Carl Gussick, Jack Morrison, Boyd Williams and Darlene Chilton.

Several club members who were involved at the provincial level were: Cliff Lee, Fred Hargreaves and Orest Schur: zone 3 directors; Jack Towle, program chairman; Dave Powell, information chairman, zone 3 director and the AFGA president; Dave Shepherd, programs and hunting chairman; and Grant Creasey, programs chairman.

The Lacombe Fish and Game Association has and will continue to play a significant role in the operation and history of the AFGA and in wildlife management and conservation in Alberta.

Leduc Fish and Game Association
1967-present

In April 1967 Dennis Neiman and Gerry Lefebvre spearheaded the formation of a local fish and game association in Leduc. An organizational meeting was held May 4, 1967 in the Leduc Junior High school gym. Thirty-three people from Leduc and district became charter members that evening. Karl Walters was elected president, George McLeod as secretary, Dennis Neiman as treasurer

and Gerry Lefebvre as membership chair. The membership fee was set at $2. The objectives of the club were to host fishing derbies, a gun safety course, instruction in fishing procedures and the conservation of fish and wildlife. After a month of operation, the club had a membership of 80 people.

In 1975 a committee was struck to formulate the club's first bylaws and objectives. After approval by the membership, the association applied for and received registration under the *Alberta Societies Act*.

Projects
- Clean-up of debris and installation of a screen at the Leduc Reservoir to prevent trout escaping downstream.
- Initiated newspaper recycling in 1974 which prompted the construction of an eight-foot by 20-foot trailer and the purchase of two box trailers to haul the papers to Edmonton. This activity continued until December 1996 when the City of Leduc took over the operation while acknowledging the club for its invaluable contribution to recycling initiatives in the city.
- The purchase of 160 acres of land in conjunction with the Canadian Historical Arms Society to develop a full-service shooting range.
- The capture of 22 Canada geese, which were later transported and released at Saunders Lake just east of Leduc, which started the goose-nesting project.
- The purchase of four separate parcels of property totalling 635 acres to maintain and improve habitat.
- Supplied posts and wildlife warning reflectors at two sites to prevent wildlife collisions.
- Purchased two lots and a building in Leduc to serve as the clubhouse.

- Continues to conduct annual hunter success surveys for the Alberta Fish and Wildlife Division.
- Continues to supply boats and manpower (since 1977) for the physically challenged fish derby at Camp He Ho Ha at Lake Isle. The club also sponsors the lunch for all of the volunteers and participants.
- Frequently holds Hunter Education and Canadian Firearms Safety Courses.
- Has sponsored many youth to various outdoor education camps and conferences.
- Participated in a pheasant raise-and-release program.
- Provided goose- and duck-nesting platforms, boxes and tunnels throughout the Leduc County area.
- Built and distributed birdhouses all over Leduc County, many of these for the mountain bluebird.
- Supplied birdhouse kits to schools for children to participate in enhancing the outdoors and local wildlife.
- Built and supplied many bat houses to be erected in Leduc as well as the surrounding areas.
- Loaned club mounts of animals to schools so the children could learn about wildlife close-up.

In 1987 the club began working bingos in Leduc, along with a few casinos in Red Deer and St. Albert, to acquire funds to purchase the above-mentioned lands, the shooting range, clubhouse and to assist other clubs and organizations (e.g. the provincial association for purchase of its head-office building, Leduc Scouts to relocate into a new building, STARS, Santa's Helpers, the Leduc Food Bank and the AFGA Wildlife Trust Fund, to name a few).

In 1984 the club hosted the AFGA annual conference at the Convention Inn South in Edmonton and again in 2004 at the Executive Royal Inn in Leduc.

Annual Events

The club holds a few annual functions, such as a family swim or bowling with a pot-luck dinner afterward, a family sleigh-ride and picnic, a winter fish derby with a fish fry afterward, summer fish derby with a campout and barbecue as well as the annual wild game banquet and trophy night.

Club Awards

Since 1976 the club has sponsored the mallard duck trophy for the AFGA's yearly trophy competition.

Special People

Over the years, the club executive has awarded life memberships to those members who, through long service or other contributions, have promoted and upheld the aims and objectives of the club and merit special recognition. Life members include: Gilbert Magnan, Norm Henry, Les Yaceyko, Robert Arnholtz, Jack Careless, Dieter Aumuller, Alan Baker, Gene Goudreau, Lydia Aumuller, Joe Horvath, Norm McKay, Laurette Magnan and Karl Maceyovski.

Past presidents include: Karl Walters, Dennis Neiman, Walter Schnick, Jim Gormley, Lawrence Roth, Alan Baker, Les Yaceyko, Joe Dearborn, Gerry Macinnis, Gilbert Magnan, Karl Maceyovski, John Kyndesen, Ron Torgerson, John Gazankas, Bob Brewster, Jack Careless, Conrad Fennema, Robert Hoffman and Real Chalifoux.

Millet Fish and Game Association
1986-present

The Millet Fish and Game Association began back in the summer of 1986 when Al Dionne, Dennis Dziuba, Patrick Glimm, Dennis Peters, Norm Arnholtz and Dave Gursky discussed the idea of having a club for individuals who enjoyed the outdoors, primarily hunters and anglers. These people took it upon themselves to arrange for a public meeting to see if there were others interested in forming a club. That meeting was held on Sept. 4, 1986 at the Legion Hall in Millet. The 17 people present decided there was enough interest to proceed with forming a club and being part of the AFGA.

At a meeting in December, the following people were voted to serve on the first executive committee: Howie Clamp, Bill Hamburg, Al Dionne, Dan Kilborn, Dennis Dziuba, Brian McDonald, Dave Gibson, Ron McKinney, Jim Gibson, Alex Milburn, Pat Glimm, Dennis Peters, Dave Gursky and Rod Salem. Many of these people are still with the club. The club has grown considerably over the past 13 years from the original 17 members to the December 2006 membership of 180.

Education

Many club members are trained as outdoor education instructors, big-game scoring officials and fishing education instructors. The club offers annual first-time hunter training, and sponsors two youths each year to attend the zone 3 youth education camp.

Projects

Over the years the club has been very active in many areas of conservation, education, wildlife and fisheries-related issues and activities. Each year there are various activities that stand out and are memorable, including:
- Land acquisition: Miller Gravel Pit (147 acres), Pigeon Lake property (160 acres), Chain Lakes property (78 acres), the AFGA Habitat Trust Fund.
- Clubhouse development: 99-year lease from the Town of Millet in 1990, grand opening, June 8, 1991.
- Tree planting: lagoon site, MFGA property, several member-owned properties.
- Habitat projects: big-game range improvement, walleye spawning beds, beaver control, noxious weed control.
- Wildlife and fisheries management: big-game surveys, deer mortality investigation, hunter surveys, walleye management at Pigeon Lake, pheasant-raising and release, duck and goose nests.
- Special events and activities: campouts, archery tournaments, turkey shoots, annual awards banquet, volunteer appreciation events, trophy competition, parades, bingos, donation and local participation in special events.

Placemat from a Ponoka Fish and Game Association elk dinner.

Ponoka Fish and Game Association
1955-present

The Ponoka Fish and Game Association was established in 1955 by Dr. Barry Backus.

Education

As a result of the declining numbers of hunters, both provincially and nationally, about 25 years ago the club decided to try to reverse the trend. The annual midsummer conservation camp is a week-long event where members give basic instruction to get youth aged 11-14 involved in shooting long rifles and trap, archery and canoeing, and wilderness survival skills training. Nearly all students pass their conservation and hunter education exam at week's end. The club hopes this program will ensure the club prospers for another 50 years. It is most gratifying to see the earlier participants now returning as instructors, teaching their own and other children.

Projects

Not long after the club was started, Mr. Edward Bailer donated to the club 5.9 acres of land northwest of Ponoka through which

Ponoka Camp Pofianga.

flowed the seasonal Maskwa Creek. The club members cleared the brush from the ravine bottom and built a dam to create a four-acre lake on this site. Their efforts were rewarded by having the dam wash out in both 1961 and 1962. In 1964, with the help of

Ponoka Camp Pofianga.

the County of Ponoka, the provincial government and some heavy equipment located half a mile away (constructing what was to become the Queen Elizabeth II Highway), a properly engineered dam with a concrete spillway was finally completed. A contest was held for local school children to name the pond and 50 years later the facility is still known as Lake Pofianga. Over the years, the club has purchased four adjacent parcels to bring the total habitat area to 200 acres on the property. Included in these purchases was a particularly scenic 20 acres adjacent to the Queen Elizabeth II Highway that the provincial government decided not to develop as a rest stop.

While paying for this land, the club also began providing various amenities on the property. The property now boasts a 3,200-square-foot clubhouse complete with showers and a commercial kitchen, pistol range, rifle range, archery trails, ball diamond, horseshoe pits and a dozen canoes for use on the stocked lake. Weekends from May to September are usually booked for groups of up to 200 people for events such as weddings and family reunions; the club offers its use for free to many non-profit groups.

In 1991 the Ponoka Mental Health Hospital (as it was known at the time) decided to divest itself of 50 acres on Berdine (North Chain) Lake east of Ponoka. Offered first to non-profit groups, the club stepped up to the plate and for the assessed value of $80,000 secured perpetual public access to the lake. The club also partnered with the Lacombe and Millet fish and game clubs to purchase 74 acres on Centre Chain Lake. In 2005 it assumed responsibility for a 99-year lease from the County of Ponoka on 40 acres on the northeast corner of Gull Lake.

Annual Event

The annual Rifleman's Rodeo on the Labour Day weekend is a three-day event that sees competitors from all over the province testing their skills on five different targets. Competitors in both open sight and scope classes fire at silhouettes of animals that range from a running fox at 80 yards to a mountain goat at 300 yards.

Red Deer Fish and Game Association
1938-present

The Red Deer Fish and Game Association was organized on April 21, 1938 at a meeting in the Corona Motors show room, with the election of the first club officers. Association dues were set at an annual fee of 50 cents per member with a total of 34 charter members in attendance. The membership has since increased substantially to 301 in 2006.

Concerns in the early years of the club history were centred on fishing, stocking streams and lakes in the area, "snaring" and netting of fish by poachers, etc. There were crow and magpie concerns with suggestions of bounties being placed on these birds. Minutes of the meetings in the 1930s and '40s mention the need to greatly reduce the population of these birds.

COURTESY OF RED DEER FISH AND GAME ASSOCIATION
The Red Deer Fish and Game Association goose-nesting project.

Education
Members of the club promote a junior shooting program for air rifle, air pistol and .22-calibre rifles and in past years have held fly- and bait-casting seminars for youngsters. There is also an active archery club and black powder club with annual shoots held on club property.

The Red Deer Fish and Game Association provides two annual $500 scholarships to Red Deer College students, donates $150-$200 in books to the city library, annually sponsors three to four students to the zone 3 conservation academy, and sponsors one of the local Junior Forest Warden groups.

Projects
Pheasant-stocking with birds sent from the Brooks provincial pheasant hatchery was being done by the club in the Red Deer area

starting in 1943. The club was later involved in raising pheasants in the 1970s and '80s, with pens built on Lorne McArthur's property. The pens were turned over to Lorne in the 1980s and the program was cancelled by the club because the birds were being taken by coyotes before the hunters had a chance at them.

COURTESY OF THE RED DEER FISH AND GAME ASSOCIATION
The Red Deer Fish and Game Association indoor range.

Over the years the club has been active in various programs in the area. The placing of flax bales for goose-nesting in co-operation with the Alberta Fish and Wildlife Division was a major project in the 1980s.

The Physically Challenged Fun Fishing Day was an ongoing major project for 17 years, and ended when the nursing-home residents became too frail to attend this event, and the club was unable to get residents within the city at large to take part in it.

The largest consistent club project over the years has been the Annual Sportsman's Show. The 41st show ran March 2-4, 2007. This has been a major fundraiser for the organization put on solely by the Red Deer club. The show runs on a weekend between the Calgary and Edmonton boat and sportsmen shows.

The Red Deer organization has been active in other money-raising ventures, such as monthly bingos and some casino nights over the years. Funds raised by the club have allowed it to purchase two quarter-sections of land east of Red Deer, primarily for wildlife habitat, which includes a camping area complete with kitchen facilities, a stocked fish pond, a walk-through archery range, hiking trails along with several other amenities.

The club owns over 11 acres west of the city, which houses a well-equipped outdoor range for rifle and handgun use. It also owns a 25-yard indoor range within Red Deer and leased from the school board.

Annual Events
Some of the club's annual activities include the smoker and awards night in April, family campout in June, hunter survey in December and horn measuring in February.

Special People
Life members of the Red Deer Fish and Game Club include Clayben Hood, Archie Whammond, Ward Robinson, and Venny Chocholacek.

COURTESY OF THE RED DEER FISH AND GAME ASSOCIATION
The Red Deer Fish and Game Association outdoor range.

The following people served as presidents of the club: R.H. Blades, 1938–40; E. Wiggins, 1941–49; Geo Roth, 1950–52; A. Allen, 1953; L. Kalbfliesch, 1954–55; Henry Lembicz, 1956–57; J. Munro, 1958–59; H. Lembicz, 1960–61; C. Head, 1962; J. Hanson, 1963–64; E. Aronitz, 1965–66; G. Olson, 1967–68; R.H. (Bob) Scammell, 1969–70; H. Rasmussen, 1971–72; Lloyd Graff, 1973–74; W. Robinson, 1975–76; W. Brown, 1977–78; C. Hood, 1979–80; T. Turner, 1981–82; V. Chocholacek, 1983–84; R. Temchuk, 1985–86; C. Ploof, 1987; E. Miller, 1988–89; J. Dyck, 1990; H. Wright, 1991–92; L. Houghton, 1993–94; A. Hogberg, 1995–98; R. McCoy, 1999–2002; H. Wright, 2003–04; G. McCoy, 2005–06; S. Bauer, 2007.

Over the years, many of the club members have gone on to hold various positions with the parent organization. Some even held the presidency of the AFGA such as: Henry Lembicz, R.H. (Bob) Scammell, and Douglas Rumsey.

Rocky Mountain House Fish and Game Association
1940s-present

The origin of the Rocky Mountain House Fish and Game Association dates back prior to the 1940s. Some of the early founding members were Henry Stelfox, Stan Hooker, Bob Ross, Ed Stenback, Bill Street, and Melvin and Jim Cowie. Membership in the club in those years was around 20. Bob and Tom Titford were presidents in the late 1940s and early '50s.

Over the years, the club became inactive and subsequently resurrected itself several times. A diehard group of local outfitters, including Chester Sands, Ed Mackenzie, Jim Colosimo, Clayton Grosso, Sam Sands and Sam Kostynuk, kept the annual trophy night and banquet alive until the club could regroup.

In 1989 Gerry Gibson was instrumental in bringing the club back to what it has become today. Unfortunately, Gerry passed away in 1992 as a result of an industrial accident.

Projects
The club became involved in stocking fish into the local streams and the occasional lake. In one particular stocking episode from the early 1950s, a few members were hauling fish in cream cans in the back of their trucks from transport tanks to the stream to be stocked. Since the trail to the intended stream had deteriorated with no alternate way to the stream and there was concern that their fish in the cream cans were in transit too long and could soon expire, a decision was made to deposit them in a nearby lake. The next year, local residents noticed fish jumping in that lake and wondered from where they had come. The lake habitat turned out to be ideal for growing trout and it was not long before there were good-sized fish. As a result, the club decided to hold a fishing derby there. As luck would have it, one of the members who had helped stock the lake won the derby with a rainbow trout weighing six-and-three-quarter pounds. He still has the prize he received in his shed, a Westbend 2-¾ hp outboard motor.

With few access roads into the west country, wild game was plentiful so no habitat projects were needed or undertaken.

COURTESY OF BOB SCAMMELL

Martha Kostuch, vice president of the AFGA, 1990.

Hunters reported seeing two separate herds of elk of over 100 animals each. Several local hunters reported filling their elk tags during each of 16 successive years. Hunting for large antlers was not their priority as they only took "spikers" and antlerless elk. Few wolves lived in the eastern slopes area at the time. These conditions, combined with the limited access to prime hunting areas, undoubtedly contributed to the plentiful elk population.

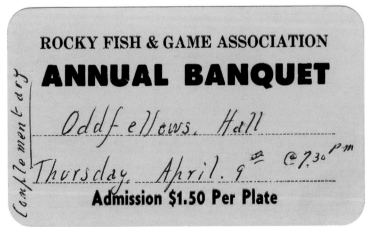

COURTESY OF HENRY LEMBICZ

The present club has been involved with the following projects:

- Moose habitat enhancement, in consultation with the local Fish and Wildlife Division biologists and with the help of the Buck for Wildlife program, the club chose areas concentrated with old willows. Either using a chainsaw or a hydro axe driven by a Caterpillar tractor, members cut old growth willow trees to get new willows to sucker and provide fresh browse for moose.
- Gap Lake. The club adopted the trail into this favourite fishing spot to manage the access of off-highway vehicles (OHV). The goal was to keep these machines out of wet areas and improve access for everyone.
- Children's fish pond. Originally the club held a lease on this pond. However, when the club became inactive in the 1980s, the Alberta Fish and Wildlife Division took over the lease and stocked the pond each year. They installed an aeration windmill to over-winter the fish. The club still looks after the fish pond site and holds an annual children's fishing derby. Weather permitting, the club invites the local seniors to come out for the day to fish and visit with the new generation of anglers.
- Baptiste River and Chambers Creek bridge project. In an effort to keep OHV-riders out of these streams and to slow down stream-bank erosion and stream siltation, the club constructed three bridges over the river at popular crossing areas. It turns out elk are also using the bridges to cross the river.
- Rocky Youth Fish and Game club. Over the last several years there has been a very active youth group. This club has been involved in bluebird house building and setup, roadside cleanup, a Pheasants Forever hunting day, and an annual fly-in fishing trip to a local mountain lake.

Annual Event

The banquet and awards night is still a mainstay of the club and is its only fundraiser. The banquet is held the first weekend in March every year. Tickets are limited, and every year it is a sellout.

Special People

A memorial trophy in Gerry Gibson's name is presented at the trophy night and banquet to a member of the club who contributes to the club. Members who have received this trophy are: Frank Spruyt, Dale Kleinschroth, Greg Mallo, Philip Lacerte, Ernie and Barb Shaw, Dale McKenelley, Greg Taylor, Robert Anger and family, Bryan Anger, Benita Anger, Kelly Drolet and Ashley Hall.

Sundre Fish and Game Club
1980-present

The Sundre Fish and Game Club was formed in 1980 to promote fishing, hunting and proper management of the fish and wildlife resources and habitats for today and tomorrow.

Projects

The Ungulate Fund is designed to help improve the depleting ungulate population between highways 1A and 54 and west of Highway 2. Financial support for this program has been received from the Iowa Chapter of Foundation for North American Wild Sheep as well as the Northwest Michigan Chapter of Safari Club International.

The fish pond is established on member Billy Knapp's land. The pond is stocked yearly. This has been a great success as it allows young people the opportunity to have a first-time fishing experience. In 2003 trees were planted, outside toilets erected, and picnic tables and fire rings built. A watering system for the trees was put in place. Lots of volunteer man hours will continue to go into this project.

Water-well project: It was brought to the attention of the Sundre Fish and Game Club that the Panther River campground did not have any fresh water supply. Once again the club took the initiative to raise the funds to drill a well and supply a pump. This project is being enjoyed by many families.

Fencing project: The fencing project on Schroeder Creek has been very beneficial to the stream and the fish in it as it keeps livestock from access to the creek.

Walking bridge project: The people living on the south side of Prairie Creek in Sundre had no foot access to the IGA and mall and surrounding area. The Sundre Fish and Game Club raised the money and supplied the manpower to build the bridge that is used by many.

Sylvan Lake Fish and Game Association
1959-present

The Sylvan Lake Fish and Game Association was formed in January or February of 1959. The club's first president was Ray Albert, who was supported by an executive committee of Bill Lund, B.C. Learned, Fred Walker and Mike McLean.

In the beginning, the club's meetings were held in private homes. The club presently meets in the Sylvan Lake Friendship Centre. One of the club's first projects was the construction of a gun and archery range. However, the insurance became so high that the project had to be abandoned.

Projects

In 1969 the club decided to build the Niemela Fish Dam to improve fishing opportunities. A fundraising campaign was launched. The Alberta government made two grants for the project of $3,000 and $1,000. The club had to match these amounts with either cash or labour. To raise the required funds, the club held raffles, auctions, banquets and accepted private donations. The dam and reservoir were constructed, and over the years the reservoir has had to be deepened and the spillway rebuilt a couple of times. The dam and reservoir have also been made wheelchair accessible and are enjoyed by all who fish there.

The club has embarked on several projects over the years, including a crow and magpie control campaign, a hunter training program, placing goose nesting bales in the southwest Sylvan Lake area, holding a fly-tying course, sponsoring curling bonspiels, and building the Aspen Ring-Neck Pheasant Farm on the John Charles farm.

Annual Events

The club started an annual trophy and awards banquet about 1972. The banquet is no longer held but the annual trophy night still takes place.

In 1987 three club members, Byron Soley, Dean Vig and Brian Nelson, took a scoring course for measuring horns and antlers. This course was taught by Jack Graham from the AFGA, and as a result, the club holds a measuring clinic on the first Saturday in January of every year. The club has participated over the last 10 years in the annual hunter survey for the Alberta Fish and Wildlife Division. Sylvan Lake Fish and Game also sponsors the annual fish and game campout and pancake breakfast that is usually well-attended by members and friends.

Club Awards

The Sylvan Lake Fish and Game Association won the following awards from the AFGA: Quota Busters Award for a membership of 250, 1975; Guy Blake Memorial Award for the best club project, 1978; and the J.B. Cunningham Award for the most improved club, 1979.

Special People

In 1981 John Charles received the AFGA Darwin Cronkhite Award for building the pheasant pens on the John Charles farm. In 1996 Doris Anderson was presented the AFGA Lady Conservationist of the Year Award. Ron Barry won the AFGA J.B. Cunningham Award for membership sales in 2002; as well, he was recognized for donating material from Ipsco Steel to make the wheelchair ramp at the Niemela Fish Dam.

The local club has given its own Exemplary Awards twice to Fred Walker, and once each to Lily Walker, Esther Soley and Byron Soley.

Thorsby and District Fish and Game Association
1966-present

The Thorsby and District Fish and Game Association was formed at the Thorsby Legion Hall in March 1966 by interested people concerned about habitat and conservation. The membership in 1968 was 187. Meetings were moved to the nearby town of Sunnybrook in October 1968 because of its central location. Members came from Thorsby, Warburg, Strawberry, Telfordville, Pigeon Lake, Sunnybrook, St. Francis, Genesee and Breton. One of the first club projects was the hunter education program taught by member instructors. The club started a monthly newsletter called *The Moose Call* in April 1969 to keep its members up-to-date on club happenings.

Projects

Club members developed an access road and campground at Sardine Lake in Brazeau Country. The lake is stocked with rainbow trout. The club built 25 recreational spaces in the Ashland Dam Park. The dam reservoir is stocked yearly with 13,000 rainbow trout.

Another project started in August 1969 was the Predator Control Program (both birds and pests) whereby a bounty for magpie and crow feet was awarded. This program has been discontinued.

A registered rifle range was established on Peter Free's land in 1971. The lease was terminated in 1980 because the land changed owners. Currently, the club is trying to re-establish a range at a new location. This is of utmost importance in the teaching of gun safety for students taking the conservation and hunter education program.

Other concerns in the past have been cleanup and pollution at Brazeau Dam, Pigeon Lake, Buck Lake, Twin Lake, and parking at Wabamun Lake.

Continuing items of concern are pollution, the changing of wildlife habitats by various developments (i.e. Odyssey, Brazeau Timber and Edmonton Power) and the danger to any critical wildlife areas in the province. Future club projects will involve pheasant rearing, hunter education, rifle range development, wildlife week in schools, the AFGA Lottery, and conservation camp participation.

Annual Events

The major event of each year is the annual trophy ball (wild game dinner), where members receive their trophies for fish and big-game entries.

Special People

One of the prized trophies given each year, sponsored by Arnold Kruger and Sons, is the Arlin Farms' Presidents Award, started in 1971. The recipient of this trophy is chosen by the president of the club for the most dedication to the club's betterment and purpose. Only the president knows who shall receive this award, which is given out the night of the annual trophy ball. Arlin Farm's Presidents Award recipients are Pete Free, 1971; Ben Grohn, 1972; L.C. Mottl, 1973; Deanna Grohn, 1974; F.V. Tomaszewski, 1975; Roy Burnett, 1976; Bill Greenhough, 1977; Albert Gunsch, 1978; Joe Herregodts, 1979; Bruce Morden, 1980; Wayne Prier, 1981; Wally Mertz, 1982; Ruth Harrison, 1983; Albert Gunsch, 1984; Pete Free, 1985; Ivan Johnston, 1986; Arlene Tomaszewski,

COURTESY OF THE THORSBY FISH AND GAME ASSOCIATION
The Thorsby Fish and Game Association outdoor range.

1987; Phil Mundy, 1988; Pete Free, 1989; Doreen Herregodts, 1990; Stan Tomaszewski, 1991; C.R. Harrison, 1992; Frank Tomaszewski, 1993; Ruth Harrison, 1994; Pete Free, 1995; Bruce Morden, 1996; Lorraine McKay, 1997; Wally Carstairs, 1998; Mike Tomaszewski, 1999; Susie Szepesi, 2000; Vivian Morden, 2001; Pat Drewniak, 2002; C.R. Harrison, 2003; Carol Valade, 2004; Tracy Musson, 2005; and Ken Hamilton, 2006.

Lifetime achievements are given to members who have served in an active capacity on the executive for a long time. Award recipients include: Stan Tomaszewski, 1999-2001; Peter Free, 1999; Bruce Morden, 1999; William Greenhough, 2000; Lumir Mottl, 2000; Wally Mertz, 2000; Michael Tomaszewski, 2001-04; Frank Tomaszewski, 2001; Walter Carstairs, 2002; Clifford (Russ) Harrison, 2007.

Wimborne and District Fish and Game Association
1970s-present

The Wimborne and District Fish and Game Association has been active for about 40 years. Mr. J.O. Smith organized a meeting at the Crossroads Hall with the desire of forming a club to lobby the government to prevent the use of motorized boats on the newly constructed Bigelow Reservoir which was built in 1971. The club then moved in to the Wimborne Hall and the membership increased with J.O. Smith as president, Alex Benedict as secretary, and Dick Vickery as treasurer.

The club's next project was the construction of the Kraft Fish Pond. This was dug in January 1973 and stocked with 300 trout that spring. "Mr. J.O.," as president Smith was know by everyone, got the provincial government to put in another 1,000 fish in June. In 1973 the membership had increased to 132 members.

The club was founded with the goal of providing family activities and this remains so to 2007. There have been many highlights over the years from participation in parades, curling and dances to Clarence Brown's record book elk. The club remains active with an annual wild game supper held in Wimborne every March and a campout and fishing derby at the Kraft Pond in July. Membership has varied over the years with the present enrolment at 130 and growing.

Mountain goat.

COURTESY OF DON MEREDITH

Zone 4

Zone 4 covers an area from the City of Edmonton to British Columbia to the west, and is bordered on the north by zone 6 and on the south by zone 3, and includes the area from Whitecourt to Drayton Valley. Some zone 4 clubs are in the City of Edmonton. The area is a mixture of parkland, foothills and mountain landscapes.

The 19 clubs in zone 4 are:
- Alberta Clipper Hunting Retriever Association
- Barrhead Fish and Game Association
- Busby District Fish and Game Association
- Devon Fish and Game Gun Club
- Edmonton Old Timers Fishing Club
- Edmonton Police Department Fish and Game Association
- Edmonton Trout Fishing Club
- Evergreen Shooting Club
- Fisheries Enhancement Society of Alberta *
- Mayerthorpe and District Fish and Game Association
- Morinville Fish and Game Association
- Onoway and District Fish and Game Association
- Pioneer Gun Club *
- Spruce Grove Fish and Game Association
- St. Albert and District Fish and Game Association
- Spruce Grove Fish and Game Association
- Stony Plain Fish and Game Association
- Whitecourt Fish and Game Association
- Wildwood and District Junior Rod and Gun Club *
  * clubs that did not submit histories

Zone 4/5 Youth Conservation Camp (see zone 5)

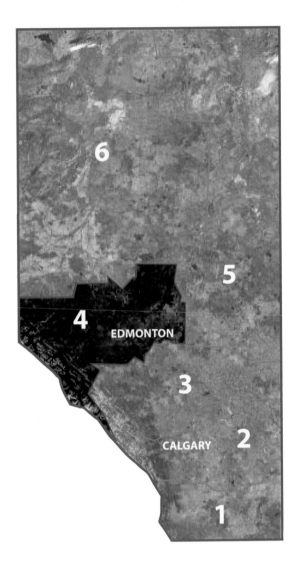

Club Histories of Zone 4

Alberta Clipper Hunting Retriever Association
1991-present

In the spring of 1991 a small group of dog retriever enthusiasts in the Edmonton area decided to form a club whose main focus was to promote and preserve the hunting instincts of retriever breeds. A meeting was held and in May of 1991 the Alberta Clipper Hunting Retriever Association was incorporated.

The Alberta Clipper Hunting Retriever Association is a non-profit organization intended to promote and preserve the hunting instincts of the retriever dog breeds. The club promotes a social environment that encourages families to be involved in the handling and training of retrievers. It educates handlers, owners and the general public to promote quality in the breeding of hunting retrievers. The club encourages the use and training of hunting retrievers as a conservation tool for the sound management and use of wildlife resources.

Initial activities of the club included training groups and education sessions so members could share their knowledge and skills with each other. Training was primarily done at gravel pits on the outskirts of the city.

The club became an affiliate of the North American Hunting Retriever Association (NAHRA) to use its standards to test and evaluate members' dogs as their skills are developed. NAHRA was created in 1983 as a non-profit organization to preserve the hunting instincts of the retriever dog breeds and to conserve game through the development of trained retrievers.

The NAHRA program was developed on the premise that hunting retrievers need improvement. Many hunters have never seen good retriever work and do not know the potential of their dogs. Hunters need a structure in which they can learn to train and evaluate their dogs off season. They also need a system of formal tests so their dog's working accomplishments can be demonstrated and recorded.

Under the NAHRA program, dogs do not compete against one another for placements but rather their performances are judged individually against a hunting standard. There are four levels of testing (beginner, started, intermediate and senior). Each level provides a variety of challenging hunting scenarios and tested skills that challenge both dog and handler.

COURTESY OF RAY MAKOWECKI

Hinton area wetland.

In the early years of the Alberta Clipper Hunting Retriever Association, NAHRA tests were held on a variety of sites in the Keephills area with the permission of TransAlta Utilities. The evenings were always concluded with the presentation of ribbons to the qualifying dogs and a social meeting and meal afterwards at the Sundance ball diamond.

Eventually access to the gravel pits became restricted and the club felt that it needed its own property where members could take their dogs and give them the experience of training on a variety of land and water situations. In 2000, the club leased a quarter section of property near Wabamun.

The club continues to use this property as its central area for training and tests. It also makes the property available to other organizations dedicated to preserving its natural state, such as the Junior Forest Wardens. In 2006, the club started the construction of a large shelter to be used as a meeting place.

Currently, the club has a membership of about 40 people.

Annual Events
The club promotes itself through training classes for novice handlers and retriever demonstrations at the Edmonton Boat and Sportsmen's Show. Every summer, the club holds at least one picnic test for its members. This is a fun and informal training session where handlers can identify and address dog training issues with the assistance and guidance of other club members. The club holds one NAHRA test and several Canadian Kennel Club sanctioned tests yearly on the club property.

Barrhead Fish and Game Association
1963-present

The Barrhead Fish and Game Association was started in September 1963 and was affiliated with the AFGA on Feb. 27, 1964. The first president was Gotlieb Schuman, secretary was Ed Hornsby, treasurer was Shorty Schilling; directors were Dave Serner, Ray Hindmarsh, John Baron and Tom Wolfinger.

Education
Conservation and hunter education courses are held every two years with over 200 students having completed the course. Three qualified instructors are club members.

Projects
The club stocked fish at the following lakes: Schuman Lake, 1965, rainbow trout; Peanut Lake, 1968, rainbow trout; Dolberg Lake, 1971, rainbow trout. Pheasant-raising and goose-nesting bales projects were started in 1981. The club built fencing along the north shore of Thunder Lake in 1998.

The club has a permanent gun range located 17 kilometres west of Barrhead. It includes trap and pistol shooting ranges, and a 300-metre rifle range.

Annual Events
Antler-and horn-measuring occurs on the first Saturday in February each year. An annual wild game supper, trophy night and dance is held the first Saturday in March with attendance ranging from 110 to 140 people.

Busby and District Fish and Game Association
2002-present

On Jan. 9, 2002 Fred Stamper of Morinville approached the AFGA to take over the trust fund of the Pembina River Fish and Game Association, as that club had become inactive. He then approached previous members of the Pembina club to form the Busby and District Fish and Game Association.

The first executive included Fred Stamper, president; Mike Edwards, vice president; Dianne Edwards, secretary; Tilly Yagos, treasurer; Brian Yagos, membership chair; Richard Edwards, fishing chair; Daryl Denman, hunting chair; Joanne Edwards, publicity chair; and Colleen Stamper, program chair. The club is family-oriented and tries to support its local communities.

Education

Over the last four years, the club has sent youths to the zone 4/5 Narrow Lake Conservation Education Centre camp. The club has hosted the largest recorded horn measuring school and a boat licensing course.

Projects

In support of habitat, the club and its members have constructed and placed birdhouses, bird feeders, bat houses, goose nests and duck tunnels. Thanks to Wayne and Maureen Mirus, the club has developed a stocked trout pond, at which a fishing derby was hosted.

The club has contributed financial aid to the zone 4/5 Conservation Education Centre, Ducks Unlimited Canada, the Camp He Ho Ha disabled fishing derby and the Family Community Support Services Christmas program in Westlock. In 2006 the Busby and District Fish and Game Association received the Dennis Hindbo Predator Award for magpie traps, built by the club and used in the surrounding area.

COURTESY OF DUANE RADFORD

Fred Stamper, zone 4 AFGA director, 2007.

COURTESY OF HENRY LEMBICZ

Devon Fish and Game Club float in Devon Days parade.

The club has put on four very successful annual banquets. Mrs. Correna Simmons was a guest at the 2005 annual banquet, where her husband, Bill Simmons, was honoured by giving her a plaque and roses. Bill was instrumental in getting some land set aside as a natural area over in the Tawatinaw area. The Busby and District Fish and Game Association is a steward of the Tawatinaw Natural Area.

Club Award

The Busby and District Fish and Game Association received the AFGA Guy Blake Memorial Award for their support in helping to purchase the Wabamun/Whitewood conservation properties.

Devon Fish and Game Gun Club
1950s-present

The Devon Fish and Game Club was among the first voluntary groups to emerge from the town and area around Devon. The town was originally built to accommodate the oil boom of 1947 after the discovery of the Leduc Woodbend oilfield by Imperial Oil. Peopled by workers of spirit and enterprise, the town was a natural home to a good many who liked to hunt and fish. The area had good populations of game animals, fish, and both waterfowl and upland birds. The club founders, in the early 1950s, were also concerned about the conservation of their wildlife resources.

One of the first members of the club was Mr. R.A. (Bob) Bailey. A veteran of World War II, Mr. Bailey commanded a militia group, a platoon of the 19th Alberta Dragoons, for whom he had set up a rifle range in 1953 on his property edging onto the north bank of the North Saskatchewan River. In 1955 he decided to turn this range, approved by the Department of National Defence, over to the club, with the proviso that it still be accessible to shooters from the ranks of militia, cadets, police and prison guards. Indeed, the RCMP's K-Division used the range to qualify its members in shooting for many years.

The range was improved in numerous ways over the next 40 years. Backstops and target boards were upgraded; shooting benches were built; and, for the trap range, concrete pads for the shooters, an automatic clay-pigeon thrower, and a bunker to house it. With the increasing popularity of archery during the 1980s, the club built a shed to house archery butts and a tower from which to practice hunting from a tree stand. In addition, 3-D targets (simulated wild-game figures) for archery-hunting practice were purchased. Much of this equipment and work was funded by community lottery grants.

From late spring to early autumn, club members keen to break clay pigeons met at the range to compete. However, the range was closed in 2002 because of a pending sale of the land. Since then, the club's trap shooters, somewhat fewer in number, have used the Edmonton gun club's range off Highway 19 between Devon and Nisku.

Education

The Alberta conservation and hunter education course has been offered by the club since the 1960s. To date, some 400 local people have become qualified to hold an Alberta hunting licence as a result of the club's instruction.

Since firearms safety testing became mandatory in Canada in 1993, the club's certified instructors have provided the Canadian firearms safety course to local residents, often in conjunction with the conservation and hunter education course.

Projects

Over its half-century of existence, the Devon club has performed many habitat projects for the enhancement of wildlife. Goose-nesting rafts were constructed during the 1970s for numerous wetland sites in the region north and west of Devon, and maintained for many years. Shelter belts were planted on the gun range property during the 1980s to reduce erosion and provide cover for bird species. Club members helped in a Parkland County project to remove purple loosestrife, an alien species that chokes out natural plants in the wetlands.

In the 1990s the innovation of duck-nesting tunnels came into vogue throughout the province, and the Devon club installed some 30 of these in the region. It had become clear by then that ducks, in contrast to geese, whose numbers had increased hugely, were much more in need of conservation efforts. The nesting tunnels have shown increasing use by ducks, in large part for the protection from predators they provide. The club maintains them to this day.

The club has been active in the AFGA habitat steward program, in which local residents are recognized for their efforts in reserving parts of their properties for wildlife habitat. Over a dozen acreage owners in the area have been so recognized.

The club has collected big-game hides for the AFGA's hide collection program since the inception of this laudable initiative.

From the 1970s to the 1990s, the club took part in the provincial pheasant-raising and release program, maintaining pens, feeding the birds, and releasing them into the wild each year.

With the loss of their shooting range in 2002, club members turned their attention to a major project in angling and habitat. A lease was secured of a plot of land near the junction of highways 60 and 39, about six kilometres south of Devon. A pond on the property, surrounded by a grove of trees and brush, became the focus of the Jim Nelson memorial trout pond. Honouring one of the club's prominent early members, his successors built a wharf and stocked the pond with rainbow trout. This site has proved so popular with local residents that the entire stock of fish had been caught by the late fall of 2005. Work is to continue on the site, with construction of toilets, improvement of the parking area and of course restocking the pond with trout.

Although the Jim Nelson memorial trout pond has been a notable success, there is no escaping the fact that the loss of the club's own shooting range has led to a serious decline in membership over the past four years. The membership roster, which extended to well over 200 members during the 1990s, has shrunk to only a quarter of that. A search thus began for either a new range or access to another club's range. In the spring of 2006, the search finally bore fruit. An agreement with both the Leduc Fish and Game Association and the Canadian Historical Arms Society was achieved, by which the club was allowed to use the Genesee range, southwest of Stony Plain. Although some distance for many members to travel, this range includes a handgun course, a trap range, and rifle courses from 100 metres out to 700 metres.

Annual Events

A measure night, when trophies are scored, is held during the first week of December. The club's annual wild game banquet, trophy night and silent auction occurs early in March. Trophies are awarded to members who bagged the best heads of game, caught the largest fish, and scored highest in the club's shooting contests, among other categories. The Sportsperson of the Year is honoured at this time, and the President's Award is also conferred on another member who made an outstanding contribution to the club during the preceding year.

Club Awards

The Devon club has sponsored the AFGA Non-typical Mule Deer Trophy for Alberta since 1975.

Edmonton Old Timers Fishing Club

In 1992 Wally Warawa, a well-known senior Edmonton fisherman, was concerned about other senior fishermen who wished they had someone to go fishing with and some way to travel to Alberta's beautiful lakes. He realized he had to find a way to get these older anglers together to combine resources to go fishing, learn from each other, socialize and otherwise improve their retirement years. Wally talked the idea over with Dave and Darrell Johnston, owners of the Fishin' Hole stores. They both agreed to put up posters in their stores, asking anyone over 55 years of age to sign up if they were interested, and almost immediately there were 35 to 40 names on the list.

The Edmonton Old Timers Fishing Club was officially incorporated on March 25, 1993 as an organization providing activities for seniors with the motto "Seniors Helping Seniors." The club held its first meeting on April 13, 1992. Everyone was

Wally Warawa (centre) enjoying St. Michael's School fishing day at Lake Wabamun.

asked to bring a friend and the club logged 39 charter members. The first officers of the club were: Wally Warawa, president; and Jack Belland, Harry Daniels, Steve Drew, Tom Ferguson, Ed Fox, Gord King, Don Millwood, and Howard Stewart, directors.

Education

Weekly workshops are held on Mondays at 1 p.m., and fly-tying and lure-making are taught and fishing matters are discussed.

Projects

The club is involved in the annual Edmonton Boat and Sportsmen's Show and the Outdoor Show and Sale, the latter sponsored by The Fishin' Hole and Campers Village. The club, along with other fishing clubs in the Edmonton area, participated in the Muir Lake trout rehabilitation project and the Spring Lake aeration project.

The club invites guest speakers to present at its monthly meetings and holds a fundraising auction each April. It produces a monthly newsletter that keeps members informed and up to date about club events, such as weekly fishing outings, meetings, speakers, equipment and supplies for rent and sale, etc. A telephone committee ensures club members are informed. As well, a "sick-and-visiting" representative keeps members informed about the well-being of all members.

Annual Events

Each year the club holds a family outing where members and their families enjoy a day of fishing and winter activities, including a fish fry, hotdogs, chili, hot chocolate and doughnuts.

The club holds a competition each year, sponsored by an outdoor business, for the largest pike, perch, walleye, trout and lake whitefish caught, plus a catch-and-release category.

Club Awards

The club sponsors the provincial AFGA Lake Whitefish Award for the largest lake whitefish taken in a year. In 2005 the Edmonton Old Timers Fishing Club received the AFGA *Outdoor Edge* communication award for its newsletter being the best to inform its membership.

Special People

The club promotes the Wally Warawa President's Award, which is presented to a member who "exemplifies unselfish commitment to the Old Timers Fishing Club." The past winners are Jack Belland, Bill Lee, Jack Graham, Gordon Lamoureux and Don Millwood. As well, the following have been granted life memberships for their service to the club: Ivan Johnston, Bill Lee and Gordon Lamoureux.

Past presidents of the club are Wally Warawa, Don Millwood, George Wigley, Dave Derworiz, Jack Graham and Doreen Batterham.

Edmonton Police Department
Fish and Game Association
1968-present
a memoir by Mike Chetek

Early in 1968, I attended a meeting of the Edmonton Fish and Game Association. There were approximately 250 to 300 members present and all seemed to know each other, except me. The only person I recognized was George Mitchell, who I later learned was on the executive of the club. That spring, I entertained the idea that surely there were enough fellow members of the Edmonton Police Service who were active in the outdoors and who might be interested in coming together to share stories about hunting and fishing.

In the summer, I headed to a reported "hot" fishing spot along the McLeod River with two other members of the police service. We had stopped along the side of the highway to catch some grasshoppers for bait when I heard a loud voice coming from the

COURTESY OF THE EDMONTON OLD TIMERS FISHING CLUB

Otto Hammermeister fishing on the Red Deer River.

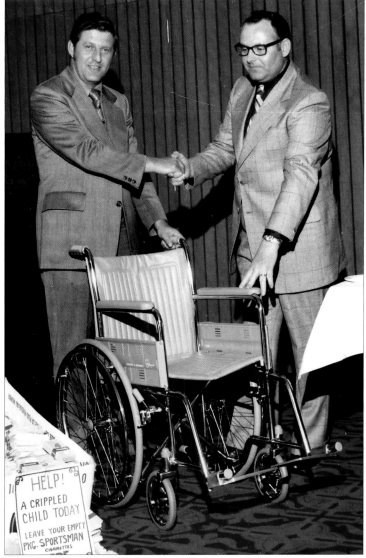

SUPPLIED

Don Miller (L), Rothmans Tobacco Products. Mike Chetek, president, Edmonton Police Fish and Game Association. Empty packs of Sportsman tobacco products were donated and contributed to the purchase of a wheelchair, circa 1977.

COURTESY OF THE EDMONTON OLD TIMERS FISHING CLUB

Emil Naharnik (L), Doreen Batterham, Bob Sangster and Jack Graham of Edmonton Old Timers Fishing Club at Gull Lake, winter 2005.

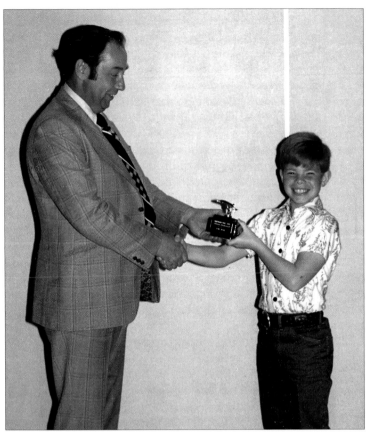

COURTESY OF CAROLE ROMANIUK

Kevin Romaniuk receiving the largest fish award from trophy chairman Vern McIntosh.

Edmonton Trout Fishing Club
1953 - present

Members of the Edmonton Trout Fishing Club share a common interest and passion for the outdoors and the sport of trout-fishing. Club members are particularly interested in fly-fishing and the practices of fly-tying and rod-building. The club also engages in conservation and educational projects and encourages efforts to preserve, maintain and enhance the trout fishery in Alberta.

Established in 1953, the Edmonton Trout Fishing Club is one of the oldest fishing clubs in Canada. The 14 original members were Earl Barefoot, Ray (Chip) Chisholm, Art Craig, Gordon Gould, Art Graham, Cal Keys, Dr. Lipsey, Lyall MacLagan, Harry McDermott, Andy McNally, Stewart Morrison, James Robertson, Robert (Bob) Thurston and Fred Turnbull. The club grew quickly, reaching some 42 members by the end of 1953. Annual membership fees at that time were $5 and there was a big demand for the club's instructional classes.

In the 1950s, the availability of fly-fishing equipment and materials was very limited in the city. As a result, the club became the primary means of ordering this equipment and fly-tying materials from catalogue suppliers during the 1950s and '60s. In more recent times, a variety of local, commercial sources of fly-fishing and fly-tying equipment and supplies have become established, in large part because of the club creating the demand for such businesses.

Coincidental with the formation of the club, the fisheries branch of the Alberta Fish and Wildlife Division initiated an experimental trout-stocking program in a number of lakes around Edmonton. Club members and staff from the fisheries branch quickly established a mutually supportive relationship that was to benefit not only club members, but also Alberta anglers in general. Club members helped sample experimental pothole lakes where trout had been planted to confirm survivability and growth. This resulted in the establishment of many fine trout fisheries around the city.

In 1954 the club executive decided to establish a fishing facility on one of the newly stocked lakes. Fred Turnbull and Lyall MacLagan purchased a lot at Edmonton Beach on Spring Lake [aka Cottage Lake]. The club began its annual barbecues at the lake in the fall of that year. In 1955 a fireplace and barbecue were built on the lot. Club members erected a picnic shelter in 1956 and a second lot was purchased to provide members with vehicle and boat access to the lake.

The club regularly organized fishing trips and fishing events, either at local lakes or to destinations farther afield. Regular annual derbies were held, which often included barbecues or picnics for the whole family. Two such events usually occur each year, one in the spring (early June) and one in the fall (usually September). Prizes or trophy awards recognize the members able to land the largest trout during these events. The spring derby and picnic has generally been held at Spring Lake.

riverbank below, one that I will never forget. "George, you lost another one. I told you your drag is set too tight." It was the voice of Joan Mitchell, wife of George, and whose voice I would hear at lakes, streams, hunting fields and social gatherings for years to come.

It was my first trip for stream fishing, so I just stood and watched how it was done by Joan and George. Joan soon approached me, a stranger to her, and asked, "Your first time?" I said, "Yes." She then gave me some instruction about stream fishing. This act of kindness by a stranger further convinced me that we should start a group of police service members who would meet and educate ourselves in the art of fishing. I spoke with several others about the idea and all were excited about it and offered to help. In the fall of 1968, we met and organized the Edmonton Police Service Fish and Game Association. We all had a common background as police officers and felt comfortable in the group. We viewed many fishing and hunting films, and had guest speakers and discussions. When we left the meetings, we felt we were a closer-knit group.

Our first banquet was held in early 1969 and was very successful. Everyone who attended looked forward to the next.

We soon affiliated with the AFGA, and became active in various projects, including: going to schools to teach students to fish; taking handicapped people fishing; assisting in various AFGA activities; and assisting in various community activities.

In 1974-75 the club was officially affiliated with the AFGA. This was a mutually beneficial arrangement. For example, for many years, the AFGA raffle tickets were a significant revenue generator for both the club and the AFGA, with members actively engaged in ticket sales. In 1976-77, the club presented the AFGA with a trophy to be awarded annually for the "largest trout caught in Alberta on a fly" at the annual AFGA Wildlife Awards banquets held in April.

In 1975 a trophy was established to annually recognize the club member who had the distinction of catching the largest trout caught in Alberta that year. The trophy was established in honour of the original group of 14 founders of the club, and was called the Edmonton Trout Fishing Club Founding Members Trophy.

Two other fishing trophies were established in association with the club's two annual fishing events: The Edmonton Trout Fishing Club Trophy for the largest fish caught at the annual fall derby, and the Art Graham Trophy for the best trout caught on a fly at the annual club barbecue and fishing derby held at Spring Lake each June.

In 1992 the club established its library, an extensive collection of fishing-related books and videos for members to borrow. The club held its first annual auction in the winter of 1980 as a fundraising program. It has been very successful and is held each March.

Education

Fly-tying has been one of the club's core activities throughout its long history. During the 1950s, several of the club's charter members, notably Fred Turnbull and Lyall MacLagan, organized these activities. Both beginner and advanced fly-tying classes were taught.

In the 1950s and '60s, rod-building was another important and popular skill taught by club members, particularly given the limited equipment available at that time. Over the years, there have been a number of excellent rod builders in the club, including Doug Kilburn, Eric Sohnle and Bill Miller.

Projects

Club members become involved in many different conservation, community support and related activities sponsored by many different organizations. These range from eastern slopes stream bank rehabilitation and fencing initiatives, to support of the Camp He Ho Ha fishing outings for disabled people, to donations to worthy causes like the Women's Fly Fishers (for women recovering from breast cancer). In recent years, the club has met annually with the minister responsible for fisheries management in Alberta to talk about improving the quality of trout and other fisheries in Alberta.

In 2000 members of the club began looking at ways to commemorate the 50th anniversary of the club. A decision was made to establish a new trout lake fishery in the Edmonton area that would provide a higher quality of fishing experience and would promote

COURTESY OF THE EDMONTON TROUT FISHING CLUB

Welcome to Muir Lake Trout Enhancement Project signage. Tim Doskoch (L), Joe Sykes and Tak Shimizu. Partly sponsored by the Alberta Conservation Association.

Moms and kids stocking trout at Muir Lake.

the practice of catch-and-release fishing, particularly for the benefit of youngsters learning to fish. Tim Doskoch led the initiative. The club approached other area fishing clubs, including the Edmonton Chapter of Trout Unlimited, the Northern Lights Fly Tyers [sic] and Fly Fishers, and the Edmonton Old Timers Fishing Club. These organizations bought into the concept and agreed to supply both funding and volunteers. The outcome of these efforts was the Muir Lake Trout Rehabilitation Project, an initiative to re-establish a trout fishery at Muir Lake located just northwest of Spruce Grove. With the co-operation of the provincial government, the club established regulations for the lake that encouraged a "delayed harvest" of fish. These included only the use of artificial lures, a winter-fishing ban from November 1 to April 30, and a restricted daily catch limit of one fish over 50 centimetres.

The project also included the creation of a "Walk of Fame," honouring individuals who have significantly contributed to the protection and enrichment of angling habitat in Alberta, and an education centre where people of all ages could learn about the relationships between fish and other aquatic life, as well as angling strategies.

The Muir Lake fishery opened in May 2004, quickly proving to be a very popular local angling destination. It was made possible through a variety of fundraising efforts and the combined contributions of many people representing hundreds of volunteer hours. Support was received from many organizations, including the County of Parkland for the use of a parking and day use area at Muir Lake, and donations of equipment, supplies and grants from the Alberta Conservation Association, Community Initiatives Program, Trout Unlimited Canada, and Canadian National Sportsmen's Shows.

Special People

Starting in 1967, the club began to recognize its members who had made major contributions to the club and its services by designating "life members," or memberships for life with the waiver of annual dues. The following are life members of the club: R. Campbell, Fred Turnbull, W. Bissell, D. Clayton, Andy McNally, Gordon Gould, Lyall MacLagan, Doug Kilburn, Loftus Goodall, Cal Keyes, Eric Sohnle, Carl Schroder, Ed (Buzz) Hunter, Art Graham, Ron Tucker, Gordon Raymond, Clary Wilson, Roy Fitzsimmons, Malcolm MacCrimmon, Martin Paetz, Bill Miller, Lloyd Shea, Ed Lefebvre, George Ainsley, Wally Warawa and Tak Shimizu.

In 1992 the club established the Distinguished Service Award, named in honour of Eric C. Sohnle, a long-time life member who had passed away earlier that year. This award is presented to a member who is judged to have made the most significant contribution to the betterment of the Edmonton Trout Fishing Club. The following are the recipients of this award: Lloyd Shea, Ed Lefebvre, Terry Leskiw, Peter and Darolyn Mapplebeck, Dick Slobodian, Ray Kelsey, Bill Miller, George Ainsley and Tak Shimizu.

The provincial government recognized Lloyd Shea for his many contributions to conservation by presenting him with the Order of the Bighorn Award in 1985.

Presidents of the Edmonton Trout Fishing Club include H. McDermott, 1953-54; R. Thurston, 1954-55; F. Turnbull, 1955-56; L. MacLagan, 1956-57; C. Keys, 1957-58; A. Graham, 1958-59; B. Kuechler, 1959-60; D. Kilburn, 1960-61; E. Sohnle, 1961-62; W. Jeandron, 1962-63; N. Blakey, 1963-64; R. Nelson, 1964-65; L. MacLagan, 1965-66; L. Shea, 1966-67; W. Warawa, 1967-68; T. Wagler, 1968-69; A. Butt, 1969-70; G. Kent, 1970-71; C. Tebby, 1971-72; G. Raymond, 1972-73; L. Shea, 1973-74; B. Miller, 1974-75; B. Gillyean, 1975-76; E. Sohnle, 1976-77; G. Ainsley, 1977-78; R. Cramp, 1978-79; F. Cramp, 1979-80; B. White, 1980-81; P. Bentley, 1981-82; L. Shea, 1982-83; B. White, 1983-85; L. Stefanyk, 1985-87; R. Kelsey, 1987-88; J. Van Veen, 1988-89; T. Leskiw, 1989-91; M. Knopp, 1991-93; T. Leskiw, 1993-95; B. Miller, 1995-96; L. Campbell, 1996-97; D. Slobodian, 1997-99; R. Kelsey, 1999-2001; E. Lefebvre, 2001-03; T. Doskoch, 2003-05; A. Sopczak, 2005-07; R. Sohnle, 2007-08.

Evergreen Shooting Club
Drayton Valley, 1975-present

The Drayton Valley Shooting Club was started in 1975. Ken Wardrow and Joe Kokas acquired a lease on approximately 58 acres of land from the Alberta Department of Lands and Forests. The club now has developed at that location a 75-yard pistol range, a 200-yard rifle range, a 300-yard rifle range, and a trap-shooting range. The range is used by the Royal Canadian Mounted Police, provincial Fish and Wildlife officers, air cadets and local schools for basic firearms handling instruction.

The club regularly has competitions in black powder, pistol and rifle. There are approximately 200 members in the club.

Grande Cache Fish, Game and Gun Association
1971-present (not affiliated)

The Grande Cache Fish, Game and Gun Association was registered Nov. 25, 1971. Members of the first executive committee and other people involved in getting the club started were Ray Bruntjen, Clark Wolff, Stan Wall, Don Gillies, Bruce Morrison, Robert Krewsik, Jim Manning and many others. The late Ray Bruntjen had donated a lot of time to get the club going and build the clubhouse. Stan Wall and Jim Manning are still in Grand Cache and continue to be members of the club.

The 1,500-square-foot clubhouse was built in 1972, and a few years later a 25-yard indoor shooting range was added. The club also has a 100-yard outside range, trap-shooting facilities and is presently trying to develop a 200-yard range. In the early years there were many trap-shooting and black-powder competitions as well as some handgun competitions.

The club used to have banquets and trophy presentations every year. In 1983 Francois Lambert received a trophy for the largest moose taken that year by a club member, which scored 208 6/8. As a result, he was invited to the provincial AFGA awards banquet and received the trophy for the largest moose taken that year in Alberta. He is now vice president of the club.

Over the years the number of members dwindled with people moving, but the club has remained involved in teaching hunter education to youth and new hunters, and there seems to be renewed interest in club affairs. The club promotes the education and safety for youth interested in hunting, fishing, the environment and outdoor life. Some of the local Fish and Wildlife Division officers are also members of the club and have held information meetings for the club to keep everyone up-to-date on the ever-changing rules and regulations.

The club plans to organize more functions, especially for the youth. Last fall, it held its first annual pig roast and trophy presentations. This year the club is planning to hold a bear awareness meeting, a Father's Day barbecue, a fishing derby, hikes, shoots, its second annual pig roast, and a float for the Canada Day parade.

Hinton Fish and Game Association
1957-present (not affiliated)

The Hinton Fish and Game Association had its beginnings in 1957-58 as a shooting club that used an indoor rifle range in the Athabasca Valley Development Corporation warehouse in Hinton. The range was confined to the use of .22-calibre rifles and the shooting was done mostly on weekends. The second manager of the pulp mill, Mr. Harry Collinge, presented the fledgling club with two Remington .22-calibre rifles, which were greatly appreciated. The first president was Robert C. Hallam.

Some of the early members of the club were Vern Truxler, Vic Worobetz, Ben Meier, Bob Backman, Bill Switzer, Art Dunn, Harvey Cook, Tets Kitaguchi, Dave Kopas, Mike Wisla and Bill Shepeley.

Projects
The club had a need for an outdoor range where larger calibre firearms could be used. Shortly after the club was formed, Mr. Hallam looked for and found a safe, secure location just off Highway 16, where the range is today. The first lease was signed by Ernest Manning. Joe Rochip and Ernie Muldoon donated heavy equipment to install the range. In 1985 the club expanded the lease and the gun ranges. Today, the ranges include shooting distances of 100, 200 and 500 yards. As well, trap and archery ranges have been added, the latter operated by the Yellowhead Arrow Launchers. A 3-D archery trail is also available. All are handicap accessible.

In the early 1960s, the club installed an air compressor at Millers Lake over the winter to help prevent winterkill of fish. In 1968 and '69, the club helped put gravel on the winter road bridge over Jarvis Creek to enhance walleye spawning beds. In 1972 the club helped install a weir at Mary Greg Lake to raise the water level 18 inches. The club created a trout-fishing pond in 1979 south of Highway 16, near Cold Creek, to promote youth fishing. In 1984 the club helped place round bales in Obed Lake for geese nesting.

In 1986 the club assisted a program to improve wildlife habitat by fertilizing areas on Folding Mountain. Billy Dunn, Gerry Wilde and Steve Witiuk from the AFGA were instrumental in this project. From 1987 to '88, the club helped to improve habitat on Summit Lake by planting wild rice. The club helped clean the spawning beds on Emerson Lake in 1989.

Annual Events
Since 1962 the club has held annual competitions for the largest fish and big-game animals harvested during the year. Trophies are presented at an annual dinner. The club holds an annual turkey shoot on the Sunday before Thanksgiving. The club holds an annual raffle with some of the proceeds going to the programs sponsored by the Foothills Model Forest, including studies on fish, elk and grizzly bear.

Club Awards
Since 1975 the club has sponsored the AFGA provincial award for best mountain goat presented at the AFGA Fish and Game Awards dinner.

Special People
Some of the past presidents of the club include: Robert Hallam, 1957-60; Vern Truxler, 1960 (and later); Jim Wilson, 1963; Blaine Sornberger, 1977-80; Bill Dunn, 1980; Ron Hellum, 1994-2000; Ron Croot, 2001-05; Eric Rosendahl, 2006.

Jasper Place Fish and Game Association
(inactive) a memoir by Lois Argue

The Jasper Place Fish and Game Association, although disbanded, should never be forgotten. We are not sure when the club was formed but it disbanded sometime in the 1960s, perhaps when Jasper Place joined the City of Edmonton. It was a very active club, and certainly a great asset to the young people and the community of Jasper Place. The following account is from 1965. That year, the officers were Ron Wheeler, president; Chuck Meyer, past president;

George Ewanchuk, vice president; Denis Luchkovich, secretary; Larry Rekdal, treasurer; Angus MacDonald, fish committee; and Bill Tanisichk, newsletter editor.

One of the club projects was a birdhouse contest under the leadership of Chuck Meyer. The contest was a great success, with birdhouses displayed at the Meadowlark Shopper's Park. Awards were given for best all-around birdhouse, most original birdhouse, best workmanship, most original (age 11-14), and best workmanship (age 11-14). Prizes were donated by McBain Camera, Carlings Brewery and Zellers.

The club constructed a float entered in the Klondike Days parade; and established a fish pond in one of the city parks (with assistance from the City Parks Department) for children.

Another club project was the running of a Junior Forest Wardens club under the leadership of Bill Burtenshaw. At the time, the Junior Forest Wardens were for boys ages 10 to 16.

The fish committee organized derbies, trophies and instructional classes such as fly-tying and casting. Carlings Brewery donated trophies.

In the fall of 1965 a wild game supper and dance was held and reported as follows:

"Those of you who missed the wild game supper and dance missed a good do. The food was fantastic. The music was great. The jokes were terrible. Kidding aside, the supper was a great success, thanks mainly to Hubert Pesch and his wife, Frances. … Thanks must also go to that great hunter, Lois Argue, who was kind enough to donate that great hunk of moose meat (she'd had success in big-game hunting out by Edson). We hope that Lois won't go hungry until next September."

The newsletter reported very interesting and informative articles on such items as biological aspects of fish, Canadian fishing records and world records by Bill Brown, lures and tackle by Rod Edwards, and fly-fishing by Al Butt. Well-known Alberta fisheries biologist Martin Paetz gave a brief summary of the lake situations. He reported, "We expect at least a partial kill on Cottage Lake (Edmonton Beach), and that Muir Lake was borderline. Star Lake should pull through if we are lucky, and they were doing running tests on Sauer Lake and Chichako Lake and that Whitewood Lake was in very poor shape and certainly would not justify restocking then."

For a few years this was a very enthusiastic group in the Jasper Place community of west Edmonton. We seemed to do so much in those years with the clubs in Calgary and the Raven Fish Hatchery, attending conventions and so many interesting activities across Alberta. They left wonderful memories.

Mayerthorpe and District Fish and Game Association
1988-present

In the early 1980s, a sizeable group of Mayerthorpe and area residents were looking to join a fish and game club. The nearest club was in Whitecourt. The main fundraiser for that club was their annual trophy night held in the Whitecourt Legion. It included supper, movies and a dance and had about 100 people in attendance. Because a large number of attendees at these meetings and events were from the Mayerthorpe area, it was decided one year to host the annual supper in Mayerthorpe at the Diamond Centre. Over 400 people attended. It was not long after that a motion was brought to the floor of a meeting of the Whitecourt club to divide that club and start a fish and game club in Mayerthorpe. The motion passed and the Whitecourt club gave the new club its blessings and split the bank accounts down the middle. In 1988 the Mayerthorpe and District Fish and Game Association became a reality.

One of the first projects of the new club was to develop a shooting range. However, the plan always seemed to hit a roadblock of some kind. The club had to contact the local people residing around the proposed range site (within three kilometres) and obtain their permission to use the location for a gun range. No one would give permission. Local MLA Peter Trynchy offered a piece of Crown land just south of town below the Paddle River Dam. The provincial government refused that site and another site was chosen above the dam. The county turned down that site. This went on for seven years until the club finally exhausted all of its options.

The club held two large gun rallies in Mayerthorpe in opposition to the federal gun control legislation. The club brought in the AFGA counterparts to speak in conjunction with the Responsible Firearms Owners of Alberta. Cliff Breitkreiz, Member of Parliament, attended in support of the club's efforts. When the legislation became law and required that everyone

COURTESY OF THE STONY PLAIN FISH AND GAME ASSOCIATION

Keephills School and their birdbox-building program. Grades 1 through 3, assembling birdboxes supplied by Stony Plain Fish and Game Association and Wabamun Gun Club.

who wished to obtain firearms take the firearms safety course, the club sent three members (Thad Buckler, Doug Wynnyk and Greg Hritzack) to be trained as instructors. As a result, the club has trained many people who want to keep their right to possess and carry firearms.

Mayerthorpe and District Fish and Game held two separate courses to train new Alberta antler and horn measurers under the guidance of the AFGA's Jack Graham. The club trained 32 students in the first class and 47 students in the second with the assistance of Jack Reader and Curtis Siegfried. Students came from as far away as Bonnyville and Rocky Mountain House.

The club has donated to the local Ducks Unlimited Canada chapter since it began in Mayerthorpe. The club has also annually donated to the annual Camp He Ho Ha Fun Fishing Day for the Disabled and many other events and organizations.

Members of the club have set out flax bales for goose-nesting sites and donated time to help the Alberta Fish and Wildlife Division in its helicopter grid-counting of moose in the area. In one day, as many as 114 moose were sighted. When the local Fish and Wildlife Division biologists needed a hand at Shiningbank Lake to net and count spawning fish, the club provided volunteers to help. As well, each year members have performed the hunter surveys in the area for the Alberta Fish and Wildlife Division.

In 1998 the Mayerthorpe and District Fish and Game Association hosted the 35th annual Alberta trophy ball in Mayerthorpe, with just under 400 people in attendance. It was rated as one of the most profitable suppers the AFGA had ever hosted.

Membership in the Mayerthorpe and District Fish and Game Association has dwindled over the last few years. Regular members are aging and not able to take on the same roles as they previously had in the club, and fewer younger people are joining. If this club is to survive it needs a younger generation to take the reins and keep the organization strong.

Morinville Fish and Game Association History
1989-present

In approximately 1989, shortly after the Griesbach club shut down, Greg Moffatt, Bob Valk and some other individuals talked over coffee about the need to form a fish and game club in Morinville. A small group of people started meeting at LaMaison Hotel and Restaurant. This informal group elected Bob Valk as the first president. In December 1989 the Morinville Fish and Game Association (MFGA) was meeting at Primeau High School in Morinville. However, the first "formal" meeting of the club was held in February 1991 and Bob Valk remained as president. The MFGA was incorporated in August 1991. At this time the club members started looking for a more permanent place to hold meetings and activities.

As a result of the hard work of club members such as Frank Ricard, Ray Souliere, Gerald Foster and Jack Reader, a site was leased from the Town of Morinville. The site is located at the north end of town and is a beautiful location that includes a stocked fish pond, 800 metres of paved trail, two wheelchair-accessible docks and a picnic area with a fire pit. A portable classroom was obtained from the former CFB Namao, and a deck as well as a dock on the pond were constructed.

This vibrant club, while only having approximately 160 members, is a giant in the local conservation scene. In 2007 the MFGA invested Ray Souliere with a life membership in the MFGA; sadly a couple of months later Ray passed away from a battle with cancer.

Special People
Presidents of MFGA include: Bob Valk, 1992; Neil Halonen, Ray Souliere*, Dave George, Len Smith, Gerald Foster, Quentin Bochar and Dave Wulff (2005-present). * Deceased.

Onoway and District Fish and Game Association and Gun Club
1960-present

The Onoway and District Fish and Game Association was first organized in 1960 by a group of people concerned with conservation of fish and wildlife. In 1962 a gun club was also formed. Although these were two very active clubs at the time, they gradually died out. In January 1982 a few people decided to see if enough interest could be generated to start up anew. A member of the AFGA came out and a discussion took place with approximately 20 people in attendance. It was decided to re-activate a club combining the interests of both previous clubs. By the end of the year, the club boasted a membership of over 100 people.

Projects
One of the first projects the newly formed club did was to publish and sell a wild game recipe cookbook. The funds raised by this endeavour enabled the club to move forward into other areas of interest.

Another early project was a pheasant-rearing program, where several members volunteered to have rearing pens located on their properties. For several years members took an active interest in this project. However, after a number of years, members could see no signs of the pheasant population increasing in the area and it was decided to discontinue the project.

In 1982 the club discovered a parcel of land east of Onoway could be obtained and would be a suitable location for a gun range. Work began on this project, and by May 1985 the land was acquired, a committee set up to oversee the development, and to this day the gun range is still in operation at this location. Members have worked with diligence to make sure this range meets and exceeds all pertinent regulations and safety requirements.

A goose-nesting program was the next project undertaken by the club. This project generated a lot of interest among the general public, and many local farmers volunteered to locate nesting platforms on their properties.

COURTESY OF THE ONOWAY FISH AND GAME ASSOCIATION

Onoway Fish and Game members show off some of their birdboxes.

Over the years, bluebird birdhouse building has been a yearly event, much-anticipated by the general public. With funding assistance from the Alberta Conservation Association (ACA) the club constructed over 100 birdhouses annually. Members are sighting more bluebirds in the area, indicating the project's success.

In 1990 the Onoway and District Fish and Game and Gun Club became stewards of Imrie Park, adjacent to Devil's (Matchayaw) Lake. For the next number of years, members volunteered many hours developing the park for use by the public. When the first building was constructed, the club obtained permission to use it for its meetings.

COURTESY OF THE ONOWAY FISH AND GAME ASSOCIATION

The Onoway pancake breakfast at Heritage Days.

A project that started in 1999, and that is ongoing at the present time, is the rehabilitation of Salters Lake, one mile south of the town of Onoway. With financial assistance from the ACA, the club has purchased an aerator, which has been installed to raise the oxygen levels, so that this lake can once again become a trout fishery. Through grant applications, enough funds have been raised to continue improvement of the facility. In May 2004 the club purchased 750 rainbow trout to release into Salters Lake, and in May 2005 the Fish and Wildlife Division stocked 16,000 rainbow trout from the Cold Lake Hatchery. In 2005 the club was very pleased to accept the Neville Lindsey Award for this project.

Each year members assist the Fish and Wildlife Division with its hunter survey. In the new year the club invites the local Fish

Salters Lake Fish Project. Norm Fibke, Onoway president (R) accepting cheque (2005).

COURTESY OF THE ONOWAY FISH AND GAME ASSOCIATION

and Wildlife Division officer to attend a meeting to discuss items of interest to the general membership. Over the years the club has had many interesting and informative guests at its monthly meetings, as well as a variety of interesting films or videos.

Annual Events

For a number of years, the club hosted the annual pancake breakfast at Onoway's Heritage Days weekend, where members have served in excess of 500 breakfasts. Over the years, the club hosted a wild game supper and trophy awards night where members who won the club's hunting and fishing competitions received awards. The wild game supper tradition has changed, and awards are now presented at the annual barbecue. More award categories have been added, including trophies available for youth and a category for wildlife photography.

The club holds an annual barbecue, silent auction and trophy awards in June. Local businesses sponsor some of the trophies and the club sponsors others.

Another annual event the club sponsors is the Christmas tree burn, held about the middle of January. It is enjoyed by the public.

In 2004 the club decided to sponsor an annual Fun Fishing Derby on Devil's Lake. This is a catch-and-release derby and has just begun to gain the public's interest.

Onoway and District Fish and Game Association and Gun Club continues to take an active role in promoting conservation and public awareness of fish and wildlife. The club continues to encourage young people to become involved in these worthwhile projects.

Pembina River Fish and Game Association
Westlock, Alberta
1970-1997 (inactive)

The Pembina River Fish and Game Association was formed in April 1970 by Jim Edwards and Des Sutton, with Bob MacKenzie as president and Lyle Birnie as secretary treasurer. Other members involved on the executive and in the club at that time were Bill Maclean, Bill Gault, Phillip Ashton, Gary Kruger and Bill Simmons. Meetings were held monthly with a guest speaker or the presentation of a film rented from the AFGA main office. Many of the speakers were local Fish and Wildlife Division officers, biologists or some other government of Alberta official; there was always a large turnout of club members to these meetings. The club found that if it kept the business session short, more members would attend. The club also held an antler measuring night. A well-attended banquet with an interesting guest speaker was hosted every year.

The PRFGA was instrumental in creating the Westlock Borrow Pit that became a useful trout fishery for the community. This was part of the Buck for Wildlife program and was partnered by the Lions Club, Alberta Transporter and the Fish and Wildlife Division.

COURTESY OF DUANE RADFORD

Children attending Berkley's Pathway to Fishing course.

Later in the 1980s, attendance at meetings dropped, as some members turned the meetings into complaint sessions about commercial fishermen, government regulations and anything else on their minds. Despite this discouraging trend, president Bill Simmons kept the club going with the help of people like Gerald Van Ruskenveld, Ron MacIntyre, Richard Edwards, Walter Kostiw, Ken Hemeon, Verdun Baxandall, Fred Stamper, Brian Yagos, Robert Ashton and Mary Ashton. Bill Simmons was instrumental in getting some land set aside as a natural area over in the Tawatinaw. However, despite their best efforts, the Pembina River Fish and Game Association became inactive in 1997. (See Busby and District Fish and Game Association.)

Spruce Grove Fish and Game Association
1982-present

The Spruce Grove Fish and Game Association was formed in 1982 when an advertisement in the local newspaper drew a core group of local sportsmen, assembled by town Coun. Larry Walker. December 1982 saw an executive chosen among a membership of 20. Membership has fluctuated between 60 and 120. Nine members have remained active since the club was formed in 1982.

Projects

The club organized a fishing derby at Devil's Lake in February 1983. During May-June 1983, a pheasant-rearing facility was constructed. That autumn pheasants were locally released into the wild and from then to 1993 some 100-150 pheasants were raised and released annually.

During 1985 the club developed a goose-nesting project at Whale Lake, where 23 round flax bales were placed; 68 Canada geese were released at this lake by Ducks Unlimited Canada. That winter, five deer feeders were built and situated to assist deer survival in the local area.

During 1987 the club was incorporated under the *Societies Act*. The primary purpose of the club is to promote education; protection and establishment of wildlife interests; and recreational development and entertainment in the area. This area is bounded by Highway 37 to the north, Parkland County boundary to the west, the North Saskatchewan River to the south and the St. Albert and Edmonton City limits to the east.

Also during 1987, the club erected duck-nesting boxes at Muir Lake and floating nesting rafts at Whale Lake during the winter.

COURTESY OF DUANE RADFORD

Randy Collins assisting Fun Fishing Day participant at Camp He Ho Ha, 2007.

Additional nesting structures were placed at the Chickakoo Recreation Area during 1988 and Mallard Lake during 1993. At present, the club inspects and maintains about 80 waterfowl nesting structures each winter.

In 2005 the club won second prize in the local category with a float in the Spruce Grove Agri-Fair parade. The club became stewards of 1.3 hectares of land affiliated with the AFGA Wildlife Trust Fund north of Spruce Grove.

The club initiated a cribbage tournament and chili cook-off during 1991. In later years this event was combined with trophy measuring.

In 1992 club members built a dock for the Muir Lake Recreation Area and became stewards for two Parkland County properties located at Keephills and Kapasiwin. The club partnered with the county in a Wildlife Reflector Program, with the club being responsible for purchase of the reflectors and posts and the county for installation and ongoing maintenance of these reflectors at three locations.

In 1993 firearms, hunting and fishing issues were front and centre. During 1994, the club revised its bylaws where access management and native hunting rights were the key issues. In 1995 the club also made its first contribution to the AFGA Wildlife Trust Fund and the Chip Lake Habitat Conservation Property was purchased.

In 1998 the Ambrose Property was purchased; the George and Joan Mitchell Memorial Property was purchased in 2001 after this couple died tragically in a highway accident. The club became stewards of the Atim Creek Buck for Wildlife Property in 1999. In 2004 the club contributed to the purchase of the Wabamun Whitewood Conservation Properties.

The Spruce Grove club has supported many community events (e.g. City of Spruce Grove 10th Anniversary, Kinettes Christmas Hamper and Parkland Palliative Care Facility). The club also financially supports and participates in the annual Camp He Ho Ha handicapped fishing derby.

Annual Events

During the summer of 1984, the club held its first annual Family Fun Fishing event, which continues to this day. Lakes visited over the years include Fawcett, Beaver and Iosegun.

In 1985 the club held the first annual wild game dinner and trophy presentation at the Golden Age Drop-In Centre. The wild game dinner has since become an annual event.

The club began participation in the Fish and Wildlife Division's annual telephone hunting survey in 1989, which continues to this date.

Special People

Presidents of the club over the years include Everet Elzenaar, Gordon Bedard, Dallas Pasula, Wayne Wendell, Randy Strocki, Bill Moar, Brian Rufiange, Byron Liddell, Bill Clark, Harry White, Bill McKeeman, Bert Reed, Trevor Patterson and Mark Feist.

COURTESY OF THE STONY PLAIN FISH AND GAME ASSOCIATION

Stan Kozyra with the bluebird and tree swallow nesting box program he runs for the Stony Plain Fish and Game Association.

COURTESY OF DUANE RADFORD

Disabled fishing derby participants (2007) at Camp He Ho Ha, 2007.

St. Albert and District Fish and Game Association
1967-present

The St. Albert and District Fish and Game Association originated with a meeting on Nov. 27, 1967. Charter members included: Gordon Kirby, D. O'Connell, R. Rix, J. Roberts, Don Hayden, Claude Valliere, D. Richardson, J. Mitchell, A. Rapiti and E. Schmidt. The aims and goals of the club were to develop a hunter-training program, construct a rifle range and develop a recreation area at Big Lake.

The first general meeting was held in the St. Albert Community Hall, Dec. 12, 1967, where meetings are still held to this day. The above charter members acted as the interim executive, with seven new members in attendance, one of whom was Arnim Zimmer, who is still a club member today. General meetings usually had a guest speaker. To maintain member interest, no long, drawn-out business sessions were conducted at these meetings. This style appears to have worked as this format is still used to this day.

By September 1968 the club had grown to 210 members when the population of St Albert was much smaller than it is today.

Education

Numerous students have graduated from the club's conservation and hunter education courses, conducted once or twice each year until the present time. The club also has participated in junior rifle courses which taught many children safe firearm handling. However, this course was dropped when federal gun legislation made it difficult to continue. The club has also conducted a course called Pathways to Fishing in conjunction with Riverside Honda and Berkley to teach youngsters about the fundamentals of fishing.

Projects

Club members have been involved in birdhouse building projects, where children build birdhouses to install at their homes or lake properties.

COURTESY OF DUANE RADFORD

Line-up of disabled people at the disabled fishing derby (2007) at Camp He Ho Ha .

Stony Plain Fish and Game Association showing school kids how to assemble bluebird boxes.

COURTESY OF DUANE RADFORD

Camp He Ho Ha disabled fishing derby participants. Kelly Fair and Cathy Steeves in back of boat; boat operators are Scott Arthurs and his son Tyler.

COURTESY OF THE STONY PLAIN FISH AND GAME ASSOCIATION AND WABAMUN GUN CLUB

Mrs. Elsie Scheideman (L) receiving the club's conservation award on behalf of her husband Harry from Stan Kozyra.

The St. Albert and District Fish and Game Association raised pheasants for release from 1969 until 1993, at which time the cost of pheasant chicks became prohibitive.

Club members assisted the St. Albert Community League with renovations to the community hall and with monthly bingos until the bingo hall was closed. From the beginning, the club published a monthly newsletter, which contained many outdoor tips and articles written by executive members. Unfortunately, high postage costs forced its cancellation.

The club is presently involved in bank improvement on the Sturgeon River with the hope of improving the water quality in this river.

Annual Events

The club has held summer and winter fishing derbies for members and friends from its beginning until the present time. Annual chili-making contests have allowed members and their spouses to display their culinary prowess, and the final products are fun to eat. The club has participated in the Fun Fishing Day for the Physically Challenged and are presently hosting this special event with assistance from other clubs in the area.

In 2006 the club held its 38th annual wild game dinner and trophy ball. Local merchants sponsor the trophies.

Special People

Members of the St. Albert and District Fish and Game Association have held positions in the provincial AFGA executive since the club was established. The club is very proud that Don Hayden, Andy von Busse and Randy Collins, all past presidents of the AFGA, have been members of the St. Albert and District Fish and Game Association.

COURTESY OF THE STONY PLAIN FISH AND GAME ASSOCIATION AND WABAMUN GUN CLUB

Edgar T. Jones (L) presenting Earl Erickson with the club's conservation award for approximately 45 years dedicated to promoting habitat for bluebirds and tree swallows.

COURTESY OF THE STONY PLAIN FISH AND GAME ASSOCIATION AND WABAMUN GUN CLUB

One of Stony Plain Fish and Game Association's ten bulletin boards in the area.

Stony Plain Fish and Game Association. Entrance to the SPFG and Wabamun Gun Club rifle range.

Stony Plain Fish and Game Association and Wabamun Gun Club fundraising supper, Uli Naef cooking a wild pig.

Stony Plain Fish and Game Association. Duck nesting tunnel program; Bill Demchuk, (L) and Stan Kozyra.

Stony Plain Fish and Game Association builds two types of bluebird boxes. To date, Stan Kozyra has distributed over 1,000 boxes to those who request them, free of charge.

Stony Plain Fish and Game Association. Silent auction display at the annual fundraising supper.

Stony Plain Fish and Game Association. The club's trophy cabinet in the Provincial Building, Stony Plain.

COURTESY OF THE STONY PLAIN FISH AND GAME ASSOCIATION AND WABAMUN GUN CLUB
Stony Plain Fish and Game Association. The club's pheasant program in 1979.

COURTESY OF THE STONY PLAIN FISH AND GAME ASSOCIATION AND WABAMUN GUN CLUB
Stan Kozyra of Stony Plain FGA carrying out the hide collection program.

COURTESY OF THE STONY PLAIN FISH AND GAME ASSOCIATION AND WABAMUN GUN CLUB
Manning the information booth at Stony Plain annual trade fair are Dale Althiem, (L) Greg Kulak, Grant Kulak and Stan Kozyra.

COURTESY OF THE STONY PLAIN FISH AND GAME ASSOCIATION AND WABAMUN GUN CLUB
The George and Joan Mitchell Conservation award. Leah Kenchington (L), Kathleen Williams (recipient), D.F. Snip Loblick (president, Wabamun Gun Club) and Mike Veitch (president, Stony Plain Fish and Game), 2005.

The past presidents of the St. Albert and District Fish and Game Association are Gordon Kirby, 1967-69; Don Hayden, 1970-72; Mac Anderson, 1973-74; Andy Anderson, 1975, 1976; Phil Ficht, 1977-79; Lome Zallas, 1980; Gary Edwards, 1981-83; Phil Ficht, 1984; Dave Sawich, 1985-86; John Paul, 1987-88; Pat Sawich, 1988; Andy von Busse 1989-91; Vern Kalnychuk. 1992-93; Randy Collins, 1994-96; Doug Hrynkiw, 1997-99; Jim Hutchison, 2000-01; and Rene Lamoureux 2002-06.

Stony Plain Fish and Game Association and Wabamun Gun Club
1952-present

Hunters, anglers and others interested in fish and wildlife conservation in the Stony Plain area have been organized as the Stony Plain Fish and Game Association for at least 56 years. That is as far back as the club's records (a 1952 membership card) go; but old timers say the club was started well before 1952. The club has been very active over the years, helping conserve fish and wildlife, keeping

COURTESY OF THE STONY PLAIN FISH AND GAME ASSOCIATION AND WABAMUN GUN CLUB
Stan Kozyra (L) putting up mallard duck coils on local lakes.

COURTESY OF THE STONY PLAIN FISH AND GAME ASSOCIATION AND WABAMUN GUN CLUB
Bright Bank community kids with boxes they assembled to take home.

COURTESY OF THE STONY PLAIN FISH AND GAME ASSOCIATION AND WABAMUN GUN CLUB
The not-so-common Common Sea Buckthorn in full fruit in the Kilini Creek Natural Area.

members informed of issues and programs, and informing the general public about the value of their fish and wildlife resources.

Firearms enthusiasts in the Stony Plain and Wabamun Lake area organized the Wabamun Gun Club in 1959-60. The club established and maintained a gun range to practice safe gun handling. Because many members of the Stony Plain Fish and Game Association also belonged to the Wabamun Gun Club, the two clubs combined in 1998.

At present, the club has 250 members which come from the Stony Plain, Spruce Grove, Wabamun, Onoway and Edmonton areas. The club is a member of the Stony Plain Chamber of Commerce.

Education

The club has provided conservation and hunter education and firearms safety courses to its members and the public since the courses were first offered in 1964.

Projects

In 1967 the club started the bluebird trail program to encourage mountain bluebirds to nest in the area. This project was initially spearheaded by Earl Erickson and Harry Scheideman. Currently

the club cares for more than 1,200 bluebird houses on 220 miles of road allowances. The club also builds birdhouses for area residents to put up. As well, members go to schools in Parkland County and present workshops. Students in grades 1 and 2 assemble 20 to 80 pre-cut boxes per school, often with the help of junior high school students. The students and their parents put up and maintain the boxes.

COURTESY OF THE STONY PLAIN FISH AND GAME ASSOCIATION AND WABAMUN GUN CLUB
Stony Plain Fish and Game Association and Wabamun Gun Club approved this 200-yard rifle range.

COURTESY OF THE STONY PLAIN FISH AND GAME ASSOCIATION AND WABAMUN GUN CLUB
Stan Kozyra holds up almost a keeper at the Stony Plain Fish and Game Association annual fishing derby!

Since the early 1970s, club members have assisted the Alberta government in stocking fish into local lakes: Spring Lake, Star Lake, East Pit Lake. This project was initially spearheaded by Peter Mapplebeck.

Since 1975-76 club members have planted trees and shrubs on reclaimed land near Wabamun Lake as part of a land reclamation program that was started by John Stelfox, Glen Davis and Larry Anderson.

In 1976 the club constructed and installed goose- and duck-nesting platforms at several locations throughout Parkland County. The project was spearheaded by John Stelfox.

In partnership with the Department of National Defence, the club became stewards of the Kilini Natural Area in 1989, largely through the efforts of Dale Loosemore and Stan Kozyra. The 320 acres of very sensitive natural habitat is located west of Lake Eden and contains numerous forms of plant life that are present only in the Kilini Natural Area and nearby Wagner Bog Natural Area. The area is maintained in conjunction with Alberta Parks and Protected Areas.

The club developed the Sundance boat launch located on the south side of Wabamun Lake back in the early 1990s in partnership with TransAlta Utilities. The site includes a picnic area, bird-viewing site and washroom.

Spearheaded by Greg Kulak and Glen Davis in 1992, the club began the Wildlife Reflector program, where a series of reflectors are placed on posts in ditches along highways at wildlife crossings to prevent wildlife/vehicle collisions. The reflectors flash the light from oncoming headlights into the woods in the form of a band of light. Studies have shown such reflectors significantly reduce collisions. The program is done in partnership with Parkland County, TransAlta Utilities, Parkland Bowbenders and the Spruce Grove Fish and Game Association. The clubs provide the reflectors and the County of Parkland is responsible for installing them.

Starting in 1995, the club acquired 312 acres of habitat property around East Pit Lake, a 40-acre man-made lake near Wabamun. The lake and surrounding land are part of a reclaimed coal mine. East Pit Lake is stocked annually with approximately 11,500 rainbow trout. In co-operation with TransAlta Utilities, the club has developed the property as fish and wildlife habitat, including the provision of bird-nesting structures, fish shelters, and tree and shrub plantings. As well, the club constructed a 20-car parking lot surrounded by a five-foot chainlink fence to prevent vehicles from driving to the lake. The club also provided a garbage dumpster, toilet facilities and signage about the lake.

In co-operation with the town of Stony Plain and the Community Lottery Board, in 1999 the club placed 10 bulletin boards about the town to reduce unsightly bulletins and signs placed on lawns and green areas.

In 2003 the club acquired 531 acres of prime wildlife habitat, known as the White Wood Conservation Properties, located north of Wabamun. This acquisition was realized through the generous financial assistance of the AFGA Wildlife Trust Fund, the Government of Alberta, TransAlta Utilities, and numerous fish and game clubs and other organizations. The club has received a number of prestigious awards for undertaking this conservation program.

The club has a lease from TransAlta Utilities on a quarter-section of land near Wabamun Lake for its 200-yard gun club range. The range is federal-government certified and is open to members only.

Annual Events

Since its beginning, the Stony Plain Fish and Game Association has offered big-game horn measuring each year. Club members and the public are invited to bring their trophies for official measurement on one Saturday in February.

The club has presented 50 annual wild game suppers and trophy balls over the years as one of its major fundraising programs. As well, members help conduct the Annual Hunter Survey for the Fish and Wildlife Division to earn funds for the club.

In 1991 the club started the annual Hide Collection Program, largely through the efforts of Stan Kozyra. Drop-off locations are provided for hunters to donate big-game hides and shed antlers to the provincial AFGA fundraising program.

The club participates in the annual Christmas bird count in conjunction with the Edmonton Nature Club. The club first became involved in 1994 largely through the efforts of Dale Loosemore.

The club supplies boats and members to assist in operation of the handicapped fishing day at Camp He Ho Ha, which is run by the St. Albert and District Fish and Game Association.

Club Awards

The club periodically presents the George and Joan Mitchell Award to one of its members in recognition of outstanding contributions toward conservation and wildlife habitat enhancement. In 1985, the club received the Order of the Bighorn Award for its work enhancing wildlife habitat at the Wabamun TransAlta Utilities property, a reclaimed portion of a coal mine.

Special People

Past presidents of the Stony Plain Fish and Game Association (since 1954) are Jack Mayer, 1954-58; Norris Bamber, 1959-61; Ken Ewart, 1962; Norris Bamber, 1963; Harold McLaughlin, 1964-65; Dan Edmonton, 1966-67; Bill Greenhough, 1968-69; Murray Byers, 1970-71; Harry Scheideman, 1972; Jack Webster, 1973-74; Dr. John Stelfox, 1975-76; George Miller, 1977; Larry Anderson, 1978-79; Jack Webster, 1980; Larry Anderson, 1981; Jack Shaver, 1982-83; Peter Marchuk, 1984-86; Norman Holt, 1987; John Lammers, 1988; Eleanor Martin, 1989; Dale Loosemore, 1990-91; Glen Davis, 1992; Sharonne Albert, 1993-94; Dale Loosemore, 1995; Bernie Letourneau, 1996-98; Blair Crites, 1999-2000; Bernie Letourneau, 2001-02; Joe George, 2003-04; Leighton Stewart, 2005; and Michael Veitch, 2006.

The current Wabamun Gun Club president is D.F. (Snip) Loblick, 1998-2007.

Whitecourt Fish and Game Association
1959-present

The Whitecourt Fish and Game Association is situated in the heart of one of Alberta's finest hunting and fishing areas. It was first organized by a group of sports-minded people in 1959, headed by Ross Quinn and Ben Carr. The membership has grown to 223 members in 2005. The club contributes in many ways to the community, as well as the provincial AFGA.

The objectives of the club are many, including working and co-operating with the Alberta Fish and Wildlife Division, the Alberta Forest Service, the Department of Tourism, Parks, Recreation and Culture, and all youth groups interested in the great outdoors.

Education

The club has offered a conservation and hunter education course for the last 10 years. There have been approximately 250 graduates. It has contributed money, labour, and materials to the Narrow Lake Conservation and Hunter Education Camp. As well, the club sponsors one to four youths to attend the camp annually.

Projects

The association has developed and maintained a rifle and pistol range for the convenience of members. The range is also used by the local Fish and Wildlife Division and the RCMP. It includes a 100-yard rifle range and a handgun range at various distances. The club's archery range has 10-, 20-, 30-, 40- and 50-yard backstops as well as a 3-D course. In the autumn of 2005 a cabin was constructed on the range and future developments are being considered.

The club works with the Fish and Wildlife Division to stock local lakes, including assessing lakes for potential stocking. It has also assisted the division in other ways including helping with aerial wildlife surveys and telephone hunter surveys to determine hunter success rates.

The club has established a scholarship for post-secondary education given to two Whitecourt and area students annually. In previous years, the club purchased portions of farmers' crops to provide forage and cover for a variety of wildlife species.

Annual Events

The Whitecourt Fish and Game Association holds the McLeod (Carson) Lake ice fishing derby each year. The club has a youth fishing day held annually at the Whitecourt Rotary Pond in conjunction with the Rotary Club. It also holds a birdhouse/feeder building event for kids and a wild game banquet, dance and silent auction.

COURTESY OF THE WHITECOURT FISH AND GAME ASSOCIATION

Whitecourt archery, 1996. Gerald Mannweiller (L), Alberta Fish and Game Association programs chair, 2002-03.

Zone 5

Zone 5 covers an area from the City of Edmonton to the Saskatchewan border to the east, and is bordered by zones 4 and 6 on the west, zone 3 on the south, and the Northwest Territories on the north. It is the largest zone by geography, membership and number of clubs. The boreal forest covers a large portion of the zone, along with some fringe farming areas, and the remnants of the parkland region. Alberta's Lakeland is in this zone, the area where the largest percentage of angling takes place in the province. Excellent goose populations are present in the eastern part of the zone in the parkland and agricultural areas, with large numbers of white-tailed and mule deer, along with good moose numbers in the northern regions.

The 20 clubs in zone 5 are:
- Athabasca Fish and Game Association
- Beaver River Fish and Game Association
- Clandonald and District Fish and Game Association
- Edmonton Fish and Game Association
- Edmonton Springer Spaniel Club *
- Fort McMurray Fish and Game Association
- Fort Saskatchewan Fish and Game Association
- Innisfree and District Fish and Game Association
- Irma Fish and Game Association
- Lamont Fish and Game Association
- Lloydminster and District Fish and Game Association
- Mundare Fish and Game Association
- St. Paul Fish and Game Association
- Sherwood Park Fish and Game Association
- Spedden Fish and Game Association
- Two Hills and District Fish and Game Association
- Vegreville Wildlife Federation
- Viking Sports and Wildlife Society
- Vilna Fish and Game Association
- Wainwright Fish and Game Association
- Willingdon and District Fish and Game Association
     * clubs that did not submit histories

Zone History

Prior to the creation of the zoning system in 1968, the AFGA clubs often worked together regionally on projects and concerns of common interest. For example, clubs in southern Alberta banded together as did those in the central/northern area. In the early 1960s, clubs in what became zones 4 and 5 often found common ground, as many residents in one area often hunted and fished in the other. The directors of this early association included Ben Rosnau and Gordon Peel.

Once created in 1968, zone 5 was led by the following directors: Hugh Bossert, Don Appleby, George Ford, Roy Ozanne, Charlotte Drake, Steve Witiuk, Eve Ozanne, Eileen Christensen, Maurice Nadeau and Dave Doonanco. Steve Witiuk was the zone 5 director for 20 of the 40 years in which the zone operated.

Although zone 5 was very active in the AFGA, in 1992 it changed its name to the North Eastern Alberta Fish and Game Association (NEAFGA), with the intent of withdrawing from the

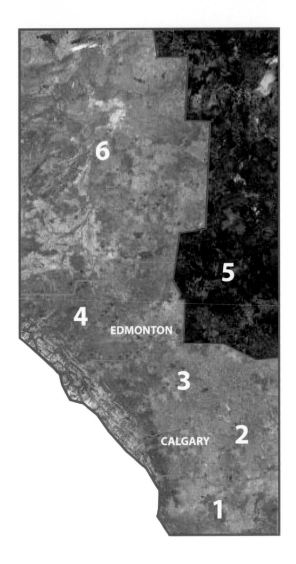

AFGA. Dennis Perka drafted a set of bylaws and the zone was incorporated under the *Societies Act*. However, continued discussions between the groups averted a separation, although zone 5 kept its new name.

The NEAFGA has been involved with several environmental issues over the years including the ESSO heavy oil development in the Cold Lake area, the Beaver River Water Management Plan, the review of the Range Improvement Plans, the Provincial Park Classification System, the Assessment of Northern Pike Regulations, Alberta Pacific Timber Harvesting Operations, Chronic Wasting Disease and the Marie Lake Seismic Operations; the list continues.

The zone has been instrumental in contributing towards the purchase of fish and wildlife habitats and contributing to the AFGA Wildlife Trust Fund. As well, the zone has supported many of its clubs participating in Buck for Wildlife projects.

The NEAFGA has taken strong leadership in hosting four conferences for the provincial AFGA. It has operated five casinos over the years, earning over $300,000 for various fish and wildlife projects.

Before the zone system was developed, clubs in northeast Alberta came together to foster their mutual interest in conservation education. They were part of the start of the alberta hunter education program in 1964, led by the Edmonton Club. The development of youth conservation education camps at both Marie Lake and Narrow Lake (see below) further illustrated this commitment.

Zone 4/5 Youth Conservation Camp

Initially, the AFGA plan was for each zone to administer and operate an independent camp for instructing youth about conservation, hunter training and firearms safety. Zones 4 and 5 of the AFGA decided to combine their resources and build a camp for both zones.

The first youth camps occupied a hodgepodge of venues and it was obvious the camp needed a permanent home. In April of 1986, Don Appleby acquired an AFGA lease on 170 acres of property adjacent to Marie Lake. A committee assessed the prospects for access, shooting ranges and other facilities on the site. Given enough time and resources, Marie Lake would have resulted in an outstanding facility. However, there were a number of caveats associated with the development permitted on the leasehold, and it became evident that the Marie Lake Youth Camp was going to be a long-term project. In the interim, the zone obtained permission from the Fish and Wildlife Division to use its Narrow Lake Hunter Education Camp. In 2003 this facility became zones 4 and 5 youth conservation camp, the zone 4 and 5 Narrow Lake Conservation Education Centre.

The curriculum for the conservation camp was based on a prototype camp developed and implemented by Martha Kostuch in the Rocky Mountain House area. Representatives from zone 5, especially Sam Smolyk and Art Ripley, worked under Martha's tutelage to acquire the necessary expertise.

Martha's curriculum was based on the Alberta Conservation and Hunter Education program. The AFGA Firearm Safety Program and subsequently the Canadian Firearm Safety course were also incorporated into the zone 4/5 program.

The staffing plan usually comprised a core complement of full-time personnel who were expert, or willing to acquire expertise, in at least one of several modules (e.g. firearms, archery, survival, first aid and fisheries). The remaining staff were specialists in at least one module and attended the camp as the schedule dictated. There were dozens of individuals who served as core staff over the years, including Sam Smolyk, Jack Easterbrook, Dave Schumacher, Jim Agnew, Bibiane Foisy, Bill MacLean, Molly Molloy, Dave Scobie, Robert Ashton, Evan Simmons, Vern McIntosh, Twyla MacDonald, Roy Ozanne, Eve Ozanne, Brent Nichols and Yvonne Deboer.

The camp also solicited help from outside experts in their fields. Examples include first aid instructor Jim Owens and Captain Molly Molloy who added orienteering to the survival program. Others included Janice Johnson (Green) and John Dyke from the Alberta Federation of Shooting Sports, Staff Sgt. John Dickinson and Bruce Wilson of the RCMP crime lab, William Hare of the Alberta Handgun Association and Ryk Visscher, an archer. As the camp evolved, a policy of appointing junior instructors from the previous year's graduating class was implemented. Evan Simmons, Robert Ashton, Yvonne DeBoer, Twyla MacDonald and Jenna Boyd were some of the junior instructors. Camp attendant Peter Zachoda, wildlife biologist Blair Rippin, fisheries biologist Hugh Norris, Athabasca district fish and wildlife officer Doug Slatnik, regional director Ray Makowecki and others from the Fish and Wildlife Division also participated frequently in the conservation camp. The camp concluded with a visit from a guest speaker, usually a member of the AFGA hierarchy. Examples include zone directors Don Appleby, Eileen Christensen, Steve Witiuk and AFGA presidents Jack Shaver and Roy Ozanne.

Fish and Wildlife Division hunter education course instructors Lionel Dunn and Red Hasay far exceeded their job requirements in administering workshops for the benefit of the camp's hunter-education instructors. As Lionel became aware of the difficulties the camp faced in staffing its programs, he advised that any time there were 10 instructors interested in further training he would personally schedule a workshop.

In terms of finances, the camp was intended to be self-sufficient. Fees were initially $150 per student. Within a year or so this was increased to $200. However, revenue from fees was never enough to pay for much more than the catering. The Fish and Wildlife Division was generous in donating shotgun shells, a few bricks of .22 cartridges, targets and clay birds. However, this contribution amounted to a fraction of the ammunition used. Fortunately, zones 4 and 5 considered the camp an important investment and never questioned the necessity to underwrite shortfalls.

Over the years many volunteers have worked at the camps and provided wonderful experiences for the youth. Some of the key people included: Sam Smolyk, Bibiane Foisy, Jack Esterbrook, Steve Witiuk, Ed Scarlett, Mike Hanzel, Eileen Christensen, Gordon Christensen, Dennis Grover, Gerald Foster, Fred Stamper, Ken Schlachter, Lloyd Hakes, Brian Rudyk, Jack Reader, Garry Kalyn, Gilbert Gomez, Allan Baker, Dave Doonanco and Allan Wright, Robert Loewen, Gord Thorpe, Jim Hill, Gary Damon, Robert Kutash, Brian Tatarin, Vern McIntosh, Harry White, Randy Collins, Rene Lamoureux and Andy von Busse.

Aerial view of Slave River rapids.

The zone spent over $200,000 on making improvements to the Narrow Lake Conservation Education Centre. The funds came from the hard work of many dedicated volunteers. The centre represents the strong commitment of the NEAFGA towards conservation education.

Club Histories of Zone 5

Athabasca Fish and Game Association
1945-1995

On Saturday, May 19, 1945, a group of dedicated individuals met in Athabasca and committed themselves to the preservation of fish and game in the Athabasca district by forming a branch of the AFGA. Otis Nelson was unanimously elected president and Dr. E.K. Wright was elected as secretary treasurer.

Over the years, the association has seen monumental changes to laws governing fish and game and people's hunting and fishing habits. The club has been instrumental in ensuring that a balance in hunting practices and the conservation of fish and game received the highest priority.

Education
In 1972 the club started hunter-training classes.

Projects
The first project for the Athabasca Fish and Game Association was the release of pheasants in the Athabasca area to improve hunting opportunities. The club contacted the AFGA and arranged to have 100 pheasant eggs delivered from the newly constructed Brooks Pheasant Hatchery on May 26, 1945. The eggs were given to a number of farmers in the area to raise and later release.

COURTESY OF VERN MCINTOSH

Georgia Otway (L) and Marlene McIntosh with a great catch from the Athabasca River, circa 1979.

In 1949 the AFGA, along with the managers of the Brooks Pheasant Hatchery, established a plan for school children to collect pheasant eggs for the hatchery. A total of 14,000 eggs were collected across the province. The hatchery paid two cents per egg and later raised the rate to four cents. Eighty percent of the eggs hatched. The Athabasca Fish and Game Association received 100 of the pheasant chicks, which they raised for 14 to 16 weeks and released in the south Athabasca district. This program was repeated throughout the following years.

The club held its first fish derby on July 2, 1950 at Baptiste Lake. Also in 1950, Dexter Champion and Ernie Ferguson helped restore beaver to the Calling Lake area to help water conservation in aid of forest protection and to help the people whose existence depended on trapping.

On Feb. 4, 1956, as a result of the efforts of the club lobbying both the federal and provincial governments, 26 elk from Elk Island National Park were transplanted five miles north of Calling Lake. On Feb. 27, 1956 an additional 29 elk were released in the Long Lake area.

In March 1962 Pat Buchanan won first place in the 1960 Boone and Crockett North America Big Game competition for moose (score: 225). The Boone and Crockett Club is the recognized organization that keeps records of North American trophy heads. Pat said the Boone and Crockett Club had held competitions for 74 years and never had as perfect a moose trophy as the one he presented. The moose was shot Nov. 10, 1960. Later the government purchased the head and it is now on display at the Fish and Wildlife Division headquarters office in Edmonton.

In 1968 the club membership was 340. The club requested the Fish and Wildlife Division do an aerial big-game survey of this area. Some 1,320 miles of transect were flown in the Athabasca area, showing the largest moose densities in the province: 2.72 per square mile. The club started its big-game trophy competition and the following people donated memorial trophies: Dorothy Evans, Effie Labrie, Rita Birkigt, Fern Nelson and Michael Stychin. The club established a boat-launching site with parking and garbage facilities at Narrow Lake and were looking at stocking of rainbow trout in some waters.

In 1968 approximately 700 elk were present in the Calling Lake and Fish Creek areas from the 56 elk transplanted there in 1956.

The first trophy night of the Athabasca Fish and Game Association was held April 11, 1969. Randy Schulte was the first to receive the club's Dr. E.K. Wright Memorial Trophy for conservation.

In 1970 the club was instrumental in establishing Calling Lake Provincial Park when Dr. J. Donovan Ross was wildlife minister. On June 6, 1970 the club held its 25th anniversary supper and invited all the original members.

The club received 333,000 eastern brook trout from the Alberta Fish and Wildlife Division in 1971 and transplanted them to Ghost Lake where many fish had died.

COURTESY OF DUANE RADFORD

Adrienne Radford with a Cornwall Lake pike, 1974.

In 1972 the club wanted guiding stopped in wildlife management unit 510, as members felt the non-resident alien hunters were causing a serious overkill of game animals. A petition was circulated and when completed was 60 feet long with over 2,000 signatures. The club presented the petition to Dr. Allan Warrack, Minister of Lands and Forests, on Aug. 28, 1972. Dr. Warrack subsequently presented the petition to the provincial cabinet on Aug. 30, where the government agreed to close big-game hunting by non-resident aliens (guided hunters) in that area.

The club planted approximately 159,000 fingerling trout in Ghost Lake in 1977 and 55,000 in Lower Chain Lakes. The club was instrumental in getting a fish ladder at Bolloque Lake.

On Thanksgiving Day in 2002, 12 members of the club along with Ray Makowecki, the AFGA senior vice president, met with local MLA and Minister of Alberta Sustainable Resources Development, Mike Cardinal at his constituency office to discuss a proposal to check off a dollar for each licence sold to go to the AFGA. Cardinal indicated he might be able to provide a grant to the AFGA. In 2003 he presented the AFGA with a cheque for $150,000. This action is an example of the political impact local fish and game clubs can have in support of the AFGA.

The club purchased a lease on a piece of land at Long Lake with profits from a lottery in 1979; in 1980 the club started working on the lease. In 1982 the club along with the Forfar Community Club received a $100,000 initial grant to develop Forfar Recreation Park. The club purchased a quarter-section of land along Long Lake and started working on the park in June.

In 1985 the club stocked a number of dugouts in the area with rainbow trout, and then released them into Chain Lake in October. Forfar Recreation Park opened on May 15, 1985. There are 27 overnight stalls, 20 day areas, eight walk-in tenting areas, four piers, two change rooms, 13 washrooms, four wells, a sewer dump, park warden's cabin, a wood and equipment compound, a boat launch, two fish-cleaning tables and a children's play area.

The fish and game park lease is located on Long Lake across the road from Forfar Park. It is patrolled by park and fish and game members and is open free of charge to fish-and-game members and their guests. It contains a ring-road with 12 overnight stalls, one pier, four washrooms, picnic tables, barbecue pits and a wood splitter.

In 1992 the Athabasca Fish and Game Association hosted an open public forum with First Nation groups to discuss the impact of aboriginal rights on the fish and wildlife resource. This was the first meeting of this kind in Alberta. Chairman Doug Slatnik stated that the meeting was productive and more meetings would help opposing sides understand each other better.

In 1993 the club, in conjunction with the County of Athabasca and the Athabasca Recreation Board, undertook a project to identify municipal and environment reserves adjacent to lake developments. Plastic markers on steel posts were installed along boundaries of municipal and environmental reserves. Those boundary markers serve to distinguish private property from municipally owned reserves. The markers were installed on Baptiste Lake, Amisk Lake, Crooked Lake, North Buck Lake, Skeleton Lake and Tawatinaw Lake. This project was done with funds from the Environmental Partners Fund, the Buck for Wildlife program, the County of Athabasca and the Athabasca Fish and Game Association.

Club Awards

The club received the provincial government's prestigious Alberta Order of the Bighorn Award in November 1983 for its work in wildlife conservation projects in Alberta.

In 1984 the Athabasca Fish and Game Association received the AFGA Neville N. Lindsay Memorial Award for best fisheries project in the province of Alberta. Neville's family designed and handcrafted this award to commemorate his service to the association and to recognize the achievement of its members.

The Athabasca Fish and Game Association won the AFGA Guy Blake Memorial Award for the best habitat project, the 1987-89 elk seismic line-seeding project. The club seeded approximately 30 miles of cutline in the Narrow Lake and Long Lake areas.

Special People

Gordon Christensen won the AFGA Gerry Gibson Memorial Hunter Training Rural Award. Gordon was one of the first hunter education instructors in the province; he was certified in 1971 and has taught classes every year since with approximately 40 graduates per year. In 1986 Eileen Christensen was awarded the AFGA Lady Conservationist of the Year Award.

Past presidents of the Athabasca Fish and Game Association were Otis Nelson,1945-46; E.K. Wright, 1947-52; Doug Harold, 1953-54; A.O. Evans, 1955; E.K. Wright, 1956-57; A.O. Evans, 1958-59; E.K. Wright, 1960-62; Glen Osment, 1963-64; Cec Hyde, 1965-67; Gus Deisting, 1968-69; Peter Marchuk, 1969-70; Gordon Christensen, 1970-75; Alex Pacholok, 1976-79; Leo Beller, 1980-82; Hal Harrison, 1983-84; Nick Rubik, 1985; Eileen Christensen, 1986-90; Sharon Van Hout, 1991-93; and Gordon Christensen, 1994-95.

COURTESY OF GORD POIRIER

Beaver River Fish and Game Association. Gord Poirier (provincial fish chair) and daughter Kristy celebrate a successful elk hunt, 2006.

Beaver River Fish and Game Association
1988-present

The Beaver River Fish and Game Association was founded in 1988 when some people got together in La Corey to discuss whether to establish a local sportsmen club or a shooting club. Outdoorsmen attended from La Corey, Iron River, Crane Lake, Bonnyville, Cold Lake and the surrounding area. At the close of the meeting it was clear a sportsmen club would materialize. At a subsequent meeting it was decided to establish a club and name it after the main river in the area, the Beaver River Fish and Game Association. The first club meeting was held at the Willow Prairie Hall, north of La Corey. The following people were involved in establishing the club: Jerry (founding president) and Jackie Maruniak, Dave Fehr (secretary treasurer), Al and Pat Espetveidt, Scott Dudley, Don Hutchison, Andy Koshykar (vice president), Rick and Rhonda Young, Louise Lapointe, Ron Maruniak, Donny Maruniak, Morris and Shirley Kolody, Al Carr, Mike Mytrash, Mitch Sylvestre, Edward Duchesne, Norm Jubinville, Lou Preteau, Don Solowonuik and Steve Witiuk, the AFGA zone 5 director.

Club membership averages about 380 and peaked at 438.

Education

At its new educational facility the club offers the Alberta Conservation and Hunter Education course, the federal Safe Firearms course, Alberta trapping course, a safe boating course, and any other course of interest to the membership. About 20 people per year take the hunter education course, 30 per year the firearms safety course and youth archery program. Indoor archery is provided on Sunday and Wednesday nights during the six months of winter, with 15-25 youth members attending. The group of instructors is lead by life member Rodger Browatzke, with help from Rollie Inman, Gordon Poirier, Dan McCury, Neil Adams, Dennis Ozaruk, Cynthia Pawluik, Gary Hill, Kristy Poirier, and Matt Janz. The club sponsors youth to the Narrow Lake Conservation Camp annually.

Projects

In 1995 the club leased 1,000 square feet in the Remax building in Bonnyville for a place to meet and store gear. As a result of a growing interest in archery, the membership wanted its own facility to accommodate an indoor archery range and store the club assets. In the fall of 1998, the club moved to the Action Bam east of Bonnyville.

From 1989 to 2001, the club held annual raffles along with walleye tournaments to raise funds to build its own clubhouse and educational facility. In the fall of 2002 a steak supper and auction was held as the final event to obtain funding from the community. This was combined with a government grant to make this dream a reality. Construction of the new 6,000-square-foot building began that autumn in Bonnyville. The Beaver River Fish and Game Association Educational Centre was completed in 2006, a clubhouse and archery lanes. The club has rented the building out to junior forest wardens at no cost, to farmer's markets, dog clubs, and for small weddings and Christmas parties.

The club has participated in numerous conservation projects including lakeshore cleanup, goose nesting, weed abatement, turkey vulture nest protection and many others. Some of these projects received the AFGA awards and plaques. In addition, funds were donated by the club to help purchase wildlife habitat, the most recent donations being $5,000 toward the Vilna property and another $5,000 to the Partridge property south of Elk Point. Previously, the club was the steward of the Beartrap Lake Buck for Wildlife property.

In 2005 a presentation by then president Gordon Poirier to the Municipal District of Bonnyville resulted in a letter of support and the expansion of Sunday hunting into WMUs 500, 501, 502 and 514 in 2007.

Annual Events

The club holds an antler/horn-measuring night on the first Friday night after the close of the November hunting season. However, this may have to change as more and more seasons extend into mid-December.

The club's awards and wild game banquet is traditionally held on the first Saturday in February. This banquet is a major fundraiser for the club. It has always been sold out with people purchasing tickets well in advance.

COURTESY OF TRAVEL ALBERTA

A meadow of wildflowers near Peace River.

In 2007 the club brought back its boat raffle after a three-year hiatus. A $71,000 boat was raffled with only 100 tickets offered, each at $1,000. The raffle sold out in weeks!

Each year the club holds the popular Moose Lake Walleye Classic. This tournament is limited to 100 boats and features over $20,000 in prize money. The local business community lines up to sponsor the entire prize pool. As a result, all of the revenue from the entries goes to the club to be used for various projects such as sending kids to camp, sending voting and youth delegates to the annual AFGA conference and zone meetings, and providing donations to the AFGA Wildlife Trust Fund. The Moose Lake Walleye Classic is a major fundraiser, but it takes a lot of hard work and dedication from volunteers to achieve this mark.

Club Awards

The club sponsors the provincial rainbow trout AFGA trophy and award. The Beaver River Fish and Game Association received the best fisheries project award in 1994 and 1995.

Special People

Some of the club members who have made a difference over the years are Rodger Browatke, life member and awarded the AFGA Gerry Gibson Award for outstanding work in teaching hunter training; Don and Heather Hutchison, the AFGA Distinguished Service Award for their volunteer and fundraising efforts; Arthur Carr, life membership; Maurice and Nadine Nadeau, life memberships.

Presidents of the Beaver River Fish and Association include; Jerry Maruniak, 1988-91; Rick Young, 1991-93; Scott Dudley, 1993-95; Morley Hancock, 1995-97; Maurice Nadeau, 1997-99; Dennis Ozaruk, 1999-2002; Gordon Poirier, 2002-05; and Matt Janz, 2005-07.

Clandonald and District Fish and Game Association
1955-present

The Clandonald and District Fish and Game Association was established in April 1955 in the hamlet of Clandonald, located east of Highway 41, north of Vermilion. The club serves the hamlet and surrounding district. The founding president was Henry Schneider and the vice president was Louis Garnier. Other founding members were John Forsyth, Harold Schoonmaker, Matt Kada, Hugh Logan, Roderick McDonald and Philip Zaph.

Education

The club had conservation and hunter education courses every year for 20 years. About 10 or 12 students would complete the course each year.

Projects

The club raised pheasants and released them in the autumn for 10 years. A trout pond was dug on the club's gun range, where members fished it out every fall and stocked it in the spring. Club members put flax bales out around the shore of some local water bodies for goose-nesting, but the geese have become too plentiful lately, so the program was stopped.

The club held fishing derbies at Laurie Lake for about 10 years, including ice fishing. These derbies were quite popular.

The gun range was constructed around 1982 on land donated to the club by Louis Garner. The range has trap shooting, target and a rifle shooting range. The RCMP used the range for about eight years until they acquired their own.

Annual Events

The club held wild game suppers and trophy nights for about 20 years. They were always well attended. Auctions were also held to raise money to support club activities.

The club reached a peak in membership in 1982 when there were 342 regular and 131 associate members for a total of 473 overall. At present, the average annual membership is about 40. It is getting more difficult to attract new members. Nobody seems to have the time anymore.

Edmonton Fish and Game Association
(1908) 1920-present

There is some controversy as to when the Edmonton Fish and Game Association was initially formed. The Provincial Archives of Alberta has a record that indicates the AFGA was established in Edmonton on Feb. 20, 1908 as the Northern Alberta Game and Fish Protective League. However, that record appears to be unsubstantiated and has been challenged as being incorrect by the AFGA Heritage 100 Committee. What is substantiated is that on March 3, 1920, Edmonton and district sportsmen held a meeting to form an association to look after the fish and game interests in the Edmonton area. Those present at the meeting unanimously adopted the name: "Northern Alberta Game and Fish Protective League." Whether this was a resurrection of a previous organization of the same name or the creation of a new organization with a new name is not known for certain.

Mr. B.J. Lawton, Provincial Game Guardian, addressed the 1920 meeting, speaking generally on the need for such an association, outlining the work to be done and the advisability of having game sanctuaries, among other matters pertaining to game protection. The following people formed the club's first executive committee: A. H. Esch, president; P. E. Bowen, vice president; W. Holmes, secretary treasurer; P. Anderson, big-game chair; A. Hine, feathered-game chair; C. W. Boon, fish chair.

In the beginning, the Edmonton Fish and Game Association served the greater Edmonton area. Over the years, several other fish and game clubs arose to serve this area, many having splintered from Edmonton Fish and Game. Records indicate peak membership for the Edmonton Fish and Game Association was reached in the early 1960s when membership topped at about 6,200. One of the main attractions of membership was the club's shooting range. However, when the range closed, membership dropped. Today the club's membership is 200–250.

COURTESY OF DUANE RADFORD

Edmonton Fish and Game Association horn measuring day, 2007.

COURTESY OF DUANE RADFORD

Mike Masse, Edmonton Fish and Game Association horn measuring day, 2007

Education

The clubhouse, at 13710 - 104 Street in Edmonton, is where the club meets and offers conservation and hunter education, firearm and the occasional taxidermy course.

Projects

Over the long history of the Edmonton Fish and Game Association, there have been a number of conservation projects. There was the introduction of the Hungarian (grey) partridge to Alberta. Numerous goose-nesting projects were also undertaken throughout the club's history. The club had a duck-nesting project in Hawrelak Park, which is located along the North Saskatchewan River in the city of Edmonton. Predator control, whether it was shooting coyotes, magpies, gophers, etc., was one of the club's conservation efforts. A hide collection program was begun and eventually turned into a very successful program for many AFGA clubs across the province. The Edmonton club started an annual sportsmen's show, which is still going

COURTESY OF DUANE RADFORD

Gerald Foster at Edmonton Fish and Game Association horn measuring day, 2007.

strong today. It promotes the conservation, education and stewardship of hunting and fishing sports.

Club Awards

At the provincial AFGA wildlife awards banquet, the Edmonton Fish and Game Association sponsors the Master Big Game Trophy, which recognizes the largest big-game animal harvested in Alberta in the past hunting season.

Annual Events

The club holds its trophy measuring night at the clubhouse in early February. It is well-attended. The trophy awards banquet is where members who have won awards receive a trophy and two tickets to the dinner, dance and silent auction. This event is well-attended with numbers ranging from 260 to 300. About 25-30 percent of the people attending dinner do not hunt or fish, but come specifically to sample and experience the wild game dishes. The 2007 banquet was the club's 43rd wild game awards dinner.

COURTESY OF HENRY LEMBICZ

Edmonton Fish and Game Association float, summer of 1964.

COURTESY OF DUANE RADFORD

Bob McDonald (L) and Wes Voogd, Edmonton Fish and Game Association horn measuring day, 2007.

Special People

The following are some of the members who made significant contributions to the club and the AFGA over the years. With the club's long history, it is possible that some members were missed.

Past presidents of both the Edmonton club and the provincial AFGA include C. E. (Buster) Brown, Jack Graham, Budd Traver, Ron Gladish and Gordon Peel. Other past presidents of the Edmonton club are Steve Germaniuk, Denis Grover, Eve Ozanne, Frank Pickering, Jim Shewfelt, Ed Tremblay, Alan Wright, Colin Murphy, Brent Nichols, Lawrence Iley, Steve Stephens and Morris Komonasky.

Other significant members of the club include Ray Bellamy, Chuck Burghardt, John Czar, Marcel Droessaert, Jack Easterbrook, Cliff Enfield, Ben Farnham, Frank Grismer, J. Hamilton, Herb Lutz, L. McRae, Sylvia Miles, George Mitchell, Brent Nichols, Monty Nichols, Tom Morris, Art Ripley, Ruth Shewfelt, Ivan Wakaruk, Albert Young, Frank Latour, Don Rowe, Bert Thackray, Dan Schindler, Steve Stephens, John Eglinski, Art Miles, Frank Nichols and Don Cameron.

Looking Ahead

With 100 years behind the AFGA, it is time to look at the next 100. Youth participation in hunting and fishing activities is crucial to the future of those activities and the conservation of the resource. Encouraging youth to participate in these activities and not to be ashamed of being hunters and anglers should be the top priority of all the AFGA clubs. If more youth become involved in fish and game clubs, they will become good stewards of the land and will provide the leadership society needs to ensure there will always be fish and game.

COURTESY OF DUANE RADFORD

Derrick Voogd at the Edmonton Fish and Game Association horn measuring day, 2007.

Fort McMurray Fish and Game Association
1968-present

The Fort McMurray Fish and Game Association was started in 1968 by four local sportsmen who recognized the need for an organization dedicated to the conservation of the flora and fauna in the Fort McMurray area. The other primary goal of the club was the promotion of ethics in the shooting sports. Current membership of the club is about 500 members. The club encourages members to include their families by charging the same for an individual as a family.

Education

Over the years, the club has held a number of courses including conservation and hunter education and firearms safety and Range Safety Officer courses. Juniors shoot free in both trap and biathlon.

Projects

The club originally used shooting ranges at the present-day site of the Valiant Memorial Motor Cross Park. In 1984 the club purchased the lease for its current facility from Contact Airways, 148 acres of land situated 17 kilometres south of Fort McMurray on Highway 63. After purchasing the lease, the club immediately began fund raising to build a year-round shooting facility. A ground-breaking ceremony occurred in 1984 and construction started in 1986. However, with limited funds and volunteer labour, progress was slow. In the spring of 1989, with the building 75 percent complete, a fire completely destroyed the structure. Fortunately, insurance money helped start the building again on the original site. By the fall of 1990, both the clubhouse and the indoor range were completed. The facility includes seven ranges: a .22-calibre range, a high-power rifle range to 1,000 yards, a black-powder range, seven handgun bays, three trap houses and a skeet house, a biathlon range with 20 targets and 2.5 kilometres of cross-country ski trails, and an archery range. There is also an indoor range.

The clubhouse is well-used by members who stop in for coffee and a game of cards in front of the wood-burning stove. AltaCan Tours rents the facility from September to April to bring Japanese tourists to view the northern lights from 10 p.m. until 4:30 a.m. most nights.

The shooting range has been the site of many major shooting competitions. In 1980 the Canadian Black Powder National Shoot was held there. The club hosted the shooting sports for the Alberta Summer Games in 1985. The Alberta Provincial Skeet Championship was held at this range in 1989. Club member George Ford won that championship and went on to win the Canadian championship in Winnipeg.

The club's trap and skeet ranges have produced a number of champions, both junior and senior. Greg Crosland Jr. was Canadian Junior Champ in 1998, as was Andrew Stepanuk in 2002. Ron Crockford and George Ford have taken many trophies and awards for skeet and trap shooting.

Biathlon became the seventh event at the facility in 1998. In 2004 the range hosted first the Alberta Cup and then the Arctic Winter Games. The club's athletes took eight medals in the ski and snowshoe biathlon events that included athletes from Russia, Finland, Alaska, the Northwest Territories, northern Quebec, Greenland, Nunavut and Numavik. The range hosted the Biathlon Alberta Championship in 2005.

The Hanging Stone Ravens have hosted a four-to-five day Black Powder Rendezvous for the past four years at the range. Competitors come from the prairie provinces, B.C. and the northern United States.

The club heavily supports the local biathlon team, supplying ammunition, rifles, transportation and accommodations to all competitors. It also supplies targets and shotgun shells to junior trap shooters.

In 2002 the club acquired a lease of 27 acres at Engstrom Lake to maintain the campground and the lake. The lake is known for its excellent stocked rainbow trout taken by fly in the summer and through the ice in winter. Robert Jameson, the club's environment chair, spearheaded this project.

In the early 1970s the club was instrumental in developing the fish ladders for Arctic grayling on Hanging Stone Creek that minimized the effect of Highway 63 construction on the grayling population of the creek. The association, in conjunction with the Alberta Fish and Wildlife Division, helped stock Engstrom Lake and the Texaco freshwater pond. For the last five years the club has been a funding partner of the Fish and Wildlife Division's Bear Aware program.

The club has transplanted pheasants, wild turkeys and partridges into the Fort McMurray area with limited success. The club had a game-bird feeding program but it was felt the program was doing more to support the coyote population than help establish game bird populations.

Annual Events

The club holds a big-game scoring night at the clubhouse each year, which includes a potluck supper. Any member is eligible to enter horns, antlers or skulls into the scoring competition. The annual general meeting is held the first Sunday in December.

Fort Saskatchewan Fish and Game Association
1958-present

The first club organized under the name of Fort Saskatchewan Fish and Game Association was founded in 1958 in the home of Chester Simmons with the help of Herman Hennig and an assembly of a dozen interested people. Mr. Simmons was elected president and the membership quickly grew to 150.

From 1959-63, Fred Young held the position of president. Unfortunately, the club became dormant until it was revived in 1969 with an initial membership of 43 under the presidency of Bob Wilson with Henry Visscher as secretary. The formative years were ambitious ones with the establishment of a trophy award system, a rifle range, and a fish pond. In 2005, membership numbered 575.

Education

Over the years, the club has presented courses in conservation and hunter education, fishing education, fly casting and fly-tying, predator control (magpies and crows), and taxidermy. Norman Dahl and Chuck Meyer put on some of the earliest hunter training courses anywhere, going as far back as the 1950s, and continuing for many years.

Projects

Many of the events established in the club's early years are still carried on today. For example, the club has supported a minor hockey team from 1970 to this date. The first Rifleman's Rodeo was held in the autumn of 1971. This event became the main expenditure of club effort until the establishment of the spring fish derby. Howard Johnson, a teacher from Ponoka, introduced the club to the idea of the Rifleman's Rodeo and helped the club establish it here. The rodeo consisted of five events: men's senior (open to all male shooters), ladies' senior (open to all female shooters), junior open (shooters under 18 years of age), family event (one adult and one junior from each family), and team event (one adult male and female plus one junior shooter). Five targets were used, two mobile and three pop-up, consisting of a running antelope at 100 yards, a pop-up goat at 150 yards, a pop-up sheep at 200 yards, a running deer at 250 yards, and a pop-up bear at 300 yards. The club awarded a formidable array of trophies and prizes down to fifth place in each event. These rodeos brought shooters to Fort Saskatchewan from all over Alberta and some entries from Saskatchewan and British Columbia. The annual rodeos continued until the loss of the gun range in 1978.

While the gun range dominated activities through the early 1970s, the fishermen were not forgotten. The club stocked a fish pond with fingerling trout as early as 1971 at a Steel Brothers gravel pit near Fort Saskatchewan. The pond was a great diversion for children and old-timers, but was later lost. The club held family gatherings at North Buck Lake. Fishing was the main attraction, but horseshoe pitching, foot races and egg-throwing contests were also on the agenda.

A well-organized fish derby was re-established in 1977. This was held at North Buck Lake the long weekend in May until 1982, when it moved to Moose Lake, where there were a more comfortable campsite and better facilities. By 1987 this derby was about the third largest in the province organized by an individual club. The event included prizes and trophies for men, women and children for catching northern pike, walleye and perch.

Other activities of the club in its earlier years included the Junior Conservation Program, and the raising and release of pheasants; 575 pheasants were released by 1987.

Goose-nesting was also a major program and many flax bales and later floating structures were set out in area wetlands. Other events from the club's early years are unknown as all the club records and archives were lost in a fire in the home of Al Dimmer in Evergreen Trailer Park.

In more recent times (1990 forward), the club continued to grow. A much-sought-after rifle range was finally established in 1989, in conjunction with the Mundare Fish and Game Association. The club finished another five-year pheasant-rearing program, with 1,000 birds released. Other programs were the building and placing of mallard duck-nesting cones, nesting tunnels, cavity nesting boxes, and scores of bluebird houses.

In the late 1990s, the club, spearheaded by Leo Cams, obtained a long-term lease with Strathcona County on 80 acres near Elk Island Park. A cabin was erected with the help of Real Bibeau and friends, and a trout pond dug: the Chuck Meyer Memorial Trout Pond. Many of the club's activities now occur at this location.

Annual Events

Doug MacLean was the main driving force behind the first wild game supper held in the old Legion hall in 1969. The event eventually moved to Josephburg, where it has occurred each year since.

The club's Andrew Young Memorial Junior Trap Shoot is held every September. Andrew Young was the son of Bill and Mary Young of Sherritt Gordon Mines. Andrew died tragically in an auto accident at the age of 16. At the time of his death, young Andrew was chairman of the bird committee of the Fort Saskatchewan Fish and Game Association. He is remembered as an avid outdoorsman, a graduate of the Alberta conservation and hunter education program, and an enthusiastic butterfly collector. The Andrew Young Trophy, donated by his family, was established in 1970 and recognizes the club's junior trap shooting champion each year.

The club's summer fish derby (now a family weekend campout and catch-and-release derby) has gained in fame and moved to lakes such as Cross Lake and recently Fawcett Lake.

The Fort Saskatchewan club also established a kids' ice fishing derby, recently named "The Bill Kostenuk Memorial Kids' Ice Fishing Derby," held every winter at various locations, including Hanmore Lake, Lac St. Anne, Nakamun Lake, Lac La Nonne, Long Lake and also at the club's trout pond. The first derby was put on by Gerald Inkster and John Appleton at Bonnie Lake in the early 1970s.

The club's annual wild game dinner and trophy banquet is held every March and is second to none and the envy of many. The 2009 event will be the 40th on record. At these events, the club honours the year's trophy winners and provides a social gathering for the members. It is also the club's biggest fundraiser of the year. With help from many sponsors, the club has 36 major trophies awarded on an annual basis. Most trophies date back to the 1969-70 era; however, some new ones have been added over the years.

Club Awards

The Fort Saskatchewan club has sponsored the provincial AFGA grizzly bear trophy since 1975.

Special People

The main contributing members in the early years included Al Dimmer (former president) Marshall Melnyk, Jim Skillen, Doug MacLean, John Thompson, Jack Lundberg, Marcel Letawsky, Brian Bilan, John Appleton and Walter Bablitz. Through the late 1980s and 1990s, influential club members included Eric Mickailyk, Doug Urichuk, Len Gransch, Roger Gamache and Doug and Robyn Butler, to name but a few. Current active members include Real Bibeau, Colin McLean, Dennis and Pat Hluschak, Dan Roth, Gord Blize, Doug and Robyn Butler among many others.

Innisfree and District Fish and Game Association
1968-present

The Innisfree and District Fish and Game Association was founded in the fall of 1968. Members of its first executive committee were Howard Ferguson, president; Mike Strynadka, vice president; Tom Saik, secretary treasurer; and board members-at-large Fred Gizowski, Art Kostynuk, Joe Sobchyshyn, Alex Paranych, John Teierle, Walter Paranych, John Melnyk, Mike Pichota, Nestor Kozma and Morris Paranych. Since the club began, it has had an annual membership of approximately 140 people.

Education
The club sponsors conservation and hunter education courses for youth in the community and first-time hunters. It annually sponsors youth to attend the zone 5 Narrow Lake Conservation Camp.

Projects
The club maintains a fish pond, picnic tables, restroom facilities and camp shelter. The pond is stocked annually with rainbow trout for public enjoyment.

Annual Events
Innisfree Fish and Game hosts an annual supper and dance the third Saturday in February. The event sells out each year at 550 tickets, and is widely attended by members and friends from across the province. The club also holds an annual horn and antler scoring event each December that is enjoyed by all who participate. An annual trout pond derby is held during the summer months, and enjoyed by all, young and old alike. The club's annual general meeting is held in March.

Irma Fish and Game, Rifle and Gun Club
1955-present

The Irma Fish and Game, Rifle and Gun Club was started in May 1955. It serves Irma and the surrounding area. Some of the founding members of note were Fred Clumstad, Milt Fahner, Jack Ballantine, Gus Prosser, Charlie Milne, Ole Raasok, Bob Hanson, Charlie Allan, Torlief Larson, Ole Nissen, Donald Gunn and Ted Hill. The club's highest membership was in 1975 when there were 140 members. Currently, the membership is around 50.

Education
The club sponsors the Irma High School hunter education course, with 150 to 200 students having taken the course. It has sponsored firearms courses with about 75 graduates. The club runs a pistol course for its pistol shooting members a small-boat course for anglers. It sends youths to the Narrow Lake Conservation Camp.

Projects
Some of the club's conservation projects over the years have included goose-nesting platforms and bales, pheasant-raising, trout ponds at three separate locations at different times, and the club holds an annual crow, magpie and gopher shoot. The club has

sponsored public forums with Fish and Wildlife Division district officers and gives out a stewardship award. At this time the club has a fish pond, a pistol range and a trap range.

When the club first started it met at members' homes. Over the years meetings have been held in such places as the local hotel, the Cub Hall and the school. Now the club meets the first Monday of the month at the Irma Elks Hall. Some of the activities the club is involved with are an annual turkey shoot, a fish derby every Father's Day weekend, annual trophy night which is held in conjunction with the spring gopher, magpie and crow shoot. Some activities from past years include wild game suppers, turkey dinners, gun shows and guest speakers such as Al Oeming and his cheetah. To raise funds the club has raffled off everything from rifles to televisions.

The club's annual fish derby started in 1975 as an outing for grade 9 students, many of whom had never been out fishing before. The event culminated with a fish fry on Saturday night. It was so successful that by 1979 so many people were coming that feeding them all became a problem and the event was cancelled. It has since become a members-only outing with a small but faithful following.

Special People
Club presidents were Mervin MacKay, Lorne Anquist, Len Skori and the current president, who has served admirably for the last 20 years or so, Brad Hill.

Lamont Fish and Game Association
1950s-present

The actual origin of the Lamont club is unknown but is thought to have been sometime in the late 1940s or early 1950s. According to current members Ed Koroluk and Marvin Letwin (who both joined in 1957), Ben Rosnau and Alex Mitchell were the founders. An early executive committee consisted of Paul Nychka as president, Alex Mitchell as vice president and Tom Small as secretary. Paul was an original club member and remained an active member until his death in 2006 at 93 years of age.

According to Bob Mitchell (Alex's son), the club once had 500-plus members when membership costs were $1 per year. In recent years the club has maintained a membership of approximately 100 members.

Projects
The club has always had both winter and summer fish derbies, with locations including Floating Stone, Pinehurst, Beaver, Goodfish, Fawcett, Long, North Buck and Baptiste lakes.

Lamont's old water reservoir was turned into a trout pond and the club has looked after and maintained the site since about 1976. In addition to an excellent trophy competition, the club sponsors both youth and women to summer camps and puts a float in Lamont's Canada Day parade.

Annual Events

An annual wild game dinner is the club's biggest fundraiser and is held in conjunction with the trophy awards each January.

Special People

The club's past presidents include Alvin Heigh, Marian Seminuk, George Kuzyk, Mike Zazula, Chuck Varga and present-day president Vince Hallisky.

Lloydminster and District Fish and Game Association
1927-present

Unfortunately, all documentation for the early history of the Lloydminster and District Fish and Game Association was lost in a house fire in 1963. According to J.A. (Archie) Miller, who was with the club from the beginning (and who recently passed away), the club started in 1927 as the Lloydminster Gun Club. The first executive committee was J.W. (Jack) Swift, president; Jack Lister, secretary; and Archie Miller, treasurer; with Dr. Lindley, Alan Young, Joe Greupner, and Fred Dunstan as directors. Jack continued to lead the club for at least 20 years.

Records indicate that by 1947 the name of the club had become the Lloydminster and District Fish and Game League. The club had become affiliated with both the Saskatchewan Fish and Game League and the AFGA.

The location of Lloydminster on the border between Alberta and Saskatchewan always necessitated affiliating with both provinces. As a result, the club divided its contributions to provincial programs, such as youth programs and camps, the hide programs, and the provincial habitat lands programs, between the two provinces. However, club minutes show that by Nov. 12, 1969, the cost of affiliating with both provinces was becoming a burden.

In negotiations with both the Saskatchewan Wildlife Federation and the AFGA, the club was able to half its affiliation fee with each provincial organization.

In 1957 a splinter group, interested more in serious competitive shooting than in broader conservation issues, separated from the club under the name of the Lloydminster Fish and Game League Gun Club. That club purchased six acres of land from Reg Salt south of the city and built a gun range and clubhouse. The following year, due to legal complications, their name was changed to the Lloydminster Gun Club. This club is still very active and has produced some highly respected shooting champions. The remainder of the original club eventually became known as the Lloydminster and District Fish and Game Association.

COURTESY OF LLOYDMINSTER AND DISTRICT FISH AND GAME ASSOCIATION
Orienteering at the Lloydminster and District Fish and Game Association youth day, June 2007.

COURTESY OF LLOYDMINSTER AND DISTRICT FISH AND GAME ASSOCIATION
Thirty-nine youths with instructors at Lloydminster and District Fish and Game Association Youth Day, June 2007.

As a result of interest in the Kenilworth Goose Project (see below) and the purchase and development of the club's indoor and outdoor shooting ranges on 80 acres of scenic habitat, membership increased during the 1970s. It reached an all-time high of 993 in 1976. For the last 15 years, the club has maintained a membership of between 600 and 700.

Education

Over the years, thousands of students have graduated from the club's Conservation and Hunter Education courses. Instruction was provided by volunteers such as Archie Miller, D. Mark, Ken Anderson, Brian Sheppard, Ralph Conlon, Gerald Johnson, Larry Chambers, Bill Luchyski, Dean Hotchkiss, Dale Forland, Eric Rounce and Jack Kienlen.

The club has sent students to summer camps since 1975. These camps help young people develop a better understanding of conservation, of the interdependence of humanity and the natural world, and the value of healthy populations of fish and wildlife. The students go to either the Saskatchewan camp in Prince Albert or the Alberta camp at Narrow Lake, all expenses paid.

In 1986 the club started a scholarship program. Over $15,000 in scholarships have been awarded to students in the membership area. Up to two $750 scholarships are presented annually to post secondary students studying conservation or wildlife management - an investment in the future.

In recent years, the club has organized a Youth Fun Day at the end of June. Young people are introduced to archery, the use of compasses, and camp skills.

Projects

Predator control was an important program in the early years. A group of club members organized the Gun and Crow Club in the spring of 1936 to eradicate such pests as crows and magpies. One colourful figure who had a lot to do with maintaining this program over the years was Joe Greupner, affectionately known as "The Crow Man" because of his prowess in hunting crows. Joe put up a "handsome shield" each year to be awarded to the individual who shot the most crows. Thousands of birds were removed over the years and presumably benefitted the game and songbird populations.

Coyote drives were also popular in the late 1940s to early '60s. Dozens of men would walk through bush and ravines, where coyotes were thought to inhabit, toward shooters posted at the end. This method did not remove as many coyotes as the poisoning programs extant at the time but avoided some of the controversial issues, such as the unintentional poisoning of non-target species.

The club tried a pheasant-stocking program for 10-15 years. However, the program was discontinued because a viable population failed to develop.

The club has constructed two very successful trout ponds available for the public along the Yellowhead Highway; one in Alberta and the other in Saskatchewan. In the past the club stocked these ponds, but both are now stocked by government.

In the early 1970s goose populations were low. As a result, the local fish and game clubs at Lloydminster, Marwayne, and Vermilion got together and conceived the Kenilworth Goose Project in 1972. Bill Wishart, wildlife biologist with the Alberta

Archery at Lloydminster and District Fish and Game Association (LDFGA) youth fun day, 2007.

COURTESY OF LLOYDMINSTER AND DISTRICT FISH AND GAME ASSOCIATION

The Lloydminster and District Fish and Game Association cleanup work bee crew at the Gordon Leslie Property, 2005.

COURTESY OF LLOYDMINSTER AND DISTRICT FISH AND GAME ASSOCIATION

Outdoor cooking at the Lloydminster and District Fish and Game Association youth day, 2006.

COURTESY OF LLOYDMINSTER AND DISTRICT FISH AND GAME ASSOCIATION

The Lloydminster and District Fish and Game Association took seniors from Pioneer Lodge fishing for the day, July 2006.

Fish and Wildlife Division, provided the technical expertise and arranged the propagation permit from the Canadian Wildlife Service. Stan Daniel was a driving force in the project, along with Gordon King of Lloydminster, Gerald Colton of Vermilion, and Mike Hamernyk of Marwayne.

Kenilworth Lake on Highway 16 between Lloydminster and Vermilion was chosen for the project because it was a migratory bird refuge, closed to hunting in the fall. The goal of the project was the preservation and propagation of the greater Canada goose through the imprinting of the young geese to the general area so they would return for nesting. Mr. and Mrs. Lyle Anson provided the necessary land for the 500 x 500-foot chainlink-fenced enclosure. A reservoir was dredged and a building was donated for winter shelter. Husky Oil donated much of the pipe and sucker rod for the fence. Geese for the project were provided by the Alberta Fish and Wildlife Division and Mr. and Mrs.

Bill Bowthorpe of Round Hill. These geese soon multiplied and added to the abundance of Canada geese seen today.

Annual Events

Probably the best known and widely attended function of the club is the wildlife supper and awards night. It started in 1936 as a Father and Son banquet. From its inception, it has had crowds of 250-350 attend. By the 1970s it became the Family Wildlife Banquet where spouses and the whole family were encouraged to attend. This event continues today on the last Saturday of January and now involves fundraising events such as raffles, silent auctions and displays. The selling of corporate tables has increased attendance to 450 in the last two years.

Club Awards

The Lloydminster and District Fish and Game Association sponsors the Alberta Provincial Scenic Photography trophy and the Saskatchewan Provincial Brook Trout trophy.

In 1973 the club won the AFGA J.B. Cunningham Memorial Award for having the highest increase in membership sales in Alberta. The club was awarded the prestigious AFGA Guy Blake Memorial Award in 1973-74 for the best conservation project in Alberta, the Kenilworth Goose Project.

In 2003 the club won the AFGA's J. D Munroe Outdoor Activities Award and the Saskatchewan Best Branch Project for its Walleye Micro-Rearing Pond Project. The project sought to develop methods and materials needed to inexpensively and significantly improve the survival rate of walleye larvae to a healthy fry stage up to one inch. The club has been successful in releasing large numbers of fingerlings in only two out of five years (at Peck and Little Fishing Lakes).

Special People

The AFGA and the Saskatchewan Wildlife Federation honoured Ab England with distinguished service awards in 2004 for his exemplary service as an official wildlife trophy measurer. Ab has been measuring for the club since 1981 and has been keeping the Alberta records since 1986. In 2001 Ab was one of only two Canadian judges who sat on the North America Boone and Crockett Awards panel in Springfield, Missouri. He again sat on this panel in Kansas City in 2004.

Larry Chambers was awarded the AFGA Distinguished Service Award and the Saskatchewan Wildlife Federation Gordon Lund Memorial Award for his many and continuous years of service to the ideals of conservation.

Many directors served faithfully on the executive for years. The following are some of the directors from the early years: Roger Jones, Alan Young, Les Foote, Les Leer, Art Nicholson, Gordon Davidson, Desmond Evans, A. B. (Alex) Tingley, W. A. (Slim) Thorpe, Dave McGladdery, Joe Greupner, Fred Dunstan, Reg Dobson, Charlie Fisher, John Goodwin, H. Aston, Harry Anderson, D. Mark, Art Clemens and Keith DeLeeuw. Long-serving directors in more recent years include Wayne Burzinski, Gerald Johnson, Dean Hotchkiss, John Kerr, Gordon Davidson, Ab England, Adrien Beauvais, Bob Corpe, Jack Kienlen, Gunther Henglehaupt, and Jerry Russell.

The club confers life membership status to those who have given many years of dedicated service and have made significant contributions to the objectives of the club. Members who have received life members include the following: Archie Miller (also given a life membership by the AFGA and the Saskatchewan Wildlife Federation), Nick Fuchs, Howard Bygrove, Dave McGladdery, Les Leer, Gordon Garner, Peter Dribnenky, Stan Daniel, Bill Luchinski, Gordon King, Frank Bexson, Larry Chambers, Norris Edwards, Lorne Topley, Walt Backer and Rick Knight.

The following are some of the presidents of the Lloydminster and District Fish and Game Association: J. W. (Jack) Swift, 1927-47+; Fred Wallace, 1962-63; Russ Drury, 1964-65; Al Jardine, 1966-67; Keith Pawsey, 1968-69; Peter Dobranski, 1970-71; Gordon King, 1972-73; Stan Daniel, 1974-75; Bill Luchinski, 1976-77; Larry Chambers, 1978; Gordon Garner, 1979; David Fisher, 1980-81; Kevin Mark, 1982; Jim Kenyon, 1983-84; Lorne Topley, 1985-86, Rick Knight, 1987-88; Norris Edwards, 1989-91; Lyle Gardiner, 1992-93; Eric Rounce, 1994-95; Bill Armstrong, 1996-98; Larry Chambers, 1999-2000; Earl Kaye, 2001-02; Curly Hallan, 2003; Garry Cunningham, 2004-05; and Tyler Verabioff, 2006.

COURTESY OF TRAVEL ALBERTA

Canada geese at Beaverhill Lake, Tofield.

Mundare Fish and Game Club
1950s-present

The Mundare Fish and Game Club originally started in the 1950s but dismantled in 1968. There is little information about the old club, but members remember wild game suppers, trophy nights, annual curling bonspiels and the club being active around the community. In 1977 a group of local sportsmen discussed re-establishing the Mundare club and in the winter of 1977-78, an organizational meeting was held in the Mundare Recreation Centre. An executive committee was elected: Bob Shelast, president; Ed Kuhn, vice president; and Ken Ferleyko, secretary treasurer. In the first year, there were roughly 50 members, mostly from the Mundare area.

Education
Each year the club sends two to three youths to the Narrow Lake Conservation Camp, where they learn outdoor, hunting and fishing skills.

Projects
The first order of business for the new club was to resurrect the wild game supper and trophy night, similar to what the old club had done. The response from the community was great and helped generate funds towards a pheasant-rearing project, one of the key initiatives the club had in the early years. The wild game supper and trophy night was an annual event for several years until interest faded and it was difficult to find a cook who knew how to prepare wild game for large numbers of people.

At a meeting in 1981, the need for a gun range was discussed. The club acquired a 25-year lease from Charlie Soleski on about 15 acres of land. The club designed and built rifle ranges of 50, 100, 200 and 300 yards; a pistol range, a skeet range, and an archery lane. Once the gun range was completed, the club decided to restock a trout pond adjacent to the range for the benefit of members and their families. The trout pond was a great success. It was not uncommon to see a family fishing and having a barbecue at the pond on a Sunday afternoon.

In the late 1980s, the Fort Saskatchewan Fish and Game Association approached Lynn Soleski, vice president of the Mundare club, and asked if the club would consider sharing the gun range with the Fort Saskatchewan club. The offer was discussed at a Mundare club meeting and the membership decided to allow the Fort Saskatchewan club to use the range, which it continues to do to this day.

Throughout the years the club has had numerous social events for its members and the community; they've had summer and winter fish derbies, Christmas parties, Family Day events, curling bonspiels, buck scoring nights, open houses and skeet competitions. They've also participated in different projects throughout the years such as pheasant rearing, the AGT bird nesting program, and planting fruit trees at the gun range.

In 1998 the club started to work satellite bingos to raise money for upcoming projects. This has turned out to be a great fundraiser,

COURTESY OF ST. PAUL FISH AND GAME ASSOCIATION

Crow shoot near St. Paul in 1953. Top row: Frank Gordy (L), Fred Baron. Middle row: Jack Dupuis (L), Prosper Foisy, George Chamberlain, Jean Lupul. Front row: Vix Laboucane (L), Alec Tannas, Vianney Joly, Phil Germain, Ted Generoux and Tony Joly.

The first zone 5 youth conservation camp was held at Lake Bellevue in the St. Paul district in 1983. Officer Wayne Brown and Bibiane Foisy, along with numerous members from other clubs, were instrumental in organizing the camp.

Projects

During the 1940s and 1960s, there were bounties on crows and magpies to reduce their populations. Crow and magpie feet sold for five cents a pair. The club organized hunts that provided entertainment and raised funds for the club. As well, hawks, snowy owls and great horned owls had bounties of 25 cents for a pair of feet. The bounties on the birds of prey were discontinued in 1954.

Pheasant chicks were brought from the provincial Brooks Pheasant Hatchery in the spring, raised and released to the wild. Unfavourable weather conditions and predators often took a toll on the released pheasants.

COURTESY OF ST. PAUL FISH AND GAME ASSOCIATION

Bibiane Foisy, goose-nesting project, St. Paul, 1984.

From 1954-56, in conjunction with Parks Canada and the Alberta Fish and Wildlife Division, the club helped transplant elk from Elk Island National Park to Ardmore, and then to Worm Lake.

In June 1955 the club helped plant 81,000 rainbow trout fingerlings into Thoben Lake. In October of the same year, trout ranging in weight from seven to nine ounces were caught out of the lake. Unfortunately, in the following year, all were winter-killed.

In 1956 the club reported seeing the first turkey vultures ever recorded in the St. Paul area. Other activities recorded during these years were fish derbies, crow shoots, turkey shoots, egg hunts and gopher shoots.

COURTESY OF ST. PAUL FISH AND GAME ASSOCIATION

Bibiane Foisy receiving the Darwin Cronkhite Award from Ed Kubash in St. Paul, 1986.

The club helped plant over 73,000 lake trout fingerlings into Lac Sante from 1960-61. At the same time the club helped with the transplanting of 100 adult perch and 25 adult pike from Long Lake into Lake Bellevue. Another 40,000 perch fingerlings came from Mann Lake.

In 1964 the club constructed a quarter-mile damn to cut off a bay from the main waterbody at Lake Bellevue and create a trout pond. Six thousand rainbow trout were released. However, the damn eventually broke and the project was abandoned.

The club purchased land east of St. Paul in 1983 for a gun range. The land was purchased for one dollar from Maggella and Yvonne Pelchat.

In 1984 the club placed goose bails in several key locations to establish a goose population in the area. Under the Environment 2000 program, the club hired five students and supervisors to restore spawning beds in streams.

allowing the club to purchase the gun range land when the lease expired in 2006 and build new shooting benches.

One of the goals of the Mundare Fish and Game Club was to sign up 100 members, which had not been done in the history of the club. In 2006 the goal was finally reached with 116 members.

Annual Events

In 1978 the club started the Mundare Fish and Game mixed curling bonspiel as a fundraiser for projects. The bonspiel has been a great success ever since and continues to be an annual club event.

The club began an annual horn scoring and open house night in 2003, which has been very successful. Ron Borowski of Borowski Taxidermy has generously donated to Mundare Fish and Game Club a white-tailed deer-mount for the biggest white-tail taken each year and a fish-mount for the biggest fish taken.

Club Awards

From 1986 to 1994, the Mundare Fish and Game Club sponsored the AFGA provincial award for the biggest white-fronted goose taken in the year. In 2001 the club began sponsoring the provincial AFGA lake trout award for the biggest lake trout taken in the year.

Special People

Pete Dziwenka has been on the executive for the past 25 years and Dale McCarty for 23 years. Pete was the president in 2006. Both members have been a great asset to the club.

The Mundare Fish and Game Club acknowledges the following members for their assistance and support over the years: Leonard Babin, Norm Choma, Brenda Dziwenka, Lloyd Dziwenka, Pete Dziwenka, Ken Ferleyko, Darryl Hackman, Harvey Hrynyk, Dave Ilkiw, Ed Kuhn, Dale McCarty, Lloyd Sereda, Bob Shelast, Lynn Soleski, Blair Talaga, Marvin Walinski, Bill Zelen.

St. Paul Fish and Game Association
1940s-present

Over the last 60 or more years, the St. Paul Fish and Game Association has actively supported the conservation of Alberta's natural resources for the benefit of future generations. Although the club became affiliated with the AFGA in 1946, letters from G.M. Spargo, provincial secretary of the AFGA in 1946, indicated the St. Paul club was quite active prior to 1946. Unfortunately no records are available from that time. Records do indicate that in the mid-1940s a number of people were involved in establishing the St. Paul club, including: W.H. Acton, George Julien, A.J. Tremblay, George Cyr and J. Amable Lapierre.

Education

The club sponsored a hunter education course in 1971, with 23 graduates. Although the program was discontinued for a few years, it was reinstated by Alberta Fish and Wildlife Division district officer Wayne Brown. Wayne received a special award from the St. Paul club and the AFGA for his work beyond the call of duty.

COURTESY OF ST. PAUL FISH AND GAME ASSOCIATION

St. Paul Club on a 1953 crow, snowy owl, hawk and horned owl shoot. Hawk and owl shoot discontinued in 1954.

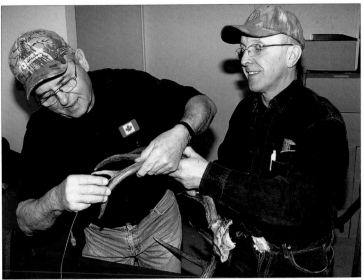

COURTESY OF DUANE RADFORD

Steve Witiuk and Gaetan Richard at the 2007 Sherwood Park horn measuring day.

Habitat chairman Ed Kubash and his crew fenced, cultivated and seeded five-acre lots in the community pasture to restore upland bird nesting sites in 1985. The club prepared a rebuttal to game ranching, representing its 350 members, and submitted it to the provincial government. Unfortunately, the government chose to allow game ranching in the province. The club received funding through the provincial Fish and Wildlife Division Buck for Wildlife program to place flax bales and cone nests for goose-nesting. Bales were set up in several locations throughout the region.

The gun range was upgraded in 1987 with two shooting shelters, a flagpole, storage shed, cement walks, gravel, seeding, tree planting, concession booth, rules and regulation signs. The work was done by club members and the project concluded with a pig roast for all who participated. The club hosted the trap, pistol and silhouette shoots at the Northeastern Summer Games.

The club organized a public forum against firearm registration in 1996, with 650 people in attendance.

Annual Events
Annual events play a big part in keeping club members active. They require a lot of planning and dedication. Some annual events include: fish derbies (discontinued in 1989 due to fish decline), trophy measuring day, wild game supper and trophy ball, hunter telephone survey, hunter education courses, firearm safety courses, sending students to youth conservation camps, heritage farmstead awards, habitat steward awards, spring barbecue, trap and pistol shoots.

Club Awards
In 1985 the club won the AFGA Henry Lembicz Award for its Environment 2000 Project. In 1986 the AFGA awarded the St. Paul Fish and Game Association the Darwin Cronkhite Award for its upland bird-nesting site restoration project.

Special People
In 1985 Bibiane Foisy won the AFGA Outstanding Service Award and Alvin Drapaka won the AFGA Hunter Education Award. Bibiane Foisy received an AFGA Certificate of Merit in 1989. The AFGA also presented her with Lady Conservationist of the Year Award in 2000.

Presidents and representatives of the St. Paul Fish and Game Association include W.H. Acton and George Julien, 1946; A.J. Tremblay, 1947; George Cyr, 1948-50; J. Amable Lapierre, 1951-52; Phil Germain, 1953-55; Terry Laboucane, 1956; Ken Tenove, 1957-58; Gerry St. Jean, 1959-60; Nick Tymofichuk, 1961; Joe O'Driscoll, 1962; Lloyd Cartier, 1963-64; Marcel Belzil, 1965-66; Lawrence Scheffelmiar, 1967; Ray Basaraba, 1968-69; Walter Billey, 1970-71; Dave Powell, 1972-74; E.T. Dubois, 1975; Henry Foisy, 1976; Ray Bell, 1977; Bill Gamier, 1978-80; Ed Kubash, 1981-83; Bibiane Foisy, 1984-86; Ron Dovell, 1987-88; Dan Yake, 1989-91; Hal Brodiak, 1992-93; Bibiane Foisy, 1994-95; Dave Doonanco, 1996-98; Ken Gerlinsky, 1999-2001; Shannon Leskiw, 2002; Ken Gerlinsky, 2003; Francis Hachey, 2004-05; Walter Cardinal, 2006.

Sherwood Park Fish and Game Association
1962-present

The Sherwood Park Fish and Game Association was founded in the fall of 1962 with a complement of 30 members. Some of the founding members were Dr. John Woytuck, Reg Gray, Jim Robison, Don Atha, Dave Voss, Roy Stannard, Willy Kadetz and Paul Morck. In November 1962 the club amalgamated with the Sherwood Park Pistol and Rifle Club, including the range facilities four miles south of Sherwood Park. This property was provided by the County of Strathcona and was enjoyed until encroaching development forced it to be closed in 1972. In 2006 the club's membership was over 1,200.

Education
The conservation and hunter education program has been a large part of the club's activities through the years. Instructors who have taken the executive chair and run the courses are Keith Burrows, Don Chapman, John Hendricksen, Clarence (Bill) Middleton, John Dickinson, Jim Lukion, Ken Lengert, Ed Tremblay and Zeta Sawchuk.

Projects—Gun Range
As a result of the closure of the gun range in 1972, there was a strong desire to find a permanent, secure recreation area where a new range could be built. In 1974 George Page found a quarter-section of land for sale south of Hastings Lake in Beaver County. The land contains the main headwaters of Ketchamoot Creek. George and Steve Witiuk inspected the area and mounted a campaign to convince members to acquire it. To purchase the land for $23,000, the club took out a mortgage of $18,400.

In 1986 Frank Lee, then president, started a personal venture to purchase for the club as much of the surrounding land as possible and create an area around the gun range as a cushion or buffer from encroaching acreage development and to conserve wildlife habitat. It took a few years and considerable effort in negotiating the land deals and the money to make the purchases. Most of the land was secured by 1990, but the final parcel didn't fall into place until 2005, when prices had increased significantly.

Frank worked with Brad Fenson, the AFGA habitat development co-ordinator, to strike a deal with the landowner and raise the $208,000 for the final 160 acres. The Alberta Conservation Authority, Ducks Unlimited Canada, zone 5 of the AFGA and individual members of the Sherwood Park club all contributed funds to complete the purchase. As a result there is a solid block of 720 acres of prime conservation land at the Ketchamoot Creek Recreation Property.

Back in 1974, George Page spearheaded a group, including Clarence (Bill) Middleton, Steve Witiuk and others, to apply and receive grants to build a road, clear trees and construct a rifle range on the original quarter-section. A fish pond was dug, followed by the construction of a clubhouse and pistol range. In 1986 Frank Lee applied for a grant and supervised construction in 1987 to bring the rifle range up to the recommended standards as set out by the federal Attorney General.

In 1988 Frank Lee applied for and received a grant from Alberta's Buck for Wildlife program to develop nature trails, that could be used for biathlon, on the club's conservation land. Garnet Anthony and Ken Steinhouer headed up a group that laid out and cleared a black-powder trail in 1989. Ron Kalaitis secured a substantial community facility enhancement grant ($58,000) in 1990 to upgrade the facilities as well as construct a new camp site.

Upon completion of the handgun range in 1980, Alex Scharzer hosted the Canadian Metal Silhouette Handgun Championships. In 1987 the club hosted the .22-rifle metallic silhouettes shoot as well as the big-bore handgun demonstration shoot at the Strathcona 1987 Summer Games.

Garnet Anthony hosted the first-ever Western Canada Black Powder Championships at the club's property in 1989. For his endeavour, Garnet was presented the 1990 member of the year award by the Alberta Black Powder Association. Rick Crossen headed up a group in 1991 that hosted the Alberta Cup biathlon race and in 1992 the Western Canadian Biathlon Championships at the club's range.

Other Projects

The club helped sponsor surplus elk transplants from Banff to Spirit River in 1965. Member Keith Burrows was instrumental in starting the first Junior Forest Wardens chapter in Sherwood Park in 1968.

COURTESY OF THE AFGA
Paul Morck and Pat Frederick. Sherwood Park Fish and Game Awards, 1988.

COURTESY OF THE AFGA
Frank Lee, (L) recipient of a provincial award. Jack Graham, Cliff Enfield and Phyllis Graham.

Pat Frederick spearheaded the creation of the club's pheasant raise-and-release program in 1975. He applied for funding from the AFGA to build pens and organized a group of club members—George Page, Steve Witiuk, Bill Middleton, and Chris van der Meer—to construct the pens on the properties of Martin Smigelski, Walter Saruk and Adalbert Missel. The Alberta government's Fish and Wildlife Division supplied the birds and shipped them free of charge to the clubs. The club raised and released pheasants in the region for the next 10 years.

The club hosted AFGA conventions in 1977 and 1982. Steve Witiuk organized the 1977 convention and George Bull organized the 1982 convention. Steve Witiuk also hosted the 1996, 1999 and 2008 conventions on behalf of zone 5.

In 1986 Pat Frederick spearheaded the raising of funds ($21,700) to pay for transporting excess elk and moose out of Elk Island National Park to the wild. The club ran this program under Pat and later Frank Lee until the Rocky Mountain Elk Foundation took it over in the mid-1990s.

From 1989-91, Frank Lee planned and implemented a ruffed grouse habitat enhancement project with the help of students from the Biological Science Tech program of the Northern Alberta Institute of Technology. They clear-cut small two-and-a-half-acre plots and planted 6,300 trees acquired through the Fish and Wildlife Division's Buck for Wildlife program.

From 1989-93 the club, in co-operation with the County of Strathcona and the Alberta Fish and Wildlife Division, took part in the "ConservACTION" program to improve local wildlife habitat. The program was funded by the Government of Canada's Environmental Partners Fund and involved 617 projects and over 4,000 volunteer hours for a cost of $417,000.

The club became the lead partner in the purple loosestrife eradication and awareness project from 1994-98, in co-operation with Alberta Agriculture and Ducks Unlimited Canada. Seven locations were eradicated of purple loosestrife, with over 5,400 volunteer hours involved.

Over the years the club has built a multitude of birdhouses. Bill Middleton built birdhouses almost continuously in his basement until he moved out of his home in Sherwood Park. In 2003 Frank Lee received a grant from the Alberta Conservation Association (ACA) for $1,500 and oversaw the building of 164 birdhouses and three large colony bat houses. In 2006 Frank again received an ACA grant for $1,020 and headed up a work party that built four 12-compartment purple martin houses, including metal poles.

Annual Events

Frank Lee involved the club in the annual Alberta Fish and Wildlife hunter harvest survey in 1986 and headed this up until 2000. Lyall Kortzman has carried on since.

A dinner and awards night is held in March of each year. The winners of the club's trophy competition receive their prizes and club members are recognized for special service to the club.

Club Awards

The club sponsors the Non-Typical White-tail Trophy for the annual provincial AFGA awards. The club received an Alberta Emerald Award in 1996.

Special People

Paul Morck, a founding member of the club and president from 1964-65, served as secretary manager of the AFGA, a paid employee position, from 1967 to 1988.

Steve Witiuk has been a very active member of the club since he joined in 1966. He joined the executive committee in 1972 and was president in 1977 and '78. With the exception of four years, he has served as zone 5 director since 1982, and has represented the AFGA on many issues.

Andy Boyd has held an executive position in the club since the late 1980s, including a term as president for 1990-91. He has served as the political action chair or the environment chair in the ensuing years to the present. As well, he has represented zone 5 and the AFGA on many committees on a variety of issues.

Garnet Anthony received the Order of the Bighorn in 1985 and a Special Minister's Award in 1995 for work on the Bull Trout Task Force. Reg Gray was the recipient of the Strathcona County Award of Excellence—Reeves Metal in 1989. Frank Lee was presented with the Strathcona County Award of Excellence in 1997. Ed Scarlett received the Order of the Bighorn in 2004.

Life members of the Sherwood Park Fish and Game Association as of 2006 are Reginald Gray, Paul Morck, Steve Witiuk, William Tenetiuk, George Page, Alex Schwarzer, Fred Wolfe, Clarence Middleton, Frank Lee, Lloyd Hakes, Andy Boyd, Al Wagner, Dennis Perka, Al Giacomazzi, Garnet Anthony, Steve Ujvarosy, Ed Scarlett, Norman Honish, Robert Lowen, Bill Abercrombie and Lyall Kortzman.

The presidents of the Sherwood Park Fish and Game Association include: Dr. John Woytuck, 1962-63; Paul Morck, 1964-65; Jim Pollock, 1966-67; Dave Voss, 1968-69; George Allenbrand, 1970; Don Chapman, 1971-72; Clarence (Bill) Middleton, 1973-74; George Page 1975-76; Steve Witiuk, 1977-78; Alex Schwarzer,

COURTESY OF DUANE RADFORD

A bull moose sniffs through the muskeg on the lookout for food.

COURTESY OF THE SHERWOOD PARK FISH AND GAME ASSOCIATION

Sherwood Park club conservation project setting out goose rafts.

COURTESY OF THE SHERWOOD PARK FISH AND GAME ASSOCIATION

Sherwood Park Fish and Game trap shooting.

COURTESY OF THE SPEDDEN FISH AND GAME ASSOCIATION

Spedden Fish and Game and their birdhouse-building project for local youth.

1979-80; Ted Hendriks, 1981; George Bull, 1982-83; Alex Schwarzer, 1984-85; Frank Lee, 1986-87; Lloyd Hakes, 1988-89; Andy Boyd, 1990-91; Dennis Perka, 1992-94; Norman Honish, 1995-97; Lee Schurman, 1998-2000; Lyall Kortzman, 2001-03; Lloyd Hakes, 2004-05; Ken Sobkiw, 2006-07.

For more information about the Sherwood Park Fish and Game Association, please visit the website: www.spfga.org.

Spedden Fish and Game Association
1954-present

The Spedden Fish and Game Association was started in 1954 by founders John Tchir and Fred Leskiew. The club started with approximately 60 members.

The club held a barbecue every fall and a fish fry each spring. The fish were caught and donated by members. At the fish fry, children could bring in their gopher tails, magpie and crow's feet for which the club would pay 10 cents per tail. Games like horseshoes for the adults, and tug-of-war and different races for children were also held.

Marksmen competitions were held with .22-calibre rifles and targets at a distance of 25 feet. Prizes were awarded to the best marksmen. Ice fishing derbies were also held. A bottle of whiskey was raffled off at most events as a fundraiser for the club.

The first few events were held near North Bay, which is the north side of Garner Lake and at that time had lots of water. When John Tchir moved to his present farm, the events were held south of the old landfill site near his farm. After the meeting was over, some of the members would often go fishing at the Owl River, north of Lac La Biche. They often had a fish fry on the spot and returned home in the wee hours of the morning.

Trophies were handed out for the largest fish of each species. Later on dances and wildlife suppers were organized and enjoyed by the members and community.

For several years pheasants were raised by different members of the club. Once the pheasants were fully grown, they were released in the wild in different areas.

Two Hills and District Fish and Game Association
1950s-present

(as told by Sylvester "Sylver" Lakusta to Ray Makowecki)

As I listened to Sylver Lakusta recall the history of the Two Hills Fish and Game Association, I could not help but think this man really was a big part of the history of the Two Hills club for the past 40 years. There were not too many others who could tell the story. We held our discussion on a sunny March 2007 day at his home near the Two Hills Trout Pond, his over 80 years clearly reflecting the past.

Tony Volk was one of the organizers back in the 1950s and early 1960s but the minutes from those days could not be found. The club members at that time were interested in getting together with people having similar interests and socializing around hunting and fishing activities. After 1968, the records are extant. Mr. Lakusta kept records of meeting minutes, pictures, newspaper clippings and special project information.

The membership of the club has ranged from 80 to 130 and one year there were 202 members. The price of membership was once $2 per year.

Education

Several members have instructed Alberta Conservation and Hunter Education courses to young hunters and anglers in schools and in special classes provided by the club.

Projects

In the early years many members participated in crow and magpie hunts in an attempt to manage these predators of duck eggs and ducklings.

The club developed a public access site and campground on Lac Sante. This was a special project that involved numerous volunteers. The land was owned by the town of Two Hills and the club operated the campground for over 10 years until 1982.

During the 1970s, the club created the Two Hills Trout Pond. Ken Zelt, then Edmonton regional fisheries biologist, and Ray Makowecki, then fisheries habitat biologist, examined the site and the project on behalf of the Fish and Wildlife Division. They assessed the biology and provided a design to the club. The club took over and proceeded to obtain funding and solicit contributions from club members. Sylver Lakusta was a major organizer of the project. This fish pond has provided countless hours of recreation for the community and has been a place for young people to learn about fishing and to spend special time with their parents and grandparents.

A contingent of club members that included Peter Orlecki, Nestor Hryciw and Sylver Lakusta went to Edmonton to meet with Dr. Martin Paetz, the director of fisheries for the Fish and Wildlife Division, to request the transplant of yellow perch to

Two Hills horn measuring school graduates. Instructor: Jack Graham (front, centre); participants: Allan Mathes, Ken McIntosh, Richard Bidulock, Kelly Kassian, Rod Marcichiw, Michael Tarkouski, Dan Toohey, Dean Bromberger, Brian Zayak, Gordon Mathes, Robert Kutash and Ken Tyler, 1993.

COURTESY OF VEGREVILLE WILDLIFE FEDERATION

Vegreville Club goose-nesting project. Gordon Gresiuk (L), Barney and Rodger Welsh taken on Oct 17, 1979.

COURTESY OF VEGREVILLE WILDLIFE FEDERATION

Lawrence Yakimchuk (L), Sam Smolyk, Blair Rippin and Peter Samoil inspecting a goose-nesting project near Vegreville in 1975.

lakes such as Lac Sante. Martin Paetz said, "I cannot kill your enthusiasm," and approved the project. The club made a number of perch transplants from Upper Mann Lake, Lac St. Cyr and Vincent Lake to Lac Sante and other lakes.

The club spent numerous volunteer hours placing nesting islands in wetlands for Canada geese. These projects contributed to increased numbers of Canada geese in the area.

Club members monitored dissolved oxygen levels in 32 waterbodies during the mid-1980s as part of a pothole monitoring project. George Walker and Dick Brown of the Fish and Wildlife Division provided the equipment in support of the program.

Club Awards

Two Hills sponsors the AFGA Burbot Fish Award. The club received the Archie Hogg Award for important work in publicizing environmental issues.

Special People

Many people have served on the executive of the club. Some of the prominent ones over the years include: Don Basaraba, Peter Orlecki, Nestor Hryciw, Ernie Psikla, Ron DeSmit, Gordon Forbes, Andy Gorgichuk, Bob Blad, Nick Wysocki, Allan Hohol, Robert Kutash, Dan Toohey, Marshall Taranko, Arnold Romaniuk, Lorry Gordeyko and Sylver Lakusta.

Past presidents of the Two Hills Fish and Game Association include: Sylver Lakusta, 1974-77; Nestor Hryciw, 1978-79; Ron DeSmit, 1980; Ernie Psikla, 1981; Hall, 1982; Bob Blad, 1983; Sylver Lakusta, 1984-87; Bob Blad, 1988; Tim Shchurek, 1989; Robert Kutash, 1990-92; Dan Toohey, 1993; Lorry Gordeyko, 1994-98; Robert Kutash, 1999; Lolly Kutash, 2000-01; Brian Kutash, 2002-03; Ted McLuckie, 2004-05; Lorry Gordeyko, 2006-07.

During his interview, Mr. Lakusta made the following observations: 1) The loss of anglers over the last few years is the result of too many size and limit restrictions and government management. 2) Gill nets in Winefred Lake were a factor in reducing the fish stocks of that lake. 3) The loss of walleye in Vincent Lake in 2003 was a real disappointment in the restrictive management of fish harvest by the government. 4) The recent Calling Lake management has also made the angler lose confidence in government fisheries management.

Vegreville Wildlife Federation
1968-present

The Vegreville Fish and Game Association was registered on April 29, 1968 as a society. At the time, the organization was also known as the Vegreville Fish and Game and Gun Club. The club was organized for people in the Vegreville area interested in all facets of the outdoors. In 1996 the name of the club was changed to the Vegreville Wildlife Federation. Members of the club come from Vegreville and the surrounding area, as well as Willingdon, Two Hills, Red Deer and Edmonton.

Education

The club provides firearm safety courses, conservation and hunter education courses, fishing, boat safety and shooting courses.

From April 11 to May 23, 1995, the club sponsored a Wonders of Wildlife program at the Alberta Environmental Centre in Vegreville. It included conservation and hunter education with wildlife identification and an introduction to nature photography.

Projects

In 1974-75 the club became involved in a goose-nesting project through the Buck for Wildlife program. However, the costs to run the project mushroomed in 1980 and the club has struggled to monitor and maintain the Buck for Wildlife property located west of Vegreville off Highway 16.

In 1984 and 1985 wild game suppers were organized by Steve Savoy and David Saganiuk, with Lillian Yakimchuk as caterer. Lawrence Yakimchuk and Sam Smolyk were also involved in the suppers as well as the Akasu (Sickman) Lake goose-nesting bale program in 1979 and 1980.

The late Rube Johnston was instrumental in activating the local Rube Johnston Mountain Bluebird Trail, where bluebird nesting boxes are placed and monitored. It is currently monitored by Robert Hughes and sponsored by the club.

In the early 1990s, Ernie Preuss, along with Carl Grosfield and Nick Tyzuk, modernized the outdoor range, the project being spearheaded by Sam Smolyk. They called on other members of the club to assist, spending many volunteer hours. The members and guests have enjoyed trap and target shooting, as well as sighting-in rifles and shotguns, at the range. The club has held several June meetings at the range including a barbecue dinner. Alberta Sustainable Resource Development and local members of the RCMP have used the outdoor range for their qualifying tests and competitions.

David Beaudette, fishing chair, has spent many hours over the last few years with the VALID group (Vegreville Association for Living in Dignity) who are mentally/physically challenged people, helping them take special fishing trips to Camp He Ho Ha on Isle Lake and Moose Lake. Some club members have assisted at these events which have brought much delight to these individuals.

Trophy nights were held on March 7, 1987, March 28, 1992 and April 24, 1993. On March 28, 1999 the club held a family fishing day at Upper Mann Lake. A turkey shoot was held Dec. 6, 2002 and Dec. 8, 2006.

Annual Events

Gun and hobby shows started in February 2003 and have become an annual event. The club has participated in the annual hunter survey through the Fish and Wildlife Division. The club has been involved in zone 5 meetings and helped fund wildlife projects in the zone.

Club Awards

In 1976 the club initiated its sponsorship of the Johnny Weleschuk Memorial Trophy as an AFGA provincial award for the northern pike competition. Jim and Donna Drury of Cold Lake were commissioned in November 1976 to produce this unique award. The carving, standing 32 inches in height, is made of rare jelutong wood imported from Malaysia. The trophy was completed in January 1977 and Mr. John Weleschuk, Sr. agreed to buy the tro-

COURTESY OF THE VEGREVILLE WILDLIFE FEDERATION

John Radesh of Vegreville with the Smork Award for the best hunting story, June 26, 1979.

Vegreville
FISH & GAME ASSOCIATION
Annual
Wildlife Supper
—DANCE & TROPHY AWARDS—
SAT., FEB. 13th   6:30 p.m.
Legion Hall
Refreshments   Tickets $2.00

COURTESY OF HENRY LEMBICZ

phy and donate it to the Vegreville Fish and Game and Gun Club as a living memorial to his son, the late Johnny Weleschuk. The trophy is presented at the AFGA Trophy Awards each spring to the person who caught the largest northern pike registered in Alberta in the previous year.

Special People

The late Sam Smolyk left a memorial fund of $100 to be used each year towards the sponsorship of youths wishing to attend the Narrow Lake Youth Camp. The fund has been used several times to date.

The late Carl Grosfield, who was also on the zone 5 and AFGA executive committees, made a big difference to the club. He wrote a nature column, "Wildscape," in several newspapers, both locally and nationally, and had his own website. He was also involved in the goose-nesting project and kept track of the Rube Johnston Mountain Bluebird Trail. He was a range officer and instructor in the conservation and hunter education and firearm safety courses. He was a strong, committed member who helped the club continue after a few rough times during

COURTESY OF THE AFGA

Vegreville Wildlife Federation life member Sam Smolyk.

the late 1980s and early '90s and until his death on Nov. 14, 2004. A special commemorative plaque is implanted on a huge fieldstone at the local outdoor gun range in his memory.

The late Nick Tyzuk, as club treasurer, helped to set up a modern-day financial program for the club. He was a dedicated member who spent countless hours improving the outdoor range, especially the yardage backstops and trap shooting. He was also a very active member assisting at the gun shows, turkey shoots and the Buck for Wildlife project. The club has a memorial fund in his memory.

Some of the presidents of the Vegreville Wildlife Federation include: Johnny Weleschuk, 1968; Rodney Tymchyshyn, 1976; Sam Smolyk, 1977-79; Mike D. Lynn, 1979; Sam Smolyk, 1980; John Radesh, 1982; Alan Carter, 1984; Michael Mills, 1985; Sam Smolyk, 1985; Lee George, 1989; Geoff Norgard, 1992; Ken McKay,

1993; Lee George, 1994-95; Ron Anderson, 1996; Ernest Preuss, 1998; Charles Nagey, 1999; Ernest Preuss, 2000; Peter Varga, 2001-02; Ernest Preuss, 2003; and Daryl Sapp, 2003-06.

Vermilion and District Fish and Game Association
1970s - present (not affiliated)

Although an earlier fish and game club in the Vermilion area was in existence in the 1970s and '80s, spearhead by Keith Baker and others, it disbanded. On Aug. 21, 2002 some residents of Vermilion area came together to form the Vermilion and District Fish and Game Association and to develop a shooting range. The organizers included Kevin John (president), Dave Moore (treasurer), Cindy Usenik (secretary), Bob Chowolski (membership chair), Bernard Yonkman (chairman), and Claire Schielke (fundraising chair). The fundraising committee included Patrick Willis, Len Chetter, Erin Tate and Eric Ganton.

A local farmer, Danny Farkash, donated land for the development of a gun range. The land is located about 12 kilometres south of Vermilion. The facilities were developed in an old gravel pit with 25-, 50-, 100-, 200- and 250-yard ranges. It was completed in 2002-03 by Gourley Construction and Snelgrove Construction.

The number of memberships over the few years the club has been in existence has averaged between 125-160 annually. With the addition of a trap range in 2006, the number of members is increasing. Shooters using the range enjoy the various activities, including cowboy action, trap, pistol, and rifle shooting. The club offers all with the family spirit in mind. A local 4-H shooters club also participates in range activities.

The range is in a long sweeping valley with all kinds of wildlife nearby. Access in the winter is limited. April to November finds shooters at the range on a daily basis. The addition of a clubhouse has made the facility very attractive and has attracted the attention of shooters from all over Alberta for its peaceful setting.

Vermilion and District Fish and Game and Gun Club promotes the education of youth; hunter-training and gun-safety courses are offered yearly. The club is a family affair, promoting good sportsmanship.

Viking Sports and Wildlife Society.

COURTESY OF THE VIKING SPORTS AND WILDLIFE SOCIETY

Viking Sports and Wildlife Society
1944-present

The first organizational meeting of a fish and game club in Viking was held on June 22, 1944. This club was called the Viking Fish and Game Protection Association. The 16 men present elected the following executive committee: R.R. Gilpin, president; R.H. Brooke, vice president; G.T. Loney, treasurer; and S. Lefsrud, secretary. The annual membership fee was set at $1 per member and for another 50 cents, a member could subscribe to the magazine *Game Trails*. The meetings were held at various businesses throughout town. Members were involved in various activities, such as stocking of fish in local lakes, such as Camp Lake, and raising pheasants and releasing them in the surrounding areas. They were also involved in the campaign to control crow and magpie populations as well as coyote problems. The club was in charge of paying for the bounty for these pests. Unfortunately, there are no records on file from 1962-86.

In March, 1986 the Viking Sports and Wildlife Society was incorporated. Eighteen people attended the organizing meeting and elected an executive committee, including Sam Klontz, Rod Mattinson, Marshall Tymofichuk, Lil Anderson and Irvin Arndt. The membership fee was $10. Meetings were held once a month, except during July and August. The highest number of members for any one year has been 148.

Education

The club has offered firearms safety courses and sponsored members going to the youth conservation camp at Narrow Lake.

COURTESY OF TRAVEL ALBERTA

Elk Island National Park.

COURTESY OF RANDY COLLINS

Award winners at Vilna's 50th Anniversary trophy night. Marilee Sklerek (L), John Gordey, Adam Piwowar, Don Stefaniuk and John Goruk.

Projects

The club has sponsored various events over the years such as trap shoots, turkey shoots, dances, annual trophy scoring day for birds, big-game and fish. It has held several fishing derbies at various lakes and the club's own Castaway Fish Pond, which is located in Viking. The club holds an annual banquet.

Viking Sports and Wildlife Society has donated funds to many other clubs and charities in the Viking area, such as sponsoring minor hockey tournament trophies, Raise the Roof for the Viking Arena, Viking Cubs and Scouts, Mammography Fund, day care and other groups.

The club has placed flax bales for goose-nesting, and provided nests for other waterfowl and built and maintained a trout pond in town. The club also stocks the pond every year. Fishing is enjoyed by local people and others during the summer and winter.

In 2001 the clubhouse was moved from the country to its present location by the Castaway Fish Pond.

Special People

The current executive consists of Del Kirchmayer, Ken Johnston, Pat Tkaczyk, Fred These and Irene These.

Vilna Fish and Game Association
1940-present

The Vilna Fish and Game Association was organized in 1940, and charged a membership fee of $1. From the beginning the club has always been active in the community. In the early days, the club succeeded in having some land donated to it; members cleared the land to build a ballpark near the beach at Bonnie Lake, two miles east and one mile north of Vilna.

Projects-Early Years

Picnics were held in the summer months on Sundays at the park. The club constructed boats and rented them on weekends for fishing. With the ball games, children's games and prizes for fishing, everyone who attended had a good time and the events were good fundraisers for the club.

The club raised pheasants that were hatched at the provincial pheasant hatchery at Brooks. It was quite an experience for the members involved. The chicks arrived from the hatchery and were successfully raised and released into the wild two weeks before bird season opened.

A crow shoot was another successful event the club hosted in the early days. Many members looked forward to the shoot held in late spring with prizes for different categories. Crow eggs and feet, magpie eggs and feet, and gopher tails were collected and used in a point system to calculate the winners. The shoot always ended with a wiener roast at Bonnie Lake and plenty of refreshments.

The club annually cleaned the beach at Bonnie Lake and prepared it for swimming lessons. Working closely with Polly Karpysyn of the Canadian Red Cross, the club provided swimming lessons to all children from the community. Today, lessons are offered through schools at indoor pools, but those who took their lessons at Bonnie Lake have fond memories of their experiences.

The club hosted an annual fun day picnic each July at the ballpark which included ball games and a concession selling hotdogs, hamburgers, ice cream and pop. Each winter, a fish derby was held at Bonnie Lake, Goodfish Lake or Garner Lake. The derby was open to everyone and prizes were awarded in several categories.

Recent Projects

As you travel down Highway 28 near Vilna, you will notice there is an abundance of birdhouses on the fence lines. This is a club project that has increased the bluebird population in the Vilna area. Every year the students of grade 4 at Vilna School receive a birdhouse and a visit from Don Stefaniuk, who volunteers his time to make the birdhouses for the club and explain the program to the students.

The club has set out several flax round bales for goose nests. In conjunction with Ducks Unlimited Canada, duck nests were set up in local wetlands and lakes.

The club co-sponsors youth members to attend Narrow Lake Conservation Camp. Several youth have enjoyed the benefits of this wonderful camp located near Athabasca.

Most recently the Vilna club completed another successful habitat conservation program, the "Vilna Project." The club put up half the funds and the following fish and game clubs donated the rest: Beaver River, Edmonton, Fort Saskatchewan, Lloydminster, Innisfree, Sherwood Park, Spedden and Willingdon. John Gordey spear headed fundraising for the Vilna club.

Club Awards

The club received the AFGA Guy Blake Memorial Trophy for the best club project in 1998 for the Jackpine Project. The club worked with Smoky Lake county to preserve a quarter-section of land to be left as a natural habitat area for birds and other wildlife. Bird watchers, naturalists and hikers can also enjoy the property as it has several meandering trails.

Annual Events

The Willingdon fish and game club together with the Vilna fish and game club organize and run the WillVil Fish Derby held annually at Pinehurst Lake the third weekend in June. Proceeds from this successful event are divided between the two clubs. Vilna's share is designated for habitat projects and Willingdon's share is designated for a fish pond.

The club's biggest fundraiser is the annual trophy night held in either February or March. The Vilna club celebrated its 65th anniversary in 2005 at the annual event. The event includes a supper featuring wild game dishes, guest speakers and a silent auction. As well, trophies and plaques are presented to members in recognition of their achievements whether it is for hunting or fishing or photography. All trophies are on display in the Vilna Cultural Centre. Local businesses and residents generously sponsor these trophies.

For the past 12 years the Vilna club has participated in the annual hunter survey organized by the Department of Sustainable Resource Development. Volunteers gather information from local hunters and submit the information to the Fish and Wildlife Division. The division then pays the club for each hunter contacted, another fundraiser for the club.

The club participates in the annual AFGA Hide Collection Program. The club collects big-game hides from hunters for the AFGA. The hides are sold and the dollars raised are put into the AFGA's Wildlife Trust Program to preserve wildlife habitat.

Special People

Current club officers include: Jerry Tchir, president; Carl Tatarin, vice president; and Marilee Sklerek, secretary treasurer and membership chair. The club executive may change but dedicated members are the backbone of the club. For the last number of years, they included John Gordey, Adam Piwowar, John Goruk and Don Stefaniuk.

Wainwright Fish and Game Association

The Wainwright Fish and Game Association was an extremely active club in the 1970s and 1980s. The club was one of the major contributors to conservation projects and annual convention.

They were involved in several Buck for Wildlife program projects, including the Shuster Lake stabilization and rehabilitation project, as well as the development of the Wallace Park fish pond and goose-nesting bale projects in the town of Wainwright. They were active in discussions regarding CFB Camp Wainwright hunting

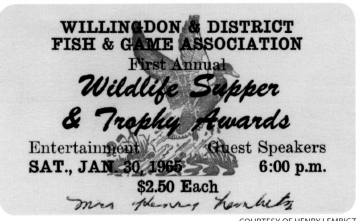

Willingdon and District Fish and Game Association
1961-present

The original Willingdon and District Fish and Game Association was formed on Feb. 6, 1961. The "district" included the areas surrounding Willingdon, Andrew and Hairy Hill. Camille Ethier was elected president, N.W. Shandro as secretary, and Paul Von Borstel as treasurer. Mr. Joe Fedechko, an AFGA representative, spoke at the first meeting about the importance of conservation, sportsmanship and relationships with both the farmers and the provincial government. As well, he urged the newly formed group to admit as many young people in to the organization as possible, recognizing they are the future leaders. The new board, its members and their successors over the next 45 years would continue to use that message and their wildlife conservation mandate to ensure the club's ultimate success.

The club had 400 members at its peak and was once the fourth largest fish and game organization in Alberta. Today the membership is about 70. The decline in membership is at least in part the result of a shrinking community. However, the membership has been steady for the last five years.

seasons; they were also involved in habitat protection issues in the community and in the province. They provided excellent awards evenings and dinner banquets for the local community to enjoy.

Some of the key people in the club included Ken and Jean Anderson, Al Higgins (famous banjo player at annual conventions), Ray Pierce, Addie Coleman and many more. The efforts of club members should not be forgotten.

Canoeing on Maligne Lake in Jasper National Park.

Education

On March 5, 1964 a motion was passed that the association would take a leading role in adopting a youth-training program in the area. In 1964 the association held a birdhouse competition. Students from Andrew, Hairy Hill and Willingdon competed for trophies and prizes.

In 1978 the club held an essay contest, "What we can do to preserve our wildlife" to encourage students to consider the importance of wildlife conservation. In conjunction with the County of Two Hills, the club provided lifesaving instructions at Sandy Lake. Today the club is very active with 4-H clubs and sends a minimum of two and as many as six youths to the Narrow Lake Conservation Education Centre.

Projects

On May 7, 1961 a special meeting of the executives of Willingdon club and the Fish and Angling Committee was held to decide whether to purchase property at Sandy Lake and develop a campsite and public beach. The two groups agreed on the purchase, and a campsite and public beach were opened in 1978. It consisted of cabin sites, a boat ramp, diving boards, a pier, a club building, a baseball diamond, a pavilion, a kids' playground and a concession stand. The County of Two Hills and various government grants were instrumental in the creation and subsequent improvements at the Sandy Lake site over the years. In keeping with its mandate to act as habitat stewards of the Sandy Lake site, the club successfully lobbied for restrictions on outboard motors on the lake, released as many as 300 pheasants per year, and stocked the lake with pike and perch.

COURTESY OF TRAVEL ALBERTA

A sleepy owl in a tree.

The club built and maintained birdhouses and goose nests, and planted trees. Conservation efforts were not only directed at the club's Sandy Lake property but also to other lakes in the area and the community as a whole. Throughout the years the club participated in various conservation programs, including contributions towards wolf-control programs, habitat steward awards and various wildlife projects. In conjunction with the AFGA, the club became strong supporters of the Buck for Wildlife program. The Kachuk family designated three-quarters of land to create the Kachuk Habitat Development Area.

In 1961 the club held its first annual sports day at Sandy Lake. The day's events included fastball, tug-of-war, horseshoes, kiddy races, fishing derby, canoe races, pony rides, swimathons, rowboat races, nail-driving competitions, wiener- and kielbasa- (Polish sausage) eating contests. These family-oriented events were enjoyed by the community. The club also held fundraisers like Family Fun Day at Primrose Lake and a Family Fishing Derby at Goodfish Lake. These fundraisers contributed to various projects like the Marie Lake project and eventually the Willingdon Fish Pond.

In 1993 the club asked the Village of Willingdon for its support in the creation of a fish pond and park. The village was very supportive of the idea and a 12-acre parcel of land was donated to the organization by Metro Karbashewski. As a result, the park became the Metro Karbashewski Memorial Park. After extensive fundraising, the pond and park were developed and are attractions today. The club stocks the pond with a minimum of 300 fish per year. The residents of Willingdon and district enjoy it immensely.

Annual Events

The first sportsman dinner and trophy night was held in 1965 on the last Saturday in January. The plates sold for 60 cents each. Today the plates are $30 each. The annual wildlife supper and trophy ball replaced the sportsman dinner and trophy night in 1981. Various organizations and individuals in the community donate trophies for this fundraiser. The supper and ball is the club's major fundraiser and is strongly supported by the community.

Special People

The honorary life members of the Willingdon and District Fish and Game Association include the following: Camille Ethier, William G. Lazaruk, Paul Von Borstel, Kost Kelba, Metro Karbashewski, Metro Romanko, George Soprovich, Mike Kapicki, Toder Hauca, Mike Matwichuk, Alexandra Matwichuk, Nick P. Hawrelak, George Dary, Mike Radesh, Paul A. Luchek, William T. Kokotailo, Victor Kowalchuck, Henry Smilar, and Lloyd Babiuk.

The Willingdon and District Fish and Game Association presidents include Camille Ray Ethier, 1961-64; Camilla Swiderski, 1965-66; Victor Ethier, 1967-69; Camille Kowalchuck, 1970; George Ethier, 1971; Allan Soprovich, 1972; Nick P. Mulek, 1973; Mike Hawrelak, 1974-75; Ed Matwichuk, 1976-77; Stan Stefaniuk, 1978-79; Ed Hamaliuk, 1980-81; Marvin Stefaniuk, 1982; Ed Toma Hrudey, 1983-84; Robert Babiuk, 1985-86; Kenneth Schlachter, 1987-88; Brian Tatarin Virgil, 1989-90; Kenneth Huculak, 1991-92; Virgil Schlachter, 1993-94; Brian Huculak, 1995-96; Kenneth Tatarin, 1997-98; Schlachter, 1999-2006.

Zone 6

Zone 6 covers the Peace River block, from the Northwest Territories border in the north to Fox Creek and zone 4 in the south, British Columbia to the west and zone 5 to the east. Agricultural land in the fertile Peace area is predominant, with boreal forest covering the rest of the zone. Bear, white-tailed deer, geese and moose are popular game species, along with some excellent fishing opportunities in lakes such as Sturgeon and Lesser Slave.

The 10 clubs in zone 6 are:
- Dunvegan Fish and Game Association
- High Level Sporting Association *
- High Prairie Fish and Game Association
- Mighty Peace Fish and Game Association
- Monkman Fish and Game Association *
- Peace Country Fish and Game Association *
- Red Earth Creek Rod and Gun Club
- Slave Lake Rod and Gun Club *
- South Peace Fish and Game Association *
- Swan Hills Outdoor Recreation Club
    * clubs that did not submit histories

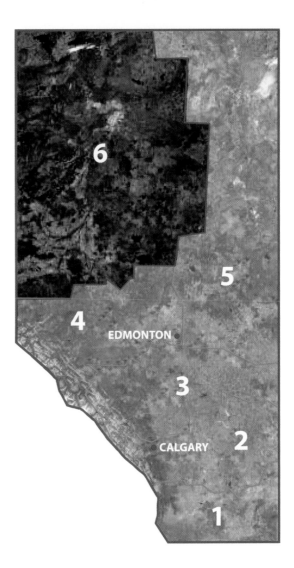

Club Histories of Zone 6

Dunvegan Fish and Game Association
1946-present

The Dunvegan Fish and Game Association was founded in 1946 and soon became affiliated with the AFGA. In 1948 the club formed a skeet club which was reorganized into a gun club in 1954. The original gun range was located west of Fairview but was closed in the late 1990s. The club has since developed a new range six miles northeast of Fairview. The range has facilities for rifle, trap, small bore and handguns. In 2002 the club merged with the Fairview Archery Club and the gun club to form one organization with a variety of interests.

One of the yearly highlights of the club continues to be the annual wild game supper that over the years has been well-attended and appreciated by the community. The club continues to provide hunter-training courses for first-time hunters. For many years, the club has helped the Alberta Fish and Wildlife Division with its surveys of big-game harvests.

Hunting opportunities have increased in the area with the success of the 1960s and '70s transplants of elk into the Saddle Hills and Chinchaga areas, respectively. As a result, the Fish and Wildlife Division has established increasingly generous seasons for elk over the last few years. As well, the population of Hungarian (grey) partridge, which were originally brought into the Sexsmith area by local fish and game clubs, seems to be on the increase.

The Dunvegan Fish and Game Association offers the outdoorsman the fellowship of like-minded individuals who care for and influence decisions regarding wildlife, hunting and fishing in the province.

COURTESY OF DON MEREDITH

Beaver pond in the Valleyview area.

High Prairie Fish and Game Association
1981-present

The High Prairie Fish and Game Association began in 1981. Founding members included Stanley Rowe, Bob Langenhahn, and Lloyd Stevens. The club includes members from the High Prairie, Joussard, Valleyview, Driftpile, Grande Prairie, McLennan, and Donnelly areas. Club members are mostly interested in firearms and shooting activities and the club is not currently active in hunting or conservation efforts. At present, club membership is 70 individuals. In the past five or six years, Dennis Hazen has been instrumental in driving the club forward by introducing members to trap and silhouette shooting at the club's gun range. He and Tammy Kaleta have been a driving force behind the yearly successful gun shows for the club.

The club has a quarter-section lease approximately 12 kilometres north of High Prairie on Highway 749, where it has its small clubhouse and cook shack, and holds its shooting activities. There is a trap-shooting field, a big-bore handgun range, silhouette shooting, 200-yard rifle range, and a 25-yard .22-calibre rifle and handgun range. Future improvements will include an archery walk and range. The club also co-ordinates firearms licence qualification training courses.

Since 2002 the High Prairie Fish and Game Association has hosted a gun show which has now expanded to a Gun and Sportsman Show. During the gun show weekend, the club hosts a supper and silent auction, which has been a very successful fundraiser.

Kinuso and District Fish and Game Association
1967-present (not affiliated)
by K.A. Thorburn
(excerpts from a piece originally published in Sodbusters [1979, Kinuso History Book Committee] reprinted here with the permission of Mr. Thorburn)

The organization was first formed in the spring of 1967 but fizzled out in the fall of 1968 when part of the organizing committee moved away. It was strongly reorganized on April 16, 1969 and a membership of 60 was attained that year. Membership in the succeeding years has always been over 100.

In December 1969 the final lease papers were executed so that a shooting range could be constructed east of Kinuso on Prichuck Hill. The first annual Fish and Game banquet was held on Jan. 16, 1970 in the Legion Hall. It was a tremendous success then and has continued to be each year since.

In the summer of 1970 the association reached a high when they blew the whistle on the oil industry in the Swan Hills. Under our pest and pollution committee chairman Keith Kepke, a brief was compiled and submitted to the Alberta government, describing negligence by some in the oil industry. On July 3, 1970 a CBC television crew arrived in Kinuso, with reporter Dwayne Erikson, to tour the Swan Hills oilfield with regard to the brief submitted. The story was aired on local television and picked up and shown

COURTESY OF DUANE RADFORD
Anglers on Lesser Slave Lake.

nationally. We also received excellent coverage by other papers and local radio stations.

An excerpt from an article printed in the *Edmonton Journal* [July 10, 1970] by reporter Bob Bell, stated: "On the basis of the pictures of 15 well sites contained in a report made public by the Kinuso Fish and Game Association last week, the spills 'are difficult to justify from an operating standpoint and they are not typical of the industry,' said Health Minister J.D. Henderson Thursday."

As a result, the Kinuso Association was awarded the AFGA Henry Lembicz Trophy for Pollution Control – Clean Air – Clean Land – Clean Water at the Annual Fish and Game Convention, held in Medicine Hat in February 1971.

In the summer of 1973 pheasant-rearing pens were built on the farm of George Gallagher. Our association has since raised and turned loose approximately 200 mature pheasants. There are still a few around and hopes are to raise more birds in the future.

Interest in the association fluctuates with the passing seasons and different tasks. But the main thing is that the base is there, and the backing, should the need arise.

COURTESY OF DUANE RADFORD
Darryl Smith, long-time zone 6 director, with an Arctic grayling from the Kakwa River.

Mighty Peace Fish and Game Association
1991-present

The Mighty Peace Fish and Game Association was established in April 1991 and is based out of La Crete (located approximately 56 kilometres southeast of High Level) and represents the surrounding area. La Crete is located in the Municipal District of Mackenzie No. 23, the largest rural municipality in Alberta that covers an area of 30,500 square miles. The original officers of the Mighty Peace Fish and Game Association were Larry Neufeld, Aaron Foulkes, Johnny Weiler, Jack C. Peters and Jim Friessen.

SUPPLIED

Darryl Smith, life member, past provincial fishing chair, zone 6.

The club created a fish pond in 2000 for the enjoyment of local residents, La Crete Pond (10-106-16-W5). The pond is stocked annually with about 1,500 rainbow trout. The club owns 80 acres of land where it maintains a trap-shooting and large-bore gun range. It is also affiliated with the Alberta Bowhunters Association.

Red Earth Creek Rod and Gun Club
1989-present

The Red Earth Creek Rod and Gun Club is based in the town of Red Earth Creek, north of the town of Slave Lake. The club was originally organized in 1989. Founding members were Allan Twigge, Ron Sahlin and Robert Werney. At present the executive members are Shane Parsonage, Bey Schriever and Chris Schriever.

The club has a membership of approximately 20-30. It has its own gun range with a range house. Presently the membership is raising funds for community services in Red Earth Creek, such as a Victim Services Unit in the town and upgrading the club's shooting range.

The club reinstated its annual wild game dinner on Feb. 24, 2007. It hopes to make this an annual event. It has also reinstated its contest for the biggest fish taken annually in two categories, walleye and northern pike. Each winner receives a trophy at the annual dinner. Each year the club sponsors a major fishing derby with terrific support from the community, including prize donations and volunteers to register participants and record entries.

The club plans to educate the community about wildlife and protection of the environment, as well as to support important causes in the community.

COURTESY OF DUANE RADFORD

Paddling on the Kakwa River.

Special People

Doug Etherington spent countless hours doing volunteer work in every aspect of club affairs since its inception. Also, Sandy Bell was an active participant of the club for a long time. Ron Sahlin was not only involved in establishing the club but is also still an active member and has been involved in various affairs throughout the club's history.

COURTESY OF TRAVEL ALBERTA

A pronghorn antelope normally found in southern Alberta.

Swan Hills Outdoor Recreation Club
1977-present

In 1977-78 the Swan Hills Recreation Club revived the old gun club by developing a trap and archery range in co-operation with the AFGA. The range is located southeast of the town of Swan Hills.

In 1981 the club moved the range to the old Home Oil air strip, and moved the clubhouse from the town site to the range. A skeet field and a trap field were constructed during the summer. In the winter, an indoor pellet-gun range was built for youth members, as well as an archery range for both youth and adult members.

A skeet league began in 1982 during the winter months. By the summer, there were up to 25 shooters, with 10 members travelling to out-of-town competitions as far as the United States.

A hunter training program was initiated by the club in 1982-1983. The club planted wild rice in some of the smaller local lakes as a food source for waterfowl, as well as installing round bales for goose nesting during these years.

In 1984, the club started testing barren lakes for levels of dissolved oxygen during the winter months to evaluate their potential for fish stocking. This project was done with help from the local Fish

Muskeg.

COURTESY OF DON MEREDITH

and Wildlife Division fisheries technician in Slave Lake, Martin Brilling.

The club stocked yellow perch fry from Lesser Slave Lake into Roche Lake in 1985-87 with assistance from Federated Pipeline.

In co-operation with the Fish and Wildlife Division staff in Slave Lake, the club planted yellow perch from Goose Lake into two small lakes west of the town of Swan Hills from 1988 to 1989. One of these lakes now has a population of small perch; however, the other lake suffered a winterkill during the third year after the perch were planted.

In 1990-91 spawning-age yellow perch were stocked into Roche Lake twice. Within three years, good size perch were being caught along with northern pike.

Duane Radford with a Lesser Slave Lake walleye.

Arctic grayling were trapped in 1994-'95-'96 at Freeman Lake and artificially spawned; fertilized eggs were shipped to the Sam Livingstone Trout Hatchery in Calgary for grayling enhancement in Alberta. During this time period, four local lakes that were barren of fish were stocked with trout for the first time.

The gun range continued to be developed over the years; a covered shooting stand was constructed along with backstops up to 500 yards, with additional mounds at 25-, 50-, 75-, 100- and 250-yards. There is also one trap field and four skeet fields, along with a sporting clays field.

Spruce Point Marina on Lesser Slave Lake, 2000.

Kakwa River.

Northern forest.

Barrow Lake north of Lake Athabasca, 1966.

Alberta Fish & Game Association

36th ANNUAL

CONVENTION

Capri Motor Hotel, Red Deer

SATURDAY, FEBRUARY 6th, 1965

Under the Auspices of

The Alberta Fish and Game Association

AND

The Red Deer Fish and Game Association

"MAY YOU ENJOY THE GREAT OUTDOORS"

•

Town and Association History and "Menu" by Kerry Wood

Chapter Three

Conferences

The annual conference of the Alberta Fish and Game Association (AFGA)—or convention, as it used to be called prior to 1973—is a major event. In the most recent decades, delegates would meet on Thursday, Friday and Saturday in late February to listen to presentations on issues of concern, to address resolutions from the various clubs, zones and provincial executive, and to elect the provincial executive for the following year. The past president would preside over the election of officials and explain the nomination and election process. Elections are held if more than one member contests a position, otherwise nominees (selected by a nomination committee) are appointed by acclamation.

The first annual convention was held in Calgary in 1929 and the 78th conference, the last one prior to the AFGA centennial year, was held at the Medicine Hat Lodge Hotel and Conference Centre in Medicine Hat on Feb. 22-24, 2007. Prior to conferences in recent years, the AFGA staff set up a registration-information booth in the main lobby of the hotel hosting the conference. As well, they open a working office off the foyer to handle administrative and financial matters arising from the conference—this office is a beehive of activity during each conference.

On the Wednesday evening prior to the start of the conference, the staff hold a training and orientation session for both the AFGA staff and volunteers. Registration of delegates and guests begins the next morning, prior to the opening of the conference on Thursday afternoon and continues through the second and third days.

The following description of the 2007 Medicine Hat conference is an example of what occurs at a typical AFGA conference. At the opening session on Thursday afternoon the conference committee chair, Deb Kopp from the Medicine Hat club, gave a welcoming address, followed by opening remarks by the mayor of Medicine Hat. The 2007 conference committee consisted of Deb Kopp (chair), Sandie Buwalda (AFGA communications co-ordinator), Scott Kultgen, Len (Leonard) Mitzel (MLA for Cypress Hills – Medicine Hat), Kerry Mckenzie and Boyne Lewis.

During that first afternoon, AFGA staff presented habitat and environmental reports to the delegates. This was followed by a program report on matters of interest to the delegates; in 2007, the presentation dealt with the AFGA insurance coverage.

There was a companion program for spouses of delegates or others not directly related to the conference. It featured local attractions and events. Also featured was a youth program with entertaining activities.

The life members of the AFGA met during the first evening. This was followed by a "meet and greet" zone night with a host bar, providing an opportunity for all delegates to socialize. There was also a hospitality suite open throughout the conference where delegates could discuss matters in a casual atmosphere.

On the second and third days of the conference, the executive committee held breakfast meetings while the delegates fared for themselves. A guest speaker was featured during the morning session on the second day (Friday) of the conference. This was followed by reports from the provincial fisheries and wildlife branches regarding important issues and activities, which ran into the afternoon session.

Just prior to lunch on the second day, Ted Morton, Minister of Sustainable Resource Development (the sitting minister responsible for the Fish and Wildlife Division) made a presentation to the delegates and guests (this is often followed by a question and answer period, time permitting). On Friday evening a semi-

AFGA dance, circa 1970.

COURTESY OF JACK GRAHAM

AFGA conference. Tom O'Keefe (L), Ernie Psikla and Andrew McPherson.

formal dinner was held, followed by some entertainment. A silent auction was held in conjunction with this dinner, as a fundraiser for the AFGA. In earlier conferences, a dance was held on either or both Friday and Saturday nights.

The annual general meeting of the AFGA was on Saturday, the third day of the conference, at which time resolutions were debated and voted on. The conference appointed a Parliamentarian who administered rules of order for the meeting and especially with regard to the discussion and voting of resolutions. Gerry Pittman from the Lethbridge club held this position at the last two conferences (2006 and 2007). The AFGA operates under the meeting procedures of Roberts Rules of Order. At this meeting there was also a traditional "parade of donations," during which various clubs and delegates formally donated money to the AFGA, some of which was earmarked for specified purposes. The association is a not-for-profit organization and provides charitable donation receipts to individuals.

On Saturday evening there was a president's dinner, including AFGA awards presentations. At the 2007 conference, the

COURTESY OF HENRY LEMBICZ

Horst Fauser and Paul Morck, past AFGA manager, hamming it up at a conference in the 1970s.

Hon. Rob Renner, Minister of Environment and MLA for Medicine Hat, made a presentation to the dinner guests.

Each delegate at a conference is provided a conference yearbook, which includes the minutes of the annual general meeting of the previous conference, including the outcome of the resolutions; a list of the proposed resolutions for the current year; a budget report; reports from the AFGA executive committee on the preceding year's events and highlights; and staff reports on their projects and activities.

The annual AFGA conference is an important meeting place where the delegates address matters of mutual interest and interact with the executive and other officials; it is also an occasion where election of the executive takes place by secret ballot. For most members, it represents an opportunity to recharge their batteries in support of conservation of Alberta's fish and wildlife resources and to renew acquaintances in a collegial setting.

During the 2007 AFGA conference, co-authors/editors Don Meredith and Duane Radford interviewed the following past presidents in attendance, as well as Randy Collins, the sitting president, to obtain their perspective on the annual conference.

Bob Scammell 1973-75

At his first conference in Banff in 1966, Bob Scammell was greatly impressed with the passionate arguments that occurred during the debate on whether or not AFGA conferences should be held in national parks. He was especially impressed with Joe Balla from Lethbridge, who was a very strong individual and who made effective arguments. As a result, a resolution was passed at that conference which banned the AFGA from holding all future conferences in national parks. This later came back to haunt the association when the Jasper club wanted to host a conference in Jasper National Park. Because of the no-national park policy, the bid was refused and the Jasper club subsequently withdrew from the AFGA.

COURTESY OF BOB SCAMMELL

BOB SCAMMELL

Scammell observed that over time there has been less attendance at conferences. When he was president there were maybe 125 clubs, with close to 25,000 members and very substantial attendance at conferences. He said he believes much is done now that prevents delegates from getting to know each other. For example, there are fewer hospitality rooms, when in the past each zone had one. Also, there is less time at the formal social events for delegates to socialize. He believes the chief benefit of having conferences is meeting other like-minded people and creating lasting friendships and meaningful alliances; and those opportunities are getting fewer. "Conferences are not as much fun as they used to be," he said.

George Mitchell (L) presenting the Distinguished Service Award to Carole and Nestor Romaniuk

Past president (1973-75) Bob Scammell (L) and Paul Morck, with the trophy for the most outrageous white-tail story, 1979.

The one minister who stands out for Scammell is Dr. Allan Warrack, the minister when he was president. "There's nothing like being a president when there's a really good minister," said Scammell, "and that doesn't happen very often." He remembered Warrack as a well-educated man and a great listener who impressed Scammell by personally looking at the resolutions the AFGA passed at conferences. According to Scammell, that was how the Buck for Wildlife program came into being (see Epilogue).

Scammell said he believes the presentations made by biologists and other experts are valuable for the delegates. However, he felt the time to consider and debate resolutions and policies is less than it used to be and that is unfortunate. Annual conferences energize, Scammell said, and the AFGA would "flat-out die" if the annual conferences were cancelled.

Tony Ferguson *1977-79*

The first conference Tony Ferguson attended was at Banff in 1966 when he was a member of the Wainwright club. He made some statements on the floor about issues of concern, and remembers Archie Miller approaching him to say that he should serve as president. Ferguson declined because he didn't feel he knew enough yet. He also remembers a great battle when the membership chairman presented his report. For some reason the motion to accept the report was defeated, and to Ferguson's knowledge, was never accepted. He remembers that sort of set the tone for the rest of the discussions.

Of all the ministers Ferguson saw over the years, Dr. Allan Warrack stood out as one who did the most for conservation. In those days, the executive used to meet regularly with government to discuss issues and how to address them. Al "Boomer" Adair was another good minister who seemed to understand the concerns of the AFGA.

Ferguson remembered there being good working relationships with the Saskatchewan Wildlife Federation and B.C. Wildlife Federation in the 1960s and 70s, where those organizations would send representatives to AFGA conferences and the AFGA would send representatives to theirs. The groups also held joint executive meetings on a three-year rotation, where each province took turns hosting the meeting. These events fostered a close working relationship. As Ferguson remembers it, B.C. was issue-oriented, Alberta was business-management-oriented, and Saskatchewan was membership-oriented. These alliances worked very well on national and regional issues.

Ferguson felt that some of the fun and games at conferences have changed for the worse over the years. Conference-hosting clubs and zones used to make their own entertainment for the delegates. Now, the entertainment is hired—not a good way for people to meet and learn from each other. He also believes there is a need for more input into resolutions. Delegates often do not have enough information to make well-informed decisions.

Ferguson did not have a favourite conference site, unless it was Medicine Hat where he became president. "Each site has its own attributes," he said. However, distance is a factor for a lot of delegates.

Past presidents Roy Ozanne 1981-83 (L); Horst Fauser 1993-95; Ron Gladish 1983-85.

Carole Romaniuk (L) and Eve Ozanne, winner of the Lady Conservationist Award in 1983. The 54th annual conference was held for the first time in Grande Prairie in the Peace River country, hosted by zone 6.

"If annual conferences were cancelled," Ferguson stated, "it would be a disaster." Conferences allow clubs to see what others are doing, who has similar problems, and how they are solving them. A good conference has interesting speakers, good programs, and good information that delegates can take back to their clubs.

Don Hayden *1979-81*

Don Hayden remembered his first conference in Calgary, sometime in the early 1960s. "Tom O'Keefe was president," Don recalled with a smile. "He was known as 'All Mighty Voice' because he didn't need a public address system." Hayden was impressed with the organization and was glad to see it existed and was working for conservation.

Hayden felt that conferences have lacked continuity from one year to the next. When he became president, he wanted things to be done differently. He made sure that something was always happening at a conference, that the major players from the executive were always at the front table so that delegates could see they were doing something, and being listened to.

Shortly after Hayden became president, he arranged a get-acquainted luncheon meeting with the new minister, Bud

DON HAYDEN

Miller. The two got along well. Later, when he was looking for a sponsor for the next conference luncheon, he convinced Miller that his department should do it, and Miller agreed. To this day, the government department responsible for fish and wildlife conservation sponsors the Friday luncheon at each AFGA conference. "All you have to do is approach people the right way," said Hayden, "and they want to help."

Hayden said he had no particular favourite conference site. However, he did feel that distance becomes an issue any time a conference is held outside the Queen Elizabeth II Highway corridor from Calgary to Edmonton.

With regard to changing the conference agenda, Hayden felt there should be a president's report on Saturday before the President's Banquet. Ray Makowecki did this, and it went over well. The report did not have to be long, hitting only the highlights. Also, Hayden said he would like to see a few more words from the committee chairs (big game, fishing, etc.) before they bring the specialists up for presentations.

Doug Rumsey (L), Carole Romaniuk with the Lady Conservationist Award, 1987, and Niels Damgaard.

Hayden believed Dr. Allan Warrack was the best minister he had seen. He remembered Bob Scammell being president at that time and that he got along well with Warrack. Bud Miller also stands out for Hayden because of the relationship he had with Miller.

He stated the most memorable conferences were those that were most controversial. Hayden remembered a conference in Banff in 1966 where there was much discussion about having a fishing and hunting conference in a national park. Joe Balla from Lethbridge became so incensed about the location that he decided to run for president from the conference floor against the previously nominated candidate who defended the conference site. Balla won.

Jack Graham *1988-90*

Jack Graham's first AFGA conference was in Calgary—he said he had a great time, and recalls the lineups at the podium during

SUPPLIED

Niels Damgaard (L), Penny Damgaard and Ike Johanson at the AFGA conference in Red Deer, February 1992.

resolutions as a battle royal, often pitting the north against the south. Graham always found the conferences to be very informative, with a long-standing focus on protecting wildlife. He said that the respect for the AFGA and the resource has remained strong over the years, and believed that almost every conference has had some kind of highlight – for example, the dams that were being built, land and water conservation issues, or keeping a place for wildlife in Alberta's forests.

Graham said he didn't have a favourite conference site but as a past president admitted that for economic purposes either Calgary or Edmonton made better sense, financially. "People don't care, but when you start looking at where you can save money, the location is pretty damn important," he claimed. He noted the conference was essential in order for the AFGA to maintain its charitable status, and run the business of the day – any member is entitled to see their financial records.

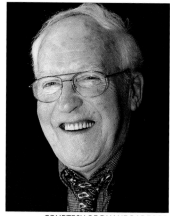

COURTESY OF DUANE RADFORD

JACK GRAHAM

Dr. Allan Warrack, Don Sparrow and LeRoy Fjordbotten were Graham's favourite ministers, top-notch guys in his opinion. He said they could have a meeting with any of these ministers at any time and if they wanted a breakfast meeting all it took was a phone call; they were never refused an audience. He recalled Sparrow telling him, "I don't want any surprises from you and you won't get any surprises from me!"

A good turnout of delegates is necessary for a good conference so they can't be overpriced, he said, along with an agenda that's of interest to the members, with a balance of issues and lots of visuals to accompany presentations.

Horst Fauser *1993-95*

Horst Fauser remembered his first conference, held at the Highwayman Motor Inn in Edmonton in 1977 and hosted by the Sherwood Park club. "I was very taken and impressed with the conference," he said, "and it sort of got me involved. The atmosphere and discussions and the whole bunch of people that were there—hunters and fishermen—and so that was my first convention and impression, and because of that I became fairly active later on."

He noted that the style of the conferences has changed over the years but with the emphasis still on hunting and fishing. "In the early years when I took part in conventions, we had more fun. One club came with a band and played. On Friday night we roasted each other. I know in Grande Prairie, we got kicked out of one corner because we were singing all night and we moved to another corner. It was a more fun-type affair, where now it seems to [have] become fairly serious and involved... the fun part has kind of disappeared."

In terms of conference highlights, Fauser said his election to serve as president stands out in his memory—running against another senior member on the executive. He first thought he had a favourite conference site but on reflection, he saw a lot of value in moving the conference around Alberta—at one time it was felt the conference should be held in Red Deer for travel purposes, but he saw a lot of benefits to moving it around the province to expose the conference to various parts of Alberta. "I feel it is good for exposure, and I feel it is good for the members and for the various zones in the regions where the conference takes place."

He said he would like to see the agenda changed with more seminars and workshops, so that people go home with new ideas and even more knowledge. Fauser suggested that the conferences were essential to the business of the AFGA. He was very

SUPPLIED

Archie Hogg (L), Sylver Lakusta and Chris van der Merwe receiving a provincial award.

impressed with Don Sparrow as a minister [Forestry, Lands and Wildlife], because Sparrow came from private business and he made things happen; he also provided the AFGA with a Buck for Wildlife co-ordinator and 10 acres of Crown land for hunter training camps in each zone.

"One item that's important is that the meals are good," Fauser laughed, "and of course the organization and to give people a chance to ask questions and get them more involved in the proceedings. The organization is now pretty well in place; each convention has a certain rhythm. But at the good conventions you should have fun. In the early years, Martha Kostuch and myself, we made sure we had a dance on Friday night, and a dance on Saturday night – and there was a lot of dancing going on, and now people don't dance anymore!"

VERN MCINTOSH

Morton [appointed Minister of Sustainable Resource Development in 2006] presented the most positive speech at any convention I have ever attended. LeRoy Fjordbotten was pretty good and so was Don Sparrow but nothing has been as positive as Morton's speech—it really gives you hope."

When asked what makes for a good conference McIntosh said, "The right people are necessary to organize it and get it off the ground; for instance, a guy like Steve Witiuk [incumbent zone 5 chair in 2007], who has more or less been responsible for organizing four different conferences. He's got it down to a science; he does a dandy job. It's a voluntary thing with him. He's the right person to get involved." He also mentioned that George Belter, zone 3 director, did a tremendous job organizing the previous conference in Red Deer. "Those volunteers make or break a conference," concluded McIntosh.

Horst Fauser's acceptance speech as president at the 1993 conference while Murray Rush and Niels Damgaard listen.

Vern McIntosh *1995-97*

Vern McIntosh couldn't recall his first conference, which he attended many years ago. He was of the opinion that the AFGA conferences were getting better, with a lot of high-quality presentations, compared with early conferences which were sometimes routine without a lot of variety to draw interest. A highlight of one conference he remembered was when Ty Lund, then Minister of Environmental Protection, handed him a cheque for $250,000 for the AFGA.

McIntosh liked Red Deer as a conference site because of its central location—compared with extreme locations—although he said it was nice to have conferences in different locations because it heightens the interest of the local fish-and-gamers. He said he wouldn't make many changes in the agenda for the annual conference which was very tight due to time constraints.

"It would be disastrous if the annual conference was cancelled," remarked McIntosh, "simply because it's the only opportunity we have for direct interaction with clubs from all over the province. Otherwise it's email, telephone and zone meetings and they're not broad enough to include everybody." McIntosh said "Ted

Dave Powell *1998-2000*

The first conference Dave Powell attended was in 1981 in his home town of Red Deer. It was an eye-opening experience for him because he started to learn how the process works, how the AFGA goes about getting things done. As Powell put it, "It became obvious to me that 'the world is run by those who show up' and those people who were running the world (in terms of Alberta conservation) were there." Powell felt the conference sets the direction of what the executive does, especially how it pressures government. "We may not win all the battles [with government]," he said, "but what would the world look like if we hadn't been in the fight?" In other words, Powell believes that over the years the AFGA has influenced key government decisions for the better of fish and wildlife conservation, even though the organization may not have achieved all that it hoped for. The conference demonstrates that this organization is run by the grassroots. He felt that without the annual conference, "Fish and Game" would not survive and the clubs would not "hang together."

Powell's favourite conference site was Red Deer, but he admitted he was biased; he lived there. However, Red Deer is a central site; there is always good attendance at conferences there because it is easy for most people to get there. Going to places like Medicine Hat and Grande Prairie are nice, he said, you get to see more of Alberta, but central conferences attract more people.

With regard to changes to conferences, Powell said he would like to see more emphasis on fundraising, how local clubs can raise money in their areas. He believes delegates would appreciate working sessions on just how to run a club—how clubs should be administrated, attract new members, etc. He would also like to see

COURTESY OF DUANE RADFORD

Past presidents attending the 2007 conference in Medicine Hat. Back row: Don Hayden (L), Vern McIntosh, Dave Powell, Rod Dyck, Randy Collins and Gerry Pittman. Front row: Tony Ferguson (L), Bob Scammell, Ray Makowecki, Jack Graham and Horst Fauser.

the public invited to fundraising events at conferences. This would help raise funds and increase the profile of the AFGA. As well, Powell believes the AFGA has to find ways to attract the news media to conferences.

Powell believed the best conferences occur when there's a key issue to discuss. He believes the AFGA's finest moments happened when conferences determined the need for a Buck for Wildlife program to enhance habitat and Minister Allan Warrack picked up the idea and ran with it. Similarly, Minister LeRoy Fjordbotten expanded the Buck for Wildlife program into the Fish and Wildlife Trust Fund as a result of resolutions debated at conferences.

Gerry Pittman *2000-01*

Hon. Mike Cardinal at the 2003 AFGA annual conference.

COURTESY OF BOB SCAMMELL

Gerry Pittman's impression of his first conference was "that there's a whole lot of digesting to do here! I think it's a revelation to people to go to conferences the first couple of times and realize how much goes on behind the scenes— how much work the executive of a provincial association actually does—and that's a big load for people to get into. And, I think you go home renewed and revitalized; and all gung-ho. You always learn something new, and you meet the friends who have a like-minded outlook compared to yourself."

COURTESY OF DUANE RADFORD

GERRY PITTMAN

COURTESY OF DUANE RADFORD

Bob Transtrom, Martin Sharren and Wayne Lowry at the 2007 conference.

COURTESY OF DUANE RADFORD

Laurie Kerestes at the 2007 AFGA conference display.

Pittman believed that, in the past, conferences were a little more interactive than at present; he felt that while today's presentations are high quality there just isn't enough time for the delegates to get the feedback they require, as a result of lack of time. "I believe they have changed a little. I do believe the conferences were better in the old days," he said.

One of the most controversial conference agenda items Pittman recalled was the closure of the caribou season in northern Alberta due to a high Indian harvest and predator depredation. Pittman strongly believes that every conference should be held in Red Deer. "Absolutely, no question in my mind," he said emphatically. "It's central to the province. It's a very big conference city. Everybody can get there quite easily." He noted that attendance drops off when the conferences are held elsewhere, such as Grande Prairie and Medicine Hat.

Pittman said he would like to change the format of the annual conference to get more interaction; he feels a wider variety of interactive opportunities, displays, with shorter presentations would enhance attendance. "I think old-timers, like me, would miss it if the annual conference was cancelled; the general rank-and-file members wouldn't miss it that much," Pittman noted, "provided one was held every other year."

Pittman dealt with the Hon. Ty Lund, then Minister of Environmental Protection, when he was president and he credits Lund as being a good listener, and remarked that David Coutts, Minister of Sustainable Resource Development, was "extremely approachable." Pittman said, "I really liked Dave Coutts; I think he did a fine job for us."

He concluded: "What makes for a good conference is not too much regimentation. Not too much soldier volunteer stuff... being able to talk to people. As much as anything, it's a meeting place and that's what makes a good conference when you get out and meet with other people."

COURTESY OF DON MEREDITH

Ted Morton, Minister of Sustainable Resource Development, at the 2007 AFGA conference in Medicine Hat.

Rod Dyck 2001-03

Rod Dyck remembered his first conference in Calgary in the mid-1980s, which he found overwhelming. "Conferences were quite a bit different then than they are now," he remarked. "At that time we had speakers come in from all the provincial departments. The fish guy would be there. Forestry would be there. I took it quite seriously; I wrote a lot of notes. When I was done with that conference, I had a lady in Drumheller who typed up those notes so I could

COURTESY OF THE AFGA

ROD DYCK

present them to my club and give a report. The report was over 50 pages long."

Dyck remembered his first conference as a much more formal event than later conferences. "In the evenings it was suit and ties, with a big brass band at the president's ball. It was a pretty posh event that has been toned down over the years. It was an eye-opener to see just how involved members are throughout this province in managing the resources and working with government."

Dyck remembered there being a lot more information being disseminated at the earlier conferences he attended, with a choice of regional meetings which were informative and interactive, not that the more recent conferences lacked information. He also noted that an older crowd attended the conference in Medicine Hat, compared with a younger crowd at many of the previous meetings.

"They gave me the mike hog award last year [2006]; I don't think I deserved it," he laughed when recalling conference highlights. Dyck remarked that there had been some important announcements at conferences, especially during the minister's presentations. "One of the key ones was when Mike Cardinal [former Minister of Sustainable Resource Development] came in and announced that he was giving us a $150,000 annual grant," he noted.

Dyck said Red Deer was probably his favourite conference site, due to its central location. "I really think the association should limit conferences to the Calgary-Edmonton corridor, and try and keep them more in the central part of the province, to get better turnouts." He said Red Deer has been a good place to have conferences, maybe because of the better turnouts. He'd also like to see the youth get more involved in conferences and be directly involved in fish and game business. "They went bowling yesterday," he remarked, "and maybe they should be sitting in on some of the meetings." He'd also like to see some practical seminars on outdoor products, such as how to use a GPS [global positioning system], how to set up a camp in the outdoors—some hands-on courses—how to run successful meetings, sessions with head office staff, for example.

2007 AFGA conference question period: Heinz Plontke (L) and Garnet Anthony (standing).

It would not be a good thing if the annual conference was cancelled, he said, and the AFGA membership would fall. Dyck thought that the Hon. David Coutts was a very good minister, who was onside with the AFGA interests. Also, he had good discussions with the Hon. Mike Cardinal and said that Halvar Jonson seemed very reasonable. He commented that the various ministers had always been very honest with the AFGA, and noted that Gary Mar "…didn't pull any punches, he told us the way it was going to be." Dyck felt that good interaction makes for a good conference—input from other groups—and one-on-one discussions to make good decisions.

Ray Makowecki *2003-05*

Ray Makowecki recalls attending his first conference in the early 1970s where he gave a talk about northern pike in Seibert Lake in Alberta's Lakeland Country. He remembers the conferences having a strong similarity over time; he said some of the passion of committed members remains, with a continuity provided by many dedicated members—people like Roy Ozanne, Ben Rosnau, Jack Easterbrook, Norm Ferguson and Sam Smolyk—who were outspoken advocates for fish and game for many years. "These were very dedicated people who always got up to the microphone to speak their minds; as these people phased out we now have people like the Pittmans [Gerry and Ron, of Lethbridge] who come up to the microphone to speak, and others like Rod Dyck, Tony Ferguson and Vern McIntosh, who have moved in as well, and provide the real backbone of the organization," he said. "These people have such strong convictions they kind of carry the ball from decade to decade."

RAY MAKOWECKI

In terms of conference highlights, "Obviously the years that you are president are pretty profound," he noted. "In fact, when I first became elected many years ago, I can remember when Bill Morton, a southern Alberta AFGA member, and then Ted Morton who's currently the sitting Minister of the Department of Sustainable Resource Development, both came up to me and asked me if I was a priest or minister, after I gave an election speech for junior vice president. Another classy event was when the commercial fishermen attended with their booth and burbot tasting, and when we [co-author/editor Duane Radford and Ray Makowecki] were regional directors for the Fish and Wildlife Division and we had the feeling of serving the AFGA as clients."

Makowecki said the Grande Prairie conferences stood out in his mind because they were fun events, filled with excitement. He remembered one in Lethbridge when Henry Kruger, Coronation MLA, poured a pitcher of water on a table during his presentation to demonstrate what he thought about the importance of dams regarding water management.

Makowecki said it's much cheaper to hold conferences in Edmonton, from purely an administrative perspective, even over Calgary, simply because of the location of the AFGA head office, but there was value in visiting other locations in Alberta. He said it was very important to get the agenda out to members as soon as possible and to attract high-profile keynote speakers to generate media interest and draw attention to conservation issues. He thought that the conferences were very important to unite the membership, and the resolution process was of fundamental importance to the membership.

Dr. Allan Warrack stood out as notable minister, but he also said that Ted Morton had a very profound presentation at the Medicine Hat conference. Don Sparrow was another notable minister, as well as Mike Cardinal who started the contribution of an annual grant of $150,000 to the AFGA. He felt that elections made for a good conference, along with good food, the right venue to create a good atmosphere, and quality presentations with lots of visual aids.

Randy Collins 2005-07

Randy Collins joined the AFGA because he loved the outdoors and wanted to do more to conserve fish and wildlife. He felt a need to speak out on things that could be changed. The first conference he attended was at Medicine Hat in 1993. He was impressed with the number of people who travelled from all over Alberta to attend the conference in the southeast corner of the province, and the passion those people brought, especially on Saturday when resolutions were discussed.

For Collins, "each conference has had its own feel." Grande Prairie's northern setting differs from Medicine Hat's prairie feel, where local issues and concerns can be quite different. His most memorable conference was at Grande Prairie in 2005 where he was elected president. He remembers the beautiful drive home, passing by Mayerthorpe, just days before the tragic death

COURTESY OF DUANE RADFORD

Randy Collins, president (2005-07) at the 2007 AFGA conference.

COURTESY OF DUANE RADFORD

2007 AFGA conference Parade of Donations. Doug Butler (with microphone) and Robyn Butler with Randy Collins.

of the four RCMP officers, and then Wabamun Lake where later that summer a train wreck and oil spill occurred. These two events would soon impact his presidency where the AFGA had to take stands against gun control on one hand and the lack of environmental protection on the other.

Collins remembered many conference highlights, such as Ted Morton's speech in 2007—the first angling/hunting minister in a long while who knew his audience and what they needed to hear. Indeed, it is individuals who stand out as highlights for Collins—people who demonstrated their passion for the AFGA and conservation, such as Jack Easterbrook, Rod Dyck and Niels Damgaard, just to name a few. He especially remembers a presentation Ray Makowecki gave to a conference on the Interim Métis Harvest Agreements. "It brought the members together," Collins said, to fight a deal that wasn't going to be good for anyone.

Collins said he felt that distance is the major factor affecting whether a certain location for a conference is good or not. Conferences need to have good participation from across the province to reflect all viewpoints. Of course, conferences held in Calgary, Red Deer or Edmonton are more likely to get the largest number and widest variety of delegates. However, he also felt that every corner of the province should get a chance to see what an AFGA conference is all about.

Of the various government ministers whom Collins has seen at conferences, he was most impressed with Ted Morton (see above). He feels Mike Cardinal stepped up when it was needed to support the grizzly bear hunt. He thinks Gary Marr was a good politician who made a lot of friends with his honesty when he spoke at the conference, admitting he did not hunt or fish but that he would seek to understand the AFGA and its issues.

Collins said he believed annual conferences are what keep the organization together and viable. They showcase the AFGA, and without them the organization would soon disintegrate. He believed a good conference is one where there is full participation from all the delegates and there is a good crowd.

2007 AFGA Conference
Medicine Hat, Feb. 22-24

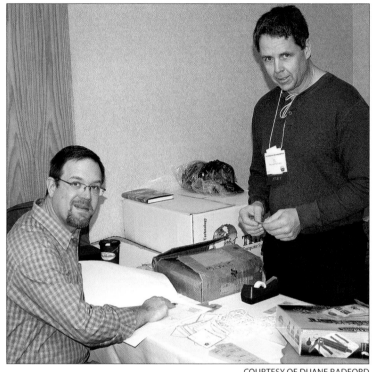

COURTESY OF DUANE RADFORD

Brad Fenson (L), AFGA habitat co-ordinator and T.J. Schwanky, habitat facilitator.

COURTESY OF DUANE RADFORD

François Blouin, AFGA Operation Grassland Community co-manager.

COURTESY OF DUANE RADFORD

Martin Sharren (sitting L), Sandie Buwalda, Yvonne Baxter and Lee Bell.

COURTESY OF DUANE RADFORD

Lee Bell, controller.

Heritage 100 Book Committee at the 2007 annual conference in Medicine Hat. Back row: Vern McIntosh (L), Randy Collins, Martin Sharren, Don Hayden. Front row: Tony Ferguson (L), Bob Scammell, Carole Romaniuk, Ray Makowecki, Jack Graham. Missing: Maurice Nadeau, president 2007-08.

AFGA youth group attending the annual conference in Medicine Hat, Feb. 22-24, 2007. Front row, third from left: Maurice Nadeau, president, 2007-08.

2007 AFGA conference coffee break. Bob Scammell, Bibiane Foisy, Trevor Rhodes, Dave Powell and Andy Boyd.

Deb Kopp, 2007 AFGA conference chair.

Martin Sharren, AFGA executive vice president.

Rocky Mountain bighorn sheep on a steep cliff in the Rockies.

Chapter Four

Wildlife Awards Competitions *by Brad Fenson*

The genesis of the Alberta Fish and Game Association (AFGA) originated in 1908 from a group of grassroots individuals who belonged to a fledgling organization in Calgary. From these early members, the idea of developing clubs for anglers and hunters interested in fish and game resources, and how they were managed, expanded to communities across the province. In 1928, the local clubs affiliated to form a single voice for the sportsmen and woman and the resources they cherished. The association expanded and drew members from all sectors of the hunting, fishing and conservation communities.

Today, the AFGA is recognized as the oldest conservation organization in the province. It continues to work on behalf of the fish and wildlife species across Alberta and the habitat that they depend on. It is made up of members with a wide variety of interests in our fish and wildlife resources. One of the well-documented activities of fish and game clubs from across Alberta is the annual trophy competition to determine the largest fish and game species harvested by local hunters and anglers. With clubs in over 100 communities there are a number of local competitions that highlight the incredible trophies our province continues to produce.

The friendly province-wide competition started in 1962 when a group of dedicated sportsmen from the Edmonton Fish and Game Association embarked on a club project to organize an Alberta trophy competition, which would try to find and recognize the largest specimens of big game, birds and fish legally taken in Alberta. They formulated a scoring system based on the Boone and Crockett Club and standardized minimum scores for species hunted in Alberta.

Records have been tabulated since 1963 in order to recognize the incredible fish and wildlife our province has always produced. In 1975 the AFGA took over the record-keeping tasks of this project. They continue to compile records that come in from affiliate clubs across the province that hold annual trophy competitions at a local level.

The Alberta trophy competition winners dating back to 1963, and animals meeting the minimum score requirements, were compiled to form the *Alberta Record Book*. The first hard-covered record book was produced in 1985. It provided a snapshot of Alberta's diversity and superior genetics for all species of fish, birds and big game. The record books offer exciting stories about the largest fish and big-game animals

taken by sportsmen. The listings provided insight into regions that produce trophy-calibre fish, birds and big game animals. In general, the records prove that Alberta is home to incredible trophies in all classes, offering sportsmen and woman some of the best hunting and angling in North America.

In addition to the previous competition records, the *Alberta Wildlife Records – Official Records of the Alberta Fish and Game Association*, Second Edition 1963-2001 contains all Alberta big-game species ranked by size in accordance with the minimums set out in the Big Game Awards of Boone and Crockett. This information was obtained from the AFGA, affiliated clubs, the Boone and Crockett Club and Pope and Young records up to and including 2001 entries. Jack Graham, Steve Witiuk and Ab England, in particular, played a key role over the years as chairs of the trophy committee.

The competition records include 15 species of "big game," as well as "largest big-game taken with bow and arrow," "largest big-game with black powder," a "non-current" class which covers all big-game species taken or found prior to the current year and not previously entered, and a "master trophy," given to the largest big-game specimen taken each year.

It also includes six species of game birds, including Merriam's turkey, white-fronted goose, Canada goose, snow goose, pheasant and mallard duck.

Fifteen Alberta fish species are recognized, as well as "largest trout taken with a fly," a "master fish trophy" for the largest fish taken that year, and the "provincial fish derby" for the physically disabled. This publication also includes catch-and-release records for the province.

The objectives of the trophy competition are:
- To have a stronger tie between affiliated AFGA clubs throughout the province.
- To have all hunters and fishermen become members of a fish and game association in their communities.
- To obtain greater recognition of the wildlife found in the province of Alberta.
- To have qualified people to recognize and score the trophies, a course was developed to certify Official Alberta Measurer's.

The course has evolved to a level that covers the scoring procedures for each species to the understanding of all pupils. There are now qualified measurers in almost all communities in Alberta. Courses are still offered on a regular basis to increase the number of qualified measurers required in our province.

Trophy records have been an important part of the AFGA for close to half a century. New records are continually coming out of Alberta in all classifications. The *Alberta Wildlife Records* book is a testament to the trophy quality, diversity and positive game

management that continues to offer Alberta sportsmen and woman the unique opportunity to harvest a trophy-class animal or fish.

COURTESY OF DUANE RADFORD

Adrienne Radford with an Athabasca River walleye.

Annual Awards Banquet by Duane Radford

*T*he 44th Annual Wildlife Awards Banquet was held on April 21, 2007 at the Polish Hall in Edmonton to recognize the AFGA trophy winners for 2006 in the big game competition, fish competition, catch and release fish winners, bird competition and also the photography competition. Various clubs sponsor awards for each particular species or photography event.

While there were many outstanding trophies taken in 2006, notable is the non-typical whitetail deer taken by Blair Cote of Plamondon which won the Master Big Game Trophy Award with a score of 258 4/8 scoring 139.7 percent above the minimum entry; this trophy is sponsored by the Edmonton Fish and Game Association. The Provincial Fish Derby for the Physically Disabled trophy was for a 5 pound 7 ounce northern pike taken by Warren Wallace of Edmonton at Lake Isle; this trophy is sponsored by the Edmonton Police Department Fish and Game Association. The Largest Trout Taken with a Fly trophy was a 7 pound 2.9 ounce rainbow trout taken by Ted Kelter of Cochrane in Kananaskis Lake; this trophy is sponsored by the Edmonton Trout Fishing Club. The Master Fish Trophy was for a 16 pound 15.7 ounce brown trout caught by Vince Rasmussen of Delburne in Swan Lake; this trophy is sponsored by the Sarcee Fish and Game Association.

The dean of the AFGA Wildlife Awards, Mr. Jack Graham, presided over the 44th annual banquet.

Willow Valley Trophy Day by Don Meredith

*I*f you hunt or fish in Alberta, it is not long before you hear about Willow Valley Trophy Day. The annual event comes up in a conversation around a campfire or over a beverage at a favourite watering hole, often in reverent tones. It is an event whose reputation is known across the province and in many of the States south of the border. Although there are other provincial fish and game trophy competitions, including the AFGA's own annual competition, the Willow Valley competition is the longest-standing in the province (since 1949). As well, Willow Valley not only matches trophies from the previous year, it also matches those trophies against winners from past years. Because many Willow Valley big-game trophies hold Boone and Crockett Club status as some of the largest taken in North America, winning the "Trophy Day Challenge" for a specific species of big game is an accomplishment indeed. Although the day itself occurs on the second Saturday in January, things really get started the night before. Pickup trucks line the parking lot of the Pincher Creek Community Hall and hunters from across the province stand in line just inside the doors, waiting to enter their trophies in the competitions. Meanwhile, the official trophy measurers are busy with tape measures and calipers as they assess the many attributes of the various entries of big game, game birds and game fish trophies. In the main hall, club members set up displays of previous years' winning trophies and the plaques listing the winners of the various competitions from previous years.

Saturday begins early as the parking lot fills with vehicles and soon even the streets leading to the hall are lined with parked cars and pickup trucks. Although the official program does not start until 1 p.m., more competitors

line up early in the morning to enter their trophies, and visitors arrive early to get a look at the trophies and peruse the displays set up in the associated trade show. After each trophy entered is measured and tagged, it is placed on display in the main hall with the hundreds of other entries lining the walls. The whole community comes together to make this a welcoming event.

As show time approaches, entries are closed and the judges begin comparing score sheets in each category. Meanwhile, the main hall fills with 1,000 or more people. The show includes a presentation by a guest speaker about a topic of interest. For example in 2007, Dr. Brad Stelfox, wildlife biologist, spoke about the effects of multi-land-uses on southwest Alberta landscapes; and Ted Morton, new Minister of Alberta Sustainable Resource Development, made a surprise visit to the show and gave his maiden speech about what he would like to accomplish as minister. Following the presentations, the various awards are given for the best trophies in the show. For anyone who has ever dreamed about what is possible to hunt in Alberta, the Willow Valley Trophy Day is an unforgettable experience.

The course has evolved to a level that covers the scoring procedures for each species to the understanding of all pupils. There are now qualified measurers in almost all communities in Alberta. Courses are still offered on a regular basis to increase the number of qualified measurers required in our province.

Trophy records have been an important part of the AFGA for close to half a century. New records are continually coming out of Alberta in all classifications. The Alberta Wildlife Records book is a testament to the trophy quality, diversity and positive game management that continues to offer Alberta sportsmen and woman the unique opportunity to harvest a trophy-class animal or fish.

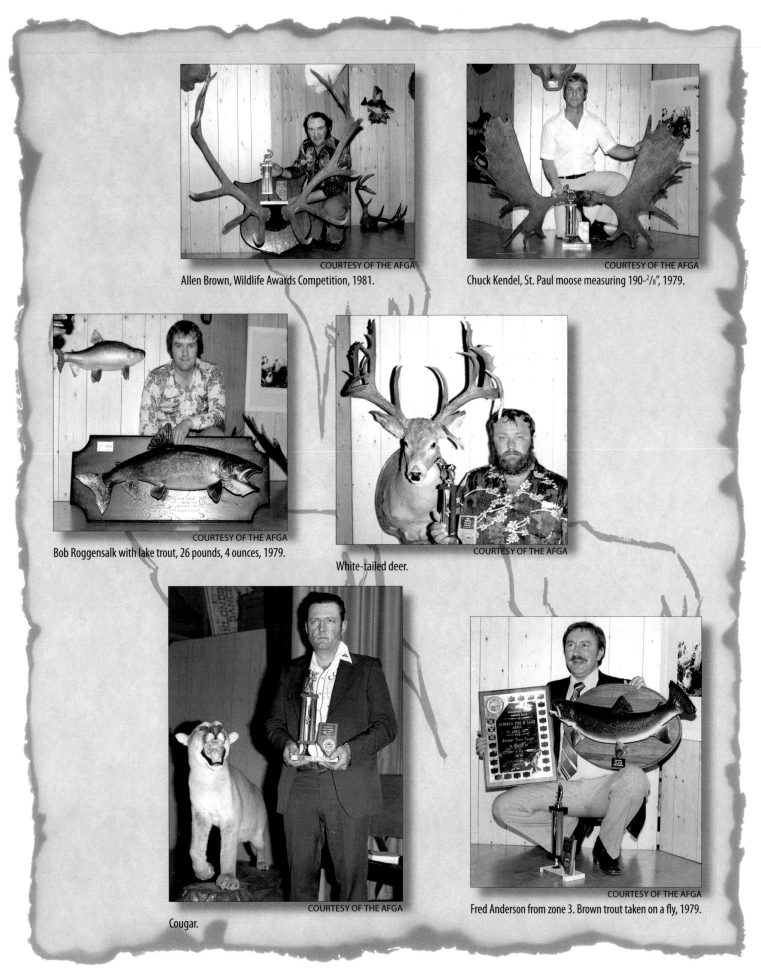

COURTESY OF THE AFGA

Allen Brown, Wildlife Awards Competition, 1981.

COURTESY OF THE AFGA

Chuck Kendel, St. Paul moose measuring 190-^{2}/$_8$", 1979.

COURTESY OF THE AFGA

Bob Roggensalk with lake trout, 26 pounds, 4 ounces, 1979.

COURTESY OF THE AFGA

White-tailed deer.

COURTESY OF THE AFGA

Cougar.

COURTESY OF THE AFGA

Fred Anderson from zone 3. Brown trout taken on a fly, 1979.

Minor Chawrun with perch, 2.07 pounds.

SUPPLIED

Fred Dobirstien (L), Cory Key, Dave Powell, John Powell and Mike Vanson at the 1990 WAC trophy ball.

COURTESY OF THE AFGA

Tim Harbridge, 1978 moose winner, 226-7/8.

SUPPLIED

Dave Vogel, winner of the 1982 non-typical mule deer trophy.

COURTESY OF THE AFGA

Al Higgins (L) receives trophy from Norm Ferguson for largest goldeye at 1981 Wildlife Awards banquet. Jack Graham (centre) as MC.

COURTESY OF JACK GRAHAM

The Crousen ram officially scored 208 3/8 points by a Boone and Crockett panel of judges in 2001.

COURTESY OF BOLAND TAXIDERMISTS

Alberta's legendary buck, the Broder buck taken by Ed Broder that scored 355 2/8 non-typical, 1926.

COURTESY OF VERN MCINTOSH

Vern McIntosh with pronghorn antelope (84-6/8") bagged near Jenner, Alberta, 1988.

COURTESY OF DUANE RADFORD

2006 moose winner by William Penner at Wildlife Awards banquet, 2007.

COURTESY OF DUANE RADFORD

Blair Cote (L) and long-time wildlife records co-ordinator Ab England at the 2007 Wildlife Awards banquet.

COURTESY OF DUANE RADFORD

Peter Mappleback, Edmonton Trout Fishing Club, winner of the AFGA largest trout caught in Alberta trophy. Wildlife Awards banquet, 2007.

COURTESY OF JOE GORE

Joe Gore of High River took this new Alberta record cougar in 2005 scoring 16-2/16. It weighed 225-1⁄2 lbs. and measured 96-3⁄4 inches from nose to tail. The taxidermist, who was familiar in doing African lions, told Joe its size was comparable to that of a lioness.

COURTESY OF DUANE RADFORD

Jack Graham, trophy chair at the 2007 Wildlife Awards banquet.

COURTESY OF DUANE RADFORD

Head table at 2007 Wildlife Awards banquet: Maurice Nadeau (L), Jack and Phyllis Graham, Conrad and Hilda Fennema, Nadine Nadeau, Karen and Quentin Bochar, Brad Pickering and Paul Leeder.

Peter Mappleback holding the Master Trophy for largest northern pike, sponsored by Vegreville Wildlife Federation at the 2007 Wildlife Awards banquet.

Robyn (L) and Doug Butler at the 44th Annual Wildlife Awards banquet in Edmonton, April 21, 2007.

Robert Sydenham, Edmonton: Cougar winner 2007, measuring 15-5/16 on the Boone and Crockett scale.

Tim McKinnon shows off his winning bighorn after taking the AFGA's minister's raffle in 2006.

Mule deer.

Big bull moose!

COURTESY OF HEINZ PLONTKE

Deb Clarke (nee Plontke) with trophy antelope shot in WMU 106 in 1989.

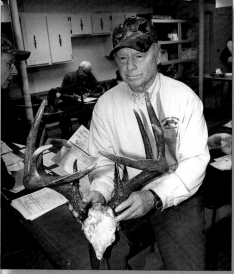

COURTESY OF DUANE RADFORD

Chris Weintz at Sherwood Park FGA horn measuring day.

COURTESY OF THE AFGA

AFGA president Maurice Nadeau (2007-09) on a successful bow hunt in 2003.

SUPPLIED

Gordon Kerr (L), being presented with the Sherwood Park Fish and Game Association Antelope Trophy by Roy Sylyski of LoTech Manufacturing, 2006.

COURTESY OF CURTISS MCLEOD

Curtiss McLeod with moose, 2006.

SUPPLIED

Mighty big moose!

**Norm Shaddock,
recipient of the
Fulton Trophy, 1966.**

Encased in glass on the right hand side of the
trophy are fossilized seeds of the Ginkgo tree,
which is one of the oldest tree species
in the world that is still growing today.
The donor wanted the trophy to
commemorate the old and
the new; thus the Ginkgo seeds
and the vibrant young bull elk.

Chapter Five

Service Awards

Following is a list of the prestigious Alberta Fish and Game Association (AFGA) Service Awards that are bestowed upon members or clubs who have shown great initiative and effort in serving Alberta's wild. They are awarded annually at the provincial conference. The annual deadline for submission of nominees to the AFGA office is Nov. 30.

Fulton Award

The highest award of the association and not necessarily awarded each year. This award is given to the person having made the most outstanding long-term contribution to conservation and the well-being of the AFGA.

Life Membership

Awarded by the executive, such memberships to be restricted to members of the AFGA who, through long service to the AFGA or through other contributions to the aims and objects of the association, merit in the opinion of the association, special recognition for their services. Every life member of the AFGA is permitted to attend, participate in and vote as a delegate at conferences.

Henry Lembicz - Clean Air, Clean Land, Clean Water Award

Awarded to the club or individual who has done the most outstanding job towards pollution control or clean-up of our environment.

J.B. Cunningham - Memorial Award

Awarded to the club or individual who has contributed the most to membership of the AFGA either by increasing membership or providing important membership services.

G.M. Spargo - Memorial Award

Awarded to the club that has the best program for children, resource, education, outdoor education, and/or has given great support to children's groups in their area of interest such as Junior Forest Wardens.

Guy Blake Memorial Award

Awarded to the club with the best project such as habitat improvement, Buck For Wildlife, or for preparing and delivering briefs at public hearings.

Lady Conservationist of the Year

Awarded to the sports lady of the year who has contributed the most to conservation, and/or the AFGA.

Archie Hogg Memorial Award

Awarded to the club or individual which has promoted the best publicity program to bring environmental issues to the public attention.

Budd Traver Outdoors Observer Award

Awarded for contributions made to aiding in the prevention of game law violations.

Junior Conservation Award

Awarded to a junior citizen or a junior group for an outstanding effort in conservation.

George E. Watt Memorial Award

Awarded to the club or individual who makes the highest financial contribution or raises the most funds towards fish and wildlife projects, habitat enhancement or donates such funds to organizations that do that kind of work.

J.D. Munroe Outdoor Activities Award

Awarded to the club or individual with the best project to ensure the future of healthy fish and game populations.

Darwin Cronkhite Award

Awarded to the club that has done the best job in regard to bird rejuvenation, such as habitat enhancement, stocking, introduction of species or disease research.

Urban Hunter Training Award

Awarded to the urban club or person that has done an outstanding job teaching and graduating hunter training students.

Gerry Gibson Memorial Award for Rural Hunter Training

Awarded to the club or person that has done an outstanding job in teaching and graduating hunter training students in rural areas.

Outdoor Ethics Award

Presented to club or individual who makes a significant contribution to promoting hunting and/or fishing ethics through education, programs, landowner hunter relations, field signage etc.

Dennis Hindbo Predator Award

Awarded to the club or individual who has made an outstanding contribution to predator control.

Outdoor Edge Communication Award

Awarded to the club who uses the best method of informing their membership, such as newsletters, club handbooks and local newspapers.

Neville Lindsay Memorial Award

Given to the club or individual who has the best fisheries project.

G.E. Stevens Memorial Award

Awarded to club/individual who has contributed the most to the AFGA Firearm Safety Program.

Distinguished Service Award

Awarded to individuals contributing to the welfare of the AFGA in any way for outstanding work.

AFGA Support Award

Given to the group, corporation or individual who has made a significant financial or other contribution to the operation of the AFGA.

Deer in Waterton Lakes National Park.

Chapter Six

AFGA Habitat Programs

One of the most important contributions the Alberta Fish and Game Association (AFGA) makes to fish and wildlife conservation is its habitat programs. The programs secure and protect critical wildlife habitat throughout the province and leave lasting legacies for future generations of Albertans.

WILDLIFE TRUST FUND

In the AFGA 78th annual conference report, Brad Fenson, habitat development co-ordinator, reported that the Wildlife Trust Fund (WTF) had another tremendous year with outstanding support from affiliated clubs and zones from across the province. He noted that the WTF managed to acquire additional critical habitat for fish and wildlife throughout Alberta and more importantly, continued to manage existing habitat properties for fish and wildlife benefits. Prior to Fenson taking over as WTF co-ordinator in 1989, both Lyle Fullerton and Grant Nieman were AFGA officials who worked on the WTF during its formative years. T.J. Schwanky assisted Fenson in the capacity of a habitat facilitator.

Established in 1983, the WTF celebrated its 25th anniversary in 2008; the WTF has been responsible for the acquisition of over 1,000 acres per year since it was established – the equivalent of over two acres per member based on current membership statistics. The WTF board of directors reviews all project proposals and makes decisions on purchases to be pursued or completed by the AFGA; the board functions separately from the AFGA executive and outside of the regular AFGA business operations. WTF funds are raised through the AFGA hide collection program, various annual raffles—one of which featured the opportunity for a combination hunt for four species of big game in the Yukon Territory—and donations from clubs, zones and individuals. Fenson reported that the raffle was the largest single source of income the AFGA had ever generated for the WTF in 2006. Grassroots funding is multiplied by finding conservation partners and by developing funding proposals to generate matching funds.

According to Fenson, the collaborative effort of the AFGA membership allowed the WTF to secure one of the largest conservation properties ever in central Alberta: the Wabamun-Whitewood Conservation Properties (just north of Wabamun Lake and Highway 16) to the east of Edmonton. The area is a

COURTESY OF THE AFGA

Zone 1, Peigan Creek Conservation Property.

COURTESY OF THE AFGA

Jackpine Property in Vilna/Smoky Lake area.

Walt Backer putting up a bluebird house at the Gordon Leslie Property.

transition zone between aspen parkland and the boreal forest, providing a unique blend of habitats that benefit a wide range of wildlife and provide incredible biodiversity. The terrain is gently rolling with densely wooded uplands and productive sedge wetlands. The properties border the Whitewood Mine, used for coal extraction, enabling TransAlta to produce electricity at their Wabamun facilities.

This wasn't the first property the WTF secured on this landscape. In 1997 TransAlta helped secure the East Pit Lake property for conservation by working with the AFGA and local affiliate clubs. The 312 acres comprising the East Pit Lake property provide recreational angling, nesting cover for birds, wintering range for ungulates and a wide range of other benefits for conservation. In early 2003, the Stony Plain and Spruce Grove clubs brought a referral to the WTF for a property neighbouring East Pit Lake. Fenson assessed the property and its values and sent a referral to the trust fund board for review. The project was seen as a positive initiative and staff and volunteers went to work raising funds to move forward with the purchase. The half-section contained 251 acres of native habitat with white spruce, aspen, willow, Saskatoon, chokecherry, wild rose, sedge meadows and wetland basins. There were not enough funds to complete the purchase and a request was sent to affiliated clubs to support the project. The response was incredible. Funds came in from 20 different sources including 18 AFGA clubs and zones. Funds were also contributed from the Stony Plain Elks, TransAlta and the Department of Sustainable Resources Development. The incredible support allowed the WTF to secure the property and before long the AFGA was working on additional properties on the landscape. In total, the AFGA WTF now owns or has secured some 844 acres in the Wabamun area.

Fenson also reports, "The AFGA Wildlife Trust Fund has been extremely successful due to its strong conservation partners.

The provincially based program has always worked closely with affiliated clubs and zones to secure critical habitats throughout Alberta. However, we have also formed strong partnerships with other conservation groups and Ducks Unlimited Canada (DUC) has been one of our strongest allies to date."

As of 2007, the WTF had 26,930.98 acres under management for habitat values to help ensure a healthy future for Alberta's natural resources, amounting to 72 different properties throughout the province. Fenson reported that the AFGA managed to acquire the following four new properties in 2006, comprised of 656.5 acres.

• **The Faust Property** - a unique 14.5-acre parcel of land located on the south shore of Lesser Slave Lake, where a critical heron rookery that supports a large breeding colony of great blue herons was located. The WTF and the Alberta Conservation Association (ACA) purchased the land. The WTF also acquired a donation for this purchase through the Sawridge Inn and Conference Centre in the town of Slave Lake.

Ray Makowecki, the AFGA president from 2003-05, at Wabamun Whitewood Conservation Properties opening ceremony at East Pit Lake, May 2004.

• **The Vilna Property** - acquired in 2006 - a 160-acre parcel of native aspen parkland located east of Smoky Lake on Highway #28. This project was developed through a referral from the Vilna club and was purchased by the WTF with funding from the zone in northeastern Alberta, and the Vilna, Beaver River, Sherwood Park, Fort Saskatchewan, Innisfail, Lloydminster, Spedden Fish and Game associations, as well as the Vegreville Wildlife Federation. Fenson advised that these clubs and the zone rallied behind this project to get it done in a relatively short period of time.

• **The Buffalo Meadows Property** - a 160-acre parcel of native parkland and tame pasture purchased in partnership with the Alberta Conservation Association (ACA), DUC and the AFGA. The Rocky Mountain House, Dickson and Millet clubs contributed funds to allow the WTF to work as a valued partner on this acquisition. The Buffalo Meadows Property is adjacent to the Buffalo Lake Moraine Conservation Area and several other conservation properties managed by other organizations. The protected landscape will help ensure that the native parkland in central Alberta will continue to support the vast diversity of flora and fauna.

• **The Karpo Property** - a 320-acre parcel of Peace River area parkland located within the riparian corridor of the Smoky River. Fenson noted that the WTF was continuing to work on the possible acquisition of a 320-acre grazing lease that could be managed with the Karpo lands. DUC and ACA were partners in this purchase and additional funding came from the Canadian Wildlife Federation and Rocky Mountain Elk Foundation. The property supports a wide variety of wildlife.

Fenson advised that the WTF continued to be strongly supported by affiliated clubs and members of the AFGA. The provincial association delivers the Hide Collection Program and the Dream Hunt and quad raffles in order to help raise funds for WTF activities. He advised clubs that were not involved in the fundraising program that now was the time to consider being a part of the successful activities associated with the WTF. A complete listing of properties secured under the WTF up until 2006 is provided on the AFGA website and was also included in the 78th annual conference book for clubs and members as a reference guide.

Fenson noted that ongoing management of properties included the following activities: grazing leases, oil and gas development, fencing, access issues, livestock management, noxious weed control, property inspections, neighbouring landowner relations, volunteer stewards-liaison with other conservation groups, fundraising, education and information, referrals, and habitat assessment and evaluation.

Noteworthy is that some of the following WTF properties are legacy projects in honour of members of the AFGA:

• **The Potiuk Memorial Property** was originally purchased by the Brooks club, in partnership with Ducks Unlimited Canada and the Brooks Pheasant Festival. It is named in memory of Vern Potiuk, an active member from the Brooks club.

• **The Gordon Leslie Memorial Property** was willed to the AFGA by the late Mr. Leslie, an avid outdoorsman who lived in the parkland region. He grew up on the family farm near Marwayne where his parents had homesteaded. He was a member of the Marwayne club and loved to fish, hunt and trap. Gordon was familiar with the AFGA habitat programs and when the WTF was established he made plans to leave part of his estate to the program. The native parkland habitat on the family farm provided a lifetime of recreation, not to mention a livelihood. The AFGA found out about Mr. Leslie's estate planning when it received six quarter-sections of land from the Gordon Leslie Estate. The planning and progressive thinking arising from this estate will allow the wildlife and people of Alberta to perpetually benefit from the lands that Gordon and his family carefully managed for years. At the time, this was the single, largest donation ever received in the WTF. The AFGA gratefully acknowledged the Gordon Leslie Estate for the generous donation of land and the spirit in which it was openly given.

• **The Roy Ozanne Memorial Property** was dedicated in recognition of Mr. Ozanne as one of the founders of the WTF. The Alberta Conservation Association partnered with the AFGA in purchasing the 320-acre property.

• **The George and Joan Mitchell Memorial Property** (160 acres) was established to recognize the activities and commitment of this couple in the history of the AFGA, affiliated clubs, and with other members of the conservation community in Alberta. This property is located west of Pigeon Lake along Tide Creek, the major spawning tributary for walleye, northern pike and suckers in Pigeon Lake. Partners were the zone 3 AFGA clubs, Alberta Fish and Wildlife Division and Alberta Sport, Recreation, Parks and Wildlife.

COURTESY OF THE AFGA

Roy Ozanne Memorial Property.

Alex Kurash and the Gordon Leslie Six Quarter-Sections of Property Bequeathal

by Ray Makowecki, past president of the AFGA

Gordon Leslie was an avid outdoorsman who lived in the eastern parkland region of Alberta. He grew up on the family farm near Marwayne where his parents had homesteaded, and was a devoted outdoor enthusiast who loved to fish, hunt and trap and share the outdoors with friends and family.

Gordon became familiar with the AFGA's commitment to habitat programs and left a portion of his estate to the Wildlife Trust Fund. The family farm, made up of native parkland habitat, consisting of trees, shrubs, indigenous and tame grasslands, provided both a livelihood and a lifetime of recreation for him and his family. He became most familiar with the work of the AFGA through Alex Kurash, a farmer, a community member, an AFGA member, and a former president of the Clandonald AFGA club. Alex was full of energy and ideas and one of his passions was pheasants and the conservation of wildlife habitat. Alex's enthusiasm inspired others in the community, including Gordon Leslie. As the regional director for the northeast region of Alberta, I was impressed with the dedication of Alex and the support from his wife Louise and his father-in-law Emil (Pooch) Leroux, who was an active member of the St. Paul AFGA club.

Alex died much too young on March 15, 1990. He was at the microphone at the Edmonton Inn on March 3, 1990, speaking to a walleye fish resolution, when he had to sit down because of a sudden headache, probably caused by a brain aneurysm that was not diagnosed until after his death. It is important to note that his enthusiasm and hard work inspired Gordon Leslie to provide such a gift to the AFGA.

This was the single largest land donation ever received in the history of the Wildlife Trust Fund. Therefore, the AFGA recognized the Gordon Leslie estate for the generous donation of land and the spirit in which it was

ALEX KURASH

openly given. On behalf of all Albertans, the AFGA is grateful for Mr. Leslie's stewardship, planning and vision to ensure that the land values will remain as a lasting legacy. The AFGA will also be forever grateful to the dedicated volunteers and enthusiasm in which they inspire others. To Mr. Alex Kurash, I say thank you on behalf of all Albertans who will be able to share in the use of these lands forever.

OPERATION GRASSLAND COMMUNITY

It is one thing to preach about conserving fish, wildlife and their habitats but it is quite another to actually put boots on the ground and do something about it. Like the Wildlife Trust Fund and the Parkland Stewardship program, Operation Grassland Community (OGC) is an AFGA conservation program that puts the preaching to work in the grasslands of southeast Alberta.

Developed in 1989, Operation Grassland Community was first known as Operation Burrowing Owl, a program to protect the endangered burrowing owl on the prairie. It was renamed Operation Grassland Community to reflect the broader need to conserve native habitats for all wildlife, especially species at risk. OGC is a grassroots stewardship program that works directly with landholders in Alberta to secure and enhance prairie wildlife habitats for species at risk. OGC operates on the premise that prairie habitats can be wisely used, ensuring the sustainability of both wildlife habitats and agricultural livelihoods.

The grassland region of Alberta is among the most intensively developed landscapes in the world. Over the past century, human land uses have caused the loss and degradation of more than 75 percent of native mixed grass prairie. Not surprisingly, 24 of the 31 (77 percent) species at risk in Alberta rely on grassland habitats. Because over 95 percent of the land base in the prairie region is

COURTESY OF THE AFGA

Zone 4, Ray and Perry Ambrose Property.

privately owned or managed for agricultural use, landowners are crucial to developing sustainable land-use practices that provide long-term protection for species at risk, while at the same time ensuring a sustainable livelihood from agriculture. Such land management will also prevent the decline of game and other non-game wildlife. Operation Grassland Community works with

COURTESY OF DON MEREDITH

Operation Grassland Community's Lindsay Tomyn at a burrowing owl nest.

Burrowing owl.

landowners and managers to build the foundation for a sustainable prairie landscape through direct landholder contacts, voluntary land stewardship agreements, environmental on-farm planning and range management workshops.

As of 2007, OGC has more than 340 members who steward land throughout the grassland region of Alberta. Each year, OGC seeks new members who have species at risk located on their lands or have significant parcels of native prairie habitats. Each new member signs a voluntary stewardship agreement to protect these species at risk and native prairie habitats. Membership is voluntary and strictly confidential—no information about a member's land is shared with third parties without express permission from that landholder. Members also retain all rights to their land and how to use their land. Membership is renewed every five years, ensuring members are kept abreast of the habitat needs on their land, and renew their commitment to protect such habitat.

Knowledge Exchange

The members of Operation Grassland Community are a diverse and passionate group of land stewards who have provided OGC with unique insights and knowledge on balanced approaches to protecting and enhancing prairie habitats. This knowledge has enabled OGC to produce socially and economically balanced fact sheets, natural resource inventories and management plans for species at risk. Using this knowledge-building as a base, OGC

has been able to work closely with several members to implement larger habitat-enhancement projects.

Operation Grassland Community produces a semi-annual newsletter, *Prairie Acres*, presenting articles about species, habitat and land management. The *OGC Conservation Toolbox* is a series of fact sheets on topics ranging from badgers and ground squirrels to beneficial management practices for species at risk, and impacts of oil and gas development. The following is a list of fact sheets available from OGC in 2007, either in print form or from the OGC website in portable document format (pdf): Badgers, Burrowing Owls Nesting in Your Cropland?, Best Management Practices for Grassland Birds, Chamomile, Conservation Easements, Knapweeds, Leafy Spurge, On-Farm Conservation Planning, The Prairie Gopher, Not All Grasshoppers are Pests, Oil and Gas Development, The Species at Risk Act, Thistle, Wheatgrass.

Natural Resource Inventories

This comprehensive habitat inventory is designed to assist landholder members in recognizing significant natural resources on their land, as well as key habitat features. Natural resource inventories provide significant background information to assess habitat quality, potential risks of further habitat degradation and establish conservation goals for possible habitat improvement.

Management Plans for Species at Risk

Operation Grassland Community works with the landholder to develop a management strategy for the habitat of a particular species. Management plans are developed to create awareness about the status of the particular species, its biology and habitat requirements, and to provide detailed recommendations for managing that habitat.

Public Presentations

Operation Grassland Community reaches out to community groups, industry and schools through public presentations throughout southern Alberta. As well, OGC partners with the Science Alberta Foundation to distribute the education crate: "Burrowing Owls and Cows," which includes instructional materials about how the burrowing owl can co-exist with agriculture. As part of the important work done by the Science Alberta Foundation, this crate is lent to schools and youth groups across the prairie region.

Operation Grassland Community is a good example of how people who are interested in protecting and developing habitat for species at risk and other wildlife can work together with landowners and managers on the ground to steward the land in a mutually beneficial way. Such a program points the way to how conservation should be done for the benefit of us all.

PARKLAND STEWARDSHIP PROGRAM

Land stewardship is key to maintaining fish and wildlife habitat. Like Operation Grassland Community in the Alberta prairie, the Parkland Stewardship Program promotes good land stewardship in the parkland of the province, the transition zone between prairie and forest.

The Parkland Stewardship Program is designed to ensure both the conservation and enhancement of native parkland habitat within the intensely managed landscapes of central Alberta. It is a grassroots program that works directly with landholders to secure and enhance wildlife habitats on their lands. The program uses a strategic approach to identify locally significant habitats and evaluate the risk of future habitat loss both at the farm and in the municipality. It provides educational and on-farm services to help its members understand how they can protect habitat within working landscapes. Participation is voluntary, and there is no fee. Members receive free on-farm planning support, and may be eligible for additional financial assistance with specific farm or habitat conservation projects. All members receive a gate sign and wall plaque recognizing their important contribution to wildlife conservation in Alberta.

COURTESY OF YVONNE KELLER

Wild chives.

Community Based Stewardship

By working co-operatively with individuals, community groups, and local municipalities, the Parkland Stewardship Program provides the framework for making informed land-use decisions. Whether members are interested in learning more about ways to include wildlife habitat on their farms or would like to see their communities come together to clean up a local stream or wetland, the Parkland Stewardship Program has a variety of important resources to offer.

Project Planning

The Parkland Stewardship Program is involved in conservation planning on many levels: provincial, municipal and local farm planning. On the provincial level, the Parkland Stewardship Program is involved in conservation initiatives such as Alberta Water Quality Awareness (AWQA) Day (www.awqa.ca). This is a province-wide, community-based water-monitoring program that allows participants to gather water quality data in their area and compare it to data gathered in other parts of the province. This education tool gives a "snapshot" of water quality in the province every year.

On the municipal level, the Parkland Stewardship Program is involved in such projects as the Beaver Hills Initiative (www.beaverhills.ab.ca), a partnership between several counties, provincial and federal governments, as well as a number of non-government conservation organizations. The award-winning Beaver Hills Initiative promotes environmentally, socially and economically sustainable development and land use within the Beaver Hills, just east of Edmonton.

On the farm, the Parkland Stewardship Program helps its members with planning and provides technical resources to turn plans into practice. These services can increase the ecological value of a member's land. By taking part, a member demonstrates due diligence in addressing environmental issues on the farm. Services available to members include:

- An aerial photo of the member's land to help link the farm with other environmental values in his or her community.
- A natural resource inventory of the habitats and wildlife species on their land.
- Farm WaterWatch tools for monitoring surface water quality in farm runoff, streams, and wetlands.
- A custom-prepared Farm Conservation Plan for improving fish and wildlife habitats on the farm.
- Farm-specific development of environmental Best Management Practices.

Natural Resource Inventory

A natural resource inventory is conducted on a member's farm to identify habitat or community types, understand how plant and wildlife species interact and develop lists of plant and wildlife species unique to the farm. This comprehensive habitat inventory assists the landholder in recognizing significant natural resources on his or her land, as well as key habitat features. Upon completion, the member has significant background information to assess habitat quality, potential risks of further habitat degradation and establish conservation goals for possible habitat improvement.

COURTESY OF ALBERTA CONSERVATION ASSOCIATION

Buck for Wildlife was a program started by the AFGA.

Best Management Practices

Best Management Practices (BMP) are a set of guidelines a producer can use to mitigate the environmental impact of his or her operation. Agricultural best management practices may include: nutrient (manure and fertilizer) management, integrated pest management, erosion control, pasture management, conservation tillage, and riparian area conservation. Producers evaluate which BMP would be most valuable on their farm, based on their environmental, social, and economic goals. The Parkland Stewardship Program helps producers develop BMPs for their farms, tailored to their individual needs.

Farm WaterWatch

The Farm WaterWatch program was developed by the AFGA in response to producers' questions about their impact on surface water quality. The program emphasizes a farm-specific approach that gives landowners the tools and support they need to go from awareness of water quality issues to the planning of best management practices specific to their farm.

Program participants have the opportunity to gather information on how their agricultural activities may be affecting surface water quality. The on-farm service provides a confidential and practical way for producers to collect and analyze surface water runoff from individual fields and pastures, or monitor the changes in water quality within a creek on their lands. Participants will have the opportunity to analyze samples from a number of sites on their land during several runoff events.

Participants develop a watershed map and runoff supply model of their farm. On farm consultation is provided to assist the producer in identifying potential risks to surface water quality, and planning best management practices which would improve riparian habitat or mitigate impacts on water quality. The program can also play an important role in developing an environmental risk management strategy.

The Parkland Stewardship Program is another example of how conservationists and landholders have come together to steward the land for the benefit of all.

COURTESY OF DUANE RADFORD

Jack Shaver, past president 1985-86 at the Antelope Creek Ranch opening ceremony in October 1986.

COURTESY OF DUANE RADFORD

Don Sparrow, Minister of Sustainable Resource Development, 1978-87 at the Antelope Creek Ranch opening ceremony in October 1986.

ANTELOPE CREEK RANCH
by Duane Radford, as the official Alberta Fish and Game Association representative on the Antelope Creek Ranch Management Committee

The Antelope Creek Ranch (ACR) is located several miles west of Brooks and is managed co-operatively in partnership with the AFGA, Ducks Unlimited Canada (DUC), Alberta Sustainable Resource Development–Fish and Wildlife Division and Wildlife Habitat Canada (WHC). While not an official partner, Alberta's Public Lands Division also plays a major role in ranch operations and range research.

The ACR celebrated its 20th anniversary in 2006, testament to a success story that it is possible for ranching, oil and gas operations and wildlife to co-exist on the same property. The ranch is managed for livestock and wildlife amid long-standing EnCana Corporation (formerly Pan Canadian Energy Corporation), and relatively new Pengrowth Energy Trust (formerly Murphy Oil), oil and gas operations, a work-in-progress to promote the wise use of native mixed grass prairie in southern Alberta, and elsewhere in western Canada. Crested wheatgrass, irrigated pasture and native rangeland are all incorporated into a complimentary, deferred-rotation grazing system to achieve overall ACR management goals and objectives.

The year 2005 marked a watershed in ranch operations and saw the following key changes:

1. Management Committee Membership
- Ron Bjorge (then southeast regional head of the Alberta Fish and Wildlife Division and currently wildlife director) replaced Ken Crutchfield as chairperson of the management committee
- Duane Radford replaced Gerry Pittman as the AFGA representative
- Dave Kay replaced Morgan Stromsmoe as the DUC representative
- Lynn McIntyre became the WHC representative replacing the late Nestor Romaniuk
- Andy von Busse remained as the ACR finance chair, and sits as an ex-officio member of the ACR management committee

Entrance signage at the Antelope Creek Ranch.

2. Technical Committee Membership
- Joel Nicholson (Medicine Hat Fish and Wildlife Division non-game biologist) replaced Lorne Fitch as the chairperson of the technical committee
- Gerry Pittman became the AFGA representative replacing Dave Scobie
- Morgan Stromsmoe became the DUC representative

3. Ranch Managers
- Neal Wilson and Shannon Burnard became the new ranch managers, replacing Bob Kaufman, on Nov. 1, 2005.

Research related to crested wheat field production and utilization, irrigated flood/pivot field production and native range has been ongoing since the purchase date. In 2004, overall "range health" was measured for the first time, however, and clearly demonstrated that the new rotational grazing system has benefited both cattle and wildlife.

The 5,500-acre property, formerly part of the Ward Ranch, was purchased through a partnership including the Alberta Fish and Wildlife Division, AFGA, WHC and DUC in 1986 under a 25-year, joint miscellaneous lease. Ranch operations are subject to an official management agreement that expires in 2015 which is subject to amendment in 2010. Officially, the joint miscellaneous lease was

Jack Shaver (L), Elmer Kure and Stu Morrison at the Antelope Creek Ranch opening ceremony in October 1986.

issued to AFGA. Upon termination of this lease, the provincial government is required to issue a new lease, consistent with the intent respecting the overall objectives of the original lease.

All revenues received from ranch operations by the lessee (AFGA) are to be held in trust and are not to be disposed of except in accordance with the original management agreement. These revenues are to be held in a separate account called the Antelope Creek Trust Account. The lease is subject to agreements with then-Pan Canadian Energy Corporation (currently EnCana Corporation) oil and gas interests in place at the time of the contract signing date, Feb. 4, 1986.

The acid test of the aforementioned management agreement will hinge on whether sufficient revenues are on-hand at the termination of the lease to perpetuate current ranch operations. In 2006, approximately $650,000 was in a trust account as low-interest money-market investments that have a small financial risk. Subject to an investment policy that was developed and approved by the ACR board of directors, these funds, along with any future identified surpluses, have been invested with a professional investment advisor to enable the Antelope Creek Trust Account to reach as high a return as feasible, and still stay within conservative guidelines of the investment policy. The investment policy is subject to an annual review by the board of directors.

Annually, the approximate revenue line is $175,000 with a budget of $125,000 for ranch operations. It has been estimated that roughly $3 million will be required to sustain operations when the lease expires, in the context of present-day ranch operations. There are draft guidelines for funding projects in support of wildlife habitat conservation from the Antelope Creek Trust Fund; appropriations subject to these guidelines are being held in abeyance pending completion of a long-term financial plan, which is contingent on completion of a strategic plan for the ranch, currently in draft form. While some oil and gas revenues have been previously disbursed for wildlife conservation purposes, at present the priority is to grow the trust account to ensure the long-term sustainability of the ranch. Financial statements are subject to an annual, independent audit.

The official sod-turning ceremony for the ACR occurred on Oct. 4, 1986. Jack Shaver represented the AFGA at this ceremony, as president of the AFGA. The late Mr. Shaver deserves much of the credit for orchestrating the purchase of the ranch.

A management plan for the ranch was developed in 1987 to ensure that livestock operations, in particular, would continue as part of the ranch business plan to demonstrate multiple and compatible land-use principles. Key management objectives for the ACR are listed below:
- Protect, enhance and develop key wildlife habitat for upland birds, waterfowl and non-game species.
- Manage livestock grazing to benefit both wildlife and livestock, in order to demonstrate the benefits of complimentary grazing systems and gain community support for overall management objectives through integrated land use.
- Integrate petroleum and natural gas activity with wildlife habitat, recreation and grazing components.

Antelope Creek Ranch management committee tour in June 2006. Dave Kay (L), Ron Bjorge, Gerry Pittman, Martin Sharren, Neal Wilson, Joel Nicholson and Andy von Busse.

- Provide primarily non-mechanized recreational opportunities.
- Provide education and research opportunities.
- To use all the "assets" of the property to the highest and best use and to ensure self-sufficiency.

In 1989, government legislation, subject to the *Wildlife Act*, was used to establish what is termed the Antelope Creek Habitat Development Area to regulate public access and activities on the ranch. Regulated access on the ACR benefits local wildlife such as white-tailed deer, antelope, foxes, coyotes, upland birds and waterfowl.

Initially, the ranch was managed by the technical committee under the direction of the management committee with members of both groups coming from the partners who were party to the original purchase agreement. Management by committee was seen as a non-starter, in the long run, and the founding members realized that eventually this would have to change to include a ranch manager who would live on the ranch. Many people have represented the member organizations on the management committee and the technical committee.

Management Committee:

Fish and Wildlife Division (chairperson) – Ken Ambrock, Gerald (Gerry) Thompson, Fred Moffat, Ken Crutchfield, Ron Bjorge
AFGA – Niels Damgaard, Jack Shaver, Horst Fauser, Gerry Pittman, Duane Radford
Ducks Unlimited Canada – Gordon Edwards, Jay Bartsch, Morgan Stromsmoe, David Kay
Wildlife Habitat Canada – Elmer Kure, Nestor Romaniuk, Lynn McIntyre, Doug Stewart
Finance Chair (all from the AFGA) – Gordon Peel, Frank Lee, Andy von Busse

Antelope Creek Ranch management committee tour in June 2006.

Technical Committee:

Fish and Wildlife Division (chairperson) – Lorne Fitch, Joel Nicholson
AFGA – Gordon Peel, Frank Lee, Rick Martin, Dave Scobie, Gerry Pittman
Ducks Unlimited Canada - Bob Kaufman, Ed Houck, Morgan Stromsmoe, Stacey Wabick
Public Lands Division – Barry Adams

Bob Kaufman was hired as the first ranch manager in 1994 to oversee the management objectives for the ACR and provide day-to-day continuity of all on-ranch operations. He resigned in 2005 to pursue other interests and was replaced by Neal Wilson and his wife Shannon Burnard. In co-operation with members of the technical committee, Mr. Kaufman was responsible for setting livestock-carrying capacity, developing an annual grazing schedule, coordinating livestock entry and exit dates, roundups, weighing -movements and salting. He was the go-to person for local authorities, such as livestock patrons, the Eastern Irrigation District and grazing associations. He maintained and operated pivots and the irrigation water delivery system, flood irrigation cells for integrated use by livestock and wildlife. He took care of soil testing and fertilizer application of irrigated fields to maximize forage production. Extension services also fell under his purview; he was the front-line contact with the oil and gas industry respecting their operations on the ranch. He was also responsible for maintenance of shelterbelts for wildlife and operation of wetland basins to benefit wildlife – primarily waterfowl.

The 2004 Antelope Creek Ranch annual report paints a positive picture of range health in the four native pastures, as well as in a control field and "…demonstrates that range improvement through specialized grazing systems benefits both livestock and wildlife." The number of cow/calf pairs pastured on the ranch was 260 in 2004. The native fields are grazed in a complimentary, deferred rotational system, with certain pastures left idle; grass production tends to increase or decrease depending on annual precipitation. An ungrazed enclosure traditionally has the highest amount of litter while a control field – grazed continually – has the lowest levels. Litter has increased in the native pastures under the deferred rotation grazing, which benefits the native prairie grasses. All the forage indicators were rated as being satisfactory. However, the footprint of the oil and gas industry on the ranch is huge: at least 10 percent of the surface area of the ACR has been impacted by this industry since 1985. These disturbances take the form of pipelines, battery stations, roads and well sites. There has been ongoing reclamation activity of various disturbances but much remains to be done.

COURTESY OF YVONNE KELLER

Canada geese and goslings.

While the ACR is a success story, there are some nagging concerns: will it be able to stand on its own two feet when oil and gas revenues expire, with enough money in the bank for it to remain viable? Only time will tell, since a new ACR Habitat Development Area Investment Policy was approved by the management committee in 2005 in support of this goal. An objective of the management committee is to contribute approximately $50,000 in revenue annually towards the ACR endowment fund; the intent is for the endowment fund to support ranch operations in 2016, when oil and gas revenues are expected to decline.

The ACR is the flagship of all AFGA habitat properties and is unique in that it is the only one that is used on an ongoing basis for educational purposes. The ranch represents the first major venture of the AFGA as a partner in wildlife habitat management and protection in Alberta's native prairies. It has been used extensively to educate the public about prairie conservation values associated with good range management. Some of the revenues from ranch operations have been used to purchase wildlife habitat for the AFGA which has been a voice for conservation since it was founded in 1908, as a secondary benefit.

Ranch Location:

Go west from Brooks along Secondary Highway 542 (Cassils Road) and cross Highway 36, continuing west on the paved road until you reach a T-intersection. Turn left across the railway tracks and proceed south on a gravel road for one kilometre, then turn right onto another gravel road, driving west approximately five kilometres to the ranch entrance. Visitors are always welcome but are encouraged to stay on trails and park in designated areas.

Oil and Gas Operations:

Pan Canadian Energy Corporation changed its name to EnCana Corporation following a merger with the Alberta Energy Corporation in 2002. Their head office is in Calgary and they have a field office in Brooks, responsible for their play on the ACR. Approximately 600 acres of the ranch has been disturbed by oil and gas operations during the past 10 years—which represents about 10 percent of the area of the property—consequently landscape fragmentation and cumulative impacts on native range are an issue. These disturbed lands are a liability and it is incumbent on EnCana Corporation to satisfactorily reclaim them. More recently, Pengrowth Energy Trust has also developed both oil and gas plays on the ACR.

Prairie sunrise.

Antelope Creek Ranch Technical Committee, Brooks:

The principle is, if it works on the Antelope Creek Ranch, why not everywhere else as well? The ranch is a 5,500-acre working concern in the dry, mixed-grass prairie west of Brooks. Managed by the technical committee—comprised of members from Alberta Sustainable Resources Development, Ducks Unlimited Canada, and the Alberta Fish and Game Association—it looks for ways to integrate often competing land-uses to maintain landscape health, biodiversity and economic use. It applies sound land management practices that demonstrate the benefits of diverse land-use integration, and then communicates its findings to wider audiences: landowners, livestock producers, industry, conservationists, academia and

government. The ranch also hosts annual field days, provides applied research opportunities and training to post-secondary students, and gives presentations to a wide range of interested groups.

LANDOWNER RECOGNITION HABITAT PROGRAM

With Alberta's land base being almost 30 percent privately owned, the AFGA realizes the importance of retaining wildlife habitat on private land. In August 1985, the association initiated two landowner recognition habitat programs to assist local fish and game clubs throughout the province in recognizing landowners for retaining habitat.

The programs, entitled "Habitat Steward" and "Heritage Farmstead," were developed to recognize landowners who have a life-long interest in preserving wildlife habitat and who also carry out responsible land-management practices.

Local fish and game clubs throughout the province have the opportunity to thank these important stewards of the land and, by doing so, educate other landowners of the need and encourage them to maintain wildlife habitat on their land.

The two programs were initially funded from the association's Conservation Lottery. However, with the discontinuation of the lottery in 1987, other funding sources have been sought.

The Alberta Conservation Association, the Alberta Sports, Recreation, Parks and Wildlife Foundation and the Buck for Wildlife program have all contributed to the successful continuation of the two programs.

COURTESY OF LILLA PFERSCHY

A nest in a barren birch tree.

COURTESY OF TRAVEL ALBERTA

The intense gaze of a snowy owl.

The following outlines the program's accomplishments since their inception back in August 1985. In total, the Habitat Steward and Heritage Farmstead Programs encompass in excess of 400 landowners and 85,000 habitat acres. This includes more than 178 kilometres of riparian habitat. Landowners participating in these two programs own more than 203,293 acres of land across Alberta.

Habitat Steward Program: Approximately 400 volunteer stewards have participated in the program, encompassing more than 85,000 acres of various habitat types.

Heritage Farmstead Program: More than 50 farmsteads, involving approximately 450 acres of habitat, are presently part of the program.

Signing Up

The Habitat chairperson or competent member of the local fish and game club is required to complete the application forms for the Habitat Steward Program or the Heritage Farmstead Program.

Include as much information about the lands as possible, as opportunity may also exist for doing habitat-enhancement projects or with the association's Wildlife Trust Fund. A rough sketch of the site (on the reverse side of the application form) will assist habitat staff in evaluating the application.

The co-ordinator will review all applications. He will contact the local club, do a field inspection if possible, and in many cases, receive aerial photographs to learn more about the existing habitat type.

Applications approved through the Habitat Steward program will receive an 18" x 24" yard sign, along with a wall plaque. The landowner's name will appear on the sign and plaque.

Approved applications for the Heritage Farmstead program will also receive an 18" x 24" yard sign to be installed at the abandoned farmstead site. The current landowner's name, as well as the pioneering family's name, will appear on the yard sign.

There is no binding contract with the landowner involving these programs. If the habitat is destroyed or seriously altered in any way, we ask that the landowner return the yard sign to the AFGA. There is no financial compensation offered to the landowner for being involved in these programs.

For more information, contact the AFGA at www.afga.org.

COURTESY OF DUANE RADFORD

Down the Whaleback Ridge road.

The Edmonton Riverboat Queen on the North Saskatchewan River.

Chapter Seven

AFGA Edmonton Office

An organization the size of the AFGA cannot function without strong headquarters office and staff. In 2007 the AFGA head office was located in a two-storey office building at 6924 104 St. in Edmonton. Head office administrative staff consisted of Yvonne Baxter (secretary receptionist), Lee Bell (controller), Sandie Buwalda (communications co-ordinator), Brad Fenson (habitat co-ordinator), Laurie Kerestes (membership and data entry co-ordinator), Kerry Grisley (operations grassland community co-manager) and Martin Sharren (executive vice president). The purpose of this chapter is to describe the nature of the head office administrative staff who generally work behind the scenes on behalf the membership. Additional staff worked outside of head office: François Blouin (Operation Grassland community co-manager), T.J. Schwanky (habitat facilitator) and Tim Schowalter (Operation Grassland community stewardship co-ordinator).

Sharren has been a resident of St. Albert for 23 years, and prior to that lived mostly in the Edmonton area. He worked as the executive vice president for just over six years in 2007. This position is accountable for all the AFGA paid staff and reports to the AFGA president. Basically, Sharren sees his job as a consultant in the organization, to make suggestions and recommendations. The AFGA executive creates a business plan, based on the strategic direction of the organization, with input from the members, clubs and zones. "It's a grassroots approach," said Sharren in an interview. "A three-year work plan is established based on the wishes of the membership as a whole that focuses on the association's mission; the staff also have some input into this plan." Once the business plan has been approved—it is subject to change and revision once a year—it's handed off to Sharren and it is up to him to make sure the various objectives are achieved.

"With any non-profit organization, especially one that is of a special-interest nature, such as the AFGA which has approximately 15,000 members, there are a lot of divergent opinions," Sharren noted. Although the organization has set policies formulated by its members, not everybody necessarily agrees with them, and he said it's a challenge to "keep the boat going in the right direction." He said another challenge is to make sure there is an adequate budget to keep the AFGA financially solvent. It's a special-interest organization so it's always a challenge to find new sources of money in a highly competitive marketplace.

The AFGA is a volunteer organization and is heavily dependent on its volunteers to carry out its objectives. During the hot Alberta economy of 2007 many of the volunteers were so busy with their day jobs they had special challenges assisting the AFGA. Sharren has seen financial stability come to the organization since he started working for the AFGA, and he has seen growth in some of their programs, as well as some growth in membership. When he started working for the AFGA there were some rather bleak prognostications, to the point where some people were saying that come March 2002 the doors were going to close because they were running out of money. The AFGA executive has taken on more of a governance style in recent years, as opposed to a hands-on management approach.

COURTESY OF DUANE RADFORD

The AFGA head office staff: Martin Sharren, Sandie Buwalda, Yvonne Baxter and Lee Bell.

In terms of the budget process, Sharren reviews the financial situation each October—in conjunction with the finance chair —relative to progress related to their business plan goals and objectives. Some fine-tuning of the proposed budget takes place at that point prior to a final budget being approved by the executive at a January meeting to take forward to the annual general meeting, at which point the membership votes on it.

Sharren meets with the AFGA president on an as-needed basis but he does most business with the president by email or telephone. The AFGA executive meets five times a year, quarterly, with the exception of January/February, when they have the annual conference. The AFGA executive vice president is ultimately responsible for all paid staff. Sharren says his attitude is: "Get good people, put them in their place, and let them do their job. Don't micromanage them."

He says that one of the strengths of the AFGA is that it takes a big-picture approach and he feels that a holistic approach is the best way to address conservation issues, rather than taking a fragmented, single-species approach. He feels there's a good reason that the AFGA has been in existence for the past 100 years and that it's necessary to be a voice of reason in striking a balance with conservation and resource development. He sees the AFGA as being the best organization to provide a connection between people and Alberta's land and resources in Alberta's future.

COURTESY OF DUANE RADFORD

The AFGA executive vice president Martin Sharren in his office.

As secretary receptionist, Yvonne Baxter is the face of the AFGA for many members and the general public in the head office. She was born in Estevan, Saskatchewan, but grew up in southwest Manitoba, moving to Edmonton in 1979. She started working for the AFGA in 2005. She works the front counter where licences, hunting-draw applications, magazines, books and merchandise (prints, clothing, map books) are sold. She handles incoming posted mail and club mailouts. She also handles incoming emails and refers them to proper authorities, as well as photocopying, drafting letters, filing, co-ordinating of raffle ticket sales/sellers, conference registrations, and various duties related to the annual Wildlife Awards Banquet and more.

COURTESY OF DUANE RADFORD

Receptionist Yvonne Baxter at the AFGA head office mail slots.

The AFGA office has a large photocopier, postage machine, fax machine, flatscreen scanners, computers, printers, cash register, credit card and draw application licence machines.

Keeping up with the current issues is one of Baxter's greatest challenges and learning about all the different facets that the

AFGA must address. "I really enjoy working here. I enjoy the people. I enjoy the variety of work and the direction that AFGA is going, and I agree with their concerns about wildlife. It's been a really good job for me," said Baxter in an interview.

Laurie Kerestes is responsible for memberships and data entry records. She was born in Edmonton, grew up in Sangudo, a small town 80 miles northwest of Edmonton, and currently resides in Leduc. She started working for the AFGA as a receptionist in 2001 and took over as membership co-ordinator shortly thereafter. She grew up with a family background of avid hunters and anglers and married into the same kind of family, consequently the business of the AFGA is close to her heart. Having this kind of background and hands-on experience helps her better understand the challenges facing the organization. Kerestes says it's important for the clubs to submit their membership lists to head office as soon as possible and get them into the data system so that the members receive the *Outdoor Edge* magazine right away as a benefit of their membership in the organization. She said, "This way the members are aware of the issues that the AFGA speaks about on their behalf to government officials and also for the members to read the reports about issues from each member of the executive."

Another challenge is record keeping, due to steady growth in membership over the past couple of years. She noted the passion of new executive members and advises "...they will fight tooth and nail to speak for the members within the province," but expressed concerns about the decline in volunteers. "Resolutions that are brought forth by these clubs that speak for the individual hunter or fisherman wouldn't be there if not for the volunteers of each club." She spoke highly of the many wonderful people she has met at the head office and conferences during the past several years and the enjoyment of working with a great head-office team.

Sandie Buwalda has moved through the head office ranks from secretary receptionist to communications co-ordinator. She was born and raised in Calgary and has been a resident of Edmonton since 1999. She started working for the AFGA in 2002. Her primary communications activities involve maintenance of the AFGA website, planning for the annual conference and co-ordinating input for the bimonthly newsletters in the *Outdoor Edge* magazine. Once the executive reports are sent in for the *Outdoor Edge* newsletter, Buwalda works with the publisher on the newsletter layout to ensure it conforms to editorial standard. The AFGA president reviews the finished product before it is sent to the publisher for publication. This magazine is also used for advertising the AFGA Dream Hunt and quad raffles, arranged through her office, although Sharren also handles some ads.

She sees the new website as one of the most important communication tools to keep the members informed about ongoing activities and any changes in the organization. "Keeping the website up to date, and making it current, using it… that's a form of communications that's just going to really move forward," she said.

Sandie Buwalda also prepares the annual conference guidebook, another key communication vehicle. She said, "I really like what AFGA stands for – conservation and education. It's important for us to have a voice on so many issues that we've taken on. There are so many passionate people in the organization and I really enjoy working with the volunteers." She also sends out news releases by email and through club mailouts.

Financial accounts are handled by the controller, Lee Bell, who was born in Campbellford, Ontario, but grew up near Toronto before moving to Alberta and taking up residence in Sherwood Park. Bell began working for the AFGA in 2004. He is responsible for all financial matters in relation to accounts receivable, bank deposits, payroll, writing cheques – he's a one-person financial officer. He also prepares all financial reports and works with an auditor to ensure they conform to accounting practices in time for the annual general meeting (i.e. the annual conference). The AFGA is a charity and not-for-profit-organization.

Bell says the donors must have faith and trust in the accounting system and the AFGA is obligated to conform to granting procedures. "I've found it a great delight to work for the organization," said Bell, "and I've enjoyed it right from the beginning." One of his greatest challenges is the fund accounting system in the AFGA: Wildlife Trust Fund, Operations Grassland,

Antelope Creek Ranch, Parkland Stewardship, which all have to be kept separate but are under the umbrella of the AFGA. "It's a lot of detail to look after, but I'm a bit of a detail person and I enjoy that challenge."

Bell feels that the AFGA is getting busier by the year, doing more and covering more and more bases. The fiscal year of the AFGA has been Jan. 1 to Dec. 31, but will change in 2007 to Oct. 1 to Sept. 30 if approved by government to facilitate financial reporting in time for the annual general meeting in February in the future.

The charitable status means that the AFGA does not pay property taxes on its building but is subject to a local improvement levy spread out over 20 years. The organization does not pay tax on revenue because it is a charity and is refunded 50 percent of the federal Goods and Services Tax. The AFGA can also issue income-tax receipts to donors as a not-for-profit charity, for financial gifts or gifts in kind. "Conservation is more in the minds of people than it ever has been in the past…and I think that the AFGA has a bright future," Bell concluded in an interview.

COURTESY OF DUANE RADFORD

Controller Lee Bell at the AFGA head office.

COURTESY OF DUANE RADFORD

Communications co-ordinator Sandie Buwalda at the AFGA head office.

COURTESY OF DUANE RADFORD

Membership co-ordinator Laurie Kerestes at the AFGA head office.

Former AFGA Staff
by past president Vern McIntosh

The AFGA has been fortunate to have had a number of long-term managers and loyal, dedicated secretarial and habitat staff, directing day-to-day operations.

George M. (Marshall) Spargo was honoured for his 38 years service as secretary-manager at the 1962 annual convention of the AFGA, at which time he was awarded a life membership in the AFGA. The association had grown mightily according to 1961 president, Gordon J. Cummings— through Spargo's enthusiasm, his devotion and his wise guidance—until it had become the second largest in Canada in 1961. Spargo received the Fulton Trophy in 1957. His contribution to conservation had also been recognized by the Western Canada – Yukon Fish and Game Council and by Ducks Unlimited, both organizations having conferred Life Memberships on him. In his historian report to the 1968 AFGA conference Darwin Chronkhite referred to George Spargo as "Mr. Fish and Game." He was categorized by Neville R. Lindsay, Sr. of Edmonton, who worked long and hard for the Northern Alberta Fish and Game Protective Association, as being a very efficient person. There is a monument at the Raven Brood Trout Station, near Caroline, in commemoration of Mr. Spargo, the only such tribute in the history of the association bestowed upon one of its members. The inscription on the monument reads as follows:

GEORGE M. SPARGO
SECRETARY- MANAGER
ALBERTA FISH AND GAME ASSOCIATION
1925-1962
A PIONEER CONSERVATIONIST

Bruce Stewart was the manager from 1960-66. He was followed by Paul Morck who took over in 1968 until 1985. Paul was privileged to have had the assistance of Wendy McLeod from 1973-75, followed by Gwen Wahlstrom from 1975 to 1983. Paul described these ladies as absolutely wonderful people, capable of running things by themselves when he was absent from head office. Lorraine MacPherson took over from Gwen Wahlstrom in 1983.

Elmer Kure, past president of the AFGA from 1958-60 and Director of Environmental Government Public Relations from 1973-86 has deservedly been called Mr. Fish and Game for his long-standing service and commitment to the organization. Always the diplomat, Mr. Kure had a knack for making compromises and achieving win-win situations in the face of difficult and controversial decisions. He would be go down as one of the most consummate AFGA member in its first 100 years as an organization. Budd Traver, vice president at large in 1974, paid Kure a great tribute in his report to the 1975 conference, advising "Without a person like Elmer Kure in his capacity as Director of Environmental Public Relations, I would not be able to consider the presidency of this Association." After 38 years of service to the AFGA Mr. Kure retired in June 1986 as the Director of Environmental Public Relations. At the 50th anniversary conference of the AFGA in 1979 senior vice president Don Hayden reported: "Our advice and council is not only welcomed by many but eagerly sought after by some. When you have a man with the integrity and knowledge of an Elmer Kure in your organization this is easy to rationalize." In the 1992 annual AFGA conference report, Andy Boyd, long-time environment chair, characterized Mr. Kure by reporting: "His steadfast, patient, long-term work on our behalf is invaluable." He received a Distinguished Service Award in 1957, a life membership in 1971, and the Fulton Trophy in 1964 which is awarded to an individual who has made the most outstanding and unrewarded conservation contribution to the AFGA. Elmer Kure also served on the Board of Directors of Wildlife Habitat Canada.

Lyle Fullerton, a competent person with extremely good knowledge of wildlife, habitat and conservation issues served as the AFGA manager from 1986 to 1990. He is presently employed by the Fish and Wildlife Division, who are very fortunate to have him on staff. Our own Brad Fenson filled the management position temporarily when we were between permanent managers. His working knowledge of the AFGA served him well.

Ron Hauser was hired in 1991 and served until 2000. He lived "Fish & Game," putting in long hours and even full weeks for the AFGA. He was supported by Kim Foo who was with us from 1989 to 2000. Mary Crinkelton was yet another fine secretary who suffered a serious illness and passed away too young; Wendy Horning was an additional short term secretarial employee.

Colleen MacDougall was appointed as the chief executive officer/ executive vice president of the AFGA on June 15, 2000 replacing Ron Hauser and was employed by the AFGA for about one year, after which Martin Sharren took over her position.

Following conferences in bygone days, it had been a practice to take the office staff for a day's fishing with a meal of chili and goodies on the ice – a day they thoroughly enjoyed!

Of late, staff numbers have increased and conditions have changed to present day modern standards and practices. We will always require loyal and dedicated staff at the AFGA to carry out our conservation goals and objectives.

COURTESY OF JACK GRAHAM

Alberta Fish and Game Association staff and friends at Gull Lake: Jack Graham (L), Mary Crinkelton, Wendy Horning, Kim Foo and Graham van Tighem.

Dusk at Sylvan Lake.

Waterton River near Waterton Lakes National Park.

Chapter Eight

Other Conservation Organizations

Although the Alberta Fish and Game Association (AFGA) is the oldest and largest wildlife conservation organization in the province, much of the work it does would not be possible without the assistance, co-operation and partnership of many other organizations from within and outside the province. The following are brief histories of some of these organizations.

ALBERTA PROFESSIONAL OUTFITTERS SOCIETY

~

THE HISTORY OF OUTFITTING IN ALBERTA FROM THE 1880s to 2007

by Susan Feddema-Leonard and Bob Heyde,
president of the Alberta Professional Outfitters Society

The first six paragraphs of this chapter are taken directly from Susan Feddema-Leonard's recently published book entitled *People and Peaks of Willmore Wilderness Park, 1800s to mid-1990s* Willmore Wilderness Foundation & Whitefox Circle Inc. (2007) 456 pp.

Outfitting in Alberta is synonymous with the very fabric that built this great province. By 1880, the Canadian Pacific Railroad (CPR) was moving west towards Calgary and there was a need for experienced trail men and packers to move supplies to the survey camps. Originally, the CPR line went through Calgary, later Banff and Laggan-Lake Louise. The expansion of the railroad resulted in tourists wanting to travel deeper into the mountain wilderness. "Necessity is the mother of invention," and it wasn't long before a profession called outfitting was born in the Banff region of the Alberta Rockies. "The first outfitter who stands out in history is Tom Wilson who, in 1881, joined the survey of what is now the Stoney Indian Reserve near Banff. He quickly learned how to pack a horse and followed old Indian trails up the Bow Valley. Tom Wilson befriended a group of Stoney Indians. One young man by the name of 'Gold Seeker' guided Tom to a beautiful lake that became known as Lake Louise. Tom believed that he was the first white man to have ever seen the lake," (Hart, 1979).

In 1887 development of Lake Louise commenced and the CPR began advertising unlimited opportunities for hunting, fishing and mountain wilderness scenery. Tom Wilson officially began a new career that autumn in Banff. He guided a party on a 30-day hunting trip, which established the new profession of guiding and outfitting. By the late 1890s, Tom was a major outfitter employing men to outfit mountaineering groups, explorers and hunting parties. For example, men like Billy Warren, Jimmy Simpson, Bill Peyto, Fred Stevens and Jack Otto worked for Wilson learning the trade. Fred Stevens and Jack Otto would also shortly play a big role in the outfitting business in the Jasper and Willmore areas.

In 1901 and 1902 A.O. Wheeler, a surveyor by trade, was placed in charge of surveying various peaks in the Alberta Rockies. Wheeler had been trained in photogrammetry, which was a method of conducting camera-assisted surveys. Photographs had to be taken from the summits of mountains in order to carry out a triangulation of images. As he climbed, he developed a passion for the Canadian Rockies. This love of the mountains was a motivating factor in his forming of the Alpine Club of Canada. In order to get the club off the ground in 1906, Wheeler depended on the generosity of Banff-based outfitters, Bill Brewster and Tom Wilson, to volunteer their horses, equipment and guides. The Alpine Club of Canada was successful because of the generosity of the outfitting community, specifically Tom Wilson. Mountaineering, not hunting, was in demand during the early 1900s affording outfitters lucrative opportunities guiding those who sought to conquer the summits of the Canadian Rockies.

By the turn of the century, Fred Stephens left Tom Wilson's employment and ventured out on his own. In 1901 and 1903, he headed north from Lake Louise to explore the Yellowhead country. This route proved to be unsuccessful for pack horses but in 1905, by travelling west from his home in Lacombe, he became the first man to investigate the Yellowhead region. He continued to visit the area on a regular basis for many years and, in later times, outfitted from a location near Entrance, Alberta.

By 1902 the Banff-based outfitting business was expanding and Wilson had competitors by the name of Jim and Bill Brewster. As adolescents, these brothers were known to have skipped school, spending time hunting and fishing with William Twin, a Stoney

Indian who had befriended them. By 1904 "Brewster Brothers" had outfitted a party in the country north of where the Sunwapta River joins the Athabasca River. This trip put pressure on the outfitting industry to explore what was then the undeveloped North Country, now known as Jasper National Park and Willmore Wilderness Park.

In 1905 the Brewster's Banff operation had expanded to 250 head of horses and their business was growing by leaps and bounds. "This company's reputation and success as outfitters was mainly attributable to the guiding talents of Jim and Bill Brewster, but after 1905 neither could afford much time to personally lead parties on the trail," (Hart, 1979). The "Brewster Brothers" business dissolved at the same time that Jasper was coming to life with the prospects of two competing railways, the Canadian Northern Railway and the Grand Truck Pacific (GTP). As the railroad pushed west, many young men came with it: men such as Donald McDonald, John Yates, James Shand-Harvey, Alex Wylie and Tom Groat. The dissolution of the "Brewster Brothers" business would make way for a host of new operators in the outfitting industry.

Outfitters such as the Hargreaves brothers, Bill Peyto, Jim Simpson, Fred Brewster, Jack Brewster, Curly Phillips and others continued outfitting during the pre- and post-World War I and World War II eras. These outfitters embarked on 30-day hunts which afforded an opportunity to take different species, including grizzly bear, black bear, bighorn sheep, mountain goats and antlered game.

During the 1920s mountain outfitters felt the need to organize and create a unified voice to lobby government. In May 1922 the various guides and outfitters formed the Rocky Mountain Outfitters Association. Their objective was to have one official body to negotiate with the dominion and provincial governments. This association operated through the 1920s with an amended name of Rocky Mountains Guide Association; however, it was disbanded in the late 1920s.

In 1932 the Alberta Outfitters Association (AOA) was formed to represent the interests of trailmen and set standards for their industry. Members were required to have a certain number of horses and specified equipment. The organization sought to collectively market their product and lobby the government on common issues.

During the 1920s and 1930s, outfitting of hunters evolved into a big business. More and more journalists, such as the famous American outdoor writer, Jack O'Connor, took advantage of outfits like Roy Hargreaves, who was based out of Mt. Robson Ranch and hunted the Alberta/B.C. border. Hargreaves guided O'Connor on a lengthy hunting trip in 1943. Jack and other journalists wrote articles in various outdoor magazines, making Alberta an increasingly popular hunting destination. Hargreaves had previously made a name for himself when he personally guided Bill Chadwick on a 1935 bighorn sheep hunt from Mt. Robson Ranch to Sheep Creek Valley in what is now Willmore Wilderness Park. Chadwick was pleased with this hunt and invited Roy Hargreaves to accompany him on a Stone sheep hunt in B.C.; this expedition became one of the most memorable in history when they took the world-record "Chadwick Ram" in 1936 in the Muskwa Valley, arguably one of the world's greatest big-game trophies (Feddema-Leonard, 2007).

COURTESY OF THE WILLMORE WILDERNESS FOUNDATION

Hunting camp.

Prior to 1970, there was no limit on resident and non-resident big-game tags. Outfitters were free to take as many hunters as they pleased. In 1970 the Alberta government decided there was a need to limit bighorn sheep allocations for non-residents to conserve the resource. Most of the active outfitters of that day were allotted six non-resident permits each, which were later cut down to four. Some of these outfitters included Tom Vinson Sr., Roy Trimble, Jim Colosimo, Dave Simpson, Jim Simpson, Charlie Stricker, Bazil Leonard, Chester Sands, Myrtle Ravio, Ed McKenzie, Sammy Sands, Randy Babala and George Kelley. Up to this point in time, no restrictions had been placed on other big-game species.

As the 20th century marched on, hunting in Alberta was gaining in popularity. More and more outfits were being born in the parkland and prairie areas, making Alberta a choice destination for American and international hunters alike. During the late 1970s, Travel Alberta sought to gain a piece of the action and approached the AOA to use their 50-plus years of expertise to co-market Alberta as a tourist destination. They were philosophically against promoting hunting, but actively focused on promoting the summer outfitting business. Travel Alberta and the AOA subsequently jointly hit the trade-show circuit across Canada and the U.S.

While the AOA was a strong voice for horse-oriented outfitters, several other outfitting organizations were formed to represent the interests of outfitters who operated outside of the mountain regions. By the late 1980s, the Professional Outfitters Association of Alberta (POAA) was created under the direction of LeRoy Fjordbotten, Minister of the Department of Forestry, Lands and Wildlife. He sought to bring the six or seven divergent outfitting groups under one umbrella. [Editor's Note: Mr. Fjordbotten had always been of a mind that it was fundamentally important for government departments to work with provincial organizations that represented the interests of their members, not unstructured, fragmented groups.] In a private meeting with outfitters Bobby Turner, Dennis Potter and others, Fjordbotten advised that he believed the outfitters could be self-governed, which would include licensing and disciplining their own members. The new organization called a duly constituted election, resulting in Dave Simpson being chosen as the founding president.

The POAA laboured through a tumultuous time; 100 years of minimally regulated outfitting had created serious problems. Resident hunters were unhappy with the escalating number of non-resident hunters they encountered in their favourite hunting spots. Each new outfitter required an area to hunt, and competition for the premiere locations ultimately created conflicts. Disgruntled clients had no recourse with fly-by-night outfitters who made promises they never kept. These issues frustrated the government and reputable outfitters alike.

Under the direction of Bob Andrews, then-wildlife director for the Alberta Fish and Wildlife Division, bold steps were taken to address these concerns. In 1989 an Outfitter Guide Policy was created to limit non-resident harvest opportunity. A previously unlimited harvest was replaced with a fixed number of resident licences available for each species in each Wildlife Management Unit (WMU). A sealed bid—for a three-year term—was the mechanism for distributing these allocations.

Outfitters, many with generations of history in the business behind them, found themselves competing for the right to ply

A collections of Hargreaves' trophies.

their trade. No one knew who might be bidding against them or what the fair market bid price might actually be in a bidding war. However, everyone understood that losing the bid meant an end to their career. The outfitting stakes, so to speak, had never been higher.

On that day when successful bidders were awarded their allocations, the dreams of literally hundreds of unsuccessful outfitters were shattered. The size of the outfitting industry was effectively cut in half. Bitterness, disillusionment, and resentment were shared by veteran and aspiring outfitters alike, many of whom now found themselves on the outside looking in.

When the initial three-year term expired in 1992, there was strong resistance to another sealed bid. Instead, allocations would be auctioned off for a 10-year term; allocation numbers were to be reviewed in the fifth year to ensure they were in compliance with the Guide Outfitter Policy. Once again, outfitters found themselves in a desperate struggle to defend their occupation—this time face-to-face with their fellow outfitters. Not surprisingly, emotions ran high. Also, not surprisingly, many more outfitters were separated from their chosen vocation.

The creation of limited allocations had been a bitter pill to swallow but it did resolve two major issues. First, it placed limits on the number of non-resident hunters, thereby addressing concerns of Alberta resident hunters. Secondly, it helped ease the congestion of outfitters, effectively reducing those conflicts. "Recreational outfitting" was replaced by outfitters who now had made a serious financial commitment to the industry.

However, because membership in the POAA was not mandatory, control over outfitter behaviour was still ineffective. There were also some other problems. For example, as in most organizations, operational funding was an issue. Furthermore, of equal significance, the stress that had been created through the sealed bid and auction had eroded confidence in the POAA. Another step was needed to rectify these problems. It took the form of a government-appointed Delegated Administrative Organization (DAO)—co-ordinated by outfitters George Page and Sven-Erik Janssen—which would operate independent of government but remain quasi-regulated by virtue of enabling provincial legislation.

Consequently, on March 31, 1997, five outfitters signed an application to create the Alberta Professional Outfitters Society (APOS). The POAA was absorbed by APOS; the new body was charged with the responsibility of managing the outfitting industry on behalf of the government of Alberta.

The APOS mission statement best describes the role of this new organization. "The Alberta Professional Outfitters Society will provide leadership and direction in the continuing development of Alberta's outfitted-hunting industry. The society will strive for long-term sustainability in its approach to wildlife management, business opportunities and global competitiveness."

It would be difficult to conceive of a more challenging situation than to give birth to such a new organization that regulated outfitting in Alberta. Outfitters and guides are, by their very nature, independent people; they're generally inclined to prefer solitude to working in a structured organization. Their tolerance for each other had been rubbed raw by forcing them to bid against each other for their very existence. They were presented with a new template of rules, and then instructed to put aside all hostility, and assemble, organize and formulate a new vision and direction with the best interests of the industry to guide them. What a daunting task!

It is a credit to the human spirit that when challenges seem impossible, individuals still rise to meet and beat those challenges. During the era of the POAA, Owen Voaklander had been hired as a managing director. His contributions to the evolution of the outfitting industry for the next decade would be monumental. Mabel Brick was hired from the Alberta Fish and Wildlife Division – her knowledge of the people and industry as well as licensing mechanisms was indispensable.

The wisdom of seasoned outfitters like Bobby Turner, Dave Simpson and Bazil Leonard, coupled with the energy and enthusiasm of people like Ryk Visscher, Kelly Semple, Gordon Burton, Terry Birkholz and Don Ayers, accelerated the development of APOS. Policies, programs and guidelines were hammered out with amazing efficiency. Task forces and committees were struck with roles and responsibilities being defined; budgets stretched to maximize the impact of each dollar the society acquired. A code of ethics was created to which all outfitters would comply or face the consequences: potential disbarment from the association.

With the mandatory purchase of an outfitter's licence, all outfitters would now have to become members of APOS. In addition, APOS would now collect the annual allocation user fee all outfitters paid on each allocation. A percentage of this sum would be retained to fund the daily operations of managing the industry; the remainder remitted to the provincial government.

In 1999 one more indispensable piece of the puzzle was added when Bob Gruszecki replaced Kirk Andres as the ministerial representative on the APOS board of directors. Gruszecki's passion for enhancement of the hunting world was matched only by his keen eye for detail. As the catalyst for creation of the WISE Foundation, the Alberta Hunters Education Instructors Association (AHEIA) and the Hunting for Tomorrow Foundation (HFTF), Gruszecki's knowledge and experience helped ensure that APOS policies were fundamentally sound.

In its brief 10 years of existence, APOS has now emerged as the international poster child of the outfitting industry. Within the province, outfitting now contributes in excess of $100 million annually to the Alberta economy. However, only five APOS staff are employed to facilitate the decisions from the member-driven APOS board of directors. Eighteen committees and task forces—staffed by APOS outfitters—address everything from public relations, discipline, marketing, annual conventions and more. Surely, the vision of Minister Fjordbotten of a self-governed industry has been surpassed, to his credit.

Alberta's outfitters have always understood the relationship between their success and the health of the wildlife. This respect has manifested itself in two separate funds created by outfitters to reinvest into wildlife conservation and the sport of hunting. A legacy fund supports initiatives that benefit outfitting, hunting, habitat and animals. Its main source of income is derived from proceeds of the APOS annual convention. Since 2001, APOS has distributed over half a million dollars through the APOS Legacy Fund in many worthwhile projects.

An Allocation Management Fund, worth over $1 million, was created through negotiations in the 10th year renewal of allocations. This money has been earmarked to supplement aerial big-game surveys and inventories, and to provide funding for studies of specific wildlife species.

It's been over 120 years since Tom Wilson provided the first guided hunting excursion on Alberta soil. So much has changed, and yet so much remains the same. Tom would still appreciate the aroma of wood smoke, freshly baked bread and pure mountain air. He'd be mesmerized by the whistle of an elk, the smell of gunpowder on a frosty morning, and the warmth of the sun in a quiet meadow. Tom would recognize a well-mannered horse, a hunter with scruples and a

guide with a sense of humour. He would be charmed by the satellite phone, awed by the global positioning system (GPS), and seduced by a helicopter. No doubt he'd struggle to understand 9-11 – the destruction of the World Trade Centers in New York by terrorists on Sept. 11, 2001. One could only guess at his response to gun control, passports and export permits! A credit card would foul his banking program, and the Goods and Services Tax (GST) would irritate his western spirit. However, Tom would be humbled by the sophistication that can trace its roots to his first Alberta hunt.

Today, Alberta's guided hunting industry is stronger than ever. Clients can expect the high level of service that is demanded of all outfitters under the APOS code of ethics. The interests of Alberta resident hunters are protected twofold: (1) Allowing non-resident hunting in Alberta reciprocates opportunities for Alberta residents to hunt elsewhere. (2) By limiting the harvest of non-residents to a small percentage of the total allowable take, resident opportunities are virtually unaffected. APOS's commitment to promoting the sport of hunting and maintaining healthy animal populations through the Legacy Fund and the Allocation Management Fund speak for themselves.

The passion of early pioneers like Tom Wilson continues to motivate Alberta's modern outfitters. This passion has been seasoned with the development of APOS's professional leadership. When matched with spectacular scenery and abun-

Packing up.

Foliage at Carson Pegasus Provincial Park near Whitecourt.

dant and diverse wildlife, it's no wonder Alberta continues to remain atop the world's destination of choice for professionally guided hunting experiences.

In 2007 as we prepare to celebrate the 100-year history of the (AFGA), ten years of APOS, and 120 years of outfitting in Alberta, it is appropriate that we reflect on the significance of that history. Although 100 years is relatively short compared to the history of North America, the commitment of those who lived during that time frame form the foundation upon which these organizations exist.

It would be naïve to suggest that the relationship between the outfitting community and the AFGA has always been harmonious. At times, each organization has rigorously defended its turf – one in defense of the rights of Alberta resident hunters, the other in defense of the industry. While Alberta's economy has always been dependent on the export of natural resources, Alberta's sportsmen hold a special passion for the sport they dearly love. And to define what is an acceptable non-resident harvest has had its struggles. The outfitter/guide policy established in 1989 provides a framework through which APOS and the AFGA negotiate every five years to address this issue.

Recently, what have become clearer to both groups are not their differences, but rather the concerns they share. Alberta's booming economy poses many challenges for the hunting community. Mega oilsands projects, sprawling urbanization and the imposition of new provincial parks all impact land use. There is the increasing gap between those who recognize and support the recreational value of "sport hunting," and those who are either oblivious or totally opposed to it. While eastern Alberta struggles with chronic wasting disease (CWD), the west wrestles with a near-epidemic infestation of mountain pine beetles.

One can't help but wonder what misgivings Tom Wilson might have had as he witnessed daily railroad progression into the pristine wilderness he first set foot on. There was no stopping progress then, anymore than today. Like Tom, our challenge will be to steer that progress in a direction that embraces the reverence we as hunters hold for the air, water, landscape and wildlife.

The legacy of our collective histories must motivate organizations like AFGA, APOS, and other like-minded conservation groups to rise above our personal agendas. Instead, we must seek a path which affords those who come after us the finest blessings nature has to offer.

CANADIAN WILDLIFE FEDERATION

The AFGA is the official provincial affiliate of the Canadian Wildlife Federation (CWF) for Alberta. As such, the AFGA and the CWF have a common goal in the pursuit of wildlife conservation in Canada and have a history of working together on important wildlife issues.

The CWF was formed in 1962 in order that sportsmen might have a voice in Ottawa. Since its formation, the CWF has advocated the protection of Canada's wild species and spaces. Currently representing over 300,000 members and supporters, the federation is one of Canada's largest non-profit, non-governmental conservation organizations. The CWF has a board of directors that includes two members from each province and territory; it also has nine elected directors-at-large from across Canada.

The CWF is dedicated to fostering awareness and enjoyment of Canada's natural world; their objectives include:
- encouraging an understanding of the impact of human activities on the environment;
- promoting the sustainable use of our natural resources;
- conducting and sponsoring research relating to wildlife and the environment;
- recommending legislative changes to protect wildlife and its habitats; and
- co-operating with organizations and government agencies with similar objectives.

Through extensive education and information programs, the CWF encourages a future in which Canadians may live in harmony with the natural order as a stated goal.

The first annual meeting of the CWF was held Nov. 8-9, 1963 at the Chateau Laurier Hotel in Ottawa with Ben Rosnau, Bruce Stewart and Elmer Kure representing Alberta. There were provincial delegates from British Columbia, Alberta, Saskatchewan, Manitoba, Ontario, Quebec, New Brunswick and Prince Edward Island at the inaugural meeting. There had been an earlier, founding meeting of the organization; during the previous year the organization had been incorporated and attained tax-free status. A national office had also been established in Ottawa.

The first president of the CWF was T.S. Hodgkiss from Ontario; Quebec's E.D. Glendening and Alberta's Gordon Cummings were vice presidents. Hodgkiss advised the delegates at the inaugural meeting that Nov. 8, 1963 was probably the most important day in the brief history of the CWF in terms of setting a course for the future of the organization with respect to educational and financial matters.

One of the first orders of business was to create a wildlife stamp to raise capital to fund the organization and be self supporting. The organization also approved a motion to put out a newsletter, with no more than four issues per year, to increase public awareness regarding conservation of Canada's wildlife. Other items of business dealt with opposition to the proposed construction of a dam at Rampart, Alaska on the Yukon River; hunting of sandhill cranes in Saskatchewan and Manitoba; funding for wetland preservation; federal-provincial cost-sharing in fisheries and wildlife research and management; management of waterfowl by species; biocides and their impact on wildlife; development of wildlife propagation programs with respect to implementation the Agricultural Rehabilitation and Development Act (ARDA) inventories; parks for Canada's centennial, and a "Good Outdoor Manners" campaign carried on by the Canadian Forestry Association.

The CWF sponsored National Wildlife Week for the first time in 1964. Since 1964, the CWF has provided leadership in various conservation programs; for example, they sponsored various conservation education programs, in addition to National Wildlife Week.

A traditional farm scene near LaGlace.

President Ted Glendening presided over the fifth annual meeting of the CWF in March 1969, and reported on what he saw as an outstanding year of growth and achievement for the federation. The organization established its first commercially leased office space in Ottawa and hired bilingual secretarial support and an assistant to the executive director, Dick Passmore at the time. The National Wildlife Week program was expanded as well as work in conservation education through the schools. A brief was presented to the minister of Indian Affairs and Northern Development, regarding Indian hunting rights under the *Migratory Birds Convention Act*. The federation also made representation to the federal government on the subject of firearms legislation which resulted in what was seen as much-improved legislation proposed in Bill C-150. Glendening noted, "One of the truly significant achievements of this past year lies in the field of conservation education, the field which we have all agreed from the beginning was the major concern of the Canadian Wildlife Federation." Teacher education was a priority, and as an example, arrangements were made with the University of Calgary to offer a six-week summer program for teachers at the university's Kananaskis Environmental Sciences Centre in 1969. This program would accommodate up to 20 teachers from the prairie provinces.

In 1971 Allison Bugden, president of the CWF, had a glowing account of the federation in her seventh annual meeting report. "Our work in such fields as conservation in northern Canada, ecological training for teachers and preservation of endangered wildlife has established us as recognized leaders in these several fields. The name of our organization has appeared with surprising frequency in the pages of Hansard, and the content of that official record of the Parliament of Canada shows clearly that we have influenced the nature and outcome of many debates. Our organization is now known to a substantial proportion of Canadians and is looked to for leadership and guidance in conservation matters by many groups and sectors of Canadian society." The most serious issue of the day, however, was the financial viability of the organization which had incurred a substantial deficit in the 1970 fiscal year and was in urgent need of increased funding from affiliated clubs or its own supporting membership.

Thanks to the efforts of Elmer Kure, who requested aid from the White Owl Cigar Company, the CWF was awarded the White Owl Conservation award of $10,000 in 1972. This award was given annually at the time to the organization that did the most toward conservation.

Official opening of Canadian Wildlife Federation head office in Ottawa, 2000. Colin Maxwell (L), executive vice president; George Clavelle, past president; Jack O'Dette; Guy Lesage; Nestor Romaniuk, president; Jim Hook, past president; Carl Shier; Yves Jean; Ron Gladish; Richard Leitch, general manager.

COURTESY OF HARQUAIL PHOTOGRAPHY

Official opening of the Canadian Wildlife Federation head office in Ottawa. CWF president Nestor Romaniuk, 2000.

Gordon Peel had urged delegates at the 44th annual conference in Lethbridge in 1973 to establish some sort of gun control before gun control was determined by non-hunters, and stressed that it was up to the sportsman to take direction.

In his president's report at the 1973 annual meeting of the CWF in Saskatoon, Saskatchewan, Jack O'Dette heaped even greater praise on the organization: "This past year will long be remembered as the one in which the Canadian Wildlife Federation became a powerful force in the conservation and environmental movement in Canada and in North America." He spoke about winning the White Owl Conservation Award and strides in their educational program "...that has helped ecology to assume a more important place in the indoor and outdoor curricula of Canadian schools," as well as the presentation of briefs on impending environmental legislation. Finances, however, continued to dog the organization as well as what was seen as waves of anti-firearm legislation sweeping back and forth across the country.

At the 45th annual conference of the AFGA in 1974, president Robert H. (Bob) Scammell noted that former AFGA president Gordon Cummings had gone on to become president of the CWF; a tribute to the respect of such AFGA past presidents on the national scene. Ron Gladish would later also hold this distinction.

Don Hayden, another past president of the AFGA, was elected president of the CWF at their annual meeting held in Calgary May 31-June 1, 1985. At the time, Hayden was residing in Calgary. He had been a member of the CWF board of directors from 1979 to 1983. Hayden was first elected to the executive of the CWF in 1983 and served as president from 1985-87. He also held posts of treasurer and secretary with the CWF during his term of office. Hayden received the Canadian Outdoorsman of the Year award from the CWF in 1999.

In 1986, the CWF hosted the World Sustainable Development conference in Ottawa with 114 countries in attendance.

In his 1972 report of the president at the eight annual meeting of the federation, Jack O'Dette advised, "This past 12 months might be considered as the year in which the Canadian Wildlife Federation came of age. I say this for two reasons. First, the provincial affiliates have finally realized that they must contribute a sum of money that will cover the general operating expenses of the CWF, and I honestly believe that they all have or are working out schemes that will allow them to meet this commitment. Second, the CWF had the nerve to join in a suit against the Secretary of the Interior of the United States of America asking for an injunction halting the issuing of a permit to build the Trans-Alaska Pipeline, until such time as alternative routes and systems had been fully considered and impact on Canada's environment taken into account."

In the late 1960s sportsmen, in particular hunters, had been branded with a bad name because they used guns; proposed federal gun-control legislation became a joint concern of the CWF and the AFGA in subsequent years. The AFGA past president

COURTESY OF CAROLE ROMANIUK

The AFGA received the Canadian Wildlife Federation Memorial Award for outstanding conservation projects. Nestor Romaniuk (L), Jack Graham, Doug Rumsey and Ron Gladish, 1990.

Elmer Kure (L) receiving Canadian Wildlife Federation Award from president Lorne Yeo for the further of conservation of Canada's natural resources, 1990.

While president of the AFGA in 1986-87, Nestor Romaniuk was a representative on the board of directors of the CWF. In 1988, he became a director at large on that board and became the CWF president in 1999. In 1991 Romaniuk became the CWF representative on the board of directors of Wildlife Habitat Canada and served as chairman of the board from 1993-95. He returned to the board of directors of Wildlife Habitat Canada in 2003 as the CWF representative.

Over the years a few Albertans have been elected and have served as directors at large for the CWF including Jack Graham, Nestor Romaniuk, Dave Powell and Ray Makowecki. Two of Alberta's AFGA executive members serve as CWF board directors during their time on Alberta's elected executive.

Bob Barton (L) and Nestor Romaniuk receiving the Canadian Wildlife Federation Stan Hodgekiss Canadian Outdoorsman Award of the Year, 2000.

The CWF addresses many issues of concern on behalf of its membership at the national level, such as invasive species, advertisers' depiction of sport utility vehicles and all-terrain vehicles in natural environments, species at risk, oil spills, climate change, the impact of wind turbines on bird mortality, chronic wasting disease (CWD), game farming, predation by cormorants and the need to encourage youth programs. It sponsors WILD Education, an umbrella of CWF education programs including: Below Zero, Project WILD, Oceans Way, Fish Ways, National Wildlife Week and Hinterland Who's Who. The CWF also partners with organizations such as Wildlife Habitat Canada and matches funding for worthy habitat projects.

DUCKS UNLIMITED CANADA

by Ron Montgomery, former Ducks Unlimited Canada Lethbridge area manager

Our Province:

As Ducks Unlimited Canada (DUC) enters their 70th year of operations in Alberta, the vision and mission of their founders has never been more relevant. The conservation of wetlands and associated habitats are critical to the benefit of waterfowl, wildlife and people from the boreal forests of the north to the prairie grasslands of the south.

This international, private, non-profit conservation organization, aptly known as "Canada's Conservation Company," began its mission in Alberta in 1938, in the semi-arid grasslands of southern Alberta. Here, the lack of reliable water supplies was a common issue with both DUC and the ranching community. By employing a series of dykes and ditches, water was distributed throughout dry wetland basins, allowing more efficient use of rangeland and ensuring more stable nesting conditions for waterfowl.

Sustaining a vibrant agriculture industry is integral to both the economic well-being of Albertans and the health of waterfowl resources. Recognizing that agriculture has a large influence on land-use practices in many of Alberta's landscapes, DUC works diligently with the agriculture community on many fronts to achieve mutually beneficial production practices.

The boreal forest of northern Alberta has been under intense pressure from industries such as forestry, oil and gas developments and agriculture expansion. Habitats within these resource-rich areas have become an urgent focus of DUC's conservation efforts. A healthy forest results in a healthy watershed, which in turn benefits everyone. By working with various industry stakeholders in Alberta's boreal forest, DUC is helping to mitigate these impacts through the development of industry best management practices. These creative programs and partnerships will help to ensure the long-term well being of the forest boreal region.

Fostering public awareness of the importance of wetlands and the key role they play in ensuring a healthy environment has always been a key component of DUC's conservation efforts. Greenwing programs, teacher resource programs, interpretive centres, informational brochures and staff participation in a wide variety of workshops and other venues are ongoing commitments in this regard.

The formation of community-driven watershed groups are a testament to the concern and awareness of water quality shared among farmers, ranchers, towns, industry, government and others. DUC has been an active participant in these groups over the past number of years, in support of Alberta's Water for Life Strategy, a provincial government program.

Conservation of natural landscapes is a complex and oft-times sensitive issue. Joint ventures, wherever possible, make good business sense as mutual goals can be realized through the sharing of public input, financial and technical resources. DUC's conservation efforts in Alberta are founded on partnerships between land-owners, industry and govern-ment agencies in support of these joint ventures.

DUC History:

At the turn of the century sportsmen in both the United States and Canada expressed concern over the dwindling numbers of waterfowl and game birds. Numerous organizations and individuals embarked upon various studies and initiatives to address these concerns. In 1928 one such U.S. organization called "Wildfowlers" sent two investigators to Alberta to study nest depredation by crows on the "duck breeding grounds."

The 1930 formation of "The More Game Birds in America Foundation," organization led by Joseph Knapp, ultimately evolved into Ducks Unlimited Incorporated in 1937, which in turn led to the inception of Ducks Unlimited Canada (DUC) in 1938.

A book entitled *Ducks and Men* published in 1977 and authored by W.G. (Bill) Leitch, chief biologist for DUC for 26 years, chronicles DUC's history to that date. It contains an apt passage in the forward section that reads in part: "It's a story of people who through dedication and innovation applied the theoretical concepts of game management to practical problems." Some 30 years later, this passage still applies.

COURTESY OF DUCKS UNLIMITED CANADA
Kids enjoying a DUC wetlands outing.

COURTESY OF DUCKS UNLIMITED CANADA
Another successful DUC marsh exploration.

Thomas C. (Tom) Main, a surface water engineer for Canadian National Railways, was persuaded to take the position of DUC's first general manager in 1938. Although born in England, Tom was brought up in Pincher Creek in southwest Alberta in the shadow of the Canadian Rockies. E.S. (Ed) Russenholt was hired as assistant manager. Bert Cartwright joined the organization as chief natural-ist. A contingent of capable support staff was immediately assembled for DUC's head office in Winnipeg, Man.

That same year (1938), it was decided that DUC would initially undertake to build one large project in each prai-rie province. To carry out this objective, provincial staff were also being assembled. The first Alberta supervisor was Col. T. Newcomen, who was respon-sible for constructing Alberta's first DUC project on a portion of the 8,360-acre Many Island Lake located east of Medicine Hat. Surveys were completed on Aug. 25, 1938 and work started on Sept. 29 of that same year. Total cost upon Nov. 3 completion for this 700-acre project was $4,609.06.

In 1938 Ed Russenholt organized a volunteer force of field men named Kee-Men to assist with waterfowl census ground surveys. Census forms were distributed to 1,200 of these volunteers with a remarkable 1,089 completed reports being completed and returned. At their peak in November 1938, the Kee-Men corps numbered 3,200. Although the Kee-Men roles were eventually phased out, members such as the late Ralph Michelson of Lethbridge continued to be great ambassadors for DUC.

In January 1939 Angus Shortt joined the organization and played a major role for over 34 years in DUC's public relations program. A skilled writer and artist, his talents combined with those of Main, Russenholt and Cartwright resulted in an aggressive and innovative public relations program. *The Duckological* or *Ducko* was a tremendously successful publication distributed in both Canada and the United States. "Jake the Drake" then "Jake the Drake and Mary the Mallard" became well-known characters through the combined verse of Bert Cartwright along with the cartoons of Ed Russenholt. In those early years DUC was also interested in managing sanctuaries. The Latter Day Saints' Church Ranch in southern Alberta was briefly a game preserve under DUC's watch.

Ministik Lake Bird Sanctuary, located approximately 50 kilometres east of Edmonton, was also managed by DUC. In 1938 Francis Williams was hired to manage the sanctuary. His brother, long-time and well-known DUC staffer Keith Williams, eventually took over in 1954. DUC apparently also had Francis' horse on payroll at $20 per month. Also, the horse had an expense account for oats!

The Gordon Lake project, located approximately 100 kilometres east of Fort McMurray, was established as a game preserve under DUC's watch in 1939. The remoteness of the site and other complications led to a cancellation of the lease in 1943, however.

DUC's land and air waterfowl census efforts were nothing short of amazing in those early years. Aerial surveys, which began in 1938, produced many a harrowing tale of near misses and hardships, but they also produced highly valuable data on waterfowl population's numbers and trends.

The concept of donor projects came about in 1941. This program honours individuals, groups, organizations or others that choose to fund a particular DUC project. The first true donor project in Alberta was Lake San Francisco-Cassils Lake near Brooks. Constructed in 1942, funds were donated specifically for that purpose by the Pacific Rod and Gun Club in San Francisco from money raised through trap and skeet shooting competitions.

During World War II, DUC was in a situation where contractors were scarce. In 1941 while on a speaking engagement in California, Tom Main received the offer of a crawler tractor, bucket and dozer, a truck to transport it and a trailer for the crew. Christened "The Major" in honour of the donor, Major Max Fleischmann, this caravan of equipment allowed DUC to conduct construction business more independently of contractors until the end of the war years. Operated by Joe Kokinsky, "The Major" built many projects around the Hanna area.

DUC also went though a critical funding period in 1940 when a ban was placed on the transfer of money out of the U.S. This nearly shut down Canadian operations, but somehow DU Inc. was granted the necessary permission to transfer budget dollars, narrowly averting a serious financial crisis at DUC.

Initially DUC's conservation projects took place in southern and central Alberta, where wetlands were deemed to be most at risk. Southern Alberta was also home to 13 irrigation districts where many large-scale, multi-use, multi-benefit projects were constructed. However the Peace River and western boreal forest areas were soon included in DUC's conservation efforts.

Fundraising events evolved into an important part of DUC Alberta's activities with the trademark banquet becoming a premier annual community social outing. These banquets also provided an opportunity for DUC to inform the public of their conservation programs and create a tremendous amount of goodwill between conservationists and the local community. Many projects have originated as the result of a referral from one of these banquets.

In 1986 the North American Waterfowl Management Plan (NAWMP) was signed between Canada, the United States and Mexico. Waterfowl population goals were established and key habitats requiring restoration and protection were identified. This ambitious program continues to be managed and delivered through the Alberta NAWMP Partnership, an award-winning consortium of provincial and federal government partners and non-government organizations (NGOs).

DUC had for several years recognized that direct habitat conservation programs alone would not achieve their aggressive waterfowl conservation goals. In 1999 DUC staff—in collaboration with their sister organization DU Inc.—developed and adopted a conservation vision for a large area that included much of Alberta known as the prairie pothole ecoregion. A strategic plan was eventually compiled forming the foundation that provides current direction for influencing policy initiatives and guiding program delivery on a landscape basis. The goals and guiding principles of this plan are:

Goals:
1. No further loss of natural uplands.
2. Restore hydrological function to wetlands in areas with suitable nesting habitat.
3. No further loss of wetlands.
4. Restore function to uplands in areas with high wetland density.

Guiding principles:
1. Focus on areas that benefit waterfowl populations.
2. Target conservation of existing natural habitats.
3. Work with other users of the land.
4. Conserve ecological function.
5. Broaden impacts and awareness; build new partnerships.
6. Minimize long-term management costs.
7. Continue to improve conservation programs.

DUC Accomplishments:

DUC's science-based conservation programs are diverse, from direct incentives to change land-use practices to extension and policy-related initiatives. In support of these habitat conservation programs, DUC utilizes a number of innovative education and fundraising initiatives. This multi-faceted approach is critical to ensuring the long-term success of waterfowl production in Alberta.

The organization has always been committed to fostering public awareness about the importance of wetlands and the key role they play in a healthy environment. Recognizing that today's youth are tomorrow's wetland conservation leaders, DUC's long-running and popular Greenwing program offers educational materials and hands-on opportunities for youth age 17 and under. Project Webfoot is another key youth education program. This program is focused on grade 4-6 students, providing classrooms with kits of exciting and engaging in-class learning material, as well as wetland field trips.

COURTESY OF DUCKS UNLIMITED CANADA

Maeco-Ministik Lake project near Sherwood Park.

Since 1938, when DUC constructed the inaugural Many Island Lake project, DUC has invested over $300 million in wetland habitat conservation in Alberta. This has resulted in over 1,900 habitat conservation projects with 5,400 landowner partners and various government and industry allies. Over one million acres of wildlife habitat have been secured through various co-operative agreements.

One example of these projects is the Tyrrell-Rush Lakes complex located north of Warner and completed in 1987. A co-operative effort between the Alberta government, the County of Warner, local landowners, DUC and the St. Mary River Irrigation District (SMRID) was behind this multi-use, multi-benefit project which provides both water and nesting habitat for waterfowl, songbirds, pheasants, Hungarian (grey) partridge, sharptailed grouse and deer.

Another example is the Contra Costa Project, located approximately 25 kilometres southeast of Brooks. This project represents the largest and most diversified mixed-grass wetland/upland complex ever undertaken by DUC in Alberta. Originally named the Tilley-Louisiana Complex, DUC first began work on this project in 1943. Over the next 30 years more than 35 wetland segments were added to the original six segments. Located on about a 60-square-mile tract of native grassland used primarily for grazing and belonging to the Eastern Irrigation District (EID),

this was always deemed a highly productive DUC project. The size of this complex is staggering:

- Over 70 kilometres of canal reconstruction, 53 water-control structures and numerous dykes (damsites) supply and impound water for 46 segments of managed wetlands totalling over 2,950 hectares (7,280 acres) in combined size.
- Complementing these wetlands are eight segments of managed upland nest cover totalling over 25,600 hectares (63,200 acres).

Historically, a key component of DUC's fundraising efforts in Alberta has been their trademark banquet and dinner auctions. Many years of experience have streamlined these events into highly anticipated social outings for the entire community and surrounding area. Approximately 130 community-based events are organized and hosted by over 2,000 dedicated volunteers throughout Alberta.

DUC Future:

The economy of Alberta is currently vibrant, and an increasingly vigilant public is aware that environmental stewardship and the conservation of our natural resources is a priority. But whether it's agriculture, oil and gas developments, forestry or mining industries, those that apply good environmental practices must also maintain profitability in order to survive. This challenge is a fact of life that DUC readily recognizes in its mission to help provide practical solutions in pursuit of its waterfowl conservation goals and objectives.

Although wetland loss is a primary concern, suitable upland nesting cover is also necessary for healthy and diverse waterfowl and wildlife populations. Achieving a healthy balance of wildlife habitat on working landscapes requires a team approach, which involves many partners.

Roughly 10 million acres of native prairie still exist in Alberta. Since wildlife conservation and grazing management goals are closely linked, DUC and the ranching community often partner to improve the quality of the native grassland.

For many years DUC has recognized the waterfowl benefits attributed to fall-seeded crops. Land-use changes over the past 30 years have resulted in a significant loss of breeding habitat for pintail and other waterfowl. Consequently, agriculture-friendly programs, which promote environmental sustainability, will remain a priority.

Addressing the problems associated with wetland drainage is a big challenge. From an agricultural perspective there may appear to be economic advantages to drainage in order to increase the amount of farmland. In the past this drainage was often driven by subsidies. Expanding urban development also has a major impact on wetland losses.

It has been estimated that over 70 percent of Alberta's wetlands have been drained or otherwise altered under the justification these are deemed "wastelands" or "unimproved lands." This degradation continues today, in spite of overwhelming evidence that wetlands play a major role in the overall health of our land and everyday requirements of daily life.

Fortunately, this view is quickly changing. A prime example is the formation of community-driven watershed groups throughout Alberta. Born out of a shared concern and awareness of water issues, farmers, ranchers, towns, industry and government are working together to improve the quality and quantity of water in their communities.

Wetlands, streams, lakes, groundwater and riparian areas are recognized as vital to healthy watersheds.

DUC's Institute for Wetland and Waterfowl Research (IWWR) continues to provide scientifically backed statistics that clearly emphasize the value of our wetlands. In addition to the now widely recognized obvious benefits of wetlands, DUC is also investigating the impact of wetland retention or loss relative to climate change and the current global warming trend. The storage potential of wetlands and riparian areas for carbon and greenhouse gases has been scientifically acknowledged.

Climate change will also negatively influence wetlands. DUC, in partnership with the Government of Canada and others, is examining the environmental linkages between wetlands, riparian areas and agriculture relative to carbon sequestration (storage) and greenhouse gas emissions.

DUC Conservation Efforts:

In the mid-1970s, 60 percent or more of the continental breeding population of northern pintails settled in the southern Canadian prairies. But the drought-ridden 1980s saw Alberta's pintail populations drop dramatically. Even with the return of water in the 1990s on much of the prairie landscape, pintail populations never recovered. Ongoing studies and agriculture statistics indicate a direct correlation between the increase in intensive land-use practices and pintail declines. Native prairie grasslands are being lost and continuous cropping is on the increase. Wetlands throughout Alberta are also still being lost.

Roughly 10 million acres of native prairie still exist in Alberta, however. Beef producers play a critical role toward ensuring these grasslands remain intact. Without the beef industry and the value they place on the health of native rangelands, many of these landscapes could be converted to cultivation. In addition to waterfowl, a vast array of wildlife relies on this native prairie habitat.

Recognizing that this loss of habitat is likely to continue, various land-protection options and extension programs offering economically sustainable production alternatives are delivered in various key focus areas of Alberta.

Habitat retention programs involve the direct purchase of key lands at imminent risk of loss and also working with landowners on securing lands through conservation easements or short-term conservation agreements. These tools are also used to enhance DUC wetland restoration programs through providing the financial

COURTESY OF DUCKS UNLIMITED CANADA

Biology component of Ducks Unlimited Canada's work.

incentive to landowners to restore wetlands on their property. "Land-Use-Exchange" is another innovative program where DUC offers landowners the use of its property for haying or grazing in exchange for restoring wetlands on a landowner's property.

Cropland conversion programs include incentives for conversion of annual cropland to forage and adoption of winter wheat as a component of normal cropping rotations.

From an extension and policy perspective, Alberta's Water for Life Strategy has been integral to increasing the awareness of wetlands and their role in maintaining healthy watersheds. DUC has been involved at many different levels in the development and implementation of this strategy, and looks forward to its success.

Further, on the policy front, the agreement between Alberta and the federal government to encourage environmental friendly farm practices under the Alberta Environmental Farm Plan (AEFP) has provided another tool for responsible environmental stewardship. Voluntarily prepared by farm families, these plans identify environmental strengths and weaknesses of their operations. Most important, however, is the action plan that identifies opportunities for improvement. A number of qualifying improvements are eligible for funding by AEFP, which DUC supports, including wetland restoration and the enhancement of riparian areas.

On the educational front, DUC is continually seeking to offer programs which benefit both youth and the general public. Besides the popular Greenwing and Project Webfoot programs, another unique example is DUC's partnership with the Government of Alberta in developing a world-class, educational "eco-park" in the heart of Calgary.

The Bow Habitat Station (BHS) is an integrated attraction, encompassing the largest indoor trout hatchery in North America —the Sam Livingston Fish Hatchery—a large visitor centre, and a unique collection of constructed aquatic habitats, treatment wetlands and interpretive features called the Pearce Estate Park Interpretive Wetland. DUC constructed the interpretative marsh and provides an interpreter as a member of the team delivering education programs.

Several agencies, in partnership with DUC, offer high quality wetland and wildlife education programs, with classroom and field-trip opportunities throughout Alberta.

Although some of DUC's "traditional" conservation programs are being modified, as research directs, the underlying goal is still to maximize benefits to waterfowl and other wildlife. DUC's supporters and volunteers can rest assured that efficient use of their financial support will continue to be a priority.

DUC Partners:

"That duck gliding slowly and quietly across a still pond portrays a picture of serenity. But nice below the surface and out of sight is a pair of churning legs propelling it along." Conservation organizations in Alberta also rely upon many "legs" to help move their projects forward. Partnerships, whether formal or informal, are quite common, but like the duck analogy are not always visible or readily recognized. DUC is proud of the many successful partnerships it has forged over the past 70 years.

When a DUC project is initiated, field staff rely upon and interact with a large number of agencies and individuals. The very success of a project is often dependent upon the efforts of individual staff members within each respective agency.

As an example only (this could be any project in Alberta with a different scenario and participants), let's take project "x" located within an irrigation district in a pintail focus area that will involve wetlands and upland nesting cover on both public and private lands. A quick overview of the necessary approvals and permits will show that several agencies are likely to be involved: an irrigation district; the department of Alberta Agriculture Food and Rural Development - Public Lands Division; a county or municipal district, a grazing association, one or more utility companies and private landowners.

COURTESY OF HENRY LEMBICZ

Fred Sharpe, Ducks Unlimited Alberta delegate, from "*Alberta Sportsmen*" March/April 1967 edition.

The irrigation district itself will, of course, play a major role, since their water is the very lifeblood of a wetland project. DUC has enjoyed a successful working relationship with irrigation districts in southern Alberta since the early 1940s. Their boards of directors, staff and water users are instrumental in making these projects a reality. The Alberta Irrigation Projects Association (AIPA), an umbrella organization for the many irrigation districts, has also been most supportive of DUC's conservation efforts.

The Alberta government's Public Lands Division personnel play an important role in DUC projects throughout Alberta. Large tracts of native prairie are home to many species of waterfowl and other wildlife. The Public Land Division's management of this habitat to fulfill the needs for both wildlife and agriculture requires co-operation, support and dedication from local staff within their respective regions. DUC recognizes and appreciates the tact and diplomacy on the part of these staff that is required to meet this challenge.

Counties and municipal districts have been quite supportive of DUC's works. Their approval process may involve having DUC

staff make a presentation to appropriate governing councils of these agencies. In many instances their agricultural staff will also work directly with DUC on projects of common interest.

Grazing associations have also been key partners in many DUC projects. Large tracts of lands are now successfully managed to serve both wildlife and cattle on such grazing association lands. Their co-operation is greatly appreciated, as these lands provide habitat for many species of wildlife.

Today it's a rarity not to have some form of public utility be associated with a particular landscape. Gas or oil pipelines and wellsites, telephone and power lines are the most common of these utilities. Approval from the utility companies and subsequent co-operation during the time of actual project construction is an important component of most DUC projects. This co-operation is returned many times during the life of the project. Numerous utility applications are processed every year by DUC staff, ensuring that industry can thrive while ensuring the integrity of the project.

Working co-operatively with farmers, ranchers or other land managers has been and still is paramount to ensuring the success of Alberta's conservation programs because a typical project relies upon a mix of both water and adequate upland nest cover.

Alberta Sustainable Resource Development-Fish and Wildlife Division are long-time supporters of DUC's conservation efforts. Their advice and expertise have made some truly difficult and complicated project proposals become a reality.

Water licensing is required on many runoff-related DUC projects in Alberta. Though this can sometimes be perceived as a daunting process, co-operation from Alberta Environment staff has been excellent in licensing various projects.

Various departments with the Government of Canada have also been long-time partners with DUC throughout Alberta. Such partnerships may be research-related, funding-related or simply sharing technical advice and support.

Organizations such as the AFGA, with their many affiliated local clubs, have supported DUC both financially and through project partnerships. The Alberta Conservation Association (ACA) has also partnered with DUC on several unique projects in southern Alberta.

The Nature Conservancy of Canada (NCC) and DUC have confirmed their long-standing partnership by embarking on a number of collaborative Alberta initiatives. Both DUC and NCC are core program delivery partners for the Alberta North American Waterfowl Management Plan (NAWMP), an international program to restore waterfowl populations.

Where possible, partnering with peer conservation groups makes good business sense for both parties. In many instances the parties can achieve mutually advantageous goals through the sharing of financial, staff expertise and technical resources.

In the autumn of 2006, four of Alberta's most active habitat conservation agencies initiated an agreement that makes it easier for them to pool resources and conserve valuable tracts of wildlife habitat. A memorandum of understanding (MOU) signed by DUC, the AFGA, Alberta Conservation Association (ACA) and the Nature Conservancy of Canada (NCC), provided a formal framework for future collaboration.

DUC Supporters:

DUC receives financial support from three primary sources, with roughly a third coming from each. First is DUC's sister organization, Ducks Unlimited Inc. of the United States, which funds DUC's conservation work for the benefit of North America's waterfowl in general. The second funding source is the federal government in the United States. Under the North American Wetlands Conservation Act of Congress, the U.S. government provides money to organizations that conserve wetlands. In order to be used in Canada, this money must be matched by non-federal U.S. dollars. The final third comes from Canadian industry and government partners and from DUC's own fundraising activities in Canada. Memberships, donations and DUC fundraising events generate funds to conserve Alberta's wetlands. Of every dollar that DUC receives, 88 cents is reinvested into conservation programs, research and wetland-education initiatives.

As mentioned earlier, a key component of DUC's fundraising efforts are the trademark banquet and auction events. Many years of experience have streamlined these events into often sold-out crowds; guests look forward to these social outings, which draw from the entire community and surrounding area. As a matter of record, the first official DUC fundraising event was held in Ontario in 1974. The program includes doorprizes, raffles, a silent and live auction and of course, a great meal. Local talent and support for these events has always been outstanding. In many instances the various donated crafts and artwork have become much sought-after items by banquet attendees. Community business and individual contributions of both merchandise and cash bolster the evening's net income.

Other special events hosted by volunteers have included golf tournaments, sporting events such as clay pigeon shoots or fishing derbies, curling bonspiels and other innovative activities.

Another successful fundraising initiative in many Alberta communities has been the "Wildlife Art Sealed Bid Auction." Ducks Unlimited artwork is displayed by business partners in the various communities. Local volunteers maintain the sites and bids are placed in a sealed box for a pre-determined time, generally a couple of weeks. On the closing date the highest bidder receives the print and the process starts over again with another new print.

Corporate partners also support DUC in numerous ways. Many of Canada's industry leading private-sector corporations,

manufacturers, retailers, media and key foundations with offices in Alberta, are partners in DUC's conservation efforts. They may have sponsored specific projects through financial contributions, participated in national sponsorships or merchandising and more.

George Freeman, Mr. DU

George Freeman, or Mr. DU as he is also so fondly known, is an Alberta Ducks Unlimited Canada icon. A World War II and D-Day veteran, George started his career with DUC on May 3, 1948 and officially retired in 1984, but continues his association with DUC to this day. It's nothing short of remarkable to trace the footsteps of this individual over his lengthy career. The impact he's had upon waterfowl conservation is evidenced by comments from many "grown children" who have gone on to become influential individuals who credit their success to those early teachings from Mr. DU.

George is well-known throughout Alberta, Canada and the U.S. for his enthusiasm, quick wit and outstanding achievements in the world of waterfowl and wildlife conservation. A tireless DUC ambassador, he made life-long friends with many DU Incorporated staff, directors and other dignitaries from government and organizations in the United States. DUC's Greenwing program benefited immensely from his boundless enthusiasm and dedication to education. He initiated and participated in waterfowl banding programs, population surveys and other research projects foregoing many of DUC's current programs.

George and wife Helena are life-long residents of Strathmore. Their home is a living testament to their remarkable commitments to nature, youth and their community in general. Their home was also home to many of DUC's early pioneers and remains a welcome stop for any of the DUC family today.

A recipient of the prestigious Alberta Order of the Bighorn Award in 1995, and the Queen's Jubilee Medal, George has also been bestowed with several other awards. DUC board of directors had recognized his contributions to American youth education through the presentation of a cherished Greenwing teal decoy. Also, a dedication ceremony held in 2001 at the George Freeman Marsh (formerly known as the Thirwell project) east of Strathmore also paid a fitting tribute to this friendly and outgoing individual.

Partnerships with peer conservation groups have also been a win-win situation for all parties. DUC has undertaken cost-share arrangements with numerous organizations such as the AFGA, ACA and the NCC to name a few such organizations.

DUC People:

Given the diversity of conservation programs delivered by DUC, a correspondingly rich cross-section of employees has come and gone over the past 70 years. A more dedicated and ambitious bunch of folks has never been assembled in one place before or since, and our staff resources continue to be our key strength.

Much of our program activity prior to NAWMP revolved around extensive wetland creation and restoration projects.

Standing: George (L), Larry and Debbie Freeman, Roger and Gina Wozney and Helena. In front: Roger and Gina's kids Tim and Anne and Sarah Wozney.

As a result, staff capacity was heavily skewed to engineering, surveying and construction supervision roles. Area offices were established in Brooks and Strathmore in 1944 to accommodate the extensive work DUC was undertaking in the local irrigation districts. In 1954 an office was established in Hanna to conduct wetland creation in the Special Areas of Alberta. Offices in St. Paul and Peace River were added in 1977.

The mid-1960s saw a dramatic increase in funding that in turn required reorganization and expansion. D. Stewart Morrison became executive vice president in 1977 and led DUC through this challenging era.

Additional area offices were eventually located throughout Alberta. Biologists, engineers, and construction supervisors comprised most of the initial staff contingent, given the focus on wetland creation and restoration. Agrologists were hired to complement DUC's growing involvement in influencing and securing upland nesting habitat. As DUC's conservation strategies were adjusted, so too were staff expertise, roles and office locations. Education and communication became a higher priority; consequently provincial staff was bolstered by specialists in those respective disciplines. Increased technology required the hiring of technical staff to fulfill such needs. The Western Boreal Forest program required additional staffing.

Fundraising in Alberta has been ongoing for several years now with some local fundraising committees exceeding the 25 year mark. A large volunteer base organizes and hosts these events. A number of DUC staff are dedicated to support these fund raising activities, including fundraising managers and their able assistants.

DUC is governed by a board of directors with member representation from across Canada and the United States. Although not as visible to the general public as rank-and-file DUC employees, these directors play an integral role in assuring that funds are expended in the manner intended.

Answering to the board of directors is an executive vice president located at Canada's head office at Oak Hammock Marsh in Stonewall, Manitoba. Jeff Nelson was appointed as DUC's executive vice president (EVP) effective February 2008 succeeding Gordon Edwards, who retired in October 2007 after an impressive 31-year career with DUC.

Over the past seven decades, many unique and colourful characters have been part of the DUC family. Ted Burkell, Keith Williams, Fred Sharpe, Bill Leitch, Angus Gavin, Bill Campbell, George Freeman, Bruce McGlone, Keith Pugh and Al Burns are but a few familiar formative Alberta DUC people. Even the most dedicated and hard-working DUC staff was also well-known for their sense of humour and practical jokes.

DUC currently has approximately 70 employees in Alberta, with offices in Calgary, Brooks, Medicine Hat, Lethbridge, Hanna, Donalda, Red Deer, Camrose, Wainwright, St. Paul, Edmonton and Grande Prairie. The extended DUC family includes over 1,800 volunteers and 24,500 supporters.

It's fitting that this chapter on DUC's Alberta history should close with a statement from the "Ducks and Men" book, that's still quite applicable to DUC today. "Although the techniques have changed, the objective has not. It remains steadfastly committed with a "singleness of purpose" to the preservation and increase of the waterfowl resource, through maintaining and developing habitat and influencing, for the benefit of waterfowl, all factors affecting them. What the company has stimulated others to do is intangible, but of much greater importance, through their activities the value of waterfowl as a resource has become recognized, as it never would have been otherwise. Attitudes thus developed toward waterfowl have stimulated similar attitudes toward all wildlife species."

The public is encouraged to visit DUC's website at www.ducks.ca. You can also call toll free 1-800-665-DUCK (1-800-665-3825) or contact the Edmonton headquarters office at (780) 489-2002 for additional information about Alberta operations.

FISH AND WILDLIFE DIVISION

Officials in Alberta's Fish and Wildlife Division have historically worked very closely with the AFGA; in fact, the AFGA can take credit for the formation of the Fish and Wildlife Division as a result of persistent lobbying of the government to create such an agency solely responsible for management of Alberta's fish and wildlife resources.

The purpose of this chapter is to provide a glimpse into the historical liaison between staff of the Fish and Wildlife Division and the AFGA through the eyes of a representative number of employees of the former agency, who had (have) long careers with this organization or were key employees at important points in time. It is by no means exhaustive but should serve to illustrate an important historical context during the latter part of the 20th century when the Fish and Wildlife Division was a prominent division of the Alberta government. Many staff in the Fish and Wildlife Division were career professionals who chose their job as a lifestyle, in pursuit of an avocation with a paycheque.

The Fish and Wildlife Division is relatively young as an arm of government, having been created on Jan. 1, 1959 with Curt P. Smith as director, according to information in *Fish, Fur & Feathers* (2005). Although Alberta created its first provincial game branch under the federal Department of Agriculture administration with the appointment of Benjamin J. Lawton as the first chief game guardian in 1906. Records from the AFGA annual conference yearbooks indicate the Fish and Wildlife Division was established in 1958, however, as a separate entity from the Alberta Forest Service and information in *Fish, Fur & Feathers* (2005) notes that "between 1958 and 1963, total staff numbers in the Division

COURTESY OF GERRY THOMPSON

Gerry Thompson at the Bistcho Lake Fish and Wildlife cabin in 1986.

COURTESY OF DUANE RADFORD

Report-a-Poacher program signage.

grew from 78 to 121, including a director, three section chiefs, 10 biologists, two hatchery superintendents, seven conservation officer IIs, 56 conservation officer Is, and 42 other staff."

In Memoriam:

There is an inherent risk associated with many field activities involving fish and wildlife operations and studies; some district officers have been badly beaten (and even hospitalized) and several biologists and technicians have lost their lives while engaged in field work.

This chapter is dedicated to the memory of the following employees of the Fish and Wildlife Division who died in the line of duty. It is a tribute to these individuals that they died while engaged in activities in pursuit of sound management of Alberta's fish and wildlife resources.

- Roger Schmitke, Edmonton wildlife biologist, who drowned in a boating accident on the North Saskatchewan River in 1965.

- Cal Bohmer, Des Smith and Barry Young, Edson wildlife biologists and technicians, all three of whom died in a plane crash flying big-game aerial surveys near Edson in 1978.
- Orval Pall, Calgary wildlife technician, who died on June 6, 1986 in a plane crash while surveying bighorn sheep in Kananaskis Country, along with several rescue workers and pilots.
- Gordon Gresiuk and John MacNeill, Lethbridge fisheries technicians, who died in a boating accident while electro-fishing on the inlet canal to Lake McGregor on Oct. 13, 1983.

Report-A-Poacher Program by Robert (Bob) J. Adams, former director of the Enforcement-Field Services Branch

"Well, Bob, what do you think of this facility?" I was deep in thought and more than a little peeved when I heard the familiar voice address me. I had been searching for some material in the information centre on the main floor of the Bramalea Building [currently named the Great West Life Building] in Edmonton and had finally found it at the back of the room. I turned and faced the minister of the day, who was responsible for the then Ministry of Forestry, Lands and Wildlife.

"Oh, to be sure, it's a very impressive place," I replied, "but you know sir, I was just thinking, it's a good thing there's a back wall with a back shelf, and a back table with a bottom drawer."

"And why is that?" he asked giving me a funny smile.

"Well sir, without them, I dare say there'd be no place for Fish and Wildlife…," I replied and I did not smile.

"How can you say that?" he asked. "Did you not see the large moose head that hangs just outside the door where you enter the room, you walked right under it? And, what about the full mount of the grizzly just inside the door? You had to see that, didn't you?"

"I did, sir! I did!" I assured him. "But to me that's just a teaser, sugar candy, to bring people in. Look around, sir, everything else regarding Fish and Wildlife can only be found at the back of the room." [Editor's note: With that background, the genesis of the following Alberta's Report-a-Poacher program can be put in the proper context.]

The REPORT-A-POACHER (RAP) program in Alberta actually had its beginning in 1981. It was around the same time as the government was creating the multi-department mobile radio system (MDMRS), primarily to meet the demands of the Fish and Wildlife Division officers. Expectations were high for both programs.

The AFGA had been lobbying the government for years for a program, like RAP, that would improve on the Outdoor Observer program. They wanted the opportunity to become more involved in the Fish and Wildlife Division enforcement program and they had put forward a number of suggestions on how this could be done.

It was known at the time that there was little-to-no political will or divisional support for a RAP program. However, with the strong support of the AFGA we charged forward. After all, the MDMRS program was well on its way to implementation, why not RAP? We put the wheels into motion. Numerous fish and wildlife enforcement agencies across North America had programs in place to assist them in their enforcement efforts. Meetings were held with many of them. We carefully reviewed and assessed every program we had access to. There were good points as well as bad. We learned from them all and we used the best of them to develop Alberta's RAP program. During our meetings three main issues were constantly being brought forward as having negative or limiting impacts on every reward-type program. The first was political acceptance, both from the legislators and also from within the agency itself. Without this support we knew our program was doomed to die a horrible death. The second issue was the "need to know." Only those persons who were in a position of needing to know what was happening on each specific case could have that knowledge. The third, of course, was money. Every agency identified the fact that there was never enough money to allow programs to function properly, let alone to grow. Even if the first two issues had been resolved, the program was doomed to failure if it was not adequately funded.

Armed with this wealth of information the branch began the task of developing a RAP program for Alberta that we felt would fly. In 1982 the original draft of the RAP program was developed and funneled through the channels. MDMRS was steam-rolling ahead like gangbusters and it was obvious that for one of the few times in history Alberta's fish and wildlife officers were going to be the big winners. Could we be so lucky with RAP? We crossed our fingers. It didn't take long to receive the inevitable response. Our program flew alright, but not the way we had expected, and with the much-anticipated response it came back, bouncing through the door as if it were a rubber cheque. The answer was a very clear definite: "NO!" "Why?" I asked. The reply: "We don't pay money to people for information about people shooting people and we will never pay money to people for information about people shooting animals."

There was no need for a back shelf, a back desk, a back drawer or a back wall for RAP. A simple back door from which the program should be tossed out would suffice. For all intents and purposes RAP was dead and buried, but to those of us who realized its value, it was not forgotten. The MDMRS system kept rolling along gathering no moss. By 1985 they agreed to handle phonecalls that originated through the Outdoor Observer program.

However, all this took place before LeRoy Fjordbotten became the minister responsible for the department. That's when there was a change in attitude towards the Fish and Wildlife Division and in particular, for the Enforcement-Field Services Branch. Good things began to happen. One of those things would be the resurrection of the RAP program. Mr. Fjordbotten was a strong advocate for the division and in particular the enforcement program. Suddenly, RAP had the crucial political support it needed. After Mr. Fjordbotten became minister we dug up the RAP casket and dusted off its bones. The program was massaged to reflect the times.

The "need to know" concern was addressed and the proper security provisions developed to ensure the integrity of the program and the anonymity of the people involved. Provision of the necessary funding for the program was critical to ensuring its success. We felt we had the ideal solution to this matter. We advanced the position that RAP could be adequately financed by using dedicated funds from the sale of hunting and fishing licences. For this to happen, we needed to have both politicians and sportsmen buy into the concept. Mr. Fjordbotten sold his colleagues on this initiative. The AFGA was approached and asked if they would support this idea. They did. The three key issues had all finally been resolved.

In 1990 Mr. Fjordbotten announced the RAP program at the AFGA's annual conference. RAP became a reality on April 1 of that year. It was no April Fool's joke! Suddenly there was a program in the Fish and Wildlife Division that no longer needed the back wall, the back shelf, the back table or the back drawer. RAP was taking a front seat. An advisory board with membership from many outdoor-related organizations was appointed by the minister to review each file and assess rewards. Jack Graham, one of the original members, represented the AFGA on the review board for many years. Alberta's RAP program was considered by many, and in my mind undoubtedly was, and is, the best program of its kind in North American.

RAP quickly became the benchmark by which all other similar programs would be measured. And why not? Darryl Kublik, the program co-ordinator from its inception, reports that there have been in excess of 20,000 enforcement actions stemming from 60,000-plus calls to the program. Rewards as high as $1,000 have been paid and in the past 17 years more than $714,000 has been paid out. RAP calls have included some very high-profile special investigation cases; one such case led to the charging and conviction of 30 or more individuals with fines totaling $300,000 plus jail time.

What gave the program its instant success was the political will and of course the money. The funds were provided from a $1 levy added to the cost of each hunting licence (excluding the pheasant stamp) sold in the province. It was a windfall, an unprecedented commitment of funds for any reward-type program. From April 1, 1990 until April 1, 1997, those dedicated dollars were placed into a separate fund, housed in the Fish and Wildlife Division's Buck for Wildlife program and controlled by the division. However, as with so many programs that have been properly designed and adequately funded, RAP, and in particular RAP's funding, quickly became a target. Not unexpectedly, greedy eyes began to covet RAP. Sadly in 1997 RAP and its much sought-after funding were transferred out of the division, away from the people who knew its purpose and its value to the fisheries and wildlife resources in the province and the need to maintain its integrity. In its new home, the Alberta Conservation Association (ACA), a not-for-profit charitable organization, RAP did continue to receive the dedicated funds. However, as we move along to the year 2007, 10 short years after the move, we find that things have changed. Gone, like the passenger pigeon, is the review board. Gone are the dedicated funds, today they go into one pot and are allocated based on something called management priority.

Oh, Alberta's sportsmen are still paying their dollar and RAP still exists; however, it is not the same program it once was.

I trust that someone will have the foresight to save space on the back wall, the back shelf, the back table or the back drawer. That would be merciful before RAP is shown the dreaded back door. For I have a feeling that RAP could soon be in need of a new home.

Alberta's Conservation Education History

by Tom Bateman, former chief conservation education officer

In the 1950s the rather large supply of war surplus firearms, which were available at a low price, made recreational hunting an attractive activity to many thousands throughout North America. Many of the participants in hunting were not familiar with basic firearm safety and hunting-related injuries and deaths were quite common. Governments throughout North America responded by creating "Hunter Safety Courses." The first course was in New York State in 1949. Some of these programs were a prerequisite for a hunting licence. Alberta's program was launched in 1964. Numbers of accidents began to decline almost immediately. In 1985, Alberta eliminated the regulation that required hunters to wear scarlet or blaze orange outer clothing while hunting. Many predicted a huge increase in numbers of firearms-related accidents but records after 1985 revealed that numbers of accidents continued to decline.

Today, hunting in Alberta is a very safe activity. That is a tribute to Alberta's hunters and to the ongoing success of the Alberta Conservation and Hunter Education programs and the thousands of volunteer instructors.

COURTESY OF DUANE RADFORD
Tom Bateman (L) and Bob Stevenson with John MacNeill's blown-out rifle. Just a reminder to always check your barrel!

In 1983, the Alberta Conservation and Hunter Education course was selected by a panel of experts as the most outstanding of its kind in North America.

In 1988, the Alberta Fishing Education program was separated from the conservation and hunter education program and a separate course was created.

Outdoor Camps: A lot of Alberta schools were using the conservation and hunter education course as part of their curriculum. Teachers began asking Fish and Wildlife Division staff to act as resource people on field trips. Such subjects as wilderness survival, fisheries and wildlife identification, firearms safety, archery, map and compass orientation, and other topics became so popular that in 1970 the Fish and Wildlife Division established an outdoor camp at Narrow Lake, near Athabasca. Schools and other groups booked a three-day time slot and attended the camp where they received instruction and were able to practice some of the topics contained in the Conservation and Hunter Education course. In 1973, a second camp was added; it was located just west of Caroline and is called the Alford Lake Camp.

The camp programs were very popular with Alberta schools, scouts, Junior Forest Wardens, the military, church groups, aboriginal groups and others. Travel was a problem for some groups, consequently in 1983 a portable camp was developed and operated during the spring and summer months in southwestern Alberta.

Camp programs include archery, firearms safety, including live firing, wilderness survival, wildlife and fisheries identification, use of maps and a compass, fishing, outdoor cooking and others. Each group spends three days at camp including their travel time. The students have opportunity to cook their food over an open fire and sleep in a plastic shelter they have built.

Privatization: Albertans experienced a lot of changes during the 1990s and provincial budgets were tight during this time of fiscal restraint. During this time, Bob Gruszecki, president of the Alberta Hunter Education Instructors' Association (AHEIA), made a proposal to provincial authorities that would see this association take over responsibility for administering all the Fish and Wildlife Division Conservation Education programs. This proposal was finally accepted and the details worked out with government officials. On April 1, 1996 Conservation Education programs were turned over to the Alberta Hunter Education Instructors' Association and the Conservation Education WISE Foundation. The WISE Foundation would raise the money to support Conservation Education and the Instructors' Association would be responsible for all assets and program administration.

Sam the cat and Mary Anne and Frank Bishop.

The next years were very exciting as enough money was raised to purchase a 14,000-square-foot building that became the Calgary Conservation Education Centre for Excellence. The Edmonton Conservation Centre for Excellence was added later. A couple of years later the Calgary Trap and Skeet Club asked AHEIA to take over their property near Calgary and the Calgary Firearms Centre was added to the facilities. The Narrow Lake camp was closed and the AFGA now operates this site.

The cost of operating camps is quite significant. In 2002 a decision was made to bring all the camp operations together at the Alford Lake Conservation Education Centre for Excellence. AHEIA had completely rebuilt this camp with enough winterized cabins to accommodate 70 people. There are toilets, showers, and classrooms, meeting rooms and a modern kitchen and dining area on site. The facility also includes world-class shooting ranges, archery ranges, map and compass courses, an excellent fishing program and hiking trails. The camp is very popular and is often booked more than a year in advance.

In June 2002 the Justice Department of the Canadian Government approached AHEIA and asked if they would also administer the Canadian Firearms Safety (CFS) courses in Alberta. These programs relate to hunting so an agreement was negotiated and the CFS courses were added as elements of the Alberta Conservation Education program.

Privatization of fish and wildlife conservation education programs has resulted in a significant increase in public involvement and a corresponding increase in commitment to the conservation of Alberta's wildlife and fisheries resources.

The Future: The greatest challenge facing fisheries and wildlife resources is urbanization. More than 80 percent of Albertans now live in cities. City living is inclined to disconnect people from the realities of natural systems. People are removed from most of the realities related to food production and distribution. The same applies to the distribution of water, energy and the disposal of waste. People who are protected from natural realities often have little interest in wildlife and what wildlife needs in order to exist.

Concerns about wildlife in Alberta cities often result from a coyote killing a family pet or too many geese on the golf course, or deer killed by vehicles on city roads. In Calgary recently, a school was locked down because someone spotted a coyote near by.

The challenge related to urbanization of Alberta and its impact on fish and wildlife resources is very large. Alberta's conservation education system responds with financial resources to address the things Albertans care about. Somehow wildlife, fish and the places where these resources live must become more important to Albertans who must be made aware of the marvelous contribution wildlife and fish make to the quality of our lives. Alberta is a better place to live because we have wildlife. May it always be so…

Regional Fisheries Management in Two Very Different Regions

by Frank Bishop, former regional fisheries biologist at Peace River and Lethbridge

I had the good fortune to work for the Alberta Fish and Wildlife Division as a regional fisheries biologist and manager for some 28 years. During that time I had the opportunity to help manage fisheries resources in two dissimilar regions in Alberta. I started work at Peace River in the newly created Peace River region in October, 1967 and worked there for 13 years before transferring to Lethbridge in December 1980 which was the headquarters of the southern region. While both regions had some similarities, they had quite different fish species, topography, climate and the management approaches found therein.

The Peace River region was very large, some 86,000 square miles; at the time I arrived little biological information had been collected. Initially much basic fisheries inventory was required to determine the fish species, their distribution, growth rates and utilization by fishermen. Some part-time summer help was available some years until Don Schroeder and later Dave Walty were hired on a permanent basis. Fortunately the region was made up of smaller enforcement districts under the supervision of regional officer Bud Johnston. The local district officers often accommodated me in collecting biological data and I formed some long-lasting and solid friendships with many of these officers over the years.

The southern region was only about 20,000 square miles in area but it was much more densely populated and much of the basic biological inventory work had already been completed. More significantly the region came with experienced fisheries staff comprised of Lorne Fitch, Wes English and John MacNeill and later Glen Clements and Gordon Gresiuk. John and Gordon lost their lives in a tragic boating accident on Oct. 13, 1983 while they were tagging lake whitefish below the inlet weir to Lake MacGregor.

The Peace River region had numerous large natural lakes, but few trout-bearing streams, whereas the southern region had a number of small lakes and many trout-bearing streams, especially along the eastern slopes. Most noticeably, however, man-made reservoirs and a series of inter-connecting irrigation canals were dispersed throughout the southern region. The irrigation system was managed primarily for agricultural purposes and not necessarily for fish. Surprisingly, most of the reservoirs contained lake whitefish which had been stocked years ago from the lake whitefish hatchery in Canyon Creek on Lesser Slave Lake!

Generally, the productivity of the waters in the south was higher than those in the colder north. Commercial fisheries management absorbed much staff time in both regions. Regular meetings between us and commercial fishermen to set quotas, opening and closing dates of fisheries were often heated and clamorous. Credit must be given to the few brave AFGA representatives who attended these meetings to express their concerns that sportfish species must be protected.

Lake whitefish were the target species of the commercial fishermen, both in the north and in the south. Many of the northern whitefish were infected with *Triaenophorus crassus*—a parasite which lowered their commercial value—but southern whitefish were free of this parasite. Monitoring infection rates of this parasite was a time-consuming and laborious aspect of our job in the Peace River region.

Lesser Slave Lake was the largest lake in the Peace River region and the annual harvest of cisco (tullibee) was in the neighbourhood of 2.5 million pounds from this lake alone, virtually all of it to feed a thriving mink-ranching industry.

Both regions had large rivers, but the mighty Peace River in the north was significantly larger than anything found in the south. The Peace River and the South Saskatchewan River in the south had relatively light angling pressure; however, the lake sturgeon fishery in the South Saskatchewan River attracted a small but ardent number of anglers interested in catching one of these large, unique fish. A sturgeon questionnaire was mailed out to each annually to monitor catch data to help us manage this important species.

The southern region also contained a number of high mountain lakes, some of which were stocked with another uncommon species of fish, the golden trout. Management efforts in these remote lakes were difficult but necessary to maintain fisheries in these distinctive waters. There were no high mountain lakes in the north, but a number of the larger lakes in the north did contain natural populations of lake trout, which, with one exception, were not found in the south.

My first exposure to the AFGA came at a meeting with the Dunvegan Fish and Game Association club in Fairview in November 1967. This was the first of many meetings which often dealt with members' concerns about the negative effect of commercial fishing on sport fish populations. Another topic frequently raised in both regions was that of trout stocking. By 1980 the trout stocking program in the Peace River region had doubled to almost 400,000 trout in 12 locations – this was small compared to the approximately two million trout being stocked in 35 locations in the southern region.

While walleye were present naturally in many of the northern lakes, interest in this species was relatively low until a concerted effort was made by Alberta fisheries branch officials to increase the numbers and locations of walleye by collecting eggs, raising them for release to waters in areas thought suitable to sustain them. Many of the early techniques to locate, capture and collect walleye eggs were discovered at Upper Chin Reservoir in southern Alberta. Using this knowledge, spawn-taking camps were first set up at Bistcho Lake in the Peace River region. Walleye stocking in a number of reservoirs in the southern region resulted in the creation of walleye fisheries where previously only pike fisheries had existed. Many of the AFGA members volunteered their time to assist with the distribution of walleye fry and were an integral part of the walleye enhancement program.

Although a few trout-bearing streams could be found in the Grande Prairie district of the Peace River region, there were a fair number of "blue ribbon" trout streams in the south which required specialized management. Angler use by way of creel census monitoring became a large part of our summer programs.

Irrigation canals in the south created a number of unique management predicaments, not the least of which was the efforts of the irrigation districts to control aquatic vegetation in the canals. The control of aquatic weeds led to my involvement with a study that looked into the feasibility of using biological control: triploid grass carp (*Ctenopharyngodon idella*). This study was a joint effort of Alberta Agriculture, Alberta Environment, the Lethbridge Community College and our own department. The first planting of grass carp in Alberta was on May 11, 1989, near Lethbridge. This experimental program continued in the ensuing years.

My fisheries management experiences in these two disparate regions was interesting, diverse and occasionally frustrating, but mostly it was very rewarding. It was satisfying to apply what I had learned in university but ultimately it was the collective efforts of the public and the government working together that governed the success or failure of fisheries programs. The involvement and support of groups such as the AFGA was significant in both of the regions I worked in during my career with the Fish and Wildlife Division.

Evolution of the Special Licence Draw

by Sylvia Birkholz, former head of licensing and revenue service

Special licence draws are simply lotteries people enter to obtain a hunting licence. Licences are usually specific to sex (antlered or antlerless), wildlife management unit (WMU) or area, hunting timeframe or some combination of these parameters. Hunters using a special draw licence are more restricted to what, where and when they hunt than those using a regular hunting licence. These draws are held yearly during a restricted timeframe and hunters are notified of their success prior to each year's hunting season.

The special licence draws are used for many management reasons. Biologists use special draws to ensure the number or type of animals harvested will not surpass a quantity that could be harmful to the animal population in a specific area. They are also used in areas where the demand to hunt exceeds the number of animals that can be safely harvested from the population. In other areas, special draws are used to limit the number of hunters to ensure the quality of the hunting experience remains high as well as promoting an acceptable concentration of hunters to residents of the area.

In the 1960s and early 1970s draws were straight-forward lotteries for resident Alberta hunters only. Hunters picked up their free paper application forms at Fish and Wildlife Division offices, filled out their choices and sent the application accompanied by the appropriate licence fee back to the Fish and Wildlife Division. The applications had to clearly show the hunter's full name and their current wildlife certificate number. Like today, a maximum

COURTESY OF DUANE RADFORD

Fish and Wildlife Division biological lake and stream survey camp.

of four people could jointly apply in one envelope. The postmark on the envelope could be no later than midnight on the deadline date and the fee had to be a certified cheque or money order. Following the deadline date the applications were put into a large bin and envelopes were manually withdrawn until the quota was reached. Hunters whose envelopes were drawn were sent back a portion of the application marked successful that then had to be validated at a Fish and Wildlife Division office. This form became their hunting licence. Those envelopes not drawn were simply returned to the sender. A hunter might get drawn every year or once every few years or they might apply year after year and never be successful in the special draw. By the mid-1970s there were special draws for just about every big-game species in the province. Sheep, goat, antelope, deer, elk and moose all had some type of draw that hunters could enter.

In 1978 authorizations for antlerless elk, mule deer and white-tailed deer were added to the draw system. No fees were sent with the application. Following the draw, a successful hunter went to a Fish and Wildlife Division office to buy their authorization. In order for the authorization to be valid a hunter had to first purchase the corresponding male licence that allowed the hunter to hunt a male animal anywhere in the province where the season was open. The hunter could then kill either a male or female animal but could hunt the antlerless animal only in the area prescribed on their authorization. Only one animal could be harvested as there was only one tag issued with the two documents. These were also lotteries carried out during the same time as the regular special licence draws. By 1981 the authorizations were free and included both antlered and antlerless elk, moose and both deer.

During the 1980s quota licences were created for areas that were undersubscribed in the special licence and authorization draws. These undersubscribed licences were available on a first come-first serve basis at specific Fish and Wildlife Division offices. Details were advertised only in local newspapers and on radio if any licences became available.

In 1985 non-refundable $3 application fees were added for both special licences and authorizations but the applications were made more widely available than at only Fish and Wildlife Division offices. Hunters could pick up their applications at the AFGA, certain ticket outlets in Alberta and a number of private vendors throughout the province. Once hunters obtained their authorization it was free, other than the initial application fee. On completion of the special draw, unsuccessful applicants were returned their licence fees but the application fee was kept. Special licences continued to have the prescribed fee that had to accompany the application. During this time, application information started being computerized to allow for a random computerized selection rather than manually.

During the early 1990s non-residents (Canadians) became eligible to apply on antlered draws rather than merely the trophy antelope draw. To ensure that the number of non-resident in any area would never outnumber Albertans, their applications had to contain an equal or larger number of Albertans. This practice continues to be the case today.

In 1992 hunters were given a "permanent" wildlife identification number (WiN) allowing the present day "priority" process to be added to the special draw. Each time a hunter applies on an individual special draw and is not successful they are given one "priority point." Every year a hunter applies on that draw and is not drawn the points accumulate. The quota for each different type of special draw is filled by randomly picking hunters with the highest priority number. If licences are still available, the draw continues to randomly pick hunters from each subsequent lower priority number until the quota is reached. The next time an application is made on that draw by a previously successful applicant, their priority number starts at zero and the process starts again. This guarantees, where the demand outweighs the quota, a person will not have a licence every year and ensures that the person who consistently applies on the same draw receives a licence before those who are not as diligent.

By 1996 authorizations were discontinued. Everything available through the draw was in the form of a special licence. In 1995 hunters could apply via the telephone rather than directly through mail. Undersubscribed licences were first available on 1-800 lines (no toll), then 1-900 lines (toll charge) using a call centre, followed by the current system of 1-900 interactive voice recognition system.

In 1998 the current online Point-of-Sale (POS) licensing system was put into place. This did not affect the licence types or the rules that applied to the special licence draws but simply altered the processes surrounding the draws. Applications continued to be made by telephone but they could also be made at private vendors throughout the province rather than at Fish and Wildlife Division offices. The immediate electronic transmittal of a hunter's application information eliminated the extensive entry of the rising amount of data into the draw system. Hunters still had to pay the application fee but they now paid the licence fee only when they purchased their licence at any vendor.

The new POS licensing system amounted to the "privatization" of buying hunting and fishing licences in Alberta. This meant that the physical special draw processes including the associated notification processes were carried out by private enterprise. The Fish and Wildlife Division, with input from recognized hunting and fishing groups, puts forward management changes to the special licence draws, then private industry makes the required revisions to the system and manages the licensing function.

In the early 2000s refinements to the draw system continued to be implemented. The "partner licence" was added to allow hunters who were successful in the moose special licence draws to share their hunt with one other person. Only one animal could be killed as only one tag was issued but two licences could be attached to the one tag. Following that, a youth partner licence was added allowing anyone who is successful on any of the special draws to share their tag with a youth hunter. The priority of the "partner" is not affected but the priority of the successful draw applicant drops to zero. In 2003 the use of "999" as a legitimate WMU choice was added to help hunters manage their priorities with their probabilities of being successfully drawn. The code 999 allows hunters to apply on a draw to increase their priority but lets the "draw system" know that they do not want to be drawn that particular year.

Duane Radford digging out the stuck Fish and Wildlife Division truck.

In 2005 an Internet portion was added to the licensing system which affected a different aspect of the special draw. Hunters having a valid "WiN" can now sign onto an Internet site to see their current priority numbers for every licence they have applied for. They can view the applications they make and shortly following the completion of the special draws they can see whether they have been successful rather than wait for mail notification.

During the years, rules and restrictions as to which lotteries hunters could apply for were made part of the application process. The rules and restrictions changed to reflect changing management needs. Choosing between elk or moose but not both; choosing between an antlered or antlerless moose draw but not both in a given year; only having a chance to hunt goat once; not being able to apply on a trophy sheep draw if the hunter had killed a sheep the year previously or two years previously are all examples of the types of changes that have occurred. Partner licences, junior partner licences, two tags or three tags in the case of antlerless mule deer are examples of recent changes.

Hunters now have priorities in the double digits for a few significant special draws and the number of applications for big game special licence draws has risen from 80,000 in the early 1990s to over 200,000 in 2006. Each year many hunters with "0" or "1" priorities are successful in the draw but there are also hunters who have priorities as high as 10 that are not drawn. In 2006, a special licence draw was initiated for sportfishing, again exclusively for Albertans, for walleye tags on Lake Newell, Pigeon Lake and Wolf Lake. The special draw system with its associated rules, application methods and associated licences, continue to change and evolve to reflect changes in Alberta.

COURTESY OF DUANE RADFORD

Lorne Fitch (L) and Barry Adams. "Cows and Fish" program at Callum Creek, March 2000.

Cows and Fish Program

A Pathway to Watershed Stewardship by Lorne Fitch,
former provincial riparian specialist, fisheries branch

Issues about riparian use began in Alberta with a focus on fish. In the 1970s the impact of decades of unmanaged livestock use on several high-profile trout streams in west-central Alberta became apparent through biological surveys. One stream was the North Raven River, with work supported by the AFGA. Those baseline surveys provided the catalyst to galvanize restoration actions designed to improve habitat conditions for trout. Without knowledge and tools to manage grazing in riparian systems, initial efforts for recovery involved fencing programs to permanently exclude livestock from variable portions of riparian areas. Exclusion fencing can provide rapid recovery and help to demonstrate a site's

biological potential, often quickly; this was the case for the initial riparian management program in west-central Alberta.

However, as the program to use exclusion fencing as the riparian management tool expanded, some issues related to the narrow focus became apparent. Initial fencing costs were high and the associated maintenance of fences in close proximity to an area prone to flood damage often exceeded the original cost. Stream-bank fencing was also seen to be a loss of abundant forage and a perception that this limited the opportunity for livestock watering. Acceptance of fencing as a solution and adoption by landowners became problematic in other areas of the province. As well, streams, the adjoining riparian zone and watersheds function as units and are inseparable; exclusion fencing doesn't allow the opportunity to find the solution to a riparian grazing problem in the adjacent uplands and to manage on a landscape basis.

Riparian areas are the transition zones between aquatic ecosystems and the adjacent upland terrestrial ecosystem. Riparian areas are "wetter than dry", but "drier than wet." This is a landscape type strongly influenced by water, small in size and ecologically diverse. "Healthy" riparian areas support unique plant communities that establish watershed function, provide diverse habitats for fish and wildlife, and a highly productive forage supply for livestock. Because of their magnetic attraction for agriculture, recreation, industry and residential development these landscapes are under stress. Despite their small size, riparian areas are the most valuable, productive and vulnerable areas we have in the overall scheme of varied Alberta landscapes.

In the United States the use and abuse of riparian landscapes by livestock grazing has been a focal point of more than four decades of debate. That situation provided an example of a riparian grazing issue characterized by deeply entrenched conflict among interest groups and legislated solutions. The Alberta Cows and Fish program initiative began as a recognition that resolution of the impasse over riparian areas and their management would be accomplished with a range of solutions, including, but not exclusively, stream-bank fencing. Very early it was recognized that co-operative solutions utilizing the experience and knowledge of livestock producers and others would be more effective than legislation. In 1992 six groups and agencies sat around a rancher's kitchen table and established what would eventually become the Cows and Fish program.

What made Cows and Fish effective is its somewhat unique approach. As a general rule the approach of agencies (and agency staff) to resource management issues is regulatory or prescriptive, or incentive based. Phrased differently, "this is what you must do," or "this is best and you should do it this way," or "here is some money,

Refuelling the helicopter in a field during an aerial wildlife survey.

please co-operate." These delivery mechanisms tend to be centralist or top-down in nature; a consequence of this approach is products from it tend to be viewed with suspicion and distrust by those who are the intended recipients of the advice, direction and resources.

The Cows and Fish program began (and continues) as a different way to engage people, especially livestock producers and other owners of riparian areas, and move beyond suspicion, denial and conflict toward trust, acceptance and co-operation. Engagement begins with ecological awareness, a non-threatening, non-confrontational extension effort to help people understand some of the ecological processes that shape the landscape they live on and make a living from. Part of that critical, initial message is that there are choices and alternatives to current management practices. Cows and Fish encourages the formation of watershed or community groups, composed of technical, producer and other local interests, to engage with each other and drive the process. Acceptance is enhanced because people perceive that the initiative is internal, as opposed to being externally driven. Message deliverers go where the community invites them and the messages are given more prominence. This working relationship helps assemble diverse experience, talents, perspectives and resources in a collaborative way.

Ecological awareness, a place to begin sensitizing individuals at a community level to recognize elements of their environment, leads to ecological literacy. Literacy is the ability to see and respond to choice, opportunity or option in land-management decisions. Changes to land management are driven by informed decisions that are, in part, based on a greater appreciation of ecological function and process. Individuals, in making ecologically appropriate land-management decisions, can minimize risk, avoid liability and maintain future options. Cows and Fish assists in the assemblage of technical advice and tools for management changes to provide options and alternatives to

current practices. These can include riparian grazing strategies, off-stream water development and restoration of riparian areas with rest. Information sources include those innovative, progressive or practical solutions already being used by a limited group of landowners.

Riparian health evaluation became a useful tool to allow people to critically observe, measure and assess the status of ecological functions on their own property or within their communities. Riparian health reflects the ability of a riparian area to perform certain key ecological functions. These functions include sediment trapping, bank building, water storage, aquifer recharge, water filtration, flow energy dissipation, maintenance of biodiversity and primary production. If these functions are impaired so too will be the ability to sustain agricultural operations or maintain fish and wildlife populations. Health evaluation is not just an ecological measuring stick; it becomes a communication device to allow people with differing backgrounds and experience to "see" a riparian area and its status through the same set of eyes. Arguments about riparian condition are minimized and a much more productive discussion about how to restore damaged areas can begin to take place. The current status of watersheds within a community can then become a catalyst for action based on health evaluations and forms a benchmark useful to chart progress, both on individual properties and within watersheds.

Cows and Fish assists in community-based conservation through a process of engagement that creates opportunity to move from conflict to co-operation. It is the transfer of responsibility for action to the community that is in the best position to make the changes and benefit from them. Riparian (and by association, watershed) actions need to be community-based, locally driven and largely voluntary. To help a community to arrive at this point of stewardship requires knowledge building, motivation, acknowledgement of problems and empowerment. The reasons for positive action may result from enhanced awareness, motivated self-interest, and concern about legislation, marketing opportunity or altruism. The net effect has been a return to a landscape that maintains critical ecological functions and provides a greater measure of support for agricultural operations. Cows and Fish has been about building a cumulative body of knowledge that we all should know including how riparian systems function and link us, how watersheds work, the vital signs of landscape health, the essentials of how people need to work together, how solutions need to benefit us all and the kinds of information that will enable us to restore or maintain natural systems and build ecologically resilient communities and economies.

Concerns about riparian areas in Alberta began over fisheries issues. The more the microscope focused on this seemingly insignificant landscape the greater our understanding became about the disproportionate importance of riparian areas. Issues of biodiversity, economics and water quality now crowd the media; all relate to landscape use, especially the use of riparian areas. Long-lasting solutions will have to engender thoughtful application of initiatives that are accepted and effective at a community level. Inevitably this is where we will succeed or fail, based on our approach.

Southern Alberta Big-Game Surveys

by Leo Gudmundson, former regional wildlife technician, southern region, Lethbridge

Buckle-up, we're going flying. Aerial surveys to determine wildlife abundance and distribution have been conducted for approximately 50 years in Alberta. In their infancy, sporadic aerial flights were undertaken in the southern prairie region and foothills to assess general abundance and concentrations of deer and elk primarily on winter ranges. Fixed-winged aircraft were generally utilized. Antelope population trend counts were taken on a number of survey lines located throughout the short grass prairie region.

My first experience with wildlife survey work followed shortly after obtaining a position with the Fish and Wildlife Division as regional wildlife technician in Lethbridge in 1971. As I recall, the local biologist and myself were picked up at the Lethbridge airport to accompany two Edmonton wildlife staff who flew down in a twin engine fixed-winged Dornier aircraft to undertake a deer population survey along the Milk River. I was somewhat concerned and a bit overwhelmed with what followed. The larger twin engine aircraft necessitated flying at a relatively high airspeed and maintaining considerable elevation above ground level making deer observations and identification very difficult, and in some instances giving deer the appearance of ants scampering across the rugged Milk River terrain. A bouncing aircraft as a result of strong Chinook winds did not help matters. I was not overly comfortable with the ability to make animal observations and accurate herd counts but no member of the crew admitted any difficulties so neither did I. Eventually the flight had to be called off. Employment of appropriate aircraft during future surveys made things much easier, resulting in the collection of much improved information.

Initial wildlife population surveys which were designed during the mid to late 1960s utilized a series of blocks or straight-line transects scattered throughout the various wildlife management units (WMUs). Deer surveys were conducted on blocks of habitat normally representing areas of known higher animal concentrations while antelope population trend information was assembled by conducting animal counts on line transects. This population trend information was considered sufficient during the time of general season harvest formats under which most harvest programs of the day were designed. With substantial increases to the Fish and Wildlife Division resources and personnel during the late 1960s and early 1970s aerial surveys became common place especially with access to a fleet of four or five government helicopters. The helicopter fleet was set up primarily for the Alberta Forest Service to assist with forest-fire suppression programs during the summer months but shortly thereafter became available to the Fish and Wildlife Division to conduct wildlife survey programs during the winter months. Also, at this time provincial and regional wildlife survey programs were taking on a new complexion with the establishment of a provincial survey team. During the period 1971-81 regional wildlife survey programs were normally jointly implemented with the employment of two individuals from the survey team and one regional staff member. During this same time period a substantial modification and updates to survey designs were being undertaken to meet the ever increasing need for more in-depth WMU population data, especially associated with expansion of species draw-harvest systems. Prairie deer, antelope and foothills moose population survey formats were redesigned using a system of sampling stratified habitat as a means of developing reasonably accurate WMU species population estimates. Progress over time has seen further changes to the administration, funding and implementation of regional wildlife survey programs especially following creation of the Alberta Conservation Association in 1997.

Involvement and interest in wildlife management projects and population studies has been a major focal point of Fish and Game Clubs and their membership. Over the years this interest has resulted in various meetings and in some cases regularly scheduled information exchanges between the Fish and Wildlife Division personnel, the AFGA representatives as well as other interested stakeholder groups. One such information exchange meeting which has had a history of nearly two decades brought together the AFGA representatives as well as various other interest groups to review results of recent species population surveys and recommended up-coming animal harvests and permit allocations. Support of the AFGA and local clubs has been a substantial force over the years, recognizing the need for collection of adequate and current population information in support of wildlife species management.

Coming Full Circle

by Gordon Kerr, former assistant deputy minister Alberta Fish and Wildlife Division

I caught my first rainbow trout in a north tributary to the Oldman River, near the Whaleback Ridge, when I was five years old. I attended my first AFGA meeting in 1948, when I was nine years old.

My grandfather, John Kerr, came to the Northwest Territories, Rupert's Land, in 1903, two years before Alberta was declared a province. He and his brother William (Bill) were ardent conservationists and active hunters and fishermen. My father, James Runcimen Kerr, born in 1905, was raised at Passburg, a ghost town near Burmis, in the Crowsnest Pass with an ardent appreciation of wildlife, fishing and the great outdoors.

We moved west of Coleman to a ranch and motel business in 1950 when I was eleven years old. Our ranch was a half-mile from the provincial Forest Reserve, which gave me a backyard of thousands of square miles of semi-wilderness. The 1950s was pre-seismic petroleum exploration, pre-dirt bikes, quads and snowmobiles. Even 4x4 trucks were rare. We, however, had 23 saddle horses so if my brothers and I followed game trails or searched out old half re-grown logging trails, we could have the country largely to ourselves.

In the summer of 1951, when I was 12, there were some issues resulting in a major AFGA meeting in the Crowsnest area. Mr. George Spargo, secretary manager of the AFGA, was there and he stayed the night with our family. He and my dad and I, with a couple of other men, went fishing the next day and we had a great time on Racehorse Creek. When Mr. Spargo left he gave me his fishing rod, which I still have 56 years later. My winter pastime, aside from hockey and curling, was to watch deer, elk, and moose and bighorn sheep with a spotting scope from our living room window in Star Creek. Trapping and hunting coyotes on the ranch was an ongoing event.

My grandfather and father made many trout stockings in the southern foothills by volunteering to relocate fingerling from both the Waterton Lakes National Park and the Banff National Park hatcheries, all at their own cost. My father and brothers and I continued that activity with trout from the provincial hatchery at the Burns Brewery at Calgary in co-operation with the local wildlife officers. I recall many trips but the one which stands out was to Window Mountain Lake in the Allison Creek drainage.

Porcupine Hills of the Livingstone Range, west of Longview.

We took fry (about one inch long) by pack horse to timberline and then backpacked them ourselves the last half-mile. That half-mile seemed straight up, and we were completely spent when we got to the lake. Three years later though it proved worthwhile when marvelous trout were caught by many friends in the area.

My memories from childhood to late teen years included pheasant transplants, beaver relocations with an old forest ranger named Jack Morden (stationed at the Gap Ranger Station and in the Porcupine Hills) and all the people who were active in the fish and game clubs in the Crowsnest Pass in Coleman, Blairmore, Frank, Hillcrest and Bellevue. One notable success of the fish and game clubs was the reconstruction of the Allison Creek Reservoir in which my dad played an overseeing role for the Coleman Fish and Game Association. A second trout-lake development on McGillivray Creek was also successful.

When I graduated from high school it was a forgone conclusion that I would pursue a career in wildlife management. Degrees from Montana University in Missoula and the University of Alberta in Edmonton paved the way for employment with the Alberta Fish and Wildlife Division. When I joined as a summer student, Curt P. Smith was then the first Fish and Wildlife Division director, fresh from his role as president of the AFGA. When I became the chief wildlife biologist in 1967 it had become standard practice to work co-operatively with the AFGA. We had our differences between the two groups but we worked past them for the good of the wildlife and fisheries resources and use by Albertans.

Working groups like the Fish and Wildlife advisory council, with members from the AFGA, trappers and outfitters, were positive and productive. Communications were excellent and we all worked together on various issues. One joint undertaking stands out in my memory. The AFGA executive and those of us in the government spawned the idea of a habitat program which came to be known as the Buck for Wildlife program. We sold it to government and they sold it to their members and then Minister Dr. Allan Warrack made it happen. This joint program became a model for many other areas in North America. Wildlife Habitat Canada and the whole North American Waterfowl Management Plan took a similar approach, in fact. The hunter training program, complete with training camps for school-aged people, was successful only because of the energies and work of instructors from the AFGA.

During my time as assistant deputy minister of the Fish and Wildlife Division we jointly developed the Report a Poacher program, expanded the Fish and Wildlife advisory council, jointly drafted the AFGA resolutions and moved money to the AFGA so that with volunteer labour, various projects were completed less expensively than otherwise would have been the case.

I recall many hours of discussion with Elmer Kure, director of environment of the AFGA, together with Dr. Martin Paetz, director of fisheries, and David Neave, director of wildlife, and others of both groups where problems were discussed and solutions found. Those were great co-operative times where all concerned could take pride in progress.

Over that course of time the ranks of the Fish and Wildlife Division grew from about 100 staff to over 350, with budgets from about $1 million to over $26 million, plus capital allocations for facilities like the Brooks Wildlife Centre, the Sam Livingston Fish Hatchery facilities in Calgary, trout brood stock station on Allison Creek, rejuvenated brood fish stock facilities on the Raven River and walleye rearing facilities in the Lac La Biche area. Alberta had the most advanced and effective fish and wildlife program in Canada at the time.

The political climate changed between 1977 and 1980. It seems that public servants working closely with public groups began to be viewed with some suspicion. The political agenda and appointments seemed more and more the order of the day. The plans for a broad multi-species wildlife station at Brooks were over-ruled and it was ordered to become solely a pheasant hatchery (a long-term opportunity lost). Kananaskis Country plans that had integrated wilderness experience with conservation and intensive recreation were bypassed in favour of alpine villages and golf courses. And on it went to the frustration of many employees of the Fish and Wildlife Division.

I decided I had maybe been in the same game for too long, with no desire to keep playing the professional versus political interface. I left the Government of Alberta and joined the Canadian Wildlife Service, where I hoped to reconnect with more wildlife research and science. That proved to be a good move for me but, unfortunately in late 1981, with the National Energy Policy the economy took a downturn and the Alberta Fish and Wildlife Division, not unlike other departments, experienced a number of years of downsizing and budget cuts. Many programs of value were lost, offices closed, staff reduced, the Buck for Wildlife program was quasi-privatized, the Fish and Wildlife Advisory Council disbanded and fisheries facilities lost. In some ways I was glad I wasn't there to have to deal with all the disappointments. More importantly, however, as economic times recovered and improved, the old joint working relationship with the AFGA and most other conservation groups of Alberta were not re-established. Even the "wildlife" part of the government-created Recreation, Parks and Wildlife Foundation lost its way when consolidated with the Alberta Sports Council. Fish and wildlife management seemed to no longer have a priority in government.

Since the late 1970s and through the 1980s many new wildlife-related organizations have been formed in Alberta. Some examples are Trout Unlimited Canada, The Alberta Conservation Association, The Rocky Mountain Elk Foundation, Hunting for Tomorrow, WISE Foundation, Pheasants for Tomorrow, and a number of conservation focus groups which don't foster hunting such as Canadian Parks and Wilderness Society (CPAWS), Federation of Alberta Naturalists (FAN) and other groups not so attuned to wildlife management, but rather to preservation without provision for harvest use. While the formation of these groups is encouraging, it has in many ways diluted the impact of any one group in working with provincial and federal governments. Some form of overall co-ordinating process would seem desirable.

Changes within a broad cross-section of wildlife are the best indicator or measure of the state of the environment. Intensive land uses interfere with natural ecological processes and can cause decreases in less adaptive species such that predation or habitat competition can cause some isolated pockets of a species to be lost. Harvest of more adaptive species can assist those species which may be threatened. That harvest effort can most economically be done through informed public hunting. Organized hunters must be seen as part of the management team within our modified environment.

Petroleum exploration and forest management have developed access to all corners of everywhere and the onslaught of ATVs of all kinds have opened the land to intensive use. Society on the other hand has become rapidly urbanized with organized sports such as golf, tennis, etc., displacing hunting, trapping and fishing. Hunter numbers have declined as have fish and game memberships. With all the competing uses of land it is essential that wildlife populations be managed within the carrying capacity of the habitat. The least expensive tool of population management is hunting, an honourable tool unrecognized by non-hunters.

In 1994 I retired from government and formed a consulting company with a focus on sustainable landscapes. In 1999 I ceased professional employment (except for management of a family farm woodlot) and dedicated my time to family and volunteer work with conservation organizations. I work with the Woodlot Association of Alberta and the Land Stewardship Centre of Canada to foster sustainable landscape management and the Sherwood Park Fish and Game Association to support habitat protection and enhancement as well as population management through active harvest activities.

So I have come full circle. I began my conservation work involved in the activities of the AFGA and co-operatively worked with government. I then joined government and advanced through the ranks of the provincial and federal wildlife agencies and worked co-operatively with conservation groups like the AFGA. I have been privileged to contribute to the success in resources management through these joint efforts. It is disappointing today to observe the separation of government and society's conservation core, the AFGA. It is frustrating to see the negative views held by many who don't recognize the need for wildlife population management.

By law, wildlife and fish resources are owned by the province of Alberta but its best volunteer workers are the various fish and game association clubs and provincial body. Let us hope the working partnership of the past again sees prominence in this second century of Alberta.

COURTESY OF TRAVEL ALBERTA

An elk grazing in Jasper National Park.

Milestones associated with the Alberta Fish and Game Association during my career with the Fish and Wildlife Division

by Ray Makowecki, former head, fisheries habitat development and protection section; regional director, northeast region

As I recall the milestones of my career in government with the AFGA, I was moved by the members I was fortunate to meet over the years. These AFGA members all deserve to be honoured for their dedication and commitment to the conservation of Alberta's fish and wildlife and their habitat. The following milestones are just some of the special times during my career with the Alberta government.

Hunter Education (1960s): In late 1964-65 Alberta's hunter education program was initiated and the first training manual was produced. The training manual was developed by a team of government officials that included Paul Presidente, Lionel Dunn and Joanne Hewko. The manual was government-produced and the delivery was to be completed by volunteer-trained instructors. I was a student in one of the first Alberta Hunter Education Instructor's courses in 1966 and was a certified instructor while I taught high school for a few years. Almost all of the instructors were volunteers who belonged to the AFGA and they became the delivery force throughout the province. By 1967 there were 875 certified instructors and even members of the provincial legislative assembly took the hunter training test. This was a major function of the AFGA at the time. The AFGA had an opportunity to manage the Hunter Education Program in the 1990s; however, this function was taken over by the WISE Foundation and it is now operated by the Alberta Hunter Education Instructor's Association (AHEIA) and delivered by many AFGA members.

Trophy Pike of Seibert Lake: During the early 1970s several AFGA clubs including those from St. Albert, Lac La Biche, St. Paul, Stony Plain, Wainwright and Two Hills invited me to be a guest speaker at their meetings. Don Hayden was the president of the St. Albert and District Fish and Game Association at that time. The clubs wanted to provide members with fish population information and interesting stories about what fish eat and where they live. I found the members to be very interested in the biology of the various fish species and I saw the members as true conservationists.

Buck for Wildlife program: The Buck for Wildlife program was introduced into Alberta in 1973 with a mandate to maintain an abundance of fish and wildlife throughout the province by means of various habitat development and improvement techniques. The funds for this program were mainly derived from the sale of resource development stamps in conjunction with the sale of angling and hunting licenses. I was the first fisheries habitat development biologist with the Alberta government and Brent Markham was the first wildlife habitat development biologist. Several regional fisheries biologists were also very active in habitat development, such as Duane Radford in Lethbridge, Gerry Thompson in Calgary, Mel Kraft in Red Deer, Carl Hunt in Edson, Ken Zelt in Edmonton, Doug Lowe in St. Paul and Frank Bishop in Peace River. The AFGA was

COURTESY OF BRIAN MAKOWECKI

Ray Makowecki with a mule deer.

instrumental in the establishment of this program. The association basically asked to be taxed $1 from the sale of each angling and hunting license. In 1978-79 the contribution from each license increased to $2. Several fish and game clubs were involved in Buck for Wildlife program activities in the 1970s:

- The Wainwright club—Ken and Jean Anderson, Al Higgins and Ray Pierce—was involved in the Shuster Lake Stabilization and Rehabilitation Project and in the development of Wallace Park (Town of Wainwright) fish pond.
- The Ponoka Fish and Game Association was involved with the Ponoka Pond Rehabilitation Project.
- The Ponoka Fish and Game Association and the Bashaw Club—with Bill Moltzan—was involved in the Windsor Lake Stabilization and Access Project.
- Vern Simpson and the Iron Creek club was involved in the Coronation Pond Development project and other pond assessments in the area.
- Sylver Lakusta and the Two Hills Fish and Game Association club was instrumental in the development of the Two Hills Pond.
- The Picture Butte Fish and Game Association was involved in the Lehto Reservoir Improvement Project; Bill Vogt was a key member.
- The Cardston Rod and Gun Club was involved in the Little Beaverdam Lake Improvement Project.
- The Coaldale Fish and Game Association was involved in the McQuillan Reservoir Improvement Project.
- The Brooks Fish and Game Association, along with a local citizens group, was involved in the Stonehill Lake Improvement Project.
- The Endiang and Byemoor Fish and Game Association clubs, along with Frank Sommerville, were involved in the Boehlke's Pond Improvement Project.
- The Athabasca Fish and Game Association—Leo Beller, Nick Rubik, Eileen Christensen, Gordon Christensen, Alex Krawec, Steve Krawec, Steve Shwaga, Thorel Edmundson, Bill Besaylo and Dan Peredery, along with a local seniors group—was involved in the Boyle Pond Development Project.
- The North Raven River (Stauffer Creek) Streambank Protection Project was initiated by the Red Deer, Eckville and

Rocky Mountain House AFGA clubs as one of the first projects intended to protect stream banks from various agricultural practices including livestock grazing. Several fish and game members were involved with this project including Elmer Kure, Lloyd Graff and Bob Scammell. The initial fish habitat assessment work was conducted under the direction of Mel Kraft, who was the local fisheries biologist at the time in Red Deer who confirmed many of the problems that had been identified by AFGA. The project was later turned over to me and I began negotiations with the local landowners to develop streambank protection plans and mitigate the conflicting agricultural uses. Individual quarter-sections of private land were subsequently fenced and suitable alternate watering sites provided to allow livestock watering.

- Several watercourses including Prairie Creek, Ware Creek, Raven River and Dogpound Creek were subsequently included in the stream bank fencing and rehabilitation program.

- In the 1980s and 1990s, the Millet, Thorsby, Leduc and the Wetaskiwin AFGA clubs banded together to develop fish spawning habitat on Tide Creek. Walleye spawning beds were laid down and beaver dams were removed. Some benefits arising from this project to the walleye population bore fruit in the 2000s. AFGA members who worked hard to make this project a reality were Ray Courchesne, Gilbert Magnan, Dave Gibson, Ruth Harrison and Wally Carstairs.

Chemical rehabilitation of Carson (McLeod) Lake: This project was supported by the Whitecourt AFGA club, zone 4 and the provincial AFGA. This project involved the chemical treatment of the lake with rotenone, a natural fish toxicant derived from the root of a plant (Derris sp.). A large predator population of northern pike and competing white suckers was eliminated in favour of rainbow trout.

Prior to the treatment of the lake in September 1976, four fish barriers were constructed to reduce the possible re-introduction of the unwanted fish species. Some pre-treatment salvage fishing was conducted by some fish and game members and subsequently approximately 25 personnel from the Fish and Wildlife Division assisted in the chemical rehabilitation of the lake.

The success of the treatment and the maintenance of the rainbow trout fishery in the absence of predatory and competing species for the past 30 years is a remarkable story. Carl Hunt and Ray Makowecki co-ordinated the project and supervised the government personnel under the direction of Dr. Martin Paetz and worked effectively with the AFGA volunteers to make the project a success.

Amadou Lake Elk Transplant Athabasca AFGA Club (1980-82): Leo Beller, Nick Rubik, Gordon Christensen, Eileen Christensen, Steve Shwaga, Steve Krawec, Alex Krawec, Hal Harrison, Thorel Eymundson and Dan Peredery were instrumental in arranging elk transplants north of Athabasca. I remember the celebration that was held at the Athabasca annual trophy banquet when the local MLA, Frank Appleby, Dennis Surrendi, assistant deputy minister of the Fish and Wildlife Division, and I attended a packed hall of 300 or more people. There was a strong feeling of accomplishment and the entire community was thinking wildlife because of the Athabasca AFGA club's involvement with this project.

The Athabasca AFGA club was honoured with an Alberta Order of the Bighorn Award in 1983 in recognition of their determination and efforts in this transplant program.

COURTESY OF TRAVEL ALBERTA

Pelicans enjoying the water at Elk Island National Park.

Big Bend Integrated Resource Plan: The proposed sale and agricultural expansion of some 46,000 acres of public land northwest of Athabasca was on paper, awaiting public comment, by government officials. The government was endorsing this land-use change and Frank Appleby, the local MLA, was holding some public meetings to solidify the plan. This plan was a concern for wildlife and habitat resource managers and biologists because of the potential loss of a considerable amount of wildlife habitat and accessible lands for public use were also at risk.

The January 1983 night when the first public meeting was scheduled was cold at -35 C and I was not sure who was coming to the meeting. I needed some support to retain fish and wildlife and the habitat in the Big Bend area northwest of Athabasca.

I called Leo Beller and Nick Rubik and they pulled together a group of Athabasca club members in two loaded cars as I recall, which came to the Flatbush Hall on this cold winter night. They made their concerns known to Frank Appleby and a decision was made to put on hold the proposed future developments. Many thanks go to the dedicated volunteers of the Athabasca AFGA club for forestalling this sale of public land.

The only thing I could do was to invite them over to my vehicle after the meeting, near midnight, in the cold winter night, and I poured and we shared a strong camaraderie that I shall always cherish. For no personal gain, these people came out to speak for wildlife and I thank them.

In 1981-82 Roy Ozanne was a volunteer who worked closely with the Northeast region of the Alberta Fish and Wildlife Division in attempting to minimize the impact of range improvement on wildlife populations. He would often come to the St. Paul regional office and discuss specific plans and strategies to ensure that the biologists' recommendations were heard in the meetings. Mr. Ozanne worked closely with George Hamilton, Dr. Wayne Nelson and Ray Makowecki to obtain the best deal for wildlife habitat. His volunteer efforts and dedication were very much appreciated by the government officials. The milestones are highlighted by the causes that we believe in and this involves the fish and wildlife resources and their habitats. These resources values unit biologists and the AFGA members. The strongest memories of my career are of people who have given of themselves for the natural resources, such as Hank and Dennis Holowaychuk from Smoky Lake and their personal sacrifices in speaking out for the fish and wildlife resources. Both should always be remembered.

The Evolution of Alberta's Modern Game Management Program

by Brent Markham, former assistant director, wildlife management and director of wildlife

The management of the province's game species—big-game, upland birds and waterfowl—has come a long ways since the early 1900s when Alberta became a province. Market hunting, which had depleted many big-game and waterfowl populations, was

COURTESY OF DUANE RADFORD

Brent Markham with a brace of Canada Geese.

prohibited in the 1920s. The 1930s saw Aldo Leopold's principles of game management—inventory, productivity and limiting factors—introduced. Since the first provincial wildlife biologists were hired in the 1950s, there have been major advances in the knowledge needed to apply these principles in Alberta.

As a shared, international resource, the management of waterfowl harvest in Alberta has a somewhat different template than that for other game species under strictly provincial jurisdiction. The establishment of the flyway (Pacific, Central, Mississippi and Atlantic) system in the 1940s provided a formal framework for federal (Canada and U.S.), provincial and state wildlife management agencies to discuss seasons and bag limits. Because the majority of ducks and geese produced in and migrating through the province winter in the Pacific and central flyways, Alberta participates in discussions within these two flyways.

Over the years, the Canadian Wildlife Service and Alberta Fish and Wildlife Division have collaborated on waterfowl surveys, research and various programs to enhance duck and goose populations in the province. The Canada goose translocation program, initiated by the province in the 1960s, has been a major waterfowl management success story in Alberta. The trapping and movement of goslings and adults to water bodies without breeding geese has resulted in a significant expansion in size and distribution of resident Canada goose populations. Another major partner, Ducks Unlimited Canada, has spearheaded efforts to create and enhance waterfowl habitat since it was founded in 1938.

Today, these efforts are co-ordinated through an international partnership, the North American Waterfowl Management Plan.

The management of native upland birds received little attention in the first half of the 20th century and was largely limited to setting bag limits based on the perceived abundance of these cyclical species. As interest increased in the hunting of these birds, particularly sharptailed and ruffed grouse, in the 1950s and '60s, more effort was put into understanding their biology and status. In the late 1980s stabilized bag limits were adopted regardless of population cycles. This decision was facilitated by the general decrease in hunting pressure on these species that continues today. Alberta's sage grouse population of only a few hundred birds is restricted to the southeast corner of the province. The season on this large prairie grouse was closed in 1996 after annual lek counts documented a serious decline in numbers of breeding birds.

Some members of the hunting community expressed early interest in certain exotic game-birds. Through the efforts of various fish and game clubs, Hungarian partridge and ring-necked pheasants were introduced in the first decade(s) of the 20th century. While Huns enjoyed early success in becoming established (the first season was opened only five years after the initial introduction), it was 1939 before pheasants were well enough established in the irrigation districts to provide a hunting season. The Brooks Pheasant Hatchery, built in 1945 to further augment wild pheasant populations, was expanded to the state-of-the-art Brooks Wildlife Centre in 1978. While this centre was sold to private interests in the mid-1990s, it still provides cocks annually for put-and-take releases. The release of Merriam's turkeys in the 1960s, first in the Cypress Hills, and later in the Porcupine Hills and near Burmis, rounded out the introduction of exotic game birds to the province. The latter population eventually became well enough established to provide a limited-entry spring hunt beginning in 1990.

Big-game management in the early part of the 20th century focused on preservation to rebuild populations decimated by market hunting and liberal regulatory regimes. Today, management strives to allocate these now-recovered populations for the greatest benefit of resource users with sustainability of the resource as the paramount guiding principle. The framework for this management, the Wildlife Management Unit (WMU) system, first introduced in the 1960s, has undergone continual refinement to allow for more precise management of populations and hunting pressure.

The one thing that has defined the evolution to today's big-game management program has been a movement from general seasons to limited-entry draw seasons. This change has been encouraged by both the desire to more closely manage harvest at the WMU level and the expectations of the hunting public for increased hunting opportunity and variety. Many of the current hunting opportunities available can only be offered through a limited-entry draw approach. This system applies hunter success rates to allowable harvests to determine a specific number of hunters in each WMU. Knowledge of hunter success and monitoring of harvests is obtained through the hunter survey program established in the mid-1980s. This telephone-based survey of hunters following each hunting season is completed through the participation of many AFGA clubs and other hunting organizations.

COURTESY OF TRAVEL ALBERTA

Ranchland along Hwy 22, between Lundbeck and Longview.

Forestry Lands and Wildlife Advisory Council, circa 1992.
Standing: E. Millard Wright (oil and gas industry) (L), unknown, Cleve Wershler (Alberta Wilderness Association), Larry Sears (Western Stock Growers Association), unknown, Dave Simpson (Alberta Outfitting/Guiding), unknown, Jim Robison (Alberta Trappers Association), Les Cooke (assistant deputy minister, Fish and Wildlife Division), Lewis Ramstead (co-ordinator, Fish and Wildlife Division), Cliff Smith (deputy minister, Forestry, Lands and Wildlife), Jack Graham (AFGA), Charles Navratil, Joe Smith (Alberta Association of Municipal Districts and Counties)
Sitting: Margot Hervieux (L), Betty Bateman (Alberta Commercial Fishermen's Association), Brian Evans (chairman MLA Cochrane-Banff), Hon. LeRoy Fjordbotten (Minister of Forestry, Lands and Wildlife), Helen Curr (secretary).

Management objectives and strategies for individual big-game species have been enunciated in species management plans. An estimate of population size at the WMU level is a basic requirement for successful management. For most species this information is acquired through an annual aerial survey program. Moose received extra effort in this regard in recent years. In the early 1990s concern was being expressed in various quarters over apparent decreases in moose numbers throughout northern Alberta. Because of the importance of moose for both recreational and subsistence purposes, a major initiative, the Northern Moose Management Program, was undertaken. The largest component of this five-year effort was an extensive aerial survey program to develop reliable moose-population estimates, including bull:cow:calf ratios. The information collected, together with input from the hunting public, was used to create the current split-season regime, designed to optimize hunting opportunity while controlling harvest of breeding bulls.

An additional outcome of this detailed look at moose management was the creation of the partner licence. This licence allows increased hunter participation without increasing harvest by allowing two hunters to "share" a moose. Another licensing change intended to encourage participation of young hunters and help offset the ongoing decline in hunter numbers was the creation of youth hunting licences at a reduced cost. More recently the partner and youth licence concepts have been combined to expand opportunity for young hunters in all draw hunts.

Another significant change in the management of Alberta's big-game occurred in 1989 when a new outfitter-guide policy was established. The basis of the new policy, intended to address conflicts that had developed between resident and non-resident

hunters and within the outfitting community itself, is an allocation system, that limits the percentage of the allowable harvest of each species that can be taken by outfitted hunting in each WMU.

The management of Alberta's rich and varied wild game resource remains a challenge. Coupled with the basic conservation needs of our game species are the desires and expectations of the users of the resource and those that may be affected by it. All of these factors have contributed to the establishment of Alberta's current game-management program.

Aquatic Pollution Research Section

by Paul Paetkau, Alberta's first pollution control biologist

"To address the increased demands on the fisheries research section and to study land management practices alongside several water bodies, an Aquatic Pollution Research Section was established in 1968-69. The new section, directed by Paul Paetkau, continued to monitor fish in the Oldman River for accumulated pesticide residues. They also initiated a new study to look at the effects of cattle grazing on fisheries in the Red Deer River. In addition, the group examined coal mining in the Crowsnest Pass and Coal Branch areas, oil spills, seismic operations, and land clearing adjacent to rivers. As a result of their activities, several companies and individuals were prosecuted for their actions, and increasing time was devoted to the inspection of coal, gas and other industrial operations." (*Fish, Fur & Feathers: Fish and Wildlife Conservation in Alberta 1905-2005*, Chapter Six, 2005).

We did all that? Wow! I remember starting this job in 1968 and thinking, "Where do I start? This is a big province." That first winter, an *Edmonton Journal* photographer caught that frustration and impatience to get going on my part, when he snapped a photo of me at -30C chopping a hole in the ice on the North Saskatchewan River, sweat running down my face as I tried to figure out how to sample those macro invertebrates that I knew were crawling on the bottom of the river just waiting to tell me their pollution story. But how to get at them and where to start, that was the question?

Fortunately, Dr. Martin Paetz, the head of the Fisheries Branch, knew the province from front to back and knew the people who were interested in helping with this work. One of those was Henry Lembicz from the AFGA. I remember him as always being ready to pitch in and do his part. And help was needed. At first there was just myself and Vic Gillman, an excellent wildlife technician. Other biologists and officers in the Fish and Wildlife Division were of course also involved but they all had other jobs to do as well.

Industry, I remember, wasn't much better staffed or knowledgeable. I remember regular meetings with the vice president of Shell as the representative of the oil and gas industry. There seemed to be no one between him in industry and me, a relatively young biologist, in government, who was directly involved in aquatic pollution work in industry or government at that time. That has changed.

Many people helped make that change. People in organizations such as the AFGA, people in industry, the general public and people in government, like Dennis McDonald, the regional fisheries biologist in Calgary at the time.

I remember Dennis organizing a fish-tasting test in Calgary. In typical McDonald fashion, he had every organization, the city and as much press as he could find, totally involved. We, the tasters, sat around a big table at the local gas companies headquarters and were given little pieces of cooked but unspiced

COURTESY OF TRAVEL ALBERTA

A hidden gem, Kakwa Falls can be found in Kakwa Wildland Park.

and unlabelled fish to taste. The object was to see if we could pick out trout from the Bow River below Calgary, that is below the sewage outlets. No problem!

With that knowledge, and that knowledge widespread, Dennis, the Aquatic Pollution Section, the city representatives and others could start putting pressure on those who needed it to get the City of Calgary to upgrade their sewage treatment facilities. They did. Of course, population pressure soon made that necessary to do again and again.

In my opinion, that is how the best pollution work is still done today. Get the knowledge, obtain the co-operation and continue the vigilance. Good luck with that to the AFGA!

Pine trees cover a spectacular mountain view.

COURTESY OF LILLA PFERSCHY

The role of the AFGA in the development and implementation of the Outdoor Observer program

by Ernie J. Psikla, former district and regional fish and wildlife officer and executive director of regional operations

During my career with the Alberta Fish and Wildlife Division, I found the AFGA was invariably the lead non-government organization that supported and promoted fish and wildlife law enforcement initiatives with the government. In fact, enforcement program development and growth in officer services was largely influenced by the representation made to government by the AFGA. Law enforcement was never a major priority of the department or government. For that reason, those of us involved in managing the law-enforcement program depended upon the AFGA for meaningful external support that simply was absent within the organization and department.

The Outdoor Observer program was a direct product of an aggressive AFGA initiative led by Budd Traver. The association through Mr. Traver asked the department to undertake a citizen involvement program similar to one which had recently been introduced in the state of Washington, called the Civilian Wildlife Patrol (CWP). In that state, the Fish and Game Commission supported a program concept that allowed members of the CWP to be involved in the enforcement of game and fishery-related offences to the extent that included confronting violations in progress.

My initial reaction to the AFGA initiative was that, if my understanding of the operation of the Washington State program was correct, I could not recommend a similar program for our situation in Alberta. To assure that we had a clear understanding of the Washington state "patrol," permission was obtained to travel to Washington for the purpose of interviewing state officials and members of some local clubs that were involved in the "Patrol."

The visit to Washington proved to be beneficial. I found there were two different strong positions. The Fish and Game Commission headquarters people and the local club members involved with the program were highly enthusiastic and supportive. On the other hand, local game wardens, regional enforcement personnel and others actually involved in the enforcement of laws and the justice system overall were skeptical in that the program had many weaknesses and they were very worried about the perception of a vigilante patrol and how well the court system would react should that perception prevail.

The information obtained from my visit to Washington was helpful and confirmed some of the reservations I had about the CWP program. It was apparent that issues such as citizen involvement in confronting violators, seizures and arrest situations, personal and possibly departmental legal liability, training and screening volunteers was not well thought out in the Washington program.

What Mr. Traver wanted to achieve was simply to encourage more citizen awareness of possible illegal actions that involved the fish and wildlife resource. In addition, he wanted to increase the contact with local officers in the reporting of environmental pollution. To achieve these objectives the Washington state Civilian Wildlife Patrol concept was probably not the way to go in Alberta. There were simply too many avenues for problems to surface.

Within the Fish and Wildlife Division, there was support to do something but there were a few qualifiers that came via the director. There would be no new money in the current or future year's estimates, no staffing and the program would have to be low profile.

From a financing perspective, anything that we did would require adjusting existing operating budgets. In the enforcement section we were never "flush" in that about 85 percent of our budgets each year were taken up by fixed costs. There was never enough money to become really creative and break new ground, in fact.

The issue we had to address was to develop a reasonable and responsible program concept, within the guidelines provided, that would achieve the understanding and support of the AFGA and the fish and wildlife officer staff who would ultimately have to make the concept work in the field.

It was a case of going back to the basics of doing law enforcement work. Regardless of what kind of law enforcement work a person is involved with, it is a long-recognized fact that to be successful you must have the support and help of the community you are serving. A network of trustworthy contacts and informants is an absolute essential if you are to be successful as a game warden.

As I saw it at that time, what the AFGA was promoting to government was a formalized extension of an officer's feedback and contact network. The idea of expanding citizen involvement in the reporting of violations made a great deal of sense when one considered the small warden staff we had and the size of the districts they were responsible for serving.

The end product was the development of a slide presentation that encouraged individual people to become an "outdoor observer." The name was chosen in keeping with the guideline of being low profile. The slide presentation was not costly to produce and would be made available to officers upon request. The program simply encouraged people who observed violations in progress, found evidence of infractions or noticed problems such as pollution, to report their observations without delay.

Guidance was provided on how to collect information, accurately recording details with a strong emphasis on reporting the information as quickly as possible. The key to successful apprehension of violators was timely and accurate reporting of the necessary information.

During the process of developing the concept of the Outdoor Observer program, an effort was made to keep Mr. Traver informed on any progress we were making and what kind of program was unfolding. It was also important that he be made aware of the downside analysis of the Washington state civilian patrol concept. In that regard, he supported our position and pointed out that his objective overall was simply to encourage more people to report infractions and become more aware of what was taking place in their community. Above all, he did not wish to create a system that could be perceived as a vigilante group.

Because the concept was intended to support the local district fish and wildlife officers, it was important that there be input from the officers' perspective. Lewis Ramstad and James Struthers were involved in this process both having expressed interest in developing a violation-reporting mechanism.

Lastly, the concept of becoming an Outdoor Observer was factored into the annual summary of big-game, bird-game and angling regulations. As in the slide presentation, emphasis was placed upon timely and accurate reporting of information. A list of all Fish and Wildlife Division offices and telephone numbers was included in the regulation brochures in support of this initiative.

The AFGA endorsed and supported the Outdoor Observer concept to the extent that the association even brought into effect an annual award for the best club Outdoor Observer program in the province. Mr. Traver, who was the main driving force to encourage more citizen involvement in reporting wildlife, fishery and environmental crime incidents, was of the opinion that the Outdoor Observer program would satisfy this particular objective. There was now a formal means for anyone who observed an incident or violation in progress to take action without the risk of becoming personally involved in confronting individuals.

It would be difficult to accurately measure the effectiveness of the Outdoor Observer program in that it was, in many instances, an extension of existing information networks that were already in place at the district officer level. Regardless, it was a progressive move forward and would likely serve as a basis for future program enhancement, while generating more contact with officers at the district level would be a plus factor.

The Report-a-Poacher program eventually replaced the Outdoor Observer program under the leadership of R.J. (Bob) Adams. His work to put an effective reporting infrastructure into place without the necessity of huge new funding was quite remarkable and that particular achievement should not go unnoticed.

10,000 POSTERS FOR ALBERTA
. . . distributed by Alberta Fish and Game Association

Blair Rippin with largest male black bear caught at Cold Lake bear study.

Alberta Fish and Wildlife Advisory Committee

by Lewis Ramstead, former district and regional fish and wildlife officer, and executive officer to the Assistant Deputy Minister

The AFGA has reached a significant milestone, 100 years of dedicated service to Alberta which is commendable. I salute and thank the many AFGA members who I had the opportunity to meet and work with during my career (1962-93) as a Fish and Wildlife officer and executive officer in the assistant deputy minister's office. I served throughout Alberta, in Claresholm, High Prairie, Rocky Mountain House, Medicine Hat, Ponoka, Calgary, Lethbridge and Edmonton.

From 1983-93, while serving in the assistant deputy minister's office, I co-ordinated the Alberta Order of the Bighorn Awards and the Alberta Fish and Wildlife Advisory Committee. Since the Bighorn Awards inception in 1982, this prestigious award for outstanding contributions to fish and wildlife conservation has been awarded to the AFGA and many of its clubs and members from various locations in Alberta. This is an example of the conservation efforts that have been put forth by the dedicated AFGA and its members.

The Fish and Game Advisory Council was created in 1943 by Fish and Game Commissioner Eric Huestis. The council was originally composed of three members from the AFGA and two members from the University of Alberta. The council was soon enlarged to include members from the farm organizations, Western Stock Growers Association, natives, fur dealers, trappers and outfitters. The advisory council dealt with a multitude of issues that were confronting fish and wildlife management at the time, including legislation, hunting seasons and policies.

Over the years there were numerous membership changes in the original Fish and Game Advisory Council as the provincial scene changed, and various public interest groups requested representation on the council. The name of the council was later changed to the Alberta Fish and Wildlife Advisory Committee.

While assigned as the co-ordinator of the Fish and Wildlife Advisory Committee (1983-93) there was tremendous industrial development in the province (e.g. forestry/oil and gas industry). There were many requests to the ministers (Hon. Don Sparrow, Hon. LeRoy Fjordbotten and Hon. Brian Evans) for representation on this committee, and it eventually increased to 19 groups, as follows: Alberta Cattle Commission, coal industry, commercial fishery, commercial wildlife, education, environmental groups, farming industry, forest industry, forest associations, Indian community, Métis community, motorized recreation, municipal government, petroleum industry, recreational fishing and hunting, tourism and wilderness associations. The AFGA representing sport fishing and hunting had two members on the committee and they did outstanding jobs representing the sportsmen of the province. They always came prepared and were well-versed on the issues and provided sage advice at the meetings.

In addition to the meetings that were held as required (two to three a year), three-day field trips were organized and the members were taken to all parts of the province to acquaint them with Alberta, the departmental staff and operations, and the committee met with various industry and community groups. There was a major change in the advisory committee under the leadership of Hon. LeRoy Fjordbotten in 1988, when he appointed Mr. Brian Evans (MLA for Banff-Cochrane) as chairman of the committee, which historically had been chaired by a member of the council/committee selected by the membership.

A wide range of fish and wildlife issues during my tenure resulted in a great deal of debate and ministerial advice requirements. Some major projects that were reviewed were the new *Wildlife Act*, game ranching, outfitting allocation system, commercial fishery changes, and many discussions regarding the increased industrial growth affecting the environment and fish and wildlife management.

The Fish and Wildlife Advisory Committee was a valuable forum which gave stakeholders direct input to the minister. Unfortunately in the mid-1990s it was disbanded, and hopefully the government will see its value and the advisory committee will be revived.

Stages in a Wildlife Biologist's Career

by Blair Rippin, former regional wildlife biologist in St. Paul

The following is a summary of my recollection and a regional perspective of my time as a regional wildlife biologist in northeastern Alberta from 1973 to my retirement in 1998 and post-retirement until 2007. I was born and raised in northern Alberta and took a BSc in geology (1962) as well as a BSc and MSc (1970) in zoology all at the University of Alberta.

Prior to returning to Alberta in 1973, I worked as a wildlife biologist in the NWT out of Yellowknife from 1970-72.

In 1973 I was hired by the Alberta Fish and Wildlife Division as northeast regional wildlife biologist in St. Paul. My hiring was part of a major acquisition of trained biologists in the late 1960s and early 1970s by the province of Alberta. The hirings were in response to new funding and demands from the general public and specifically from the AFGA for modern management of the province's diverse wildlife and fish resources.

Most new recruits received minimal direction in their new roles. It was loosely determined that I would use the first year or so to become familiar with the region, its wildlife, and the problems facing their management. I certainly relished that sort of freedom after the restrictive regime I left in the NWT. I travelled extensively and visited nearly every nook and cranny of the region. During that time I also made contact with the numerous organized fish and game clubs in the region.

I inherited two research projects from my predecessor Gerry Kemp: the Cold Lake black bear project, investigating various aspects of bear biology and ecology; and the Rochester deer project, investigating white-tailed deer population dynamics. Thus my first three or four years on the job were very much like what I was lead to believe was the ideal life of a wildlife biologist, discovering interesting things about wildlife and how to manage wildlife.

Although that aspect of my job continued to a certain degree thereafter, major changes in land-use beginning in the mid-1970s resulted in significant changes in the role of biologists. I consider that period to represent the beginning of Alberta's amazing economic boom that continues to this day. Major changes occurred in the petroleum industry, not only for conventional reserves but with increased interest in both mineable and subsurface oilsands.

Agriculture was also expanding at a great rate. As a result, biologists became increasingly involved in habitat and land-use issues rather than with individual wildlife species. Although our main task of keeping a handle on hunted and trapped species was still being addressed to some degree, our time was increasingly being taken up by inspecting land-use proposals and on planning teams for major projects such as oil sands development in the Cold Lake and the Fort McMurray areas. In addition, the economic changes resulted in new initiatives to establish special public recreation areas. Planning for both Lakeland [Provincial] Park and the Cooking Lake-Blackfoot Recreation Area became major time consumers in the early 1980s.

Our changing role was further complicated by periodic reorganizations within the governmental system. The Fish and Wildlife Division was tossed around like a ping-pong ball among various departments over the years. With each change there were different reporting systems, work plans, and inter-departmental staff relationships.

During my tenure, major changes occurred in the abundance and distribution of many wildlife species. For example, in the 1970s our division, in co-operation with many AFGA clubs such as in Vegreville, Cold Lake and many others, placed flax-straw bales and gravel islands into local wetlands in an effort to expand the nesting range of Canada geese.

The Vermilion and Cold Lake FGA clubs even undertook to raise geese locally for release. Once we solved the puzzle of transplanting geese so they stayed put, these structures and supplemental stocks played important roles. The increase in that species in the past two decades has been phenomenal. It is now somewhat ironic that in 2006 and 2007 Strathcona County has embarked on an extensive program to decrease the number of geese nesting in that area. We originally thought that strong territoriality in geese would limit their use to about one nest per island. However, Strathcona County workers recorded 69 active nests on a one-half acre island in Sherwood Park in 2007.

COURTESY OF DUANE RADFORD

Fly-fishing for brown trout on the Bow River.

White-tailed deer and more recently mule deer have also made amazing increases in numbers. I recall telling the Clandonald AFGA club in the mid-1970s that increased land clearing in their area would soon result in the demise of that species. Little did I know that white-tails could adapt so well to a fairly intensively developed agricultural environment. Our Rochester study in the early 1970s predicted that we could not expect densities of more than one deer per square mile. Today we commonly see densities in excess of 10 times that over large areas.

Although moose densities over much of their northeast boreal forest range slowly declined over the past three decades, moose began to appear in ever-increasing numbers in the parklands and northern prairies in the 1980s, likely in response to light hunting pressure and the absence of wolves. Today about one half of our total moose population occurs in those unlikely habitats.

In the 1970s, we considered cormorants as a threatened species and made considerable efforts to learn how to increase their numbers. Little did we suspect we would later be dealing with cormorants as serous competitors for fish stocks in the area that previously provided anglers with superior opportunities to catch walleye, perch and pike.

On the other hand our woodland caribou did not fare as well. Unfortunately, their strong adherence to bog habitat that is presently under siege by oil companies will likely result in their eventual doom. Although we learned much about their ecology through considerable research using new technologies such as satellite radio telemetry, GPS [global positioning system] and GIS [geographic information systems] in the Lac La Biche-Fort McMurray area in the 1990s and early 2000s, their survival in the current industrial regime remains tenuous.

Our efforts to establish viable elk populations in the northeast were similarly without success. Considerable work with Elk Island National Park wardens and various AFGA clubs resulted in hundreds of animals being released at several locations over the past three decades but with no long-term survival. Even with a "soft" release from temporary corrals in the Calling Lake area, in co-operation with the Athabasca AFGA club, the released elk eventually disappeared.

Hunting in the northeast region also underwent major changes during the latter part of the 20th century. A number of special hunts were developed to take advantage of specific harvest opportunities as they arose over the years. The CFB Wainwright grouse and deer hunts began in the late 1960s and continue today. The Long Lake moose hunt was established to allow harvest of a rapidly expanding moose population in the fringe agricultural area; thus began a periodic opening of parkland and northern prairie units as the moose population expanded southward. The Strathcona County deer and moose hunts by shotgun were an effort to allow recreational harvest in a dense suburban area adjacent to Edmonton, while addressing a serious vehicle collision hazard. Deer and moose licensing went through major changes in response to fluctuations in game abundance and hunter numbers. Measures to restrict or extend opportunity included sex, age and area-specific tags, a draw system, multiple tags, partner tags and quota hunts.

Pheasant hunting underwent considerable changes ranging from general seasons in the 1960s, to more restrictive seasons in a number of release areas targeting birds from raise-and-release landowner operations and transplants from the Brooks hatchery; to the much more restrictive put-and-take regime of the 1980s. Today, because of the harsh environment, habitat loss, and the loss of pheasant rearing facilities, that species is essentially absent from hunters' bags in this part of the province.

Hunters and the general public have also had to deal with a significant increase in several wildlife diseases over the past few decades. Rabies of the 1950s was one of the very few disease

Horsethief Canyon near Drumheller.

concerns of that era. However, fowl cholera, botulism, West Nile and Newcastle's disease in birds; tularemia, parvovirus and Hanta virus in rodents; and tuberculosis, brucellosis, moose ticks, giant liver flukes, and more recently chronic wasting disease in ungulates, have become serious threats to our wildlife and human health.

The traditional strong consumptive user regime prior to the 1960s experienced gradual erosion, reflecting a general change in public attitudes toward wildlife and the natural environment over the past few decades. Although the change was a difficult transition for many members of the AFGA, it resulted in wildlife biologists having a greater focus on non-consumptive regimes with initiatives such as the Watchable Wildlife program, Special Area development, and endangered species recovery programs. In the northeast region, peregrine falcon recovery operations in Edmonton and near Fort Chipewyan, as well as piping plover protection projects at Reflex and Muriel Lakes, became prominent work items. In addition, the advent of commercial use of wildlife such as in big-game farms was a particularly difficult change to accept. In retrospect, vocal opposition to the latter by the AGFA and others was well-founded with respect to the introduction of disease to wildlife.

Regional Operations

by Gerald (Gerry) Thompson, former regional fisheries biologist and regional director for the eastern slopes, Peace River and southern regions

Born and raised in rural B.C., I grew up with a natural love of the outdoors. My interest in wildlife was piqued in 1954 when at age 14 my uncle Elmer Thompson introduced me to big-game hunting, an introduction that ultimately lead to my career in fisheries and wildlife management. In 1965 at the University of British Columbia, Dr. James Bendell gave a course in wildlife management. My notes from the day of his last lecture to his 24 students said: "If I have convinced only one of you to choose a career in the administrative and/or political aspects of fish and wildlife management, I will consider my job to have been accomplished more successfully than if all of you become world renowned biologists." Those words and a number of personal discussions with him guided my career approach to fish and wildlife management.

After a two-year stint as a wildlife biologist in Ontario, I joined the Alberta Fish and Wildlife Division of the Department of Lands and Forests as a fisheries biologist in Calgary on Jan. 13, 1969. Two days later I attended a fish committee meeting of the Calgary Fish and Game Association; my first of many such meetings with the AFGA clubs throughout Alberta. I registered for my first AFGA convention in Calgary on Feb. 27, 1969. While at the convention I met Gordon Cummings and Tom O'Keefe, two past presidents of the AFGA who were instrumental in raising my awareness and understanding of, and support for, the AFGA. They encouraged me to "tap into" the human resources that the AFGA had to offer to assist in resource management. In fact, during my 26 years with the Fish and Wildlife Division, numerous members of the AFGA passed on their experiences and

COURTESY OF GERRY THOMPSON

Gerry Thompson, Fish and Wildlife Division, attending the Calgary AFGA annual dinner, 1978.

knowledge to help make my job so much easier; such as Elmer Kure coming and spending a day on the Bow River to teach a rookie fish biologist how to operate a 26-foot jet boat. A memorable day indeed!

In 1972 I became the regional fisheries biologist for what was then called the Calgary Region and in 1978 took on the role of directing the Fish and Wildlife Division's capital development program in Kananaskis Country. In 1980 the Fish and Wildlife Division fully regionalized and I became the regional director for the eastern slopes region headquartered at Rocky Mountain House. In 1985 I transferred to Peace River as the regional director and in 1992 relocated to Lethbridge as the regional director, a position I held until retiring in 1995. I also held the regional director position in Red Deer for one year (1994) simultaneously with Lethbridge. Consequently, my experiences with the AFGA span the width and breadth of Alberta in many different capacities.

One of the objectives of the Fish and Wildlife Division's 1980 regionalization was to initiate and maintain regular communications with fish, wildlife, and environmental groups/publics in the region to understand the issues, determine their expectations of the fish and wildlife programs, and enlist their support for Fish and Wildlife Division programs. The AFGA was by far the most active provincial outdoorsmen group that I had the pleasure to interact with over all those years. Whether it was at the local club level, the twice-yearly zone meetings or the annual meeting, their support was unequivocal. We may not have agreed on every issue within the region but I never left any meeting without a feeling of mutual respect and a request to return at my convenience. That unqualified support I had from the AFGA members throughout my career was a partnership that stood the test of time and still is one of my fondest memories.

The first zone meeting I attended as a regional director was held on Oct. 26, 1980 at Sylvan Lake. We discussed the concept of the Fish and Wildlife Division approach to regional operations and how we would like to continue to work together to ensure the long-term management of Alberta's fish and wildlife resources in the best interests of all Albertans. In total, I attended 32 such meetings in four different regions; all meetings were productive dialogues and decisions between committed partners. A recollection I must mention in those early years was being invited and eating fish chowder prepared by the Eckville Fish and Game Association for their annual chowder night; I have never eaten better fish chowder!

The first annual AFGA convention I attended as a regional director was in Red Deer from Feb. 26-28, 1981. The behind-the-scenes discussions between all parties in attendance were eye-opening, intense and riveting. The lobbying by AFGA members of senior bureaucrats of the Fish and Wildlife Division and the minister responsible were at times fractious, but always productive. The hosting by the various zones of evening "get to know you" sessions were particularly enlightening. I believe it was at that first convention when the regional directors were volunteered by the AFGA president to act as auctioneers to raise money for the AFGA habitat fund. I have never felt more inadequate for anything I've done before or since!

One of the saddest events I attended as a regional director was the funeral on June 26, 1986 of Nyal dee Hirsche of Warner. Nyal was piloting his airplane when he crashed and died on his farm. Nyal and his wife Linda were members of the Foremost Fish and Game Association and one of the most active couples for the AFGA at the club, zone and provincial levels. Nyal received the Order of the Bighorn award in 1986 for his outstanding work for the conservation of Alberta's fish and wildlife resources.

I would be remiss if I didn't mention some of the AFGA zone directors that I worked with in each of the three regions. When I moved to Rocky Mountain House, Dr. Martha Kostuch introduced herself and welcomed me to the eastern slopes. She was and still is an inspiration that over the years I came to appreciate more and more. I recall a public meeting in Red Deer when there were allegations of someone delivering brown envelopes [confidential government information sent in plain brown envelopes without a return address] from government officials to the public. Knowing this and being aware the deputy minister was watching, Martha threw her arms around one of the directors and gave him a big kiss. As I looked at Martha and the deputy, she had a look of impish delight while he looked utterly upset and confused!

When I was in Peace River, Dr. Darryl Smith from Valleyview was a tireless worker and supporter of the Fish and Wildlife Division. At the zone level perhaps no other person that I worked with gave more of himself/herself than did Darryl. He even took time to repair a tooth for me after my retirement when I was passing through Valleyview on a moose hunting trip.

In Lethbridge, Heinz Plontke knocked on my door within the first week of my arrival and gave me his support in every way he could. Heinz made it a point to drop in about once a month to ensure I was up to date on what the AFGA was doing and how they were interacting politically. I cherished those meetings with Heinz and in fact he still keeps in touch by dropping by occasionally to my residence in Wynndel, B.C. on his way to Kootenay Lake.

Since I retired in 1995 and moved to British Columbia I have not kept in touch with the operations of the AFGA except for brief discussions with close friends. One of those close friends and a regional director peer during the formative years of regionalization, Ray Makowecki, joined the AFGA and became its president in 2003. Perhaps no other event I can mention can explain the camaraderie and respect between the regions of the Fish and Wildlife Division and the AFGA during the 1980s and 1990s.

Upon his retirement from the Fish and Wildlife Division Ray felt compelled to continue his fish and wildlife resource management work and what better way to do it than join Alberta's foremost fish and wildlife conservation group, the AFGA!

Wildlife Habitat Canada

by Dave Bracket, former executive director, Wildlife Habitat Canada

Wildlife Habitat Canada (WHC) is a national, non-profit organization that was established by the federal and provincial governments in co-operation with the conservation community in 1984. WHC funds habitat conservation projects across the country, promotes conservation action, and fosters co-ordination among conservation groups. The organization was formed to invest money paid for by waterfowl hunters for the Wildlife Habitat Conservation Stamp in habitat conservation, restoration and enhancement initiatives. As well, WHC raises additional funds from a variety of other sources.

WHC works in partnership with landowners who have an interest in habitat conservation and stewardship; farmers and ranchers on the working agricultural landscape; provincial and municipal governments; and other non-governmental organizations. Since 1984, WHC has invested about $52 million in projects and activities related to the conservation, restoration and enhancement of wildlife habitat. Of this amount, about $32 million has come from the Wildlife Habitat Conservation Stamp program, primarily through purchase of a waterfowl stamp by waterfowl hunters to validate their federal migratory game bird hunting permits.

The main focus for WHC support is projects that deliver direct on-the-ground interventions related to habitat conservation, restoration or enhancement for waterfowl in wetlands or areas of importance for wetlands-associated species. There is a continuing loss of wildlife habitats throughout Canada; conservation initiatives that WHC supports are aimed at mitigating these losses.

WHC has contributed to wildlife conservation in Alberta primarily through its grant program and board of director's representation.

Antelope Creek (formerly part of the Ward Ranch): WHC provided a total grant of $450,358 to this initiative in 1985-86. The objective was to acquire a large area of mixed prairie habitat in the Eastern Irrigation District near Brooks (part of the 5,490-acre Ward Ranch). This project was deemed to be significant to WHC as the ranch contained critical wetland habitat with substantial waterfowl production capability and involved integrated management of wetland and upland habitat, and grazing and cultivated land for both consumptive and non-consumptive users. Along with other conservation partners (e.g. province of Alberta, Ducks Unlimited Canada, the AFGA), WHC was a signatory to the 30-year Ward Ranch Management general agreement that was signed in February 1986; the purpose of this agreement is to allow "arrangements for undertaking wildlife habitat projects for the implementation of management plans through subsidiary agreements for the enhancement and conservation of wildlife and wildlife habitat in Alberta for a broad range of public benefits."

Over the years, WHC has been represented on the Antelope Creek Ranch management committee by former board members from Alberta:

- Elmer Kure, who is a past president of the AFGA. Elmer was a director on WHC's board of directors from 1984-89, and chaired the board's Agricultural Landscape Committee from 1986-89.

- Nestor Romaniuk, also a past president of the AFGA. Nestor was a director on WHC's board of directors from 1992-95, and again from 2001-04. He was chair of the board of directors in 1994, co-chair of the program review committee in 2001, and chair of the nominating committee in 2003.

WHC's representation on the Antelope Creek Ranch Management Committee continues with the involvement of Doug Stewart, a former member of WHC's board (and former chair of the program review committee in 2003 and 2004) who currently resides in Alberta.

Astotin Lake in Elk Island National Park.

AFGA Conservation Initiatives

WHC has supported several AFGA conservation initiatives over the years, such as:

Operation Burrowing Owl

WHC provided a grant of $30,000 to this project over a three-year period from 1993-94 to 1995-96. This project was a private stewardship program which aimed to protect habitat of the burrowing owl—listed as an endangered species by the Committee on the Status of Endangered Wildlife in Canada—in Alberta, as well as raise public awareness and monitor population trends.

Operation Grassland Community

WHC contributed a total of $28,000 as a grant for this project in 1996-97 and 1997-98. The project focused on voluntary habitat protection for the burrowing owl in the grassland ecosystem of Alberta, through public education and awareness.

Parkland Stewardship Program

In 1997-98 and 1998-99, WHC provided a grant of $40,000 to this project which aimed to foster a habitat stewardship ethic among landowners within Alberta's parkland region. The project's goal was to slow the rate of habitat loss and preserve the unique parkland habitat through communication about biodiversity conservation, landscape ecology, and sustainable agricultural practices, and the public recognition of farm families' conservation efforts.

AFGA Habitat Stewardship Series

WHC provided a grant of $54,869 to this initiative over a period of three years, from 1999-2000 to 2001-02. The goal of this project was to promote the conservation and enhancement of native parkland and grassland habitats through encouraging participation in private land stewardship, increasing rural landowners, community groups and industry awareness of parkland and prairie ecosystems, and developing habitat enhancement projects that would improve the landscapes surrounding native parkland and grassland.

In total, WHC has provided grants totalling approximately $1,876,518 to 41 different conservation initiatives in Alberta from 1985 to present.

Another link that WHC has to conservation initiatives in the province of Alberta is the organization's founding executive director, David Neave. Dave previously worked as Alberta's wildlife director for the Fish and Wildlife Division for many years and brought his habitat conservation and land stewardship ethic to Ottawa when he started WHC in 1984. He led WHC for 16 years and was instrumental in communicating about habitat (e.g. via a series of reports on The Status of Wildlife Habitat in Canada), as well as developing the organization's national stewardship award programs, Countryside Canada and the Forest Stewardship Recognition Program.

WHC is proud to have partnered with various groups to enhance conservation efforts in Alberta, and is hopeful that there will be many more opportunities to do so in the future.

Fish and Wildlife Division
Scrapbook

SUPPLIED

John Stelfox (L), Bill Wishart and Morley Barrett, 1997.

SUPPLIED

Gordon Kerr, 1983.

SUPPLIED

Martin Paetz (L) and Ray Makowecki, 1997.

Stuart Smith, 1983.

Bryant Bridgood (L), Ron Boyer, Duane Radford and Frank Cardinal, 1983.

Don Meredith (L) and Ken Crutchfield, 1997.

USE
RESPECT

NO MOTORIZED
VEHICLES WITHOUT
PERMISSION

FOR PERMISSION CONTACT

NAME

GC8-2.64.

PHONE

One four

LOCATION

FOOT ACCESS
PERMITTED
AT OWN RISK

Posted through cooperation of
concerned landholders and sportsmen

Alberta

ENERGY AND
NATURAL RESOURCES

Chapter Nine

Summary

This book commemorates the history of the Alberta Fish and Game Association (AFGA) during its first 100 years as an organization from 1908-2008. It was written and edited by award-winning writers Don Meredith and Duane Radford, both of whom are members of the Outdoor Writers of Canada as well as the AFGA. They worked under the direction of the AFGA Heritage 100 Committee, consisting of the following individuals, which functioned as an editorial board reviewing and approving various segments of the book:

Past presidents
Tony Ferguson, Jack Graham, Don Hayden (chairman 2003-07), Ray Makowecki, Vern McIntosh and Robert H. (Bob) Scammell

Life membership representative
Carole Romaniuk (chairperson 2007-08)

Executive vice president
Martin Sharren

Ex-officio members
2005-07 president, Randy Collins
2007-08 president, Maurice Nadeau

The Heritage 100 Committee members developed the terms of reference for the history book and oversaw its preparation and publication.

Two sections of the book were assigned to Robert H. (Bob) Scammell—the prologue and the epilogue—the award-winning dean of Alberta outdoor writers, a member of the Outdoor Writers of Canada and the Outdoor Writers of America.

The chapter on Wildlife Awards Competitions was written by Brad Fenson, provincial habitat co-ordinator for the AFGA and award-winning member of the Outdoor Writers of Canada. Material in this book prior to 1945 was obtained primarily from a summary report of archival information from the Provincial Archives of Alberta on Roper Road in Edmonton and Glenbow Museum in Calgary, researched by Kandice Sharren in 2005.

The committee directed the co-authors and editors to summarize information on the history of the association on the basis of 10 decades as well as six zones and approximately 100 clubs.

Partner organizations, such as Ducks Unlimited Canada, which have enjoyed a long and close relationship with the AFGA, and the Alberta Professional Outfitters Society as well as Wildlife Habitat Canada, were asked to contribute supporting material for the book. There is also a section on the Canadian Wildlife Federation, and the role that the AFGA played in its development and ongoing operations.

Some of the key milestones associated with the history of the association are as follows:

1905 Alberta became a province in the dominion of Canada.

1907 First provincial hunting legislation passed in Alberta, the *Game Act (1907)*, superseding the Northwest Territories Game Ordinance (1903).

1908 Calgary Fish and Game Protective League formed in 1908.

1920 Northern Alberta Game and Fish Protective League (NAGFPL) organizational meeting held March 3 in Edmonton; first record of NAGFPL songbirds committee chaired by Mr. Hilton.

1927 At the Dec. 6 meeting of the NAGFPL there was a discussion regarding a letter received from Mr. Hayden, Calgary, regarding the formation of a provincial game protective association. Dr. Wilson and Mr. Nicholls recommended that the league approve this plan.

1928 First province-wide organizational meeting of the AFGA held in Calgary on July 11, 1928.

1929 First annual convention of AFGA held in Calgary.

1930 *Natural Resources Transfer Act* legislated, transferring authority to manage fish and wildlife from the federal government to Alberta.
Second AFGA convention held at the Macdonald Hotel in Edmonton on July 18.

1938 Ducks Unlimited Canada established.

1945 The first AFGA wild game dinner for members of the Alberta government was held in the Macdonald Hotel in Edmonton on March 15.

1946 The AFGA was incorporated as a society on November 13.

1954 The 25th Silver Jubilee convention of the AFGA was held at the Palliser Hotel in Calgary.

1961 Wildlife Crop Damage Insurance law was legislated by the Alberta government, based on a $1 surcharge on hunting licences to cover waterfowl crop damage claims, after years of lobbying by the AFGA.

1962 Formation of the Canadian Wildlife Federation. The 33rd annual conference was named the George Spargo Convention to honour the former secretary manager for his 38 years of service.

1964 A fledgling hunter training program was established under Paul Presidente in the Fish and Wildlife Division, based on the AFGA program. For the first time, the Canadian Wildlife Federation sponsors National Wildlife Week.

1966 The Livestock Indemnity Fund, long an objective of the AFGA, became a reality after years of lobbying the Alberta government by the association.

1967 In Canada's centennial year, the 38th annual conference was held at the Macdonald Hotel in Alberta's capital, Edmonton. A new AFGA zone system was implemented with six zone chairmen elected.

1968 The AFGA head office was moved from the Inglewood Bird Sanctuary in Calgary to Edmonton.

1969 25th annual game dinner for the premier of Alberta, cabinet and honorary members of the Alberta legislature in Edmonton hosted by the AFGA.

1970 For the first time, all the policies of the AFGA were printed in the annual conference yearbook.

1972 A resolution was carried that the parent body of the AFGA discontinue the offering of cash prizes for the destruction of pests or predators at the annual convention; this resolution marked a major turning point in policy for the association regarding predators.

Bridge over McLeod River near Whitecourt.

1973 Membership Quota program initiated, with 31 clubs breaking their quota.

1975 The AFGA introduced Operation Respect program, which later evolved into the Use Respect program. Wildlife awards program was introduced using affiliated clubs as sponsors, rather than using commercial sponsors. The AFGA produced their first professional conservation program film, "Land – A Question of Values"

1976 Membership numbers reach an all-time high: 24,501. *Western Canada Outdoors* newsletter launched: a joint newsletter of the AFGA and Saskatchewan Wildlife Federation.

1978 Alberta's Fish and Wildlife Division Outdoor Observer program announced after years of lobbying by the AFGA. The first edition of the *Alberta Trophy Book* was published.

1979 50th annual conference of the AFGA held at the Mayfield Inn in Edmonton. Publication of *To Conserve a Heritage*, written by Margaret Lewis for the AFGA, about the history of the conservation movement in Alberta in commemoration of the 50th anniversary conference.

1980 The first year with a new AFGA executive council in place and fully functioning zone vice presidents. The 10th anniversary of the province-wide Conservation Lottery of the AFGA. The last MLA wild game dinner sponsored by the AFGA was held at Edmonton's Old Timers Log Cabin in November.

1981 The first Alberta measuring school was held in April, and it proved to be very popular with great club interest.

1982 The AFGA was the first ever organization awarded the Alberta Order of the Bighorn Award (Alberta's most prestigious award for fish and wildlife conservation) by the Alberta government; this award was established in 1982.

1983 The AFGA Wildlife Trust Fund became fully operational.

1984 The Alberta Hunter Education Instructors Association (AHEIA) was formally established.

1985 President Jack Shaver and past president Ben Rosnau presided over a ribbon-cutting ceremony for the new AFGA head office on Nov. 29; the AFGA officially opened its new provincial headquarters in Edmonton.

1986 The AFGA published the *Alberta Wildlife Trophy Book 1963-1985*. The government's Outdoor Observer program (featuring a new toll-free number to report fish or wildlife violations) became operational after years of lobbying by the AFGA.

1987 The AFGA initiated a hide collection program to raise money for their Wildlife Trust Fund for the purchase of habitat. The association also held its first fundraising casino.

1988 Alberta Fish and Wildlife Division announced the launch of a new Fishing Education program in Alberta.

1990 A Wildlife Policy for Canada was adopted by the Wildlife Ministers' Council of Canada, the first of its kind in Canada, at its meeting on Sept. 26-27.

1991 A new magazine, *The Outdoor Edge*, was created as a voice for the AFGA, with the inaugural issue published in April.

1996 The Alberta Hunters for the Hungry program had a successful pilot project in the autumn of 1996, the donation of wild game for the Edmonton food bank. This program eventually evolved into the Alberta Hunters Who Care Program.

1997 Sept. 5-7 marked the first Becoming an Outdoor Woman (BOW) program seminar for Alberta, sponsored by the AFGA.

1998 The AFGA wild game cookbook, *Cold Lake Fish and Game Association, Revised Edition* (1998) was published.

1999 The AFGA youth scholarship applications distributed across Alberta; the first scholarship awarded in April.

2003 *Alberta Wildlife Records 2nd Edition* published by the AFGA (edited by T.J. Schwanky).

2004 75th annual AFGA conference held at the Executive Royal Inn Hotel and Conference Centre in Leduc.

2005 Alberta celebrates its centennial.

2007 78th annual AFGA conference held at the Medicine Hat Lodge and Conference Centre in Medicine Hat; the AFGA membership exceeds 17,000.

2008 25th anniversary of the AFGA Wildlife Trust Fund; over 32,000 acres of critical wildlife habitat purchased since program inception.
The 79th annual AFGA conference held at the Mayfield Inn and Suites in Edmonton Feb. 21-23, celebrating a century of conservation, hosted by the Northeastern Alberta Fish and Game Association, zone 5.

The North Saskatchewan River flowing through central Alberta.

Epilogue

Toward Better New Days *by Robert H. (Bob) Scammell*

The obvious, if superficial, measure of the achievement of the Alberta Fish and Game Association (AFGA) in its first century is to compare the volume of the hunting regulations today with that one-page sheet tacked to post office walls in 1908. The *2007 Alberta Guide to Hunting Regulations* is 96 pages and the *2007 Alberta Hunting Draws* booklet (unheard-of in 1908) is 54 pages. Add in the 94 pages of *2007 Alberta Guide to Sportfishing Regulations*, and you could paper the walls of the main lobby of most of those rural post offices with the regulations that now govern hunting and fishing in Alberta.

From the start, the organizing sportsmen of Alberta who built the AFGA were primarily concerned with regulating the free-for-all that prevailed in hunting and fishing in Alberta back then, which had resulted in desperately low populations of most of our fish and wildlife. To this day and into the foreseeable future, the AFGA continues working for sound management of our fish and wildlife resources and wise regulations governing the consumption and use of our fish and game. In the last few years of its first century and as the AFGA moves into its second, outdoors people can be heard wondering if perhaps we might be over-regulated and whether or not we haven't succeeded too well in the sense that today we might have too many of certain species of fish and wildlife, debates that would amaze and amuse the founding fathers of the AFGA.

But there are other more substantial ways of looking at what the AFGA does and has achieved in its first century. Active members today, many of whose personal involvement with the AFGA goes back at least a half century, have long memories, including what they remember from parents, grandparents, aunts and uncles who have also been active AFGA members. Ever since it became known that the AFGA was preparing a book of its history to celebrate its centennial, veteran members could be heard debating what has been the greatest AFGA achievement in its first century. That there are so many worthy nominations is in itself a tribute to the achievements of the organization. Was it the hunter training and testing program that would eventually become mandatory for first-time hunters? The AFGA worked hard for that accomplishment. But there are other program achievements: Report a Poacher, and a wildlife damage and crop depredation program, a livestock indemnity fund and the Operation Respect program. What about fish and game introductions: the Hungarian partridge, the pheasant, and elk transfers? Or is the greatest achievement fighting the good fight, even though frequently losing, against the Bighorn Dam on the North Saskatchewan, the Dickson Dam on the Red Deer and the Three Rivers Dam on the Oldman? A frequent contender is the never-ending battle of the AFGA for public access to public land and against government disposal of public land by sale and lease.

All of the above are important and worthy achievements, but the one you hear most about, not just from AFGA members but also from members of the public generally, is in the area that everyone thinks is basic and crucial: acquiring, maintaining and improving the habitats, the wild places so essential to our fish and game, and to our people too. For those reasons, the people with long memories frequently nominate Alberta's Buck for Wildlife program as the greatest accomplishment of the AFGA in its first century. Certainly there is no accomplishment of the AFGA in the past century that more clearly illustrates how such a group, at its best, accomplishes great things for fish and wildlife, hunters and anglers and the public generally.

Nobody knows precisely where the idea originated, but when it started to take on a life of its own is well-known and a story in itself. Long-time AFGA members have the impression the idea was around forever, and maybe so. However, it surfaced in black and white as something quite novel for the first time in 1969, among the resolutions passed by the club delegates at the annual conference, or convention as they were called in those days. Resolution No. 16, generally recognized as the genesis of Alberta's Buck For Wildlife program, asked that the government establish a "Habitat Stamp," compulsory for all purchasers of deer and bird-game licences for a minimum of $2, matched by the government and that the revenues derived be specifically directed to a program of Habitat Retention and Improvement, etc. Strangely, the resolution did not indicate its origin, as they generally do, stating whose idea it was, whether an affiliated club, or the executive, an omission of some considerable historical interest, as will be seen.

Some perennial conference resolutions go nowhere at all, or make glacial progress, such as two that have been with the AFGA from the very start: asking for Sunday hunting and more fish and wildlife enforcement officers. But the Habitat Stamp resolution of 1969 got virtual instant action when the Progressive Conservatives ended the long reign of Social Credit in Alberta in 1971, which might tempt a cynic to suggest we should change governments in Alberta more often than we do. In any event, Dr. Allan Warrack, a University of Alberta professor of Agricultural Economics, had been appointed Minister of Lands and Forests in the first government of Premier Peter Lougheed. Studious, serious, many in the AFGA say the best minister we ever had, Dr. Warrack had been reviewing the AFGA convention resolutions to the government for the past several years and was so impressed with the 1969 Habitat Stamp resolution. He called the AFGA head office and said that if he could announce it at the next AFGA Legislative dinner as his—or the new government's—idea, he was prepared to bring in the Habitat Stamp program, even to the extent of personally guiding through the legislature the amendments to *The Wildlife Act* that would be needed to permit the "earmarking" of funds taken from the public to a specific purpose, rather than just lumping them into general revenues.

Then-AFGA president Tom O'Keefe—volatile, outspoken, shrewd, and hard-nosed—was outraged. But part of the duties of the AFGA executive is to simmer the president down occasionally, and Tom was convinced to accept the offer on the basis that if an idea is good enough, it matters not whose it was. At the very next Legislative game dinner, Dr. Warrack was as good as his word. No, the stamp would not be a minimum of $2 and the government would not match it; but because the stamp would cost $1, the fund would be called the Buck for Wildlife Fund, and the minister then and there donated the first dollar. The next session of the legislature passed amendments to *The Wildlife Act* establishing the Wildlife Habitat Trust Fund to hold the $1 sportsmen's contributions and to use them for the acquisition, maintenance and improvement of fish and wildlife habitats in Alberta.

The AFGA fish committee, chaired by Hugh Douglas of Calgary, a member of the then-affiliated Hook and Hackle Club, had persuaded the AFGA to make a substantial donation toward a stream study on Stauffer Creek, as it was then called, a central Alberta spring creek that had been all but destroyed as a trout stream by careless agricultural practices. That pioneering stream study, the blueprint for the little creek's restoration, became Alberta's first Buck for Wildlife project.

The project was difficult because Stauffer Creek flows entirely through private land. The AFGA seconded Elmer Kure, executive assistant to the president, to the government. Elmer was a former AFGA president himself, had farmed for years in the vicinity of the creek, and was of great assistance to Mel Kraft and Carl Hunt, the biologists, and other government workers on the project, in working with the streamside landowners and ultimately securing easements for public access. He even secured an Order-in-Council changing the name of Stauffer Creek to North Raven River, because that is what local residents wanted.

Work "on the ground and in the water" progressed quickly—stabilizing banks and bends, fencing cattle away from them, planting willow, narrowing the channel—and very quickly anglers were noticing that the good old days had returned to the little river. Electro-fishing surveys confirmed vast increases in the biomass of trout and their individual size within a few years of the work being done. Anglers started to come from all over the world to fish the heavy aquatic insect hatches and for the huge, ultra-wary brown trout in what is really a tiny creek. Leigh Perkins, then president of the storied Orvis tackle company of Manchester, Vermont, fished the North Raven several times in its first decade as a Buck for Wildlife project. This world-ranging angler was so delighted with the project and the first-class fishing it provided that he once said he'd like to buy the North Raven and move it to Vermont. Instead, Perkins wrote the Hon. Bud Miller, then Minister of Lands and Forests, complimenting Alberta on what he said was the best stream-restoration project he had ever seen in all his angling travels.

There were and still are many important Buck for Wildlife projects in Alberta, including many miles of fence protecting stream banks on private land, but never on public land for some reason. But ultimately and strangely, there was too much money and not enough projects. The trust fund's $11 million surplus in the bank was more than the new Klein government, obsessed with debt reduction, could resist. Then-president Vern McIntosh consulted the AFGA legal counsel about a sudden government threat simply to transfer the huge surplus to general revenue. That clearly would have been an actionable breach of trust, so the government achieved the same goal by getting seven "stakeholder" groups, including the AFGA, to form a "delegated authority organization," the Alberta Conservation Association (ACA), to which would be transferred the $11 million, the "Habitat Stamp" would be discontinued, but "levies" on hunting and sportfishing licence fees would be paid to the ACA. The catch was that Fish and Wildlife Division budgets and staff were gutted and cut to the bone in the process. So, the ACA's many critics in the AFGA maintain, the ACA—essentially funded by the hunters and anglers of Alberta—found itself fund-

COURTESY OF BOB SCAMMELL

Leigh Perkins fishing on the North Raven River.

ing many programs and division activities involving non-fish and game species that should properly be paid for by all the taxpayers of Alberta out of general revenues.

A substantial number of the AFGA members contend the organization should withdraw from the ACA, but others argue that would be "taxation without representation," leaving their members with no voice in how their money is spent. Fortuitously, in 1983 the AFGA established its own Wildlife Trust Fund that now owns, controls, or manages more than 30,000 acres of prime, some critical, fish and wildlife habitat in many parts of Alberta, all open for the lawful enjoyment of the general public. But there is never enough money, and some AFGA members, ironically, are starting to say the government must re-establish a habitat stamp for sportfishing and hunting licences. Perhaps the ultimate sad irony is that recent ACA electro-fishing surveys reveal that the numbers and biomass of trout in the North Raven are so suddenly and mysteriously "down" that some angler advocates are starting to worry the numbers will soon be worse than they were before the little creek became the first Buck for Wildlife project.

Nobel laureate in literature William Faulkner once observed "the past is never dead; it's not even past." There is never a final victory in conservation wars, it seems, just battles that must be fought, over and over. Yet the AFGA has been victorious in many battles over the years; it never gives up, employing the patience and tenacity of the good hunter. In 1908 the pioneers of the AFGA started a movement of organized anglers and hunters that has largely dominated and shaped fish, wildlife and other renewable resource conservation in Alberta for a century. George Orwell wrote, "who controls the past controls the future." If "what's past is prologue," as Shakespeare wrote in *The Tempest*, then the epilogue must be the future. What is in the future for the AFGA?

Alberta in 2008 is a very different place from what it was in 1908 and although some of the challenges for the AFGA today are the same, most are totally different from what our founders faced. The organization still battles for Sunday hunting in this supposedly free and democratic modern society, and the struggle for more fish and wildlife regulation enforcement never ends. Waterfowl populations are still good—some say too good when it comes to Canada geese—and deer populations, especially white-tailed deer are virtually out of control and causing problems, as are beaver, more abundant in Alberta now than at the height of the fur trade. The AFGA-introduced Hungarian partridge and pheasants have flourished the past two seasons as never before since the '40s and '50s. There are huge new problems, such as chronic wasting disease and ending its cause and game ranching, both unheard-of issues in 1908. In 1908 and well into the AFGA's first century, public, or Crown land was regarded as wasteland. The negligent, mindless disposal and abuse of this vast treasure, the fifty percent of Alberta that is public land, will become a critical issue in the next century.

Ironically, as the population of the province burgeons, the number of hunters and anglers shrinks. That fact has resulted in a decrease of about 10,000 in AFGA individual membership from its peak of near 25,000 in the late '60s and early '70s, to a steady 15,000 more or less today. The current AFGA executive knows the organization must address and reverse the membership drop as a priority. Is the way to more members simply increasing the numbers of hunters and anglers through a program of educating, training and mentoring them? Some informed and concerned conservationists who may or may not be AFGA members, and who should be heard from at the 100th anniversary annual conference, believe that money, not members, should be the priority.

Certainly there are conservation organizations in Alberta with far fewer members than the AFGA that seem to have much more money, derived from big fundraising events and corporate sponsorships. Yet, somehow, probably because of high fundraiser fees and staff salaries, the rich organizations do not seem to put as much of that money "on the ground" as does the AFGA, with its huge army of dedicated volunteers. The big challenge for the AFGA as it enters its second century is to solve the member-money conundrum of the modern conservation organization, ideally through a combination of raising big bucks and big membership. The problems of fish and wildlife in 2008 are different, but every bit as difficult as those faced by the AFGA founders in 1908. Anyone familiar with the organization and its history will be confident that today's AFGA leaders are up to the challenges; for the sake of better new days for our fish and wildlife resources, Albertans generally better hope so.

COURTESY OF BOB SCAMMELL

One happy past president Bob Scammell (1973-75) with a Red Deer brown trout.

Fun Fishing Day derby at Lake Isle.

Appendices

The following are lists of some of the prominent members of the Alberta Fish and Game Association and its associated local clubs. The name spellings are based on AFGA records, and every attempt was made to be accurate and consistent. The Heritage 100 Committee apologizes if a name was misspelled or a person missed.

1.0 Alberta Fish and Game Association Past Presidents

Adam H. Esch (1920-1921), A. Kinnaird (1922-1923), Dr. R.A. Rooney (1924-1926), E.P Hall (1927), C.A. Hayden (1928-1929), Dr. W.A. Wilson (1930), Frank Farley (1931), A.P. Burns (1932), Norman Frazer (1933-1934), H.L. Wyman (1935), H.L. Wyman and L.E. Wise (each in part-1936), L.E. Wise (1937-39), William Fisher (1940-41), Dr. R.A. Rooney (1942-43), J.A. McGhee (1944-46), George E. Watt (1946-50), C.E. Brown (1950-52), Floyd E. Mitchell (1952-54), Curt P. Smith (1954-56), J.E. (Earle) Carr (1956-58), Elmer Kure (1958-60), Gordon Cummings (1960-62), Ben Rosnau (1962-64), Henry Lembicz (1964-66), Joe Balla (1966-69), Gordon Peel (1969-71), Tom O'Keefe (1971-73), R. H. (Bob) Scammell (1973-75), Lewis T. (Budd) Traver (1975-77), A.G. (Tony) Ferguson (1977-79), Don Hayden (1979-81), Roy Ozanne (1981-83), Ron Gladish (1983-85), Jack Shaver (1985-86), Nestor Romaniuk (1986-88), John M. (Jack) Graham (1988-90), Doug Rumsey (1990-90), Dr. Niels Damgaard (1990-93), Horst Fauser (1993-95), Vern McIntosh (1995-97), Andy von Busse (1997-98), Dave Powell (1998-2000), Gerry Pittman (2000-01), Rod Dyck (2001-03), Ray Makowecki (2003-05), Randy Collins (2005-07), Maurice Nadeau (2007-08).

Note: The past president records from 1920-27 are for the Northern Alberta Game and Fish Protective League, which eventually became the Edmonton Fish and Game Association; no other records are available for this position during this period of time.

2.0 Alberta Fish and Game Association Life Members

Don Appleby (Grande Centre), Fell Balderson, D.B. Blacklock, C.E. Brown, Bryce Chase (Calgary), W. Clark, J.B. Cross, Gordon Cummings, Niels Damgaard (Innisfail), Rod Dyck (Drumheller), John Eglinski, Horst Fauser (Lethbridge), Norman Ferguson (Lethbridge), Tony Ferguson (Edmonton), Gerald Foster (Rivière Qui Barre), Ron Gladish (Penticton, B.C.), Jack Graham (Edmonton), Don Hayden (Calgary), Stan Henders, A. L. Hogg, E.S. Huestis, Them Kjar, Elmer Kure (Spruce View), Nils Kvisle, Frank Lee (Sherwood Park), Henry Lembicz, Neville Lindsay, Grant MacEwan, Ray Makowecki (St. Paul), Vern McIntosh (Ardrossan), Jack Munro, Tom O'Keefe (Calgary), Eve Ozanne (Edmonton), Roy Ozanne, George Page (Sherwood Park), Gordon Peel, Gerry Pittman (Lethbridge), Heinz Plontke (Raymond), Dave Powell (Lacombe), Jim Robison, Carole Romaniuk (Edmonton), Nestor Romaniuk, Ben Rosnau, Toni Rosnau (Bruderheim), Doug Rumsey (Red Deer), Bob Scammell (Red Deer), Vic Scheuerman, Gene Scully, Jack Shaver, Darryl R. Smith (Crooked Creek), Sam Smolyk, Bruce Stewart, Bob Tanghe, N. E. Tanner, Budd Traver, Andy von Busse (St. Albert), Steve Witiuk (Sherwood Park), Ken Yank, Urban Young.

3.0 Fulton Trophy Winners

The *Calgary Herald* (1950), F.E. Mitchell (1951 and 1952), Calgary Brewing and Malting Company (1953), W.C. Fisher (1954), Ed Jeffries (1956), George M. Spargo (1957), Gordon Cummings (1959), Ducks Unlimited Canada (1960), Henry Stelfox (1961), Bill Bowthorpe (1963), Elmer Kure (1964), Henry Lembicz (1965), Norm Shaddock (1966), Art Miles (1968), Joe Balla (1971), Archie Hogg (1972), Tom O'Keefe (1974), Earle Carr (1975), R.H. (Bob) Scammell (1976), Gene Scully (1981), Alberta Wilderness Association (1982), Elmer Kure (1988), John Stelfox (1989), Jack Graham (1992), Carole (spelled "Carlena" on the plaque) and Nestor Romaniuk (1993), Gordon Peel (1994), Roy Ozanne (1995), Horst Fauser (2000), David E. Powell (2001), Don Hayden (2002), Tony Ferguson (2004), Rod Dyck (2005).

4.0 Alberta Fish and Game Association Clubs and Members Awarded the Order of the Bighorn Award

1982: Alberta Fish and Game Association; Archie Hogg; Emma and Bill Bowthorpe

1983: Alva Bair; Athabasca Fish and Game Association

1985: Lloyd Shea; Vic Scheuerman; Stony Plain Fish and Game Association

1986: Ted Blowers; Lawrence D. Halmrast; Nyal dee Hirsche

1987: Bryce Chase; Brooks Fish and Game Association

1989: Ben and Toni Rosnau; Elmer Kure; Ken Kultgen

1992: Alex Kurash; Darryl Smith

1995: George Freeman

1998: Bob Gruszecki; Dr. Martin Paetz
2000: George Loades; Robert Tanghe; R. H. (Bob) Scammell
2002: Dave Powell; Andy Russell
2004: Garry Hackler, Ed Scarlett
2006: Rod Dyck
2008: Neil Downey, Merv Kopperud

5.0 Alberta Fish and Game Association Management Personnel

George Spargo (1930-1962); Bruce Stewart (1960-1966); Paul Morck (1968-1985); Danny Woytiuk (1985), Lyle Fullerton (1986-1990); Ron Hauser (1991-2000); Colleen MacDougall (2000-2001); Martin Sharren (2002) variously termed "secretary", "Alberta Manager", "Chief Executive Officer" and "Executive Vice-President" during the history of the association. [NOTE: Spargo stayed on as AFGA secretary from 1960-62, while Bruce Stewart commenced employment as general manager in 1960.]

6.0 Summary of the Numbers of Anglers and Hunters in Alberta 1960 to 2004 relative to membership in the Alberta Fish and Game Association and Alberta's Population

LICENCE TYPE

Year	Wildlife Certificate	Resident Angler	AFGA Members	Alberta Population
60-61		138,837	17,207	
61-62		119,773	17,228	
62-63		122,123	17,233	
63-64		129,244	17,561	
64-65	118,843	124,747	16,549	1,425,543
65-66	109,593	122,537	17,044	
66-67	106,132	133,092	18,170	
67-68	124,028	136,693	23,754	
68-69	119,978	139,253	22,933	
69-70	117,408	150,225	21,536	1,576,549
70-71	128,708	145,491	19,847	
71-72	132,451	156,575	19,580	
72-73	131,837	171,863	19,616	
73-74	132,476	180,847	18,599	
74-75	121,409	206,331	22,651	1,758,260
75-76	124,804	214,283	23,798	
76-77	136,497	252,790	24,494	
77-78	150,107	264,657	24,457	
78-79	155,749	272,228	23,070	
79-80	161,117	285,087	20,860	2,294,212
80-81	166,191	303,356	22,751	
81-82	164,527	323,775	23,356	
82-83	162,573	343,275	23,784	
83-84	162,304	345,265	23,386	
84-85	149,838	340,197	23,135	2,318,408
85-86	146,413	337,416	22,574	
86-87	151,708	345,809	19,296	
87-88	148,621	337,630	17,675	
88-89	144,738	327,559	16,550	
89-90	140,115	303,571	14,100	2,469,069
90-91	130,206	245,431	12,156	
91-92	114,208	245,374	12,222	
92-93	104,945	233,689	11,678	
93-94	100,257	236,170	11,450	
94-95	98,760	250,676	10,932	2,615,873
95-96	93,424	239,600	11,593	
96-97	90,059	223,551	13,375	
97-98	90,419	224,447	12,991	
98-99	97,519	210,166	13,717	
99-00	93,721	205,256	13,773	2,871,271
00-01	87,961	208,364	14,169	
01-02	87,089	205,304	14,432	
02-03	86,345	209,783	13,602	
03-04	84,873	213,659	14,345	
04-05	87,025	202,185	14,885	

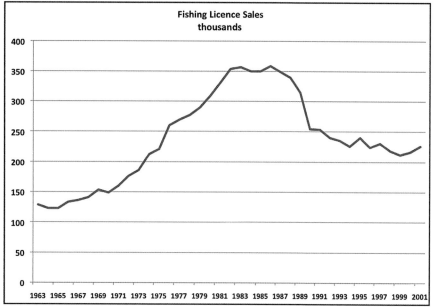

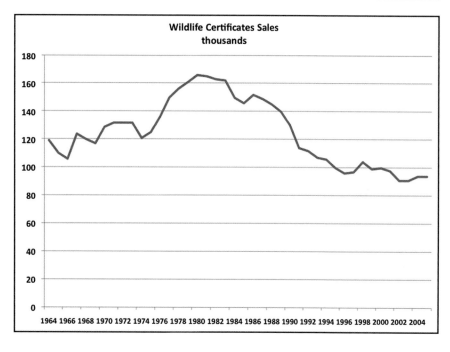

7.0 Provincial Executive of the Alberta Fish and Game Association and Alberta Fish and Game Association Staff (1945-2007)

The provincial executive and the AFGA staff lists are generally presented as given in the records, hence the variation in formatting. Secondly, there are some differences in the actual name in these lists based on records from pre-conference handbooks and conference yearbooks which are probably as a result of changes during the year, hence some years with two different lists. The spelling of the names are as taken from the records.

1944-45 Executive List

Officers
President	J.A. McGhee
Vice president	George E. Watt
Vice president	R.H. Routledge
Vice president	K.J. Webb
Vice president	G.J. Keltie
Secretary treasurer	G.M. Spargo

Regional Representatives
Foothills region	Henry Stelfox
Foothills region (south)	W. Beaubier
Irrigation region	Vacant
Shortgrass	C. Pattinson

Council
	Dr. W.A. Wilson
	Frank L. Farley
	A.P. Burns
	L.E. Wise
	Wm. C. Fisher
	Dr. R.A. Rooney
	C.A. Hayden

Committees
Legislative and constitutional	Neville R. Lindsay
	Austin de B. Winter
	L.E. Fairbairn
Big game chairman	Wm. C. Fisher
Fish and angling chairman	V.A. Newall
Upland game birds chairman	Austin de B. Winter
Migratory bird chairman	A. Hogg
National parks chairman	W. J. Selby Walker

Scientific	
Mammals	Dr. Wm. Rowan
Fish	Dr. R. Miller
Advisory council	
Game and game birds	J.A. McGhee
	G.E.Watt
Fish	H. Stelfox
	G. J. Keltie

1945 Executive List

Officers
President	J.A. McGhee
Vice president	George E. Watt
Vice president	G.J. Keltie
Vice president	R.H. Routledge
Vice president	K.J. Webb
Secretary treasurer	G.M. Spargo

Regional Representatives
Foothills region	Henry Stelfox
Shortgrass	W.D. Ingram
Foothills region (south)	Wilfred Beaubier
Irrigation region	T. Evans
Bush country	J.E. Wiggins
Northern region	Dr. T.F. MacDonald

Council
	Dr. W.A. Wilson
	Frank L. Farley
	A.P. Burns
	L.E. Wise
	Wm. C. Fisher
	Dr. R.A. Rooney
	C.A. Hayden

Committees
Legislative and constitutional	Neville R. Lindsay
	Austin de B. Winter
	His Honour Judge
	L.E. Fairbairn
Big game chairman	Wm. C. Fisher
Fish and angling chairman	K.J. Webb
Upland game birds chairman	Austin de B. Winter
Migratory bird chairman	A. Hogg
National parks chairman	W.J. Selby Walker

Scientific	
Mammals	Dr. Wm. Rowan
Fish	Dr. R. Miller
Advisory council	J.A. McGhee
	George E. Watt
	G.J. Keltie

1946-47 Executive List

Officers
President	George E. Watt
Vice president	G.J. Keltie
Vice president	T. Evans
Vice president	K.J. Webb
Vice president	J.E. Wiggins

Past president | J.A. McGhee
Secretary treasurer | G.M. Spargo

Regional Representatives

Central prairies | J.A. Williams
Bush country | Vacant
Edmonton district | Dr. T.F. MacDonald
Foothills region (south) | C.B. Cheeseman
Foothills region (central) | Henry Stelfox
Irrigation district
  (Cranford-Medicine Hat) | H. Grigsby
  | T.C. Williams
Mountain country | R. Sicotte
Shortgrass region | W.D. Ingram

Council of Past Presidents

  | C.A. Hayden
  | Dr. W.A. Wilson
  | Frank L. Farley
  | A.P. Burns
  | L.E. Wise
  | Wm. C. Fisher
  | Dr. R.A. Rooney
  | J.A. McGhee

Standing Committees Chairmen

Legislative | Austin de B. Winter
Big game | Wm. C. Fisher
Fish and angling | K.J. Webb
Upland game-birds | C.E. Brown
Migratory birds | A. Hogg
Finance and membership | George E. Watt
Constitutional and bylaws | Neville R. Lindsay
Scientific committee | Dr. Wm. Rowan
Predatory animals
  and birds committee | Vacant
Educational committee | Vacant

1947 Executive List

Officers

President | George E. Watt
Vice president | G.J. Keltie
Vice president | T. Evans
Vice president | K.J. Webb
Vice president | J.E. Wiggins
Past president | J.A. McGhee
Secretary treasurer | G.M. Spargo

Regional Representatives

Bush country | G.T. Loney
Central prairies | J.A. Williams
Crowsnest pass | Jim Kerr
Edmonton district | Dr. T.F. MacDonald
Foothills region (south) | C.B. Cheeseman
Foothills region (central) | Henry Stelfox
Irrigation district | H. Grigsby

Irrigation district
  (Cranford-Medicine Hat) | T.C. Williams
Mountain country | R. Sicotte
Shortgrass region (east) | Dr. Milton Moore
Shortgrass region (west) | W.D. Ingram

Council of Past Presidents

  | C.A. Hayden
  | Dr. W.A. Wilson
  | Frank L. Farley
  | A.P. Burns
  | L.E. Wise
  | Wm. C. Fisher
  | Dr. R.A. Rooney
  | J.A. McGhee

Standing Committees Chairmen

Legislative | Austin de B. Winter
Big game | H.F. Herron
Fish and angling | K.J. Webb
Upland game birds | C.E. Brown
Migratory birds | J. Williams
Predators | W.G. MacGillivray
Educational | W.R. H. Mason
Finance and membership | George E. Watt
Constitutional and bylaws | Neville R. Lindsay
Scientific committee | Dr.Wm. Rowan
General | Hugh C. Farthing

1948-49 Executive List

Officers

President | George E. Watt
Vice president | G.J. Keltie
Vice president | T. Evans
Vice president | K.J. Webb
Vice president | J.E. Wiggins
Vice president | Dr. Milton Moore
Vice president | G.J. Cummings
Vice president | C.E.Brown
Past president | J.A. McGhee
Secretary treasurer | G.M. Spargo

Regional Representatives

Alder Flats-Buck Lake Reserve | B.W. MacGillivray
Central prairies | J.A. Williams
Edmonton district | R.B. MacKenzie
E.I.D. district | W.D. Ingram
Foothills region (central) | Henry Stelfox
Foothills region (south) | C.B. Cheeseman
Irrigation district No. 1 | T.C. Williams
Irrigation district No. 2 | H. Grigsby
Mountain country | R. Sicotte
Northeastern prairies | G.J. Loney
Peace River | H. Thomson
Shortgrass region | H.H. Bateman

Council of Past Presidents

C.A. Hayden
Dr. W.A. Wilson
Frank L. Farley
A.P. Burns
L.E. Wise
Wm. C. Fisher
Dr. R.A. Rooney
J.A. McGhee

Standing Committees Chairmen

Legislative	Austin de B. Winter
Big game	H.F. Herron
Fish and angling	K.J. Webb
Upland game-birds	C.E. Brown
Migratory birds	J. Williams
Predators	Wm. Hedley
Educational	W. R. H. Mason
Finance and membership	George E. Watt
Constitutional and bylaws	Neville R. Lindsay
Scientific committee	Dr. Wm. Rowan
General	Hugh C. Farthing

1949-50 Executive List

Officers

President	George E. Watt
Vice president	G.J. Keltie
Vice president	T. Evans
Vice president	K.J. Webb
Vice president	J.E. Wiggins
Vice president	Dr. Milton Moore
Vice president	G.J. Cummings
Vice president	C.E.Brown
Past president	J.A. McGhee
Secretary treasurer	G.M. Spargo

Regional Representatives

Alder Flats-Buck Lake Reserve	B.W. MacGillivray
Central prairies	J.A. Williams
Crowsnest Pass	Jim Kerr
Edmonton district	R.B. MacKenzie
E.I.D. district	W.D. Ingram
Foothills region (central)	Henry Stelfox
Foothills region (south)	C.B. Cheeseman
Irrigation district no. 1	T.C. Williams
Irrigation district no. 2	H. Grigsby
Mountain country	R. Sicotte
Northeastern prairies	G.J. Loney
Peace River	H. Thomson
Shortgrass region	H.H. Bateman

Council of Past Presidents

C.A. Hayden
Dr. W.A. Wilson
Frank L. Farley
A.P. Burns
L.E. Wise
Wm. C. Fisher
Dr. R.A. Rooney
J.A. McGhee

Standing Committees Chairmen

Big game	H.F. Herron
Constitutional and bylaws	Neville R. Lindsay
Educational	W. R. H. Mason
Finance and membership	George E. Watt
Fish and angling	K.J. Webb
General	Hugh C. Farthing
Legislative	Austin de B. Winter
Migratory birds	Geo. Danyluk
Predators	Wm. Hedley
Scientific committee	Dr. Wm. Rowan
Upland game birds	C.E. Brown

1950-51 Executive List

Officers

President	C.E. Brown
Vice president	G.J. Keltie
Vice president	K.J. Webb
Vice president	J.E. Wiggins
Vice president	H.H. Bateman
Vice president	G.J. Cummings
Vice president	Wilfred Beaubier
Past president	George E. Watt
Secretary treasurer	G.M. Spargo

Regional Representatives

Alder Flats-Buck Lake Reserve	B.W. MacGillivray
Battle River district	Walter Vassar
Calgary district	F.E. Mitchell
Central prairies	J.A. Williams
Crowsnest Pass	Jim Kerr
Drumheller district	R. Siddons
Edmonton district	R. B. MacKenzie
E.I.D. district	W.D. Ingram
Foothills region (central)	Henry Stelfox
Foothills region (south)	C.B. Cheeseman
Irrigation district no. 1	T.C. Williams
Irrigation district no. 2	H. Grigsby
Mountain country	R. Sicotte
Northeastern prairies	G.J. Loney
Peace River	H. Thomson
Red Deer district	H. C. Farthing
Shortgrass region	W. Clark

St. Mary's irrigation district — F.F. Balderson
Waterton Lake district — C.S. Buchanan
Wostok district — Herman Hennig

Council of Past Presidents

C.A. Hayden
Dr. W.A. Wilson
A.P. Burns
L.E. Wise
Wm. C. Fisher
Dr. R.A. Rooney
J.A. McGhee
George E. Watt

Standing Committees Chairmen

Big game	J.E. (Erle) Carr
Fish and angling	K.J. Webb
Finance and membership	George E. Watt
General	Hugh C. Farthing
Legislative	Austin de B. Winter
Migratory birds	Geo. Danyluk
Predators	H. Cornwell
Scientific committee	Dr. Wm. Rowan
Upland game birds	G.T. Loney
Vice chairman	George Roth

1951-52 Executive List

Officers

President	C.E. Brown
Vice president	G.J. Keltie
Vice president	K.J. Webb
Vice president	H.H. Bateman
Vice president	G.J. Cummings
Vice president	Wilfred Beaubier
Past president	George E. Watt
Secretary treasurer	G.M. Spargo

Regional Representatives

Alder Flats-Buck Lake Reserve	B.W. MacGillivray
Battle River district	Walter Vassar
Calgary district	F.E. Mitchell
Central prairies	J.A. Williams
Crowsnest Pass	Jim Kerr
Drumheller district	R. Siddons
Edmonton district	W. Crawford
E.I.D. district	W.D. Ingram
Foothills region (central)	Henry Stelfox
Foothills region (south)	C.B. Cheeseman
Irrigation district no. 1	T.C. Williams
Irrigation district no. 2	H. Grigsby
Mountain country	R. Sicotte
Northeastern prairies	Sig Lefsrud
North Saskatchewan border district	G. Cyr
Peace River	H. Thomson

Red Deer district — Vacant
Shortgrass region — W. Clark
St. Mary's irrigation district — F.F. Balderson
Waterton Lake district — C.S. Buchanan
Wostok district — Herman Hennig

Council of Past Presidents

C.A. Hayden
A.P. Burns
L.E. Wise
Wm. C. Fisher
Dr. R. A. Rooney
J.A. McGhee
George E. Watt

Standing Committees Chairmen

Big game	J.E. (Erle) Carr
Finance and membership	George E. Watt
Fish and angling	K.J. Webb
General	Hugh C. Farthing
Legislative	Austin de B. Winter
Migratory birds	Geo. Danyluk
Predators	H. Cornwell
Scientific committee	Dr. Wm. Rowan
Upland game birds	G.T. Loney
Vice chairman	George Roth

1952-53 Executive List

Officers

President	F. (Floyd) E. Mitchell
Past president	C.E. Brown
Vice president	R. Wood
Vice president	K.J. Webb
Vice president	J.E. (Erle) Carr
Vice president	H.H. Bateman
Vice president	G.J. Cummings
Vice president	Wilfred Beaubier
Vice president	G.T. Loney

Regional Representatives

Alder Flats-Buck Lake Reserve	B.W. MacGillivray
Battle River district	Curt P. Smith
Brazeau-Edson district	G.L. Davidge
Calgary district	W.J. Ross
Central prairies	J.A. Williams
	J.G. Pearson
Central Saskatchewan border district	J.A. Miller
Dinosaur district	R. Siddons
Crowsnest Pass	Frank Sickoff
Edmonton district	J.P. Gow
	J. Hamilton
	W. Crawford
E.I.D. district	G. Philpott
Foothills region (central)	Henry Stelfox

Foothills region (south)	C.B. Cheeseman
Irrigation district no. 1	T.C. Williams
Irrigation district no. 2	H. Grigsby
Mountain country	R. Sicotte
	D. Hunt
Northeastern prairies	Sig Lefsrud
	D. Osterberg
North Saskatchewan border district	G. Cyr
Peace River	H. Thomson
Red Deer district	Lafond Kalbfleisch
Shortgrass region	W. Clark
St. Mary's irrigation district	F.F. Balderson
Waterton Lake district	C. S. Buchanan
Whitford Lake district	Herman Hennig

Council of Past Presidents

	C.A. Hayden
	A.P. Burns
	L.E. Wise
	Wm. C. Fisher
	Dr. R.A. Rooney
	J.A. McGhee
	George E. Watt
	C.E. Brown

Standing Committees Chairmen

Big game	J.E. (Erle) Carr
Finance and membership	George E. Watt
Fish and angling	C.S. Buchanan
General	J.P. Gow
Legislative	Wm. C. Fisher
Migratory birds	Roland Brooke
Office secretary	Dorothy Keays
Predators	G. Riach
Scientific committee	Dr. Wm. Rowan
Secretary treasurer	G.M. Spargo
Upland game-birds	C. P. Smith
Vice chair	J. Hamilton
Vice chair	G. Graf
Vice chair	Bob Arlt
Vice chair	Ken Watts
Vice chairman	George Roth
Vice chair	G.J. Cummings
Vice chair	H. Cornwell

======

1953-54 Executive List

Officers

President	F. (Floyd) E. Mitchell
Past president	C.E. Brown
Vice president	R. Wood
Vice president	J.E. (Erle) Carr
Vice president	H.H. Bateman
Vice president	G.J. Cumming
Vice president	Wilfred Beaubier
Vice president	G.T. Loney
Vice president	G. Roth

Regional Representatives

Alder Flats-Buck Lake Reserve	B.W. MacGillivray
Battle River district	Curt P. Smith
Brazeau-Edson district	Vacant
Calgary district	W.J. Ross
Central prairies	J.A. Williams
Central Saskatchewan border district	J.A. Miller
Crowsnest Pass	Frank Sickoff
Dinosaur district	R. Siddons
Edmonton district	J.P. Gow
	J. Hamilton
	W. Crawford
Foothills region (central)	Henry Stelfox
Foothills region (south)	C.B. Cheeseman
Shortgrass region	W. Clark
Lethbridge irrigation district	H. Grigsby
	D. Hunt
	D. Osterberg
Mountain country	R. Sicotte
Northeastern prairies	Sig Lefsrud
North Saskatchewan border district	G. Cyr
Peace River	Paul Appleton
St. Mary's irrigation district	F.F. Balderson
Red Deer district	Lafond Kalbfleisch
Waterton Lake district	C.S. Buchanan
Whitford Lake district	Herman Hennig

Council of Past Presidents

	C.A. Hayden
	A.P. Burns
	L.E. Wise
	Wm. C. Fisher
	Dr. R.A. Rooney
	J.A. McGhee
	George E. Watt
	C.E. Brown

Standing Committees Chairmen

Big game	J.E. (Erle) Carr
General	J.P. Gow
Finance and membership	F.E. Mitchell
Fish and angling	C.S. Buchanan
Legislative	Wm. C. Fisher
Migratory birds	Roland Brooke
Office secretary	Dorothy Keays
Predators	Sorren Norre
Scientific committee	Dr. Wm. Rowan
Secretary manager	G.M. Spargo
Upland game birds	C.P. Smith
Vice chair	J. Hamilton
Vice chair	G. Graf
Vice chair	W.R. Wolley-Dod
Vice chair	Ken Watts
Vice chair	G.J. Cummings
Vice chair	H. Cornwell

1954-55 Executive List

Officers

President	C.P. Smith
Past president	F. (Floyd) E. Mitchell
Vice president	J.E. (Erle) Carr
Vice president	G.J. Cummings
Vice president	Wilfred Beaubier
Vice president	G.T. Loney
Vice president	Urban Young
Vice president	W. Clark
Vice president	L. Kalbfleisch
Vice president	Dr. L.H. Mason

Regional Representatives

Alder Flats-Buck Lake Reserve	B.W. MacGillivray
Battle River district	E. Schielke
Brazeau-Edson district	Dewey Miller
Calgary district	Guy Blake
Central Saskatchewan border district	J.A. Miller
Central prairies	J.A. Williams
Crowsnest Pass	Frank Sickoff
Dinosaur district	K. Creighton
Edmonton district	R. Wood
	J. Hamilton
	W. Crawford
E.I.D. district	G. Philpott
Foothills region (central)	Henry Stelfox
Lethbridge irrigation district	H. Grigsby
	D. Hunt
	D. Osterberg
Mountain country	R. Sicotte
Northeastern prairies	Sig Lefsrud
North Saskatchewan border district	G. Cyr
Peace River	Vacant
Red Deer district	Art Allen
Shortgrass region	Roy Eden
St. Mary's irrigation district	F.F. Balderson
Waterton Lake district	Andy Russell
Whitford Lake district	Herman Hennig

Council of Past Presidents

	C.A. Hayden
	A.P. Burns
	L.E. Wise
	Wm. C. Fisher
	Dr. R.A. Rooney
	J.A. McGhee
	George E. Watt
	C.E. Brown
	F.E. Mitchell

Standing Committees Chairmen

Big game	J.E. (Erle) Carr
Farmer sportsman relations	G.J. Cummings
Finance and membership	F.E. Mitchell
Fish and angling	G. Hinde
General	A. McRae
Legislative	Wm. C. Fisher
Migratory birds	Ken Watts
Office secretary	Dorothy Knechtel
Predators	Sorren Norre
Scientific committee	Dr. Wm. Rowan
Secretary manager	G.M. Spargo
Upland game-birds	R. Arlt
Vice chair	W.R. Wolley-Dod
Vice chair	Roland Brooke
Vice chair	J.A. Miller
Vice chair	H. Cornwell
Vice chair	O. Uggen
Vice chair	G. Graf

1955-56 Executive List

Officers

President	C.P. Smith
Past president	F. (Floyd) E. Mitchell
Vice president	J.E. (Erle) Carr
Vice president	G.J. Cummings
Vice president	Wilfred Beaubier
Vice president	G.T. Loney
Vice president	Urban Young
Vice president	W. Clark
Vice president	L. Kalbfleisch
Vice president	Dr. L.H. Mason

Regional Representatives

Alder Flats-Buck Lake reserve	B.W. MacGillivray
Battle River district	E. Schielke
Brazeau-Edson district	Vacant
Calgary district	Guy Blake
Central prairies	J.A. Williams
Central Saskatchewan border district	J.A. Miller
Crowsnest Pass	Frank Sickoff
Dinosaur district	K. Creighton
Edmonton district	R. Wood
	J. Hamilton
	W. Crawford
E.I.D. district	Vacant
Foothills region (central)	Henry Stelfox
Lethbridge irrigation district	H. Grigsby
	D. Hunt
	D. Osterberg
Mountain Country	R. Sicotte
Northeastern prairies	Sig Lefsrud

North Saskatchewan	
border district	G. Cyr
Peace River	Dr. F. H. Sutherland
Red Deer district	Art Allen
St. Mary's irrigation district	F.F. Balderson
Shortgrass region	Roy Eden
Waterton Lake district	Andy Russell
Whitford Lake district	Herman Hennig

Council of Past Presidents

C.A. Hayden	
A.P. Burns	
L.E. Wise	
Wm. C. Fisher	
Dr. R. A. Rooney	
J.A. McGhee	
George E. Watt	
C.E. Brown	
F.E. Mitchell	

Standing Committees Chairmen

Big game	J.E. (Erle) Carr
Farmer-sportsman relations	G.J. Cummings
Finance and membership	F.E. Mitchell
Fish and angling	G. Hinde
General	A. McRae
Legislative	Wm. C. Fisher
Migratory birds	Ken Watts
Office secretary	Dorothy Knechtel
Predators	Sorren Norre
Secretary manager	G.M. Spargo
Upland game-birds	R. Arlt
Vice chair	O. Uggen
Vice chair	G. Graf
Vice chair	W.R. Wolley-Dod
Vice chair	Roland Brooke
Vice chair	J.A. Miller
Vice chair	H. Cornwell
Vice chair	E. Kure

1956-57 Executive List

Officers

President	J.E. (Erle) Carr
Past president	C.P Smith
Vice president	C.W. Johnson
Vice president	G.J. Cummings
Vice president	G. Blake
Vice president	G.T. Loney
Vice president	Urban Young
Vice president	W. Clark
Vice president	L. Kalbfleisch
Vice president	Dr. L.H. Mason

Regional Representatives

Alder Flats-Buck Lake Reserve	B.W. MacGillivray
Battle River district	G. Burnstad
Brazeau-Edson district	J. Pike
Calgary district	D. Morgan
	H. Snowden
Crowsnest Pass	Vacant
Central prairies	J.A. Williams
Dinosaur district	W. Bauer
Edmonton district	J. Gow
	W. Crawford
	S. Germaniuk
E.I.D. district	Vacant
Foothills region (central)	M. Reed
Guide's representative	S. Burrell
Lethbridge irrigation district	Roy Brewer
	D. Hunt
	D. Osterberg
Little Bow district	S. Dixon
Mountain country	R. Sicotte
Northeastern prairies	Sig Lefsrud
North Saskatchewan border	
district	J.A. Miller
Oilfields district	A. McRae
Peace River	Dr. F.H. Sutherland
Red Deer district	H. Scragg
Representative (at large)	Ken Watts
Shortgrass region	H. Ronnenberg
St. Mary's irrigation district	F.F. Balderson
Taber district	M. Bartrum
Waterton Lake district	Andy Russell
Whitford Lake district	Herman Hennig

Council of Past Presidents

C.A. Hayden	
A.P. Burns	
L.E. Wise	
Wm. C. Fisher	
Dr. R.A. Rooney	
George E. Watt	
C.E. Brown	
F.E. Mitchell	
C.P Smith	

Standing Committees Chairmen

Big game	U. Young
Good and welfare	A. McRae
Farmer-sportsmen relations	G.J. Cummings
Finance and membership	F.E. Mitchell
Fish and angling	G. Hinde
Legislative	Wm. C. Fisher
Migratory birds	Ken Watts
Office secretary	Dorothy Knechtel
Predator	S. Henders
Secretary manager	G.M. Spargo
Upland game-birds	R. Arlt

Vice chair	O. Uggen
Vice chair	B.W. MacGillivray
Vice chair	W.R. Wolley-Dod
Vice chair	Roland Brooke
Vice chair	J.A. Miller
Vice chair	H. Cornwell

1957-58 Executive List

Officers

President	J.E. (Erle) Carr
Past president	C.P. Smith
Vice president	C.W. Johnson
Vice president	Urban Young
Vice president	G.J. Cummings
Vice president	G. Blake
Vice president	G.T. Loney
Vice president	W. Clark
Vice president	L. Kalbfleisch
Vice president	Dr. L.H. Mason

Regional Representatives

Alder Flats-Buck Lake Reserve	B.W. MacGillivray
Battle River district	G. Burnstad
Brazeau-Edson district	J. Pike
Calgary district	D. Morgan
	H. Snowden
Central prairies	J.A. Williams
Crowsnest Pass	Vacant
Dinosaur district	W. Bauer
Edmonton district	J. Gow
	W. Crawford
	S. Germaniuk
E.I.D. district	G. Philpott
Foothills region (central)	M. Reed
Guide's representative	S. Burrell
Lethbridge irrigation district	Roy Brewer
	D. Hunt
	D. Osterberg
Little Bow district	S. Dixon
Mountain country	R. Sicotte
Northeastern prairies	Sig Lefsrud
North Saskatchewan border district	J.A. Miller
Oilfields district	A. McRae
Peace River	Dr. F.H. Sutherland
Red Deer district	H. Scragg
Representative (at large)	Ken Watts
Shortgrass region	H. Ronnenberg
St. Mary's irrigation district	F.F. Balderson
Taber district	M. Bartrum
Waterton Lake district	Andy Russell
Whitford Lake district	Herman Hennig

Council of Past Presidents

	A.P. Burns
	L.E. Wise
	Wm. C. Fisher
	Dr. R.A. Rooney
	George E. Watt
	C.E. Brown
	F.E. Mitchell
	C.P Smith

Standing Committees Chairmen

Legislative	Wm. C. Fisher
Big game	U. Young
Vice chair	Andy Russell
Fish and angling	G. Hinde
Vice chair	B.W. MacGillivray
Upland game-birds	R. Arlt
Vice chair	W.R. Wolley-Dod
Migratory birds	Ken Watts
Vice chair	Roland Brooke
Predator	S. Henders
Vice chair	E. Kure
Public relations	G.J. Cummings
Vice chair	A. McRae
Finance and membership	F.E. Mitchell
Secretary manager	G.M. Spargo
Office secretary	Dorothy Knechtel

1959-60 Executive List

Officers

President	Elmer Kure
Past president	J.E. (Erle) Carr
Vice president	Urban Young
Vice president	C.W. Johnson
Vice president	G.J. Cummings
Vice president	R.M. Osterberg
Vice president	G.T. Loney
Vice president	W. Clark
Vice president	L. Kalbfleisch
Vice president	J.A. Miller

Regional Representatives

Additional representatives	Colin Buchanan
	Brian Kelly
	Ken Dezall
	Ben Rosnau
Alder Flats-Buck Lake Reserve	
Battle River district	G. Burnstad
Brazeau-Edson district	J. Pike
Calgary district	D. Morgan
	H. Snowden
	G. Blake
	N. Shaddock
Central prairies	F. Hargreaves
Claresholm district	E. Warren

Crowsnest Pass	Wm. Kovach (MLA)
Dinosaur district	W. Bauer
Edmonton district	W. Crawford
	J. Beck
E.I.D. district	Geo. Philpott
Foothills region (central)	Vacant
Foremost district	P. Hagen
Goose Lake Line district	W. Petrick
Guide's representative	S. Burrell
Grassy Lake district	F. Brewin
Lethbridge irrigation district	E. Dykes
	D. Hunt
	Joe Pisko
Little Bow district	S. Dixon
Mountain country	R. Sicotte
Northeastern prairies	Sig Lefsrud
North Saskatchewan border district	
Oilfields district	J.A. Miller
	A. McRae
	J. Ramsey
Peace River	Dr. F.H. Sutherland
Porcupine Hills district	H. Janis
Representative (at large)	Ken Watts
Red Deer district	H. Scragg
	H. Lembicz
Shortgrass region	G.R. Monkman
	H. Ronnenberg
Taber district	George Powell
Waterton Lake district	Andy Russell
Whitford Lake district	Herman Hennig

Council of Past Presidents

	A.P. Burns
	L.E. Wise
	Wm. C. Fisher
	Dr. R.A. Rooney
	George E. Watt
	C.E. Brown
	F.E. Mitchell
	C.P Smith
	J.E. (Erle) Carr

Standing Committees Chairmen

Big game	U. Young
Finance and membership	F.E. Mitchell
Fish and angling	D. Gibson
Legislative	Wm. C. Fisher, Q.C.
Migratory birds	J. Fedechko
Office secretary	Dorothy Knechtel
Predator	S. Henders
Public relations and membership	G.J. Cummings
Secretary manager	G.M. Spargo
Upland game-birds	R. Arlt
Vice chair	Ken Dezall
Vice chair	D. Cronkhite
Vice chair	Roland Brooke
Vice chair	H. Cornwell
Vice chair	U. Young

1960-61 Executive List

Officers

President	Gordon J. Cummings
Vice president	Urban Young
Vice president	C.W. Johnson
Vice president	R.M. Osterberg
Vice president	W. Clark
Vice president	Henry Lembicz
Vice president	J.A. Miller
Vice president	Guy Blake
Hon. vice president	Goddard Loney
Hon. vice president	Lafont Kalbfleisch
Alberta manager	Bruce Stewart
Secretary	G.M. Spargo
Advisory council	Gordon Cummings
	Elmer Kure
	Urban Young

Regional Representatives

Brazeau-Edson district	Vacant
Calgary district	Doug Morgan
	Norman Shaddock
	Ross Laycock
	Herb Snowden
	Darwin Cronkhite
	F. Hamilton
Carstairs district (east)	Wilbur R. Reider
Central prairies	Fred Hargreaves
Claresholm district	Kai Hansen
Coleman district	Jim Kerr
Crowsnest Pass	Wm. Kovach (MLA)
Dinosaur Valley	Vacant
Edmonton district	Tom Burkett
	W. Crawford
	J. Beck
	Norman Lee
E.I.D. district	George Phillpott
Foremost district	A. Hagen
Foothills region (central)	Frank Crutchfield
Goose Lake Line district	W. Petrick
Guide's representative	S. Burrell
Lac La Biche (north)	Vacant
Lethbridge irrigation district	Dave Hunt
	Joe Pisko
	Harry Mosher
Little Bow district	Steve Dixon
Mountain district	Ralph Sicotte
Northeastern prairies	Sig Lefsrud
North Saskatchewan River	Ches Simmons
Oilfields District	J. Ramsey
Peace River	Vacant
Peace River	Bernard Hamm
Porcupine Hills district	H. Farriss
Pincher Creek area	Colin Buchanan
Raymond district	George Turner

Red Deer district	H. Scragg
	Jack D. Munro
Representative (at large)	Ken Watts
Rimbey-Buck Lake district	John Anderson
Short grass region	Lee White
	Colby Reeser
	Bob Monkman
Stettler-Big Valley	Harvey Beck
St. Mary's irrigation district	F.F. Balderson
Taber district	Jack Kinniburgh
Vegreville district	Joe Fedechko
Wetaskiwin-Battle Lake district	Vacant
Waterton Lake district	Andy Russell
Whitford Lake district	Herman Hennig
Waskatenau	Andrew Kinish

Standing Committees Chairmen

Big game	Ken Dezall
	J.E. (Erle) Carr
Finance	Floyd Mitchell
Fish	Fred Hargreaves
Vice chair	Jack Chesney
Membership and public relations	Chuck Johnson
Vice chair	Urban Young
Migratory birds	Joe Fedechko
Vice chair	W. Kalancha
Predator	Stan Henders
Vice chair	Brian Kelly
Upland game birds	Darwin Cronkhite
Vice chair	Alvin Scheer

Special Committees

Big game recommendations:	Ovar Uggen
	Bruce Stewart
	J.E. (Erle) Carr
	Henry Lemibicz
	Elmer Kure
	Kai Hansen
Wilderness area	Elmer Kure
	Urban Young
	J.E. (Erle) Carr
	Ross Laycock
Water and pollution	Sig Lefsrud
	Jack Balla
Constitution	Neville Lindsay
	C.V. Bennett
Legislative	Wm. C. Fisher, Q.C.

Council of Past Presidents

	A.P. Burns
	L.E. Wise
	Wm. C. Fisher (Q.C.)
	Dr. R.A. Rooney
	George E. Watt
	C.E. Brown
	F.E. Mitchell
	C.P Smith
	J.E. (Erle) Carr
	Elmer Kure

Directory of Officers - 1961

Officers

President	Gordon Cummings
Vice president	Urban Young
Vice president	C.W. Johnson
Vice president	W. Clark
Vice president	Henry Lembicz
Vice president	Ben Rosnau
Vice president	J.A. Miller
Vice president	Guy Blake
Hon. vice president	Goddard Loney
Hon. vice president	Lafont Kalbfleisch
Alberta manager	Bruce Stewart
Secretary	G.M. Spargo

Advisory Council

	Gordon Cummings
	Elmer Kure
	Urban Young

Regional Representatives

Battle River	Garnet Burnstead
Calgary district	Doug Morgan
	Norman Shaddock
	Ross Laycock
	Herb Snowden
	Darwin Cronkhite
	F. Hamilton
Carstairs district (east)	Wilbur R. Reider
Claresholm district	Kai Hansen
Coleman district	Jim Kerr
Crowsnest Pass	Wm. Kovach (MLA)
Edmonton district	W. Crawford
	J. Beck
Foothills region (central)	Frank Crutchfield
Foremost district	A. Hagen
Goose Lake Line district	W. Petrick
Guide's representative	Stan Burrell
Hinton-Edmonton district	James C. Wilson
Lethbridge irrigation district	Joe Pisko
	Harry Mosher
Legislative	W.C. Fisher, Q.C.
Mountain district	Ralph Sicotte
Northeastern prairies	Sig Lefsrud
North Saskatchewan River	Ches Simmons
Oilfields district	J. Ramsey
Peace River	Bernard Hamm
Pincher Creek area	Colin Buchanan
Porcupine Hills district	H. Farriss
Raymond district	George Turner
Red Deer district	H. Scragg,
	Jack D. Munro
Rimbey-Buck Lake district	John Anderson
Representative at large	Ken Watts
St. Mary's irrigation district	F.F. Balderson
Stettler-Big Valley	Harvey Beck

Short Grass region	Colby Reeser	Calgary	Bob Nugent
Vegreville district	Joe Fedechko	Calgary	Don Piche
Waterton Lake district	Andy Russell	Calgary	Ron Schmitke
Whitford Lake district	Herman Hennig	Carstairs	Alvin Scheer
Waskatenau	Andrew Kinish	Carstairs	Wilbur R. Reider

Council of Past Presidents

A.P. Burns
L.E. Wise
Wm. C. Fisher (Q.C.)
George E. Watt
C.E. Brown
F.E. Mitchell
C.P Smith
J.E. (Erle) Carr
Elmer Kure

Standing Committees Chairmen

Big game	Ken Dezall
Membership and public relations	R.W. (Chuck) Johnson
Migratory birds	Joe Fedechko
Predator	Stan Henders
Upland game birds	Darwin Cronkhite
Vice chair	J.E. (Erle) Carr
Vice chair fish	Jack Chesney
Vice chair	Urban Young

Note: There is no actual list of standing committee members in the 1962 convention yearbook. The above list is taken from various committee reports.

Directory of Officers - 1962

Officers

President	Ben Rosnau
1st Vice president	Henry Lembicz
Vice president	Urban Young
Vice president	C.W. Johnson
Vice president	W. Clark
Vice president	Elmer Kure
Vice president	Dave Hunt
Vice president	Norman Shaddock
Vice president	Bill Bowthorpe
Alberta manager	Bruce Stewart
Office assistant	Ash Clifton

Advisory Council

Ben Rosnau
Gordon Cummings
Elmer Kure

Regional Representatives

Brant	Steve Dixon
Bruderheim	Herman Hennig
Calgary	Ross Laycock
Calgary	Darwin Cronkhite
Calgary	Stan Henders

Calgary	Bob Nugent
Calgary	Don Piche
Calgary	Ron Schmitke
Carstairs	Alvin Scheer
Carstairs	Wilbur R. Reider
Coleman	Jim Kerr
Claresholm	Bob Arlt
Dickson	Them Kjar
Edmonton	Don Forsland
Edmonton	J. Beck
Edmonton	Chuck Burghardt
Edmonton	"Slim" Layley
Edmonton	Lawrence A. McRae
Foremost	A. Hagen
Fort Saskatchewan	Aale Passe
Hanna	Harry Holmes
Hartell	Jim Ramsay
Hinton	Jim Wilson
Hillcrest	W. Kovach, M.L.A.
Lacombe	Ed Tulley
Langford Lake	Norris Bamber
Lethbridge	John Bobinec
Lethbridge	Joe Balla
Lethbridge	Joe Pisko
Lloydminster	Archie Miller
Lundbreck	Hilton Farriss
Magrath	Fels Balderson
Milk River	Frank Madge
Medicine Hat	Colby Reesor
Medicine Hat	Archie Sullivan
Olds	Ralph Sicotte
Oyen	W. Kalancha
Raymond	C.D. Watson
Red Deer	Cec. Head
Red Deer	Dr. C.A. White
Pincher Creek	Jerry Gibson
Provost	Elmer Schielke
Red Deer	Eddie Aronitz
Rimbey	Frank Barry
Rocky Mountain House	Frank Crutchfield
Round Hill	Garnet Burnstead
Spirit River	Ted Scott
Spirit River	C.R. Vanderford
Stettler	Art Apperley
Stavely	Kai Hansen
St. Paul	Dr. Ken Tenove
Sundre	Stan Burrell
Taber	Ron Petrie
Vegreville	Joe Fedechko
Viking	Sig Lefsrud
Waterton Lakes National Parks	J. Attwell
Waskatenau	Andrew Kinnish
Wetaskiwin	Russ Cotterill
Willington	Camille Ethier

Council of Past Presidents

A.P. Burns
L.E. Wise
Wm. C. Fisher (Q.C.)
C.E. Brown
F.E. Mitchell
C.P Smith
J.E. (Erle) Carr
Elmer Kure
Gordon Cummings

Standing Committees Chairmen

Big game	Ross A. Laycock
Finance	Gordon Cummings
Fish	Jack Chesney
Good and welfare	
and public relations:	Norm Shaddock
Membership and public relations	R.W. (Chuck) Johnson
Migratory birds	Joe Fedechko
Predator	Jack Munro
Upland bird	Darwin Cronkhite
Wilderness, access and grazing	Elmer Kure

Note: There is no actual list of standing committee members in the 1963 convention yearbook. The above list is taken from various committee reports.

Directory of Officers - 1963

Officers

President	Ben Rosnau
1st Vice president	Henry Lembicz
Vice president	Urban Young
Vice president	W. Clark
Vice president	Elmer Kure
Vice president	C.W. Johnson
Vice president	Dave Hunt
Vice president	Norman Shaddock
Vice president	Bill Bowthorpe
Alberta manager	Bruce Stewart
Office assistant	Ash Clifton

Advisory Council

Ben Rosnau
Gordon Cummings
Elmer Kure

Regional Representatives

Brant	Steve Dixon
Bruderheim	Herman Hennig
Calgary	Darwin Cronkhite
Calgary	Stan Henders
Calgary	Bob Nugent
Calgary	Don Piche
Calgary	Ron Schmitke
Calgary	Ross Laycock
Carstairs	Wilbur R. Reider
Carstairs	Alvin Scheer
Claresholm	Bob Arlt
Coleman	Jim Kerr
Dickson	Them Kjar
Edmonton	"Slim" Layley
Edmonton	Lawrence A. McRae
Edmonton	J. Beck
Edmonton	Chuck Burghardt
Fort Saskatchewan	Aale Passe
Foremost	A. Hagen
Hanna	Harry Holmes
Hartell	Jim Ramsay
Hillcrest	W. Kovach, M.L.A.
Hinton	Jim Wilson
Lacombe	Ed Tulley
Langford Lake	Norris Bamber
Lethbridge	Joe Pisko
Lethbridge	John Bobinec
Lethbridge	Joe Balla
Lloydminster	Archie Miller
Lundbreck	Hilton Farriss
Magrath	Fels Balderson
Medicine Hat	Colby Reesor
Medicine Hat	Archie Sullivan
Milk River	Frank Madge
Oyen	W. Kalancha
Olds	Ralph Sicotte
Pincher Creek	Jerry Gibson
Provost	Elmer Schielke
Raymond	C.D. Watson
Red Deer	Eddie Aronitz
Red Deer	Dr. C.A. White
Red Deer	Cec. Head
Rimbey	Frank Barry
Rocky Mountain House	Frank Crutchfield
Round Hill	Garnet Burnstead
Spirit River	C.R. Vanderford
Spirit River	Ted Scott
Stavely	Kai Hansen
St. Paul	Dr. Ken Tenove
Stettler	Art Apperley
Sundre	Stan Burrell
Taber	Ron Petrie
Vegreville	Joe Fedechko
Viking	Sig Lefsrud
Waterton Lakes N.P.	J. Attwell
Waskatenau	Andrew Kinnish
Wetaskiwin	Russ Cotterill
Willington	Camille Ethier

Council of Past Presidents

A.P. Burns
L.E. Wise
Wm. C. Fisher (Q.C.)
C.E. Brown
F.E. Mitchell
C.P Smith
J.E. (Erle) Carr
Elmer Kure
Gordon Cummings

Standing Committees Chairmen

Access, grazing and wilderness	Elmer Kure
Big game	Ross A. Laycock
Fish	Jack Chesney
Good and welfare	Norm Shaddock
Membership	R.W. (Chuck) Johnson
Predator	Jack Munro
Upland bird	Darwin Cronkhite

Note: There is no actual list of standing committee members in the 1964 convention yearbook. The above listing is taken form various committee reports.

Directory of Officers - 1964

Officers

President	Henry Lembicz
Immediate past president	Ben Rosnau
1st Vice president	Dave Hunt
Vice president	Urban Young
Vice president	Elmer Kure
Vice president	C.W. Johnson
Vice president	Norman Shaddock
Vice president	Jack Munro
Vice president	Camille Ethier
Alberta manager	Bruce Stewart
Office assistant	Ash Clifton

Advisory Council

	Henry Lembicz
	Ben Rosnau
	Elmer Kure

Regional Representatives

Athabasca	Glen Osment
Brant	Steve Dixon
Brightview	Ernie Rossitter
Bruderheim	Herman Hennig
Bruderheim	Mrs. Toni Rosnau
Calgary	D. Cronkhite
Calgary	Stan Henders
Calgary	Bill Hamilton
Calgary	Bob Hobbs
Calgary	Ross Laycock
Calgary	Hugh Linge
Calgary	Bob Nugent
Carstairs	Alvin Scheer
Claresholm	Bob Arlt
Coleman	Jim Kerr
Coutts	W.R. Ford
Edmonton	J. Beck
Edmonton	C. Burghardt
Edmonton	"Slim" Layley
Edmonton	L.A. McRae
Edmonton	Tom Meters
Edmonton	R. Bellamy
Foremost	Ken Kultgen
Hanna	Harry Holmes
Hillcrest	W. Kovach
Hinton	Ken Alexander
Lamont	Paul Nychka
Langford Park	Norris Bamber
Lethbridge	Joe Balla
Lethbridge	John Bobenic
Lethbridge	Dixie Dougan
Lethbridge	Oscar Eritsland
Lloydminster	Archie Miller
Lundbreck	Stan Webber
Magrath	Fels Balderson
Medicine Hat	Archie Sullivan
Olds	Ralph Sicotte
Oyen	W. Kalancha
Pincher Creek	H. Louey
Provost	Elmer Schielke
Red Deer	Eddie Aronitz
Red Deer	Cec Head
Ricinus	J.E. (Erle) Carr
Rocky Mountain House	Frank Crutchfield
Round Hill	Bill Bowthorpe
Rycroft	Vincent Durda
Ryley	Garnet Burnstead
Smoky Lake	Frank Mitchell
Spirit River	C.R. Vanderford
Stavely	Kai Hansen
Stettler	Art Apperley
Sundre	Stan Burrell
Sundre	Them Kjar
Vegreville	G. Kassian
Wainwright	Dr. Vic Sawchuk
Waskatenau	A. Kinnash
Waterton Lakes National Park	J. Attwell
Wetaskiwin	Russ Cotterill
Whitehorse, Yukon	D. Camley
Willingdon	Ray Swiderski

Council of Past Presidents

	A.P. Burns
	L.E. Wise
	Wm. C. Fisher (Q.C.)
	C.E. Brown
	F.E. Mitchell
	C.P. Smith
	J.E. (Erle) Carr
	Elmer Kure
	Gordon Cummings
	Ben Rosnau
Legal Adviser	Neville N. Lindsay

Standing Committees Chairmen

Access, grazing and wilderness	G.S. Frizzell
Big game	Bob Hobbs
Fish	W.H. (Bill) Hamilton
Game bird	Darwin Cronkhite
Good and welfare	Frank Pickering
Indian affairs	Ben Rosnau
Membership	R.W. (Chuck) Johnson

Predator	J.D. (Jack) Munro
Public relations and publicity	Norm Shaddock
Vice chair	Philip Tompson

Note: There is no actual list of standing committee members in the 1965 convention yearbook. The above listing is taken from various committee reports.

Directory of Officers - 1965

Officers

President	Henry Lembicz
Immediate past president	Ben Rosnau
1st Vice president	Dave Hunt
Vice president	Urban Young
Vice president	Elmer Kure
Vice president	C.W. Johnson
Vice president	Norman Shaddock
Vice president	Jack Munro
Vice president	Camille Ethier
Alberta manager	Bruce Stewart
Office assistant	Ash Clifton

Advisory Council:

	Henry Lembicz
	Ben Rosnau
	Elmer Kure

Regional Representatives

Athabasca	Glen Osment
Brant	Steve Dixon
Brightview	Ernie Rossitter
Bruderheim	Herman Hennig
Bruderheim	Mrs. Toni Rosnau
Calgary	D. Cronkhite
Calgary	Stan Henders
Calgary	Bill Hamilton
Calgary	Bob Hobbs
Calgary	Ross Laycock
Calgary	Hugh Linge
Calgary	Bob Nugent
Carstairs	Alvin Scheer
Claresholm	Bob Arlt
Coleman	Jim Kerr
Coutts	W.R. Ford
Edmonton	J. Beck
Edmonton	C. Burghardt
Edmonton	"Slim" Layley
Edmonton	L.A. McRae
Edmonton	Tom Meters
Edmonton	R. Bellamy
Foremost	Ken Kultgen
Hanna	Harry Holmes
Hillcrest	W. Kovach
Hinton	Ken Alexander
Lamont	Paul Nychka
Langford Park	Norris Bamber
Lethbridge	Joe Balla
Lethbridge	John Bobenic
Lethbridge	Dixie Dougan
Lethbridge	Oscar Eritsland
Lloydminster	Archie Miller
Lundbreck	Stan Webber
Magrath	Fels Balderson
Medicine Hat	Archie Sullivan
Olds	Ralph Sicotte
Oyen	W. Kalancha
Pincher Creek	H. Louey
Provost	Elmer Schielke
Red Deer	Eddie Aronitz
Red Deer	Cec. Head
Ricinus	J.E. (Erle) Carr
Rocky Mountain House	Frank Crutchfield
Round Hill	Bill Bowthorpe
Rycroft	Vincent Durda
Ryley	Garnet Burnstead
Smoky Lake	Frank Mitchell
Spirit River	C.R. Vanderford
Stavely	Kai Hansen
Stettler	Art Apperley
Sundre	Stan Burrell
Sundre	Them Kjar
Vegreville	G. Kassian
Vulcan	Glen Dahl
Wainwright	Dr. Vic Sawchuk
Waskatenau	A. Kinnash
Waterton Lakes National Park	J. Attwell
Wetaskiwin	Russ Cotterill
Whitehorse, Yukon	D. Camley
Willingdon	Ray Swiderski

Council of Past Presidents

	A.P. Burns
	L.E. Wise
	Wm. C. Fisher (Q.C.)
	C.E. Brown
	F.E. Mitchell
	C.P Smith
	J.E. (Erle) Carr
	Elmer Kure
	Gordon Cummings
	Ben Rosnau
Legal Adviser	Neville N. Lindsay

Standing Committees Chairmen

Big game	Bob Hobbs
Fish	Bill Hamilton
Game bird	Darwin Cronkhite
Hunter training	Manfred Lucas
Indian affairs	Ben Rosnau
Membership	R.W. (Chuck) Johnson
Predator	J.D. (Jack) Munro
Public relations and publicity	Norm Shaddock

Not Mentioned

Vice chair	Philip Tompson
Good and welfare	Frank Pickering
Access, grazing and wilderness	G.S. Frizzell

Note: There is no actual list of standing committee members in the 1965 convention yearbook. The above listing is taken from various committee reports.

Directory of Officers - 1966

Officers

President	Joe Balla
Immediate past president	Henry Lembicz
1st Vice president	Bob Hobbs
Vice president	Archie Sullivan
Vice president	George Mitchell
Vice president	Norm Shaddock
Vice president	Steve Dixon
Vice president	Elmer Kure
Vice president	Jack Munro
Secretary/manager	Bruce Stewart
Office assistant	Dick Parker
Finance chairman	Gordon Cummings

Chairmen of Standing Committees

Fish	Bill Hamilton
Pest control	Jack Munro
Game birds	Gordon Merrick
Big game	Vern Arnold
Good and welfare	Dave Hunt
Access/grazing/wilderness	Ken Kultgen
Indian affairs	Ben Rosnau
Pollution	George Mitchell
Land/water conservation	Henry Lembicz
Hunter training	Manfred Lucas
Membership	Bob Hobbs
Legal advisor	Neville Lindsay
Publicity	Norm Shaddock
	Garry Cooper
	Joe Balla

Canadian Wildlife Federation

President	Gordon Cummings
Directors (Alberta)	Henry Lembicz
	Ben Rosnau
	Elmer Kure

Advisory Council

	Joe Balla
	Henry Lembicz
	Elmer Kure

Regional Representatives

Athabasca	Glen Osment
Bruderheim	Herman Hennig
Bruderheim	Mrs. Toni Rosnau
Calgary	Darwin Cronkhite
Calgary	Stan Henders
Calgary	Ross Laycock
Calgary	C.W. Johnson
Calgary	Mrs. Helen Hobbs
Calgary	Tom O'Keefe
Camrose	Don Green
Carstairs	Alvin Scheer
Carstairs	Reg Francis
Claresholm	Bob Arlt
Cold Lake	Bill Svelka
Coleman	Jim Kerr
Coutts	W.R. Ford
Denwood	A. Ferguson
Edmonton	C. Burghardt
Edmonton	"Slim" Layley
Edmonton	L.A. McRae
Edmonton	T.M. Meters
Edmonton	Dr. Graham Bowman
Edmonton	Gordon Peel
Edmonton	J.R. Robinson
Edmonton	Urban Young
High River	Archie Hogg
Hinton	Ken Alexander
Huxley	Ernie Fawcett
Innisfail	Dick Mountain
Lamont	Paul Nychka
Lethbridge	John Bobenic
Lethbridge	Oscar Eritsland
Lethbridge	Joe Pisko
Lloydminster	Archie Miller
Lundbreck	Stan Webber
Magrath	Fels Balderson
Markerville	Harold Rhodes
Mundare	Ernie Zyla
Pincher Creek	H. Louey
Ponoka	Ed Nelson
Ponoka	Garnet Fink
Provost	Elmer Schielke
Red Deer	Eddie Aronitz
Red Deer	Cec Head
Red Deer	Bob Scammell
Red Deer	Dennis Clark
Rycroft	Vincent Durda
Ryley	Garnet Burnstead
Smoky Lake	Frank Mitchell
Spruce Grove	Harold McLaughlin
Stavely	Kai Hansen
Stettler	Art Apperley
Sundre	Stan Burrell
Sundre	Them Kjar
Sylvan Lake	Fred Walker
Taber	John Shearer
Vegreville	Joe Fedechko
Vulcan	Glen Dahl

Wainwright	Dr. Vic Sawchuk
Waskatenau	A. Kennash
Waterton Lakes National Park	J. Attwell
Willingdon	Ray Swiderski
Willington	Camille Ethier

Council of Past Presidents

A.P. Burns
L.E. Wise
Wm. C. Fisher (Q.C.)
C.E. Brown
F.E. Mitchell
C.P Smith
J.E. (Erle) Carr
Elmer Kure
Gordon Cummings
Ben Rosnau
Henry Lembicz

1967 Executive List

President	Joe Balla
Immediate past president	Henry Lembicz
First vice president	Bob Hobbs
Finance chair	C.E. Brown
Vice presidents	Archie Sullivan
	Ray Bellamy
	Tom O'Keefe
	Steve Dixon
	Elmer Kure
	Jack Munro

Zone Chairmen

Zone 1	Dave Hunt
Zone 2	T.J. O'Keefe
Zone 3	Bob Scammell
Zone 4	Ben Rosnau
Zones 6	Vince Durda
Secretary manager	Paul Morck

Chairmen of Standing Committees

Fish	Bill Hamilton
Vice chair	Len Thompson
Pest control	Jack Munro
Vice chair	Jim Sutton
Game-birds	Gordon Merrick
Vice chair	Jerry Schissler
Big game	Vern Arnold
Vice chair	George Galambos
Good and welfare	Dave Hunt
Vice chair	Lawrence McRae
Access, grazing, wilderness	Ken Kultgen
Vice chair	Elmer Kure
Indian affairs	Ben Rosnau
Vice chair	Hugh Linge
Pollution	L. Iley

Vice chair	Neville Lindsay
Land, water conservation	Henry Lembicz
Vice chair	J.E. (Erle) Carr
Hunter training	Manfred Lukas
Vice chair	Ted Caswell
Membership	Bob Hobbs
Vice chair	Bill Bowthorpe
Legal advisor	Neville Lindsay
Publicity	Norm Shaddock
Vice chair	Gary Cooper
Vice chair	Joe Balla

Canadian Wildlife Federation

President	Gordon Cummings
Directors	Henry Lembicz
	Ben Rosnau
	Elmer Kure

Advisory Council

Joe Balla
Henry Lembicz
Elmer Kure

Note: There is no official record for the 1968 executive list.

1969-1970 Executive List

President (until 1969 convention)	Joe Balla
Vice presidents at large	Gordon Peel
	Vern Arnold

Zone Chairmen

Zone 1	Dave Hunt
Zone 2	T.J. O'Keefe
Zone 3	Bob Scammell
Zone 4	Ben Rosnau
Zones 6	Vince Durda
Secretary manager	Paul Morck

Chairmen of Standing Committees

Fish	Gene Scully
Vice chair	John Stratton
Finance	C.E. Brown
Membership	Art Miles
Vice chair	Mrs. A. Miles
Game-birds	John Eisenhauer
Vice chair	Bill Windsor
Big game	Dr. Lee Anderson
Vice chair	Gordon Cole
Constitution and bylaws	Neville Lindsay
Vice chair	Bob Scammell
Pollution	Henry Lembicz
Vice chair	Andy Antoniac
Pest control	Duncan Lloyd
Vice chair	Jack McMillan
Hunter training	Manfred Lukas

Vice chair	Lewis T. (Budd) Traver
Parks, access, grazing and wilderness	Ken Kultgen
Vice chair	Elmer Kure
Good and welfare	Tom Norris
Vice chair	Helen Hobbs
Publicity	Bob Scammell
Vice chair	Joe Balla
Vice chair	Garnet Anthony
Legal advisor	Neville Lindsay
Legal advisor	Bob Scammell
Legal advisor	William Abercrombie

Canadian Wildlife Federation

Past president	Gordon Cummings
Directors	Henry Lembicz
	Elmer Kure
	Joe Balla

Alberta Fish and Game Representatives

Advisory council	Joe Balla
	Henry Lembicz
	Elmer Kure

Pest	Duncan Lloyd
Hunter training	Lewis T. (Budd) Traver
Vice chair	Ted Caswell
Parks, access, grazing and wilderness	Archie Hogg
Vice chair	Lawrence Iley
Education	Lyle Fowler
Vice chair	Don Fowler
Good and welfare	Bob Scammell
Publicity	Bob Scammell
Vice chair	Joe Balla
Legal advisor	Neville Lindsay
Legal advisor	Bob Scammell
Legal advisor	William Abercrombie

Alberta Fish and Game Association Representatives

Game advisory committee	Gordon Peel
	Joe Balla
	Elmer Kure
Pollution advisory committee	Henry Lembicz
	Joe Balla
Land utilization advisory council	Bill Windsor

1969-1970 Executive List

President (Until 1971 Convention)	Gordon Peel
Vice presidents at large	Vince Durda
	Vern Arnold

Zone Chairmen

Zone 1	Vern Arnold
Zone 2	Tom O'Keefe
Zone 3	Jack Munro
Zone 4	Vacant
Zone 4 vice chairman	Bob MacKenzie
Zone 6	Ivan Mosenko
Secretary manager	Paul Morck

Chairmen of Standing Committees

(1969 – to be re-elected for 1970)

Fish	Gene Scully
Vice chair	Hugh Douglas
Finance	C.E. Brown
Membership	Art Miles
Vice chair	Mrs. A. Miles
Game birds	Don Hayden
Habitat improvement and restoration	W. Windsor
Vice chair	M.E. Sandeman
Big game	Gordon Cole
Constitution and bylaws	Neville Lindsay
Pollution	Henry Lembicz
Vice chair	J.E. Heather

1970 Executive List

President	Gordon Peel
Vice presidents at large	Tom O'Keefe
	R.H. Scammell

Zone Chairmen

Zone 1	Dave Simpson
Zone 2	Jim Heather
Zone 3	Jack Munro
Zone 4	Bob Mackenzie
Zone 6	Ivan Mosenko
Secretary – manager	Paul Morck

Chairmen of Standing Committees

Fish	Hugh Douglas
Vice chair	Orest Schur
Pollution	Henry Lembicz
Vice chair	Bob Wilson
Finance	C.E. Brown
Membership	Jack Forster
Game bird	Don Hayden
Vice chair	Corm Gates
Vice chair	Bjorn Berg
Habitat improvement and restoration	Bill Windsor
Vice chair	J.F.S. Anderson
Big game	Gordon Cole
Vice chair	Gerry Pittman
Pest	Stan Henders

Vice chair	Jim Nivins
Hunter training	Lewis T. (Budd) Traver
Vice chair	Don Chapman
Parks, access, grazing and wilderness	Archie Hogg
Vice chair	Lawrence Iley
Policy	R.H. Ozanne
Vice chair	Gordon Stretch
Objects and bylaws	Bob Scammell
Education	Lyle Walker
Publicity	Bob Scammell
Vice chair	Joe Balla
Legal advisor	Neville Lindsay
Legal advisor	Bob Scammell
Legal advisor	William Abercrombie
Tourist group	Terry Psaltis
Junior conservation	Marcel Droessaert

Alberta Fish and Game Association Representatives

Game advisory council	Gordon Peel
	Joe Balla
	Elmer Kure
Pollution advisory council	Henry Lembicz
	Joe Balla
Land utilization advisory council	Bill Windsor
Canadian Wildlife Federation	Gordon Peel

1971 Executive List

President	Tom O'Keefe
President at large	R.H. Scammell
	Lewis T. (Budd) Traver

Vice-Presidents

Zone 1	Ed Potter
Zone 2	Jim Heather
Zone 3	Harold Rhodes
Zones 4 & 5	Bob Kitchener
Zones 4 & 5	Bob Tanghe
Zone 6	Keith Moran
Secretary manager	Paul Morck
Office secretary	Pat Jensen

Chairmen of Standing Committees

Game bird	Bjorne Berg
Hunter training	Don Chapman
Vice chair	Jim Nivins
Pollution	Henry Lembicz
Vice chair	Cec Ross
Vice chair	Ed Potter
Vice chair	Sam Smolyk
Vice chair	Art Thorburn
Vice chair	Jim Robison

Parks, access, grazing and wilderness	Archie Hogg
Vice chair	Lawrence Iley
Junior conservation	Marcel Droessaert
Vice chair	Don Fowler
Policy	Roy Ozanne
Vice chair	Art Zimmer
Pest	Larry Holland
Membership	Jack Forster
Vice chair	Orest Schur
Big game	Gordon Cole
Vice chair	Dave Simpson
Fish	Hugh Douglas
Vice chair	Orest Schur
Finance	Buster Brown
Tourist	Terry Psaltis
Legal advisor	Neville Lindsay
Legal advisor	Bob Scammell
Legal advisor	William Abercrombie

Alberta Fish and Game Association Representatives

Game advisory council	Tom O'Keefe
	Gordon Peel
	Elmer Kure
Pollution advisory committee	Henry Lembicz
Canadian Wildlife Federation	Tom O'Keefe
	Bob Scammell
	Gordon Peel

1972 Executive List

President	Tom O'Keefe
President at large	Bob Scammell
	Lewis T. (Budd) Traver

Vice-Presidents

Zone 1	Ed Potter
Zone 2	Hugh Douglas
Zone 3	Harold Rhodes
Zones 4 & 5	Bob Kitchener
Zones 4 & 5	Bob Tanghe
Zone 6	Keith Moran
Secretary manager	Paul Morck
Office secretary	N.R. (Wendy) MacLeod

Chairmen of Standing Committees

Game bird	Bjorne P. Berg
Vice chair	Jim Warnock
Habitat	C. Burghardt
Hunter training	Yvonne Traver
Pollution	Henry Lembicz
Vice chair	Cec Ross
Vice chair	Jim Robison
Parks and wilderness	E.E. Scoville

Access and grazing	Archie Hogg
Vice chair	Ted Wilson
Resources education	Marcel Droessaert
Policy	Roy Ozanne
Vice chair	Arnim Zimmer
Pest	Larry Holland
Vice chair	Stan Henders
Big game	Gordon Cole
Vice chair	Dave Simpson
Fish	Hugh Douglas
Vice chair	Ben Rosnau
Finance	Buster Brown
Advisor	Gordon Bentham
Tourist	Terry Psaltis
Farmer-hunter relations	Walter Frank
Legal advisor	Neville Lindsay
Legal advisor	Bob Scammell
Legal advisor	William Abercrombie

Alberta Fish and Game Association Representatives

Game advisory council	Tom O'Keefe
	Gordon Peel
	Elmer Kure
Pollution advisory committee	Henry Lembicz
Commercial fishing advisory council	Jack Munro
	Harvey Bentley
Canadian Wildlife Federation	Tom O'Keefe
	Bob Scammell
	Gordon Peel

1973 Executive List

President	Tom O'Keefe

Committee Chairmen

Game bird	C. Burghardt
Vice chair	Jim Warnock
Hunter training	Jim Roberts
Vice chair	Russ Lonneberg
Pollution	Cecil Ross
Vice chair	Jim Robison
Parks and Wilderness	Nils Kvisle
Access and Grazing	Archie Hogg
Resource education	Jerry Kitt
Civilian wildlife patrol	Doug Belyea
Vice chair	Lorna Smith
Big game	Gordon Cole
Vice chair	John Eglinski
Fish	Gene Scully
Vice chair	Tim Rutter
Finance	Buster Brown
Vice chair	Gordon Bentham
Tourist chairman	Terry Psaltis

Hunter farmer	Elmer Schultz
Vice chair	Larry Holland
Policy	Roy Ozanne
Vice chair	Don Hayden
Vice chair	William Percy
Secretary manager	Paul Morck
Office secretary	Wendy MacLeod

1974 Executive List

President	Bob Scammell
Vice president at large	Lewis T. (Budd) Traver
	Harold Rhodes

Vice-Presidents – Zone Chairmen

Zone 1	Ken Nichol
Zone 2	Don Fowler
Zone 3	Ben Grohn
Zone 4	Bob Tanghe
Zone 5	Alex Elder
Zone 6	Keith Moran

Chairmen of Standing Committees

Game bird	C. Burghardt
Vice chair	Jim Warnock
Hunter training	Jim Roberts
Vice chair	Russ Lonneberg
Pollution	Cecil Ross
Vice chair	Jim Robison
Parks and wilderness	Nils Kvisle
Access and grazing	Archie Hogg
Resource education	Jerry Kitt
Big game	John Eglinski
Fish	Gene Scully
Vice chair	Tim Rutter
Finance	Buster Brown
Tourist	Terry Psaltis
Hunter-farmer relations	Elmer Schultz
Vice chair	Larry Holland
Policy	Roy Ozanne
Vice chair	Don Hayden
Civilian wildlife patrol	Douglas Belyea
Vice chair	Lorna Smith
Legal advisor	Neville Lindsay
Legal advisor	Bob Scammell
Legal advisor	William Abercrombie

Alberta Fish and Game Association Representatives

Game advisory committee	Bob Scammell
	Tom O'Keefe
	Lewis T. (Budd) Traver
Pollution advisory committee	Cecil Ross
Commercial fishing advisory committee	Jack Munro, Harvey Bentley

Snowmobile advisory committee John Eglinski
Canadian Wildlife Federation Bob Scammell
Lewis T. (Budd) Traver
Tom O'Keefe
Secretary manager Paul Morck
Office secretary N.R. (Wendy) MacLeod
Director of
environmental public relations Elmer Kure

1975 Executive

President Bob Scammell
Vice presidents at large Lewis T. (Budd) Traver
Ken Nichol

Vice-Presidents – Zone Chairmen
Zone 1 Mike Neilsen
Zone 2 Don Fowler
Zone 3 Ben Grohn
Zone 4 Bob Tanghe
Zone 5 Keith Edgett
Zone 6 Cecil Fowler

Chairmen of Standing Committees
Access and grazing Archie Hogg
Acting hunter training Gordon Kure
Big game John Eglinski
Bird game C. Burghardt
Civilian wildlife patrol Douglas Belyea
Co-chair Lawrence Iley
Co-chair Gerry Pittman
Finance C.E. (Buster) Brown
Fish Tim Rutter
Habitat Harold Rhodes
Landowner-sportsman
relationship Elmer Schultz
Lottery disposition Jim Robson
Parks and wilderness Nils Kvisle
Pollution Cecil Ross
Policy Roy Ozanne
Resource education Jerry Kitt
Vice chair Arnim Zimmer
Vice chair Ron Gladish
Vice chair John Shearer
Vice chair Russ Lonneberg
Vice chair Henry Christensen
Vice chair Jim Gormley
Vice chair Reg Denny

Alberta Fish and Game Association Representatives
Game advisory committee Bob Scammell
Tom O'Keefe
Lewis T. (Budd) Traver
Pollution advisory committee Cecil Ross
Commercial fishing
advisory committee Jack Munro
Snowmobile advisory committee Lewis T. (Budd) Traver
Canadian Wildlife Federation Bob Scammell
Lewis T. (Budd) Traver

Canadian Wildlife Federation
Vice President Tom O'Keefe
Cooking Lake
Moraine study committee Elmer Schultz
Environment trust Bob Scammell
Henry Lembicz
Red Deer River advisory
committee Henry Lembicz
Wilderness advisory committee Keith Moran

Secretary manager Paul Morck
Office secretary N.R. (Wendy) MacLeod
Director of
environmental public relations Elmer Kure

1975 Executive List (second list from the records)

President Lewis T. (Budd) Traver
Vice presidents at large Bob Tanghe
Ken Nichol

Zone Chairman
Zone 1 Mike Neilsen
Zone 2 Don Fowler
Zone 3 Ben Grohn
Zone 4 Don Hayden
Zone 5 Keith Edgett
Zone 6 Cecil Fowler

Standing Committee Chairmen
Access and grazing Archie Hogg
Anti-pollution Ron Gladish
Bird game Phil Ficht
Big game John Eglinski
Finance C.E. (Buster) Brown
Fish Lloyd Shea
Hunter training Gordon Kure
Lottery disposition Jim Robison
Membership Eve Ozanne
Office secretary Wendy MacLeod
Outdoor observer Karl Revenco
Parks and wilderness Nils Kvisle
Resource education Brenda Lachman

Secretary manager	Paul Morck
Sportsman landowner	Elmer Schultz
Trophy	Jack Graham
Vice chair	John Dickinson
Vice chair	Sam Smolyk
Vice chair	John Shearer
Vice chair	Doug Belyea
Vice chair	Lawrence Iley
Vice chair	Bob McPhee
Vice chair	Ron Goodfellow
Vice chair	Dave Simpson
Vice chair	Tim Rutter

1976 Executive List

President	Lewis T. (Budd) Traver
Vice president at large	Robert Tanghe
	Ken Nichol

Zone Vice Presidents

Zone 1	Bob Vair
Zone 2	Don Fowler
Zone 3	Dennis Hindbo
Zone 4	Arnold Toeppner
Zone 5	George Ford
Zone 6	Cecil Fowler

Standing Committee Chairmen

Bird game	Phil Ficht
Vice chair	John Shearer
Big game	John Eglinski
Vice chair	Dave Simpson
Vice chair	Lawrence Iley
Hunter training	Gordon Kure
Vice chair	John Dickinson
Anti pollution	Ron Gladish
Vice chair	Sam Smolyk
Parks and Wilderness	Nils Kvisle
Access and Grazing	Archie Hogg
Vice chair	Bob McPhee
Resource education	Brenda Lachman
Vice chair	Ron Goodfellow
Fish	Lloyd Shea
Vice chair	Tim Rutter
Outdoor observer	Karl Revenco
Vice chair	Doug Belyea
Finance	C.E. (Buster) Brown
Sportsman landowner	Elmer Schultz
Policy	Lloyd Graff
Habitat	Harold Rhodes
Vice chair	Neville Lindsay
Lottery disposition	Jim Robison
Trophy	Jack Graham
Membership	Eve Ozanne

Alberta Fish and Game Association Representatives

Game advisory committee	Bob Scammell
	Bob Tanghe
	Lewis T. (Budd) Traver
Pollution advisory committee	Ron Gladish
Commercial fishing advisory committee	Lloyd Shea
	Don Appleby
Snowmobile advisory committee	Lewis T. (Budd) Traver
Canadian Wildlife Federation	Bob Scammell
	Lewis T. (Budd) Traver
	Tom O'Keefe
Environment Trust	Bob Scammell
	Henry Lembicz
Red Deer River advisory committee	Henry Lembicz
Wilderness advisory committee	Keith Moran
Secretary-manager	Paul Morck
Office secretary	A.H. (Gwen) Wahlstrom
Director of environmental public relations	Elmer Kure

1976 Executive List (second list from the records)

President	Lewis T. (Budd) Traver
Vice president at large	Tony Ferguson
	Bob Vair

Zone Vice Presidents

Zone 1	Norm Ferguson
Zone 2	Don Fowler
Zone 3	Dennis Hindbo
Zone 4	Arnold Toeppner
Zone 5	George Ford
Zone 6	Cecil Fowler

Standing Committee Chairmen

Bird game	Phil Ficht
Vice chair	Bill Lewis
Big game	John Eglinski
Vice chair	Dave Simpson
Vice chair	Charles Stricker
Hunter training	John Dickinson
Vice chair	Vic Scheuerman
Anti pollution	Ron Gladish
Vice chair	Sam Smolyk
Parks and wilderness	Nils Kvisle
Access and grazing	Archie Hogg
Resource education	Brenda Lachman
Vice chair	Ross Carter
Fish	Lloyd Shea
Vice chair	Don Appleby
Outdoor observer	Karl Revenco
Vice chair	Lawrence Iley

Finance	C.E. (Buster) Brown
Sportsman landowner	Elmer Schultz
Co-vice (south)	Harold Waters
Co-vice (north)	Joe Evasiw
Policy	Lloyd Graff
Vice chair	Neville Lindsay
Habitat	Dennis Patterson
Lottery disposition	Jim Robison
Trophy	Jack Graham
Membership	Orest Schur
Secretary-manager	Paul Morck
Office secretary	Gwen Wahlstrom
Director of environmental relations	Elmer Kure

1977 Executive List

President	Lewis T. (Budd) Traver
Sr. vice president at large	Tony Ferguson
Vice president at large	Bob Vair

Zone Vice Presidents

Zone 1	Norman Ferguson
Zone 2	Don Fowler
Zone 3	Dennis Hindbo
Zone 4	Arnold Toeppner
Zone 5	Roy Ozanne
Zone 6	Cecil Fowler

Standing Committee Chairmen

Bird game	Phil Ficht
Vice chair	Bill Lewis
Big game	John Eglinski
Vice chair	Dave Simpson
Vice chair	Charles Stricker
Hunter training	John Dickinson
Vice chair	Vic Scheuerman
Anti pollution	Ron Gladish
Vice chair	Sam Smolyk
Parks and wilderness	Nils Kvisle
Access and grazing	Archie L. Hogg
Resource education	Brenda Lachman
Vice chair	Ross Carter
Fish	Lloyd Shea
Vice chair	Don Appleby
Outdoor observer	Karl R. Revenco
Vice chair	Lawrence Iley
Finance	C.E. (Buster) Brown
Sportsman landowner	Elmer Schultz
Vice chair (south)	Harold Watters
Vice chair (north)	Joe Evasiw
Policy	Lloyd Graff
Vice chair	Neville Lindsay
Habitat	Dennis Patterson
Lottery disposition	Jim Robison

Trophy	Jack Graham
Membership	Orest Schur
Junior rifle	Wally Way

Alberta Fish and Game Association Representatives

Game advisory committee	Bob Scammell
	Tony Ferguson
	Lewis T. (Budd) Traver
Pollution advisory committee	Ron Gladish
Commercial fishing advisory committee	Lloyd Shea, Don Appleby
Snowmobile advisory committee	Harry Krawchuk
Environmental conservation authority	Elmer Kure
	Tony Ferguson
Alberta Federation of Shooting Sports	John Dickinson
	Bob Vair
	Dennis Patterson
Canadian Wildlife Federation	Bob Scammell
	Lewis T. (Budd) Traver
Canadian Wildlife Federation vice president	Tom O'Keefe
Cooking Lake Moraine study committee	Elmer Schultz
Red Deer River advisory committee	Henry Lembicz
Environment Trust	Bob Scammell,
	Henry Lembicz
Secretary manager	Paul Morck
Office secretary	Gwen M. Wahlstrom
Director of environmental public relations	Elmer Kure

1977 Executive List (second list from the records)

President	Anthony (Tony) Ferguson
Vice president at large	Don Hayden
	Lloyd Graff

Zone Vice Presidents

Zone 1	Norm Ferguson
Zone 2	Don Fowler
Zone 3	Dennis Hindbo
Zone 4	Arnold Toeppner
Zone 5	Roy Ozanne
Zone 6	Cecil Fowler

Standing Committee Chairmen

Environmental quality	Lynn Davies
Fishing	Don Appleby
Vice chair	Don Anderson
Hunting (big game)	John Eglinski
Bird game	Phil Ficht
Information	Gary Hrycyk

Legislation	Neville Lindsay
Non-renewable resources	Bob Tanghe
Renewable resources	Dennis Patterson
Trophy	Jack Graham
Secretary manager	Paul Morck
Office secretary	Gwen Wahlstrom
Director of environmental relations	Elmer Kure

1978 Executive List

President	Anthony (Tony) Ferguson
Vice president at large	Don Hayden
	Lloyd Graff

Zone Vice Presidents

Zone 1	Norm Ferguson
Zone 2	Jim Jensen
Zone 3	Dennis Hindbo
Zone 4	Bob Tanghe
Zone 5	Roy Ozanne
Zone 6	Bernard Methot

Standing Committee Chairmen

Environmental quality	Lynn Davies
Fishing (commercial)	Don Appleby
Finance	Chris van der Merwe
Hunting (bird game)	Phil Ficht
Hunting (big game)	John Eglinski
Information	Garry Hrycyk
Legislation	Neville Lindsay
Lottery disposition	Jim Robison
Non-renewable	Vacant
Renewable resources	Nils Kvisle
Shooting sports (Jr. Rifle Program)	Wally Way
Trophy	Jack Graham
Vice chair (sport fishing)	Don Anderson
Vice chair (national parks)	Harry Lyseyko
Vice chair (big game – south)	Vic Scheurman

Alberta Fish and Game Association Representatives

Game advisory committee	Don Hayden
	Tony Ferguson
	Lewis T. (Budd) Traver
Pollution advisory committee	Lynn Davies
Commercial fishing advisory committee	Lloyd Shea,
	Don Appleby
Snowmobile advisory committee	Harry Krawchuk
Canadian Wildlife Federation	Tony Ferguson
	Lewis T. (Budd) Traver
	Tom O'Keefe

Environmental conservation authority	Elmer Kure
	Bob Tanghe
Alberta Federation of Shooting Sports	John Dickinson
	Lloyd Graff
	Bob McPhee
	Dennis Patterson
Environment Trust	Bob Scammell
	Henry Lembicz
Red Deer River advisory committee	Henry Lembicz
Wilderness advisory committee	Keith Moran
Secretary manager	Paul Morck
Office secretary	Gwen M. Wahlstrom
Director, environmental public relations	Elmer Kure

1978 Executive List (second list from the records)

President	Anthony (Tony) Ferguson
Vice president at large	Don Hayden
	Lloyd Graff

Zone Vice Presidents

Zone 1	Norm Ferguson
Zone 2	Jim Jensen
Zone 3	Dennis Hindbo
Zone 4	Bob Tanghe
Zone 5	Roy Ozanne
Zone 6	Bernard Methot

Standing Committee Chairmen

Director of environmental relations	Elmer Kure
Environmental quality	Tom Kostuck
Finance	Chris van der Merwe
Fishing (commercial)	Don Appleby
Hunting (big game)	John Eglinski
Information	Garry Hrycyk
Legislation	Neville Lindsay
Lottery disposition	Neil Goeson
Non-renewable	Horst Fauser
Office secretary	Gwen Wahlstrom
Renewable resources	Graham Skjenna
Secretary manager	Paul Morck
Trophy	Jack Graham
Vice chair (sport fishing)	Don Anderson
Vice chair (national Parks)	Harry Lyseyko
Vice chair (big game – south)	Vic Scheurman
Vice chair (bird game)	Mike Chetek

1979 Executive List

President — A.G. (Tony) Ferguson
Vice president at large — Don Hayden
Lloyd Graff

Zone Vice Presidents

Zone 1 — Norm Ferguson
Zone 2 — Jim Jensen
Zone 3 — Martha Kostuch
Zone 4 — Bob Tanghe
Zone 5 — Jim Owens
Zone 6 — Roy Ozanne

Standing Committee Chairmen

Disabled fish derby — Nestor Romaniuk
Environmental quality — Tom Kostuch
Finance — Chris van der Merwe
Fishing (commercial) — Don Appleby
Hunting (big game) — John Eglinski
Hunting (bird game) — Mike Chetek
Indian hunting rights — Gordon Peel
Information — Garry Hrycyk
Legislation — Neville Lindsay
Lottery disposition — Neil Goeson
Non-renewable — Horst Fauser
Renewable resources — Graham Skejenna
Shooting sports
  (firearms safety program) — Phil Ficht
Trophy — Jack Graham
Vice chair (sport fishing) — Don Anderson
Vice chair (national parks) — Harry Lyseyko
Vice chair (big game – south) — Vic Scheurman

Alberta Fish and Game Association Representatives

Game advisory committee — Don Hayden
Tony Ferguson
Lewis T. (Budd) Traver

Pollution advisory committee — Tom Kostuch
Commercial fishing
  advisory committee — Don Anderson
Don Appleby
Snowmobile advisory committee — Harry Krawchuk
Canadian Wildlife Federation — Tony Ferguson
Lewis T. (Budd) Traver
Tom O'Keefe
Environment Council of Alberta — Elmer Kure
Horst Fauser

Alberta Federation
  of Shooting Sports — Lloyd Graff
Phil Ficht
Environment Trust — Bob Scammell
Henry Lembicz

Red Deer River
  advisory committee — Henry Lembicz
Wilderness advisory committee — Keith Moran

Secretary manager — Paul Morck
Office secretary — Gwen M. Wahlstrom
Director,
  environmental public relations — Elmer Kure

1980 Executive List

President — Don Hayden
Past president — A.G. (Tony) Ferguson
Vice president at large — Roy H. Ozanne
Chris van der Merwe

Zone Vice Presidents

Zone 1 — Horst Fauser
Zone 2 — Charles Charlton
Zone 3 — Martha Kostuch
Zone 4 — Bob Tanghe
Zone 5 — Hugh Bossert
Zone 6 — Herb Cobb

Standing Committee Chairmen

Bird game — Vacant
Club manual — Hank Iwanicki
Disabled fish derby — Nestor Romaniuk
Environmental quality — Vacant
Finance — Bob Loewen
Fishing — Gene Scully
Fishing (commercial) — Don Appleby
Hunting — Les Yaceyko
Information — Garry Hrycyk
Indian hunting rights — Gordon Peel
Legislation — Neville Lindsay
Lottery disposition — Neil Goeson
Non-renewable — Horst Fauser
Pheasant co-ordinator — Phil Ficht
Renewable resources — Vacant
Shooting sports
  (firearms safety program) — Phil Ficht
Trophy — Jack Graham
Vice chair (big game – south) — Vic Scheurman

Alberta Fish and Game Association Representatives

Game advisory committee — Don Hayden
Tony Ferguson
Roy Ozanne
Pollution advisory committee — Nils Kvisle
Commercial fishing
  advisory committee — Gene Scully
Don Appleby
Snowmobile advisory committee — Open
Canadian Wildlife Federation — Tony Ferguson
Don Hayden

Environment Council of Alberta	Elmer Kure
	Horst Fauser
Alberta Federation	
of Shooting Sports	Lloyd Graff
	Phil Ficht
Environment Trust	Bob Scammell
	Henry Lembicz
Red Deer River	
advisory committee	Henry Lembicz
Secretary manager	Paul Morck
Director of	
environmental public relations	Elmer Kure
Office secretary	Gwen M. Wahlstrom

1981 Executive List

President	Don Hayden
Immediate past president	A.G. (Tony) Ferguson
Vice president at large	Roy H. Ozanne
	Chris van der Merwe

Zone Vice Presidents

Zone 1	Horst Fauser
Zone 2	Ken Yank
Zone 3	Martha Kostuch
	Doug Rumsey
Zone 4	Bob Tanghe
Zone 5	Hugh Bossert
Zone 6	Herb Cobb

Standing Committee Chairmen

Bird game	Vacant
Club manual	Hank Iwanicki
Disabled fish derby	Nestor Romaniuk
Environmental quality	Ron Gladish
Fishing	Dee Aumuller
Fishing (commercial)	Don Appleby
Finance	Bob Loewen
Hunting	Les Yaceyko
Hunter training co-ordinator	Open
Indian hunting rights	Gordon Peel
Information	Jack Easterbrook
Legislation	Neville Lindsay
Lottery disposition	Neil Goeson
National wildlife week	Open
Non-renewable resources	Open
Pheasant grant co-ordinator	Phil Ficht
Renewable resources	George Chronik
Shooting sports	
(firearms safety program)	Phil Ficht
Trophy	Jack Graham

Alberta Fish and Game Association Representatives

Game advisory committee	Don Hayden
	Tony Ferguson
	Roy Ozanne
Pollution advisory committee	Nils Kvisle
Commercial fishing	
advisory committee	Dee Aumuller
	Don Appleby
Snowmobile advisory committee	Lewis T. (Budd) Traver
Canadian Wildlife Federation	Tony Ferguson
	Don Hayden
Environment Council of Alberta	Horst Fauser
Alberta Federation	
of Shooting Sports	Steve Stephens
	Phil Ficht
Environment Trust	Bob Scammell,
	Henry Lembicz
Red Deer River	
Advisory Committee	Henry Lembicz
Secretary-manager	Paul Morck
Director,	
environmental public relations	Elmer Kure
Office secretary	Gwen M. Wahlstrom

1982 Executive List

Note: This is listed as the 1981 executive committee in the 1982 year book for the 53rd annual conference.

President	Roy H. Ozanne
Vice president at large	Ron Gladish
	Vacant

Zone Vice Presidents

Zone 1	Horst Fauser
Zone 2	Ken Yank
Zone 3	Doug Rumsey
Zone 4	Bob Tanghe
Zone 5	Don Appleby
Zone 6	Percy Hunkin
Immediate past president	Don Hayden

Standing Committee Chairmen

Environmental quality	Gordon Merrick
Finance	Bob Loewen
Fishing and physically	
disabled fish derby	Nestor Romaniuk
Fishing (commercial)	Don Appleby
Hunting	Les Yaceyko
Information	Jack Shaver
Legislation	Neville Lindsay
Non-renewable resources	Jim Agnew
Pheasant grant co-ordinator	Phil Ficht
Renewable resources	George Chronik

Shooting sports
  (firearms safety program)   Sam Smolyk
Trophy   Jack Graham

Ad Hoc Committees
Club manual   Lloyd Graff
Indian hunting rights   Gordon Peel
National wildlife week   Jack Easterbrook

Staff
Secretary manager   Paul Morck
Director,
  environmental public relations   Elmer Kure
Office secretary   Gwen M. Wahlstrom

1983 Executive Committee List

Note: This is listed as the 1982 executive committee in the 1982 year book for the 54th annual conference.

President   Roy H. Ozanne
Senior vice president at large   Ron Gladish
Vice president   Jack Shaver

Zone Vice Presidents
Zone 1   Horst Fauser
Zone 2   Ken Yank
Zone 3   Doug Rumsey
Zone 4   Bob Tanghe
Zone 5   Don Appleby
Zone 6   Percy Hunkin
Immediate past president   Don Hayden

Standing Committee Chairmen
Environmental quality   Gordon Merrick
Finance   Bob Loewen
Fishing and physically
  disabled fish derby   Nestor Romaniuk
Fishing (commercial)   Don Appleby
Hunting   Les Yaceyko
Hunter education   Sam Smolyk
Information   Norm Ferguson
Legislation   Neville Lindsay
Non-renewable resources   Jim Agnew
Pheasant grant co-ordinator   Phil Ficht
Renewable resources   Martha Kostuch
Trophy   Jack Graham
Vice chair   Ron Pittman

Ad Hoc Committees
Club manual   Lloyd Graff
Indian hunting rights   Gordon Peel
National Wildlife Week   Jack Easterbrook

Staff
Secretary manager   Paul Morck
Director,
  environmental public relations   Elmer Kure
Office secretary   Lorraine MacPherson

1983 Executive List

As listed in the 55th conference yearbook.

Senior executive
President   Ron Gladish
Senior vice president   Jack Shaver
Vice president   Nestor Romaniuk

Zone Directors
Zone 1   Horst Fauser
Zone 2   Jim Cooper
Zone 3   Doug Rumsey
Zone 4   Bob Tanghe
Zone 5   Don Appleby
Zone 6   Harold Peterson
Immediate past president   Roy Ozanne

AFGA Staff
Secretary manager   Paul Morck
Director,
  environmental public relations   Elmer Kure
Secretary   Lorraine MacPherson

1983 Chairmen of Standing Committees

Ad Hoc Committee
Indian hunting rights   Gordon Peel
Environmental quality   Gordon Merrick
Finance   Bob Loewen
Fishing   Lloyd Shea
Hunter education   Keith Baker
Hunting   Les Yaceyko
Information   Norm Ferguson
Legislation   Vacant
Non-renewable resources   Ron Goodwin
Renewable resources   Martha Kostuch
Trophy   Steve Witiuk
Vice chair   Jack Graham
1988 Winter Olympics   Darrel Skinner

Subcommittee Chairmen
Lottery disposition   Bob Loewen
Commercial fishing   Don Appleby
Physically disabled fishing derby   Carole Romaniuk

Firearms safety
  program and hunter training   Keith Baker
Shooting sports   Steve Stephens
Game ranching   Lyle Fullerton
Peasant grant co-ordinator   Phil Ficht
Club manual   Lloyd Graff
Conservation camp   Martha Kostuch
National wildlife week   Jack Easterbrook

1984 Executive List

Note: This is listed as taken from the March/April Western Canada outdoors newsletter.

Senior Executive

President	Ron Gladish
Senior vice president	Jack Shaver
Junior vice president	Nestor Romaniuk
Immediate past president	Roy Ozanne

Zone Directors

Zone 1	Horst Fauser
Zone 2	Jim Cooper
Zone 3	Doug Rumsey
Zone 4	Bob Tanghe
Zone 5	Don Appleby
Zone 6	Harold Peterson

Committee Chairs

Hunting	Lyle Fullerton
	Darrel Skinner
Hunter education	Keith Baker
Indian hunting rights	Gordon Peel
Fishing	Lloyd Shea
Sub-committee: commercial	Don Appleby
Trophy	Steve Witiuk
Environmental quality	Gordon Merrick
Finance	Bob Loewen
Renewable resources	Martha Kostuch
Non-renewable resources	Ron Goodwin
Information	Dave Powell
Membership	Venny Chocholocek
Peasant grant co-ordinator	Phil Ficht
Hunter ethics	Linda Hirsche
Fishing derby	
for physically disabled	Carole Romaniuk
Upland game bird	Don Bate
Club manual	Lloyd Graff
Winter olympics	Darrel Skinner

AFGA Staff

Secretary manager	Paul Morck
Director of	
environmental public relations	Elmer Kure
Secretary	Lorraine MacPherson
Buck for Wildlife co-ordinator	Lyle Fullerton

1985 Executive List

(from the 1986 yearbook)

Senior Executive

President	Jack Shaver
Past president	Ron Gladish
Senior vice president	Nestor Romaniuk
Junior vice president	Jack Graham
Executive vice president	Vacant

Zone Directors

Zone 1	Horst Fauser
Zone 2	Jim Cooper
Zone 3	Doug Rumsey
Zone 4	Phil Ficht
Zone 5	Don Appleby
Zone 6	Jerrold Lundgard

Chairmen of Standing Committees and Subcommittees

Environmental quality	Gordon Merrick
Fishing	Lloyd Shea
Hunter education	Terry Ferster
Hunting	Darrel Skinner
Information	Dave Powell
Membership	Stella Ferguson
Non-renewable resources	Ron Goodwin
Renewable resources	Martha Kostuch
Trophy	Steve Witiuk
Ad Hoc committee:	
Indian hunting rights	Gordon Peel
Conservation lottery	Jack Graham

Subcommittees

Commercial fishing	Don Appleby
Physically disabled fishing derby	Carole Romaniuk
Firearm safety program	Terry Ferster
Shooting sports	Steve Stephens
Game ranching	Darrel Skinner
Pheasant grant co-ordinator	
and upland game bird	Don Bate
Outdoor ethics	Linda Hirsche
Club manual	Lloyd Graff
Trophy vice chairperson	Jack Graham

AFGA Head Office Staff

Buck for Wildlife co-ordinator	Lyle Fullerton
Director, environmental and public relations	Grant Nieman
Receptionist	Julie Wilk
Newsletter editor	Trish Filevich
Administrative secretary	Connie Marlatt

1986 Executive List

Senior executive president	Nestor Romaniuk
Senior vice president	Jack Graham
Junior vice president	Doug Rumsey
Past president	Jack Shaver
Executive vice president	Lyle Fullerton

Zone Directors

Zone 1	Dwayne Johnson
Zone 2	Niels Damgaard
Zone 3	Venny Chocholacek
Zone 4	Bob Tanghe
Zone 5	Don Appleby
Zone 6	Dave Ridgeway

Chairmen of Standing Committees and Subcommittees

Environmental quality	Gordon Merrick
Finance	Ron Gladish
Fishing	Lloyd Shea
Hunter education	Terry Ferster
Hunting	Darrel Skinner
Information	Dave Powell
Membership	Stella Ferguson
Non-renewable resources	Dwayne Johnson
Renewable resources	Martha Kostuch
Trophy	Steve Witiuk
Ad hoc committee	
Indian hunting rights	Gordon Peel

Subcommittees

Hazardous waste	Dwayne Johnson
Commercial fishing	Don Appleby
Firearm safety program	Terry Ferster
Game ranching	Darrel Skinner
Pheasant grant co-ordinator and upland game bird	Don Bate
Outdoor ethics	Linda Hirsche
Club manual	Ron Gladish

AFGA Head Office Staff

Executive director	Lyle Fullerton
Buck For Wildlife co-ordinator	Grant Nieman

1987 Executive List

Senior Executive

President	Nestor Romaniuk
Past president	Jack Shaver
Senior vice president	Jack Graham
Junior vice president	Doug Rumsey
Finance chair	Ron Gladish
Executive vice president	Lyle Fullerton

Zone Directors

Zone 1	Dwayne Johnson
Zone 2	Niels Damgaard
Zone 3	Venny Chocholacek
Zone 4 (acting)	Carole Romaniuk
	Bob Tanghe
Zone 5	Charlotte Drake
	Don Appleby
Zone 6	Dave Ridgeway

Chairmen of Standing Committees

Environmental quality	Ron Dovell
Finance	Ron Gladish
Fishing	Lloyd Shea
Hunter education	Terry Ferster
Hunting	George Page
Information	Dave Powell
Membership	Stella Ferguson
Non-renewable resources	Hank Holowaychuk
Renewable resources	Martha Kostuch
Trophy	Steve Witiuk
Ad hoc committee	Gordon Peel
Upland game bird	Don Bate
Physically disabled fish derby	Carole Romaniuk

AFGA Head Office Staff

Executive director	Lyle Fullerton
Buck For Wildlife co-ordinator	Grant Nieman

1988 Executive List

Senior Executive

President	Jack Graham
Past president	Nestor Romaniuk
Senior vice president	Doug Rumsey
Junior vice president	Niels Damgaard
Finance	Ron Gladish
Executive vice president	Lyle Fullerton

Zone Directors

Zone 1	Norm Ferguson
Zone 2	Don Fowler
Zone 3	Ike Johannson
Zone 4	Vern McIntosh
Zone 5	Steve Witiuk
Zone 6	Darryl Smith

Chairmen and Committees

Agriculture	Elmer Kure
Environmental quality	Ron Dovell
Finance	Ron Gladish
Hunter education	Mark Jobson
Hunting	George Page
Information	Dave Powell
Membership	John Vogrinetz
Non-renewable resources	Hank Holowaychuk
Renewable resources	Martha Kostuch
Trophy	Ab England
Ad hoc (native affairs, Antelope Creek, technical)	Gordon Peel

Chairmen and Subcommittees

Hazardous waste	Ron Dovell
Firearm safety	John Dyck
Game ranching	George Page
Upland bird and pheasant grant co-ordinator	Don Bate
Club manual	Ron Gladish
Physically disabled fishing days	Al Bohachyk

AFGA Head Office Staff

Executive director	Lyle Fullerton
Buck For Wildlife co-ordinator	Grant Nieman
Office manager	Sharon Robinson-Jordan
Office support staff	Mary Crunkilton
Office support staff	Carol Severyn

1989 Executive List

Senior Executive

President	Jack Graham
Past president	Nestor Romaniuk
Senior vice president	Doug Rumsey
Junior vice president	Niels Damgaard
Finance	Ron Gladish
Executive vice president	Lyle Fullerton

Zone Directors

Zone 1	Ron Pittman
Zone 2	Don Fowler
Zone 3	Ike Johannson
Zone 4	Vern McIntosh
Zone 5	Steve Witiuk
Zone 6	Darryl Smith

Chairmen and Committees

Agriculture	Elmer Kure
Environmental quality	Vacant
Finance	Ron Gladish
Fishing	Eileen Christensen
Hunter education	Mark Jobson
Hunting	George Page
Information	Dave Powell
Membership	John Vogrinetz
Non-renewable resources	Hank Holowaychuk
Renewable resources	Martha Kostuch
Trophy	Ab England
Ad hoc (native affairs, Antelope Creek, technical)	Gordon Peel

Chairmen and Subcommittees

Assistant trophy	Steve Witiuk
Club manual	Ron Gladish
Hazardous waste	Ron Dovell
Firearm safety	John Dyck
Game ranching	Vacant
Upland bird and pheasant grant co-ordinator	Don Bate
Physically disabled fishing days	Al Bohachyk

AFGA Head Office Staff

Executive director	Lyle Fullerton
Buck For Wildlife co-ordinator	Brad Fenson
Contributor services representative	Del Scammell

1990 Executive List

Senior Executive

President	Niels Damgaard
Past president	Jack Graham
Vice president	Martha Kostuch
Finance	Andy von Busse
Interim executive director	Brad Fenson

Zone Directors

Zone 1	Ron Pittman
Zone 2	Fred Girdwood
Zone 3	Ike Johannson
Zone 4	Vern McIntosh
Zone 5	Eve Ozanne
Zone 6	David George

Chairmen and Committees

Agriculture	Elmer Kure
Environmental quality	Tony Ferguson
Finance	Andy von Busse
Firearms legislation	Dennis Grover
Fishing	Darryl Smith

Forestry	Don Norhiem
Hunter education	Mark Jobson
Hunting	George Page
Information	Eileen Christensen
Membership	Vacant
Non-renewable resources	Hank Holowaychuk
Renewable resources	Ted Johnson
Trophy	Ab England
Ad hoc (Antelope Creek, technical)	Gordon Peel

Chairmen and Subcommittees

Commercial fisheries	Darryl Smith
Club manual	Ron Gladish
Firearm safety	John Dyck
Upland bird and pheasant grant co-ordinator	Don Bate
Physically disabled fishing days	Al Bohachyk

AFGA Head Office Staff

Interim executive director	Brad Fenson
Habitat development co-ordinator	Brad Fenson
Contributor services representative	Del Scammell
Fundraising co-ordinator	Lyle Fullerton
Operation burrowing owl	Shannon Lord
Office manager	Mary Crunkilton
Data entry and word processing	Kimberly Foo

1991 Executive List

Senior Executive

President	Niels Damgaard
Past president	Jack Graham
Senior vice president	Horst Fauser
Junior vice president	Vern McIntosh
Finance executive vice president	Ron Hauser

Zone Directors

Zone 1	Ron Pittman
Zone 2	Fred Girdwood
Zone 3	Ike Johannson
Zone 4	Andy von Busse
Zone 5	Eileen Christensen
Zone 6	John Flynn

Chairmen and Committees

Programs	Nestor Romaniuk
Fisheries	Darryl Smith
Environment	Don Norhiem
Hunting	George Page
Life member	Don Hayden

Chairmen and Subcommittees

Agriculture	Elmer Kure
Firearm legislation	Casey Dzioba
Trophy	Ab England
Antelope Creek – technical	Gordon Peel
Physically disabled fishing day	Al Bohacyck

AFGA Head Office Staff

Executive vice president	Ron Hauser
Habitat development co-ordinator	Brad Fenson

1992 Executive List

Senior Executive

President	Niels Damgaard
Past president	Jack Graham
Senior vice president	Horst Fauser
Junior vice president	Vern McIntosh
Finance chairperson	Vacant
Executive vice president	Ron Hauser

Zone Directors

Zone 1	Ron Pittman
Zone 2	Fred Girdwood
Zone 3	Ike Johannson
Zone 4	Andy von Busse
Zone 5	Eileen Christensen
Zone 6	John Flynn

Chairmen and Committees

Programs	Nestor Romaniuk
Fisheries	Darryl Smith
Environment	Don Norhiem
Hunting	George Page
Life member	Don Hayden

Subcommittees

Agriculture	Elmer Kure
Firearm legislation	Casey Dzioba
Trophy	Ab England
Antelope Creek – technical	Gordon Peel
Physically disabled fishing day	Al Bohachyk

AFGA Head Office Staff

Executive vice president	Ron Hauser
Habitat development coordinator	Brad Fenson
Operation Burrowing Owl	Shannon Lord

1993 Executive List

Senior Executive
President	Horst Fauser
Past president	Niels Damgaard
Senior vice president	Vern McIntosh
Junior vice president	Andy von Busse
Finance chairperson	Vacant
Executive vice president	Ron Hauser

Zone Directors
Zone 1	Ross MacDonald
Zone 2	Rod Dyck
Zone 3	Dave Powell
Zone 4	Greg Kristoff
Zone 5	Steve Witiuk
Acting Director, Zone 6	Bill O'Toole

Chairmen and Committees
Programs	Sheila Ferguson-Marten
Fisheries	Darryl Smith
Environment	Andy Boyd
Hunting	Ike Johannson
Life member	Jack Graham
Life member (alternate)	Tom O'Keefe

Subcommittees
Agriculture	Elmer Kure
Firearm legislation	Casey Dzioba
Trophy	Ab England
Antelope Creek – technical	Gordon Peel
Physically disabled fishing day	Nestor Romaniuk

1994 Executive List

Senior Executive
President	Horst Fauser
Past president	Niels Damgaard
Senior vice president	Vern McIntosh
Junior vice president	Andy von Busse
Finance chairperson	Vacant
Executive vice president	Ron Hauser

Zone Directors
Zone 1	Ross MacDonald
Zone 2	Rod Dyck
Zone 3	Dave Powell
Zone 4	Ralph Leriger
Zone 5	Steve Witiuk
Acting Director, Zone 6	Bill O'Toole

Chairmen and Committees
Programs	Vacant
Fisheries	Darryl Smith
Environment	Andy Boyd
Hunting	Dave Gibson
Life member	Jack Graham
Life member (alternate)	Tom O'Keefe

Subcommittees
Agriculture	Elmer Kure
Firearm legislation	Casey Dzioba
Trophy	Ab England
Antelope Creek – technical	Gordon Peel

1995 Executive List

Senior Executive
President	Vern McIntosh
Past president	Horst Fauser
Senior vice president	Andy von Busse
Junior vice president	Dave Powell
Finance chairperson	Vacant
Executive vice president	Ron Hauser

Zone Directors
Zone 1	Gerry Pittman
Zone 2	Darwin Cronkhite
Zone 3	Dave Shepherd
Zone 4	Ralph Leriger
Zone 5	Steve Witiuk
Zone 6	Bill O'Toole

Chairmen and Committees
Programs	Mary Mitchell
Fisheries	Jim Clarke
Environment	Andy Boyd
Hunting	Dave Gibson
Life member	Jack Graham
Life member (alternate)	Tom O'Keefe

Subcommittees
Agriculture	Elmer Kure
Trophy	Ab England
Antelope Creek – technical	Gordon Peel

1996 Executive List

Senior Executive
President	Vern McIntosh
Past president	Horst Fauser

Senior vice president	Andy von Busse
Junior vice president	Dave Powell
Finance chairperson	Vacant
Executive vice president	Ron Hauser

Zone Directors

Zone 1	Gerry Pittman
Zone 2	Darwin Cronkhite
Zone 3	Dave Shepherd
Zone 4	Randy Collins
Zone 5	Steve Witiuk
Zone 6	Bill O'Toole

Chairmen and Committees

Programs	Mary Mitchell
Fisheries	Jim Clarke
Environment	Andy Boyd
Hunting	Dave Gibson
Life member	Jack Graham
Life member (alternate)	Tom O'Keefe

Subcommittees

Agriculture	Elmer Kure
Trophy	Ab England
Antelope Creek – technical	Gordon Peel

1997 Executive List

Senior Executive

President	Andy Von Busse
Past president	Vern McIntosh
Senior vice president	Dave Powell
Junior vice president	Gerry Pittman
Finance chairperson	Vacant
Executive vice president	Ron Hauser

Zone Directors

Zone 1	Heinz Plontke
Zone 2	Bev Chipchase
Zone 3	Norm Steinwand
Zone 4	Randy Collins
Zone 5	Steve Witiuk
Zone 6	Bill O'Toole

Chairmen and Committees

Programs	Mary Mitchell
Fisheries	Ivan Johnston
Environment	Andy Boyd
Hunting	Dave Shepherd
Life member	Jack Graham
Life member (alternate)	Tom O'Keefe

Subcommittees

Agriculture	Elmer Kure
Trophy	Ab England
Antelope Creek	Frank Lee

1998 Executive List

Senior Executive

President	Dave Powell
Past president	Andy von Busse
Senior vice president	Gerry Pittman
Junior vice president	Rod Dyck
Finance chairperson	Vern McIntosh

Zone Directors

Zone 1	Heinz Plontke
Zone 2	Bev Chipchase
Zone 3	Andy Hogberg
Zone 4	Randy Collins
Zone 5	Steve Witiuk
Zone 6	Barry Himer

Chairmen and Committees

Programs	Mary Ashton
Fisheries	Ivan Johnston
Environmental	Quentin Bochar
Hunting	Dave Shepherd
Life member	Jack Graham

Subcommittees

Agriculture	Elmer Kure
Trophy	Ab England
Antelope Creek	Frank Lee

1999 Executive List

Senior Executive

President	Dave Powell
Past president	Andy von Busse
Senior vice president	Gerry Pittman
Junior vice president	Rod Dyck
Finance chairperson	Vern McIntosh

Zone Directors

Zone 1	Heinz Plontke
Zone 2	Jim Isaacson
Zone 3	Andy Hogberg
Zone 4	Randy Collins
Zone 5	Steve Witiuk
Zone 6	Barry Himer

Chairmen and Committees

Programs	Mary Ashton
Fisheries	Gilbert Magnan
Environmental	Quentin Bochar
Hunting	Dave Shepherd
Life member	Jack Graham

Subcommittees

Agriculture	Elmer Kure
Trophy	Ab England
Antelope Creek	Frank Lee
Publicity	Horst Fauser

1999 AFGA Staff

Executive vice president	Ron Hauser
Operation Grassland program co-ordinator	Julie Haser
Habitat development co-ordinator	Brad Fenson
Parkland Stewardship program co-ordinator	Andrew Schoepf
Northern Alberta projects facilitator	Dave Nelson
Southern Alberta projects facilitator	Joe Baker

2000 Executive List

Senior Executive

President	Gerry Pittman
Past president	Dave Powell
Senior vice president	Rod Dyck
Junior vice president	Ray Makowecki

Zone Directors

Zone 1	Heinz Plontke
Zone 2	Jim Isaacson
Zone 3	Andy Hogberg
Zone 4	Randy Collins
Zone 5	Dave Doonanco
Zone 6	Darryl Smith

Chairmen and Committees

Programs	Dave Shepherd
Fisheries	Gilbert Magnan
Environmental	Quentin Bochar
Hunting	Maurice Nadeau
Life member representative	Jack Graham

2000 AFGA Staff

Executive vice president	Colleen MacDougall
Habitat Development co-ordinator	Brad Fenson
Northern regional wildlife facilitator	Dave Nelson
Southern regional wildlife facilitator	Yves Ouellette

Parkland Stewardship program facilitator	Andrew Schoepf
Operation Grassland community facilitator	Kerry Grisley

2001/2002 AFGA Executive and Staff List

Senior Executive

President	Rod Dyck
Past president	Dave Powell
Senior vice president	Ray Makowecki
Junior vice president	Randy Collins
Finance chairperson	Nestor Romaniuk
Executive vice president	Martin Sharren

Zone Directors

Zone 1	Heinz Plontke
Zone 2	Bev Chipchase
Zone 3	Andy Hogberg
Zone 4	Gerald Foster
Zone 5	Dave Doonanco
Zone 6	Jerrold Lundgard

Chairmen and Committees

Programs	Grant Creasy
Fishing	Vern McIntosh
Environment	Ruth Harrison
Hunting	Maurice Nadeau
Life member representative	Jack Graham

2001/2002 AFGA Staff

Executive vice president	Martin Sharren
Communications and marketing manager	Juli Best
Accounting manager	Cathy Anderson
Habitat development co-ordinator	Brad Fenson
Regional wildlife project facilitator	Dave Nelson
Regional wildlife project facilitator	Yves Ouellette
Parkland Stewardship program co-ordinator	Andrew Schoepf
Operation Grassland community manager	Kerry Grisley
Conservation education facilitator	Mike Larner
Membership co-ordinator	Laurie Kerestes
Administrative assistant	Joan Warnke

2002/2003 AFGA Executive and Staff List

Senior Executive

President	Rod Dyck
Past president	Dave Powell
Senior vice president	Ray Makowecki
Junior vice president	Randy Collins
Executive vice president	Martin Sharren

Zone Directors

Zone 1	Heinz Plontke
Zone 2	Bev Chipchase
Zone 3	Greg Mallo
Zone 4	Gerald Foster
Zone 5	Dave Doonanco
Zone 6	Jerrold Lundgard

Chairmen and Committees

Programs	Gerald Mannweiler
Fishing	Vern McIntosh
Environment	Quentin Bochar
Hunting	Maurice Nadeau
Life member representative	Jack Graham

2002/2003 AFGA Staff

Executive vice president	Martin Sharren
communications and marketing manager	Juli Best
Accounting manager	Cathy Anderson
Habitat development co-ordinator	Brad Fenson
Wildlife project facilitator	Yves Ouellette
Parkland Stewardship program co-ordinator	Andrew Schoepf
Operation Grassland community manager	Kerry Grisley
Membership co-ordinator	Laurie Kerestes
Administrative assistant	Sandie Buwalda

2003/2004 AFGA Executive and Staff List

Senior Executive

President	Ray Makowecki
Past president	Rod Dyck
Senior vice president	Randy Collins
Junior vice president	Maurice Nadeau
Finance chair	Dave Powell
Executive vice president	Martin Sharren

Zone Directors

Zone 1	Heinz Plontke
Zone 2	Cliff Deitz
Zone 3	Greg Mallo
Zone 4	Gerald Foster
Zone 5	Dave Doonanco
Zone 6	Rich Engler

Chairmen and Committees

Programs	Alan Baker
Fishing	Vern McIntosh
Environment	Quentin Bochar
Hunting	Wayne Norstrom
Life member representative	Tony Ferguson

2003/2004 AFGA Staff

Executive vice president	Martin Sharren
Accounting manager	Charlene Weissner
Communications and marketing manager	Juli Best
Habitat development co-ordinator	Brad Fenson
Wildlife project facilitator	Yves Ouellette
Parkland Stewardship program co-ordinator	Andrew Schoepf
Operation Grassland community manager (acting)	Don Meredith
Operation Grassland community	Lindsay Tomyn
Operation Grassland community	Stephanie Grossman
Membership co-ordinator	Laurie Kerestes
Administrative assistant	Sandie Buwalda

2004 AFGA Executive and Staff List

Senior Executive

President	Ray Makowecki
Past president	Rod Dyck
Senior vice president	Randy Collins
Junior vice president	Maurice Nadeau
Finance chair	Dave Powell
Executive vice president	Martin Sharren

Zone Directors

Zone 1	Heinz Plontke
Zone 2	Cliff Deitz
Zone 3	George Belter
Zone 4	Gerald Foster
Zone 5	Steve Witiuk
Zone 6	Rich Engler

Chairmen and Committees

Programs	Alan Baker
Fishing	Vern McIntosh
Environment	Quentin Bochar
Hunting	Wayne Norstrom
Life member representative	Tony Ferguson

2004 AFGA Staff

Executive vice president	Martin Sharren
Controller	Lee Bell
Communications co-ordinator	Juli Best
Administrative assistant /communications co-ordinator	Sandie Buwalda
Habitat development co-ordinator	Brad Fenson
Wildlife project facilitator	Yves Quellette
Parkland Stewardship program co-ordinator	Andrew Schoepf
Operation Grassland community manager	Kerry Grisley
Operation Grassland community	Lindsay Tomyn
Membership co-ordinator	Laurie Kerestes

2005 AFGA Executive and Staff List

Senior Executive

President	Randy Collins
Past president	Ray Makowecki
1st vice president	Maurice Nadeau
2nd vice president	Quentin Bochar
Executive vice president	Martin Sharren

Zone Directors

Zone 1	Wayne Lowry
Zone 2	Cliff Deitz
Zone 3	George Belter
Zone 4	Gerald Foster
Zone 5	Steve Witiuk
Zone 6 (acting)	Jerrold Lundgard

Chairmen and Committees

Environment chair	Andy Boyd
Programs chair	Alan Baker
Hunting chair	John Kyndesen
Fishing chair	Vern McIntosh
Life member representative	Tony Ferguson

2005 AFGA Staff

Executive vice president	Martin Sharren
Controller	Lee Bell
Communications co-ordinator	Sandie Buwalda
Habitat development co-ordinator	Brad Fenson
Wildlife project facilitator	Yves Ouellette
Parkland Stewardship program co-ordinator	Andrew Schoepf
Parkland Stewardship program co-ordinator	Dave Johnson
Operation Grassland community manager	Kerry Grisley
Operation Grassland community manager	François Blouin

Operation Grassland community	Kara Rowan
Membership co-ordinator	Laurie Kerestes
Receptionist	Yvonne Baxter

2006 AFGA Executive and Staff List

Senior Executive

President	Randy Collins
Past president	Ray Makowecki
1st vice president	Maurice Nadeau
2nd vice president	Quentin Bochar
Finance chair	Wayne Lowry
Environment chair	Andy Boyd
Programs chair	Alan Baker
Hunting chair	John Kyndesen
Fishing chair	Gordon Poirier
Life member representative	Carole Romaniuk

Zone Directors

Zone 1	Wayne Lowry
Zone 2	Cliff Deitz
	Rob MacKenzie
Zone 3	George Belter
Zone 4	Gerald Foster
	Fred Stamper
Zone 5	Steve Witiuk
Zone 6	Al Plantinga

2006 AFGA Staff

Executive vice president	Martin Sharren
Controller	Lee Bell
Communications co-ordinator	Sandie Buwalda
Membership co-ordinator	Laurie Kerestes
Receptionist	Yvonne Baxter
Habitat development co-ordinator	Brad Fenson
Wildlife project facilitator	T.J. Schwanky
Parkland Stewardship co-ordinator	Dave Johnson
Operation Grassland community manager	Kerry Grisley
Operation Grassland community manager	François Blouin

2007 AFGA Executive and Staff List

Senior Executive

President	Randy Collins
Past president	Ray Makowecki
1st vice president	Maurice Nadeau
2nd vice president	Quentin Bochar

Finance chair	Wayne Lowry
Environment chair	Andy Boyd
Programs chair	Alan Baker
Hunting chair	John Kyndesen
Fishing chair	Vern McIntosh
Fishing chair	Gordon Poirier
Life member representative	Carole Romaniuk

Zone Directors

Zone 1	Wayne Lowry
Zone 2	Cliff Deitz
	Rob MacKenzie
Zone 3	George Belter
Zone 4	Gerald Foster
	Fred Stamper
Zone 5	Steve Witiuk
Zone 6 (acting)	Jerrold Lundgard
Zone 6	Al Plantinga

2007 AFGA Staff

Executive vice president	Martin Sharren
Controller	Lee Bell
Communications co-ordinator	Sandie Buwalda
Membership co-ordinator	Laurie Kerestes
Receptionist	Yvonne Baxter
Habitat development co-ordinator	Brad Fenson
Wildlife project facilitator	T.J. Schwanky
Parkland Stewardship co-ordinator	Dave Johnson
Operation Grassland community manager	Kerry Grisley
Operation Grassland community manager	François Blouin
Operation Grassland community	Patrick Riess
Operation Grassland community	Kara Rowan

2007-2008 AFGA Executive and Staff List

Senior Executive

President	Maurice Nadeau
1st vice president	Quentin Bochar
2nd vice president	Conrad Fennema
Past president	Randy Collins
Finance chair	Wayne Lowry
Environment chair	Andy Boyd
Fishing chair	Gord Poirier
Hunting chair	John Kyndesen
Programs chair	Donald Koziol
Life members representative	Carole Romaniuk

Zone Directors

Zone 1	Wayne Lowry
Zone 2	Rob MacKenzie
Zone 3	George Belter
Zone 4	Fred Stamper
Zone 5	Steve Witiuk
Zone 6	Al Plantinga

2007-2008 AFGA Staff

Secretary/receptionist	Yvonne Baxter
Controller	Lee Bell
Operation Grassland community manager	François Blouin
Communications co-ordinator	Sandie Buwalda
Habitat development co-ordinator	Brad Fenson
Operation Grassland community manager	Kerry Grisley
Membership co-ordinator and data entry	Laurie Kerestes
Wildlife project facilitator and Parkland Stewardship co-ordinator	T.J. Schwanky
Executive vice president	Martin Sharren
Operation Grassland community	Patrick Riess
Office assistant	Shauna Wilson

ALBERTA

Arms of the Province of Alberta assigned by Royal
Warrant of H.M. King Edward VII, 30 May, 1907.

8.0 Minutes from the first organizational meeting of the Northern Alberta Game and Fish Protective League, March 1920.

1

ORGANIZATION MEETING

A meeting was called to bring together sportsmen of Edmonton and district with the object of forming an association to look after Fish and Game interests in this district, and was called to order at the Hotel Macdonald at 8 p.m. March 3rd. 1920.

On motion, a temporary Chairman and Secretary were nominated, A. H. Esch and C. Irgens respectively being named.

Object — The object of the meeting was put before those present and suggestions for a name were received. On motion, the name, "Northern Alberta Game and Fish Protective League" was adopted unanimously.

Officers Elected For 1920 — It was moved, seconded, and passed, that officers be elected to complete organization, draw up a Constitution and submit same at the following meeting for approval. On nominations being called for, the following were chosen unanimously:

President: A. H. ESCH.
Vice Pres: P. E. BOWEN.
Sec-Treas: W. HOLMES.
Chairman Big Game Committee: P. ANDERSON.
Chairman Feathered Game Committee: A. HINE.
Chairman Fish Committee: C. W. BOON.

Mr. B. J. Lawton, Provincial Game Guardian, addressed the meeting, speaking generally on the need of such an association; outlining the work before it; the advisability of having game sanctuaries, and other matters pertaining to game protection.

Mr. E. S. Leonard, of Minnesota, a visitor in the city, gave much valuable information regarding success that had been attained in Minnesota, particularly in introducing game fish into lakes in that state. The Secretary was authorized to write the Minnesota State Game and Fish Association for information.

Interest Farmers in Game Bird Protection — Dr. Hope spoke of the advisability of farmers being secured who would interest themselves in protecting and feeding game birds throughout the closed seasons, especially during the winter; and the Executive was ordered to bring before the following meeting a scheme to secure the interest of farmers and get them to take such action.

Several communications were read from parties in the United States who are dealers in game birds. These all explained the difficulty of (securing)

securing Hungarian Partridges and Pheasants at this time.

A communication from the Canadian Dept. of Fisheries regarding stocking Alberta waters, was read. This was referred to the Executive.

The meeting adjourned shortly before 10 o'clock to meet again within two weeks.

Walter Holmes, Secretary.

SECOND MEETING, MARCH 26TH, 1920

Change
to
King
Edward
Hotel

The second meeting of the northern Alberta Game and Fish Protective League was announced to be held Friday, March 26, 1920, at 8 p.m. at the Hotel Macdonald, but on account of the charge made for the use of the room the meeting place was changed to the Board-Room of the King Edward Hotel. The meeting was called to order at 8:20 p.m. President Each explained to the meeting that whereas a charge of $20 was asked by the manager of the Macdonald Hotel, the King Edward management offered the use of the room without charge. Which statement was greeted with applause.

Minutes

The minutes of the preceding meeting were read and adopted.

Constitution Adopted

The Constitution as drawn up by the Executive was submitted, clause by clause. It was adopted with one amendment. A later motion to add to the constitution was received and is dealt with in these minutes further on.

Correspondence Pine Lake Bass.

Correspondence was read and ordered filed. This had to do with a letter from the Postmaster C. E. Atter, Pine Lake, regarding Bass in that Lake; also a letter from Mrs. M. M. Case in which the writer stated he had seen Bass caught at Pine Lake during 1917; also a letter from the Fisheries Dept. stating that a report was being sought on Hastings and Ministik Lakes to ascertain their suitability to Bass; and an acknowledgment by the Parks Branch of a letter asking for permission to place Hungarian Partridges in Dominion Parks.

Vote of Thanks

A vote of thanks was passed to the management of the King Edward Hotel for the use of their Board Room.

Reports of Committees

Under reports by Committees, Chairman Boon named his appointees as Chris Jygens and J. C. McCaig to complete the Fish Committee.

Chairman Hine, named H. P. Warren and W. Wolfe to complete his Game Bird Committee. Mr. Hine also thought the ammunition makers should be asked for prizes to be offered in a Crow Shooting Contest. A crow shoot is to be organized throughout northern Alberta, a given date to be set, and the co-operation of sportsmen in smaller centres to be enlisted.

Allow Killing of Cows.

Chairman P. Anderson, of the Big Game Committee, made his first appearance before the members. He spoke very earnestly on the necessity of prosecuting violators of the closed season. Also, he spoke of the present law protecting cow moose and other big game, and expressed the opinion that each few years the shooting of cows be allowed as otherwise the natural balance was upset; many dry cows resulted from lack of sufficient bulls and this could be avoided if each few years the shooting of cows was allowed.

On motion the reports of the committees were adopted.

A recess was set by the President to allow those present to become affiliated as members of the League, E. Morris, J. Bowen and W. Mason be appointed to receive same.

Season for
Prairie
Chicken
to be
taken up.
with
Legislature

President Each referred to the season suggested by the Provincial Game Guardian for Prairie Chicken for 1920; he stated that the Edmonton Gun Club had appointed a committee to interview the friends of the sportsmen in the Legislature and also to appear before the Committee on Agriculture to see if the season could be made the full month of October or the first two weeks. As President he stated he had named a committee from the League to act in conjunction with the Gun Club committee. Mr. Rooney speaking on this matter, thought that the matter of having Sunday shooting allowed should also be brought up before the House. But as the Lord's Day Act which prevents Sunday shooting is a Dominion Act. it was said the Dominion Government would have to be approached.

Sunday
shooting.

A motion was proposed and seconded. that a committee of this League be appointed to draw up a petition, secure signatures and submit it to the proper authorities asking that Sunday shooting be allowed. This was carried.

Address by
J. H. Willson
Inspector
Of Fisheries

Mr. J. H. Willson. Inspector of Fisheries. gave a comprehensive report of the game conditions as far as fish are concerned. in this district. He spoke of difficulties, both arising from natural causes. and departmental regulations. that would have to be overcome, if the League's proposal to introduce sporting fish in local waters was to be a success. The hearty co-operation of his department was assured to the League and much appreciated.

Mr. E. S. Leonard told of the way Minnesota had overcome some of the difficulties mentioned by Mr. Willson

Against
.22 Rifles

Mr. H. Barry, of Clover Bar. suggested that the League should get in touch with the A. B. C. Auto Club of Clover Bar district. Also he thought that. the League would make friends with the farmers if the young boys were advised to leave their .22ª at home, as the farmers were much more apprehensive of damage by careless handling of rifles than of shotguns.

Song Bird Committee Proposed.

Mr. Hilton suggested that some action should be taken to teach the value of song birds to the community, and to do all possible to protect songsters. He thought this work could be taken up in the schools, by getting the school children interested in erecting bird-houses, feeding the birds, and such ways. He also suggested that a Childrens Branch of the League should be formed, with a low

School Children's Branch.

membership fee. Out of this suggestion a motion was made and carried that the Constitution be amended to allow for a Chairman of Song Birds Committee with two appointed members to complete the committee. Mr. Hilton was unanimously elected to this committee. The fee for the school childrens branch which will be under his directive was set at .10¢.

Crow Shoot.

The matter of a Crow shoot was brought up and on motion it was left for the Executive committee to work out the details.

In answer to a question, the President stated that meetings would be held from time to time as necessity arose and whenever business of general interest could be put before the members.

An active campaign for members is to be instituted, several taking books of tickets for this purpose.

The meeting adjourned at 10:45 p.m.

Walter Holmes. secretary.

COURTESY OF LILLA PFERSCHY

Sunset on Island Lake.

References

Alberta Fish and Game Association (AFGA) archival records. (1918-36). Information contained in the chapters from 1918-36 on each decade was obtained from the minutes of the Northern Alberta Game and Fish Protective League (NAGFPL), which went under the name of the AFGA in the archival records.

Alberta Wildlife Records. 2nd Edition 1963-2001. (2003) Editing by T.J. Schwanky. Published by the AFGA. Edmonton, Alberta. 272pp.

Colpitts, George W. (1994) *Fish and Game Association in Southern Alberta*. Alberta History/Autumn: 16-26.

Feddema-Leonard, Susan. (2007) *People & Peaks of Willmore Wilderness Park: 1800s to mid-1900s*. Willmore Wilderness Foundation and Whitefox Circle Inc. 456 pp.

Fish and Game, Convention Issue magazine. (January, 1957) Published by Prairie Publishing Company, Calgary, Alberta. 22pp.

Fullerton, Lyle. (1986) The AFGA presentation to Hon. Don Sparrow and Hon. Peter Elzinga regarding game farming/game ranching in Alberta. 13 pp.

Fish, Fur & Feathers: Fish and Wildlife Conservation in Alberta 1905-2005. (2005) Published by The Fish and Wildlife Historical Society and The Federation of Alberta Naturalists. 418 pp.

Gruszecki, Robert A. (1991) *The Wisdom Of The Woods*. Published by Orion Publications. Calgary, Alberta. 189 pp.

Hart, E.J. (Ted). (1979) *Diamond Hitch: the Early Outfitters and Guides of Banff and Jasper*. Banff: Summerthought, Ltd. 1st edition. 160pp.

Lewis, Margaret. (1979) *To Conserve a Heritage*. Written and compiled by Margaret Lewis for the AFGA in commemoration of the anniversary of its first convention 1929-79. Published by the AFGA. 283 pp.

Provincial Archives of Alberta. The information contained in these archives was submitted by the AFGA in October, 1987; it is all contained in the fonds entitled *The Alberta Fish and Game Association*. The accession consists of records concerning the AFGA, annual conferences, membership, administration, and committees, as well as general correspondence, circulars and publications for the period 1920-86.

Salt, W.R. and A.L. Wilk. (1966) *The Birds of Alberta*. 2nd edition, Revised. The Queen's Printer, Edmonton, Alberta. 511 pp.

Sharren, Kandice. (September 22, 2005) Summary Report of Archival Information to the Heritage 100 Committee, AFGA. Edmonton, Alberta.

Sodbusters. (1979) The (Kinuso) History Book Committee. Kinuso, Alberta. 391 pp.

The AFGA annual conference yearbooks (1945-2007). Published by the AFGA annually for their annual convention/conference.

Autumn foliage and mist on the Rocky Mountains

Index

I BEQUEATH UNTO THEE

ALBERTA FISH AND GAME ASSOCIATION
the RED DEER CLUB

I Bequeath unto You ...

In keeping with the philosophy of the FISH and GAME ASSO-CIATION, the RED DEER CLUB decided to commission the painting of this picture depicting our generation's desire to leave future generations the Great Outdoors that we have enjoyed over the years.

It is our hope that all those with these concerns and ambitions will support this project and thus help to enhance the habitat for wild life and the conservation of the same for upcoming genera-tions.

Our artist VILMA EBL has transposed onto canvas the feelings and emotions of all true sportsmen.

We wish to thank her on behalf of
the FISH & GAME ASSOCIATION.

Memories